ESTATE PLANNING

Michael A. Dalton
Thomas P. Langdon

12th Edition

3116 5th Street
Metairie, LA 70002
888-295-6023

Copyright© 2020 by Money Education. All rights reserved.

No part of this publication may be reproduced or transmitted in any form or by any means, electronic or mechanical, including photocopy, recording, or any other information storage and retrieval system, without prior permission in writing from the publisher. Requests for permission to make copies of any part of the work should be e-mailed to info@money-education.com.

This publication is designed to provide accurate and authoritative information in regard to the subject matter covered. It is sold with the understanding that the publisher, authors and contributors are not engaged in rendering legal, accounting, tax, financial planning, or other professional services. If legal advice, tax advice, or other professional assistance is required, the services of a competent professional should be sought.

CFP®, CERTIFIED FINANCIAL PLANNER™, and CFP (with flame logo)® are certification marks owned by Certified Financial Planner Board of Standards Inc. These marks are awarded to individuals who successfully complete CFP Board's initial and ongoing certification requirements.

Printed in the U.S.A.

ISBN: 978-1-946711-33-5

About the Authors

Michael A. Dalton, Ph.D., JD, CPA, CLU, ChFC, CFP®
- Former Chair of the Board of Dalton Publications, L.L.C.
- Professor Emeritus, Accounting and Taxation, Loyola University in New Orleans, Louisiana
- Adjunct professor at George Mason University (2014 - 2017)
- Adjunct professor at Georgetown University (2002 - 2014)
- Former Senior Vice President, Education at BISYS Group
- Ph.D. in Accounting from Georgia State University
- J.D. from Louisiana State University in Baton Rouge, Louisiana
- MBA and BBA in Management and Accounting from Georgia State University
- Former board member of the CFP Board's Board of Examiners, Board of Standards, and Board of Governors
- Former member (and chair) of the CFP Board's Board of Examiners
- Member of the Financial Planning Association
- Member of the *Journal of Financial Planning* Editorial Advisory Board
- Member of the *Journal of Financial Planning* Editorial Review Board
- Member of the LSU Law School Board of Trustees (2000 - 2006)
- Author of *Dalton Review for the CFP® Certification Examination: Volume I – Outlines and Study Guides, Volume II – Problems and Solutions, Volume III - Case Exam Book, Mock Exams A-1 and A-2* (1st - 8th Editions)
- Author of *Retirement Planning and Employee Benefits* (1st - 16th Editions)
- Author of *Estate Planning* (1st - 12th Editions)
- Author of *Fundamentals of Financial Planning* (1st - 6th Editions)
- Author of *Insurance Planning* (1st - 7th Editions)
- Co-author of *Income Tax Planning* (1st - 13th Editions)
- Co-author of *Cases in Financial Planning: Analysis and Presentation* (1st - 4th Editions)
- Co-author of *Dalton CFA® Study Notes Volumes I and II* (1st - 2nd Editions)
- Co-author of *Dalton's Personal Financial Planning Series – Personal Financial Planning Theory and Practice* (1st - 3rd Editions)
- Co-author of *Dalton's Personal Financial Planning Series – Personal Financial Planning Cases and Applications* (1st - 4th Editions)
- Co-author of *Cost Accounting: Traditions and Innovations* published by West Publishing Company
- Co-author of the *ABCs of Managing Your Money* published by National Endowment for Financial Education (NEFE)

Thomas P. Langdon, JD, LL.M.
- Professor of Business Law, Gabelli School of Business, Roger Williams University, Bristol, RI
- Principal, Langdon & Langdon Financial Services, LLC (Connecticut-based tax planning & preparation firm)
- Former Professor of Taxation at The American College, Bryn Mawr, PA.
- Former Adjunct Professor of Insurance and Economics at The University of Connecticut Center for Professional Development
- Former Member (and Chair) of the CFP Board's Board of Examiners
- Master of Laws (LL.M.) in Taxation from Villanova University School of Law
- Juris Doctor, from Western New England College School of Law
- Master of Science in Financial Services from The American College
- Master of Business Administration from The University of Connecticut
- Bachelor of Science in Finance from The University of Connecticut, Storrs, CT.
- Chartered Financial Analyst (CFA), Certified Financial Planner (CFP), Chartered Life Underwriter (CLU), Chartered Financial Consultant (ChFC), Accredited Estate Planner (AEP), Chartered Advisor in Philanthropy (CAP), Certified Employee Benefits Specialist (CEBS), Chartered Advisor in Senior Living (CASL), Registered Employee Benefits Consultant (REBC), Registered Health Underwriter (RHU), Associate in Life & Health Claims (ALHC), and Fellow of the Life Management Institute (FLMI)
- Associate Editor of the *Journal of Financial Services Professionals*
- Co-author of *Estate Planning* (1st - 12th editions)
- Co-author of *Income Tax Planning* (1st - 13th editions)
- Contributing author of *Insurance Planning* (1st - 7th editions)
- Faculty member for National Tax Institute

About the Contributing Authors

James F. Dalton, MBA, MS, CPA/PFS, CFA®, CFP®
- CEO, Money Education
- Adjunct professor at George Mason University (2014 - 2017)
- Adjunct professor at Georgetown University (2002 - 2014)
- Former Executive Vice President, Assessment Technologies Institute LLC
- Former Senior Vice President, Kaplan Professional
- Former President, Dalton Publications LLC
- Former Senior Manager of KPMG, LLP, concentrating in personal financial planning, investment planning, and litigation consulting
- MBA from Loyola University New Orleans
- Master of Accounting in Taxation from the University of New Orleans
- BS in accounting from Florida State University in Tallahassee, Florida
- Member of the CFP Board of Standards July 1996, Comprehensive CFP® Exam Pass Score Committee
- Member of the AICPA and the Louisiana Society of CPAs
- Member of the Financial Planning Association
- Member of the *Journal of Financial Planning* Editorial Review Board
- Author of *Money Education's Quick Sheets*
- Co-author of *Cases in Financial Planning: Analysis and Presentation* (1st - 4th Editions)
- Co-author of *Retirement Planning and Employee Benefits* (1st - 16th Editions)
- Co-Author of *Fundamentals of Financial Planning* (1st - 6th Editions)
- Contributing Author of *Insurance Planning* (1st - 7th Editions)
- Contributing Author of *Estate Planning* (1st - 12th Editions)
- Author of Kaplan Schweser's Personal Financial Planning Understanding Your Financial Calculator
- Author of Kaplan Schweser's Understanding Your Financial Calculator for the CFA® Exam
- Co-author of BISYS CFA® Study Notes Volumes I and II
- Co-author of Kaplan Schweser's Personal Financial Planning Cases and Applications
- Co-author of the Kaplan Schweser Review for the CFP® Certification Examination, Volumes I–VIII and Kaplan Schweser's Financial Planning Flashcards

Sherri Donaldson, CFP®, ChFC®, MSFS, CASL®, CAP®, EA
- Editing Princess for Money Education
- Former Author/Editor/Lead instructor, Keir Educational Resources
- Former Assistant Vice President, Senior Training Specialist, M&T Securities
- Former Associate Financial Consultant, M&T Securities
- Former Financial Sales Specialist, Nationwide Financial
- Former Financial Services Representative, Nationwide Retirement Solutions
- MSFS from The American College Bryn Mawr, PA
- BS in business, concentration in financial services, Pennsylvania State University
- Member of the Financial Planning Association
- Contributing Author of *Cases in Financial Planning: Analysis and Presentation* (4th Edition)
- Contributing Author of *Retirement Planning and Employee Benefits* (16th Edition)
- Contributing Author of *Fundamentals of Financial Planning* (6th Edition)
- Contributing Author of *Insurance Planning* (6th - 7th Editions)
- Contributing Author of *Estate Planning* (11th - 12th Editions)
- Contributing author of *Investment Planning* (2nd Edition)
- Co-Author/Editor of Keir *General Financial Planning Principles* textbook
- Co-Author/Editor of Keir *Risk Management and Insurance Planning* textbook
- Co-Author/Editor of Keir *Introduction to Financial Planning* textbook
- Co-Author/Editor of Keir *Retirement Savings and Income Planning* textbook
- Co-Author/Editor of Keir *Tax Planning* textbook
- Co-Author/Editor of Keir *Estate Planning* textbook
- Co-Author/Editor Keir *Investments Planning* textbook
- Editor Keir *Financial Plan Development* and *Practical Applications for Your Financial Calculator* textbook
- Co-Author/Editor Keir CFP® exam review books (*Core Knowledge Book 1* and *2*, *Essential Keys* book, *Case Studies* book), practice exams, flashcards, MP3 scripts, Key Concept Infograhics, and Quick Concept videos

Acknowledgments & Special Thanks

We are most appreciative for the tremendous support and encouragement we have received throughout this project. We are extremely grateful to the instructors and program directors of CFP Board-Registered programs who provided valuable comments on all the previous editions of this textbook. We are fortunate to have dedicated, careful readers at several institutions who were willing to share their needs, expectations, and time with us.

We also owe a special thanks to all of our reviewers for their constructive feedback. Their thorough editing, detailed calculation reviews, helpful suggestions for additional content, and other valuable comments, improved this text. To each of these individuals we extend our deepest gratitude and appreciation. We extend a special thanks to the following professionals for their thorough reviews.

Beth-Anne Perez Bracey is an attorney in New Orleans, Louisiana practicing in estate planning and administration. Ms. Bracey received her J.D. from Loyola University New Orleans School of Law. She lectures in the New Orleans area on successions and estate planning.

Benjamin F. Cummings, Ph.D., is an assistant professor in the Finance Department at Saint Joseph's University in Philadelphia, PA. He has taught estate planning at the graduate and undergraduate levels. Benjamin received a Ph.D. in Personal Financial Planning from Texas Tech University, and his research interests include behavioral and neural finance and the use and value of financial advice. While at Texas Tech, he volunteered as a Red to Black® financial counselor. Previously, Benjamin was the Scholar in Residence at CFP Board, and he also worked as a Summer Associate for FJY Financial, a fee-only financial planning firm in Northern Virginia.

Donna Dalton made a significant contribution to this textbook by her thoughtful and meticulous editing throughout the book. She provided many valuable improvements to both the textbook and instructor materials. We are extremely grateful for her contributions.

Andrew J. Head, MA, CFP® brings 14 years of financial services experience to his position as the Director of the Western Kentucky University CFP® Board Registered Financial Planning Programs as well as the WKU Center for Financial Success. He joined the faculty at WKU in 2010 and teaches courses on Estate Planning, Tax Planning, Risk Management & Insurance Planning among others. He is the faculty advisor to the WKU Financial Planning Association (FPA) Student Chapter as well as serving on the Board of Directors for FPA of Kentuckiana. Outside of his duties with WKU, Andrew operates a multi-state fee-based RIA.

Robin Meyer is a valuable member of our Money Education team. She worked diligently throughout this project by performing numerous reviews and revisions. Mrs. Meyer provided many valuable improvements to both the textbook and instructor materials. Robin is the joy in our office as she always works tirelessly with a great work ethic and an enormous sense of humor. We are always grateful for her contributions to our products as well as our office happiness.

Mariette O'Malley, CPA, J.D. (Tax), CFP represents the third generation in her family-owned accounting firm. The firm's focus on small, closely-held businesses and her own background naturally led Mariette to focus on the unique needs of their clients with regard to income tax, retirement and estate planning. Mariette has lectured and consulted on family business problems, mergers and acquisitions, real estate swaps, retirement and estate planning, divorce strategy and other areas that commingle taxation and law.

We would like to pay special thanks to **Donna Dalton** and **Robin Meyer** for their significant contribution to this textbook. They worked diligently with the authors and reviewers to manage the project, performed numerous reviews, and provided invaluable feedback throughout the entire project. This book would not have been possible without their extraordinary dedication, skill, and knowledge.

We have received so much help from so many people, it is possible that we have inadvertently overlooked thanking someone. If so, it is our shortcoming, and we apologize in advance. Please let us know if you are that someone, and we will make it right in our next printing.

Preface

Estate Planning is written for graduate and upperdivision undergraduate level students interested in acquiring an understanding of estate planning. The text is intended to be used in an Estate Planning course as part of an overall curriculum in financial planning or in a Masters in Tax program emphasizing tax and financial planning. The text can also be used as a reference for practicing professional financial planners.

This text was also designed to meet the educational requirements for an Estate Planning Course in a CFP Board-Registered Program. Therefore, one of our goals is to assure CFP Board-Registered Program directors, instructors, students, and financial planners that we have addressed every relevant topic covered by the CFP Board exam topic list. The book will be updated, as needed, to keep current with any changes in the tax law, exam topic list, or model curriculum.

Through this text, we hope to convey our knowledge and enthusiasm for estate and financial planning with a user-friendly approach to learning the topic at hand.

Special Features
A variety of tools and presentation methods are used throughout this text to assist the reader in the learning process. Some of the features in this text that are designed to enhance your understanding and learning process include:

- **Learning Objectives** – At the beginning of each chapter is a list of learning objectives to help you focus your studying of the material. These learning objectives will provide a preview of the important topics covered in the chapter.

- **Key Concepts** – At the beginning of each subsection are key concepts, or study objectives, each stated as a question. To be successful in this course, you should be able to answer these questions. So as you read, guide your learning by looking for the answers. When you find the answers, highlight or underline them. It is important that you actually highlight/underline and not just make a mental note, as the action of stopping and writing reinforces your learning. Watch for this symbol:

Key Concepts

- **Quick Quizzes** – Following each subsection you will find a Quick Quiz, which checks and reinforces what you read. Circle the answer to each question and then check your answers against the correct answers supplied at the bottom of the quiz. If you missed any questions, flip back to the relevant section and review the material. Watch for this symbol:

Quick Quiz 0.1

- **Examples** – Examples are used frequently to illustrate the concepts being discussed and to help the reader understand and apply the concepts presented.

- **Exhibits** – The written text is enhanced and simplified by using exhibits where appropriate to promote learning and application. Exhibits are identified with the following symbol:

- **Cases** – Several chapters contain real world case summaries to help the reader appreciate the application of particular topics being discussed in the chapter.

- **Key Terms** – Key terms appear in **boldfaced type** throughout the text to assist in the identification of important concepts and terminology. A list of key terms with definitions appears at the end of each chapter.

- **End of Chapter Questions** – Each chapter contains a series of discussion questions and a sample of multiple-choice problems that highlight major topics covered in the chapter. The questions test retention and understanding of important chapter material and can be used for review and classroom discussion. Additional problems are available at money-education.com by accessing the Student Practice Portal.

- **Quick Quiz Explanations** – Each chapter concludes with the answers to the Quick Quizzes contained in that chapter, as well as explanation to the "false" statements in each Quick Quiz.

- **Glossary** – A compilation of the key terms identified throughout the text is located at the end of the book.

> **Student Practice Portal**
> available by registering your textbook at
> money-education.com

To my wonderful grandchildren,
Jordan Catherine, Colin James,
Catherine Allison, & Caroline James
in hopes that you avoid transfer taxes
through proper planning.
MAD

To my daughter, Marykate, and
to my nephews, Keegan, Reilly,
Ryan and Kasey - my incentive for effective
intergenerational planning, and
in grateful memory of my son,
Kevin J.B. Langdon.
TPL

TABLE OF CONTENTS

Chapter 1 | Introduction to Estate Planning

Learning Objectives 2
Introduction 2
    Marriage Equality (After Obergefell) 3
    Estate Planning Reform 4
    Estate Planning Defined 5
Goals, Objectives, & Risks of Estate Planning 5
    Who Needs Estate Planning 6
    Why the Interest in Estate Planning 7
    Tools for Wealth Protection 7
The Estate Planning Process 7
    The Seven Basic Steps 7
    Establish the Client/Planner Relationship 8
    Collecting Client Information and Defining Transfer Objectives 8
The Estate Planning Team 9
    The Unauthorized Practice of Law 10
Overview of the Text 10
Key Terms 13
Discussion Questions 14
Multiple-Choice Problems 15
Quick Quiz Explanations 16

Chapter 2 | Basic Estate Planning Documents

Learning Objectives 18
Basic Documents Included in an Estate Plan 18
Wills 18
    Intestacy 19
    Advantages of Wills 21
    Limitations of Wills 21
    Types of Wills 22
    Electronic Wills 23
    Legal Capacity to Execute a Will 24
    Heirs, Legatees, and Devisees 24
    Will Contests 25
    Common Clauses in Wills 26
    Other Clauses 28
    Sample Wills 35
    Revoking and Changing Wills 39
    Side Instruction Letter 41
    Statutes Affecting Wills 42
    Avoiding Will Contests 43

Powers of Attorney & Powers of Appointment 44
    General Power of Attorney 44
    Limited Power of Attorney 45
    Springing Power 48
    Discussion of Exhibit 2.13 48
    Power of Attorney for Property 50
    Disadvantages of a Power of Attorney 51

Directives Regarding Health Care 52
    Durable Power of Attorney for Health Care 52
    Living Wills/Advance Medical Directives 54
    Do Not Resuscitate Order (DNRs) 55
    Physician Orders for Life Sustaining Treatment (POLST) 57

Other Important Documents for Estate Planning 57
    Digital Assets and Estate Planning Documents 57

Need for Documents 58

Key Terms 60

Discussion Questions 64

Multiple-Choice Problems 65

Quick Quiz Explanations 66

Chapter 3 | Types of Property Interests

Learning Objectives 68

Ownership And Transfer of Property 68
    Introduction 68

Property Interests (Title and Ownership) 69
    Sole Ownership - Fee Simple 70
    Tenancy in Common (TC) 71
    Joint Tenancy with Right of Survivorship (JTWROS) 73
    Tenancy by the Entirety (TE) 75
    Community Property and Separate Property in Community Property Regimes 76

Special Forms of Property Ownership 80
    Partial Ownership Interests (less than fee simple) 80
    Legal vs. Equitable Ownership 81

Cumulative Summary and Example 82
    Sole Ownership 82
    Tenancy in Common 82
    Joint Tenancy with Right of Survivorship 82
    Tenancy by the Entirety 82
    Community Property 83

Key Terms 87

Discussion Questions 89

Multiple-Choice Problems 91

Quick Quiz Explanations 93

Chapter 4 | The Probate Process

Learning Objectives 96
Introduction 96
    The Probate Process Defined 96
    Testate vs. Intestate Succession 96
    Transfer of Assets 97
    Advantages of Probate 97
    Disadvantages of the Probate Process 99
    Nontraditional Relationships 101
The Probate Process 103
    State Probate Laws 103
    Beginning the Probate Process - Producing the Will 103
    The Probate Court 104
    Personal Representative - Executors and Administrators 104
    Managing and Distributing the Estate 106
    Potential Problems in Distribution 107
Property Passing Through Probate 108
Property Passing Outside of the Probate Process 108
    State Contract Law 108
    State Titling Law 110
    State Trust Law 110
Calculating the Probate Estate 112
Key Terms 115
Discussion Questions 116
Multiple-Choice Problems 117
Quick Quiz Explanations 119

Chapter 5 | Gift Tax

Learning Objectives 122
The Gift Tax System 122
    Historical Background and Purpose 122
    Estate and Gift Tax Reform 123
Characteristics of a Gift 127
    Parties 127
    Definition of a Gift 127
    Elements of a Gift 127
    Consideration 128
    Types of Gifts 128
    Valuation of a Gift 132
Exclusions and Exemptions 133
    The Annual Exclusion 133
    Taxable Gifts Defined 134
    Split Gift Elections 134
    Gifts of Community and Joint Property 135
    The Applicable Credit Amount 137

Gifts of a Present and Future Interest 141
    Present Interest Gift 141
    Future Interest Gift 142
    The Crummey Provision 143
    The Five-and-Five Lapse Rule 144

Transfers Resulting in No Gift Tax 146
    Transfers to Political Organizations 146
    Qualified Transfers 146
    529 Plans 147
    Payments for Support 147
    Payments Between Divorcing Spouses 148
    Transfers within a Business Setting 148
    Gifts to Spouses 148
    Charitable Gifts 149

The Gift Tax Return 149
    Form 709 149
    Statute of Limitations 150
    Calculation of the Gift Tax 150

Income Tax Issues Related to Gifts 158
    Donee's Adjusted Basis of Gifted Property 158
    Exceptions 158

Gift Strategies 161
    Achieving Client Goals with Direct Gifts 161
    Gifts of Appreciating Property 161
    Gifts to Spouses 162
    Gifts to Minors 162
    Single Party Gift Strategies 162
    Multiparty Gift Strategies 163

Advantages of Lifetime Gifts vs. Bequests 166

Key Terms 168

Discussion Questions 170

Multiple-Choice Problems 171

Quick Quiz Explanations 173

Chapter 6 | Estate Tax

Learning Objectives 176

Introduction 177

The Gross Estate 179
    Property Owned by the Decedent (IRC Section 2033) 180
    Dower and Curtesy Interest (IRC Section 2034) 181
    Gifts Made Within Three Years of Death (IRC Section 2035) 182
    Transfers with a Retained Life Estate (IRC Section 2036) 183
    Transfers Taking Effect at Death (IRC Section 2037) 185
    Revocable Transfers (IRC Section 2038) 186
    Annuities (IRC Section 2039) 187
    Joint Interests (IRC Section 2040) 188
    Powers of Appointment (IRC Sections 2041 and 2514) 189

  Proceeds of Life Insurance (IRC Section 2042) 191
  Property for which Marital Deduction was Previously Allowed (IRC Section 2044) 193
Valuation of Assets at Death 193
  Hard-to-Value Assets 193
  Financial Securities 195
  Life Insurance 198
  The Alternate Valuation Date 199
Deductions to Determine the Adjusted Gross Estate 200
Deductions to Determine the Taxable Estate 203
  The Charitable Deduction 203
  The Unlimited Marital Deduction 203
  State Death Tax Deduction 203
  The Taxable Estate 204
Determining the Tentative Tax 204
  Post-1976 Taxable Gifts 204
  The Tentative Tax Base 204
  The Tentative Tax 204
Credits From the Tentative Tax 205
  Applicable Estate Tax Credit 205
  Exemption Portability 207
  Credit for Tax Paid on Prior Transfers 208
  Foreign Death Tax Credit 209
Estate Tax Liability 209
Paying and Reporting Estate Taxes 210
  Filing Requirements 210
  Penalties 212
Adjusted Basis to Heirs and Legatees 212
  Basis of Property Acquired from a Decedent 213
  IRD Assets 213
  Basis in the Hands of an Heir/Donor 214
  Surviving Owner 214
  Community Property 215
Cumulative Example 216
  Example Solutions 218
Key Terms 220
Discussion Questions 222
Multiple-Choice Problems 223
Quick Quiz Explanations 225

Chapter 7 | Transfers During Life & At Death

Learning Objectives 228
Introduction 228
  Lifetime Transfers 228
Arm's-Length Transactions 229
  Sale 230
  Installment Sale 230
  Exchange 233

Transfers to Loved Ones 233
    Transfers Not Subject to Gift Tax 233
    Gifts Outright and in Trust 234
    Partial Sale-Gift Transactions 235
    Full Consideration Transfers/Sales 236
    Grantor Retained Trusts 244
    Family Limited Partnerships (FLP) 252
    Summary 256
    Medicare/Medicaid 257

Transfers to Charities 261

Transfers at Death 261
    Transfers by Will 262
    Property Transferred at Death by Contract 263
    Transfers at Death by Operation of Law 263
    Charitable Transfers at Death 264

Estate Planning for Small Estates 264
    Estate Equalization 265
    Gifting Strategies 266
    Retained Interest Transfers 267
    Incapacity Planning 268
    Individuals with Small Estates Still Need to Plan 268

Key Terms 269

Discussion Questions 271

Multiple-Choice Problems 273

Quick Quiz Explanations 275

Chapter 8 | Trusts

Learning Objectives 278

Introduction 278

Definitions 279

Parties 279
    Grantor (Settlor, Creator, Trustor) 279
    Trustee 280
    Beneficiary 281

Why Use a Trust 283
    Management 283
    Creditor Protection 283
    Split Interests in Property 285
    Avoiding Probate (Living Trust) 286
    Minimizing Taxes 286

Trust Duration – The Rule Against Perpetuities 287

Accounting and Income Taxation of Trusts 288
    Income Taxation of Trusts 288
    Gift Tax as Applied to Trusts 292
    Inclusion/Exclusion from Gross Estate of Trust Assets 293

Classification of Trust Arrangements 296
    Revocable Trusts 296

Irrevocable Trusts	296
Inter Vivos Trust	297
Testamentary Trusts	297
Standby Trust	297
Pourover Trust	297
Grantor Trust	297
Funded or Unfunded	297
Simple or Complex	298

Specific Trusts Used in Estate Planning ... 298
- Inter Vivos Revocable Trusts ... 298
- Inter Vivos Irrevocable Trusts ... 301
- Life Insurance Trusts ... 305
- Bypass (Credit Shelter) Trusts ... 306
- Power of Appointment Trusts ... 307
- Qualified Terminable Interest Property (QTIP) Trusts ... 308
- Grantor Retained Income Trusts (GRITs) ... 308
- Grantor Retained Annuity Trusts (GRATs) ... 308
- Grantor Retained Unitrusts (GRUTs) ... 309
- Qualified Personal Residence Trusts (QPRTs) ... 309
- Tangible Personal Property Trusts (TPPTs) ... 309
- Dynasty Trusts ... 309
- Grantor Trusts ... 310
- Trusts for Minors – Section 2503(b) and Section 2503(c) Trusts ... 312
- Crummey Trusts ... 313
- Charitable Trusts ... 313
- Totten Trusts ... 314
- Blind Trusts ... 314
- Special Needs Trust ... 314
- ABLE Accounts ... 317
- IRAs in Estate Planning ... 318

Key Terms ... 322
Discussion Questions ... 325
Multiple-Choice Problems ... 327
Quick Quiz Explanations ... 328

Chapter 9 | Charitable Giving

Learning Objectives ... 332
Introduction ... 332
- General Issues Regarding Charitable Contributions and Taxation ... 334
- Qualifying Organizations ... 334
- Types of Charitable Organizations ... 335

Charitable Gifts During Life ... 337
- Gifts of Cash ... 337
- Gifts of Services ... 337
- Gifts of Property ... 338
- Contribution Base (Adjusted Gross Income) Limitations ... 341
- Choosing the Adjusted Basis Over the Fair Market Value (Special Election) ... 342
- Valuation, Record Keeping, and Reporting ... 345

Other Outright Gifts to Charity 346
    Bargain Sales of Property to Charities 346
    Bargain Sales of Appreciated Property to Charities 347
    Charitable Gift Annuities 347
    Charitable Annuity of Encumbered Properties (Mortgaged) 350
    Gifts of Life Insurance to Charities 352
    Group Term Life Insurance 352

Charitable Gifts of a Split Interest 352
    Pooled Income Funds (PIF) 353
    Charitable Remainder Annuity Trust (CRAT) 354
    Charitable Remainder Unitrust (CRUT) 354
    Calculation of the Gift and Remainder Interest 356
    Probability of Exhaustion Test 357
    A CRT and Life Insurance for Wealth Replacement 361
    Non-Trust Split Interest Charitable Gifts 361
    Charitable Lead Trusts 362

Testamentary Giving to Charities 363

Advanced Financial & Estate Planning Topics 364
    Tangible Property 364
    Community Property 365
    Choosing Between the CRAT or the CRUT 365
    Reformation of Disqualified Split Interests 366
    Transfer of an Interest in an IRA by Taxpayers Over the Age of 70½ (QCDs) 366

Key Terms 367

Discussion Questions 368

Multiple-Choice Problems 370

Quick Quiz Explanations 372

Chapter 10 | The Unlimited Marital Deduction

Learning Objectives 374

The Marital Deduction Defined 374
    The Single Economic Unit 374
    Advantages of the Unlimited Marital Deduction 375
    Requirements of the Unlimited Marital Deduction 377
    Limitations of the Unlimited Marital Deduction 377
    Community Property 378

Qualification for the Marital Deduction 379
    Inclusion in the Decedent's Gross Estate 379
    Property Transferred to a Surviving Spouse 379
    The Terminable Interest Rule 381

Outright Bequests to the Spouse 387
    Limiting a Direct Transfer 387

General Power of Appointment (GPOA) Trusts 388
    Qualifying a GPOA Trust for the Marital Deduction 388

Qualified Terminable Interest Property (QTIP) Trusts 389
    Qualifying as a QTIP Trust 389
    The QTIP Trust as a Lifetime Transfer Device 390

    Estate Taxes 390
    Portability 392

Planning for the Non-citizen Spouse 395
    Qualified Domestic Trust 396

Alternatives to Qualification 397
    Overqualification 397
    Underqualification 399
    Bypass Trust 400
    Common Trust Arrangements 403
    Disclaimers 404
    Irrevocable Life Insurance Trust (ILIT) 405
    Using the Marital Deduction to save State Inheritance Taxes 406

Comprehensive Example 409
    Scenario 1 409
    Scenario 2 410
    Scenario 3 412

Key Terms 414

Discussion Questions 416

Multiple-Choice Problems 417

Quick Quiz Explanations 419

Chapter 11 | Life Insurance in Estate Planning

Learning Objectives 422

Introduction 422

Objective of Life Insurance 423
    Protect Income Stream for Beneficiaries 423
    A Source of Funds for Education 424
    Provide Liquidity at Death 425
    A Source for Retirement Income 425
    To Create or Sustain Family Wealth 426
    To Fund Buy-Sell Agreements 427

Types of Life Insurance 432
    Term Insurance 432
    Universal Life 433
    Variable Universal Life 433
    Whole Life 434
    Second-to-Die 434

Parties to a Life Insurance Policy 434
    Owner 434
    Insured 435
    Beneficiary 435

Income Tax Treatment of Life Insurance 435
    General Approach 435
    Transfer for Value 435
    Settlement or Cash Surrender 438
    Policy Dividends 439
    Loans 440

    MECs...440
    Policy Exchanges 1035..442
    Accelerated Death Benefits...442
Gift Tax Treatment of Life Insurance 444
    Changing the Beneficiary on the Life Insurance Policy..444
    Outright Gift of a Life Insurance Policy...445
    Gifts of Premiums..446
    Gifts of Life Insurance to Charities..447
Federal Estate Tax Treatment of Life Insurance 448
    Life Insurance on Someone Else's Life..448
    Life Insurance on the Insured/Decedent's Life...448
    The Three-Year Look Back Rule...449
Creation of a Life Insurance Trust (ILIT) 451
    Using the Annual Exclusion...451
    Other Objectives..453
Key Terms..457
Discussion Questions..459
Multiple-Choice Problems..461
Quick Quiz Explanations...463

Chapter 12 | Special Elections & Post Mortem Planning

Learning Objectives..466
Introduction..466
Liquidity Needs...466
    Last Medical Costs...466
    Funeral Costs...467
    Transition or Adjustment Period Costs 467
    Administrative Costs...468
    Income, Estate, and Generation-Skipping Transfer Taxes 468
Liquidity Sources and Implications 469
    Sale of Assets...469
    Life Insurance..469
    Tax-Advantaged Accounts...470
    Corporate Redemption from Closely Held Businesses 471
    Distribution of Assets..473
    Loans for Payments of Taxes and Other Costs...473
Income Tax Issues and Elections on Decedent's Final Income Tax Return (1040) 474
    Joint or Separate Final Return..475
    Passive Losses...475
    Expense Elections..475
Income Tax Issues and Elections Regarding the Estate Fiduciary Income Tax Return (1041) 476
    Selection of Tax Year...476
    Expense Elections..476
    Waiver of Executor's Fees...476
    U.S. Savings Bonds and Income in Respect of Decedent (IRD) Assets...478
    Distributions and Income Tax Bracket Analysis...479

Gift Tax Issues and Elections 479
    Election to Split Gifts for the Year of Death 479
Basic Estate Planning Issues and Elections (Post Mortem) 480
    Valuation of Assets 480
    Selection of Valuation Date 480
    Alternate Valuation Date 481
    Installment Payments of Estate Tax (IRC Section 6166) 482
    Special Use Valuation (IRC Section 2032A) 483
    Election to Disclaim 485
    Qualified Terminable Interest Property (QTIP) Election 487
    Qualified Domestic Trust (QDOT) Election 487
    Portability of a Deceased Spouse's Estate Tax Exemption Election 488
    Generation-Skipping Transfer Tax Elections 488
Key Terms 490
Discussion Questions 491
Multiple-Choice Problems 493
Quick Quiz Explanations 494

Chapter 13 | Generation-Skipping Transfers

Learning Objectives 496
Introduction 496
Parties Involved in Generation-Skipping Transfers 497
    Transferor 497
    Transferee 498
    Qualified Disclaimers 503
Types of Taxable Transfers 504
    Direct Skip 504
    Taxable Termination 505
    Taxable Distribution 505
Exceptions, Exclusions, and Exemption 507
    Exceptions 507
    Exclusions 507
    Exemption 509
Applicable Rate, Inclusion Ratio, and Applicable Fraction 511
    Generation-Skipping Transfer Tax and QTIPs 513
Filing Requirement and Returns 514
An Overview of Generation-Skipping Trusts 515
Introduction to Dynasty Trusts 516
    The Rule Against Perpetuities 516
    Taxation of Dynasty Trusts 517
    Basic Structure and Types of Dynasty Trusts 517
    Dynasty Trusts and Business Succession Planning 518
    Types of Dynasty Trusts 519
    Funding the Trust 519
    General Drafting Issues for Dynasty Trusts 520
    Summary of Dynasty Trusts 521

Key Terms 522
Discussion Questions 523
Multiple-Choice Problems 524
Quick Quiz Explanations 525

Chapter 14 | Basic Estate Plan

Learning Objectives 528
The Estate Planning Process 528
    Determine the Client's Financial Situation 528
    Develop the Estate Plan 529
    Implement the Plan 534
    Monitor the Plan 534
Comprehensive Case Example 538
Benny and Martha Franklin Case 550
    Personal Background and Information 550
    Goals: Prepare a Proper Estate Plan 552
    Financial Statements 552
    Case Assumptions 554
    Directions for the Case 554
    Case Appendix 555

Appendix

Glossary 557
Index 573

1
INTRODUCTION TO ESTATE PLANNING

LEARNING OBJECTIVES

1. Define estate planning.
2. List the goals, objectives, and risks of estate plan.
3. List the risk in failing to plan.
4. Determine who needs estate planning.
5. Describe why there is interest in estate planning.
6. Identify the steps in the estate planning process.
7. Identify the members of the estate planning team.
8. Describe the unauthorized practice of law.

CFP Board Resource Document - Student-Centered Learning Objectives based upon CFP Board Principal Topics.

INTRODUCTION

Many philosophers and great thinkers have contemplated the inevitability of death and taxes. Benjamin Franklin is known for his famous saying that "in this world nothing is certain but death and taxes." Despite Mr. Franklin's words of wisdom, there is often uncertainty when it comes to both death and taxes. While no one likes to plan for their own death, the fact remains that no one lives forever. Unless we prepare for our deaths, there is uncertainty as to where our assets and liabilities will end up when we die. The best way to eliminate some of that uncertainty is by having a properly prepared estate plan that incorporates planning for the accumulation, protection, and disposition of wealth.

Estate planning is complex. Among other things, it is about planning for risks, including the risks of untimely death and its consequences, ill health, artificially sustaining life, inability to manage property, immaturity of heirs, and the application of state intestacy rules that may be inconsistent with a person's wishes. In large measure, estate planning is about the transfer of property, either during life or at death, the methods of effecting those transfers, and the risks associated with those transfers. Estate planning is also about the process of growing old, or not, and the planning for the financial consequences of each possible outcome.

If we knew exactly what we would face in the future, we would arrange our financial affairs, prepare our families and loved ones, get our financial records in order, identify who is to receive what property, advise our relatives what to do if we are unable to make our own decisions, select someone to make critical healthcare decisions for us, confide in someone about our funeral and burial wishes, select someone to care for our children, provide for our children's education, and provide for our spouse. We would evaluate whether we could, in good conscience, leave money or property outright to particular heirs or whether we need to have someone else protect them from themselves and others.

Consider what would happen if you knew you would die in exactly five years. The question that you would face is "what do I do?" As an individual, you may be young, middle age, or older. You may be married, single, or divorced. You may have no children, minor children, adult children, or a combination of both. You may have a low net worth, medium net worth, or high net worth. You may require small or large amounts of money for consumption over the next five years. You may be healthy right now or may be in poor health. You may prefer a traditional burial or cremation. You may wish to exhaust your entire financial estate by artificially sustaining your life or prefer no artificial sustainment of life. You may wish to provide for your spouse and heirs if you have any or you may not wish to provide for anyone's support. You may wish to leave money to charities or not. You may be tax averse or indifferent to taxes.

If you give some thought to the above demographics, attitudes, and goals, there are an endless number of permutations. Estate planning is concerned with addressing the different demographics that each of us face and the risks associated with them, our goals and the risks and likelihood of achieving them, and various attitudes toward planning and our motivations and the consequences of action or inaction. Estate planning involves developing a plan that fits the particular individual and meets the individual's goals and objectives.

It is easy to make the case that everyone needs estate planning. However, most people concentrate on developing a good financial plan for life. In developing a lifetime financial plan, people typically assume they will live to their full life expectancy or beyond. Unfortunately, many do not. The next step most people take is to plan for the financial risks that exist during life. They buy life insurance, health insurance, disability insurance, long-term care insurance, property insurance, and liability insurance to mitigate against these financial risks. Assuming that all of those risk management techniques are adequate, individuals then turn their attention to saving and investing to achieve both short and long-term financial goals. While estate planning is incorporated into all of these tasks, it also concerns itself with the individual person. Anyone can become unable to make their own healthcare decisions. Anyone can become unable to care for themselves physically, financially, or psychologically.

Estate planning involves the transfer of property, which will be addressed throughout this text, but it is about so much more. Estate planning is about being prepared for the expected and the unexpected while taking into consideration the individual client's demographic and family profile, both their assessment and an objective assessment of risks, their goals, their values, and their attitudes about property, heirs, taxation, charities, and life itself. A well-designed estate plan will be very much an individual plan, considering all of the issues mentioned as applied to each particular person.

Marriage Equality (After Obergefell)

In the summer of 2015, the United States Supreme Court legalized same-sex marriage. The landmark decision in Obergefell v. Hodges overturned prior policy that had allowed some states to deny marriage licenses and by default spousal benefits to same-sex couples. Same-sex couples are now able to marry and all states are required to issue licenses and recognize legal marriages of all couples.

Impact of Same-Sex Marriage on Spousal Benefits Outside of Estate Planning

Federal law provides many rights and protections to legally married couples. Marriage equality flowing from the Obergefell case simplifies benefits. Effectively, a spouse is a spouse, regardless of sex or gender. There are federal income tax benefits (e.g., joint income tax filing), retirement benefits (e.g., federal rights to spousal benefits), Social Security benefits, and employee benefits that are all affected by the Obergefell case, but are beyond the scope of this text.

Impact of Same-Sex Marriage in Estate Planning

In the estate planning area, the most obvious impacts of marriage equality at the federal level are in gift splitting (Chapter 5), the marital deduction (Chapters 6 and 10), the portability of any unused lifetime exemption to a spouse (Chapters 6 and 10), the use of charitable remainder trusts with joint spousal non-charitable beneficiaries (Chapter 9), and the use of QTIPs (Chapter 10).

However, because all states must issue marriage licenses and recognize same-sex marriages, there are other implications at the state level. For example, for those who are married, probate (Chapter 4) may no longer be seen as a risk for same-sex married couples. Documents (Chapter 2) may be more accepted as between married couples in comparison to previous documents drawn between non-married couples.

A significant issue remains in the property titling area (Chapter 3). Those states that have tenants by the entirety and community property titling will be required to make these property titling regimes available to same-sex married couples. In states where property that is held as tenants by the entirety (e.g., Florida), receives some asset protection, those same protections will be afforded to same-sex married couples.

Keep in mind as you read this text that a spouse is a spouse, regardless of sex.

Estate Planning Reform

The Economic Growth and Tax Relief Reconciliation Act of 2001 (herein referred to as EGTRRA 2001) was signed by President George W. Bush in June of 2001 resulting in a $1.35 trillion tax cut. While EGTRRA 2001 repealed the estate and generation-skipping transfer tax in 2010, the repeal was phased in over a nine year period (2001 - 2009). In 2010, there was no estate or generation-skipping transfer tax.

Exhibit 1.1 | Estate Tax Reform

Year	Details
2001	Exemption: $675,000; Top Estate Rate: 55%
2005	Exemption: $1.5 million; Top Estate Rate: 47%
2009	Exemption: $3.5 million; Top Estate Rate: 45%
2010	Estate Tax Repealed – Only Applied In 2010
2011	Exemption: $5 million; Top Estate Rate: 35%
2017	Exemption: $5.49 million; Top Estate Rate: 40%
2020	Exemption: $11.58 million; Top Estate Rate: 40%

The Tax Relief, Unemployment Insurance Reauthorization, and Job Creation Act of 2010 (herein referred to as TRA 2010), which was signed into law by President Barack Obama on December 17, 2010, extended the majority of the provisions found within EGTRRA 2001 through December 31, 2012; TRA 2010, in its pertinent parts for purposes of this textbook, reunified the gift and estate tax regime, increased the applicable exemption for generation skipping transfer, gift, and estate taxes to $5,000,000 in 2011 (this amount was indexed for inflation in 2012), and exacted a 35 percent maximum transfer tax rate on any excess transfer. TRA 2010 also introduced the concept of portability of lifetime exemptions as between spouses, and introduced a new formula for calculating previously paid gift tax, the purpose of which was to address discrepancies that resulted from the maximum estate and gift tax rates being decreased to 35 percent for years 2010, 2011, and 2012.

In 2010, there was no estate tax. However, with TRA 2010 in place, executors of estates of decedents that died in 2010 were permitted to opt into the new rates and exemptions regime that were effective as of January 1, 2011.

The American Taxpayer Relief act of 2012 (ATRA) was signed into law in January 2013. Under ATRA, unlike EGTRRA 2001, made the estate and gift tax provisions permanent. ATRA set the estate, gift, and generation skipping transfer tax rates at 40 percent, set the transfer tax exemption at $5 million (indexed for inflation), and made the exemption portability provisions of prior law permanent.

The Tax Cuts and Jobs Act of 2017 (TCJA) signed by President Donald Trump in December 2017 raised the transfer tax exemption to $11,580,000 for 2020 (subject to inflation adjustments in subsequent years), which translates to a unified tax credit of $4,577,800 (2020) as will be explained in Chapters 5 and 6.

This text presents current law, and where applicable, the impact of future changes in the law.

Estate Planning Defined

Estate planning is broadly defined as the process of accumulation, management, conservation, and transfer of wealth considering legal, tax, and personal objectives. Estate planning is planning in anticipation of a person's inevitable death. The goals of estate planning are the effective and efficient transfer of assets. An effective transfer occurs when a person's assets are transferred to the person or institution intended by the transferor. An efficient transfer occurs when transfer costs are minimized consistent with the greatest assurance of effectiveness. Some estate planning experts define estate planning more narrowly to include only conservation and transfer, ignoring the accumulation factor in the broader definition above.

GOALS, OBJECTIVES, & RISKS OF ESTATE PLANNING

Common goals and objectives of estate planning include transferring (distributing) property to particular persons or entities consistent with transferor wishes; minimizing taxes (income, gift, estate, state inheritance, and generation-skipping transfer taxes); minimizing transaction costs associated with the transfer (costs of documents, lawyers, accountants, and the probate process - the legal process of changing title to the decedent's assets from the decedent to the heirs and legatees); maximizing the transfer of assets to heirs; and providing the estate of the decedent with sufficient liquidity to pay for costs that commonly arise upon or around one's death, such as taxes, funeral expenses, and final medical costs.

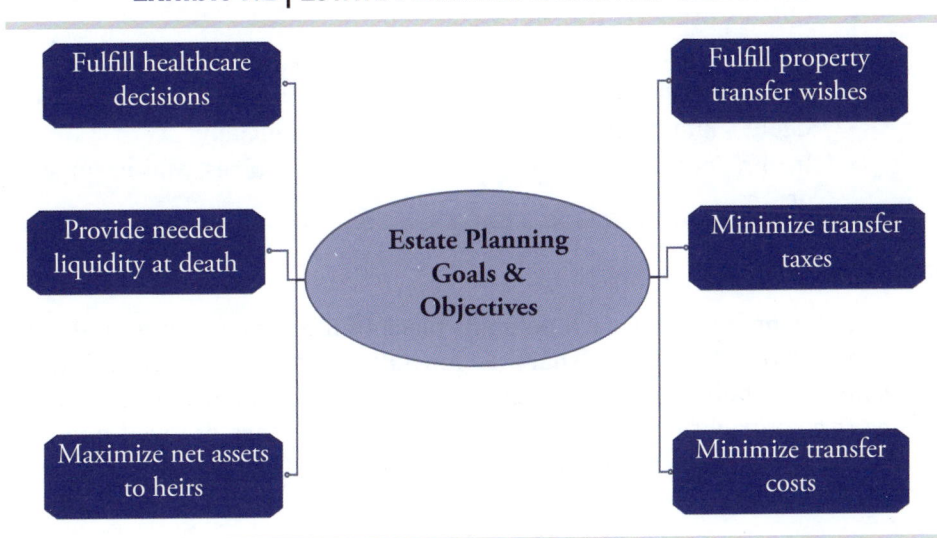

Exhibit 1.2 | Estate Planning Goals and Objectives

Everyone needs a basic estate plan to address health care issues, property management, and the ultimate transfer of property according to their wishes. Typically, the most important estate planning objective is to assure that the decedent's property is transferred to the correct person, persons, or entities in a manner consistent with the decedent's wishes.

> ### Key Concepts
>
> 1. What is estate planning?
> 2. Explain the differences between an efficient and effective transfer.
> 3. What are the common goals of estate planning?
> 4. Why do people avoid estate planning?
> 5. Identify the risks associated with failing to plan for estate transfer.

The process of estate planning requires each of us to face the inevitability of mortality. Clients tend to delay estate planning decisions for both emotional and practical reasons. Some people find contemplating their own mortality too morbid a task to engage in effective planning. Others are simply unaware of the value of their assets and/or lack sufficient knowledge about the **transfer costs** (the costs of avoiding taxes), such as the cost of document preparation, planning, and other professional fees and taxes. Still others may not realize that alternative transfer devices exist, and that each alternative transfer device bears its own costs and risks. Whatever the reason, failing to plan for an estate transfer is itself a risky proposition.

The risks associated with failing to plan for an estate transfer include the transfer of property contrary to the client's wishes, insufficient financial provision for the client's family, and the emergence of liquidity problems at the time of death. Any one of these risks could be catastrophic for the decedent's heirs (those who inherit under state law) and family. For example, the disposition of a decedent's assets could be delayed for many years in the probate court if that decedent has no will or if conflicts arise among the heirs. Another risk of not preparing an effective estate plan is exposure to excessively high transfer tax rates. The gift and estate tax structure is progressive, and rises to 40 percent for a decedent whose taxable estate exceeds $11,580,000 (in 2020).

Exhibit 1.3 | Risks in Failing to Plan an Estate

- Client's property transfer wishes go unfulfilled.
- Transfer taxes are excessive.
- Transfer costs are excessive.
- Client's family not properly provided for financially.
- Insufficient liquidity to cover client's debts, taxes, and costs at death.

Who Needs Estate Planning

Everyone needs estate planning. While each person's place in life, family status, and net worth may be different, one characteristic all persons share is mortality. Estate planning allows individuals to minimize taxes, ensure that their loved ones receive their property, and in a manner consistent with the transferor's wishes (e.g., outright or in trust) and arrange for the care of loved ones. Estate planning attempts to ensure that each person's wishes are carried out when they die.

chapter 1

Why the Interest in Estate Planning

There is significant interest in the topic of estate planning for two primary reasons. The first reason is the onerous excise taxes that are charged for transfers during life or at death (up to 40% at the federal level alone). The second reason is that everyone has an interest in making sure that when they die their worldly possessions are transferred to the persons or institutions that they choose. When a person dies, all of the assets they own will be transferred to heirs and legatees (family and friends), institutions (charities), or the government (in the form of taxes). Transfers to qualified charities are not taxed but transfers to family and friends exceeding certain thresholds are potentially subject to transfer taxes. Because the transfer tax rates are substantial, the interest in tax avoidance and planning is also substantial.

> **Quick Quiz 1.1**
>
> 1. Estate planning is the process of accumulation, management, conservation, and transfer of wealth considering only the estate tax consequences.
>   a. True
>   b. False
> 2. An effective transfer occurs when a person's assets are transferred to the person or institution intended by that person.
>   a. True
>   b. False
>
> False, True.

Tools for Wealth Protection

Since estate planning primarily focuses on wealth transfer, protecting current and projected wealth is often an important consideration in estate planning. There are many insurance products designed to protect current wealth and future income, including life insurance, disability insurance, long-term care insurance, and business disability insurance, to name a few. The government even provides some of this protection through Medicare and the provision of Social Security disability benefits. Having sufficient insurance coverage to hedge against the risks facing a person is one of the basic elements of an effective estate plan.

THE ESTATE PLANNING PROCESS

The Seven Basic Steps

There are seven basic steps in the estate planning process:
1. Gather and analyze the information necessary to understand the client's personal and financial circumstances, including the client's current financial statements and existing estate planning documents.
2. Identify and select the client's transfer objectives, including family and charitable objectives.
3. Analyze the client's current estate plan and potential alternative courses of action.
4. Develop a comprehensive plan of transfers consistent with all information and objectives.
5. Present the estate planning recommendations.
6. Implement the estate planning recommendations.
7. Review the estate plan periodically and update the plan when necessary (especially for changes in family situations).

The first two steps will be discussed in this chapter and the remaining steps are covered throughout the rest of this text.

Establish the Client/Planner Relationship

Preliminary to the seven-step estate planning process, the relationship between the client and planner must be established and defined. The client / planner relationship may arise in several different ways, but clients are often reluctant to seek out a planner to plan their estate. This reluctance may stem from several causes including concern about the expense associated with estate planning, the belief that estate planning is only for the extremely wealthy, or the desire to avoid the inevitability of the client's own mortality. Therefore, the opportunity to discuss the issue of estate planning generally arises when the planner is meeting with the client for financial planning matters other than estate planning.

> ### Key Concepts
> 1. Identify the risks associated with failing to plan for estate transfer.
> 2. Identify the seven basic steps of the estate planning process.
> 3. What is usually the most important estate planning client objective?

The estate planning engagement is the same as any other financial planning engagement. The planner should meet with the client, detail the services to be provided, and the expectations of both the client and the planner. The financial planner should then send an engagement letter to the client detailing the information discussed in the meeting.

Collecting Client Information and Defining Transfer Objectives

Collecting a client's information is essential to gain a complete financial and family picture of the client and to assist the client in identifying their financial risks. Information about prospective **heirs** (those who inherit under state law) and **legatees** (those who receive property under a will) needs to be collected to properly arrange for any transfer that the client wants to make.

To begin the estate planning process, the planner should collect:
- Current financial statements (Statement of Financial Position, Income Statement).
- A detailed list of assets and liabilities, including, for each asset, the fair market value, adjusted basis, expected growth rate, how title is being held, and the date acquired.
- Family information - information about parents and children, including the age and health of each family member.
- Copies of medical, disability, and long-term care insurance policies.
- Copies of all current life insurance policies identifying the owner of each policy, the named insured, and the designated beneficiaries.
- Copies of annuity contracts.
- Copies of wills and trusts.
- Identification of powers of attorney and general powers of appointment.
- Copies of all previously filed income tax, gift tax, and estate tax returns.
- Identification of assets previously transferred to loved ones.

After collecting the client and family information, the client's transfer objectives must be determined. Usually the client's most important objective is to transfer his assets as he wishes (an effective transfer). Next, the client generally wishes to maximize the net transfers to his heirs while minimizing the reduction in his or her estate due to taxes and transfer costs. **Exhibit 1.4** provides a list of common transfer objectives.

Exhibit 1.4 | Common Transfer Objectives

1. Transfer property as desired and minimize estate and transfer taxes to maximize the assets received by heirs.
2. Avoid the probate process.
3. Use lifetime transfers – gifts.
4. Meet liquidity needs at death.
5. Plan for children.
6. Plan for the incapacity of the transferor.
7. Provide for the needs of the transferor's surviving spouse.
8. Fulfill the transferor's charitable intentions.

THE ESTATE PLANNING TEAM

The estate planning team commonly consists of an attorney, a Certified Public Accountant (CPA), a life insurance consultant, perhaps a trust officer, and a financial planner. Each expert plays a distinct role in the planning process. The typical role of the financial planner is to help integrate the work of the estate planning team in developing the overall estate plan.

The estate planning process is complex and can be somewhat confusing to the client. A licensed attorney is always a part of the team, as the process requires explaining legal matters and drafting numerous legal documents. A CPA is usually involved as a member of the estate planning team because the process requires the identification of assets, the calculation of the related adjusted tax basis, as well as other tax issues. A life insurance specialist is usually involved to help assure liquidity at death, provide asset protection, and provide guidance as to the use of insurance to fulfill many of the client's transfer objectives. A trustee or trust officer manages the assets of trusts used in the estate plan. The financial planner sometimes serves as the team captain and assists in data collection, identification of goals and objectives, analysis, and investment decisions.

While each member of the planning team is often knowledgeable in estate planning, each specialist brings a particular and unique perspective, the combination of which is likely to produce a better result for the client. Experts who are not also licensed attorneys, should be careful not to engage in acts that could be considered the unauthorized practice of law.

The Unauthorized Practice of Law

To practice law an individual must be a licensed attorney in the jurisdiction where he or she is practicing. Simply being educated or knowledgeable in law is not sufficient to give legal advice; licensing is required by that jurisdiction (state). Certain activities are clearly reserved for a licensed attorney, such as the drafting of legal documents. A professional who is not a licensed attorney should avoid offering legal advice on any matter. Offering legal opinions or conclusions is considered the **unauthorized practice of law**. Consequently, if a matter arises that requires legal advice, the planner should refer the client to a licensed attorney. Each state determines the requirements necessary to become a licensed attorney in their state and also defines the activities that constitute the practice of law. Financial planners and other non lawyers should have an understanding of their applicable state laws before engaging in activities that may be construed as the unauthorized practice of law.

> **Quick Quiz 1.2**
>
> 1. A financial planner should consult with CPAs, attorneys, trust officers and insurance professionals throughout the estate planning process.
>   a. True
>   b. False
> 2. A financial planner may be called on to collect client information, analyze the information, and present an estate plan to the client to minimize estate transfer taxes.
>   a. True
>   b. False
> 3. To reduce the cost of estate planning, a financial planner or CPA should always draft and review all of his client's wills.
>   a. True
>   b. False
>
> True, False, False.

OVERVIEW OF THE TEXT

This text is designed for use in graduate and upper-division undergraduate classes by students interested in acquiring an understanding of estate planning from a professional planning viewpoint, and, in addition, incorporates all of the educational topics required for an Estate Planning Course in a CFP® Board Registered program.

Since estate planning is typically addressed subsequent to risk management and longer-term saving and investing planning (such as saving for a home, for retirement, and for children's education), a working knowledge of those topics is presumed. This text is not intended to be a substitute for courses in those substantive areas, and is not intended to be used as an introductory course in financial planning. The layout of this text assumes that the reader has previously been exposed to, and has developed a basic understanding of insurance planning, investment planning, income taxation, and retirement planning.

chapter 1

Estate planning is a process that matches a client's goals, needs, attitudes, and financial circumstances with available wealth transfer planning options. Effective estate tax planning requires the planner to understand:

1. The client's goals and needs (both personal and financial)
2. The client's attitudes (including risk tolerance)
3. The client's financial circumstances
4. The client's assets
5. The basic principles of insurance, investment, and income tax planning
6. The basic principles of estate, gift, and generation skipping transfer taxation
7. The details of the transfer tax rules related to client planning topics

This understanding and knowledge base can then be employed by planners to identify, recommend, and assist in the implementation of a useful wealth transfer planning strategy for the client.

The organizing structure of this text presents basic concepts and methods of wealth transfer planning (Chapters 1-4), followed by an overview of the gift and estate tax systems (chapters 5-6). After setting a base for understanding transfer taxes, the text turns to specific planning applications relevant for clients (Chapters 7-12). These chapters often review basic material covered in earlier planning courses, and discuss specific applications of the transfer tax rules to planning situations. Some of these chapters also expand on the basic tax concepts introduced in the gift and estate tax chapters (Chapters 5-6) to assist the reader in developing a deeper understanding of the planning opportunities available to clients. The last few chapters of the text deal with more advanced planning by introducing post mortem planning (Chapter 12) the generation skipping transfer tax (Chapter 13) and providing a comprehensive case study example for estate planning (Chapter 14).

Exhibit 1.5 | Chapter Summary

Chapter 1 introduces the estate planning process and covers the common goals and objections clients seek to accomplish through estate planning.
Chapter 2 introduces the typical documents used in the estate planning process, including wills, powers of attorney, durable powers of attorney for health care, living wills and do not resuscitate orders (DNRs).
Chapter 3 discusses how property titling affects the disposition of property at death, with particular reference to ownership in the form of a fee simple, tenancy in common, joint tenancy with right of survivorship, tenancy by the entirety, and community property.
Chapter 4 covers the probate process, and discusses other ways that property can pass from a decedent to a beneficiary. Basic planning techniques for titling property to accomplish estate planning objectives are discussed in Chapter 4.
Chapters 5 and 6 introduce the gift and estate tax systems. While the primary purpose of these chapters is to give the reader a view of the overall tax system (a view of the forest, to use the colloquialism), some basic planning techniques are discussed in the context of the gift and estate tax rules. Recall, as you read these chapters, that at this point in the text you want to develop a basic understanding of how these tax systems work and the formula used to calculate gift and estate tax liability. Details on specific components of the overall calculation (a view of the trees as opposed to the forest), such as the marital and charitable deductions, will be discussed in detail in subsequent chapters.
Chapters 7 and 8 explore common planning techniques used by clients to accomplish their estate planning goals. Chapter 7 looks primarily at tools, other than trust vehicles, that are used to effectuate transfers during the client's lifetime and subsequent to the client's death, while Chapter 8 provides a brief review of the operation (and taxation) of a trust followed by a discussion of the various types of trust arrangements that can be used in the estate planning process.
Chapters 9 and 10 take a deeper look at the only two deductions allowed in the estate tax calculation – the charitable and marital deductions – and review various techniques used by estate planners to take advantage of these deductions. While Chapters 5 and 6 gave you a bird's eye view of the transfer tax process (a look at the forest), Chapters 9 and 10 take a closer look at some of the trees in that forest. In practice, the game of avoiding estate or gift tax often involves use of the charitable and marital deductions, so these topics are of particular importance to an estate planner.
Chapter 11 reviews the basics of life insurance planning, with particular reference on the gift and estate tax consequences of life insurance in planning for a client. Given the popularity of life insurance in the risk-management process, understanding the transfer tax consequences of using life insurance is important for every estate planner.
Chapter 12 looks at administrative issues associated with the estate of a decedent. Some of these issues are planning oriented, such as providing liquidity for the estate and the decedent's family, while others focus on administrative steps that must be taken by the decedent's representatives after his or her death. Special elections available to the executor/administration after the death of the decedent that can limit exposure to estate tax liability are explored.
Chapter 13 introduces the Generation-skipping transfer tax, a tax designed to replace lost tax revenue for the government when taxpayers engage in very effective estate planning strategies. While the generation-skipping transfer tax is usually associated with high net worth planning, there are some implications for more modest estates as well. Clients who wish to benefit grandchildren need to take the generation skipping transfer tax rules into consideration when developing their overall estate plans.
Chapter 14 discusses various aspects of an estate plan and provides two comprehensive case studies. The Tony and Gail case includes recommended solutions. The Benny and Martha Franklin case is more open ended and does include recommended solutions in the text.

KEY TERMS

Effective Transfer - A transfer of a person's assets to the person or charitable institution intended by that person.

Efficient Transfer - A transfer in which costs of the transfer are minimized consistent with the greatest assurance of effectiveness.

Estate Planning - The process of accumulation, management, conservation, and transfer of wealth considering legal, tax, and personal objectives.

Heir - One who inherits under state law.

Legatee - One who inherits under the will.

Probate Process - The legal proceeding that serves to prove the validity of existing wills, supervise the orderly distribution of decedent's assets to the heirs, and protect creditors by insuring that valid debts of the estate are paid.

Transfer Costs - Includes the gift and estate taxes and the costs of avoiding taxes, such as the cost of documents, planning, trusts, and other professional fees.

Transferee - A person who receives a transfer (a donee receives a gift, a buyer receives property, an heir or legatee receives property from a decedent).

Transferor - A person who makes a transfer (a donor makes a gift, a seller transfers, a decedent leaves property to others).

Unauthorized Practice of Law - The proffering of legal advice or services by one who is not a licensed attorney.

DISCUSSION QUESTIONS

SOLUTIONS to the discussion questions can be found exclusively within the chapter. Once you have completed an initial reading of the chapter, go back and highlight the answers to these questions.

1. Define estate planning.

2. Explain the estate and generation-skipping transfer ramifications of the Economic Growth and Tax Relief Reconciliation Act of 2001.

3. Explain some of the potential ramifications of the extension of the EGTRRA 2001 through the Tax Relief, Unemployment Insurance Reauthorization, and Job Creation Act of 2010 (TRA 2010).

4. How did ATRA 2012 impact estate planning?

5. How did the Tax Cuts and Jobs Act of 2017 (TCJA) impact estate planning?

6. What is an effective transfer?

7. What is an efficient transfer?

8. List three common goals of estate planning.

9. List some of the reasons people avoid estate planning.

10. Discuss some of the risks associated with failing to plan for estate transfer.

11. List the seven basic steps of the estate planning process.

12. What is usually the most important client objective?

13. List the members of the estate planning team and describe their roles.

14. Why must advisors who are not an attorney be concerned with the unauthorized practice of law?

MULTIPLE-CHOICE PROBLEMS

A sample of multiple choice problems is provided below. Additional multiple choice problems are available at money-education.com by accessing the Student Practice Portal.

1. Which of the following is included in the definition of estate planning?
    1. Asset management.
    2. Accumulation of wealth.
    3. Asset preservation.
        a. 1 only.
        b. 1 and 2.
        c. 2 and 3.
        d. 1, 2, and 3.

2. Which of the following does not need estate planning?
    a. Charles, age 30, married with two minor children, and a net worth of $375,000.
    b. Sheila, age 35, never been married, one severely disabled son.
    c. Cynthia, age 45, single, has a net worth of $450,000 and two dogs.
    d. All of the above need estate planning.

3. Who on the estate planning team usually calculates the adjusted basis of assets and addresses tax issues?
    a. Licensed attorney.
    b. Certified Public Accountant (CPA).
    c. Financial planner.
    d. Trust officer.

4. Harley is a financial planner in the state of Iowa. Although he attended one year of law school, Harley is not a licensed attorney. Which of the following actions would be considered the practice of law?
    a. Drafting wills, trust documents, and powers of attorney.
    b. Reviewing wills, trust documents, and powers of attorney.
    c. Directing a client to seek legal advice from a licensed attorney.
    d. Acting as trustee for a client's trust.

5. Jimmy would like to meet with you regarding his estate plan. Jimmy is 55-years-old, and currently has an estate that would be subject to estate tax. His wife died of lung cancer last year. Jimmy has three children, ages 23, 26, and 32, and one grandchild, age 4. He does not have any dependents. Which of the following options would be the least likely reason for Jimmy to have an estate plan?
    a. Minimize estate and transfer taxes.
    b. Minimize costs.
    c. Plan for his children.
    d. Plan for his incapacity.

QUICK QUIZ EXPLANATIONS

Quick Quiz 1.1
1. False. To result in an effective transfer of assets, estate planning must first consider the goals and objectives of the client. Given the overriding goals of the client, his or her affairs should be arranged to minimize estate taxes and other transfer costs.
2. True.

Quick Quiz 1.2
1. True.
2. False. In addition to minimizing taxes, the planner must ensure that the client's wishes for asset transfers are achieved.
3. False. Unless the financial planner is a licensed attorney, he or she should not draft the client's will, since this would be considered the unauthorized practice of law.

2
BASIC ESTATE PLANNING DOCUMENTS

LEARNING OBJECTIVES

1. List and describe the basic documents generally included in an estate plan.
2. Describe a will and its essential parts.
3. Define intestacy.
4. Describe the advantages and limitations of wills.
5. Identify the three types of wills.
6. Distinguish between per capita and per stirpes.
7. Describe a side letter of instruction.
8. Identify statutes affecting wills.
9. Distinguish between powers of appointment and powers of attorney.
10. Describe the consequences of a general power of appointment.
11. Describe the durability feature used in some powers of attorney.
12. Describe a springing power.
13. Describe directives for healthcare including a durable power of attorney for healthcare, living will/advance medical directive, and a do not resuscitate order.

CFP Board Resource Document - Student-Centered Learning Objectives based upon CFP Board Principal Topics.

BASIC DOCUMENTS INCLUDED IN AN ESTATE PLAN

Effective estate planning requires the execution of some basic estate planning documents. These documents effectuate the transfer of property at the death of the testator (the maker of a will), grant powers to others for both property and health care decisions, and direct doctors and hospitals on matters concerning the artificial sustenance of the testator's life. The basic documents that are used in estate planning include:

- wills,
- side letters of instruction,
- powers of attorney for property,
- durable powers of attorney for health care,
- living wills or advance medical directives, and
- do not resuscitate orders.

This chapter will describe each of these documents, discuss their importance and clarify why an estate plan is incomplete without the appropriate documents.

WILLS

A **will** is an essential part of any estate plan. A will is a legal document that gives the **testator** (will-maker) the opportunity to control the distribution of his property at death and thus avoid his state's intestacy laws (the distribution scheme provided by each state for those individuals that die without a valid will). A will may be amended or revoked by the testator at any time prior to his death provided that the testator is legally competent. The provisions of a will are not invoked until the death of the testator. Any assets that do not automatically transfer upon the testator's death under state contract laws, state property titling law, or state trust law (such as retirement benefits with a designated beneficiary, jointly owned property, and life insurance policies) will become part of the probate estate, which is normally distributed according to the will. The will is the voice of the decedent directing how probate assets should be administered and distributed through and from the probate process.

chapter 2

Intestacy

A decedent who has a valid will is said to die "**testate**." To die "**intestate**" is to die without a valid will. A decedent who dies with a will that does not dispose of all probatable property is said to die "partially intestate." An individual may not have a valid will for several reasons, including the failure to write a will, or perhaps the will is invalid under state law. A will may be invalid under state law if:

- the decedent did not comply with the testamentary requirements of the domiciliary state at the time of the execution of the will;
- if the decedent moved to another state of domicile and failed to update his will to meet the new state law requirements (however, if the will is valid in a previous state of domicile, then it may be held to be valid in a new domicile); or
- the decedent did not satisfy the necessary requirements (such as testamentary competence) to execute a will.

> **Key Concepts**
>
> 1. What are the basic documents used in estate planning?
> 2. What is intestacy and what problems arise when someone dies intestate?
> 3. Briefly define the three basic types of wills.
> 4. What are the advantages and limitations of wills?
> 5. List and describe the common clauses in wills.

In the case of intestacy, the law of the decedent's state of **domicile** (the place where a person votes, lives, pays taxes, etc.) at the time of his death, determines how the decedent's personal property will be distributed. Personal property included in the probate estate is distributed according to the will or the laws of intestacy in the state of domicile of the decedent. Real property, on the other hand, is distributed based on the laws of the state in which the property is actually located (the **situs**). Non-domiciliary states determine who receives probatable real property in their state by applying that state's intestacy laws in the absence of a valid will. The probate process in a state other than the state of domicile is called **ancillary probate**.

The Uniform Probate Code (UPC) was introduced in 1969 as a set of model rules to serve as a guideline for many states' probate laws. The UPC was substantially revised several times, the most recent being 2019. Although state intestacy laws vary greatly from state to state, 18 states (Maine, Massachusetts, Pennsylvania, New Jersey, South Carolina, Michigan, Minnesota, North Dakota, South Dakota, Nebraska, Montana, Idaho, Utah, Colorado, Arizona, New Mexico, Alaska and Hawaii) have adopted at least part of this uniform code. Under the Uniform Probate Code, in the absence of a valid will, close relatives receive the decedent's assets. Close relatives include the surviving spouse, lineal descendants, parents, descendants of the decedent's parents (siblings, nieces, and nephews), grandparents, and descendants of the decedent's grandparents (aunts, uncles, and cousins). The Uniform Probate Code treats adopted descendants in the same manner as biological descendants and treats relatives of the half blood in the same manner as relatives of whole blood. In cases where no person is considered qualified to receive the assets, the property by default transfers to the decedent's state of domicile, or if real property is held outside the state of domicile, to the state of its situs. When a decedent has no heirs at law and the state receives the decedent's property, the property is said to **escheat** to the state. Exhibit 2.1 provides an example of how a state's intestate succession law may be phrased. Practitioners should review their own state's intestacy laws, and be aware of its provisions.

The old adage "one size does not fit all" applies to state intestacy laws since they may not distribute property in the same manner that the client would like their property to be distributed. For example, in certain states, a surviving spouse's legal statutory share of the decedent spouse's estate under intestacy laws is equal to a child's share. In these states, the surviving spouse's share who has one child would be one-half, but a surviving spouse who has nine children would only receive a one-tenth share. Other states provide the surviving spouse with a life estate (discussed in Chapter 3) with the remainder beneficiaries being any children of the decedent. Under other state laws, the surviving spouse may be forced to share with the deceased spouse's parents or siblings when the decedent had no children. In addition, although each child's needs may be quite different, children are usually treated equally and, therefore, not necessarily equitably.

Intestacy requires the appointment of an **administrator** (an estate representative appointed by the probate court), as opposed to an **executor** (an estate representative appointed by the decedent through the will). In most states, the individual with the largest share in the estate is entitled to be appointed an administrator. The probate court must approve the administrator of the estate and the administrator typically has to furnish a surety bond. In contrast, an executor is chosen by the decedent, and although he must be approved by the probate court, the executor is generally not required to furnish a surety bond, thus reducing the overall cost of administering the estate. This topic is discussed more fully in Chapter 4.

Exhibit 2.1 | Sample State Intestate Succession Law

If any part of a decedent's estate is not effectively disposed of by will, the intestate share will generally be distributed in the following order and manner:

1. A surviving spouse is generally first in line to get any assets from the intestate estate. However, the amount to which a surviving spouse is entitled varies as follows:
   - A surviving spouse is entitled to the entire intestate estate if the decedent is not survived by lineal issue (i.e., descendants such as children and grandchildren).
   - If the decedent is survived by issue, a surviving spouse gets the first $50,000, plus one-half of the remaining property in the intestate estate.

2. Any part of the intestate estate not passing to the surviving spouse as indicated above, or the entire intestate estate if there is no surviving spouse, passes as follows to the first applicable group:
   - Decedent's issue, taking by representation (per stirpes, as discussed later in this chapter).
   - Decedent's surviving parent or parents equally.
   - Issue of decedent's parents, taking by representation (brothers, sisters, nieces, and nephews).
   - If none of the above relatives are available, but the decedent is survived by one or more grandparents or immediate issue of grandparents (i.e., decedent's aunts and uncles), half of the estate passes to the paternal grandparents if both survive, or to the surviving paternal grandparent or to the issue of the paternal grandparents (taking by representation) if both are deceased. The other half passes to the maternal relatives in the same manner. If there is no surviving grandparent or issue of grandparent on either the paternal or maternal side, the entire estate passes to the relatives on the other side in the same manner as the half portion would. For purposes of this category, issue of grandparents does not include issue more remote than grandchildren of such grandparents.
   - Great-grandchildren of decedent's grandparents, split one-half to the great-grandchildren of the paternal grandparents side and one-half to the great-grandchildren of the maternal grandparents side, with per capita distributions to each side. If there are no great-grandchildren of grandparents on one side, the whole amount goes to the other half (still split per capita).

3. If there is no taker under any of the above provisions, the intestate estate passes (escheats) to the state.

Advantages of Wills

A properly drafted will can eliminate many of the problems that arise from dying intestate. An effective will also provides other benefits to the testator, including the ability to:
- select an executor as the decedent's personal representative to administer the estate
- transfer assets that do not automatically transfer at death via contract or operation of law
- designate a guardian for minor children and/or dependents
- transfer assets to a designated charity
- maximize the utilization of any marital deduction
- direct that certain people do not receive any inheritance (disinheritance)
- implement provisions to minimize any estate tax burden
- direct the payment of the estate's share of the estate tax burden as well as the designation of the source of funds to be used to pay such estate taxes

Limitations of Wills

Although a will can provide many benefits and advantages, a will also has limitations. Some of these limitations include:
- The potential for a will contest, particularly if the decedent disinherits potential beneficiaries. The estate may have to litigate if the will is contested, which will increase costs (attorney fees) and delay distributions to other heirs or legatees.
- The possibility that courts may invalidate certain restrictions and/or sections in a will that put impermissible conditions on the receipt of assets or that have too many constraints on the transfer of assets. For example, a will that requires a beneficiary/heir to commit an illegal act in order to receive the asset will be deemed invalid.
- Assets that pass automatically by contract or by law supersede the transfers provided for under the will. Property that passes by beneficiary designee (retirement plans, life insurance policies), through pay on/transfer on death clauses (bank accounts and brokerage accounts), through trust, or through property titled with a survivorship feature will be transferred directly to those named beneficiaries or joint tenants and will not be a part of the probate process and thus not distributed according to any will provisions or intestacy laws.
- A poorly drafted will that contains conflicting transfer provisions, reference to deceased heirs, or nonexistent property may become invalid or the testator's wishes may not be clearly understood.

> ### Quick Quiz 2.1
>
> 1. A nuncupative will is a handwritten will dated and signed by the testator.
>   a. True
>   b. False
> 2. A will controls the distribution of all property.
>   a. True
>   b. False
> 3. A decedent who dies without a will cannot appoint an executor.
>   a. True
>   b. False
> 4. The intestacy laws vary from state to state.
>   a. True
>   b. False
> 5. A holographic will is drawn by an attorney, complying with the statutes for wills of the domiciliary state.
>   a. True
>   b. False
>
> False, False, True, True, False.

Types of Wills

In most states, the only requirements necessary to execute a valid will are:
1. the will must be in writing, and
2. the will must be signed at its logical end by the testator.[1]

The three basic forms of wills include statutory, holographic, and nuncupative. While most wills are statutory wills (professionally drafted by an attorney), some states continue to recognize the other two types of wills.

- **Statutory wills** are drawn by an attorney, and comply with the statutes for wills of the domiciliary state. Statutory wills generally must be witnessed. Statutory wills must be typed or be in writing, be signed by the testator (generally in front of witnesses), and be signed by the witnesses. Typically, a statutory will includes a self-proving affidavit which aids in the institution of probate proceedings when the testator dies.
- **Holographic wills** are handwritten (not typed) by the testator and include the material provisions of a will. The holographic will must be dated and signed by the testator, but most states do not require a witness. Holographic wills are valid in most states.
- **Nuncupative wills** are oral, dying declarations made before a sufficient number of witnesses. In some states, nuncupative wills may only be effective to pass personal property, not real property, and the dollar amount transferred by this method may be limited. The use of nuncupative wills is restrictive and is not valid in most states. In states where such wills are permitted, the witnesses must generally submit an affidavit declaring the testator's final wishes.

Exhibit 2.2 | Types of Wills

- **Statutory Wills**
  - Drafted by an attorney and complies with the statutes of the domiciliary state.
  - Generally must be witnessed and signed by the testator.
- **Holographic Wills**
  - Generally handwritten by testator.
  - It must be signed and dated by the testator but does not usually require a witness.
  - Valid in most states.
- **Noncupative Wills**
  - These are oral, dying declarations made before a sufficient number of witnesses.
  - Generally not valid in most states and they only apply to tangible property.

---

1. It should be noted that states might have other requirements. For example, Louisiana requires that a valid will be signed on each page by the testator.

Wills may also be classified based on the function or characteristics of the will. For example, two individuals may sometimes execute identical wills that leave all assets to the other person. This type of will is generally used by spouses who want all assets to go to the other spouse at death. This type of simple will may be referred to as a **mutual** or **reciprocal will** and if executed by spouses it may be called a **"sweetheart" will** or an "I Love You" will. Reciprocal wills, like all other wills, are not permanently binding on the individuals making such will and can be changed at any time.

In some instances, two or more individuals, usually spouses, will execute one will, called a **joint will**, that transfers their common interest in property to one individual. When the first party dies and the will is probated, the will contractually binds the surviving party to dispose of their assets in the manner set forth in the joint will. The intent of this type of will is for two or more individuals, usually spouses, to agree on who will receive the property in advance of the first death and contractually bind the survivor to the agreement. This type of will is recognized in many states and is often used in situations where an individual enters into a second marriage and wants to protect his or her children from a previous marriage. This type of arrangement is generally not recommended because it binds the surviving spouse to dispose of property without considering future events (including future tax law changes) and there are other transfer devices that will more appropriately achieve the desired objective.

Electronic Wills

In 2019, The National Conference of Commissioners on Uniform State Laws adopted the Uniform Electronic Wills Act (UEWA). The intent of the UEWA is to permit testators to create an electronic will that can be executed, witnessed and notarized in a real-time audio visual meeting. States that adopt the UEWA will permit valid wills to be created without witnesses and notaries being physically present with the testator upon execution of the document. The UEWA builds on the Federal Electronic Signatures in Global and National Commerce Act (ESIGN) and the State Uniform Electronic Transaction Act (UETA) to expand the use of electronic signatures to the execution of wills. In permitting online meetings for will execution, the UETA would permit those who are unable or unwilling to travel to execute their will.

While the availability to execute a will electronically may be attractive to some, there are some valid concerns raised about this new approach. First, it may be possible that individuals executing an electronic will may be more susceptible to fraud and duress. In a traditional will execution ceremony presided over by an attorney, it may be easier to ascertain whether the testator is signing the will as their own free act and deed. In contrast, when a will is executed electronically, there could be influence from someone just out of view of the camera that is not observed by the witnesses and notary. Second, if the will is truly an electronic will and will not be printed on paper, a question arises as to where the will should be stored and whether there should be standard electronic file formats so that the will can be read on a computer many years down the road when the testator dies. Over the past few decades, some services have emerged which allow individuals to store electronic copies of their wills that can be accessed if the will is lost or misplaced, but none of these services have official recognition from probate courts as of the date of this writing. Finally, concerns may arise concerning the revocation of an electronic will. While a physical will can be revoked by defacing or destroying it, an electronic will may have to be revoked by execution of a subsequent will. Even if the electronic will is deleted, other copies may exist, which can create confusion unless the will is formally revoked in a subsequently executed will.

Nevada was the first state in the United States to permit execution of electronic wills. Beginning in 2001, Nevada permitted execution of wills using electronic signatures of the testator, witnesses, and notary, and required that only one authoritative copy of the will must be maintained and controlled by the testator. Beginning January 1, 2020 Residents of Florida are also able to execute electronic wills. Florida law accomplished this by expanding the definition of "appearing before" a notary to mean "outside the physical presence of another person, but able to see, hear, and communicate with the person by means of audio-video communication technology." As a result of the Coronavirus Epidemic of 2020, the Governor of Connecticut temporarily (from April to June of 2020) authorized, by executive order, the online execution of Wills provided that the execution of the Will was overseen by an Attorney. While, as of the date of this writing, several other states (Alabama, Colorado, Connecticut, Delaware, Georgia, Illinois, Iowa, Kansas, Minnesota, Nevada, North Carolina, North Dakota, Pennsylvania, South Dakota, Texas, Utah, Virginia, Washington, and West Virginia) permit electronic notarization of certain documents, only Nevada and Florida (and Connecticut, on a temporary basis) permit electronic execution of Wills. Perhaps, over the next decade or so, other states will also permit this using the Uniform Electronic Wills Act as a guide.

Legal Capacity to Execute a Will

To execute a valid will, the testator must have sufficient legal capacity. A will is considered valid when the will maker is the age of majority in his domiciliary state, or is an emancipated minor, and when the will maker has legal testamentary capacity. A testator has legal testamentary capacity if he has sufficient mental capacity to:
- understand the consequences of writing the will;
- understand the nature and extent of the property being disposed of by the will; and
- recognize the natural objects of his or her bounty (those friends and relatives who have any claim to the testator's assets).

It is often said that the testator must be of "**sound mind**." The "sound mind" mental capacity rules that apply to wills are not as rigorous as the capacity rules that are required to form contracts. In other words, a person who may not have the legal capacity to form a contract may nonetheless have sufficient legal capacity to execute a will to transfer his assets at death, provided that the conditions specified above are met.

Heirs, Legatees, and Devisees

Individuals who are beneficiaries of an estate are referred to by many names. **Heirs** are individuals who are eligible to receive a portion of a decedent's estate under the intestacy law of the state. Heirs are related to the decedent, and may include the decedent's spouse, siblings, children, parents, nieces, nephews, grandparents, aunts, uncles, and cousins. A **legatee** is a person who is named as a beneficiary in a will. Legatees may also be heirs (if they are related to the decedent and would be eligible to receive a share of the decedent's estate under the intestacy laws), but do not have to be heirs, and could even be non-natural persons, such as businesses or charities. A **devisee** is a person named to receive real estate under the will. As such, a devisee is always considered to be a legatee, and may also be an heir (if he or she is related to the taxpayer and is eligible to receive a portion of the decedent's estate under the intestacy laws. Some states have slightly different definitions of these terms, so it is important for an advisor to understand the rules for the state of practice. **Exhibit 2.3** summarizes the differences between heirs, legatees, and devisees.

Exhibit 2.3 | Heir vs. Legatee vs. Devisee

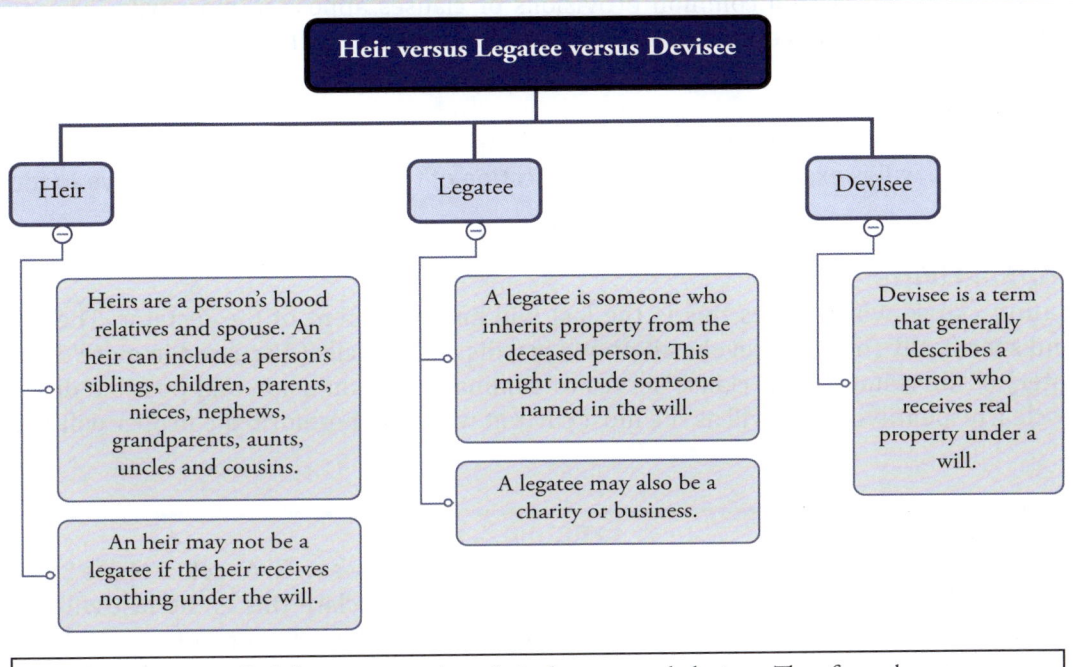

Note: Each state will define terms such as heir, legatee, and devisee. Therefore, these terms are sometimes defined differently than what is presented in this exhibit.

Note: The term beneficiary may also be used to describe a legatee or devisee, but is often used to describe someone who inherits from a contract (such as life insurance) or a retirement account.

Will Contests

All or part of a will may be invalidated by the probate court if the will was executed by a testator who did not have sufficient capacity. Invalidation may occur when an individual, usually an heir-at-law that has been excluded from the will, successfully contests the will. A will contest typically includes a claim that the testator did not have the capacity to create a will or that the testator was subject to undue influence from another person. Undue influence occurs when the decedent was susceptible to influence from a third party (such as a caregiver), the third party had the means and opportunity to exercise influence over the decedent and the decedent made a disposition because of such influence. To avoid the appearance of undue influence, attorneys and financial advisors should avoid drafting wills or assisting in distribution planning when they will be named as legatee or devisee, particularly in instances where the professional is not a related party. In some instances, attorneys and financial advisors may feel obligated to assist related parties with their estate planning, but in these cases, extra caution should be taken to avoid future will contests.

Common Clauses in Wills

All wills are unique, but certain common provisions or clauses appear in most wills. These common clauses, found in even the simplest of attorney-prepared (statutory) wills, include:

An Introductory Clause

An **introductory clause** to identify the testator. The testator's full name and residence, the state of domicile where the will is executed, and the identification of the next of kin will all serve to identify the testator.

A Declaration Clause

A **declaration clause** which states this is the last will and testament of the testator. The will should clearly and specifically (by date) revoke all previous wills and codicils (discussed in more detail later in this chapter) of the testator. This clause serves to eliminate any confusion and possible discord in the future by clearly identifying this will as the most current will and, therefore, the proper will to submit to probate.

Example 2.1

A typical introduction containing the above two clauses may say, "I, Angelica Marie Steed, living at 1000 Lovers Lane, Houston, Texas, do hereby declare this is my last will and testament. I hereby revoke all prior wills, including the will written on January 14, 1987, as well as any other papers, documents, oral declarations, writings, or anything else that may have been or could be construed as a last will and testament. I have been married only once, and then to Ryan Arthur Steed, and have two children from that marriage, namely, Delano Trey Steed and Sammy Ann Steed. I have neither adopted any children, nor has anyone adopted me."

A Bequest Clause

A specific **bequest clause** directs the distribution of specific property, whether cash, tangible personal property, or real estate. If multiple legatees are to inherit then there may be multiple bequests clauses, generally grouped together in one section of the will.

Example 2.2

A typical bequest clause may say, "To my daughter, Sammy Ann Steed, I leave my prized doll collection and $100,000 in cash."

A Residuary Clause

A **residuary clause** transfers assets not previously distributed to specific individuals or to charitable institutions through a specific bequest clause. Without a residuary clause, some assets may remain undistributed, which will pass under the laws of intestacy. When this occurs, the decedent is said to die partially testate and partially intestate.

Example 2.3
A typical residuary clause may say, "I leave all remaining property owned by me, not previously provided for in this document, herein referred to as my "residuary estate," to my wonderful husband, Ryan Arthur Steed."

An Appointment of Executor Clause
An **appointment of executor clause** identifies the executor and any successor executor. This clause may also define the extent of the executor's powers and may grant specific or general powers. For example, this clause may direct the executor to pay the estate taxes and any debts of the estate out of specific assets or to use assets at the executor's discretion (tax-apportionment clause). This clause may also waive the surety bond requirement discussed in Chapter 4, and may give the executor the option to be paid for services rendered or to decline compensation. Executor compensation is governed by state law, but typically ranges between two and five percent of the gross estate value. An executor may elect to forfeit an executor fee when the executor is also a legatee and would prefer to receive an inheritance instead of taxable compensation.

Example 2.4
A typical executor clause may say, "I name Rory Arthur Steed as my Executor. In the event Rory is unable or unwilling to serve as executor, I name Delano Trey Steed as Executor. I grant my executor the power to direct my estate as he deems reasonable to the full extent of the law. I waive any surety bond requirement imposed by any party. At my executor's discretion, he may be compensated for his services in the amount of 5% of the fair market value of my gross estate."

A Guardianship Clause
A **guardianship clause** allows the testator to identify an individual to raise minor children or legal dependents. The testator often selects successor guardians, in the event that the testator's original choice is unwilling or unable to serve as the guardian. The probate court will generally need to approve the appointment of guardians. Individuals who have few financial assets but have minor children should execute a will so that they can choose the person who will raise their children. The testator's choice will almost always be preferable to a family court determination of guardianship for minor children.

Example 2.5
A typical guardianship clause may say, "In the event that my children are minors, as defined by state law, at the time of my death, I appoint my husband, Rory Arthur Steed, as guardian of our children. In the event he is unable or unwilling to serve as guardian, I appoint my sister, Cheryl Conn, as guardian."

A Tax-Appointment Clause
A **tax-appointment clause** directing which assets will bear the payment of any debts and estate taxes. Often this clause is included as part of the residuary clause, but only when the residuary estate is directed to bear the payment of the estate taxes and debts.

> **Example 2.6**
> A typical tax-appointment clause may state, "I direct that debts and taxes be paid out of my residuary estate."

An Attestation Clause

An **attestation clause**, or witness clause, is a provision at the end of the will that is signed by at least two qualified witnesses (some states require three witnesses) who certify that the document is the testator's will bearing the testator's signature and that the testator was competent and not under any kind of duress at the time the will was executed. As discussed previously, legatees should not serve as a witness, as it could jeopardize their right to receive a bequest under the will.

> **Example 2.7**
> A typical attestation clause may say, "On this 15th day of June, 2020, the testator declared this his last will and testament and signed in our joint presence and by us in his presence."

A Self-Proving Clause

A **self-proving clause** involves the notary signing a declaration that he witnessed the testator and witnesses sign the will. The self-proving clause eliminates the need for the witnesses' live testimony during the opening of the probate process (discussed in Chapter 4).

> **Example 2.8**
> A typical self-proving clause may say, "In witness whereof, I have hereunto subscribed my name and affixed my seal on this 15th day of June, 2020, in the presence of the subscribing witnesses.

Other Clauses

More sophisticated wills often have additional clauses that dictate specific wishes regarding the administration of the estate.

Simultaneous Death Clause

A **simultaneous death clause** establishes a presumption regarding which individual died first in the event that both individuals die in the same event (such as in a plane crash, car accident, fire, etc.) when it is impossible to determine which person died first. The simultaneous death clause overrides any state law presumption determining who died first and allows the decedent's estate to move directly to probate without the possibility of the other deceased individual inheriting the estate. Many states now have incorporated simultaneous death clauses into state law which requires individuals to live a defined period, generally one to five days in order to take from the estate of a prior decedent. These state imposed rules can be superseded by including a simultaneous death clause in the testator's will. The simultaneous death clause establishes the guidelines for the disposition of the assets, eliminates the expense of two probate proceedings including identical assets, and most importantly, ensures the fulfillment of each individual's transfer desires. The simultaneous death clause also eliminates the possibility that competing heirs will fight over who died first.

Example 2.9

Kerner, age 65, is married to Kelly, age 32. They have no children. In the event Kerner dies, he wants all of his assets to go to Kelly, but if Kelly dies first, he plans to leave his assets to his only sibling, Pam. Kelly plans to leave all of her assets to Kerner, but if Kerner dies first, she plans to leave her assets to her brother, Jeff, who Kerner has always disliked. Assume that Kerner and Kelly die in a tragic car accident and it is impossible to determine who died first but doctors believe that Kelly may have survived Kerner by a few minutes. Without a simultaneous death clause, the heirs of Kerner and Kelly would be left to fight over which person died first. If Jeff could show that Kerner died first all of Kerner's assets would initially transfer to Kelly's estate which would then transfer to Jeff. Under this scenario, Jeff inherits both Kelly's estate and Kerner's estate. Kerner never intended that his assets would immediately transfer to Jeff. He only wanted his assets to transfer to his wife, if she were alive and expected to live for a substantial period of time.

If Kerner and Kelly had each included simultaneous death clauses in their wills, each including the presumption that the other died first (Kelly's simultaneous death clause assumes Kerner dies first and Kerner's simultaneous death clause assumes Kelly dies first), Pam would receive Kerner's estate and Jeff would receive Kelly's estate. In this case, both Kerner and Kelly's transfer desires would have been fulfilled.

Survivorship Clause

A **survivorship clause** is an alternative to, and sometimes eliminates the need for, a simultaneous death clause. A survivorship clause requires that a beneficiary/heir must actually survive the decedent for a specified period of time to receive the identified inheritance or bequest. Similar to the simultaneous death clause, the survivorship clause prevents property from being included in two different estates in rapid succession and ensures that a decedent's transfer objectives are met. For transfers to a surviving spouse to qualify for the unlimited marital deduction (discussed in Chapter 10), the survival period included in a survivorship clause for a spouse cannot exceed six months. If the survivorship clause requires the surviving spouse to live beyond six months, the transfer will occur if the surviving spouse survives the defined period, but the transfer will not qualify for the unlimited marital deduction. A survivorship clause overcomes problems with simultaneous death issues or close death issues and, therefore, often eliminates the need for a simultaneous death clause.

Quick Quiz 2.2

1. A residuary clause in a will transfers assets that have not been specifically disposed of through a bequest clause.
   a. True
   b. False

2. A survivorship clause always qualifies the estate to use the unlimited marital deduction.
   a. True
   b. False

3. A simultaneous death clause always eliminates the need for a survivorship clause.
   a. True
   b. False

True, False, False.

Example 2.10

Assume in the previous example that Kerner dies immediately and Kelly survives the car accident but is critically injured. She remains in intensive care for over a month and then dies. The simultaneous death clause is not relevant because of the time frame involved as it is clearly identifiable which individual died first. However, a survivorship clause would solve this problem. Assume Kerner's will had a survivorship clause which stated that in order to inherit under the will Kelly must survive him by three months. If Kelly died within the three month period, Kerner's estate would go to his sister, as he intended if his wife was not alive. Had the survivorship clause not been included in his will, Kerner's estate would have transferred to Kelly and subsequently (in one month) at Kelly's death, to her brother, Jeff.

Had Kelly survived the survivorship clause and received the property, the value of the property would have qualified for the unlimited marital deduction because the clause did not require Kelly to live beyond six months following Kerner's death.

Some attorneys advise against a long period survivorship clause because it can delay probating the will. Therefore, it should only be included with that consideration in mind.

Disclaimer Clause
A **disclaimer clause** reminds heirs that they can disclaim any bequest, while still allowing the testator to direct the distribution of disclaimed property. Some states have specific statutory provisions that deal with who receives disclaimed property. When an heir disclaims all or part of his interest in an estate, the disclaimed property will generally pass to the designated heirs, or will default to the residuary estate, as if the disclaiming party was not alive. A beneficiary, heir, or legatee can disclaim any asset, portion of an asset, or any traction of an asset. To be effective:
1. the disclaiming party cannot benefit from the property (with the exception, in certain circumstances, of the surviving spouse);
2. the disclaiming party must not direct who receives a future interest in the property;
3. the disclaiming party must disclaim the property within nine months of the decedent's date of death; and
4. the disclaimer must be in writing.

When a bequest is disclaimed, the property avoids any gift tax that would have otherwise been incurred if the disclaiming party received the property and then transferred it by gift to the intended beneficiary. Disclaimers are used to reallocate interests so that the property passes without gift tax consequences and to ensure that a decedent's estate is not **overqualified** (too much left in a qualifying way to the spouse). In such cases, disclaiming property can be an effective tool in estate planning. Beware, however, that use of a qualified disclaimer cannot be employed to avoid the generation skipping transfer tax.

Example 2.11
Arline's will leaves $500,000 to her son Brian. The will states that if Brian is unable or unwilling to take the $500,000, then the money goes to Brian's daughter Shelby. When Arline dies, Brian is still alive, but does not need the money and would prefer Shelby to have it. He properly disclaims his inheritance and Shelby receives the $500,000. Because Brian properly disclaimed his inheritance, the money passes directly to Shelby and thus avoids a gift tax on the constructive transfer from Brian to Shelby. However, the transfer will be subject to generation skipping transfer tax which is discussed in Chapter 13.

Contingent Legatee Clause

The process of distributing property may become complicated when a legatee predeceases the decedent, dies within the survivorship clause period, or disclaims property bequeathed to them. State law dictates the method of distribution for situations where there are multiple generations of surviving descendants who are entitled to some share of the property. A **contingent legatee clause** in a will allows the testator to determine in advance how their property should be distributed in the event the original legatee is no longer able or willing to inherit under the will because of death or disclaimer.

This clause may specifically designate an alternate legatee or may allow the assets to be distributed to the original legatee's heirs. Frequently, broad language is used to allow the will to meet the client objectives over time as both the client and their objectives change. The contingent legatee clause may employ several approaches to estate distribution to those with a right of representation. The most common methods are per stirpes, per capita, and per capita at each generation.

Per Stirpes

The **per stirpes** method means taking "by representation" and is also called "by the roots." Per stirpes directs equal shares to each member of a specified tier or class of relatives of a generation with the share of a deceased member divided proportionately among his or her beneficiaries (i.e., his or her children). In other words, the grandchildren represent their deceased parent. The intent is that the early death of a child will not cut off that child's children from receiving the same share of the inheritance as the deceased parent would have received.

Example 2.12
A is a widower with three adult children, B, C and D. B has two children, D has one child, and C has no children. B and D predecease A. Under per stirpes, B, C, and D are each entitled to an equal share of the estate (1/3 each) and B and D's children would simply receive their parent's shares. Therefore, C receives 1/3, B's children receive 1/6 each as they split B's 1/3 share, and D's child receives 1/3. Under per stirpes, it is irrelevant if C has children of his own, because he is still alive and there is no need to look to a younger generation.

Per Capita

The **per capita** method means "by the head" or "by total head count." Per capita directs equal shares based upon the number of beneficiaries that are living at the time of decedent's death. In other words, the descendants of predeceased children do not inherit the share that would have gone to their parents, rather all of the shares of the other members are increased or decreased accordingly.

Example 2.13
A is a widower with three adult children, B, C and D. B has two children, D has one child, and C has no children. B and D predecease A. Under per capita, the four living heirs (C, B's two children, and D's child) each receive 1/4 of the estate.

Per Capita at Each Generation

The **per capita at each generation** method directs equal shares to each living member of the same generation. This method always provides equal shares to those equally related and is typically the most preferred method of the two per capita methods.[1]

Example 2.14

A is a widower with three adult children, B, C and D. B has two children, D has one child, and C has no children. B and D predecease A. Under per capita at each generation, C still gets 1/3 but the remaining 2/3 of the property is split evenly among the three grandchildren, because they are the same generation. Therefore, each gets 1/3 of the remaining 2/3 of the property or 2/9 of the original estate.

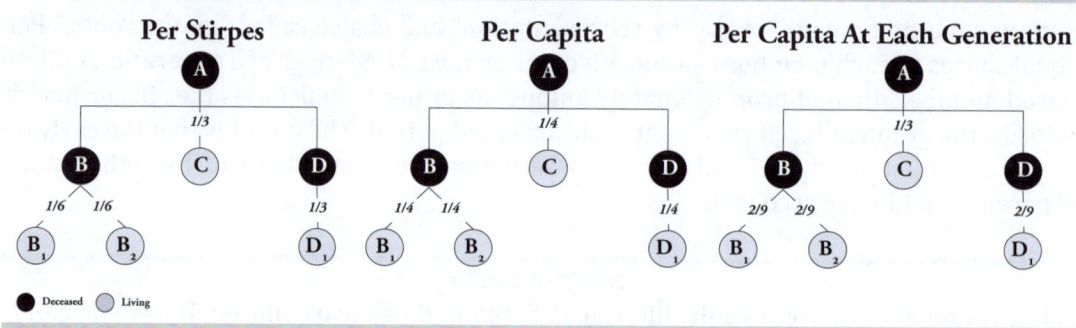

Exhibit 2.4 | Illustration of Examples 2.12, 2.13, and 2.14

Exhibit 2.5 | Systems of Representation

Per Stirpes	Per Capita	Per Capita At Each Generation
"By Representation" or "By the Roots" Directs that the grandchildren stand in for their deceased parent and get that share to split among themselves.	"By the Head" Equal shares based upon the number of living beneficiaries. Heirs of the same generation get an equal share IF they are the only heirs.	Heirs of the same generation ALWAYS get an equal share. Typically, one of the more preferred methods of leaving assets to heirs.

Sometimes the various methods yield similar results, but other times they yield dramatically different results.

---

1. Fellows of the American College of Trust and Estate Counsel survey. See Young, "Meaning of 'Issue' and 'Descendants,'" 13 ACTEC Probate Notes 225 (1988).

Example 2.15

Consider a family in which A is the intestate decedent. A has three children, B, C and D. B has three children (B_1, B_2 and B_3), C has one child (C1), and D has two children (D1 and D2).

Variation 1: All three children (B, C and D) survive A

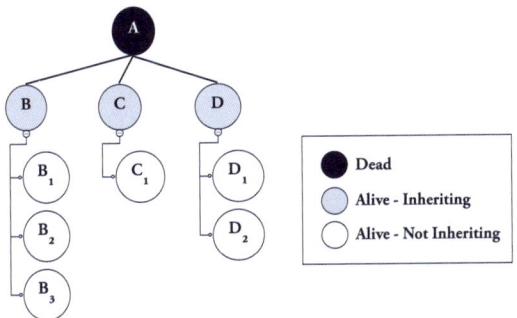

Result: All three systems would reach the same result with A, B and C each receiving 1/3.

Variation 2: B predeceases A (C and D survive A).

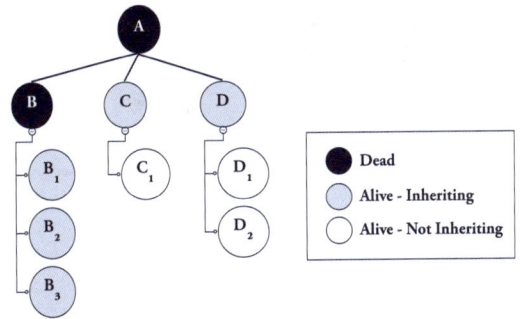

Result:
- **Per Stirpes:** C and D receive 1/3 each and B_1, B_2 and B_3 each receive 1/9 (1/3 each of B's 1/3 share)
- **Per Capita:** The five remaining living heirs (C, D, B_1, B_2 and B_3) receive 1/5 each.
- **Per Capita at Each Generation:** Same result as Per Stirpes.

Variation 3: B and C predecease A (D survives A).

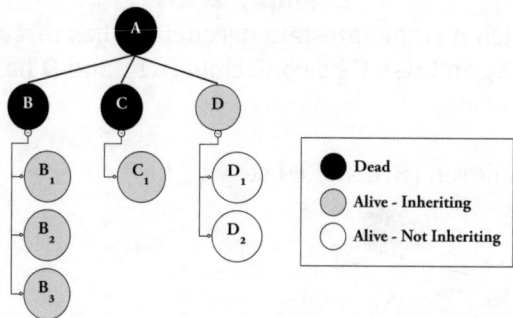

- **Per Stirpes:** D receives 1/3, C_1 receives 1/3 (C's 1/3 share), B_1, B_2 and B_3 split B's 1/3 share and each receive 1/9.
- **Per Capita:** The five remaining living heirs receive 1/5 each.
- **Per Capita at Each Generation:** D receives 1/3 and B_1, B_2, B_3 and C_1 equally share the remaining 2/3 share (1/6 each).

Variation 4: All three children predecease A.

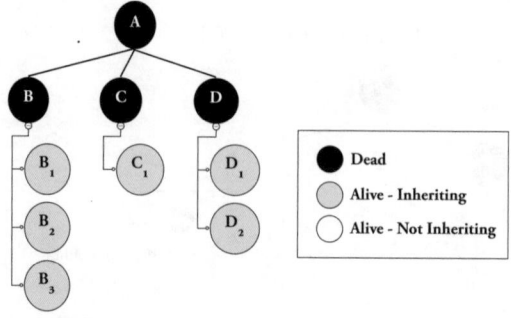

Result:
- **Per Stirpes:** B_1, B_2, and B_3 split B's 1/3 share and each receive 1/9, C_1 receives 1/3 (C's 1/3 share), and D_1 and D_2 split D's 1/3 share and each receive 1/6.
- **Per Capita:** The six remaining living heirs (B1, B2, B3, C1, D1 and D2) receive 1/6 each.
- **Per Capita at Each Generation:** The only remaining heirs are all from the same generation, therefore, all six grandchildren split the estate equally with 1/6 each.

No-Contest Clause

A **no-contest clause** (sometimes called an *in terrorem* clause) attempts to discourage disappointed heirs from contesting the will by substantially decreasing or eliminating any bequest to them if they file a formal, legal contest to the will. In the event that the disappointed heir is able to successfully invalidate the will, the no-contest clause will not apply. The key when designing a no-contest clause is to make sure that the token bequest to any heir is sufficient to create the incentive not to contest. Although no-contest clauses generally discourage contests to the will, they may not discourage disinherited parties or those who have little to lose. The no-contest clause can be broad or specific, but if the clause is too general, it may be subject to various interpretations. Enforcement of the no-contest clause depends on the interpretation of specific state laws.

Example 2.16

Harper has two children, Chris and Steven. Harper was widowed many years ago and has amassed substantial wealth. The last few years before her death, Harper required around-the-clock in home nursing care. During this time Harper became very fond of her young, handsome nurse, Beck. A few months before her death, Harper changed her will so that Beck was the sole beneficiary of her fortune instead of her two children. The will, which was drafted by Beck's lawyer brother, Pete, included a no-contest clause because Pete suspected that Chris and Steven would contest. Because of the circumstances, Chris and Steven were furious when the will was produced by Beck and they announced their intention to contest the will based on undue influence. In this instance, the no-contest clause does not provide any incentive for Chris and Steven to not contest the will. If they are unsuccessful in court then they lose nothing because they don't currently stand to inherit anything. If they are successful in court then they may get everything.

Example 2.17

Assume instead, that the will gives Steven and Chris $1,000,000 each and Beck $10,000,000. Now the no-contest clause may incentivize the children not to contest because if they lose in court then they each forfeit their right to $1,000,000, a risk they may not be willing to take.

Sample Wills

Two examples of actual wills follow. Since probate is a public process, anyone can look up a will to see what a testator has done with his or her assets. The examples that follow are of Chief Justice Warren Burger's and Elvis Presley's wills.

Exhibit 2.6 | Last Will and Testament of Warren Burger

The Will of Warren Burger

LAST WILL AND TESTAMENT OF WARREN E. BURGER

I hereby make and declare the following to be my last will and testament.

1. My executors will first pay all claims against my estate;

2. The remainder of my estate will be distributed as follows: one-third to my daughter, Margaret Elizabeth Burger Rose and two-thirds to my son, Wade A. Burger;

3. I designate and appoint as executors of this will, Wade A. Burger and J. Michael Luttig.

IN WITNESS WHEREOF, I have hereunto set my hand to this my Last Will and Testament this 9th day of June, 1994.

[Signed by Warren E. Burger]

Exhibit 2.7 | Last Will and Testament of Elvis Presley

The Will of Elvis Presley
Known as "The King," Presley sold more than 45 million records and starred in 33 motion pictures. He left much of his vast fortune to members of his family.

Last Will And Testament Of Elvis A. Presley, Deceased Filed August 22, 1977

I, Elvis A. Presley, a resident and citizen of Shelby County, Tennessee, being of sound mind and disposing memory, do hereby make, publish and declare this instrument to be my last will and testament, hereby revoking any and all wills and codicils by me at any time heretofore made.

Item I - Debts, Expenses and Taxes
I direct my Executor, hereinafter named, to pay all of my matured debts and my funeral expenses, as well as the costs and expenses of the administration of my estate, as soon after my death as practicable. I further direct that all estate, inheritance, transfer and succession taxes which are payable by reason under this will, be paid out of my residuary estate; and I hereby waive on behalf of my estate any right to recover from any person any part of such taxes so paid. My Executor, in his sole discretion, may pay from my domiciliary estate all or any portion of the costs of ancillary administration and similar proceedings in other jurisdictions.

Item II - Instruction Concerning Personal Property: Enjoyment in Specie
I anticipate that included as a part of my property and estate at the time of my death will be tangible personal property of various kinds, characters and values, including trophies and other items accumulated by me during my professional career. I hereby specifically instruct all concerned that my Executor, herein appointed, shall have complete freedom and discretion as to disposal of any and all such property so long as he shall act in good faith and in the best interest of my estate and my beneficiaries, and his discretion so exercised shall not be subject to question by anyone whomsoever.

I hereby expressly authorize my Executor and my Trustee, respectively and successively, to permit any beneficiary of any and all trusts created hereunder to enjoy in specie the use or benefit of any household goods, chattels, or other tangible personal property (exclusive of choses in action, cash, stocks, bonds or other securities) which either my Executor or my Trustees may receive in kind, and my Executor and my Trustees shall not be liable for any consumption, damage, injury to or loss of any tangible property so used, nor shall the beneficiaries of any trusts hereunder or their executors of administrators be liable for any consumption, damage, injury to or loss of any tangible personal property so used.

Item III - Real Estate
If I am the owner of any real estate at the time of my death, I instruct and empower my Executor and my Trustee (as the case may be) to hold such real estate for investment, or to sell same, or any portion therof, as my Executor or my Trustee (as the case may be) shall in his sole judgment determine to be for the best interest of my estate and the beneficiaries thereof.

Item IV - Residuary Trust
After payment of all debts, expenses and taxes as directed under Item I hereof, I give, devise, and bequeath all the rest, residue, and remainder of my estate, including all lapsed legacies and devices, and any property over which I have a power of appointment, to my Trustee, hereinafter named, in trust for the following purposes:
(a) The Trustees is directed to take, hold, manage, invest and reinvest the corpus of the trust and to collect the income therefrom in accordance with the rights, powers, duties, authority and discretion hereinafter set forth. The Trustee is directed to pay all the expenses, taxes and costs incurred in the management of the trust estate out of the income thereof.
(b) After payment of all expenses, taxes and costs incurred in the management of the expenses, taxes and costs incurred in the management of the trust estate, the Trustee is authorized to accumulate the net income or to pay or apply so much of the net income and such portion of the principal at any time and from time to time to time for health, education, support, comfortable maintenance and welfare of: (1) My daughter, Lisa Marie Presley, and any other lawful issue I might have, (2) my grandmother, Minnie Mae Presley, (3) my father, Vernon E. Presley, and (4) such other relatives of mine living at the time of my death who in the absolute discretion of my Trustees are in need of emergency assistance for any of the above mentioned purposes and the Trustee is able to make such distribution without affecting the ability of the trust to meet the present needs of the first three numbered categories of beneficiaries herein mentioned or to meet the reasonably expected future needs of the first three classes of beneficiaries herein mentioned. Any decision of the Trustee as to whether or not distribution, to any of the persons described hereunder shall be final and conclusive and not subject to question by any legatee or beneficiary hereunder.
(c) Upon the death of my Father, Vernon E. Presley, the Trustee is instructed to make no further distributions to the fourth category of beneficiaries and such beneficiaries shall cease to have any interest whatsoever in this trust.
(d) Upon the death of both my said father and my said grandmother, the Trustee is directed to divide the Residuary Trust into separate and equal trusts, creating one such equal trust for each of my lawful children then surviving and one such equal trust for the living issue collectively, if any, of any deceased child of mine. The share, if any, for the issue of any such deceased child, shall immediately vest in such issue in equal shares but shall be subject to the provisions of Item V herein. Separate books and records shall be kept for each trust, but it shall not be necessary that a physical division of the assets be made as to each trust.
The Trustee may from time to time distribute the whole or any part of the net income or principal from each of the aforesaid trusts as the Trustee, in its uncontrolled discretion, considers necessary or desirable to provide for the comfortable support, education, maintenance, benefit and general welfare of each of my children. Such distributions may be made directly to such beneficiary or to the guardian of the person of such beneficiary and without repsonsibilty on my Trustee to see to the application of nay such distributions and in making such

Last Will and Testament of Elvis Presley (Continued)

distributions, the Trustee shall take into account all other sources of funds known by the Trustee to be available for each respective beneficiary for such purpose.

(e) As each of my respective children attains the age of twenty-five (25) years and provided that both my father and my grandmother are deceased, the trust created hereunder for such child care terminate, and all the remainder of the assets then contained in said trust shall be distributed to such child so attaining the age of twenty-five (25) years outright and free of further trust.

(f) If any of my children for whose benefit a trust has been created hereunder should die before attaining the age of twenty- five (25) years, then the trust created for such a child shall terminate on his death, and all remaining assets then contained in said trust shall be distributed outright and free of further trust and in equal shares to the surviving issue of such deceased child but subject to the provisions of Item V herein; but if there be no such surviving issue, then to the brothers and sisters of such deceased child in equal shares, the issue of any other deceased child being entitled collectively to their deceased parent's share. Nevertheless, if any distribution otherwise becomes payable outright and free of trust under the provisions of this paragraph (f) of the Item IV of my will to a beneficiary for whom the Trustee is then administering a trust for the benefit of such beneficiary under provisions of this last will and testament, such distribution shall not be paid outright to such beneficiary but shall be added to and become a part of the trust so being administered for such beneficiary by the Trustee.

Item V - Distribution to Minor Children

If any share of corpus of any trust established under this will become distributable outright and free of trust to any beneficiary before said beneficiary has attained the age of eighteen (18) years, then said share shall immediately vest in said beneficiary, but the Trustee shall retain possession of such share during the period in which such beneficiary is under the age of eighteen (18) years, and, in the meantime, shall use and expend so much of the income and principal for the care, support, and education of such beneficiary, and any income not so expended with respect to each share so retained all the power and discretion had with respect to such trust generally.

Item VI - Alternate Distributees

In the event that all of my descendants should be deceased at any time prior to the time for the termination of the trusts provided for herein, then in such event all of my estate and all the assets of every trust to be created hereunder (as the case may be) shall then distributed outright in equal shares to my heirs at law per stirpes.

Item VII - Unenforceable Provisions

If any provisions of this will are unenforceable, the remaining provisions shall, nevertheless, be carried into effect.

Item VIII - Life Insurance

If my estate is the beneficiary of any life insurance on my life at the time of my death, I direct that the proceeds therefrom will be used by my Executor in payment of the debts, expenses and taxes listed in Item I of this will, to the extent deemed advisable by the Executor. All such proceeds not so used are to be used by my Executor for the purpose of satisfying the devises and bequests contained in Item IV herein.

Item IX - Spendthrift Provision

I direct that the interest of any beneficiary in principal or income of any trust created hereunder shall not be subject to claims of creditors or others, nor to legal process, and may not be voluntarily or involuntarily alienated or encumbered except as herein provided. Any bequests contained herein for any female shall be for her sole and separate use, free from the debts, contracts and control of any husband she may ever have.

Item X - Proceeds From Personal Services

All sums paid after my death (either to my estate or to any of the trusts created hereunder) and resulting from personal services rendered by me during my lifetime, including, but not limited to, royalties of all nature, concerts, motion picture contracts, and personal appearances shall be considered to be income, notwithstanding the provisions of estate and trust law to the contrary.

Item XI - Executor and Trustee

I appoint as executor of this, my last will and testament, and as Trustee of every trust required to be created hereunder, my said father. I hereby direct that my said father shall be entitled by his last will and testament, duly probated, to appoint a successor Executor of my estate, as well as a successor Trustee or successor Trustees of all the trusts to be created under my last will and testament.

If, for any reason, my said father be unable to serve or to continue to serve as Executor and/or as Trustee, or if he be deceased and shall not have appointed a successor Executor or Trustee, by virtue of his last will and testament as stated -above, then I appoint National Bank of Commerce, Memphis, Tennessee, or its successor or the institution with which it may merge, as successor Executor and/or as successor Trustee of all trusts required to be established hereunder.

None of the appointees named hereunder, including any appointment made by virtue of the last will and testament of my said father, shall be required to furnish any bond or security for performance of the respective fiduciary duties required hereunder, notwithstanding any rule of law to the contrary.

Item XII - Powers, Duties, Privileges and Immunities of the Trustee

Except as otherwise stated expressly to the contrary herein, I give and grant to the said Trustee (and to the duly appointed successor Trustee when acting as such) the power to do everything he deems advisable with respect to the administration of each trust required to be established under this, my last will and Testament, even though such powers would not be authorized or appropriate for the Trustee under statutory or other rules of law. By way of illustration and not in limitation of the generality of the foregoing grant of power and authority of the Trustee, I give and grant to him plenary power as follows:

Last Will and Testament of Elvis Presley (Continued)

(a) To exercise all those powers authorized to fiduciaries under the provisions of the Tennessee Code Annotated, Sections 35-616 to 35-618, inclusive, including any amendments thereto in effect at the time of my death, and the same are expressly referred to and incorporated herein by reference.

(b) Plenary power is granted to the Trustee, not only to relieve him from seeking judicial instruction, but to the extent that the Trustee deems it to be prudent, to encourage determinations freely to be made in favor of persons who are the current income beneficiaries. In such instances the rights of all subsequent beneficiaries are subordinate, and the Trustee shall not be answerable to any subsequent beneficiary for anything done or omitted in favor of a current income beneficiary may compel any such favorable or preferential treatment. Without in anywise minimizing or impairing the scope of this declaration of intent, it includes investment policy, exercise of discretionary power to pay or apply principal and income, and determination principal and income questions;

(c) It shall be lawful for the Trustee to apply any sum that is payable to or for the benefit of a minor (or any other person who in the Judgment of the Trustee, is incapable of making proper disposition thereof) by payments in discharge of the costs and expenses of educating, maintaining and supporting said beneficiary, or to make payment to anyone with whom said beneficiary resides or who has the care or custody of the beneficiary, temporarily or permanently, all without intervention of any guardian or like fiduciary. The receipt of anyone to whom payment is so authorized to be made shall be a complete discharge of the Trustees without obligation on his part to see to the further application hereto, and without regard to other resource that the beneficiary may have, or the duty of any other person to support the beneficiary;

(d) In Dealing with the Trustee, no grantee, pledge, vendee, mortgage, lessee or other transference of the trust properties, or any part thereof, shall be bound to inquire with respect to the purpose or necessity of any such disposition or to see to the application of any consideration therefore paid to the Trustee.

Item XIII - Concerning the Trustee and the Executor

(a) If at any time the Trustee shall have reasonable doubt as to his power, authority or duty in the administration of any trust herein created, it shall be lawful for the Trustee to obtain the advice and counsel of reputable legal counsel without resorting to the courts for instructions; and the Trustee shall be fully absolved from all liability and damage or detriment to the various trust estates of any beneficiary thereunder by reason of anything done, suffered or omitted pursuant to advice of said counsel given and obtained in good faith, provided that nothing contained herein shall be construed to prohibit or prevent the Trustee in all proper cases from applying to a court of competent jurisdiction for instructions in the administration of the trust assets in lieu of obtaining advice of counsel.

(b) In managing, investing, and controlling the various trust estates, the Trustee shall exercise the judgment and care under the circumstances then prevailing, which men of prudence discretion and judgment exercise in the management of their own affairs, not in regard to speculation, but in regard to the permanent disposition of their funds, considering the probable income as well as the probable safety of their capital, and, in addition, the purchasing power of income distribution to beneficiaries.

(c) My Trustee (as well as my Executor) shall be entitled to reasonable and adequate compensation for the fiduciary services rendered by him.

(d) My Executor and his successor Executor and his successor Executor shall have the same rights, privileges, powers and immunities herein granted to my Trustee wherever appropriate.

(e) In referring to any fiduciary hereunder, for purposes of construction, masculine pronouns may include a corporate fiduciary and neutral pronouns may include an individual fiduciary.

Item XIV - Law Against Perpetuities

(a) Having in mind the rule against perpetuities, I direct that (notwithstanding anything contained to the contrary in this last will and testament) each trust created under this will (except such trust created under this will (except such trusts as have heretofore vested in compliance with such rule or law) shall end, unless sooner terminated under other provisions of this will, twenty-one (21) years after the death of the last survivor of such of the beneficiaries hereunder as are living at the time of my death; and thereupon that the property held in trust shall be distributed free of all trust to the persons then entitled to receive the income and/or principal therefrom, in the proportion in which they are then entitled to receive such income.

(b) Notwithstanding anything else contained in this will to the contrary, I direct that if any distribution under this will become payable to a person for whom the Trustee is then administering a trust created hereunder for the benefit of such person, such distribution shall be made to such trust and not to the beneficiary outright, and the funds so passing to such trust shall become a part thereof as corpus and be administered and distributed to the same extent and purpose as if such funds had been a part of such a trust at its inception.

Item XV - Payment of Estate and Inheritance Taxes

Notwithstanding the provisions of Item X herein, I authorize my Executor to use such sums received by my estate after my death and resulting from my personal services as identified in Item X as he deem necessary and advisable in order to pay the taxes referred to in Item I of my said will.

In WITNESS WHEREOF, I, the said ELVIS A. PRESLEY, do hereunto set my hand and seal in the presence of two (2) competent witnesses, and in their presence do publish and declare this instrument to be my Last Will and Testament, this 3 day of March, 1977.

[Signed by Elvis A. Presley]
ELVIS A. PRESLEY

The above examples highlight the differences in the length and detail that can be covered in wills. Elvis Presley's will contains many of the important clauses discussed in this chapter, while Chief Justice Warren Burger's will is practically void of any of those clauses. Fortunately, the length and the number of clauses mean very little to estate planning if proper planning is not completed. **Exhibit 2.8** details that Elvis only passed 27 percent of his ten million dollar estate to his heirs, while Warren Burger passed 75 percent of his $1,800,000 to his heirs.

Exhibit 2.8 | Celebrity Estate Tax Consequences

	Estate	Taxes & Costs	Net Estate	% Passed to Heirs
Henry Kaiser Jr.	$55,910,373	$1,030,415	$54,879,958	98%
Warren Burger (estimated)	$1,800,000	$450,000	$1,350,000	75%
Walt Disney	$23,004,851	$6,811,943	$16,192,908	70%
Humphrey Bogart	$910,146	$274,234	$635,912	70%
Gary Cooper	$4,948,985	$1,520,454	$3,454,531	70%
Al Jolson	$4,385,143	$1,349,066	$3,036,077	69%
Cecil B. DeMille	$4,043,607	$1,396,064	$2,647,543	65%
Hedda Hopper	$472,661	$165,982	$306,679	65%
Earle Stanley Gardner	$1,795,092	$636,705	$1,158,387	65%
W.C. Fields	$884,680	$329,793	$554,887	63%
Clark Gable	$2,806,526	$1,101,038	$1,705,488	61%
Henry J. Kaiser Sr.	$5,597,772	$2,488,364	$3,109,408	56%
William Boeing	$22,386,158	$10,589,748	$11,796,410	53%
William Frawley	$92,446	$45,814	$46,632	50%
Marilyn Monroe	$819,176	$448,750	$370,426	45%
Frederick Vanderbilt	$76,838,530	$42,846,112	$33,992,418	44%
Alwin Ernst (CPA)	$12,642,431	$7,124,112	$5,518,319	44%
Charles Woolworth	$16,788,702	$10,391,303	$6,397,399	38%
John D. Rockefeller	$26,905,182	$17,124,988	$9,780,194	36%
J.P. Morgan	$17,121,482	$11,893,691	$5,227,791	31%
Elvis Presley	$10,165,434	$7,374,635	$2,790,799	27%

Source: www.stricklen.com

Revoking and Changing Wills

Unfortunately, creating a will is not the ultimate and final step in estate planning. Over time, heirs are born and die, property is bought and sold, and preferences regarding distributions change. Wills need to be reviewed and updated periodically. Attorneys drafting statutory wills try to draft wills that are flexible over time through the use of broad language. Nonetheless, wills may need to be changed at some point in time. The testator may change or update his will by revoking the previous will and creating a new one, or by executing a codicil (an amendment or supplement to the existing will).

Key Concepts

1. How is a will revoked or changed?
2. What is a side instruction letter?
3. What are some of the statutes that affect wills and how do they affect them?
4. How can will contests be avoided?

Revocation

Revoking a will is very simple. The testator can destroy the will, either by shredding it or burning it. The testator can also create a new will specifically revoking the previous will. Better yet, do both. In some states, the testator can revoke the will by writing "cancel" across the will. Other states provide that any defacing of the will, such as crossing out one provision, constitutes revocation of the will. The testator's state law may also provide other acceptable methods of revoking a will. When revoking and creating new wills, clients should be cautioned not to write new provisions on a previously executed will, as some state probate courts have interpreted the new handwritten provisions to be valid alterations to the will, superseding the original provisions. Any writings clients make regarding their will distribution choices should be labeled "draft" to avoid courts interpreting these documents as a last will and testament.

Codicil

A **codicil** is an amendment, or supplement, to a will. It is a separate document or attachment to the will and must meet all of the legal requirements of a will. A codicil may be executed like a statutory will, which must be signed, properly witnessed, and notarized as discussed previously. If the state allows, the codicil may also be in the form of a holographic, or handwritten, document attached to the will. The purpose of a codicil is to modify, explain, or amend a will. A codicil may be used, for example, to include additional children born after the drafting of the original will or when additional property is acquired after the drafting of the will. When admitted to probate, the codicil becomes part of the will.

Because codicils are attached to the will, they can be inadvertently or intentionally separated from the will and lost. If this happens, the testator's ultimate desires may not be fulfilled. If the codicil addresses an important issue, or addresses many issues, redrafting the will may be wiser than adding a codicil. A sample codicil is displayed at **Exhibit 2.10**.

Exhibit 2.9 | Celebrity Estate Planning Mistake

Celebrity: Michael Crichton (author)
Estimated Estate Worth: $175 million
Mistake: Failing to update estate documents

When best-selling author John Michael Crichton (Jurassic Park and ER) died in 2008, he left behind pregnant wife Sherri Alexander and a very messy estate and trust battle because he failed to update his estate planning documents. His will left most of his fortune in a trust, but the trust was not updated to include his future son. In fact, his will included language disinheriting any children not specifically named in the will. His wife, who was not an heir due to a prenuptial agreement, went to court to fight for their newborn son to be included as an heir and to be appointed as guardian of the son's property. Crichton's daughter from a previous marriage opposed the request. Eventually a judge ruled Alexander's son could inherit.

Side Instruction Letter

Another separate document from the will, the **side instruction letter**, or personal instruction letter, details the testator's wishes regarding the disposition of specific tangible possessions (such as household goods), as well as funeral and burial wishes. The side instruction letter exists separately from the will, to avoid cluttering the will with small details that may create conflicts among heirs and is not binding in the probate process. In many states, burial is required before probate can begin, and the side letter of instruction gives specific instructions to the heirs. This letter, which is given to the executor, may contain information regarding the location of important personal documents, safe deposit boxes, outstanding loans, and other personal and financial information that the executor will use to administer the decedent's estate. While the letter has no legal standing, the executor will generally carry out the wishes of the decedent.

Exhibit 2.10 | Sample Codicil

SAMPLE CODICIL

I, _____ being of sound mind and body and free will, and having full testamentary intent and capacity, do hereby voluntarily make, publish and execute this document as a codicil to my Last Will and Testament which was made on the _____ day of _____ , 20__.

I hereby amend and modify the provisions of my Last Will and Testament identified above as follows:

1.

2.

3.

Except as expressly modified by this codicil, all remaining terms and provisions of my Last Will and Testament identified above shall remain in full force and effect.

IN WITNESS WHEREOF, I have signed this document as a codicil to my Last Will and Testament identified above on this _____ day of _____, 20___.

_____
Your Signature

The foregoing codicil of _____, dated this _____ day of _____, 20___, was signed and published in our presence as a codicil to his/her Last Will and Testament. We declare that the maker was of sound mind and body and free will at that time, and we have hereto signed our names as witnesses in the presence of the maker and of each other.

_____   _____
_____   _____
(Name & Address of Witness)   *(Name & Address of Witness)*

Subscribed and sworn to before me by said
(testatrix, testator) and the said witnesses,
this _____ day of _____, 20___.

_____
Notary Public
My Commission expires:

Statutes Affecting Wills

Over the course of time, state legislatures have enacted statutes designed to protect both testators and natural heirs during the probate process. These statutes may in many instances override the preferences set forth in the will. Particular attention should be paid to the statutes in the testator's domiciliary state to determine how these statutes will affect the testator.

Forced Heirship

While the concept may be termed differently, some states have statutes requiring a certain portion of the estate to be transferred to the decedent's children. **Forced heirship** in the United States derives from French law, but the concept of forced heirship is common in civil law jurisdictions throughout the world.

Marital Share

The marital share is somewhat similar to that of forced heirship in that both require a decedent to provide for certain people. State laws concerning the marital share require the decedent to provide for his surviving spouse under certain circumstances.

Felonious Homicide Statutes

Substantial wealth has, on occasion, served to encourage heirs to intentionally participate in the death of their so called loved one. Because of this, many states now have **felonious homicide statutes** that prevent legatees and heirs who have been convicted of intentionally killing the decedent from inheriting from the decedent's will or through the intestate process. If a will has been executed, the probate court will invalidate any provisions relating to the legatee. Likewise, if a will has not been executed, the probate court will distribute assets under the intestacy scheme, pretending that the convicted heir is dead. If the testator's state does not have such a statue, a clause in the will indicating the testator's desire to exclude those individuals who intentionally caused their death will typically create the same result.

Divorce Statutes

Many times divorcing spouses fail to revise their wills in a timely fashion. To protect such individuals, many states now have statutes that invalidate any provisions in a will that leave assets to a former spouse. In the event that a testator does wish to leave assets to a former spouse, a clear indication should be made in the will to prevent the clause from being stricken by the probate court. These statutes do not apply, however, to property passing by contract, such as life insurance, pension plans, and annuities. After a divorce, the beneficiary designations on these contracts should be changed to ensure the former spouse does not receive these assets. Be aware, however, that not all states have statutes that invalidate bequests to former spouses. To effectively serve their client's estate, planners must know the specifics of their state's laws.

> ### Quick Quiz 2.3
>
> 1. When additional property is acquired after writing a will, a codicil can amend the will without having to rewrite the entire will to include provisions that dispose of the new property.
>   a. True
>   b. False
>
> 2. By using a side instruction letter, specific bequests are left out of the will and avoid probate.
>   a. True
>   b. False
>
> 3. Will contests can always be eliminated by using a no-contest clause.
>   a. True
>   b. False
>
> True, False, False.

Anti-Lapse Statutes

Some states have statutes that will presume that if a close relative, like a child or sibling, is not alive when the testator dies the testator would have wanted bequests to those individuals to pass directly to their heirs. Anti-lapse rules generally do not apply to gifts to friends, or distant relatives. In those instances, the law generally presumes the testator would have wanted the assets to go to the residuary estate. Obviously, a well drafted will can overcome these presumptions.

Avoiding Will Contests

Unfortunately, it is not possible to eliminate the possibility of all will contests. No-contest clauses (in terrorem clauses) may be used to discourage contests but, nonetheless, cannot stop them. Will contests often occur in nontraditional relationships, such as same-sex relationships or relationships where there is a substantial age difference between the partners. They also occur in cases where individuals leave substantial fortunes to nontraditional churches or other charitable organizations. Sadly, they can occur in any family. Will contests result in added time and expense incurred in estate administration. Testators can and should take action to avoid will contests. Being open and honest with heirs before death regarding will choices may alleviate some of the disagreements that may occur after the decedent's death. In addition, detailed and well-drafted wills can, in some cases, prevent will contests. For non-traditional bequests, the testator may consider lifetime gifts, trust options, or property titling as a means of avoiding will contests.

Some states allow the testator to have the will validated before death. In such cases, the testator notifies all interested parties that a hearing will be held and if they would like to challenge the will they should attend the hearing. The court will evaluate any claims and provide a judgment on the validity of the will. While this may prevent will contests, it can be expensive and time consuming as a new hearing will be needed each time the will is altered.

Exhibit 2.11 | Celebrity Estate Planning Mistake

Celebrity: Jim Morrison (Doors lead singer)
Estimated Estate Worth: $80 million (at the time of his death)
Mistake: Failing to have an adequate will or trust

Lead singer of the Doors, Jim Morrison died in 1971 from a heroin overdose, at just 27-year-old. While his estate had limited cash when Morrison died, the assets in his estate became worth approximately $80 million. His simple will left everything to his companion, Pamela Courson, and if she failed to survive Morrison by three months, then his assets would pass to his brother and sister. Even though Courson did survive Morrison by more than three months, she died only three years later, also from a heroin overdose. Because Courson died without a will, the Jim Morrison fortune was set to pass to her heirs under intestate law. Morrison's parents sued and the estate was tied up in litigation in probate court. In the end, the Morrison estate drama ended with an out-of-court settlement, with the families reportedly splitting everything 50/50. But it was the Courson family who ended up inheriting the rights to manage and control Morrison's image, music, and royalties. On a side note, Morrison's brother and sister, the alternate beneficiaries received nothing, because of the three-month survivorship clause.

POWERS OF ATTORNEY & POWERS OF APPOINTMENT

People frequently need a trusted person to make important financial or health care decisions for them when they cannot make those decisions themselves, or to execute documents on their behalf. A **power of attorney** is a legal document that authorizes a trusted person to act on another's behalf. It grants a right to one person, the **attorney-in-fact** (sometimes called the power holder or agent), to act in the place of the other person, the **principal** (the grantor of the power). Generally, any person who is legally capable to act for himself may also act as an attorney-in-fact for another. The principal must have reached the age of majority, defined in most states as 18-years-old, and be legally competent in order to grant the power. All powers are revocable by the principal as long as he is legally competent and all powers granted cease at the principal's death. A power of appointment is sometimes included in a power of attorney. A power of appointment is a power to appoint the assets of one person to another and may be either general or limited (sometimes called a special power).

General Power of Attorney

The broadest power a person can give another is a general power of attorney. The person who is given the power of attorney will be able to act in the principal's place as though he is the principal. Essentially the general power of attorney gives the agent the power to do anything that the principal could do. The general power of attorney may be revoked by the principal by giving notice, usually with a revocation form, to the agent and is automatically revoked at the principal's death.

Although the general power of attorney grants the agent the right to do anything the principal could have done, some states require certain powers, such as the power to make gifts or to engage in self-dealing, to be specifically granted to the power holder. The ability of the agent to appoint assets to himself, to his estate, his creditors, or his estate's creditors is considered a general power of appointment over the property covered by the power of attorney. Although a power of appointment or the ability to appoint assets in a general or limited way, is traditionally associated with trusts, it functions similarly when included in a power of attorney. Powers of appointment will be discussed in more detail later in the text. The following exhibit illustrates the general characteristics of Powers of Attorney and Powers of Appointment.

> ### Key Concepts
> 1. What is a power of attorney?
> 2. Identify and discuss the parties to a power of attorney.
> 3. Identify a reason to use a power of attorney.
> 4. What is a durable power of attorney, and why are they used?
> 5. What is a springing durable power of attorney?

Exhibit 2.12 | Power of Attorney vs. Power of Appointment

Power of Attorney	Power of Appointment
• A stand alone document that allows an agent to act for the principal and may include the power to appoint assets	• A power, usually included in a trust or power of attorney, allowing the power holder to direct assets to another
• A power to act	• A power to transfer or assign assets
• The power ends at the death of the principal	• The power may survive the death of the grantor
• The power may be general or limited	• The power may be general or limited
• The power may be revoked at any time by the principal	• The power may be revoked by the principal during life or at death (via last will and testament)

General Power of Appointment

If the agent dies before the principal and is holding a general power of appointment over assets of the principal, the agent's gross estate will include the fair market value of the principal's assets over which the agent held the power of appointment regardless of whether the power has been invoked. Therefore, a general power of appointment should be granted sparingly when the holder of the power will have a taxable estate. Frequently, estate planners only recommend general powers as between spouses because of the unlimited marital deduction.

Most states presume that agents do not have the power to gift assets to themselves, their estates, or pay their creditors unless such power is expressly provided for in the power of attorney. If a principal wants the holder to have this kind of power, he should be sure to have the appropriate language included in his power of attorney.

Limited Power of Attorney

A limited power of attorney, also referred to as a special power of attorney, gives the agent very specific, detailed powers. The power granted in a limited power of attorney may be extremely narrow, only authorizing the agent to act on a specific matter. For example, if the principal were purchasing a new home and was unable to attend the actual closing because he was out of the country, he can give a power of attorney to someone else specifically authorizing them to sign his name at the act of sale. Other uses for a limited power of attorney include situations where a principal gives an agent the authority to act on his behalf to pay his bills, or handle a specific business transaction.

As a written document, the limited power of attorney should state the agent's name and the powers granted to the agent. Although the powers granted under most limited power of attorney documents are quite narrow, the power granted may be more broad if the principal desires. For example, a very broad power will still be considered limited if the agent is authorized to do anything the principal can do, except appoint assets to the agent (himself), to his creditors, to the agent's heirs, or to the agent's heir's creditors.

Exhibit 2.13 and **Exhibit 2.14** graphically depict the differences between the special/limited power and general power of attorney and appointment.

Limited Power of Appointment

Like a general power of appointment, a limited power of appointment is the power to affect the beneficial enjoyment of property. Unlike a general power of appointment, a limited power of appointment is limited in some way. One of the ways in which a power of appointment can be limited is by the application of what is known as an ascertainable standard. According to the Internal Revenue Code, a power is limited by such a standard if the extent of the holder's duty to exercise and not to exercise the power is reasonably measurable in terms of his needs for health, education, maintenance, or support (or any combination of them known or referred to as HEMS). If a power of appointment is limited by an ascertainable standard, then the property subject to the power will not be includible in the gross estate of the power holder. Furthermore, the use of an ascertainable standard allows the principal to give the power holder the ability to appoint assets to himself without creating a general power of appointment.

Example 2.18
Jamie gives Corinne the power to appoint the $1,000,000 in his bank account to herself or her mother. Jamie has given Corinne a general power of appointment. If Corinne dies while holding the power of appointment, the $1,000,000 bank account will be included in Corinne's gross estate.

Example 2.19
Jamie gives Corinne the power to appoint the $1,000,000 in his bank account to herself or to her mother, but only for educational expenses. Even though Corinne can appoint the assets to herself (which would usually create a general power of appointment), she has a limited power of appointment because she is limited by the fact that the assets can only be used for educational expenses. Therefore, if Corinne dies while holding the power, the value of Jamie's bank account will not be included in her gross estate.

In determining whether a power is limited by an ascertainable standard, it is immaterial whether the beneficiary is required to exhaust his other income before the power can be exercised.

Exhibit 2.13 | Graphical Depiction of Powers of Attorney

Exhibit 2.14 | Durable Feature Graphical Depiction of Powers of Appointment

When a power of attorney is "**durable**," the agent's power does not expire upon the principal's incapacity or disability but rather expires only at the principal's death. Because the power remains in effect even after the principal becomes incapacitated, it is considered to be durable. The durability feature, which allows the agent to maintain the power granted even after the principal's incapacity, should be included if the principal intends the power to survive his incapacity or disability. The durable power of attorney is especially appropriate where the principal anticipates the need for someone to manage his affairs in the near future. For example, an elderly parent about to enter a nursing home may need to appoint his adult child to manage his existing home affairs or make health care decisions.

Springing Power

When a power of attorney is structured as a **springing power**, the agent's authority to act "springs" into existence upon some defined event or determination (i.e., at the disability of the principal). In this case even though the principal has signed the power of attorney, the agent cannot exercise the powers granted to him until the specific event occurs. Generally, the power springs upon disability or incapacity and lapses if the principal recovers. The power is always revocable by the principal, provided that the principal is competent at the time of revocation.

> ### Quick Quiz 2.4
>
> 1. A power of attorney is generally granted to a relative or person whom an individual would trust making decisions for them if they become incapacitated, disabled, or cannot perform a needed task. A power of attorney does not survive death.
>   a. True
>   b. False
>
> 2. If someone dies holding a general power of appointment over someone else's assets, the agent's gross estate will include the value of all of the assets under the general power of appointment.
>   a. True
>   b. False
>
> 3. Durable powers of attorney are irrevocable.
>   a. True
>   b. False
>
> True, True, False.

The purpose of a springing power of attorney is to make sure that someone has the power to act for the principal and handle the principal's affairs in the event that the principal becomes incapacitated or disabled. A springing power of attorney would be appropriate for someone who is currently able to handle their own affairs but would like to plan for possible future incapacity.

Discussion of Exhibit 2.15

Exhibit 2.15 is an example of a durable general power of attorney. Because it is a general power of attorney, the Internal Revenue Code dictates that the agent must include the fair market value of the principal's assets that are under the power in his gross estate if the agent predeceases the principal. Had the principal limited the power as follows: "the agent cannot appoint assets to himself, his creditors, his estate, the creditors of his estate, or to anyone else for his own benefit," this power would have become a special power of attorney (albeit a broad power) and forgo the risk of inclusion in the agent's gross estate if the agent predeceases the principal. The power of attorney is also effective as of the date of writing unless the principal chooses to make the power springing.

Exhibit 2.15 | Power of Attorney Example

STATUTORY DURABLE POWER OF ATTORNEY (Texas)

NOTICE: THE POWERS GRANTED BY THIS DOCUMENT ARE BROAD AND SWEEPING. THEY ARE EXPLAINED IN THE DURABLE POWER OF ATTORNEY ACT, CHAPTER XII, TEXAS PROBATE CODE. IF YOU HAVE ANY QUESTIONS ABOUT THESE POWERS, OBTAIN COMPETENT LEGAL ADVICE. THIS DOCUMENT DOES NOT AUTHORIZE ANYONE TO MAKE MEDICAL AND OTHER HEALTH-CARE DECISIONS FOR YOU. YOU MAY REVOKE THIS POWER OF ATTORNEY IF YOU LATER WISH TO DO SO.

I, _____ (insert your name and address), appoint _____ (insert the name and address of the person appointed) as my agent (attorney-in-fact) to act for me in any lawful way with respect to all of the following powers except for a power that I have crossed out below.

TO WITHHOLD A POWER, YOU MUST CROSS OUT EACH POWER WITHHELD.

Real property transactions; Tangible personal property transactions; Stock and bond transactions; Commodity and option transactions; Banking and other financial institution transactions; Business operating transactions; Insurance and annuity transactions; Estate, trust, and other beneficiary transactions; Claims and litigation; Personal and family maintenance; Benefits from social security, Medicare, Medicaid, or other governmental programs or civil or military service; Retirement plan transactions; Tax matters.

IF NO POWER LISTED ABOVE IS CROSSED OUT, THIS DOCUMENT SHALL BE CONSTRUED AND INTERPRETED AS A GENERAL POWER OF ATTORNEY AND MY AGENT (ATTORNEY IN FACT) SHALL HAVE THE POWER AND AUTHORITY TO PERFORM OR UNDERTAKE ANY ACTION I COULD PERFORM OR UNDERTAKE IF I WERE PERSONALLY PRESENT.

SPECIAL INSTRUCTIONS:

1. Special instructions applicable to gifts (initial in front of the following sentence to have it apply):

   I grant my agent (attorney in fact) the power to apply my property to make gifts, except that the amount of a gift to an individual may not exceed the amount of annual exclusions allowed from the federal gift tax for the calendar year of the gift.

2. ON THE FOLLOWING LINES YOU MAY GIVE SPECIAL INSTRUCTIONS LIMITING OR EXTENDING THE POWERS GRANTED TO YOUR AGENT.

   _____
   _____

3. UNLESS YOU DIRECT OTHERWISE ABOVE, THIS POWER OF ATTORNEY IS EFFECTIVE IMMEDIATELY AND WILL CONTINUE UNTIL IT IS REVOKED.

   CHOOSE ONE OF THE FOLLOWING ALTERNATIVES BY CROSSING OUT THE ALTERNATIVE NOT CHOSEN:

   (A) This power of attorney is not affected by my subsequent disability or incapacity.

   (B) This power of attorney becomes effective upon my disability or incapacity.

   YOU SHOULD CHOOSE ALTERNATIVE (A) IF THIS POWER OF ATTORNEY IS TO BECOME EFFECTIVE ON THE DATE IT IS EXECUTED.

   IF NEITHER (A) NOR (B) IS CROSSED OUT, IT WILL BE ASSUMED THAT YOU CHOSE ALTERNATIVE (A).

Power of Attorney Example (Continued)

If Alternative (B) is chosen and a definition of my disability or incapacity is not contained in this power of attorney, I shall be considered disabled or incapacitated for purposes of this power of attorney if a physician certifies in writing at a date later than the date this power of attorney is executed that, based on the physician's medical examination of me, I am mentally incapable of managing my financial affairs. I authorize the physician who examines me for this purpose to disclose my physical or mental condition to another person for purposes of this power of attorney. A third party who accepts this power of attorney is fully protected from any action taken under this power of attorney that is based on the determination made by a physician of my disability or incapacity.

I agree that any third party who receives a copy of this document may act under it. Revocation of the durable power of attorney is not effective as to a third party until the third party receives actual notice of the revocation. I agree to indemnify the third party for any claims that arise against the third party because of reliance on this power of attorney.

If any agent named by me dies, becomes legally disabled, resigns, or refuses to act, I name the following (each to act alone and successively, in the order named) as successor(s) to that agent: _____.

Signed this ___ day of _____, 20__.

_____
(your signature)
State of _____

County of _____

This document was acknowledged before me on _____ (date) by _____ (name of principal).

_____
(signature of notarial officer)

(Seal, if any, of notary)

_____
(printed name)

My commission expires:_____

THE ATTORNEY IN FACT OR AGENT, BY ACCEPTING OR ACTING UNDER THE APPOINTMENT, ASSUMES THE FIDUCIARY AND OTHER LEGAL RESPONSIBILITIES OF AN AGENT.

Power of Attorney for Property

A **power of attorney for property** is a special power of attorney designed for a specific purpose. It provides an agent with the power to manage a principal's property and finances. The power of attorney for property may be durable to provide for continuity in the management of property affairs in the event of the principal's disability and/or incapacity. A power of attorney is an inexpensive and relatively easy way for the principal to ensure that his finances will be managed by a trusted person of his choosing.

A durable power of attorney for property enables the principal to select a particular person or financial institution to act on his behalf and manage financial tasks that may arise in the event of incapacity. Examples of these tasks include paying bills, making bank deposits, handling insurance issues, and managing property and investments. In most cases, a durable power of attorney is the most practical way to handle such situations. A durable power of attorney for property may also be used to manage a business.

Consequences of Not Having a Durable Power of Attorney for Property

- A durable power of attorney eliminates the necessity of petitioning a local court to appoint a guardian of the estate to make property decisions for a person who is incapacitated or disabled. These proceedings can be expensive and embarrassing for those involved, as court proceedings are open to the public. If relatives disagree over who should be the guardian of the estate, the proceedings can become lengthy and costly.
- Although a spouse may have some authority over jointly owned property, there are limits to a spouse's right to sell jointly owned property. In most states, both spouses must agree to the sale of jointly owned property. Because an incapacitated spouse cannot consent, the other spouse without a durable power of attorney for property may be limited in what he can do with such property.

Example 2.20
Eric and Jessica have been married for 35 years. Their home is owned in both their names as joint tenants. Their only other major asset is stock that Eric bought prior to their marriage and is titled in his name only. If Eric becomes incapacitated and requires expensive medical treatment, without a durable power of attorney for property Jessica may not be able to legally sell the stock to pay for medical costs without a local court's approval.

Disadvantages of a Power of Attorney

- The agent possessing a power of attorney can abuse the powers granted to him, so the principal should give serious consideration in choosing a person to hold such a power. Unfortunate as it may be, agents may take advantage of their position for their own interest while the principal is incapacitated or disabled.
- In most cases, a person possessing a limited/special power of attorney is not permitted to make gifts to himself or other family members. In addition, if the power to gift to charitable or non-charitable donees is a desirable feature, such powers should be separately and explicitly stated in the instrument.
- In the case of a general power of attorney, if the agent dies before the principal and is holding a general power of appointment over the principal's assets, the power will cause an inclusion in the agent's gross estate of the value (but not the actual assets) of the principal's assets over which the agent had a power.

DIRECTIVES REGARDING HEALTH CARE

Directives regarding health care are probably the most controversial and difficult documents to discuss with a client. Individuals tend to have strong feelings regarding their health care and the ability of others to make health care decisions for them. This section discusses some of the alternative documents related to health care available in most states.

Durable Power of Attorney for Health Care

A **durable power of attorney for health care**, also called a medical power of attorney or health care proxy, is a legal document that appoints an agent (someone with authority to act on behalf of another) to make health care decisions on behalf of a **principal** who is unable to make those decisions for him/herself. Unlike a living will, which states the person's wishes regarding the sustainment of life, the durable power of attorney for health care puts health care decision making in the hands of a third person with the objective to get better.

> ### Key Concepts
> 1. What is a durable power of attorney for health care and why are they used?
> 2. What is a living will and why are they used?
> 3. What is a DNR and why are they used?

The durable power of attorney for health care may provide direction in terminal and nonterminal situations, such as disclosure of medical records, blood transfusions, cardiac resuscitation, organ transplants, and selection of medical support staff, but generally does not provide the right to refuse or the right to end life-sustaining treatment. (Note that in some states a power of attorney for health care may provide the right to withhold or end life-sustaining treatment.) The durable power of attorney for health care eliminates the necessity of petitioning a local court to appoint a guardian to make health care decisions for a person who is incapacitated or disabled.

The durable power of attorney for health care is typically a springing power of attorney. As discussed previously, this feature only allows the agent to act on behalf of the principal when the principal becomes incapacitated. It also lapses the power when the principal recovers from the disability. In some states, it is assumed that the power of attorney for health care is a springing power. Keep in mind the power could also be immediately effective as opposed to springing.

The advantage of the document is that it is less costly to prepare in advance than to have a guardian seek court approval at a time when a health care decision needs to be made. The durable power of attorney for health care is recognized in almost every state, although each state has different laws governing the drafting of such documents.

A durable power of attorney for health care is distinguished from a regular power of attorney (discussed above) in two ways. First, the power is specific to health care decisions, and second, the document entitles the power holder to do exactly what may be needed if the principal is incapacitated or disabled to the extent that the principal cannot make his own health care decisions. A nondurable power of attorney does not survive incapacity or disability. An example of a health care power of attorney is shown in **Exhibit 2.16**.

Exhibit 2.16 | Durable Power of Attorney for Health Care Example

MEDICAL POWER OF ATTORNEY DESIGNATION OF HEALTH CARE AGENT (Texas)

I, _____ (insert your name), appoint:

Name:_____
Address:_____
Phone:_____

as my agent to make any and all health care decisions for me, except to the extent I state otherwise in this document. The medical power of attorney takes effect if I become unable to make my own health care decisions and this fact is certified in writing by my physician.

LIMITATIONS ON THE DECISION-MAKING AUTHORITY OF MY AGENT ARE AS FOLLOWS:
Insert any limitations here.

DESIGNATION OF ALTERNATE AGENT.
If the person designated as my agent is unable or unwilling to make health care decisions for me, I designate the following persons to serve as my agent to make health care decisions for me as authorized in this document, who serve in the following order:

A. First Alternate Agent
Name:_____
Address:_____

B. Second Alternate Agent
Name:_____
Address:_____

The following individuals or institutions have signed copies:
Name:_____
Address:_____

DURATION.
I understand that this power of attorney exists indefinitely from the date I execute this document unless I establish a shorter time or revoke the power of attorney. If I am unable to make health care decisions for myself when this power of attorney expires, the authority I have granted my agent continues to exist until the time I become able to make health care decisions for myself.

(IF APPLICABLE) This power of attorney ends on the following date: _____.

PRIOR DESIGNATIONS REVOKED.
I revoke any prior medical power of attorney.

ACKNOWLEDGMENT OF DISCLOSURE STATEMENT.
I have been provided with a disclosure statement explaining the effect of this document. I have read and understand that information contained in the disclosure statement.

I sign my name to this medical power of attorney on __ day of _____ (*month, year*) at [it may be prudent to include at this point: _____ (time).]

_____
(City and State)

_____
(Signature)

_____
(Print Name)

Living Wills/Advance Medical Directives

A **living will**, also known as an **advance medical directive** or in some states, a Natural Death Declaration or Instruction Directive, is not a will at all, but rather a legal document expressing an individual's last wishes regarding the sustainment of life under specific circumstances. The living will establishes the medical situations and circumstances in which the individual no longer desires life-sustaining treatment in the event he is no longer capable of making those decisions. The document only covers a narrow range of situations, and is usually limited to decisions concerning administering artificial life support treatments when there is no reasonable expectation of recovery from extreme physical or mental disability. Examples of such life sustaining treatments include resuscitation (restarting the heart after it has stopped beating), mechanical ventilation (takes over breathing), nutritional assistance (provides fluids and nutrients intravenously or through a tube into the stomach, and kidney dialysis (waste removal from the blood). It should be noted that almost every state has legislation in place that disregards the living will if the patient is pregnant.

> **Quick Quiz 2.5**
>
> 1. A durable power of attorney for health care typically directs the termination of life-sustaining treatment.
>   a. True
>   b. False
> 2. A springing power of attorney springs into existence upon some future event.
>   a. True
>   b. False
> 3. A living will acts to transfer property during life.
>   a. True
>   b. False
>
> False, True, False.

The living may also name a person as agent to make life-sustaining decisions for the person who is incapacitated. The agent is responsible for making these decisions when the patient can no longer make the decision on his or her own.

The purpose of the living will is to allow individuals who are terminally ill to die on their own terms, or as it has been coined, "die with dignity." Many states have adopted Natural Death Acts stating that the withholding or discontinuance of any extraordinary means of keeping a patient alive, or the withholding or discontinuance of artificial nutrition and hydration, shall not be considered the cause of death for any civil or criminal purpose, nor shall it be considered unprofessional conduct, thus allowing terminal individuals the right to choose the healthcare provided to them.

The living will is also used to avoid the expense of sustaining life artificially and thus to preserve assets for the decedent's heirs. The living will is prepared in advance of an illness to (1) explicitly state the client's wishes, and (2) avoid the necessity for heirs to seek court approval for life-sustaining or termination decisions. The document, though authorized in all states, must meet the specific requirements of the individual's state statute. If the document is not drafted by a competent attorney, problems may arise with vagueness or ambiguities in drafting. Some states have developed a computerized registry of those who have filed living wills so if a person is alive solely because of life-sustaining treatments, the institution providing care can determine if the document exists, and thus comply with the wishes of the registrants. In addition, privately administered national registries have also increased in popularity in the wake of the highly publicized case of Terri Schiavo in 2005. Schiavo's case highlights the importance of having a living will regardless of age or current health. An example of a living will can be found at **Exhibit 2.17**.

Many health care providers suggest that all people, regardless of age or health, should have a living will and a durable power of attorney for health care. In addition, individuals should discuss with their loved ones their feelings regarding natural death as well as anatomical gifts (the donation of organs and tissue). A desire to make anatomical gifts can usually be declared through the state board of motor vehicles as an election printed on the driver's license, or through a notarized declaration. In addition, family members may be able to elect organ donation for an individual at death.

Do Not Resuscitate Order (DNRs)

Individuals may also have a document called a "DNR" which stands for Do Not Resuscitate. These documents declare the principals wish to avoid having cardiopulmonary resuscitation (CPR) performed in the event their heart stops beating. This is not generally prepared as part of an overall estate plan unless the individual is already terminally ill. These types of orders are generally prepared once an individual has already been admitted to a hospital and is near death, and are commonly used by patients with advanced cancer or kidney damage, or patients suffering from significant ailments relating to old age.

DNRs are generally executed on a form provided by the state and may be filed with the patient's medical records. Some states also provide statewide registries allowing these documents to be placed on file for easy access. Some states provide medical bracelets to patients with DNRs that have been sent home to spend their remaining days. The bracelet notifies emergency personnel of the individual's wish to decline CPR. In some states, the advice, consent, and signature of a physician may be necessary to execute a legally enforceable DNR.

It is crucial to understand that DNRs only apply to CPR and do not apply to any other medical treatment. DNRs are not sufficient to avoid other life sustaining treatment. As the application of DNRs vary by state, a thorough understanding of the individual state law is imperative when working with DNRs.

Exhibit 2.17 | Living Will Example

ADVANCE MEDICAL DIRECTIVE (Texas)

DIRECTIVE made this _____ day of _____ (month, year).

I, _____, being of sound mind, willfully and voluntarily make known my desire that my life shall not be artificially prolonged under the circumstances set forth in this directive.

1. If at any time I should have an incurable or irreversible condition caused by injury, disease, or illness certified to be a terminal condition by two physicians, and if the application of life-sustaining procedures would serve only to artificially postpone the moment of my death, and if my attending physician determines that my death is imminent or will result within a relatively short time without the application of life-sustaining procedures, I direct that such procedures be withheld or withdrawn, and that I be permitted to die naturally.

2. In the absence of my ability to give directions regarding the use of those life-sustaining procedures, it is my intention that this directive shall be honored by my family and physicians as the final expression of my legal right to refuse medical or surgical treatment and accept the consequences from that refusal.

3. If I have been diagnosed as pregnant and that diagnosis is known to my physician, this directive has no effect during my pregnancy.

4. This directive is in effect until it is revoked.

5. I understand the full import of this directive and I am emotionally and mentally competent to make this directive.

6. I understand that I may revoke this directive at any time.

Signed:

_____

City, County and State of Residence:

_____

I am not related to the declarant by blood or marriage. I would not be entitled to any portion of the declarant's estate on the declarant's death. I am not the attending physician of the declarant or an employee of the attending physician. I am not a patient in the health care facility in which the declarant is a patient. I have no claim against any portion of the declarant's estate on the declarant's death. Furthermore, if I am an employee of a health facility in which the declarant is a patient, I am not involved in providing direct patient care to the declarant and am not directly involved in the financial affairs of the health facility.

Witness: _____

Witness: _____

Physician Orders for Life Sustaining Treatment (POLST)

Over the past few years a new type of document impacting health care planning has emerged - the **Physician Orders for Life Sustaining Treatment**, or POLST. The purpose of the POLST is to supplement a living well and health care power of attorney by specifically addressing the treatment wishes of an individual in a standardized way. By addressing various treatment options, the POLST improves on the DNR order, which only expresses an intent to withhold cardiopulmonary resuscitation. The POLST is executed by both the individual expressing their treatment wishes, and a physician. The physician's signature on the document constitutes an order of the physician for treatment, and is included in the medical records of the individual. POLSTs are intended to be used by individuals with a serious illness who are expected to die within the a year or so. The objective of the POLST is to ensure that patients receive only those treatments they wish to receive, and to reduce the frequency of medical errors in providing such treatment. Not all states have adopted a formal POLST program, but many are considering it and the POLST will likely become a widely available option. More information on the POLST program may be found at www.polst.org.

OTHER IMPORTANT DOCUMENTS FOR ESTATE PLANNING

While these are not what is generally thought of as estate planning documents, beneficiary designation forms and entity documents, such as LLC operating agreements are extremely important documents to incorporate into an overall estate plan.

A beneficiary designation form will direct contract devices with beneficiary designations such as a life insurance or a retirement plan to pay or transfer ownership of an account after the death of the owner. These forms are often completed and are often forgotten. In some cases, someone will die with a beneficiary designation form completed with the name of an ex-spouse whom the decedent did not intend to benefit after the divorce. Like wills, beneficiary designation forms should be reviewed periodically to ensure that they adequately reflect the wishes of the owner of the accounts or contracts.

It is very common for decedents to have businesses or property owned by corporations, partnerships or limited liability companies (LLCs). Each of the entities will likely have operating documents that may impact part of an overall estate plan. For example, an LLC owning beach property might have an operating agreement that provides for transfer of ownership to a surviving LLC member in the event that one of the LLC members dies. Alternatively, the LLC operating agreement might provide that the decedent's LLC interest will transfer according to the will of the member. These documents should also be periodically reviewed as part of an overall estate plan.

Digital Assets and Estate Planning Documents

The Revised Uniform Fiduciary Access to Digital Rights Act (RUFADAA), which has been adopted by 46 states, recognizes digital assets as property interests that can be held, managed, conserved and transferred. Digital assets include information stored on a person's computer and digital devices, social media accounts, and other information in electronic form. As the use of digital assets continues to increase, estate planners should consider asking a client to provide an inventory of their digital assets, along with instructions on how those digital assets should be dealt with upon the incapacity or death of the client. Wills and powers of attorney should include provisions addressing disclosure and access to the client's digital assets so that Executors/administrators of the estate and attorneys in fact under a power of attorney can fulfill the wishes of the client when managing and distributing the client's assets to intended beneficiaries.

NEED FOR DOCUMENTS

Everyone needs some or all of the documents discussed in this chapter. Individuals often do not realize the necessity of having these documents until it is too late. Consider the following example which illustrates several different scenarios and the need for documents in each case.

Example 2.21

Bill, age 42, is married to Marsha and they have three small children. Bill also has an older child from his first marriage to Cindy. Bill has a net worth of $200,000. On his way home from work one day, Bill is in a serious accident that leaves him comatose and terminally ill where his only means of survival are life-sustaining procedures provided by the hospital. Bill does not have any of the documents discussed in this chapter. Due to the extent of Bill's injury and the means needed to keep him alive, he quickly meets his health insurance policy's maximum lifetime benefit. Thus, his own funds are then needed to continue to maintain his life. Studies show that a hospital stay where life-sustaining procedures are needed costs between $5,000 and $14,000 per day.

In this instance, Bill's family is faced with many dilemmas. Since Bill did not have a living will, his family will have to consider when, or if, to end life sustaining treatment and will likely need a court order to do so. Assume it takes one month after medical benefits run out for Bill's family to consider and obtain the authorization to end life-sustaining treatment and his hospital cost is $5,000 per day. By the end of this first month, Bill's assets will have been reduced from $200,000 to $50,000. If instead, the cost was on the high end of the estimate at $14,000 per day, his assets would be completely depleted and his estate would owe the hospital $220,000. The above chart illustrates this scenario.

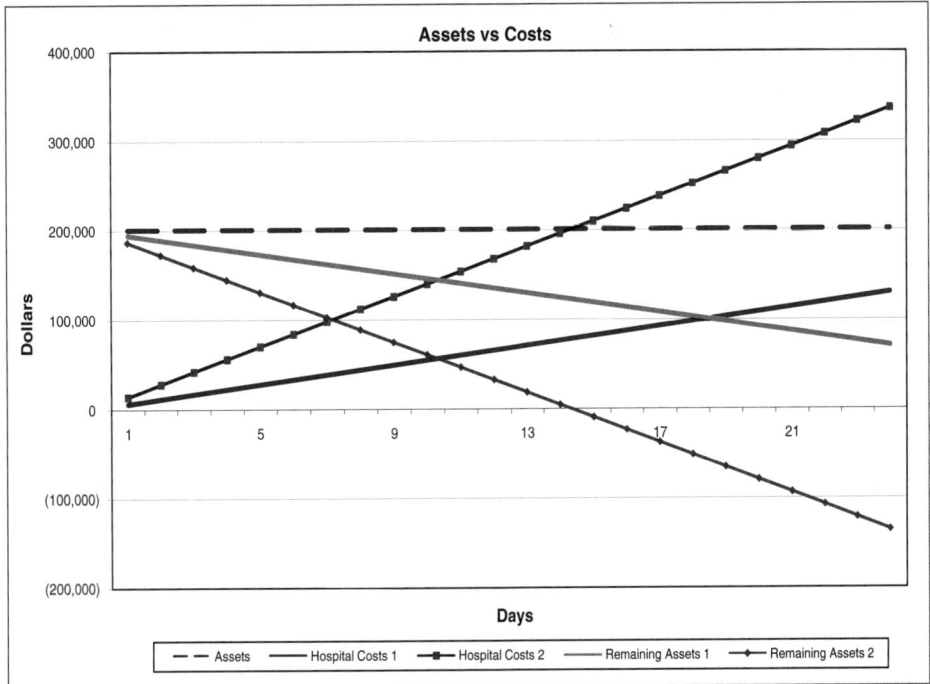

Unfortunately, this is just one of the possible negative situations. Recall that Bill does not have a Power of Attorney either. If Bill is in a common law (separate property) state (see Chapter 3) and holds all of his assets in a separate account, his family may not have access to his funds during his hospital stay. Assuming that Marsha is not employed and all funds are held in an account titled in Bill's name only, Marsha will not have immediately accessible funds. She may have to seek a court order to access his funds for his use, and for their family's use. Unfortunately, this takes time. Again, we see that poor planning on Bill's part has negatively impacted his family.

Let's now assume that Bill dies the day after his accident and his $200,000 in assets are left intact. The fact that he does not have a will may result in his assets not being distributed as he would have wished. In Bill's case this is a concern because of the blended family (i.e., the presence of a child from his first marriage). In some states, the children would inherit most, or all, of the assets with the current spouse retaining a small interest for life. This may leave Marsha with very little assets, or in some cases, the need for her to account for the assets she holds interest in on a regular basis. Such distributions can lead to animosity within the extended family.

All adults should have the appropriate documents as discussed in this chapter as part of their estate plan. While use of these documents is important to the estate planning process, documents are just one of the factors involved in proper estate planning.

KEY TERMS

Administrator - A person, usually a relative of the deceased, appointed by the probate court to oversee the probate process when an executor is not named in the will.

Advance Medical Directive/Living Will - Legal document expressing an individual's last wishes regarding life sustaining treatment.

Ancillary Probate - A probate process conducted in a state other than the state of the decedent's domicile.

Appointment of Executor Clause - A clause in a will that identifies the executor and any successor executor. This clause may also define the extent of the executor's powers and may grant specific or general powers.

Attestation Clause - Witness clause stating that the testator is of sound mind and that he signed the document in the witness' presence.

Attorney in Fact - Agent or power holder of a power of attorney.

Bequest Clause - Directs the distribution of property, whether cash, tangible property, intangible property or real property.

Codicil - A document that amends a will. A codicil is prepared subsequent to and separate from the will to modify or explain the will.

Contingent Legatee Clause - A clause in a will that names a secondary person to inherit if the original legatee is dead or disclaims the property.

Declaration Clause - A clause in a will which states this is the last will and testament of the testator.

Devisee - A person names to receive real estate under the will.

Disclaimer Clause - An heir or legatee's refusal to accept a gift or bequest. The disclaimer allows assets to pass to other heirs or legatees without additional transfer tax.

Domicile - Where one lives and intends to remain. The location of one's home.

Durable Feature - Allows a power of attorney to survive incapacity and/or disability.

Durable Power of Attorney Issued Either for Health Care or for Property - A written document enabling one individual, the principal, to designate another person(s) to act as his "attorney-in-fact." A durable power of attorney survives the incapacity and/or disability of the principal.

Escheat - The reversion of an heirless, intestate decedent's property to the state.

Executor - Estate representative designated in the will by the decedent. An executor may serve without bond if the bond is waived by the decedent.

Felonious Homicide Statute - Statute that prevents heirs who feloniously participated in the decedent's death from inheriting via the will or state intestacy laws.

Forced Heirship - A state requirement that a certain portion of the decedent's estate be transferred to a spouse and, in some instances, children.

Guardianship Clause - A clause in a will which allows the testator to identify an individual(s) to raise any minor children.

Heirs - Individuals who are eligible to receive a portion of a decedent's estate under the intestacy law of the state.

Holographic Will - Handwritten will.

Intestacy - To die without a valid will or to die with a will that does not distribute all property.

Introductory Clause - A clause in a will which identifies the testator.

Joint Will - One will executed by two or more individuals jointly that transfers their common interest in property.

Legatee - A person who is named as a beneficiary in a will.

Living Will/Advance Medical Directive - Legal document expressing an individual's last wishes regarding life sustaining treatment.

Mutual Will - Two or more identical wills that leave all assets to the reciprocal party.

No-Contest Clause - A clause in a will that discourages heirs from contesting the will by substantially decreasing or eliminating bequests to them if they file a formal legal contest to the will.

Nuncupative Will - Oral will consisting of dying declarations.

Overqualified - A decedent's taxable estate is less than the applicable estate tax credit equivalency, usually the result when too many assets pass to a surviving spouse.

Per Capita - Sometimes called "by the head" allows the deceased person's heirs to move into the generational slot of the deceased heir and inherit accordingly.

Per Capita at Each Generation - Directs equal shares to each living member of the same generation.

Per Stirpes - Sometimes called "taking by representation" directs that the deceased person's designated share of an estate is transferred to his heirs.

Physician Orders for Life Sustaining Treatment (POLST) - A document, constituting a physician's order, detailing the types of medical treatments an individual wishes to receive when they are within a year or so of death. The POLST is part of the patient's medical record, and is used to minimize the potential for medical errors in providing treatment.

Power of Attorney - Legal document that authorizes an agent to act on a principal's behalf.

Power of Attorney for Property - A special Power of Attorney designed for a specific purpose.

Principal - The grantor or giver of a power of attorney.

Reciprocal Will - Two or more identical wills that leave all assets to the reciprocal party.

Residuary Clause - A clause in a will which directs the transfer of the balance of any assets not previously bequeathed or distributed.

Self Proving Clause - A clause in a will which involves the notary signing a notarized declaration that he/she witnessed the testator and witnesses sign the will.

Side Instruction Letter - Also known as a personal instruction letter, details the testator's wishes regarding the disposition of tangible possessions (household goods), the disposition of the decedent's body, and funeral arrangements. A side instruction letter is not legally binding, but generally followed.

Simultaneous Death Clause - A clause in a will that establishes a presumption of which person died first in simultaneous death situations.

Situs - The place, generally referring to the state, where property is located.

Sound Mind - A person's mental capacity.

Springing Power - The agent's power "springs" into existence upon some defined event or determination.

Statutory Will - A will meeting state statutes generally drawn up by an attorney and signed in the presence of witnesses.

Survivorship Clause - A clause in a will requiring that the legatee survive for a specific period in order to inherit under the will. The bequest will qualify for the marital deduction if the property transfers to the surviving spouse and the time period of the survivorship clause is six months or less.

Sweetheart Will - Two wills executed by spouses that leave all assets to the other spouse.

Tax-Appointment Clause - A clause in a will directing which assets will bear the payment of any debts and estate taxes.

Testate - When a decedent dies with a valid will.

Testator - Writer of a will.

Uniform Electronic Wills Act - A Uniform Law proposed in 2019 that permits electronic execution and storage of Wills. The act attempts to modernize the will creation process by permitting the creation and storage of a valid will through electronic means.

Uniform Fiduciary Access to Digital Assets Act - A Uniform law that recognizes digital assets as a form of intangible personal property that can be held, managed, conserved, and transferred by the owner. The act provides methods for digital asset owners to grant fiduciary access to their digital assets that held by custodians even when the custodian's terms of service agreements would otherwise deny access to the assets.

Uniform Probate Code - A Uniform Law that provides rules for inheritance and the management of decedent's estates in the United States. The purpose of the act was to standardize probate court procedures across the states.

Will - A legal document that provides the testator, or will maker, the opportunity to control the distribution of property, appoint an executor and avoid the state's intestacy law distribution scheme.

DISCUSSION QUESTIONS

SOLUTIONS to the discussion questions can be found exclusively within the chapter. Once you have completed an initial reading of the chapter, go back and highlight the answers to these questions.

1. List the basic documents used in estate planning.

2. What problems arise for someone who dies intestate?

3. Briefly define the types of wills.

4. List the common provisions in a valid will.

5. Briefly list and define at least three other additional clauses found in wills.

6. What is a living will?

7. Why should a living will be prepared in advance?

8. Identify a reason to use a living will.

9. What is a power of attorney?

10. Identify and discuss the parties to a power of attorney.

11. Identify a reason to use a power of attorney.

12. What is a durable power of attorney?

13. What is a springing durable power of attorney?

14. What is a side instruction letter?

15. Identify some examples of instructions included in a side instruction letter.

chapter 2

MULTIPLE-CHOICE PROBLEMS

A sample of multiple choice problems is provided below. Additional multiple choice problems are available at money-education.com by accessing the Student Practice Portal.

1. Donald drafted his own will utilizing the "Will-Maker" software that he purchased at the local office supply store and sends it to you for a review. In your first review of the will, you look for which of the following most common provisions?
    a. A left-over clause.
    b. A statement of the domicile of the testator.
    c. A primary clause.
    d. A codicil.

2. Which of the following documents appoints a surrogate decision-maker for health care?
    a. Durable power of attorney for health care.
    b. General power of appointment.
    c. Life insurance beneficiary designation.
    d. All of the above.

3. While he was in the hospital, Emile told his wife that if he died he wanted to give his fishing tackle to his son, Joseph; his golf equipment to his son, Joshua; his truck to his daughter, Abigail; and everything else to her (his wife). Emile died the next day without writing anything that he told his wife, but a nurse and another patient were in the room and heard his declarations. What type of will does Emile have, if any?
    a. Holographic.
    b. Nuncupative.
    c. Statutory.
    d. Emile does not have a will.

4. Of the following, which is not a clause commonly found in a will?
    a. Introductory clause.
    b. Payment of debts clause.
    c. Payment of taxes clause.
    d. Conclusory clause.

5. Melissa is terminally ill. Her doctors gave her twenty-four months to live thirty-six months ago. Melissa has decided that she does not want to be placed on life support. Which document will direct Melissa's doctors to refrain from putting her on life support?
    a. Living will.
    b. Power of attorney.
    c. Durable power of attorney.
    d. General power of appointment.

QUICK QUIZ EXPLANATIONS

Quick Quiz 2.1
1. False. Noncupative wills are oral, not written, wills.
2. False. While it is possible for a will to control the disposition of all property, it is common to have some property pass by contract or by law.
3. True.
4. True.
5. False. Holographic wills are drawn by the testator and are in the testator's own handwriting.

Quick Quiz 2.2
1. True.
2. False. If a survivorship clause applies to a spouse and requires the spouse to survive the decedent by more than six months, transfers to the spouse will not qualify for the marital deduction.
3. False. While a survivorship clause often eliminates the need for a simultaneous death clause, a simultaneous death clause does not eliminate the need for a survivorship clause.

Quick Quiz 2.3
1. True.
2. False. Side letters of instruction are not binding in the probate process, but the property transfers that are covered in the side letter of instruction are probate transfers.
3. False. Will contests can never be eliminated although use of no-contest clauses can minimize the likelihood that they will occur.

Quick Quiz 2.4
1. True.
2. True.
3. False. All powers of attorney may be revoked at any time by a competent principal.

Quick Quiz 2.5
1. False. A durable power of attorney for health care does not typically direct the termination of life-sustaining treatment, although this is allowed in some states.
2. True.
3. False. A living will is concerned with the provision or withholding of life-sustaining treatment. It does not direct the transfer of property during life.

3
TYPES OF PROPERTY INTERESTS

LEARNING OBJECTIVES

1. Describe the three property interests in our legal system (real, tangible personal property, and intangible personal property).
1. Describe fee simple.
2. Describe the various legal forms of property titling and ownership including sole ownership, tenants-in-common, joint tenancy with right of survivorship, tenants by the entirety, and community property.
3. Identify the number of owners in each property regime, the right to transfer, automatic survivorship features, the portion included in the gross estate, the portion included in the probate estate, and whether or not the property is partitionable without the consent of any joint owner.
4. Describe other ownership types such as partial ownerships including life estates and interest for a term.
5. Distinguish legal versus equitable ownership.

CFP Board Resource Document - Student-Centered Learning Objectives based upon CFP Board Principal Topics.

OWNERSHIP AND TRANSFER OF PROPERTY

Introduction

In our legal system, all property interests are classified into one of three categories:
1. real property,
2. tangible personal property, or
3. intangible personal property.

Key Concepts

1. Identify the three types of property and examples of each.
2. Identify the characteristics of sole ownership.
3. Identify the characteristics of tenancy in common ownership.
4. Identify the characteristics of joint tenancy with right of survivorship.
5. Identify the characteristics of tenancy by the entirety.
6. Identify the characteristics of community property.

Real property (realty) includes land and anything permanently attached to the land (such as buildings, trees, and items permanently affixed to buildings, called fixtures). **Tangible personal property** consists of all property that is not realty (not affixed to the land and generally movable) and that has physical substance. **Intangible personal property** is property that is not real property and is without physical substance (such as stocks, bonds, patents, and copyrights). Some types of property require a state title as proof of ownership. Examples of titled property include real estate, automobiles (assuming the state has a motor vehicle title law), stocks, bonds, bank accounts, and retirement accounts. Other property, such as household goods, may not have a specific title. State law determines the forms of ownership interest available as well as the ways in which property interests can be transferred from one person to another during lifetime or at death.

Digital Assets are a special form of intangible personal property that has been increasing in importance recently. Section 2(10) of The Revised Uniform Fiduciary Access to Digital Rights Act (RUFADAA), which has been adopted in 46 states as of the date of this writing, defines a digital asset as an "electronic record of which an individual has a right or interest." Digital assets may include information stored on a user's computer and other digital devices, social media accounts, information uploaded to websites, and catalogs of the content of electronic communications. RUFADAA recognizes the existence of digital assets as property which can be held, managed, conserved, and transferred. While a custodian (such as Facebook, Twitter, Dropbox, and the like) of a user's digital assets often has a terms of service agreement (TOSA) that is very favorable to the custodian (such as Facebook's assertion in its TOSA that any items posted on the user's account becomes the property of Facebook), RUFADAA recognizes that the user has the right to decide whether the custodian of his or her digital data may disclose to a representative of the user (called a fiduciary in RUFADAA) the existence of or access to specific, or all, digital assets of the user. The custodian of a user's digital assets must honor the user's grant of access to those assets to a fiduciary named in a Will, trust, power of attorney, or the custodian's own online tool created for that purpose regardless of contrary terms in the TOSA. A court order can also grant fiduciary access to a user's digital assets. Under RUFADAA, the custodian may charge a reasonable administrative fee that a fiduciary would have to pay to gain access to the digital assets. As the use of digital assets continues to increase, protecting and guaranteeing succession of those property interests becomes an important part of the estate planning process.

Alternative types or forms of property interest vary from state to state. Thus, financial advisors need a working knowledge of the various forms of property interests and how each is transferred. Depending on the client's objectives and the way in which the client intends to transfer the property during life or at death, clients need to be properly advised as to the appropriate ownership form.

PROPERTY INTERESTS (TITLE AND OWNERSHIP)

State law classifies the interest an owner has in property based on how the property is held (referred to as legal form of ownership) by the owner. Common among these legal forms of ownership are sole ownership, tenancy in common, joint tenancy, tenancy by the entirety, and community property. In addition, some ownership interests in property represent less than complete ownership and are referred to as partial interests. Partial interests in property as differentiated from fee simple (all rights) include life estates, usufruct interests, and term interests.

Exhibit 3.1 | Property Interests

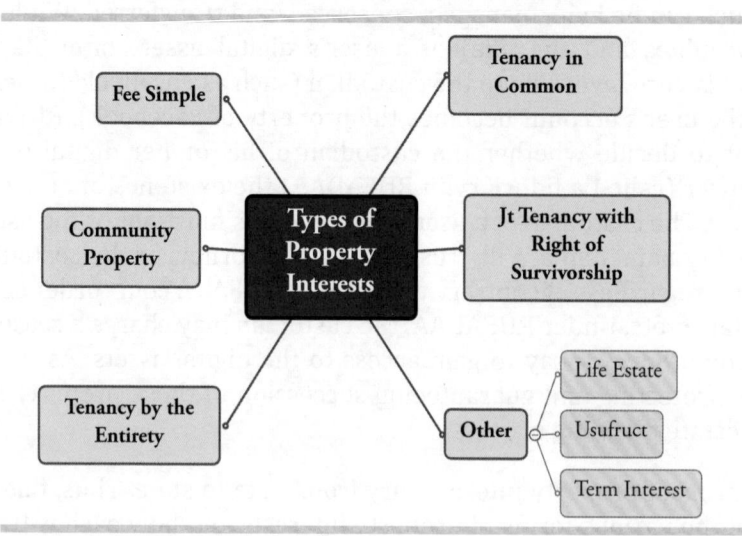

Sole Ownership - Fee Simple

Sole ownership is the complete ownership of property by one individual who possesses the property fee simple meaning all ownership rights associated with the property, including the right to use, sell, gift, alienate, convey, or bequeath the property. The key characteristic of **fee simple** ownership is that the owner has the unfettered right to transfer his ownership interest in the property during lifetime (gift, sale) or at death by a will. Fee simple ownership is the most common way to own property interests today both by a sole owner and by joint owners. It consists of the maximum rights that an owner can have.

The ability to use, consume, or dispose of one's property in the form of fee simple is often referred to as fee simple absolute. The entire fair market value of a fee simple property interest is included in the owner's gross estate for federal estate tax purposes. When a person dies owning fee simple property, that property is passed to the decedent's heirs (or whomever else the decedent specifies) through the probate process (discussed in Chapter 4) by virtue of the will or, where no will exists, by virtue of the state's intestacy laws. If, however, real property is located in a state that is not the **residence domiciliary** (decedent's state of residence) of the decedent, it will be subject to **ancillary probate** (probate in a state where the owner is not domiciled) in the state of situs.

When someone owns property in fee simple, he can mortgage that property and use it in any way he desires. Of course, jurisdictional restrictions may place reasonable limits on the use of property. For example, if someone owns land in the middle of an urban area, certain zoning laws may prohibit the owner from using the land to hunt, conduct outdoor concerts, or engage in other types of activities that could endanger others or interfere with the rights other people have to the quiet enjoyment of their own property.

Exhibit 3.2 | Sole Ownership Summary

Number of Owners	Only 1
Right to Transfer	Freely
Automatic Survivorship Feature	No, transfers at death via will or intestacy laws
Included in the Gross Estate	Yes, 100%
Included in the Probate Estate	Yes, 100%

Tenancy in Common (TC)

Tenancy in common is an interest in property held by two or more related or unrelated persons. Each owner is referred to as a tenant in common. Tenancy in common is the most common type of joint ownership between non-spouses. Each person holds an undivided, but not necessarily equal, interest in the entire property. Each co-owner does not own a designated portion of the property, instead he owns an interest in the entire property. For example, if Jim and Bill own a two story home together, Jim does not own the top floor and Bill does not own the bottom floor. Instead, they each own a percentage of the entire house, and both are entitled to use the entire property. Tenants in common typically hold fee simple titling rights.

The property interest is treated as if it were owned outright and each owner's interest can be used, sold, donated, placed in trust, willed, or transferred via the state's intestacy laws at the owner's death (unless restricted by contract or agreement). On its own, property held as tenancy in common does not avoid probate. Each party shares in the income and expenses of the property in proportion to his interest.

Usually, co-owners are not liable for the debts of the other co-owners. Thus, a creditor of one co-owner is unable to seize the entire property to satisfy a debt of one particular owner. The creditor is only able to seize the portion of the property that corresponds to the ownership interest of that debtor.

> ### 📝 Quick Quiz 3.1
>
> 1. Examples of real property are land, automobiles, and stocks.
>   a. True
>   b. False
> 2. In a sole ownership, the joint tenants must agree to sever.
>   a. True
>   b. False
> 3. Sole property owned by a decedent is included in the owner's gross estate for federal estate tax purposes.
>   a. True
>   b. False
>
> *False, False, True.*

Example 3.1

Naomi and Andrew, who are not married, own a tract of land together, held as tenants in common. The property is worth $100,000 and each of them owns 50% of the property. Andrew recently defaulted on a personal loan that was not associated with the property and the creditor has placed a lien on his property. The creditor will only be able to seize Andrew's 50% interest in the tract of land. Except in exceptional circumstances, the creditor will not be able to seize Naomi's portion. If the creditor ultimately forces Andrew's 50% interest in the property to be sold to satisfy the debt, Naomi will have a new co-tenant in the property.

Exhibit 3.3 | Tenancy in Common Ownership Summary

Number of Owners	2 or more
Right to Transfer	Freely without the consent of other co-tenants
Automatic Survivorship Feature	No, transfers at death via will or intestacy laws
Included in the Gross Estate	Usually the FMV of ownership percentage
Included in the Probate Estate	Yes, fair market value of interest
Partitionable	Yes, with or without consent of joint owner

Tenancy in common does not imply an automatic right of survivorship. At the death of a tenant in common, the other tenant in common does not automatically receive the decedent's interest. When an owner of a tenancy in common interest dies, his interest will pass through the probate process, and will be retitled in accordance with his will or the state intestacy laws. The fair market value of a tenant in common's ownership interest is included in his gross estate for federal estate tax purposes. If an owner transfers his interest to a new owner, the new owner receives the transferor's share of ownership, and holds the property with the other tenants in common.

If tenants in common cannot agree on the management of the property or no longer want to own the property jointly, they can partition, or sever, the property. If all tenants in common do not agree to sever, the right to partition can be requested of a court without the permission of the other tenants in common. Once the property has been severed, each former tenant in common will own a piece of the original property in sole ownership.

Usually, each tenant in common will have an interest proportional to his financial contribution. On occasion, however, a tenant in common's share of ownership in the property will be of greater proportional share than his pro rata contribution. In such a case, a gift has been made from one party to another.

Example 3.2

If Carla and Brian agree to purchase property for $100,000, and Carla pays $60,000 and Brian pays $40,000, but they agree to own the property tenancy in common 50% each, Carla has made a gift to Brian of $10,000 (the value of a 10% interest in the property).

Property owned tenancy in common is included in the tenant's gross estate to the extent of the tenant's ownership percentage.

Example 3.3

Kayli and Brody own a tract of land, titled tenancy in common. Kayli contributed $75,000 and Brody contributed $25,000. Assuming Brody died today, the value of the jointly held property included in his gross estate is 25% of the fair market value of the property. If Kayli died she would have included 75% of the fair market value in her gross estate. In this example, it is irrelevant whether they are married; the answer will be the same.

Joint Tenancy with Right of Survivorship (JTWROS)

Joint tenancy is an interest in property held by two or more related or unrelated persons called joint tenants. Each person holds an undivided, equal interest in the whole property. Each joint tenant shares equally in the income and expenses of the property.

A right of survivorship is implied with this form of ownership; and at the death of the first joint tenant, the decedent's interest transfers to the other joint tenants outside of the probate process according to state titling law. Because of this right of survivorship, joint tenancy is often called joint tenancy with right of survivorship (JTWROS).

Unlike tenancy in common, in some instances co-owners may be liable for the debts of the other co-owners to the extent of the property held in joint tenancy. Thus, a creditor of one co-owner may be able to seize the entire property to satisfy a debt of one particular owner.

> ### Quick Quiz 3.2
>
> 1. Tenancy in common is only available for married couples.
>   a. True
>   b. False
> 2. Tenancy in common provides an automatic right of survivorship, thus avoiding the probate process.
>   a. True
>   b. False
> 3. A tenancy in common can be severed without the permission of all of the tenants in common.
>   a. True
>   b. False
>
> *False, False, True.*

Example 3.4

Naomi and Andrew own a tract of land together, held JTWROS. The property is worth $100,000 with each of them owning 50% of the property. Andrew recently defaulted on a loan and the creditor has placed a lien on his property. The creditor may be able to seize the entire piece of property to satisfy Andrew's debt depending on the state law.

In the event joint tenants cannot agree on the management of the property, or no longer want to own the property jointly, any joint tenant can sever his interest in the property without the consent of the other joint tenants. After the property is severed, each former joint tenant will hold his interest in sole ownership if the property has been divided and there is no longer joint ownership, or tenancy in common, if joint ownership remains.

Exhibit 3.4 | Joint Tenancy with Right of Survivorship Ownership Summary

Number of Owners	2 or more
Right to Transfer	Freely without consent
Automatic Survivorship Feature	Yes, transfers at death to other owners
Included in the Gross Estate	Yes, FMV times the % contributed
Included in the Probate Estate	No
Partitionable	Yes, with or without consent of joint owner

While JTWROS property avoids the costs and delays of probate, it is still included in the decedent's gross estate to the extent of the decedent's original contribution percentage. This rule, sometimes known as "the **actual contribution rule**," does not apply to spouses who are named as joint tenants. Spouses named as joint tenants are legally deemed to have each contributed 50 percent of the financial consideration to purchase the property regardless of the actual source of funding.

Example 3.5

Tom purchased a piece of real estate and titled the property JTWROS with his son, Paul. Paul did not make any financial contribution to the purchase of the property. When this transaction occurred Tom made a gift to Paul of one-half of the value of the property. When Tom dies, 100 percent of the value of this property will be included in Tom's gross estate even though he made a gift of 50%.

Even though Tom only had a legal right to 50% of the property, and had made a gift to Paul for the other 50%, 100% of the value of the property is included in his federal gross estate due to the actual contribution rule. If Paul died first he would initially be presumed to include 100% of the value of property in his gross estate, but when his executor provides proof that Paul did not contribute to the purchase price, none of the value of the property will be included in his gross estate.

Example 3.6

Assume instead that Tom purchased a piece of real estate and titled the property JTWROS with his wife, Pauline. Again, Pauline made no financial contribution towards the purchase of the property. In this transaction Tom is deemed to have contributed only 50% because he and Pauline are married. When Tom dies only 50% of the value of the property will be included in his gross estate.

In this example, Pauline gains ownership rights to the property (50%) without ever having contributed to the overall price of property. While a gift has been made to Pauline, the unlimited gift tax marital deduction prevents it from being subject to gift tax (provided that Pauline is a U.S. citizen).

An exception to "the actual contribution rule" exists for gifts of a joint interest in a bank account or Series H bond. In these situations, a completed gift is not made until the non-contributing joint account owner takes a withdrawal from the account for his own personal benefit.

Example 3.7
If Tom creates a joint checking account for himself and his son, Paul, by contributing $10,000, Tom has not made a gift to Paul at the date of the contribution. However, if Paul later withdraws any of the money for his own personal benefit, Tom will be deemed to have made a gift to Paul equal to the amount withdrawn at the date of withdrawal.

Tenancy by the Entirety (TE)

Tenancy by the entirety is very similar to joint tenancy between a married couple. To understand this form of ownership it is important to remember the following four key components:
1. tenancy by the entirety applies to joint ownership only between married couples,
2. neither tenant is able to sever their interest without the consent of the other tenant (spouse),
3. property ownership interest is automatically transferred to the surviving spouse upon death, and
4. it may involve the ownership interest of either real or personal property.

In most respects, tenancy by the entirety is simply a JTWROS that can only occur between a married couple. Tenancy by the entirety exists throughout the length of the marriage and terminates upon divorce or death. Upon divorce, the tenancy by the entirety form of ownership ceases to exist, thus transforming the ownership interests of both parties to some form of joint ownership, usually tenants in common. Tenants by the entirety is not available to cohabitating, non-married couples.

In most states, neither tenant (spouse) is able to sever their interest in property titled tenancy by the entirety without the consent of the other tenant (spouse). If either married partner wishes to transfer their share of interest in the property to a third party (through sale or gift), both parties must join (consent) in a mutual transfer of the property. This stipulation helps to prevent any termination of the other spouse's right of survivorship by transfer of property to a third party. In such cases, the interest in the property between the remaining tenant (spouse) and the new third party owner becomes a joint tenancy or tenancy in common. Spouses may choose to convert their tenancy by the entirety ownership into a tenancy in common or a joint tenancy. The form of property ownership is simply changed without triggering any gift tax consequences.

Quick Quiz 3.3

1. Because of the implied right of survivorship, only related parties can enter into a joint tenancy.
   a. True
   b. False

2. Tom created a joint checking account for himself and his cousin, Bill, with a $50,000 deposit. Because Bill has every right to withdraw the money at anytime, for federal gift tax purposes Tom has made a gift to Bill.
   a. True
   b. False

False, False.

Exhibit 3.5 | Tenancy by the Entirety Ownership Summary

Number of Owners	2 - spouses only
Right to Transfer	Need consent of other spouse
Automatic Survivorship Feature	Yes, transfers at death to other spouse
Included in the Gross Estate	Yes, always 50% of FMV
Included in the Probate Estate	No
Partitionable	Not without consent of spouse / joint owner

For property held as tenancy by the entirety at the death of the first tenant, the decedent's property ownership is passed to the surviving spouse according to state law titling requirements. Because the state law provides for retitling upon presentation of a certified death certificate, there is no need for this property to go through the probate process to be retitled in the name of the surviving spouse. Like property owned as JTWROS between spouses, 50 percent of the value of the property held as tenants by the entirety is included in the gross estate of the first spouse to die, regardless of the amount the deceased spouse contributed to the purchase price of the property.

Community Property and Separate Property in Community Property Regimes

Community property is a civil law concept designed to protect the property interests of married women, and is followed by states in the U.S. whose early development was influenced by French and Spanish law. In states that have adopted this statutory regime, married individuals own an equal undivided interest in all property accumulated during their marriage. During marriage, the income of each spouse is considered community property. Property acquired before the marriage and property received by gift or inheritance during the marriage retains its status as separate property. However, if any separate property is commingled with community property, it is often assumed to be community property. The states following the community property regime are Arizona, California, Idaho, Louisiana, Nevada, New Mexico, Texas, Washington, and Wisconsin (see **Exhibit 3.6**). In addition, Alaska allows residents and nonresidents to enter into community property agreements permitting in-state property to be treated as community property. Community property regimes may vary slightly from state to state; thus, a thorough understanding of a client's state laws is needed for proper planning.

Quick Quiz 3.4

1. The actual contribution rule does not apply to married persons where the married couple owns property JTWROS.
   a. True
   b. False

2. Tenancy by the entirety is a tenancy in common that can only occur between a married couple.
   a. True
   b. False

3. Property owned as tenancy by the entirety does not pass through probate because of the automatic right of survivorship.
   a. True
   b. False

True, False, True.

Exhibit 3.6 | Community-Property States

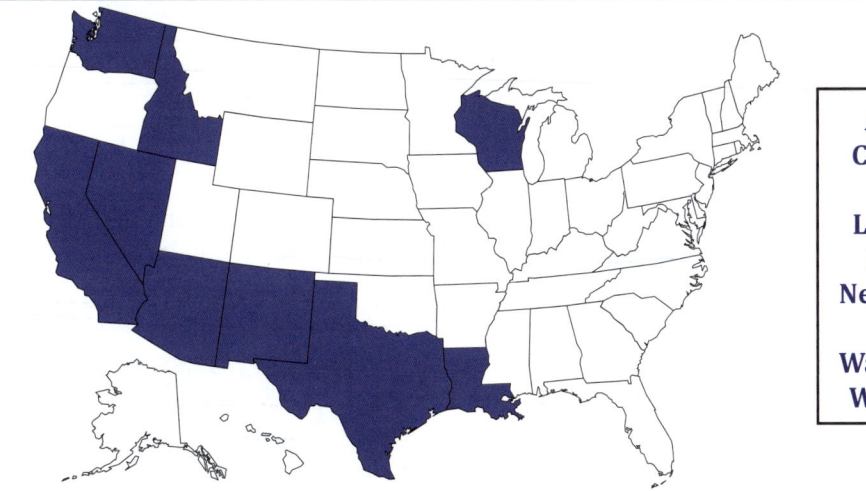

Arizona
California
Idaho
Louisiana
Nevada
New Mexico
Texas
Washington
Wisconsin

Community property does not usually have an automatic right of survivorship feature, although some states, including Texas and California, have a survivorship option. When the first spouse dies, one half of the value of the property will pass through the probate process for retitling per the direction of the decedent's will or the state intestacy law. Each spouse's one-half interest will also be included in their own federal gross estate.

Community property status can be dissolved by death, divorce, or by agreement between the spouses. Specifically, one spouse can gift his half of the community property to the other spouse, thereby creating separate property owned entirely by the donee spouse. Because there is an unlimited marital deduction for gift taxes (as discussed in Chapter 5), such a gift would not create any gift tax liability. This type of gift may occur when a couple moves from a community-property state to a common law (separate property) state in which the couple intends to make their permanent domicile. Otherwise, community property retains its community property status.

When a couple moves from a common law (separate property) state into a community-property state, the property acquired before the move retains its separate property status, unless the couple agrees to treat the property as community property. Any property acquired subsequent to the couple's move into the community-property state is considered community property unless statutory law allows, and the couple chooses, to formally opt out of the state's community property regime.

Quick Quiz 3.5

1. Both halves of property owned tenancy by the entirety in a common law (separate property) state would receive a new basis at the death of one of the owners.
   a. True
   b. False

2. Community property is a regime under which married individuals own an equal undivided interest in all property accumulated, utilizing either spouse's earnings during their marriage.
   a. True
   b. False

False, True.

Exhibit 3.7 | Community Property Ownership Summary

Number of Owners	2 - spouses only
Right to Transfer	Need consent of other spouse
Automatic Survivorship Feature	No, transfers via will or intestacy law
Included in the Gross Estate	Always 50% of community property + 100% of separate property
Included in the Probate Estate	Always 50% of community property + 100% of separate property not retitled otherwise
Partitionable	Not without consent of spouse / joint owner

In certain community-property states, a **quasi-community property** regime is recognized for a couple moving from a common law (separate property) state to that community-property state. Quasi-community property is property that would be community property had the couple been living in the community-property state at the time of acquisition. Quasi-community property is treated just like community property at the death of either spouse, or at the time of divorce. Aside from treating the property as community property at death or divorce, quasi-community property is treated as separate property.

As will be discussed in Chapter 6, a decedent's property is valued for federal estate tax purposes as of his date of death or the alternate valuation date (six months after death). Upon distribution of the property, the decedent's heirs will receive an adjusted ("step-up") basis equal to the value used in the federal estate tax calculation (date of death or alternate valuation date). When property owned jointly is included in a decedent's gross estate, the individual who receives such property will generally receive a new tax basis in the inherited portion equal to the fair market value at the date of death or the alternate valuation date (if elected) and the other joint owners will retain their original adjusted basis in the portion they owned originally.

By contrast, community property provides that at the death of the first spouse both halves of community property receive a step up in basis to the fair market value at decedent's date of death or alternate valuation date even though the decedent only owned 50 percent of the property. Generally, this new tax basis is higher than the old tax basis and will thus reduce future capital gains. Only property owned as community property is afforded this tax basis treatment. Recall that in certain situations, a married couple can own property, even within a community-property state, as separate property. Such separate property would only receive a new tax basis at the death of the separate property owner.

> ### Quick Quiz 3.6
>
> 1. There is an implied right of survivorship with community property.
>   a. True
>   b. False
> 2. Community property may be dissolved by death, divorce, or by agreement between the spouses.
>   a. True
>   b. False
> 3. When a couple moves from a common law (separate property) state to a community-property state, all of their previously owned separate property automatically becomes community property.
>   a. True
>   b. False
>
> *False, True, False.*

Example 3.8

Ann and Bill have lived in a community-property state all 32 years of their marriage. Ann and Bill purchased a home 20 years ago for $120,000 (each would have a deemed $60,000 adjusted basis in the home). The value of their home has appreciated to $2,000,000. When Bill dies, his executor will include ½ of the value of the home, equal to $1,000,000, in Bill's gross estate for federal estate tax purposes. Bill's heirs (not necessarily Ann - community property does not have an automatic right of survivorship) will have an adjusted basis in ½ of the home of $1,000,000. Ann will also receive a new income tax basis equal to $1,000,000 for her ½ of the home.

In this example, it is important to remember that Bill can bequeath his share of community property to whomever he wishes (assuming there are not any state statutes limiting his ability to do so). However, Bill could have bequeathed his ½ to Ann and she would then own the entire house with an adjusted basis of $2,000,000.

> **Quick Quiz 3.7**
>
> 1. Property acquired by gift, by inheritance, or before the marriage can retain its separate property status even in a community-property state.
>   a. True
>   b. False
>
> 2. If separate property is commingled with community property to the extent that it cannot be traced as separate, the property is automatically deemed community property.
>   a. True
>   b. False
>
> 3. Quasi-community property is property that was community property before one spouse donated his interest to the other spouse.
>   a. True
>   b. False
>
> True, True, False.

Example 3.9

If Bill and Ann had lived in a common law (separate property) state and owned the property tenancy in common, only Bill's heirs would receive a new basis in ½ of the home. Ann would continue to own her ½ of the home with a tax basis equal to her original $60,000 adjusted basis.

Example 3.10

Ronan and Mia lived in Illinois (a common-law state) since their marriage in 1989. In 2002, Ronan and Mia purchased a vacation home in California for $50,000 and titled the property joint tenancy with right of survivorship. In 2005, Ronan and Mia moved to California, but did not declare all property community property. When Ronan died in 2006, Ronan's executor included ½ of the value of the California vacation home in Ronan's federal gross estate at $150,000 (the home was valued at Ronan's date of death at $300,000). Because of the right of survivorship, Mia is the beneficiary and receives Ronan's ½ of the home with a tax basis of $150,000. Because the property was not community property, Mia does not receive a new tax basis for her original ½ of the home, but keeps her old tax basis of $25,000 ($50,000/2). Mia now owns 100% of the home but with an income tax basis equal to $175,000 ($25,000 + $150,000 = $175,000).

Had Mia and Ronan declared all the property community property, Mia would have received a new tax basis on her ½ of the home and would have a tax basis equal to

$300,000 in the property. An increase in tax basis could greatly affect any capital gains tax on a future sale of the property.

SPECIAL FORMS OF PROPERTY OWNERSHIP

Partial Ownership Interests (less than fee simple)

Certain planning scenarios call for the creation, or transfer, of less than a full and complete ownership of property under state law. Three of the most common types of property titling that represent partial ownership interests are life estate, usufruct, and term interest.

> **Key Concepts**
>
> 1. Identify the characteristics of a life estate.
> 2. Identify the characteristics of a usufruct.

Life Estate

A **life estate** is an interest in property that ceases upon the death of the owner of the interest and provides the owner of such interest with a right to the income or the right to use property, or both. Upon termination of the life estate (at the death of the life tenant), the property is transferred to the remainder beneficiary (remainderman) who owns the underlying property and any right to income or use at the death of the life estate owner. Life estate interests are generally excluded from the life tenant's taxable estate, since they have no disposition powers associated with the property. A common example of a life estate is when one person leaves another person the use of their beach property for the life of the other person.

Example 3.11
If Xavier bequeathed his vacation home to his mother for the rest of her life and then to his brother at his mother's death, Xavier's mom would have a life estate in the property, and his brother would have a remainder interest.

Example 3.12
Bill, who is 70 years old, has been dating Betty, who is only 40 years old, for the last five years. They have been living in Bill's house for the last four years and plan on living there together forever. Bill's son, Don, is 50 years old and has a daughter named Ainsley. Bill decides to leave a life estate for his house to Betty in the event of his death. After Betty's death, the house will pass to Ainsley.

Usufruct

A **usufruct** is a civil law concept (only available in Louisiana) similar to a life estate under common law rules. A usufruct provides the holder with the right to use property and/or the right to income from property similar to a life estate. At the death of the usufructuary (the person who owns the usufruct interest), the property passes to the naked owners (remaindermen) in full ownership interest.

Example 3.13
When Steve dies, he leaves his home to his children subject to a usufruct on behalf of Steve's mother. Steve's mother can enjoy the property for her life, but the children own

the home. Upon the death of Steve's mother, the complete interest in the home will pass to his children.

A usufruct may be either statutory or may be voluntary. The statutory usufruct is codified in Article 890 of the Louisiana Civil Code and states: If the deceased spouse is survived by descendants, the surviving spouse shall have a usufruct over the decedent's share of the community property to the extent that the decedent has not disposed of it by testament. This usufruct terminates when the surviving spouse dies or remarries, whichever occurs first. Therefore, unlike a life estate, the usufruct may end upon either death or remarriage, whereas a life estate will end upon death.

In addition, a usufruct could be for a specific period of time, which is a similar concept as a term interest.

Term Interest

A **term interest** is an interest in property that grants the holder the right to use the property for a definite term (number of years). A term interest may grant a right to income or use of the property or both. At the end of the term interest, the property is transferred to the remainderman.

Example 3.14
Robin, who is 55 years old, owns a home in Miami. She has been dating a younger man named Matt. Matt is only 23 years old. While drafting her will, she decides to leave Matt an interest in her home for a period of three years. Robin believes that three years is enough time for Matt to actually find a job or another "friend." After the three-year period, the property will transfer to her two children, Reese and Seth. The interest Robin has left Matt is referred to as a term interest because it only lasts for a specific term.

Legal vs. Equitable Ownership

Legal ownership implies that a party has title to the property. Generally, the legal owner possesses all rights, duties, responsibilities, and privileges associated with the property. Only the person with legal ownership of property can convey that property to others.

Equitable ownership is the economic right to enjoy the benefits of the property. Equitable ownership is a form of ownership that is typically associated with use of the property. Even though a person possessing legal ownership holds absolute title to the property, an equitable owner holds temporary title to the property for as long as he has legal use of the property. This holds true even though the absolute title may be in the name of someone else. The equitable owner reaps the rewards of property ownership through the use of the property. Benefits associated with the use of the property include:
- the right to possess the property,
- the right to enjoy the property,
- the right to use the property, and
- the right to receive income from the property.

> ### Quick Quiz 3.8
> 1. A life estate is an interest in property that ceases at a predetermined date.
>   a. True
>   b. False
> 2. A usufruct is similar to the life estate, but only applies in Louisiana.
>   a. True
>   b. False
>
> *False, True.*

Special Forms of Property Ownership

A common example of a technique that splits legal and equitable title is a trust. In the case of trusts, the trustee has the legal title to the property held in trust and acts as a fiduciary for the holder of the equitable interest or the beneficiary of the trust. We will explore this in more detail in Chapter 8.

CUMULATIVE SUMMARY AND EXAMPLE

As described in this chapter, each property ownership type has a unique combination of features and characteristics. The five most important planning questions concerning the various property ownership forms are:
1. What value or percentage of value is included in a decedent's gross estate?
2. Is the property included in the decedent's probate estate?
3. Does the property have an automatic right of survivorship?
4. Will the value of the property qualify for the unlimited marital deduction?
5. Can an interest in the property, if jointly held, or an interest in community property, be partitioned without the consent of the other joint or community owner?

Sole Ownership

Sole Ownership is full outright ownership by one person. The fair market value of property owned as sole ownership is fully included in a decedent's gross estate, but if the property is transferred to the surviving spouse, the fair market value of the property is eligible for the unlimited marital deduction. Also, because sole ownership property does not automatically pass to another person at the decedent's death, the full fair market value of sole ownership property is included in the decedent's probate estate. Most sole ownership is of fee simple rights.

Tenancy in Common

Tenancy in common is a joint interest in property between two or more individuals who can choose to partition their interests without the consent of the other owners. The fair market value of a decedent's ownership interest in tenancy in common property is included in the decedent's gross estate. If the property is transferred by probate to the decedent's surviving spouse, the fair market value of the decedent's interest in the property is eligible for the unlimited marital deduction. The decedent's interest in tenancy in common property does not automatically transfer, but must pass through probate for retitling.

Joint Tenancy with Right of Survivorship

Joint tenancy with right of survivorship is an equal joint interest in property between two or more individuals who can choose to partition their interest without the consent of the other joint tenants even when the joint tenant is a spouse. At the death of one joint tenant, his interest automatically passes to the surviving property owners, and therefore the property is not included in a decedent's probate estate. The fair market value of the decedent's interest (as determined under the actual contribution rule) in the property is included in the decedent's gross estate, but if the property is owned with the spouse as joint tenancy with rights of survivorship the value of the property is eligible for the unlimited marital deduction. In the case of a spousal joint tenant, the contribution rule will always assume a 50 percent contribution from each spouse, regardless of the amount that was actually contributed by each spouse.

Tenancy by the Entirety

Tenancy by the entirety is joint ownership of property between a married couple that cannot be partitioned without the consent of the other spouse. At the death of the first spouse, the property is automatically transferred to the surviving spouse, and therefore does not go through probate. Fifty percent of the fair market value of the property is included in a decedent's gross estate as there is a deemed 50 percent contribution rule. Because the property automatically transfers to the surviving spouse, the value of the property is eligible for the unlimited marital deduction.

Community Property

Community property is a property ownership form available only to spouses. Like tenancy by the entirety, each spouse is deemed to have contributed, and to own, 50 percent of the property. A community property interest cannot be partitioned without the consent of the other party. However, unlike the tenancy by the entirety property ownership form, community property does not have an automatic right of survivorship to the surviving spouse, and therefore the decedent's interest is included in the probate estate. Fifty percent of the value of the property is included in the decedent's gross estate, and if the property is transferred to the surviving spouse by will or intestacy, the value of the property transferred to the spouse is eligible for the unlimited marital deduction.

Exhibit 3.8 summarizes and contrasts these five key features and characteristics of each of the property ownership types.

Exhibit 3.8 | Property Ownership Key Features (Summary)

Ownership Type	Sole Ownership	Tenants in Common	JTWROS	Tenancy by the Entirety	Community Property
Number of Owners	1	2 or more	2 or more	2	2
Survivorship Feature	No	No	Yes (with certified death certificate)	Yes (with certified death certificate)	No
Included in Probate	Yes 100%	Yes % owned	No	No	50%
Included in Gross Estate	Yes	Yes	Yes	Yes	50%
Qualified for Marital Deduction	If spouse	If spouse	If spouse	Yes	If spouse
Partitionable Involuntarily	N/A	Yes	Yes	No	No
Step to FMV at Death	Yes	%	%	%	100%
Actual Contribution Rules	N/A	Yes	Yes (except spouse)	No	No
Deemed Contribution Rule	N/A	No	Yes (if spouse)	Yes	Yes

Example 3.15

Mandy and Steven had been married for six years. Three years ago, after having their only daughter, Carol, they bought their first home for $250,000. Last year, Steven was killed in a car accident. His will left everything to his daughter. The value of the home at Steven's death was $400,000. Referring to the notes below, complete the following table assuming that the personal residence was owned using each alternative ownership type. When complete, check your answers on the next page.

Property Ownership Type	Amount Included in Gross Estate? (Steven)	Amount Included in Probate Estate? (Steven)	Who receives Steven's ownership in the home?	Mandy's income tax basis after Steven's death?	Carol's income tax basis after Steven's death?	Qualifies for Unlimited Marital Deduction
Sole Ownership*						
Tenancy in Common**						
Joint Tenancy with Rights of Survivorship with Spouse**						
Tenants by the Entirety**						
Community Property***						

* Assume that Steven had purchased the home with his separate funds for $250,000.
** Assume, at the purchase of the home Steven contributed $150,000 and Mandy contributed $100,000 and held in corresponding percentages unless the method of titling assumes otherwise.
*** Assume the home was purchased with community funds.

The correct answers are provided below.

Solution to Example 3.15

Property Ownership Type	Amount Included in Gross Estate? (Steven)	Amount Included in Probate Estate? (Steven)	Who receives Steven's ownership in the home?	Mandy's income tax basis after Steven's death?	Carol's income tax basis after Steven's death?	Qualifies for Unlimited Marital Deduction
Sole Ownership*	$400,000	YES $400,000	Carol	N/A	$400,000	NO
Tenancy in Common**	$240,000	YES $240,000	Carol	$100,000	$240,000	NO
Joint Tenancy with Rights of Survivorship with Spouse**	$200,000	NO $0	Mandy	$325,000	N/A	YES
Tenancy by the Entirety**	$200,000	NO $0	Mandy	$325,000	N/A	YES
Community Property***	$200,000	YES $200,000	Carol	$200,000	$200,000	NO

* Assume that Steven had purchased the home with his separate funds for $250,000.
** Assume, at the purchase of the home Steven contributed $150,000 and Mandy contributed $100,000 and held in corresponding percentages unless the method of titling assumes otherwise.
*** Assume the home was purchased with community funds.

Sole Ownership: The full fair market value of the property, $400,000, is included in Steven's gross estate because Steven was the full, outright owner of the property. The property is included in Steven's probate estate because sole ownership does not provide a right of survivorship and will transfer to Carol as directed by the will. A legatee receives sole ownership property at an adjusted basis equal to the fair market value of the property at the decedent's date of death, which, in this case is $400,000. Mandy does not receive any interest in the property, but may have a claim to continue living in the home or some other right granted by her state because she is a spouse.

Tenancy in Common: The full ownership percentage is included in the gross estate thus 60 percent (or the ratio of the Steven's contribution to the original purchase price over the full original purchase price, $150,000/$250,000) of the fair market value at Steven's date of death is included in his gross estate, $240,000 (60% of $400,000). Per the direction of the will, Steven's interest in the property will transfer through the probate process to Carol. Carol will receive the property with an adjusted basis equal to the value reported on Steven's estate tax return, or $240,000, and Mandy will retain her original adjusted basis, equal to her original cash contribution at the purchase date, or $100,000.

Joint Tenancy with Rights of Survivorship (JTWROS): When property is owned JTWROS between a married couple, each is assumed to have contributed 50 percent of the value of the property at the original purchase date. Accordingly, Steven's gross estate will include 50 percent of the fair market value of the property at his date of death, or $200,000. With the right of survivorship, the property automatically transfers to Mandy and does not transfer through the probate process. Accordingly, Carol does not receive any interest in the property. Mandy has an adjusted basis in the property equal to her original deemed contribution, $125,000, plus the fair market value included in Steven's gross estate, $200,000, for a total adjusted basis equal to $325,000.

Tenancy by the Entirety: Property owned tenancy by the entirety is just like property owned JTWROS between a married couple for all of the matters addressed. A key point to remember, however, is that property owned tenancy by the entirety requires the consent of both spouses to partition the interest, whereas property owned JTWROS, even between spouses, can be partitioned without the consent of the other spouse.

Community Property: If the home is community property, 50 percent of the value, or $200,000, would be included in Steven's gross estate, and his interest would pass through probate to Carol per the direction of the will. Mandy would retain her 50 percent interest and would receive an increased adjusted basis equal to the fair market value of her interest at Steven's date of death, $200,000. Carol's adjusted basis in her 50 percent interest would also be the fair market value at Steven's date of death, $200,000.

KEY TERMS

Actual Contribution Rule - The value of a decedent's joint interest in property is based on the actual percentage of the original purchase price contributed by the decedent - not the decedent's ownership percentage.

Ancillary Probate - Concurrent second probate process conducted in a non-domiciliary state in which the decedent owns real property, which often requires the services of an attorney from that state, and separate court fees.

Community Property - A regime in which married individuals own an equal undivided interest in all of the property accumulated, utilizing either spouse's earnings, during the marriage.

Digital Assets - An electronic record of which an individual has a right or interest, may include information stored on a user's computer and other digital devices, social media accounts, information uploaded to websites, and catalogs of the content of electronic communications.

Equitable Ownership - Possession of the economic right to property.

Fee Simple Ownership - The ownership of property with all the rights associated with outright ownership.

Intangible Personal Property - Property that cannot truly be touched such as stocks, bonds, patents, and copyrights.

Joint Tenancy (with right of survivorship) - An undivided interest in property held by two or more related or unrelated persons, generally includes a right of survivorship.

Legal Ownership - Possession of legal title to the property.

Life Estate - An interest in property that ceases upon the death of the owner of a life interest or estate and provides a right to the income or the right to use property or both less than fee simple.

Quasi-Community Property - Property that would be community property had the married couple been living in the community-property state at the time of acquisition (applies to married couples who move from a common law (separate property) state to a community-property state).

Real Property - Property that is land and buildings attached to the land.

Residence Domiciliary - An individual's legal state of residence.

Sole Ownership - The complete ownership of property by one individual who possesses the property fee simple meaning all ownership rights associated with the property, including the right to use, sell, gift, alienate, convey, or bequeath the property.

Tangible Personal Property - Property that is not realty and may be touched.

Tenancy by the Entirety - A JTWROS that can only occur between a married couple.

Tenancy in Common - An undivided interest in property held by two or more related or unrelated persons.

Term Interest - An interest in property that ceases after a defined period of time.

Usufruct - A Louisiana device similar to a life estate which provides the holder with the right to use property and/or the right to income from the particular property.

chapter 3

DISCUSSION QUESTIONS

SOLUTIONS to the discussion questions can be found exclusively within the chapter. Once you have completed an initial reading of the chapter, go back and highlight the answers to these questions.

1. List and define the three major types of property.

2. List at least three types of property ownership.

3. Define fee simple property ownership.

4. Discuss what happens when a person dies owning property by sole ownership.

5. Define tenancy in common.

6. Discuss what happens at the death of a tenant in common.

7. Can a tenancy in common be partitioned? If so, how?

8. Discuss the consequences of two people owning property as a tenancy in common with equal interests, but one contributes 70% to the initial purchase price.

9. Define joint tenancy.

10. Define right of survivorship.

11. Can a joint tenancy by partitioned?

12. Discuss the contribution rule and how it affects inclusion in the decedent's gross estate.

13. Define community property.

14. List three common ways to own separate property in a community-property state.

15. Which states recognize community property?

16. Discuss what happens at the death of the first spouse to die when property is held as community property.

17. How can a married couple convert community property into separate property when property is held as community property?

18. Discuss the implications when a married couple moves from a community-property state to a common law (separate property) state.

19. What is quasi-community property?

20. Define life estate.

21. Define usufruct.

22. Who is a remainderman?

23. Define interest for term.

chapter 3

MULTIPLE-CHOICE PROBLEMS

A sample of multiple choice problems is provided below. Additional multiple choice problems are available at money-education.com by accessing the Student Practice Portal.

1. Which of the following statements regarding joint tenancy with rights of survivorship is correct?
   a. Each tenant may bequeath their interest in the property at their death.
   b. Joint tenancy with rights of survivorship is the same as community property.
   c. Only spouses can establish joint tenancies.
   d. Each tenant under a joint tenancy with rights of survivorship has an undivided interest in the property.

2. Of the following types of ownership, which is available for married couples?
   1. Tenancy by the entirety.
   2. Tenancy in common.
   3. JTWROS.
   4. Tenants by marriage.
      a. 1 only.
      b. 1 and 3.
      c. 1, 2, and 3.
      d. 1, 2, 3, and 4.

3. Which of the following statements regarding sole ownership is not true?
   a. Sole ownership is the complete individual ownership of property with all rights associated with outright ownership.
   b. Property owned solely passes through probate at the death of the owner.
   c. Property owned as sole ownership is excluded from the federal gross estate of the owner.
   d. Sole ownership allows the owner to use, sell, gift, alienate, convey or bequeath the property without others' approval.

4. Mateo travels quite often and wants his daughter to have access to his checking account while he is out of town. For this reason, on October 3, 2016, Mateo deposited $100,000 in a checking account. Several years passed and Mateo used the funds for normal living expenses, but his daughter never accessed any of the funds. Recently, on May 2 of this year, Mateo's daughter needed an extra $35,000 to purchase the car of her dreams so she made a withdrawal from the account with full intentions of reimbursing the account. At what date has Mateo made a gift to his daughter?
   a. October 3, 2016 (the date of the creation of the account).
   b. December 31, 2016 (the end of the year in which the account was established).
   c. May 2 of this year.
   d. May 31 of this year.

5. Which of the following would not meet the ascertainable standard requirement if it appeared in a trust document?
    a. Health.
    b. Education.
    c. Maintenance.
    d. Comfort.

chapter 3

QUICK QUIZ EXPLANATIONS

Quick Quiz 3.1
1. False. Automobiles and stocks are examples of tangible and intangible personal property, respectively. Land is real property.
2. False. If property is held solely, there are no joint owners / joint tenants.
3. True.

Quick Quiz 3.2
1. False. Tenancy in common ownership is available for spouses, related individuals, and unrelated individuals.
2. False. A tenancy in common interest is a probate asset. It does not have an automatic survivorship feature.
3. True.

Quick Quiz 3.3
1. False. Related and unrelated individuals may enter into a joint tenancy with right of survivorship.
2. False. For gift tax purposes, Tom is not deemed to make a gift to Bill until Bill withdraws money for his own use. A gift does not result when the money is deposited into the account.

Quick Quiz 3.4
1. True.
2. False. A tenancy by the entirety is essentially a joint tenancy with right of survivorship between spouses that cannot be severed without the consent of both spouses.
3. True.

Quick Quiz 3.5
1. False. Only the half interest in the property held as tenants in common that passes through the decedent's estate receives a step-up in basis. The surviving co-tenant's half interest in the property retains its original basis.
2. True.

Quick Quiz 3.6
1. False. As a general rule, there is no right of survivorship associated with community property. Some states, like Texas and California, have passed legislation to allow this.
2. True.
3. False. When moving from a common law to a community-property state, property either retains its character as separate property or is considered quasi-community property depending on the laws of the state to which the married couple is moving.

Quick Quiz 3.7
1. True.
2. True.
3. False. Quasi-community property is property that was acquired during marriage in a common-law state after a married couple has moved to a community-property state.

QUICK QUIZ EXPLANATIONS

Quick Quiz 3.8
1. False. A life estate is an interest in property that ceases upon the death of the owner of the interest.
2. True.

4
THE PROBATE PROCESS

LEARNING OBJECTIVES

1. Define the probate process.
2. Distinguish between intestate and testate succession.
3. Describe the advantages and disadvantages of the probate process.
4. Discuss the issues associated with nontraditional relationships as they relate to the probate process.
5. Describe the probate process including the duties and responsibilities of executors and administrators.
6. Define ademption and abatement.
7. Describe the property that passes through probate and that which passes outside of the probate process.
8. Calculate the probate estate.

CFP Board Resource Document - Student-Centered Learning Objectives based upon CFP Board Principal Topics.

INTRODUCTION

The Probate Process Defined

When a person dies, there are many things the survivors must do. Relatives and friends must be notified, funeral and burial arrangements must be made, and the survivors must begin to pick up the pieces and rebuild their lives without the decedent. After facing the emotional distress that naturally occurs upon the death of a loved one, the survivors must begin to look at their financial security and the process of transferring the decedent's assets from the decedent's estate to the heirs. Surviving heirs need a method to obtain clear legal title to property inherited from the decedent. The **probate process** is the legal process through which the decedent's assets that are not automatically transferred to their heirs by contract or law are retitled in the name of the heirs. The probate process can be defined as the legal proceeding that serves to prove the validity of an existing will, supervise the orderly distribution of a decedent's assets to the heirs, assure heirs that they receive clear title, and protect creditors by ensuring that valid debts of the estate are paid prior to distribution of assets to heirs.

> ### Key Concepts
> 1. Define the probate process.
> 2. Identify the main advantages of the probate process.
> 3. Identify the three main disadvantages of the probate process.
> 4. Identify the risks associated with the probate process for individuals who are in a nontraditional relationship.

Testate vs. Intestate Succession

Chapter 2 discussed in detail the basic estate planning documents including wills and their applicable provisions. The preparation of the will is often considered the first step in an overall estate plan, since it expresses some or all of the decedent's transfer wishes regarding property. In theory, every person who dies has an estate plan. If the decedent did not establish his own estate plan by executing a will, the state in which he is domiciled has created one for him under the state intestacy laws. The state intestacy laws specify to whom assets will be transferred for a person who does not validly transfer assets by will, contract law, state titling law, or trust law.

A person who dies with a valid will is said to die testate, whereas a person who dies without a valid will is said to die intestate. A person named in a will to receive property is referred to as a **legatee**, while a person who receives property under the state intestacy laws is called an **heir**. In addition, the term devisee is used to refer to a person who inherits real property under the will. Historically, the term heir was reserved only for those individuals who received property under the intestacy laws; but the term is now used more loosely and may refer to any individual who inherits property from the decedent, even under a will. A planner should understand these distinctions since there are legal differences in some states, but realize that clients and non professionals may not use the terminology appropriately in practice.

Transfer of Assets

Assets may be transferred and retitled through the probate process, by contract law, by state titling law, or by state trust law.

Advantages of Probate

Transferring assets through the probate process has several advantages over transferring assets outside of probate. The central advantage to the probate process is the protection of the individuals involved in the probate process. The advantaged parties include the decedent, the decedent's named heirs, unnamed heirs, and creditors. The following is a discussion of the more common advantages of the probate process.

Protect the Decedent

When individuals die testate (with a valid will), they are considered to have given great consideration to whom and how their assets will pass. The probate court will generally honor the wishes set forth by the decedent in the will. The exceptions include instances of proven fraud or undue influence by a legatee or third party regarding the decedent or in cases where the decedent lacked the mental capacity to execute a will. Since the probate process is the legal process used to implement the disposition objectives of the testator, the testator is assured that his desires will, for the most part, be followed.

Protect the Legatees and Heirs

The legatees and heirs are generally the parties with the largest interest in the probate process. The probate process provides for an orderly administration of the decedent's assets. Thus, it prevents one legatee or heir from having priority over another of equal rank. The following example illustrates this point.

> **Quick Quiz 4.1**
>
> 1. The probate process is a legal proceeding that serves to prove the validity of any existing will, supervise the orderly distribution of the decedent's assets to the heirs, and protect creditors by ensuring that valid debts of the estate are paid.
>   a. True
>   b. False
>
> 2. Probate is the legal process that performs the function of changing title to those properties that do not change title some other way.
>   a. True
>   b. False
>
> *True, True.*

Example 4.1

Sarah has two children, Ruth and Matthew. Ruth has lived with Sarah for many years and is known by the family to take advantage of her mother. Matthew lives far away, but has often helped both his mother and sister financially. When Sarah dies, Ruth believes that she can take all of her mother's belongings, sell them, and keep the profits for her own use, even though her mother's will bequeaths the assets equally to Ruth and Matthew. Ruth is mistaken. The probate process will protect Matthew by requiring the assets be marshalled and accounted for (as discussed below).

Transfer of Clear Title

The probate process also provides clear title to heirs or legatees. When the heirs or legatees receive property, they want to receive the property free of creditor claims and other competing ownership interests. Thus, the probate process assists the estate in satisfying creditor claims and clarifying competing ownership interests.

Example 4.2

Joelle dies leaving her car to her son, Don. Without the probate process, Don would be responsible for determining if there are any liens on the vehicle and also for clearing the liens. If Joelle did not bequeath other property or cash to Don, he would have to clear the title with his own funds. The probate process eliminates these responsibilities on the part of Don. The probate process clears all liens and provides Don with clear title to the vehicle.

The probate process provides for an orderly administration of the decedent's assets and increases the chances that all parties of interest have notice of the proceeding and, therefore, an opportunity to be heard. The probate process generally requires the executor or administrator of an estate to advertise the upcoming probate proceeding for a statutory period of time in legal newspapers and a newspaper of general circulation in the county where the decedent was domiciled. This process gives interested parties notice of the death of the decedent and an opportunity to participate in the probate process. It also allows heirs and creditors that may not have been recognized or absent legatees the opportunity to present themselves and take property under the will or via the state intestacy laws.

Example 4.3

Dylan and Kali were married for many years but never had children. Dylan, who was not always faithful in the marriage, had an affair with Chelsea while traveling to Chicago on business. After several months of carrying on the affair, Dylan broke off the affair. Unknown to Dylan, Chelsea gave birth to a boy, Blake, after Dylan ended the affair. Chelsea was certain that Dylan was Blake's father but kept it to herself. On her death bed, Chelsea revealed to Blake that Dylan was his father. When Blake finally came to grips with this knowledge, he began to seek out his father. Unfortunately, Dylan died days before Blake found him. Dylan died intestate and the probate process had already begun. The probate process may permit Blake to join the proceedings and establish his right as the biological son of Dylan; thus allowing Blake to take property under the intestate laws of the state.

chapter 4

Protect the Creditors

When a person dies they often have outstanding debts. The creditors would like to be paid the money owed to them, and the probate process protects these creditors by ensuring that the debts of the estate are paid before distributions are made to heirs or legatees.

> **Exhibit 4.1 | Advantages of Probate (Summary)**
>
> 1. Implements disposition objectives of testator.
> 2. Provides for an orderly administration of assets.
> 3. Provides clean title to heirs or legatees.
> 4. Increases the chance that parties of interest have notice of proceedings and, therefore, a right to be heard.
> 5. Protects creditors by insuring that debts of the decedent are paid.

Disadvantages of the Probate Process

The probate process also has certain disadvantages. While the advantages of probate center around protecting individuals, the disadvantages center around the losses individuals may face. The losses include time (delays), money (costs), and privacy (publicity).

The Time Cost of Probate (Delays)

The probate process is a complex legal process that takes time to complete. In order to protect the individuals involved, legal notices must be posted, hearings must be scheduled, and asset valuations must be conducted. Delays are frequently caused by the difficulty in locating and identifying property, time needed to value assets, time needed for the identification of creditors and heirs, court delays, and the filing of tax returns. All of these processes take time, with probate proceedings typically averaging from six to 24 months to complete. In addition, probate also ties up the decedent's probate assets during administration of the estate.

> **Quick Quiz 4.2**
>
> 1. The probate process often requires the executor or administrator to advertise the upcoming probate for a statutory period of time in legal newspapers to give interested parties notice to enter into the process.
>   a. True
>   b. False
> 2. The probate process protects the decedent's creditors by ensuring that the debts of the estate are paid prior to distributions to heirs.
>   a. True
>   b. False
>
> *True, True.*

Example 4.4

Imagine a nonworking spouse whose working spouse dies. The surviving spouse does not have the funds to buy food for the family because the working spouse's assets are tied up in the probate process. Frequently, surviving spouses have serious financial hardships in the immediate period after their spouse's death because they have less income while many of their expenses remain fixed and they cannot use assets that are tied up in the probate process to meet daily living needs.

Introduction 99

Monetary Cost of Probate (Costs)

Probate may also have a large monetary cost. The legal notice requirement, attorney's fees, and court costs are just a few of the expenses that are included in the probate process. The average probate process generally consumes five to 10 percent of an estate in legal fees and administrative costs, with some estates losing up to 20 percent. This can result in a significant reduction in the total dollar value of assets that will pass to the decedent's heirs. In addition, real property located in a state outside the testator's domicile requires a separate ancillary probate in the **situs** state.

Ancillary probate is a concurrent probate process conducted in the nondomiciliary state. It often requires an attorney in that nondomiciliary state and additional, separate court fees, thus further reducing the overall value of the estate that passes to the heirs. The ancillary probate process is the process by which the property in the non-domiciliary state is retitled. Another issue that can arise with ancillary probate is when the decedent dies intestate or without a will. The intestacy laws of the domiciliary and non-domiciliary states may be different.

> ### Quick Quiz 4.3
> 1. Because of the orderly administration, the probate process is private.
>   a. True
>   b. False
> 2. Because of the orderly administration, the probate process is quick.
>   a. True
>   b. False
>
> *False, False.*

Example 4.5

Chance recently died in a bizarre fishing accident. He died leaving his $1,000,000 estate to his wife, Laurie. Assume that the probate process goes rather smoothly and only 5% of the estate is consumed by fees and other costs. In this instance, $50,000 would be used to pay these expenses, leaving Laurie with $950,000 of Chance's $1,000,000.

Instead, assume that Andi, an old friend of Chance's, claims her newborn son, Rowdy, is the biological child of Chance. Although the claim proves to be false, the estate's legal fees and administrative costs are 20% of the estate. Now Laurie would only receive $800,000 of Chance's $1,000,000 estate. As illustrated, the heirs could suffer a substantial loss of assets during the probate process.

Privacy (Publicity)

One of the biggest disadvantages of the probate process is the loss of privacy. The probate process is an open court proceeding, and like any other open court proceeding, the documents filed and hearings held are open to the public. Since the files are public records, anyone can access the probate documents. In Chapter 2, Elvis Presley's and Warren Burger's wills are reprinted as examples because each document is part of a public record and open to public scrutiny.

Example 4.6

A golfer dies with a will directing the disposition of all of his assets. Because the golfer was famous, the news media and tabloids are covering the funeral and stories of his death blanket the television every evening. Soon, reporters scouring through publicly available probate court documents begin reporting the location and value of all of his homes, cars, and investment accounts. Had his assets been titled under other methods, such as a trust arrangement or property titling with survivorship, the golfer's assets could have remained confidential, and the news media would not have had access to the information.

Example 4.7

Now assume the deceased person is you and instead of the media and the tabloids, the snoopers are your nosy neighbor and the annoying busybody at work. Now imagine that they are scoring your public probate documents. It's your home's valuation they want to know and how much you had in your investment accounts. This example illustrates why many individuals do not want to go through the probate process.

Exhibit 4.2 | Disadvantages of Probate Summary

1. Can be complex and excruciatingly slow - Delays
2. Can result in substantial monetary costs - Costs
3. The process is open to public scrutiny - Publicity

Nontraditional Relationships

Nontraditional relationships require additional considerations in transferring assets, especially at death. Nontraditional relationships include unmarried couples, who are often cohabitating. These couples may be of opposite sex or of the same sex and may include couples with significant age differences. Additionally, nontraditional relationship planning may apply to any couple where there is an anticipated will contest from family members.

From an estate planning point of view, it is advisable that unmarried individuals and those in nontraditional relationships avoid probate if the goal is to pass assets to a non-traditional partner. There have been a number of cases where family members of the decedent contested the will based on undue influence by the nontraditional partner. Some courts have held the will of the first deceased partner to be invalid, thus leaving the nontraditional, surviving partner without the assets the decedent intended.

Example 4.8

One of the most famous examples of a nontraditional party will contest occurred in the estate of Robert Kaufmann. Robert had inherited substantial wealth and was the major stock holder in his family's business, Kay Jewelers. Robert had a long-term relationship with Walter Weiss from 1948 until Robert died in 1959. As part of his will, Robert left a letter to his family describing why he left his amassed fortune to his "dearest friend" Walter. The family, who had always suspected a homosexual relationship and were unhappy about the purported relationship, managed to convince two juries and an appellate court that Walter had manipulated Robert through undue influence. The end result was that Walter did not receive the assets Robert wanted him to have. Individuals in nontraditional relationships, whether they are the same sex or not, should consider avoiding the probate process or getting married.

Fortunately, nontraditional, unmarried partners can ensure that transfers will be made to each other in other ways. An annual gifting program up to the annual exclusion amount ($15,000 in 2020) may be an appropriate place to start. Additionally, nontraditional partners should make use of transfer devices that pass property outside of the probate process, such as transfers by contract, titling with survivorship features, and trusts. Each of these alternative methods offer advantages over transfers through probate for nontraditional relationships. For example, the use of JTWROS may be appropriate for nontraditional, unmarried partners where one partner is not concerned about relinquishing some control over the property during life. Alternatively, a revocable living trust may be a better alternative if the wealthier partner is concerned about relinquishing control because such a trust can be revoked by the principal at any time before death. Automatic retitling mechanisms reduce the risk of challenges from blood relatives of the decedent and increase the probability that the decedent's assets will be left as desired.

Quick Quiz 4.4

1. If a partner of a nontraditional, unmarried couple wishes to pass assets to the surviving partner, he should plan to avoid probate.
   a. True
   b. False

True.

Estate planners should focus not just on the appropriate transfer devices for nontraditional, unmarried partners, but also the tax consequences of each device, including the income, gift, estate and generation-skipping transfer taxes involved. While the Supreme Court has ruled that same sex married couples who are married may make use of the federal tax benefits available to married individuals, such as the unlimited marital deduction and portability of the estate tax exemption, will contests from family members may still be possible. As various transfer devices are discussed throughout this book, keep in mind how they may be used to benefit and protect the interests of clients in non-traditional relationships.

chapter 4

THE PROBATE PROCESS

State Probate Laws

The probate process varies among states. The discussion below focuses on the more general aspects of the probate process in order to explain how the process works.

Exhibit 4.3 | Probate Process

The Probate Process

Producing the Will
- If there are no challenges, this part should go smoothly.

Opening Succession
- This process takes place in the probate court.
- An executor or administrator is appointed.
- Court letters are issued and allow the executor/administrator to act as an agent of the court.

Managing and Distributing the Estate
- The executor/administrator must identify and take control of the decedent's assets.
- Assets must be inventoried and valued.
- All debts and taxes must be identified, valued and paid.
- Specific bequests are then fulfilled. Remaining property is distributed heirs or legatees.

Beginning the Probate Process - Producing the Will

Once a person dies, the first step in the probate process is producing a will, if one can be found. Any person can begin the probate process by presenting the will to the probate court. Generally, clients should be advised to let a trusted individual, usually the executor, know where the will is located. If the will is in a safe deposit box, banks will generally open the safe deposit box for the sole purpose of removing the will after receiving proof of death. If individuals plan to keep the will in a safe deposit box, it is wise to make a copy of the will and give this to the executor with a note stating the actual will's location. This will expedite the retrieval of the will. At this point, it is also advisable for the family to obtain multiple certified copies of the death certificate for insurance, Social Security, probate, and other purposes.

The Probate Court

Once the will has been found or it is determined that the decedent did not have a will, then the interested parties must go to the probate court to open the **estate administration** or **succession** (a term for passing property) process. The appropriate probate court in which to bring a petition will depend on the type and location of assets owned by the decedent. For a majority of individuals, the appropriate probate court will be the court where the person was domiciled at death. A person's **domicile** is the place where the person has made their home, is registered to vote, has a drivers license, filed a resident state income tax return, etc. In the event that a person holds real property located outside the state of their domicile, then an additional probate court must be consulted. This process is called ancillary probate. In most cases, a majority of the process is completed with the initial probate court, with only a few documents being filed in the ancillary probate court to change title for the real property sitused in that jurisdiction.

> **Key Concepts**
>
> 1. Distinguish between an executor and an administrator.
> 2. Identify how the probate process begins.
> 3. Determine which individuals must post a surety bond.
> 4. Distinguish between letters testamentary and letters of administration.

To begin the probate process, the petitioner (generally the executor) must provide the court with certain information, including a certified copy of the death certificate, the last will (if available), a list of the names and addresses of the decedent's heirs, and a list of the known creditors. Depending on the state, this can be rather easy. Generally the state will have a short document that can be filled out and submitted to the probate court with the necessary documents attached. A hearing will then be scheduled for interested parties to appear. The known creditors of the estate should be notified of the date of the hearing. In addition, the date of the hearing should be publicized in the appropriate legal and community newspapers. Assuming all paperwork is in order and there are no disputes among the heirs, the hearing will be rather short. The court will accept the will, it will be filed in the public records and the court will officially open the probate process. The court will then appoint a personal representative, as discussed below.

As mentioned in Chapter 2, if the will is a statutory will and has a self proving affidavit, the will is considered valid on its face without the need for witnesses to testify that the decedent did indeed sign the will and was mentally competent. If the will does not have a self proving clause, then witnesses will be needed at the initial hearing to validate the will.

Personal Representative - Executors and Administrators

When the probate process begins, a personal representative will be appointed to administer the estate. Depending on whether the decedent had a will or not, the personal representative is called the **executor** or **administrator**. When females were appointed they were historically referred to as the executrix or administratrix, but today many people use the generic terms: executor/administrator. In addition, some states now use the generic all encompassing title of personal representative and do not distinguish between an executor or administrator.

In the case of a valid will in which an executor is named, the probate court usually accepts the appointed individual as executor and provides that person with powers called letters testamentary. A grant of **letters testamentary** empowers the executor to act as the agent of the court. In the event of intestacy, or where an executor cannot be appointed by the probate court, the court will appoint an administrator (generally a family member of the decedent who has the largest interest in the estate). The court issues individuals appointed as administrator with powers called **letters of administration**. The primary difference between an executor and an administrator is that the decedent chooses the executor, and the probate court names the administrator. In some states, administrators may have to formally close the estate before the probate court while an executor may be able to close informally. Letters testamentary or letters of administration are essentially equal in power and provide the holder with the legal authority to perform the functions of executor or administrator. **Exhibit 4.4** identifies the primary duties of an executor or administrator in the probate process.

Exhibit 4.4 | Common Duties of Executor and Administrator

Duties of Court-Appointed Executor or Administrator
- Identify and produce a detailed list of decedent's property/assets
- Safeguard, manage, and invest assets
- Give legal notice to creditors and heirs/legatees
- Pay the estate's expenses
- Pay the debts and taxes of the decedent
- Collect revenues, interest, rents, etc. during the estate
- File all federal, state, and local tax returns timely
- Make appropriate tax filing elections
- Distribute assets to heirs/legatees as appropriate
- Close the estate with the court

Specific Duties of Administrator
- Petition court for appointment
- Put up security bond
- Court selects
- Court issues letter of administration

Specific Duties of Executor*
- Locate will
- Submit will to court
- Prove will with witnesses/notary
- Receives letters of testamentary

*In some states the actions of the executor/administrator must each be approved by a probate court. However, in some states there is a provision for the appointment of an independent executor who having received letter of testament has wide latitude to take actions without court approval (e.g. buy/sell property, open bank accounts, etc.).

Surety Bonds

If an administrator is appointed by the court, then the administrator must generally post a bond called a **surety bond**. Some states also require a bond to be posted if the will names an individual as executor, unless a provision of the will waives the bond requirement. Although the surety bond requirement can be waived by the will or by the heirs and legatees, states generally will not allow the bond to be waived if an executor is named that is not a resident of the state in which the probate process is occurring. The purpose of the surety bond is to protect the creditors, heirs, and legatees of the estate from financial loss in the event that the administrator or executor engages in a wrongful act. In the event that the administrator or executor misappropriates assets of the estate or is negligent and causes a loss to the estate, the surety bond company will reimburse the estate for the loss. An administrator will need a formal discharge of the surety bond before closing the estate.

Managing and Distributing the Estate

Once appointed, the executor or administrator identifies and takes control of the decedent's assets. This is referred to as "marshalling the assets." After the assets have been marshalled, the personal representative compiles an inventory list of the decedent's property. The property is then valued by a valuation specialist or appraiser. Depending on the type of assets, the valuation may be relatively inexpensive or substantial in both cost and time.

The personal representative must then identify and list all debts owed by the decedent. This includes notifying potential creditors regarding the death and requesting final payoff balances. Most importantly, the personal representative must file the necessary federal and state tax returns and pay any taxes due. Remember that the personal representative must be paid (unless compensation is waived) and the court-approved advisors to the executor or administrator must also be paid. Once the debts and taxes have been paid, the probate court will generally allow the assets to be distributed to the heirs or legatees. At this point, if ancillary probate is required, then the court order allowing disposition of property is filed in the ancillary probate court to allow title to change in that jurisdiction as well.

The personal representative will first distribute the specific personal property bequests to specific legatees (e.g., a particular piece of jewelry is left to the decedent's daughter) and then the specific real property bequests to specific legatees. Only after all debts, taxes, and costs have been paid and all specific legatees have been satisfied will the residuary heir or legatee take the remaining property. After all of the assets have been distributed, the court will officially close the probate proceedings.

> **Quick Quiz 4.5**
>
> 1. The probate court provides an appointed administrator with certain powers represented by letters testamentary.
>   a. True
>   b. False
> 2. All executors are chosen by the probate court.
>   a. True
>   b. False
> 3. Court-appointed administrators must generally post a bond.
>   a. True
>   b. False
> 4. Letters testamentary provide the holder with the legal authority to perform the functions of executor.
>   a. True
>   b. False
> 5. In the event a decedent dies without a valid will, the probate court appoints an administrator.
>   a. True
>   b. False
>
> *False, False, True, True, True.*

chapter 4

Potential Problems in Distribution

Probate is not simple. One common problem is that assets specifically bequeathed to legatees may have been disposed of prior to the decedent's death. In these cases, unless the testator has provided some alternative asset, the legatee is not entitled to any replacement asset. This extinction of the legacy is called **ademption**.

Example 4.9

In Zion's will, he leaves a 1986 convertible to Justin. When Zion dies, he has a 1999 convertible, which he acquired when he traded in his 1986 convertible. Justin receives nothing under the will, and his bequest is said to adeem.

Another frequently encountered problem during the probate process occurs when there are not enough assets in the estate to satisfy all of the decedent's specific bequests. If the estate is too small to satisfy all bequests, the court will generally reduce the amounts given to the legatees. This reduction is called **abatement**.

Example 4.10

Len leaves $100,000 to each of his four brothers, but when he dies, Len only has $250,000. If Len has not decided who takes what and in what priority, the probate court will ascertain the likely wishes of the decedent. In this case, since all four brothers have equal standing, the court would likely award each 25% of the total.

Even if there are sufficient assets to satisfy all specific legatees and create a residuary estate, there remains a question as to who will bear the cost of debts and federal estate taxes and state inheritance taxes of the estate. Should each specific legatee pay his own taxes pro rata or should the residuary legatee bear the entire burden of state and federal taxes? Most states have a default presumption if the testator fails to specify, but any presumption may or may not be consistent with the testator's wishes.

Example 4.11

Karen and Teddy were married and had two children, Josh and Kerstin. Teddy died with an estate valued at $400,000. Teddy's will left $100,000 to each child and the remainder of his estate to his wife Karen. His will did not specify how taxes should be paid, so assume the state law dictates that the estate taxes should be paid out of each bequest based on the percentage the assets bear to the estate. Also, assume the taxes were $10,000. In this instance each person will pay based on the pro rata share they received. Since Karen received $200,000 of the $400,000 estate, one half of the estate taxes will be paid from her proceeds (($200,000/$400,000) x $10,000 = $5,000). Each child's net proceeds are reduced by one fourth of the tax due because they are each receiving one-fourth of the estate (($100,000/$400,000) x $10,000 = $2,500 per child). Thus Karen will receive a net amount of $195,000 and each child will receive a net amount of $97,500.

Now assume that the will stated that the state estate taxes are paid from the residuary portion. Since Karen is receiving the residuary, her portion will be reduced by the full amount of all taxes paid. Therefore, she will receive a net amount of $190,000 and each child will receive $100,000. The point is that the will should be written in a clear way so as to avoid any possible ambiguity. The will is the voice of the decedent and the decedent's desires should be clearly expressed

PROPERTY PASSING THROUGH PROBATE

Property passing through probate includes property that can be disposed of by a will, such as sole ownership property, the decedent's share of property held as tenancy in common, and the decedent's share of community property (as discussed in Chapter 3).

Recall that sole ownership is outright ownership and does not provide for automatic retitling. Therefore, this type of property must pass through the probate process to be retitled. Similarly, there are no provisions for property held as tenancy in common or community property to automatically transfer title once the owner dies and therefore the property must be retitled through the probate process at the time of death.

> **Key Concepts**
>
> 1. Determine which types of assets go through probate.
> 2. Determine which types of assets do not go through probate.

In addition to real property, other tangible and intangible property also passes through probate for retitling. For example, automobiles and household goods are often disposed of through a will and must pass through probate for retitling. Finally, the probate process also retitles property owned at the time of death, but not disposed of through the will, such as intestate property resulting from the failure of the decedent to include a residuary clause in his will.

PROPERTY PASSING OUTSIDE OF THE PROBATE PROCESS

Property that passes outside of the probate process includes property that passes by state contract law, state property titling law, and state trust law. All of these transfers reduce the probate estate and therefore reduce probate transaction costs and may improve liquidity for the named heirs and legatees.

State Contract Law

Transfers that avoid probate by contract allow the client to select a designated beneficiary to whom the property will be transferred. The selected beneficiary will directly receive title to the property at the death of the owner. However, before the death of the owner, the selected beneficiary does not have any rights to the property; since the owner of the property can, at any time, change, amend, or revoke any revocable beneficiary selection. In all situations, if a named beneficiary is not chosen, the property is included in the decedent's probate estate. If a beneficiary or successor beneficiary that was named predeceased the testator, and there is not a living contingent beneficiary, then the property will transfer through the probate process to be retitled. In addition, if the decedent had named his estate as the beneficiary of a contract, then the proceeds would also transfer through the probate process.

Example 4.12

Jamie owns a life insurance policy on his life with his wife Barbara named as the beneficiary. At Jamie's death, the death benefit will be paid directly to Barbara, thus avoiding the probate process.

Example 4.13
Ajay owns a life insurance policy on his life. He does not have a named beneficiary. At Ajay's death, the death benefit will be paid to his estate and thus will be transferred through the probate process to his heirs.

Example 4.14
Ajay owns a life insurance policy on his life. The named beneficiary is his wife Deepha, who died last year. At Ajay's death the proceeds will be paid to Ajay's estate because Deepha is deceased. Thus, the death benefit will transfer through Ajay's probate estate.

Example 4.15
Ajay owns a life insurance policy on his life with his estate as the named beneficiary. When Ajay dies the assets will be paid directly to the estate and thus will transfer through the probate process.

Naming a beneficiary does not trigger any gift tax consequences. These contractual beneficiary designators are easy and efficient mechanisms to avoid the probate process, as there is no need for the asset to be retitled, since title is transferred automatically to the named beneficiary. The following are typical devices that use beneficiary designations to transfer property at the death of the owner under state contract law.

Life Insurance
Life insurance is a contract that allows the owner of the policy to name a beneficiary. The life insurance company contracts with the owner of the policy and agrees to pay the death benefit to the named beneficiary upon the death of the insured. The insurance company is thus acting as agent of the owner. For the beneficiary to collect the proceeds of life insurance, he simply has to provide a certified copy of the death certificate obtained from the local coroner's office to the insurer. Life insurance thus offers a fairly quick solution to help meet the many immediate liquidity needs that arise when someone dies.

Annuities
Annuities are contracts, similar to life insurance, where a named beneficiary can be selected by the owner of the annuity. At the death of the owner of the annuity, the named beneficiary will receive the annuity death benefit, which may come in the form of an annuity for life, annuity for term, or a cash payment. In some cases, the death benefit settlement option has been pre-selected by the owner, or if not pre-selected the beneficiary may choose any one of the settlement options allowed under the contract.

IRAs, SEPs, SIMPLEs, and Qualified Retirement Plans

Retirement plans also allow the owner to name a beneficiary. At the death of the account owner, the named beneficiary receives the assets from the retirement account. The custodian of the plan or account has a contract with the owner of the account and is directed upon the owner's death to pay the beneficiary upon receipt of a certified death certificate.

Totten Trusts, Pay-on-Death (POD) Accounts, and Transfer-on-Death (TOD) Accounts

Totten Trusts, named after the legendary 1904 Totten case (*In re Totten,* 179 N.Y. 112, 71 N.E. 748), are not really trusts at all, but are instead accounts designated as "held in trust for another." Totten Trusts are not joint accounts, and the named beneficiary does not have any rights to the account while the owner was alive. Instead, they are merely bank accounts with beneficiary designations. At the death of the account owner, the bank transfers the assets in the account to the named beneficiary. Most states have now codified the historical Totten Trust into what is now called **Pay-on-Death (POD) Bank Accounts** or **In Trust For (ITF) Accounts**. In addition, many states have statutorily created **Transfer-on-Death (TOD) Accounts** for investment accounts with named beneficiaries.

Most states have adopted PODs/ITFs for bank accounts and/or TODs for investment accounts to allow these types of accounts the same advantages as other beneficiary-designated accounts. The beneficiary designation is similar to naming a beneficiary for a retirement account or IRA and generally completed in a similar fashion. Most now have a similar transfer device for either bank accounts or investment accounts, with over half of the states having transfer devices for both types of accounts. Some states even have transfer-on-death registration for vehicles and real estate deeds. State laws vary and a full understanding of applicable state law is needed when selecting such designations.

> **Quick Quiz 4.6**
>
> 1. A decedent's interest in property owned "joint tenancy with rights of survivorship" with his surviving brother will not pass through probate.
>   a. True
>   b. False
>
> 2. A revocable living trust is a device that may be used to avoid the probate process.
>   a. True
>   b. False
>
> 3. Life insurance proceeds payable to the decedent pass through the probate process.
>   a. True
>   b. False
>
> 4. Property held "tenancy by the entirety" will pass through probate for retitling.
>   a. True
>   b. False
>
> 5. A bank savings account with a listed pay-on-death beneficiary avoids the probate process.
>   a. True
>   b. False
>
> True, True, True, False, True.

State Titling Law

Property held as a joint tenancy with rights of survivorship (JTWROS), or as a tenancy by the entirety (TE) pass outside of the probate process because of the automatic retitling mechanism of the survivorship feature. At the death of a joint tenant, his or her interest passes automatically to the surviving tenant, or in the case of TE, to the surviving spouse. The surviving joint tenant must produce a certified death certificate of the decedent in order to transfer title.

State Trust Law

As discussed in Chapter 8, all trust property will pass outside of the probate process per state trust law. Property in trust has already been retitled because when the grantor of the trust transferred the property into the trust, it had to be retitled as trust property. Even in the case of a revocable trust, the trust becomes irrevocable upon the grantor's death. Property in trust is managed and distributed according to the specific provisions of the particular trust and has no further need to be retitled. **Exhibit 4.5** illustrates various assets and how they pass through and around probate.

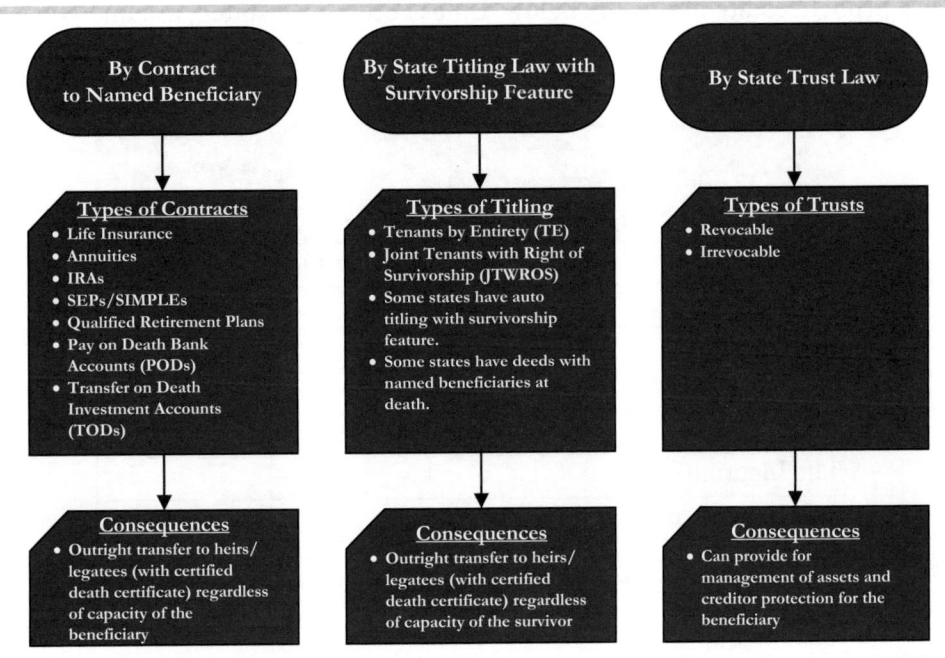

CALCULATING THE PROBATE ESTATE

Calculating the value of the probate estate is important and should be fairly easy if you can identify which assets are and which assets are not included in the probate estate. We will use the following example to work through the concepts that have been discussed in this chapter.

Cody and Reese were married years ago and had one child, Amber. Cody and his longtime friend, Kandi, were recently flying in Kandi's new plane. For a brief period Kandi was distracted and lost control of the plane. Unfortunately, the plane crashed and Kandi died instantly and Cody died a few days later as a result of the injuries sustained during the crash. When Cody died he and Reese owned the following property:

- Home valued at $500,000 held tenancy by the entirety.
- Car 1 valued at $10,000 owned solely by Cody.
- Car 2 valued at $15,000 owned as Joint Tenancy with Rights of Survivorship by Cody and Amber.
- Diamond ring valued at $50,000 held solely by Reese.
- Boat valued at $20,000 held tenancy in common by Cody and Amber.
- Life Insurance Policy 1 on Reese's life, owned by Cody. The fair market value of the policy was $100,000 and the death benefit was $200,000. The beneficiary is Amber.
- Life Insurance Policy 2 on Cody's life, owned by Cody. The fair market value of the policy was $85,000 and the death benefit was $500,000. The only beneficiary is Kandi.
- IRA account valued at $2,000,000 owned by Cody with Amber as the beneficiary.
- Irrevocable Trust by Cody for the benefit of Amber created five years ago. The trust is valued at $500,000, and Amber is the beneficiary at Cody's death.

Calculate Cody's probate estate in the box below. Unless otherwise stated, assume equal contributions were made by all parties for jointly owned property. The first asset has been completed for you. Answers are provided on the next page.

Asset	FMV at Date of Death	FMV of Cody's Interest	Included in the Probate Estate
Home	$500,000	$250,000	$0
Car 1			
Car 2			
Diamond Ring			
Boat			
Life Insurance 1			
Life Insurance 2			
IRA			
Trust			
Total			

chapter 4

ANSWERS:

Asset	FMV at Date of Death	FMV of Cody's Interest	Included in the Probate Estate
Home	$500,000	$250,000	$0
Car 1	$10,000	$10,000	$10,000
Car 2	$15,000	$7,500	$0
Diamond Ring	$50,000	$0	$0
Boat	$20,000	$10,000	$10,000
Life Insurance 1	$100,000	$100,000	$100,000
Life Insurance 2	$500,000	$500,000	$500,000
IRA	$2,000,000	$2,000,000	$0
Trust	$500,000	$0	$0
Total	**$3,695,000**	**$2,877,500**	**$620,000**

HOME

The home is owned tenancy by the entirety. Therefore, Cody owns one half and Reese owns one half. Since the property is held tenancy by the entirety, the property automatically has a survivorship feature, thus it will not pass through probate.

CAR 1

Car 1 is owned solely by Cody; therefore, he owns the entire asset outright. Since there is no survivorship feature associated with sole ownership, the property will pass through probate.

CAR 2

Car 2 is owned JTWROS by Cody and Amber. Thus Cody owns one half of the property. Since the property will pass via state titling law because of the survivorship feature, the asset will not pass through probate.

DIAMOND RING

The ring belongs to Reese (she owns it) and there is no effect on Cody regarding this asset.

BOAT

The boat is held tenancy in common and Cody owns one half. Since there is no survivorship feature, his half of the asset will pass through the probate process. Note that while only half of the value of the boat is included in the probate estate, the amount included in the gross estate for estate tax purposes will be determined by the percentage of contribution rule, since Cody owned the boat with his daughter. This illustrates one of the common differences between the probate and gross estate calculations.

LIFE INSURANCE POLICY 1

Cody owns the policy on Reese's life. When he dies the value of the policy will transfer through his probate estate. The ownership of the policy is like any other asset in that it must be transferred to

Calculating the Probate Estate

someone else. Because the death benefit is not currently payable (the policy is on Reese's life) only the FMV of the policy is included in Cody's gross estate.

LIFE INSURANCE POLICY 2

There was a named beneficiary, but the beneficiary was Kandi who died in the crash shortly before Cody. Since the beneficiary is dead, the property will transfer through the probate process like any other asset unless a contingent beneficiary had been named.

IRA

The IRA has a designated beneficiary, Amber, who is living. Therefore, the property passes by the operation of contract law and will not transfer through the probate process.

IRREVOCABLE TRUST

The trust is not part of Cody's assets and is therefore not part of Cody's probate estate. The assets in the trust pass via state trust law.

KEY TERMS

Abatement - The reduction in assets transferring to a legatee because the estate has insufficient assets to satisfy all of the legatees.

Ademption - Extinction of a legacy because an asset, specifically bequeathed to a legatee, has been disposed of prior to death.

Administrator - A person, usually a relative of the deceased, appointed by the probate court to oversee the probate process when an executor has not been named.

Ancillary Probate - Concurrent second probate process conducted in a non-domiciliary state in which the decedent owns property, which often requires the services of an attorney from that state, and separate court fees.

Domicile - Where a person lives, the location of their home.

Estate Administration or Succession - The passing of property at death to surviving heirs/legatees.

Executor - Estate representative designated in the will by the decedent. An executor may serve without bond if the bond is waived by the decedent.

Heir - One who inherits under state law.

In Trust For (ITF) Accounts - A bank account utilizing a beneficiary designation.

Legatee - One who inherits under the will.

Letters of Administration - A legal document that affirms the power of the administrator to act as the agent of the probate court.

Letters Testamentary - A legal document that affirms the power of the executor to act as the agent of the probate court.

Pay-on-Death Bank Account (POD) - A bank account utilizing a beneficiary designation.

Probate Process - The legal proceeding that serves to prove the validity of existing wills, supervise the orderly distribution of decedent's assets to the heirs, and protect creditors by ensuring that valid debts of the estate are paid.

Situs - The place, generally referring to the state, where property is located.

Surety Bond - A bond posted by the administrator or the executor of the estate to protect creditors, heirs, and legatees from losses created by the administrator or executor.

Totten Trust - Not a trust, but rather a bank account with a beneficiary clause.

Transfer-on-Death Account (TOD) - An investment account utilizing a beneficiary designation.

DISCUSSION QUESTIONS

SOLUTIONS to the discussion questions can be found exclusively within the chapter. Once you have completed an initial reading of the chapter, go back and highlight the answers to these questions.

1. Describe the probate process.

2. Describe at least three advantages and three disadvantages of the probate process.

3. Identify alternatives to probate regarding the disposition of property.

4. Discuss the main differences between an executor and an administrator.

5. List the duties of the executor and the administrator.

6. Define pay-on-death and transfer-on-death accounts.

7. Identify assets that pass outside of probate by contract law.

8. Identify assets that pass outside of probate by titling or trust law.

chapter 4

MULTIPLE-CHOICE PROBLEMS

A sample of multiple choice problems is provided below. Additional multiple choice problems are available at money-education.com by accessing the Student Practice Portal.

1. If Paula died with each of the following property interests, which will be excluded from her probate estate?
    a. Property owned as community property.
    b. Property held tenancy in common.
    c. Death proceeds of life insurance payable to a living stranger.
    d. Property owned solely.

2. Which of the following property interests of a decedent will avoid probate?
    a. Proceeds of life insurance payable to the decedent's estate.
    b. Community property.
    c. Property owned tenants in common with decedent's father.
    d. Proceeds of life insurance payable to the decedent's living son.

3. Carol's executor has located all of her property. Given the following property listing, what is the total value of Carol's probate estate?

Life Insurance	Face	$1,000,000	Beneficiary is James, Carol's son
401(k)	Balance	$350,000	Beneficiary is Carla, Carol's Daughter
Vacation Home	Value	$460,000	Titled Tenancy by Entirety with Jim
Automobile	Value	$24,000	Owned by Carol

    a. $24,000.
    b. $484,000.
    c. $834,000.
    d. $1,024,000.

4. Eric owns the following property:

Property	Joint Owner	Titling
Home	None	Sole Ownership
Stock in ABC Corp	Brother, Jim	Tenancy in Common
Beach House	Wife, Rebecca	Tenancy by the Entirety
Checking Account	None	Pay-on-Death to Son

    Which of the following is included in Eric's probate estate?
    a. Home and stock in ABC Corp.
    b. Home, beach house, and checking account.
    c. Stock in ABC Corp and checking account.
    d. Home only.

5. Parker lives in Florida and dies at age 71. He has the following assets:

Assets	Titling	Value
Home	Tenancy by the entirety with his wife, Penny	$345,000
Porshe	Sole Ownership	$65,000
Furnishings	Tenancy by the entirety with his wife, Penny	$45,000
IRA	Penny as beneficiary	$390,000
Checking Account	Sole Ownership POD to Penny	$350,000
Undeveloped Commercial Lot in Alabama	Sole Ownership	$490,000

Which of Parker's assets have to be retitled through Florida probate?
    a. The Porsche.
    b. The home and the Porsche.
    c. The home, the Porsche, and the checking account.
    d. The home, the Porsche, and the Alabama property.

QUICK QUIZ EXPLANATIONS

Quick Quiz 4.1
1. True.
2. True.

Quick Quiz 4.2
1. True.
2. True.

Quick Quiz 4.3
1. False. Probate is a public process and is open to public scrutiny.
2. False. The probate process typically takes six to twenty-four months to complete.

Quick Quiz 4.4
1. True.

Quick Quiz 4.5
1. False. An administrator receives letters of administration. An executor receives letters testamentary.
2. False. Executors are appointed by the decedent in a validly executed will. Administrators are appointed by the court when the decedent died without a will, or failed to name an executor in his will.
3. True.
4. True.
5. True.

Quick Quiz 4.6
1. True.
2. True.
3. True.
4. False. Tenancy by the entirety has automatic survivorship feature and will therefore pass to the surviving spouse by operation of law and will not pass through the probate process.
5. True.

5
GIFT TAX

LEARNING OBJECTIVES

1. Describe the historical background and purpose of the gift tax system.
2. Describe the impact of the American taxpayer relief act (ATRA).
3. Understand how to use the tax rate schedule for gifts and estate.
4. Describe the parties to a gift, the definition of a gift, and the elements of a gift.
5. Calculate any gift associated with below market rate loans.
6. Describe a net gift.
7. Determine conceptually the value of any gift.
8. Identify annual exclusions and lifetime exemptions for gifts including annual exclusions and super exclusions for non-citizen spouses.
9. Describe a split gift election and joint gifts in community property.
10. Distinguish gifts of a present and future interest and their implications as to the annual exclusion.
11. Be able to identify a taxable gift.
12. Describe a Crummey provision.
13. Describe the five-and-five lapse rule.
14. Identify transfers that are outside the gift tax regime such as transfers to political organizations, qualified transfers, payments for support, payments between divorcing spouses, transfers within a business setting, and gifts to spouses.
15. Describe the gift tax return (Form 709), the due date, the statute of limitations, and the calculation of the gift tax.
16. Calculate the donee's adjusted basis of gifted property under three different situations. (1) The fair market value of the property at the date of the gift exceeds the donor's basis. (2) The fair market value of the property at the date of the gift is less than the donor's basis. (3) The donor has paid gift tax on appreciated property that was gifted.
17. Describe gifting strategies for single party and multi-party donations.
18. Distinguish the advantages of lifetime gifts versus bequests at death.

CFP Board Resource Document - Student-Centered Learning Objectives based upon CFP Board Principal Topics.

This chapter provides an overview of the Federal gift tax system, including the requirements for making a gift, the gift tax calculation, exclusions from gift tax, and basic gift tax planning strategies. Subsequent chapters will explore some of these topics in more detail, and in the context of the overall Federal transfer tax system.

THE GIFT TAX SYSTEM

Historical Background and Purpose

The gift tax is an excise tax on the right to transfer assets gratuitously to another person during life. Like the federal estate tax, the gift tax exists as a method of raising revenue for the federal government and functions as a method of social reallocation of wealth by taxing large masses of wealth transferred from one generation to subsequent generations. The gift tax is paid from the taxpayer's wealth to the federal government and thus is reallocated to other members of society through the social programs and other expenditures of the federal government.

The gift tax system was established in 1932 to prevent individuals from avoiding the income tax (which, in its current form, was enacted in 1913), and the estate tax (which was enacted in 1915). Before the gift tax system, some individuals (donors) would transfer income producing property to family members (donees) who were in lower income tax brackets for the purpose of reducing the overall family income tax burden without incurring transfer costs. Others would transfer property during life to family members to avoid the imposition of the estate tax at their death. Congress, being ever mindful of the resolve and ingenuity of planners and clients in avoiding income and estate taxes, responded by establishing an excise tax for gifts during life. Initially, the gift tax rates were lower than the estate tax rates, and as such, individuals continued transferring property during life, paying the lower gift tax rates, and avoiding the higher estate tax rates at their death.

In 1976, Congress unified the gift and estate tax rate schedules to discourage taxpayers from transferring assets during life to avoid the higher tax on the transfer of property at death. Essentially, the unified gift and estate transfer tax system taxes the transfer of property at the same tax rates regardless of the time of transfer of property, during life (gifts) or at death (bequests). Despite the equal tax rate systems, there were some major differences between transfers made during life and those made at death. This unified system was temporarily suspended after 2003, when the **Economic Growth and Tax Relief Reconciliation Act of 2001 (EGTRRA 2001)** repealed the estate tax over a nine year period ending in 2010. At the end of 2010, the Tax Relief, Unemployment Insurance Authorization, and Job Creation Act of 2010 (TRA 2010) extended EGTRRA through December 31, 2012, reinstated the estate tax, and re-unified the gift and estate tax systems. The American Taxpayer Relief Act of 2012 (ATRA) was signed into law on January 2, 2013, and made the changes specified in TRA 2010 permanent.

Estate and Gift Tax Reform

EGTRRA 2001 resulted in the gradual, temporary repeal of the estate and generation skipping transfer tax over the period 2001-2010, and completely eliminated estate and generation skipping transfer taxes in 2010. Over the period 2001 to 2009, estate tax exemption amounts increased; and the highest marginal tax rates imposed on estates, gifts, and generation skipping transfers decreased. Under EGTRRA, no federal estate or generation skipping transfer tax was to be assessed in 2010. From 2001 – 2010, the gift tax exemption remained at $1 million while the estate tax exemption grew to $3,500,000 in 2009, which "de-unified" the Unified Credit and created planning complexity for some clients. The gift tax system remained in force in 2010, despite the repeal of estate and generation skipping transfer taxes that year. All of the tax changes in EGTRRA were set to "sunset" after December 31, 2010.

> ### Key Concepts
> 1. Understand how TRA 2010 potentially affects the estates of decedents that died during 2010.
> 2. Understand how ATRA 2012 impacted the estate and gift tax.

In the years leading up to 2010, many advisors and clients hoped that Congress would address the impending "sunset" of EGTRRA 2001 and provide clear guidance on what the future would hold with enactment of permanent estate tax reform legislation. While politicians promised to do this year after year, political fighting in Washington prevented any permanent solution from emerging. Finally, on December 17, 2010 Congress enacted, and the President later signed, the **Tax Relief, Unemployment Insurance Authorization, and Job Creation Act of 2010 (TRA 2010)**.

By extending certain provisions of EGTRRA through December 31, 2012, TRA 2010 retroactively imposed an estate tax on decedents dying in 2010, and set the estate tax exemption amount for the years 2010-2012 at $5 million adjusted for inflation. The highest marginal transfer tax rate was set at 35 percent for the period 2010-2012. The executors of estates of decedents dying during 2010 had the option of electing out of any potential estate tax imposed by TRA 2010, in which case the modified carry-over basis rules set forth in EGTRRA 2001 would apply. In addition, TRA 2010 permitted portability of estate and gift tax exemptions (but not generation skipping transfer tax exemptions) between spouses, addresses several generation skipping transfer tax concerns, and adjusted the methods of calculating gift and estate taxes. Like it's predecessor, EGTRRA, TRA 2010 was a temporary solution. All of the estate and gift provisions of the act were scheduled to sunset after December 31, 2012.

The **American Taxpayer Relief Act (ATRA 2012)** established permanent estate and gift tax rules beginning in 2013. The estate, gift, and generation skipping transfer exemption amounts were set at $5,000,000 indexed for inflation, and as of 2020 the exemption equals $11,580,000. The highest marginal gift and estate tax rate was set at 40 percent, and the portability of a deceased spouse's unused exemption amount was made permanent. ATRA 2012 retained most of the provisions of its predecessor, TRA 2010, albeit with a slightly higher gift and estate tax rate.

The **Tax Cuts and Jobs Act of 2017 (TCJA)**, signed by President Donald Trump in December, 2017, substantially increased the estate, gift, and generation skipping transfer exemption amounts, and, like ATRA, subjects those amounts to annual inflation adjustments. In 2020, the exemption amount equals $11,180,000.

Since EGTRRA 2001 was enacted, Congress has debated increasing, and decreasing, the gift and estate tax exemption amount. Like the provisions found in EGTRRA 2001, which would have reverted the estate tax exemption back to $1,000,000 after the Act sunset in 2011, TCJA 2017 increased the gift and estate tax exemption until 2025, after which TCJA 2017 sunsets and the estate and gift tax exemption reverts back to its 2017 level, adjusted for inflation. Several candidates for national office have promoted repealing the expansion of the estate tax exemption earlier than 2026, and resetting it a lower amount without inflation adjustments going forward.

Continuing uncertainty about the amount of the gift and estate tax exemption amount is problematic for planners. While some clients may not have federal estate tax concerns today due to the large exemption, many of those clients may be subject to estate tax if the exemption reverts back to the $5 million amount as indexed. Furthermore, if a client used the entire gift and estate tax exemption available today, and the exemption amount reverts to a lower level in the future, the client could potentially be subject to adverse tax consequences.

Thankfully, in November 2019, the IRS issued Final Regulations (referred to as the **Anti-Clawback Regulations**) that addressed this issue. The final regulations state that the benefit of the temporary increase in the estate and gift tax exemption that is used by a taxpayer in current planning will not be "clawed back" after TCJA 2017 sunsets in 2026. In issuing the anti-clawback regulations, the IRS concluded that Congress had intended all gifts made prior to 2026 to qualify for the higher exemptions, and the temporary increase in the estate and gift tax exemption amount over the period 2018-2025 is a use it or lose it benefit, much like the gift tax annual exclusion.

> ### Example 5.1
> In 2020, Kevin made a taxable gift of $11,580,000 to an irrevocable trust for the benefit of his family, and applied his entire lifetime exemption to the transfer. Congress did not enact any additional estate and gift tax legislation prior to 2026, and as a consequence, the estate and gift tax exemption reverts to $5 million as indexed beginning in 2026. Even though Kevin gave away more than the level of the exemption in 2026, he will not be subject to gift tax on the excess amount since the gift was made prior to 2026.

The anti-clawback regulations also addressed estate tax exemption portability for married couples where one of the spouses dies before 2026. As discussed in more detail later, upon the death of the first spouse, the deceased spouse's executor may elect to transfer the unused exemption of the deceased spouse (called the Deceased Spouse's Unused Exemption, or DSUE) to the surviving spouse on a timely filed Estate Tax Return. Since the unused exemption is fixed at the death of the first spouse, if the death occurs prior to 2026, the DSUE transferred to the surviving spouse will not be decreased if the sunset provisions of TCJA 2017 take effect.

> ### Example 5.2
> Marge died in 2020 with a taxable estate of $1 million. Her executor made an election on Marge's estate tax return to transfer Marge's unused exemption amount of $10,580,000 ($11,580,000 – $1,000,000) to Marge's husband, Pete. Pete died eight years later, and before his death TCJA 2017 sunset, reducing his gift and estate exemption amount to $6,440,102 ($5 million indexed for inflation to 2028, the year of Pete's death). While Pete's exclusion is only $6,440,102, he can still use Marge's DSUE of $10,580,000 to shield a total of $17,020,102 in assets from estate tax at his death.

While the final anti-clawback regulations provide some degree of certainty regarding lifetime gifts and estate tax portability, the IRS did not address the question of how much of the prior gifts made by a taxpayer would be included in the taxpayer's estate tax calculation upon his or her death, leaving open the possibility for a clawback of lifetime gifts in a taxpayer's estate if the taxpayer dies after 2025. Furthermore, the final anti-clawback regulations did not address whether generation skipping transfers are covered by the anti-clawback rules, and reserved this issue for further consideration.

While the gift tax regime, with all of its rules, exceptions, and exemptions, is complex, planners and clients can navigate the waters of gift taxation by answering four basic questions:
1. Is the transfer a taxable gift?
2. Do any exceptions, exclusions, or exemptions apply to avoid tax liability?
3. What is the tax due, and how is it reported?
4. Is the gift appropriate in light of the goals and objectives of the donor and the donee?

As you read this chapter, you will see the rules of gift taxation presented in the context of these questions, and the practical application of those rules to planning engagements.

Exhibit 5.1 | Tax Rate Schedule for Taxable Gifts and Estates (2020)

Over $0 but not over $10,000	**18%** of such amount.
Over $10,000 but not over $20,000	$1,800 plus **20%** of the excess of such amount over $10,000
Over $20,000 but not over $40,000	$3,800 plus **22%** of the excess of such amount over $20,000
Over $40,000 but not over $60,000	$8,200 plus **24%** of the excess of such amount over $40,000
Over $60,000 but not over $80,000	$13,000 plus **26%** of the excess of such amount over $60,000
Over $80,000 but not over $100,000	$18,200 plus **28%** of the excess of such amount over $80,000
Over $100,000 but not over $150,000	$23,800 plus **30%** of the excess of such amount over $100,000
Over $150,000 but not over $250,000	$38,800 plus **32%** of the excess of such amount over $150,000
Over $250,000 but not over $500,000	$70,800 plus **34%** of the excess of such amount over $250,000
Over $500,000 but not over $750,000	$155,800 plus **37%** of the excess of such amount over $500,000
Over $750,000 but not over $1,000,000	$248,300 plus **39%** of the excess of such amount over $750,000
Over $1,000,000	$345,800 plus **40%** of the excess of such amount over $1,000,000

Exhibit 5.2 identifies the highest marginal estate, generation-skipping, and gift tax rates for tax years (2004-2020).

Exhibit 5.2 | Estate and Gift Tax Rates and Credit Exemption Amounts for 2004-2020

Calendar Year	Applicable Estate & GST Exclusion Amount	Applicable Gift Tax Exclusion Amount	Highest Estate, Gift & GST Tax Rates
2004	$1,500,000	$1,000,000	48%
2005	$1,500,000	$1,000,000	47%
2006	$2,000,000	$1,000,000	46%
2007	$2,000,000	$1,000,000	45%
2008	**$2,000,000**	**$1,000,000**	**45%**
2009	**$3,500,000**	**$1,000,000**	**45%**
2010	Estate Tax Repealed*	$1,000,000	35% (Gift Tax Only)*
2011	$5,000,000	$5,000,000	35%
2012	$5,120,000	$5,120,000	35%
2013	$5,250,000	$5,250,000	40%
2014	$5,340,000	$5,340,000	40%
2015	$5,430,000	$5,430,000	40%
2016	$5,450,000	$5,450,000	40%
2017	$5,490,000	$5,490,000	40%
2018	$11,180,000	$4,417,800	40%
2019	$11,400,000	$4,505,800	40%
2020	$11,580,000	$11,580,000	40%

chapter 5

CHARACTERISTICS OF A GIFT

Prior to discussing the practical consequences of the gift tax, one must first determine whether a particular transfer of property meets the definition of a gift.

Parties

There are two parties involved in a gift transfer. The **donor** is the person who makes the gift. The **donee** is the person who receives the gift.

Definition of a Gift

A **gift** is a voluntary transfer, for less than full consideration, of property from one person (a donor) to another person or entity (a donee).

Elements of a Gift

In general, the elements of a gift are:
1. The donor must have the intent to make a voluntary transfer.
2. The donor must be competent to make the gift.
3. The donee must be capable of receiving the gift.
4. The donee must take delivery.
5. The donor must actually part with dominion and control over the gifted property.

> ### Key Concepts
> 1. List the elements of a gift.
> 2. List the various types of gifts.
> 3. Explain how an incomplete gift becomes a complete gift.
> 4. Define a gift loan.
> 5. Understand how real estate and securities valued for gift tax purposes.

Donative intent implies that the donor had a conscious desire to make a gift to the donee. The element of donative intent differentiates gifts from transfers received in return for consideration. Whether or not the requirements of donative intent have been met is a frequent subject of litigation in the courts. A standard that courts typically employ to determine whether or not a transfer is a gift is whether the transfer was made out of "detached and disinterested generosity." Transfers that lack donative intent include quid-pro-quo transfers, transfers occasioned by lost or stolen property, and transfers resulting in a poor economic arrangement for one or both parties.

Competence to make a gift implies that the donor:
1. has attained the legal age of majority,
2. has the mental capacity to make the gift, and
3. owns, or possesses a general or limited power of appointment over, the property that is the subject of the gift.

To receive a gift, the donee (an individual or organization) must be identifiable at the time of the gift. The requirements of legal age and mental capacity are not necessary, provided that the gift is made in trust or to a guardian for the benefit of a person who has not attained legal age or does not have the capacity to manage his/her property. For the gift to be complete, the donee (or, if necessary, the donee's trustee or guardian) must take delivery of the gift, requiring the donor to relinquish dominion and control over the property.

Example 5.3
Lakin transfers $10,000 to her grandson; her grandson has not worked for, sold, or transferred anything to Lakin in return for the $10,000. Lakin has made a $10,000 gift to her grandson.

Example 5.4
Lakin transfers $15,000 to Marques; Marques in turn transfers the title to his vehicle, with a fair market value of $15,000, to Lakin. Lakin has not made a gift to Marques, even if Lakin later discovers that the vehicle is worth less than $15,000 because of a bad engine that neither Marques nor Lakin knew of at the date of the sale. Lakin did not have any intent to transfer an amount greater than the fair market value of the vehicle to Marques.

Consideration

Consideration is the value of property transferred in return for other property. A gift arises whenever an exchange of property occurs and one of the parties does not receive full and fair consideration for their property or services. One of the parties could have made a poor economic deal, but in evaluating suspect transactions, it is always prudent to look closely at the relationship of the parties (especially if they are related) to determine if there was any donative intent and/or a lack of consideration.

Example 5.5
If Father transfers a house to his Son, and Son pays Father $1, Father has made a gift to Son of the difference between the fair market value (FMV) of the house and $1. This is not a bona fide sale for full and adequate consideration because adequate consideration was not paid for the house. For tax purposes, this will be treated a part sale ($1) and part gift (FMV less $1).

Types of Gifts

Gifts can be classified into several categories, including direct, indirect, complete, incomplete, reversionary interests, and net gifts.

Direct Gifts

A direct payment of cash or transfer of property to a donee is a **direct gift**. When a donor makes a direct gift, control of the property is transferred to the donee, and the donor does not retain any control over the property after the transfer.

Example 5.6
A transfer from George to Robin of $10,000 cash without consideration is a direct gift from George to Robin.

Indirect Gifts

Indirect gifts can take many forms, and generally occur with intrafamily transactions. One of the most common ways an indirect gift occurs is through the payment of another's debt.

Example 5.7

Joann pays her friend Susan's automobile note. While Joann has not transferred any property directly to Susan, she has made an indirect gift to Susan equal to the payment made.

Indirect gifts also occur when one person titles property in joint tenancy with another and the other person has not paid for their ownership share. Recall from Chapter 3 that certain exceptions apply when titling checking accounts and savings bonds; in this instance the gift is not yet complete until money is withdrawn by the non-contributing party (discussed later in this chapter).

Example 5.8

April buys a vacation home and titles it joint tenancy with right of survivorship with her brother, Billy. If Billy has not paid anything towards the purchase of the vacation home, April has made an indirect gift to Billy equal to one-half of the equity in the vacation home.

An interest-free or below-market loan (also known as a gift loan) is also an indirect transfer. Interest-free loans and below-market loans have special income tax treatment that requires the lender to impute the interest income as if the arrangement was a bona fide interest-bearing market loan. Imputed interest creates phantom income for the lender. The interest is included in income even though the lender did not actually receive any money. In addition to the income tax consequences, the lender is also deemed to make a gift to the borrower in the amount of the imputed interest. When calculating the gift tax consequences of the transfer, the gift of the imputed interest may be eligible for the annual gift tax exclusion (discussed below).

Although the income tax consequences of below-market loans are covered more thoroughly in an income tax course, the rules have been restated here. In general, loans of less than $10,000 are exempt from both income tax and gift tax consequences. Loans of $100,000 or less are exempt from income tax and gift tax consequences when the borrower has net investment income of less than $1,000 from any source. Loans in excess of $10,000 but up to and including $100,000 where the net investment income of the borrower (donee) exceeds $1,000 require the donor (lender) to impute interest income for income tax purposes equal to the lesser of the donee's (borrower's) net investment income or the applicable federal rate (AFR) times the loan balance. Any imputed interest will also be considered a gift for gift tax consequences. For loans in excess of $100,000 the lender imputes an amount equal to the AFR times the loan balance for income tax purposes and includes the same amount for gift tax purposes. If any loan has a stated interest rate below the AFR, the imputed interest is the difference between the AFR and the stated rate. Exhibit 5.3 summarizes the rules for imputed interest on gift and below market loans.

Exhibit 5.3 | Summary of Imputed Interest on Gift and Below Market Loans

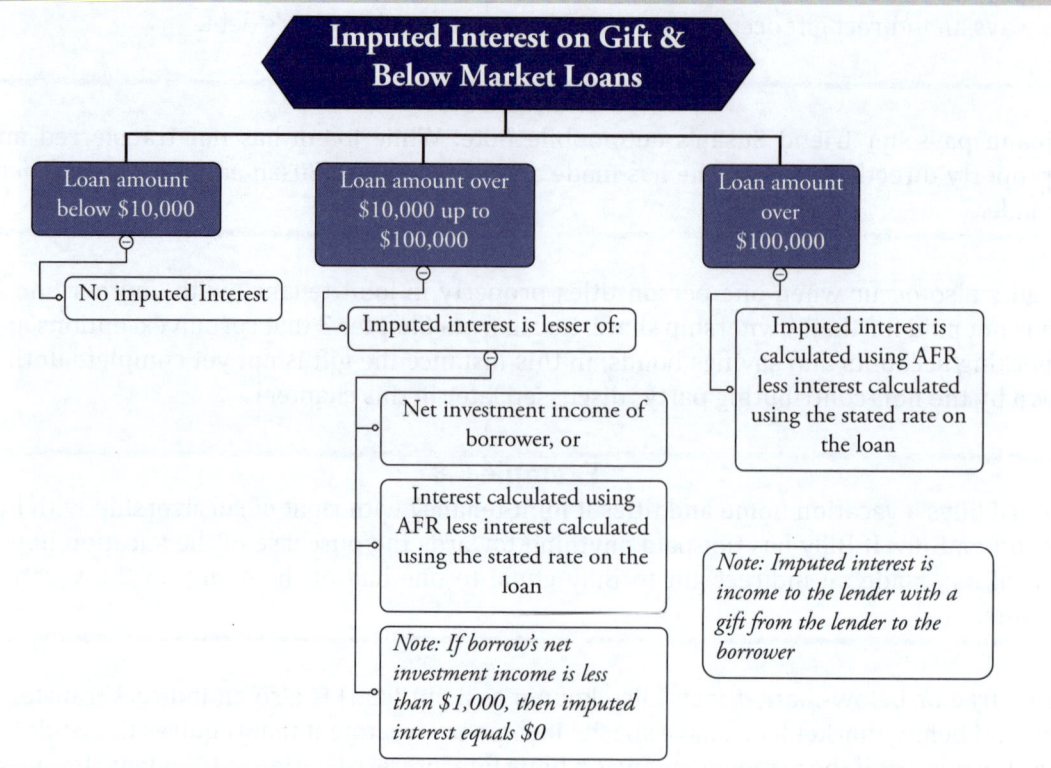

In some planning scenarios, individuals will make below-market or interest-free loans and then later forgive the debt. Forgiving such debt is also an indirect gift, even if there was a bona fide debt transaction.

Complete and Incomplete Transfers

As discussed previously, a gift is complete when the donor releases control over the asset to a donee who can be identified at the date of the gift. Naming an individual as a revocable beneficiary of an account, or making a transfer to a revocable trust (See Chapter 8) are examples of **incomplete transfers** and are not considered to be gifts for gift tax purposes. Since incomplete gifts allow the donor to direct the ultimate disposition of the property, the donor has not released control of the property, and dominion and control over the property has not been transferred to the donee. If the transferor renounces his retained or reversionary interest, or a trust becomes irrevocable (by election, death of the transferor, or by direction of the trust document), the transfer would, at that time, become a completed gift for gift tax purposes.

Example 5.9

Aadil transfers title on his Ferrari to his friend, Bob, without receiving anything in return. Bob becomes the fee simple owner of the car. The transfer of the property is complete because Aadil did not retain any interest in the car, and it is clear that Bob is the ultimate donee of the transfer.

Example 5.10

Warren transfers his home to a revocable living trust. Warren retains the right to live in his home for the rest of his life, and at his death, the home will be transferred to his daughter, Sara. Because this is a revocable trust, Warren can revoke the trust at any time and ownership of the home will return to him. Also, Warren could change or add a beneficiary to the trust at any time. This gift to the trust is incomplete, and not considered to be a gift for gift tax purposes because Warren retains control over the asset. Since this is not a complete gift for gift tax purposes, there is no gift tax consequence on the day of transfer.

The creation of joint bank accounts and the purchase of U.S. Savings Bonds are treated differently from other joint gifts. A completed gift does not occur until the noncontributing party withdraws money for his or her own benefit. The reasoning is simple; the contributing party could have withdrawn all of the money at any time prior to a withdrawal by the noncontributing party. A gift does not occur upon the creation of the joint account nor upon the notification that the joint account has been created. The gift occurs only upon a withdrawal by the noncontributing party for his or her own benefit.

Quick Quiz 5.1

1. If Kyle pays Krystal's car note, and there is no consideration from Krystal to Kyle, Kyle has made a gift to Krystal.
   a. True
   b. False
2. The lender of a $150,000 no-interest gift loan will always impute interest.
   a. True
   b. False
3. The donee of a gift is primarily liable for any gift tax due on the transfer.
   a. True
   b. False
4. Generally, gift tax is calculated based on the fair market value of the property at the date of the gift.
   a. True
   b. False

True, True, False, True.

Example 5.11

On February 14th, Barbara deposited $40,000 into a joint banking account titled with her daughter, Jessica. On April 30th, Jessica withdraws $10,000 from the joint bank account to purchase a diamond ring. The gift was not complete until Jessica withdrew the $10,000 because anytime between February 14th and April 30th, Barbara could have withdrawn the entire $40,000 and Jessica would not have been able to access any of the money.

Reversionary Interests

Reversionary interests are interests in property that have been transferred away and subsequently revert back to the grantor. A reversionary interest has both gift and estate tax consequences. The value of the gift to the donee is not the full fair market value of the property. Rather, it is the present value of the right to use the property. The value of the reversionary interest is determined using statutory tables found in the Treasury Regulations. As will be discussed in Chapter 6, a reversionary interest also has certain estate tax consequences.

Example 5.12
Chuck transfers property to a trust for five years for the benefit of Robbie. At the end of the five years, the property reverts back to Chuck. Since the property reverts back to Chuck, his interest is a reversionary interest and the value of the gift is less than the full value of the property.

Net Gifts

Ordinarily, the donor is responsible for gift tax associated with a taxable transfer. A **net gift** is a gift made on the condition that the donee pay gift tax due when the net gift is made. The donor will report taxable income to the extent that any gift tax paid by the donee exceeds the donor's adjusted basis in the gifted property. Since the taxable gift is calculated by subtracting the actual gift tax paid by the donee from the gross gift, the calculation of a net gift and its associated gift tax is a circular calculation.

Example 5.13
Assume Brianna gifts property worth $250,000 to Kenny on the condition that Kenny pay the gift tax. Brianna's adjusted basis in the property is $100,000. Brianna has already utilized her lifetime gift exemption and her annual exclusion for Kenny this year. Because Kenny must pay the gift tax, the gift is considered a net gift, and the gift tax is calculated on $250,000 less the gift tax that Kenny must pay, assumed to be $71,429 or [$250,000 - ($250,000/1.40)]. In this example, Kenny would pay the gift tax of $71,429, the taxable gift would be $178,571. The 40% is from the marginal tax bracket from Exhibit 5.1.

Exhibit 5.4 | Net Gifts Do Not Produce Gift Tax Savings

Gross Gifts		Net Gift	
Gift to loved one	$10,000,000	Net Gift	$14,000,000 (total outlay)
Gift Tax	$4,000,000	Gift Tax	($4,000,000) [NG / 1.4) x 0.40]
Total Outlay	$14,000,000	Gift to Loved Ones	$10,000,000

Valuation of a Gift

The value of a gift for gift tax purposes is equal to the fair market value of the gifted property on the date of the gift. For real estate, an appraisal is usually necessary to determine the fair market value of the property. Publicly traded securities are valued at the average of the high and low trading price for the day. The fair market value of a bond is the present value of the expected future payments. Treasury Regulations 25.2512-1 through 25.2512-8 provide detailed guidelines to calculate the fair market value of certain types of property. Valuation discounts are allowed for lack of marketability, lack of liquidity, and lack of control. A more thorough discussion of valuation as it relates to particular assets and the availability and application of valuation discounts is covered in Chapter 6.

chapter 5

CASE STUDY 5.1

In **Steinberg v. Commissioner, 145 T.C. No. 7** (September 2015), Petitioner (P) (Donor) entered into a binding gift agreement with her daughters under which P gave her daughters properties in exchange for an agreement to assume and pay gift tax and to assume any estate liability under 2035(b) [the gross-up rule - gift taxes paid on gifts made within three years of death are included in the gross estate] (See Chapter 6).

In calculating the gifts, P reduced the fair market value of the gifts by an amount representing the value of the daughters assumption of the 2035(b) estate tax liability. The value of the assumption was determined using IRS mortality tables and applying interest rates under IRC Section 7520 as a discount factor.

The Tax Court held that the assumption was a detriment to the daughters and a benefit to P such as would be considered in an arms-length transaction between a willing buyer and a willing seller.

P was 89-years-old at the time of the transfer in 2007. The total transferred to the daughters before the gift tax and the assumption of the 2035(b) estate liability was $109,449,307. Forty million was transferred to an escrow account by the daughters and $32,437,261 was used to pay the gift tax. (In 2007, the gift tax rate was 35%.) The balance $7,562,739, was set aside to pay any 2035(b) estate tax liability. The respondent (IRS) issued a deficiency notice for additional tax of $1,804,908 for 2007. Held for petitioner and against respondent (IRS).

EXCLUSIONS AND EXEMPTIONS

Once a transfer is determined to be a gift, the donor should determine whether an exclusion or exemption would transform the transfer into a nontaxable transfer. The next two sections cover the annual exclusion and lifetime exemption, and the related rules for their use.

The Annual Exclusion

All individuals may gift, transfer-tax free, up to $15,000 (2020) per donee per year to a related or unrelated party. This **annual exclusion** is a de minimis rule set by Congress to help reduce the reporting requirements for small gifts. The annual exclusion will offset the fair market value of the total gifts to each donee by $15,000. To qualify for the annual exclusion, the gift must be of a present interest (discussed in the next section). If the gift is of a future interest, it normally does not qualify for the annual exclusion and will be reported as a taxable gift. The annual exclusion is perishable and any unused amount expires at the end of each year.

Key Concepts

1. Explain how much can an individual transfer, gift tax free, each year.
2. Define a taxable gift.
3. Understand the requirements of utilizing the annual exclusion.
4. List advantages of the gift-splitting election.
5. Discuss why gift-splitting was enacted.
6. Define the lifetime gift tax applicable exclusion amount.

The $15,000 annual exclusion is indexed using the Consumer Price Index (CPI) rounded down to the nearest $1,000. The annual exclusion is available and expires at the end of each calendar year. Any annual exclusion a taxpayer might have for a particular year is lost forever if not used. Outright gifts equal to or less than the annual exclusion are also exempt from generation-skipping transfer taxes. There is a special annual exclusion for non-citizen spouses equal to $157,000 (as indexed) for 2020. For citizen spouses there is an unlimited deduction for gifts. In addition to the annual exclusion, each person has a $11,580,000 lifetime applicable gift tax exclusion (resulting in a gift tax applicable credit of $4,577,800 for 2020).

Example 5.14

Carolyn makes a present interest gift of property with a fair market value of $15,000 to Bobby. This was the only gift Carolyn made during the year. Because the gift is for property of a present interest, the transfer will qualify for the annual exclusion, and Carolyn will not owe any gift tax on the transfer to Bobby nor will Carolyn be required to file a gift tax return.

Example 5.15

Early this year, Mary made a present interest gift to Emile with a fair market value of $15,000. Later in the year, Mary made another present interest gift to Emile for $6,000. As the annual exclusion applies on a per year, per donee basis, Mary has made a taxable gift equal to $6,000 ($15,000 + $6,000 - $15,000) to Emile during this year and will be required to file a gift tax return.

Quick Quiz 5.2

1. A donor's gross estate will not include the fair market value of lifetime gifts that qualify for the annual exclusion.
   a. True
   b. False

2. If the annual exclusion is not used during the year, it does not carryover to the following year.
   a. True
   b. False

3. If a donor gifts $15,000 of community property to his niece, the donor must file a gift tax return.
   a. True
   b. False

4. An individual who gifts a total of $100,000 split equally between eleven donees is not required to file a gift tax return.
   a. True
   b. False

5. The amount of annual exclusion for transfers to a non-citizen spouse is $157,000 for 2020.
   a. True
   b. False

True, True, False, True, True.

Taxable Gifts Defined

A **taxable gift** is any gift in excess of the annual exclusion. However, a taxable gift will not produce gift tax liability until the summation of taxable gifts over a lifetime exceeds the lifetime exemption and its credit equivalency. A taxable gift does not include any qualified transfers (discussed later in this chapter).

Split Gift Elections

As will be discussed later in this chapter, gift tax returns are filed on a per donor basis, which creates some interesting issues for married individuals. If both spouses each gave one donee $15,000, then each donor spouse would use their annual exclusion, and would not be required to file a gift tax return. In many cases, one spouse would like to give property to a donee but the other spouse does not. In this case, the donor spouse, with the consent of the non-donor spouse, could use both the donor and the non-donor spouse's annual exclusion and gift $30,000 of separate property to the donee. This concept is called gift-splitting.

Therefore, if a donor is married at the time of the gift and joins with his spouse to use both annual exclusions for a particular donee, the exclusion is effectively increased to $30,000, double the annual exclusion, per donee, per year. Since the exclusion per donee expires annually, the donor spouse is essentially using the non-donor spouse's annual exclusion right for this particular donee, this particular year, even though the non-donor spouse would not have used it. When one donor makes the gift, and the donor's spouse consents to use their annual exclusion for that donee, then the gift is called a **split gift**.

A gift tax return (Form 709) is required for all split gifts, and both spouses are required to sign the gift tax return (the non-donor spouse signs an election to split gifts on the return). If no taxable gift is made during the year, (because all gifts are under the annual exclusion due to gift-splitting), only the donor who actually gifts property is required to file a gift tax return. If an election to split gifts is made, the election applies to all gifts made from both spouses during the year, regardless of the identity of the donees. If the couple married during the year, any property gifted after their marriage may be considered a split gift, but the couple cannot elect to split gifts made prior to their marriage. In addition, if they are divorced during the year and are not remarried at the end of the year then the split gift election can be used only for gifts given while married. A split gift election can also be made for gifts made in the year in which one spouse dies, but only for those gifts made while the spouse was alive.

Example 5.16
Jennifer gifts $20,000 of her separate property to her son, Alex. Jennifer's husband, Robbie, consents to split. The gift to Alex is the only gift made by Robbie or Jennifer during the year. Neither Jennifer nor Robbie will have a taxable gift as both annual exclusions, totaling $30,000, can offset the $20,000 gift. Because of Robbie's election to split the gift, Jennifer will be required to file a gift tax return and Robbie will be required to sign her gift tax return to make the gift splitting election.

Gifts of Community and Joint Property

Gifts of community property do not require gift-splitting, since each spouse is deemed to own one-half of any community property. Therefore, any gift of community property is a joint gift not subject to gift-splitting. Gift-splitting was enacted as a way to equalize to impact of the gift tax rules in community and non-community-property states. Since gifts of community property are not considered split gifts, the donor(s) are not required to file a gift tax return unless the gifts constitute taxable gifts. A comparison between gifts of separate property and gifts of community property is presented in the following example.

Example 5.17

Gift-Splitting Comparison:
Peter and Reagan, who are married, made the following gifts during the current year:

Donees	Donor From Peter	Donor From Reagan	Total
To daughter, Amber	$50,000	$3,000	$53,000
To daughter, Nicole	$50,000	$3,000	$53,000
To niece, Victoria	$30,000	$3,000	$33,000
	$130,000	$9,000	$139,000

If the gifts were from community property:

Gifts of Community Property			
	From Peter	From Reagan	Total
To daughter, Amber	$26,500	$26,500	$53,000
To daughter, Nicole	$26,500	$26,500	$53,000
To niece, Victoria	$16,500	$16,500	$33,000
Total Gross Gifts	$69,500	$69,500	$139,000
Less Annual Exclusions			
To daughter, Amber	$15,000	$15,000	$30,000
To daughter, Nicole	$15,000	$15,000	$30,000
To niece, Victoria	$15,000	$15,000	$30,000
Total Exclusions	$45,000	$45,000	$90,000
Equals Current Taxable Gifts	$24,500	$24,500	$49,000

If the gifts were from separate property and without gift splitting:

Gifts of Separate Property without Gift Splitting			
	From Peter	From Reagan	Total
To daughter, Amber	$50,000	$3,000	$53,000
To daughter, Nicole	$50,000	$3,000	$53,000
To niece, Victoria	$30,000	$3,000	$33,000
Total Gross Gifts	$130,000	$9,000	$139,000
Less Annual Exclusions			
To daughter, Amber	$15,000	$3,000	$18,000
To daughter, Nicole	$15,000	$3,000	$18,000
To niece, Victoria	$15,000	$3,000	$18,000
Total Exclusions	$45,000	$9,000	$54,000
Equals Current Taxable Gifts	$85,000	$0	$85,000

If the gifts were from separate property and gift splitting was elected:

Gifts of Separate Property with Gift-Splitting			
	From Peter	**From Reagan**	**Total**
To daughter, Amber	$26,500	$26,500	$53,000
To daughter, Nicole	$26,500	$26,500	$53,000
To niece, Victoria	$16,500	$16,500	$33,000
Total Gross Gifts	$69,500	$69,500	$139,000
Less Annual Exclusions			
To daughter, Amber	$15,000	$15,000	$30,000
To daughter, Nicole	$15,000	$15,000	$30,000
To niece, Victoria	$15,000	$15,000	$30,000
Total Exclusions	$45,000	$45,000	$90,000
Equals Current Taxable Gifts	$24,500	$24,500	$49,000

Notice where the gifts are from community property, Peter and Reagan have the same gift tax consequences as if the property were separate and they elected to split gifts.

Electing to split gifts results in a decrease in the total taxable gifts from $85,000 to $49,000. The $36,000 difference is a result of Reagan not making full use of her annual exclusion for gifts if gift splitting is not elected.

The Applicable Credit Amount

In addition to the annual exclusion, there is a lifetime gift tax applicable credit amount of $4,577,800. This applicable credit amount shelters up to $11,580,000 of cumulative lifetime taxable transfers, in excess of the annual exclusion amount, from transfer taxes. The applicable exclusion amount of $11,580,000 (also known as the applicable credit equivalency amount or applicable credit) is defined as the fair market value of taxable property that can transfer without creating a gift tax greater than the applicable credit against transfer taxes. For gifts in excess of the annual exclusion, there is a mandatory reduction in the applicable credit amount.

Example 5.18
A couple with two children who had made no previous gifts could gift a total of $23,220,000 during 2020 (one-half to each child) and not pay any gift tax by fully using each parent's annual exclusion and applicable transfer credit (2 donors x $15,000 x 2 donees = $60,000 + (2 x $11,580,000)). They could gift each child another $30,000 each subsequent year to use their annual exclusions.

Example 5.19

Celeste transfers a present interest in property with a fair market value of $32,000 to Raymond in 2020. This transfer is the only gift that Celeste has ever made and the only gift made to Raymond for the year. It qualifies for the annual exclusion because it is a gift of a present interest. $15,000 of the $32,000 is excluded under the annual exclusion and the tax on the remaining $17,000 is a taxable gift and reduces Celeste's available applicable credit ($4,577,800) by a like amount, resulting in no gift tax payable.

Example 5.20

Zeke gifts a total of $23,220,000 ($11,610,000 to each of his two children). Zeke is married to Debbie. Debbie allows Zeke to use her annual exclusion and her lifetime applicable gift tax credit by signing a split gift election. Assuming no previous taxable gifts, there would be no gift tax payable. The couple would use their annual exclusions for the year for these donees and would have exhausted each of their applicable gift tax credits ($4,577,800 or $11,580,000 credit equivalency).

For tax years beginning before December 31, 2003 and after December 31, 2010, the applicable credit for transfers during life is equal to the applicable credit for transfers at death. However, EGTRRA 2001 increased the applicable credit against estate taxes for years after 2003, while the applicable credit against gift taxes for years after 2003 remained at the same level. During the EGTRRA years, the credit amounts were not unified, so we will continue to refer to the credit against gift taxes as the "applicable gift tax credit" and the credit against the estate tax as the "applicable estate tax credit." **Exhibit 5.5** illustrates the differences in the applicable credits against gift and estate tax.

Exhibit 5.5 | Applicable Gift and Estate Tax Credits and Exclusion Amounts

Year of Death	Applicable Estate Tax Credit	Applicable Estate Tax Credit Equivalency	Applicable Gift Tax Credit	Applicable Gift Tax Credit Equivalency
1997	$192,800	$600,000	$192,800	$600,000
1998	$202,050	$625,000	$202,050	$625,000
1999	$211,300	$650,000	$211,300	$650,000
2000	$220,550	$675,000	$220,550	$675,000
2001	$220,550	$675,000	$220,550	$675,000
2002	$345,800	$1,000,000	$345,800	$1,000,000
2003	$345,800	$1,000,000	$345,800	$1,000,000
2004	$555,800	$1,500,000	$345,800	$1,000,000
2005	$555,800	$1,500,000	$345,800	$1,000,000
2006 - 2008	$780,800	$2,000,000	$345,800	$1,000,000
2009	**$1,455,800**	**$3,500,000**	**$345,800**	**$1,000,000**
2010	REPEALED*	REPEALED*	$330,800	$1,000,000
2011	$1,730,800	$5,000,000	$1,730,800	$5,000,000
2012	$1,772,800	$5,120,000	$1,772,800	$5,120,000
2013	$2,045,800	$5,250,000	$2,045,800	$5,250,000
2014	$2,081,800	$5,340,000	$2,081,800	$5,340,000
2015	$2,117,800	$5,430,000	$2,117,800	$5,430,000
2016	$2,125,800	$5,450,000	$2,125,800	$5,450,000
2017	$2,141,800	$5,490,000	$2,141,800	$5,490,000
2018	$4,417,800	$11,180,000	$4,417,800	$11,180,000
2019	$4,505,800	$11,400,000	$4,505,800	$11,400,000
2020	$4,577,800	$11,580,000	$4,577,800	$11,580,000

*TRA 2010 permits estate representatives to opt out of the TRA 2010 regime.

TRA 2010 permitted portability of a deceased spouse's gift and estate tax exemption amounts and ATRA 2012 made the portability provision permanent. Planning issues associated with portability of the estate tax exemption will be discussed in more detail in Chapter 6. The use of a deceased spouse's exemption amount for gift tax purposes permits substantial transfers to be made without triggering gift tax liability.

Example 5.21

Dermot died in January, 2020, and had a taxable estate of $1,000,000. His executor makes an election on his timely filed estate tax return to leave Kathleen, Dermot's spouse, his unused $10,580,000 unused exemption amount (via the portability feature). If Kathleen decides in December to make a large taxable gift to her children in excess of annual exclusion amounts and qualified transfers (a taxable amount of $2,000,000 to each of her 4 children, for a total of $8,000,000), the $8,000,000 transfer will not trigger any gift tax liability. Under the provisions of TRA 2010 and ATRA 2012, Kathleen's gift tax exemption amount would equal her available estate tax applicable credit amount, which, due to the executor's election in Dermot's estate, includes Dermot's $10,580,000 unused credit. Assuming that Kathleen has not made any other taxable gifts, her gift tax exemption amount would be $22,160,000 ($11,580,000 for herself as indexed, plus the $10,580,000 of unused exemption from Dermot's estate). Since her taxable gift of $8,000,000 is below the $22,160,000 credit amount, Kathleen will not owe any gift tax on these transfers, and can, in the future (2020 or 2021) make an additional $14,160,000 of taxable gifts without triggering a gift tax payment obligation.

The timing of the use of the taxpayer's exemption ($11,580,000) does not negate the portability of the deceased spouse's unused exemption amount.

Example 5.22

Assume, in our example above, that prior to Dermot's death, Kathleen had made a taxable gift of $5,000,000 to her children, but all other facts remain the same. At the end of the year following Dermot's death, she made an additional taxable gift of $3,000,000 to them to bring the total taxable gifts to $8,000,000. Kathleen will still not be liable for any gift tax on the additional $3,000,000 transfer, since her gift tax exemption amount includes Dermot's unused $10,580,000 exemption amount.

When the deceased spousal unused exemption amount (DSUEA) is used to make lifetime gifts, and the taxpayer has several deceased spouses, it may be possible for the taxpayer to use the DSUEA of each deceased spouse to increase the wealth transferred to others gift tax free.

Example 5.23

Continuing with our example, above, assume that Kathleen has made taxable transfers of $11,580,000 shielded by her gift tax exemption amount prior to Dermot's death. Shortly after Dermot's death, Kathleen makes an additional $10,580,000 in taxable transfers to her children (to use up Dermot's DSUEA). The following year, Kathleen marries Ted, a 96-year-old acquaintance with terminal cancer who has no living family members and no money. Three months after the wedding, Ted passes away, and has no taxable estate. Ted's executor elects, on a timely filed estate tax return, to transfer Ted's DSUEA of $11,580,000 to his surviving spouse, Kathleen. Subsequent to Ted's death, Kathleen can make an additional $11,580,000 in taxable transfers without triggering any estate tax liability, since the tax will be shielded by Ted's DSUEA. This brings Kathleen's total gift-tax free transfers to $33,740,000.

While this example is extreme, it could be taken farther - Kathleen could marry another poor, old, and sick suitor to get yet another DSUEA to make more tax free gifts. While non-tax decisions (i.e., marriage) can impact wealth transfer planning opportunities, it may not be in the client's best interest to make those decisions to save tax dollars when the tax savings is temporary. Furthermore, while use of multiple DSUEAs is possible when lifetime gifts are made, more severe limitations apply when the DSUEA is applied to death-time transfers. Those limitations will be discussed in more detail in Chapter 6.

To protect against the possibility of abuse, TRA 2010 extends the statute of limitations for gift and estate tax returns allocating a deceased spouse's unused exemption amount. This extension of the statute of limitations may be particularly troublesome for estates that claim valuation discounts when establishing the value of property for estate tax purposes. While the normal statute of limitations will apply to the collection of the tax, when a surviving spouse makes use of the deceased spouse's unused exemption valuation methodologies used in the deceased spouse's estate may come under attack, jeopardizing some of the unused exclusion that the surviving spouse anticipated using when making the gift.

GIFTS OF A PRESENT AND FUTURE INTEREST

Present Interest Gift

A gift can be a gift of a **present interest** or a gift of a future interest. Only a present interest gift will qualify for the annual exclusion. Section 25.2503-3(b) of the Treasury Regulations defines a present interest, in part, as "an immediate use, possession, or enjoyment of property." Gifts of cash, property, etc., where title passes immediately to the donee are common examples of gifts of a present interest. A gift in trust must be a gift of a present interest to qualify for the annual exclusion. Gifts to minors in trust under 2503(b) or 2503(c) are deemed to be gifts of a present interest and will be discussed in detail in Chapter 8. The most frequently litigated issues in the present interest context are whether notice to the beneficiaries of a contribution to a trust is required and whether it matters if the beneficiaries' other interest in the trust (in addition to their withdrawal rights) are contingent or remote. The courts have consistently answered "no" to both questions, while the IRS has maintained the opposite view. Therefore, notice is well advised to avoid such litigation.

> **Key Concepts**
>
> 1. What is the difference between a future interest gift and a present interest gift?
> 2. How does the Crummey provision convert an otherwise future interest gift to a present interest gift?
> 3. How can the problem with the 5/5 Lapse rule be solved?

Example 5.24

Erin transfers her car to her brother, Aaron. All necessary title transfers are filed with the state. This is a gift of a present interest equal to the fair market value of the car because Aaron can benefit from the car and has control over it at the date of the transfer. The gift is eligible for the annual exclusion.

Example 5.25
Sebastian transfers $15,000 to Natalia's individual bank account. Natalia has full and complete control over the current use of the money so it is a gift of a present interest. The gift is eligible for the annual exclusion.

Future Interest Gift

A **future interest** is an interest in property that comes into being at a future date or time. The donee's right to control the property will materialize upon some future date or the passage of time. Generally, gifts in trust are considered to be future interests. However, a present value gift of a mandatory income interest in a trust is considered to be a present, not a future, interest. A gift of a future interest does not qualify for the annual exclusion.

Example 5.26
Cheryl gives Billy a vacation home, but reserves for herself the right to use the property for a term of 10 years. Because Billy cannot benefit from the property at the time of the transfer, the interest transferred to Billy is a gift of a future interest.

Example 5.27
Hanna assigns (transfers) a life insurance policy on her life to an irrevocable life insurance trust and names Henri as the beneficiary of the trust. Henri cannot benefit from the transfer until Hanna dies (some time in the future), so this is a gift of a future interest.

Example 5.28
Gaynelle makes a gift of a future interest to Dylan with a fair market value of $9,000. Because the gift is for property of a future interest, the transfer does not qualify for the annual exclusion, and Gaynelle will have made a taxable gift on the transfer to Dylan. Gaynelle must therefore file a gift tax return.

Example 5.29
Jacklyn made the following gifts in the current year:

Gift	Donee	Value
Cash	Sarah	$25,000
Car	Bailie	$7,000
Bonds	Mikayla	$9,000
Stock in trust with a life estate to:	Bailie	$22,000
Stock in trust with the remainder to:	Mikayla	$25,000
Total		**$88,000**

Jacklyn's total taxable gifts for the current year equal $49,000 as determined below:

Donee	FMV	Less Annual Exclusion	Total Taxable Gifts
Sarah	$25,000	$15,000	$10,000
Bailie	$29,000	$15,000	$14,000
Mikayla - Present Interest	$9,000	$9,000	$0
Mikayla - Future Interest	$25,000	$0	$25,000
Total	**$88,000**	**$39,000**	**$49,000**

Each of Jacklyn's gifts qualified for the annual exclusion except the gift to Mikayla consisting of the remainder interest in a trust. Because Mikayla is unable to currently use the gift, it is not a gift of a present interest and therefore does not qualify for the annual exclusion. All of the other gifts qualify for the annual exclusion since they are gifts of a present interest.

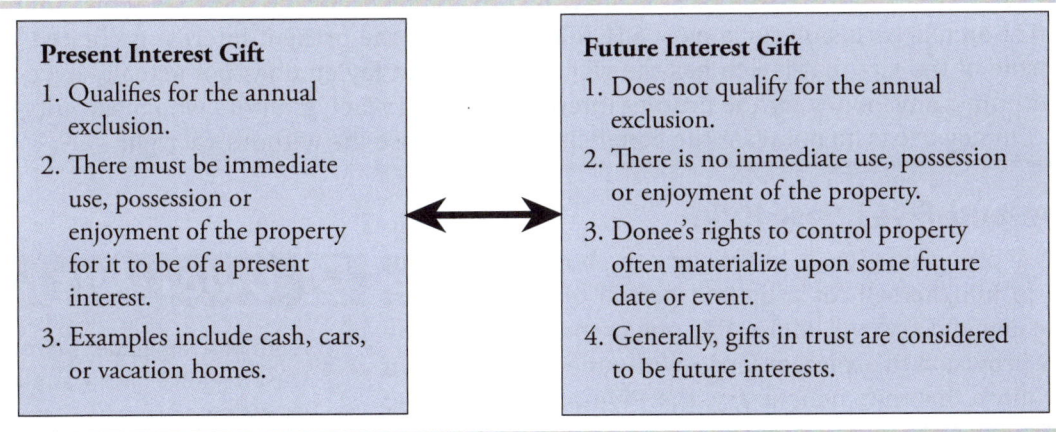

Exhibit 5.6 | Present v. Future Interest Gifts

Present Interest Gift
1. Qualifies for the annual exclusion.
2. There must be immediate use, possession or enjoyment of the property for it to be of a present interest.
3. Examples include cash, cars, or vacation homes.

Future Interest Gift
1. Does not qualify for the annual exclusion.
2. There is no immediate use, possession or enjoyment of the property.
3. Donee's rights to control property often materialize upon some future date or event.
4. Generally, gifts in trust are considered to be future interests.

The Crummey Provision

Historically, individuals struggled with a desire to limit access to gifted property by placing gifted assets into a trust while wanting the gift to qualify for the gift tax annual exclusion. A famous court case, *Crummey v. U.S.*, 397 F.2d 82 (9th Cir. 1968) eliminated this struggle to some extent. A **Crummey provision**, as it is now called, is the explicit right of a trust beneficiary to withdraw some, or all, of any contribution to a trust for a limited period of time, generally 30 days, after the contribution. A Crummey provision does two things:
1. it qualifies the transfer as a present interest gift, and
2. it creates a general power of appointment for estate tax purposes.

A Crummey provision typically limits the withdrawal right to an amount equal to the annual exclusion or less, thus, converting what might have been a gift of a future interest in trust to a gift of a present interest, which will then qualify for the annual exclusion. If the Crummey power limits the withdrawal right to an amount less than the annual exclusion, only the amount under the Crummey power is considered a present interest gift and is eligible for the annual exclusion. It is important to understand that the donee does not actually have to withdraw the money; the mere right to withdrawal creates the present interest. A recent court case, Turner v. Commissioner, reaffirmed the holding in Crummey that notice of a contribution to a trust is not required to convert the contribution to a present interest.[1] All that matters is that the trust beneficiaries have the legal right to demand the contributed property.

Example 5.30

Jeffrey created an irrevocable trust in 2020 for the benefit of his son, Jaylen. The trust document prohibits distributions to Jaylen until he reaches the age of 26. Included in the trust document, however, is a Crummey provision which allows Jaylen to take a withdrawal from the trust equal to the lesser of the annual exclusion or the amount contributed to the trust each year. In 2020, Jeffrey contributed $6,000 to the trust and in 2021, Jeffrey contributed $15,000 to the trust. Even though Jaylen cannot benefit under the trust document until he reaches the age of 26, and thus his interest is a future interest, the Crummey provision creates a present interest for the lesser of the contribution or the annual exclusion ($15,000 for 2020) each year. As such, in 2020, Jaylen has the right to withdraw $6,000 from the trust, which will qualify for the annual exclusion. In 2021, the $15,000 contribution to the trust is offset by the annual exclusion of $15,000 (assuming 2021 annual exclusion remains at $15,000). Note that the present interest is created by virtue of the fact that Jaylen has the right to withdraw. Jaylen does not actually have to withdraw any money for the present interest to apply. In fact, grantors who make gifts to Crummey trusts do not want the beneficiaries to exercise the withdrawal right.

The Five-and-Five Lapse Rule

A Crummey provision gives a beneficiary the power to appoint property to him/herself for a limited period of time. In most cases, the beneficiary will allow the power provided by the Crummey provision to expire, or lapse, without exercising it. If a trust has more than one beneficiary, the **Five-and-Five Lapse Rule** must be applied to determine if the lapse causes the beneficiary holding the Crummey power to make a taxable gift from the beneficiary holding the Crummey power to the other beneficiaries of the trust. Under the Five-and-Five Lapse Rule, a taxable gift is deemed to have been made when a power to withdraw an amount in excess of the greater of $5,000 or 5 percent of the trust assets has lapsed, or not been used by a beneficiary. These numbers are not adjusted for inflation. In a trust with multiple beneficiaries, the lapse of one beneficiary's power to withdraw assets in excess of $5,000 or 5 percent results in a taxable gift to the other beneficiaries, thus requiring the filing of a gift tax return. However, the 5/5 Lapse Rule does not apply to single beneficiary trusts for gift tax purposes (although it can cause estate tax consequences for the beneficiary) because any lapse of a power to withdraw would only result in the beneficiary essentially making a gift to himself. Since the

> **Quick Quiz 5.3**
>
> 1. A gift of a remainder interest in a trust qualifies for the annual exclusion.
>   a. True
>   b. False
>
> 2. A Crummey provision is the explicit right of a trust beneficiary to withdraw some, or all, of any contribution to a trust for a limited period after the contribution.
>   a. True
>   b. False
>
> *False, True.*

---

1. Turner v. Commissioner, T.C. Memo 2011-209.

taxable gift treatment from a lapse of the 5/5 amounts is a gift of a future interest, it does not qualify for the annual exclusion.

Example 5.31

Harry and Wendy transfer $90,000 to an irrevocable trust and name their three children, Adam, Billy, and Christopher, as beneficiaries. The trust provisions include a right to withdraw an amount equal to one-third of any contribution for 30 days for each beneficiary up to the annual exclusion limit for both spouses ($30,000 for 2020). After 30 days, Adam has allowed his power to withdraw $30,000 to lapse. Allowing the power to withdraw $30,000 to lapse violates the 5/5 Lapse Rule because $30,000 exceeds $5,000. In this case the lapse of the power to withdraw $30,000 also exceeds 5% of the value of the assets of the trust, or $4,500 (5% of $90,000).

To determine the taxable gift that Adam made to Billy and Christopher as a result of the lapse, first determine the total amount of the lapse, which in this case is $30,000. However, only the amount of the lapse that exceeds the greater of $5,000 or 5% of the trust ($30,000 - $5,000 = $25,000) is reported as a taxable gift. Divide $25,000 by the total number of beneficiaries, which in this case is three. Therefore, Adam has made a taxable gift to Billy and Christopher of $8,333 ($25,000 ÷ 3 = $8,333). Note that Adam has also technically made a gift to himself of $8,333, but this is not reported as a taxable gift. Adam's gifts to Billy and Christopher as a result of the lapse are gifts of a future interest and therefore do not qualify for the annual exclusion.

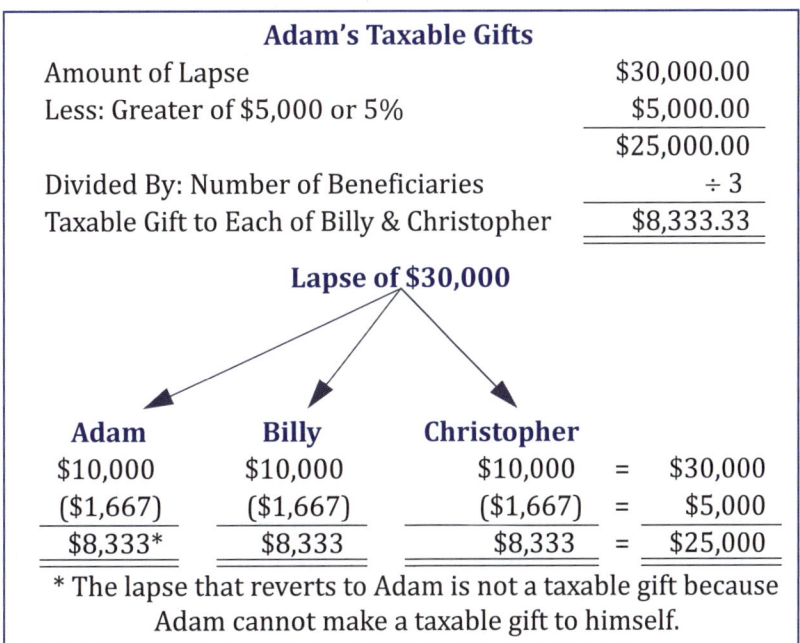

Harry and Wendy could have created a separate trust for each beneficiary or included a 5/5 lapse provision in the trust in order to avoid these intra-beneficiary gift problems. The 5/5 lapse provision would limit the withdrawal amount to the greater of $5,000 or 5% of the trust assets.

TRANSFERS RESULTING IN NO GIFT TAX

Transfers to political organizations, qualified transfers, payments for legal support, payments between divorcing spouses, and transfers within a business setting are types of gifts that are not subject to gift tax. Other transfers, such as gifts to spouses and gifts to charities, are subject to the gift tax regime but generally result in no gift tax due to their unlimited deduction.

Transfers to Political Organizations

Under Section 2501(a)(5) of the Internal Revenue Code, gifts made to political organizations are exempt from gift tax. The term "political organization" means a party, committee, association, fund, or other organization (whether or not incorporated) organized and operated primarily for the purpose of directly or indirectly accepting contributions or making expenditures, or both, for an exempt function. Under Section 527(e)(2), exempt functions include influencing or attempting to influence the selection, nomination, election, or appointment of any individual to any federal, state, or local public office or office in a political organization, or the election of Presidential or Vice-Presidential electors, whether or not such individual or electors are selected, nominated, elected, or appointed.

Qualified Transfers

Certain transfers, called **qualified transfers**, are not subject to transfer taxes. A qualified transfer is a payment made directly to a qualified educational institution (a qualified educational institution is an educational organization which maintains a regular faculty and curriculum and normally has a regularly enrolled body of students in attendance) for tuition (this does not include room and board, books, supplies, and other similar expenses which do not constitute direct tuition costs) or a payment made directly to a medical care provider for qualifying medical expenses of someone else. Qualifying medical expenses include physician expenses for the diagnosis, cure, mitigation, treatment or prevention of disease, as well as the cost of prescription drugs (generally expenses that would be deductible to the benefited taxpayer for income tax purposes if actually paid for by the taxpayer). The exclusions do not apply to the payments for unnecessary cosmetic surgery. These qualified transfers allow taxpayers to effectively transfer wealth to others (no relationship between the donor and the donee is necessary) without being subject to transfer tax. To qualify, the payments must be paid directly to the specific institution or provider.

> **Key Concepts**
>
> 1. List the requirements for a qualified transfer.
> 2. Are legal support payments subject to gift tax?

Since qualified transfers are not subject to gift tax and there is no limitation on the amount of the qualified transfer, individuals can provide assistance to other individuals without worrying about transfer taxes. This exclusion is not limited to family members. Qualified transfers do not reduce the grantor's annual exclusion and do not reduce the applicable lifetime credit. Qualified transfers can be used to minimize the overall transfer tax within a family. For example, grandparents can pay for their grandchildren's college tuition instead of making gifts to the grandchildren's parents, which may be taxable.

Example 5.32
Baker, who is single, gave an outright gift of $60,000 cash directly to her friend, Quincy, who used the money to pay for her medical expenses. Because the gift was paid to Quincy, instead of directly to the medical institution, it is not a qualified transfer. However, the gift is of a present interest and qualifies for the $15,000 annual exclusion. Therefore, Baker made a taxable gift of $45,000 and must file a gift tax return to report the gift. If Baker had paid Quincy's medical expenses directly to the medical institution, the entire $60,000 would have escaped gift taxation. In addition, Baker would have been able to gift Quincy up to an additional $15,000 during that year, which would have qualified for the gift tax annual exclusion.

529 Plans

A **529 plan** is a tax-advantaged savings plan designed to encourage saving for future college costs. 529 plans, legally known as "qualified tuition plans," are sponsored by states, state agencies, or educational institutions and are authorized by Section 529 of the Internal Revenue Code. Gifts made to 529 plans qualify for the annual exclusion. In fact, the IRC permits taxpayers to contribute five times the annual exclusion amount to a 529 plan per donee (beneficiary) in a single year and avoid gift tax. This option uses the current year annual exclusion and accelerates the use of the annual exclusion for the next four years. In the event that the donor dies prior to the end of the five-year period over which the annual exclusions were being used, the gross estate of the donor shall include the portion of such contributions properly allocable to periods after the date of death of the donor.

Example 5.33
In 2020, Seth and Anna Belle could each contribute $75,000 ($15,000 x 5 years) to a 529 plan for their newborn son Chaz. None of the $150,000 would be subject to gift tax as long as they lived for at least five years.

Example 5.34
Jack and Ann are wealthy grandparents to 28 grandchildren from 7 of their 10 children. The grandchildren are ages 0-10-years-old. Jack and Ann want to fully fund each grandchild's education in separate 529 plans. They can contribute $15,000 x 5 x 2 for each child or $150,000 per child times 28 or $4.2 million, which will be out of their gross estate. Because they expect more grandchildren, any unused amounts can be used for their other grandchildren by changing the name of the 529 beneficiary.

Payments for Support

Legal support payments or obligations are transfers to, or for, children or dependents and can be interpreted broadly. Payments of support obligations are exempt from the gift tax rules. Support obligations take many forms and do not necessarily stop at age 18 (the age of majority in most states).

Example 5.35
Graduate or professional education and the living expenses incurred while pursuing a graduate or professional education paid for by the parent of the student may or may not qualify as legal support depending on state law regarding the definition of legal support obligations.

Payments Between Divorcing Spouses

Payments made from one spouse to another pursuant to a divorce or separation decree are not gifts. Rather, they are either nontaxable property settlements with a carryover basis or alimony payments deductible for income tax by the payor and includible for income tax by the payee. A property transfer is deemed to be pursuant to a divorce decree if it occurs within one year of the termination of the marriage or is related to the cessation of the marriage.

Transfers within a Business Setting

Any transfer within a business setting between business people is presumed to be compensation for services rendered and is not a gift. De minimis type gifts are excepted from this presumption and because of the size of their amount are generally not subject to gift tax. Examples of such de minimis gifts would include token gifts at retirement or as part of a service reward program.

Gifts to Spouses

An unlimited marital deduction allows for unlimited tax-free transfers between spouses during life provided that both spouses are U.S. citizens. This is because the Internal Revenue Code considers a married couple to be a single economic unit. Note that to be eligible for this unlimited marital deduction, the donee spouse must be a citizen of the United States.

Quick Quiz 5.4

1. Qualified transfers are limited to the annual exclusion amount.
   a. True
   b. False

2. If a payment is made directly to an educational institution, the portion of the payment that applies to room and board is not excluded from gift tax.
   a. True
   b. False

3. Reimbursing an individual for medical expenses that he paid directly to the hospital is a qualified transfer.
   a. True
   b. False

4. To be eligible for the unlimited marital deduction, the donee spouse must be a citizen of the United States.
   a. True
   b. False

False, True, False, True.

Example 5.36
Travis gifts his wife $1,000,000. Travis' wife is a U.S. citizen. With the marital deduction, Travis will not owe any gift tax on the transfer to his wife.

Non-citizen spouses do not receive an unlimited marital deduction. However, a citizen spouse may transfer $157,000 annually (2020) to his or her non-citizen spouse with no transfer tax consequences. This annual exclusion is sometimes referred to as the "spousal super annual exclusion."

chapter 5

Charitable Gifts

There is an unlimited gift tax charitable deduction for transfers to the following organizations:
1. Federal, state, or local government for public use;
2. Section 501(c)(3) corporations operated exclusively for religious, charitable, scientific, literary, or education purposes;
3. Section 501(c) fraternal or veterans organizations.

Exhibit 5.7 | Transfers Exempt from Gift Tax

> Transfers to political organizations
> Qualified transfers directly to:
> - Medical institutions or doctors
> - Educational institutions (tuition only)
>
> Payments for support (legal obligations)
>
> Payments to divorced spouses pursuant to decree
>
> Transfers in a business setting
>
> Gifts to spouses
>
> Charitable gifts

THE GIFT TAX RETURN

Form 709

Any donor who makes a gift during a calendar year must file a gift tax return, unless all of the gifts are less than or equal to the annual exclusion, or are not subject to gift tax, such as qualified transfers, transfers to spouses, or transfers to charities. If a split gift election is made, a gift tax return must be filed by the spouse who makes the gift, or both spouses if both make a gift, even if after the split, the gift is under the annual exclusion. Individuals in a community-property state do not split gifts when using community funds as any gift of community property is a joint gift and therefore deemed to be one-half owned by each spouse. Thus, spouses making community property gifts would only file a gift tax return if the value of the total community property gift exceeds $30,000.

> **Key Concepts**
>
> 1. What is the due date of Form 709?
> 2. How can the IRS extend the statute of limitations for the Form 709?

The gift tax return (Form 709) must be filed by the donor by April 15 following the year of the gift. The filing date can be extended simply by extending the donor's income tax return, but similar to income tax, the time to pay is not extended and penalties will apply. In the event the donor dies in the year of the gift, the gift tax return must be filed no later than the due date, including extensions, of the estate tax return. The donor is primarily liable for the payment of gift tax, but if the donor does not or cannot pay the tax due, the IRS will seek to collect the tax from the donee.

Statute of Limitations

The **statute of limitations** for the IRS to assess any additional gift tax is three years, unless the gift is not adequately disclosed on a filed gift tax return. If the gift is not adequately disclosed, the statute of limitations will never expire. It is important to file a gift tax return where a valuation discount (e.g., a minority interest stock) may be subject to reasonable differences of opinion. When the gift tax return is filed, the statute of limitations will begin, whereas the failure to file (even when the proposed value is less than the annual exclusion) would subject the valuation to argument from the IRS without the protection of the statute of limitations.

> **Quick Quiz 5.5**
>
> 1. A donor must file a gift tax return within three and one-half months of making a taxable gift.
>   a. True
>   b. False
>
> *False.*

Calculation of the Gift Tax

The following steps are used to determine the gift tax liability for a particular donor:

1. Sum the total gifts for the calendar year.
2. Subtract the total exclusions and deductions (annual exclusions, marital deduction, charitable deductions).
3. Add the donor's taxable gifts for the calendar year (total gifts less exclusions and deductions) to the donor's previous taxable gifts for all prior calendar years.
4. Calculate the gift tax on the total gifts (current and prior year) based on the estate and gift tax rate schedule.
5. Calculate the gift tax on prior year gifts based on the estate and gift tax rate schedule.
6. Reduce the gift tax on total gifts by the gift tax on prior gifts.
7. Reduce the net gift tax by the remaining applicable credit. This amount equals the applicable credit for the current year (2020 amount is $4,577,800) less applicable credit against tax allowable for all prior periods. The applicable credit against tax allowable for all prior periods effectively equals the credit used in prior years. In the example below, the applicable credit against tax allowable for all prior periods equals $345,800 because that was the credit during 2005 and 2006, which is when the prior gifts were made.
8. The net of the gift tax less the remaining applicable credit is the amount of gift tax that must be paid in the current year.

There is no gift tax liability until the donor makes cumulative taxable gifts greater than $11,580,000. The following examples demonstrates the gift tax calculation.

Exhibit 5.8 | Gift Tax Calculation

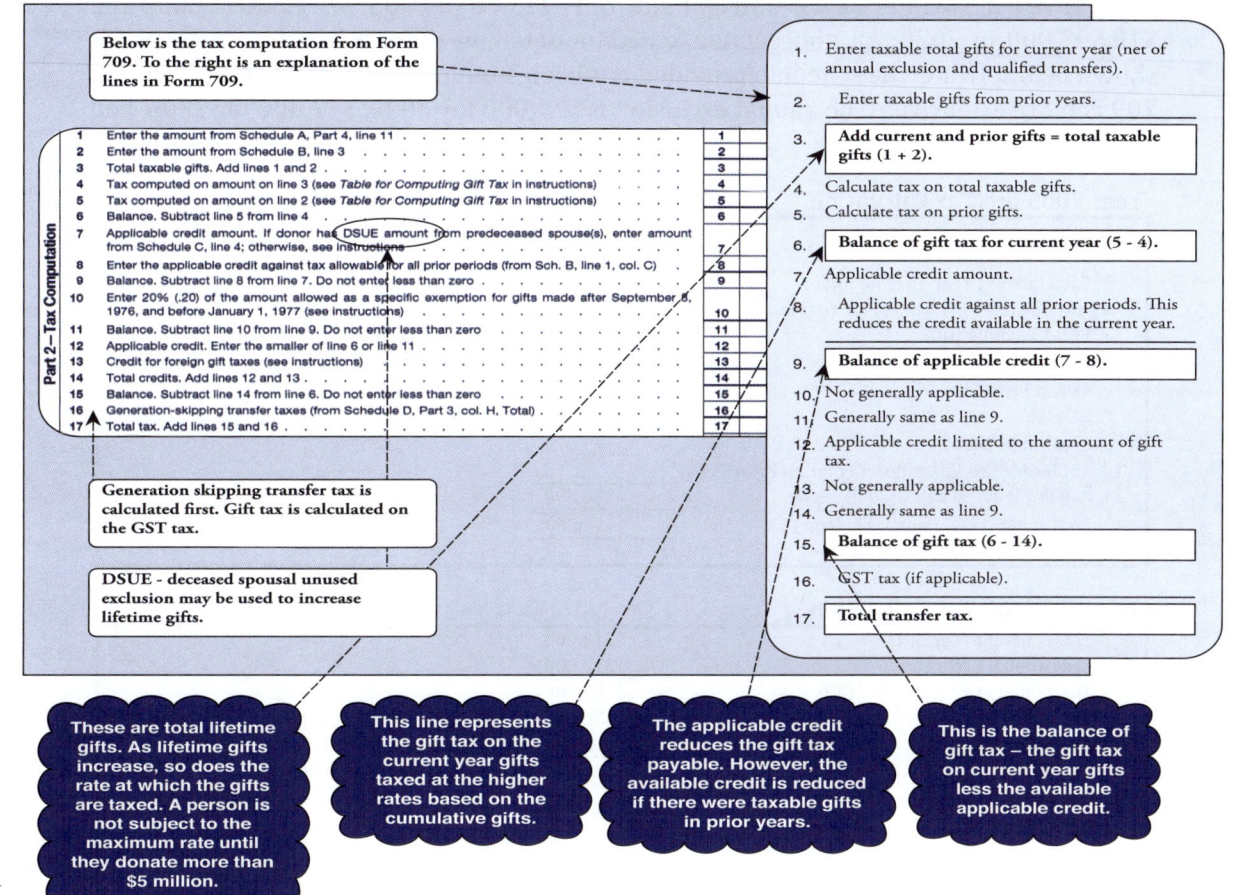

The Gift Tax Return

Example 5.37

Tracy gave his daughter Skylar outright gifts of $611,000 in 2005, $712,000 in 2006 and $10,595,000 in 2020. An abbreviated schedule detailing the gift tax due each year is shown below. (Note: the schedule provided has been simplified to ease illustration. Form 709 is more extensive.) The annual exclusion is $11,000 for 2005, $12,000 for 2006, and $15,000 for 2020.

Year 2005 Gift Tax Calculation

#	Item	Amount	Calculation
1	Total Current Year Gifts	$611,000	
2	Less Annual Exclusion	($11,000)	
3	Total Current Year Taxable Gifts	$600,000	
4	Plus Taxable Gifts from Prior Years	$0	
5	**Total Taxable Gifts**	**$600,000**	
6	Tax on Total Taxable Gifts	$192,800	($155,800 + (37% x 100,000))
7	Tax on Prior Gifts	$0	
8	Balance	$192,800	
9	Applicable Credit	$345,800	
10	Applicable Credit Against Tax for all Prior Periods	$0	
11	Balance (subtract 10 from 9)	$345,800	
12	Applicable Credit (smaller of 8 or 11)	$192,800	
13	**Total Gift Tax (8 minus 12)**	**$0**	

Year 2006 Gift Tax Calcuation[1]

#	Item	Amount	Calculation
1	Total Current Year Gifts	$712,000	
2	Less Annual Exclusion	($12,000)	
3	Total Current Year Taxable Gifts	$700,000	
4	Plus Taxable Gifts from Prior Years	$600,000	(from 2005)
5	**Total Taxable Gifts**	**$1,300,000**	
6	Tax on Total Taxable Gifts	$469,800	($448,300 + (43% x 50,000))
7	Tax on Prior Gifts	$192,800	($155,800 + (37% x ($600,000 - $500,000))
8	Balance	$277,000	
9	Applicable Credit	$345,800	
10	Applicable Credit Against Tax for all Prior Periods	$192,800	
11	Balance (subtract 10 from 9)	$153,000	
12	Applicable Credit (smaller of 8 or 11)	$153,000	
13	**Total Gift Tax (8 minus 12)**	**$124,000**	

Year 2020 Gift Tax Calcuation

#	Item	Amount	Calculation
1	Total Current Year Gifts	$10,595,000	
2	Less Annual Exclusion	($15,000)	
3	Total Current Year Taxable Gifts	$10,580,000	
4	Plus Taxable Gifts from Prior Years	$1,300,000	(from 2005 and 2006)
5	**Total Taxable Gifts**	**$11,880,000**	
6	Tax on Total Taxable Gifts	$4,697,800	($345,800 + 40% x ($11,880,000-$1,000,000))
7	Tax on Prior Gifts	$465,800	($345,800 + 40% x ($1,300,000-$1,000,000))
8	Balance	$4,232,000	
9	Applicable Credit	$4,577,800	
10	Applicable Credit Against Tax for all Prior Periods	$345,800	
11	Balance (subtract 10 from 9)	$4,232,000	
12	Applicable Credit (smaller of 8 or 11)	$4,232,000	
13	**Total Gift Tax (8 minus 12)**	**$0**	

Note: The $124,000 of gift tax paid in 2006 will be credited on the estate tax return (Form 706).

The 2005 taxable gift of $600,000 did not exceed the lifetime exemption amount ($1,000,000) and therefore, did not require Tracy to pay any gift tax. However, the 2006 taxable gift of $700,000, when combined with prior year gifts, exceeded the lifetime exemption by $300,000, which resulted in Tracy having to pay $124,000 in gift tax. During 2005 and 2006, the applicable credit equaled $345,800. The combined gifts during 2005 and 2006 depleted this amount.

For 2020, the exemption amount is $11,580,000 and the applicable credit is $4,577,800. This increase in the applicable credit amount allows Tracy to make significant additional lifetime gifts in 2020 without paying gift tax.

In the three examples, Tracy transfers a total of $11,880,000 in taxable gifts, which is the sum of the 2020 exclusion amount of $11,580,000 plus the $300,000 excess from the year 2006. He does not owe any tax in 2020 because the total consists of the exclusion amount and the amount that he paid gift tax on in prior periods.

Example 5.38

Assume instead that Tracy gave his daughter, Skylar, a total of $11,895,000 in 2020 and had not made any previous taxable gifts. Notice that the total taxable gifts is equal to the total taxable gifts over the three years given by Tracy in the previous example.[1] In this case, Tracy must pay gift tax of $120,000 on the additional $300,000 gifts above the exemption amount at the top rate of 40 percent. The other difference between the examples is that Tracy was only able to use one annual exclusion rather than three in the previous example.

Year 2020 Gift Tax Calculation (Same Taxable Gifts as Previous Example)

1 Total Current Year Gifts	$11,895,000	
2 Less Annual Exclusion	($15,000)	
3 Total Current Year Taxable Gifts	$11,880,000	
4 Plus Taxable Gifts from Prior Years	$0	
5 **Total Taxable Gifts**	**$11,880,000**	
6 Tax on Total Taxable Gifts	$4,697,800	($345,800 + 40% x ($11,880,000-$1,000,000))
7 Tax on Prior Gifts	$0	
8 Balance	$4,697,800	
9 Applicable Credit	$4,577,800	
10 Applicable Credit Against Tax for all Prior Periods	$0	
11 Balance (subtract 10 from 9)	$4,577,800	
12 Applicable Credit (smaller of 8 or 11)	$4,577,800	
13 **Total Gift Tax (8 minus 12)**	**$120,000**	

If Tracy gave the same amount of total gifts, $11,918,000, as he had given over the three years but instead gave them all within 2020, then he would have owed $9,200 more transfer tax because of his failure to use the annual exclusion for the previous two years ($23,000 x 0.40 = $9,200). Note, however, that the planner must consider the potential appreciation in the property to determine if making a gift in one installment (and foregoing some annual exclusions) makes sense. If the appreciation over the proposed transfer period exceeds the additional gift tax that is incurred by making the transfer in one year, it may make sense to incur the additional tax if the client is engaging in long-term planning.

---

1. Disregard the gifts subject to the annual exclusion in 2005 and 2006.

Example 5.39

Assume the same facts as in **Example 5.37** except that Tracy gave Skylar $11,145,000 in 2020 (instead of $10,595,000).

Year 2020 Gift Tax Calculation

1 Total Current Year Gifts	$11,145,000	
2 Less Annual Exclusion	($15,000)	
3 Total Current Year Taxable Gifts	$11,130,000	
4 Plus Taxable Gifts from Prior Years	$1,300,000	
5 **Total Taxable Gifts**	**$12,430,000**	
6 Tax on Total Taxable Gifts	$4,917,800	($345,800 + 40% x ($12,430,000-$1,000,000))
7 Tax on Prior Gifts	$465,800	($345,800 + 40% x ($1,300,000-$1,000,000))
8 Balance	$4,452,000	
9 Applicable Credit	$4,577,800	
10 Applicable Credit Against Tax for all Prior Periods	$345,800	
11 Balance (subtract 10 from 9)	$4,232,000	
12 Applicable Credit (smaller of 8 or 11)	$4,232,000	
13 **Total Gift Tax (8 minus 12)**	**$220,000**	

Note: The $124,000 of gift tax paid in 2006 will be credited on the estate tax return (Form 706).

In this example, Tracy transfers $11,130,000 in addition to the annual exclusion amount in 2020. The total taxable gifts are $12,430,000, which results in Tracy having to pay gift tax of $220,000. Consider the following summary:

Total Gifts	$12,430,000
Less Exemption Amount	($11,580,000)
Less Gifts Subject to Gift Tax in Prior Periods	($300,000)
Net Gifts	$550,000
Gift Tax at 40%	**$220,000**

Any additional taxable gifts Tracy makes will be taxed at the highest rate of 40 percent.

Exhibit 5.9 | Abbreviated Form 709

Form 709 — United States Gift (and Generation-Skipping Transfer) Tax Return
Department of the Treasury
Internal Revenue Service

▶ Go to *www.irs.gov/Form709* for instructions and the latest information.
(For gifts made during calendar year 2019)
▶ See instructions.

OMB No. 1545-0020

2019

Part 1 — General Information

1. Donor's first name and middle initial
2. Donor's last name
3. Donor's social security number
4. Address (number, street, and apartment number)
5. Legal residence (domicile)
6. City or town, state or province, country, and ZIP or foreign postal code
7. Citizenship (see instructions)

		Yes	No
8	If the donor died during the year, check here ▶ ☐ and enter date of death _____ , _____ .		
9	If you extended the time to file this Form 709, check here ▶ ☐		
10	Enter the total number of donees listed on Schedule A. Count each person only once ▶		
11a	Have you (the donor) previously filed a Form 709 (or 709-A) for any other year? If "No," skip line 11b		
b	Has your address changed since you last filed Form 709 (or 709-A)?		
12	**Gifts by husband or wife to third parties.** Do you consent to have the gifts (including generation-skipping transfers) made by you and by your spouse to third parties during the calendar year considered as made one-half by each of you? (See instructions.) (If the answer is "Yes," the following information must be furnished and your spouse must sign the consent shown below. **If the answer is "No," skip lines 13–18.**)		
13	Name of consenting spouse	14 SSN	
15	Were you married to one another during the entire calendar year? See instructions		
16	If line 15 is "No," check whether ☐ married ☐ divorced or ☐ widowed/deceased, and give date. See instructions ▶		
17	Will a gift tax return for this year be filed by your spouse? If "Yes," mail both returns in the same envelope		
18	**Consent of Spouse.** I consent to have the gifts (and generation-skipping transfers) made by me and by my spouse to third parties during the calendar year considered as made one-half by each of us. We are both aware of the joint and several liability for tax created by the execution of this consent.		

Consenting spouse's signature ▶ _____ Date ▶ _____

| 19 | Have you applied a DSUE amount received from a predeceased spouse to a gift or gifts reported on this or a previous Form 709? If "Yes," complete Schedule C | |

Part 2 — Tax Computation

1	Enter the amount from Schedule A, Part 4, line 11	1
2	Enter the amount from Schedule B, line 3	2
3	Total taxable gifts. Add lines 1 and 2	3
4	Tax computed on amount on line 3 (see *Table for Computing Gift Tax* in instructions)	4
5	Tax computed on amount on line 2 (see *Table for Computing Gift Tax* in instructions)	5
6	Balance. Subtract line 5 from line 4	6
7	Applicable credit amount. If donor has DSUE amount from predeceased spouse(s) or Restored Exclusion Amount, enter amount from Schedule C, line 5; otherwise, see instructions	7
8	Enter the applicable credit against tax allowable for all prior periods (from Sch. B, line 1, col. C)	8
9	Balance. Subtract line 8 from line 7. Do not enter less than zero	9
10	Enter 20% (0.20) of the amount allowed as a specific exemption for gifts made after September 8, 1976, and before January 1, 1977. See instructions	10
11	Balance. Subtract line 10 from line 9. Do not enter less than zero	11
12	Applicable credit. Enter the smaller of line 6 or line 11	12
13	Credit for foreign gift taxes (see instructions)	13
14	Total credits. Add lines 12 and 13	14
15	Balance. Subtract line 14 from line 6. Do not enter less than zero	15
16	Generation-skipping transfer taxes (from Schedule D, Part 3, col. G, total)	16
17	Total tax. Add lines 15 and 16	17
18	Gift and generation-skipping transfer taxes prepaid with extension of time to file	18
19	If line 18 is less than line 17, enter **balance due**. See instructions	19
20	If line 18 is greater than line 17, enter **amount to be refunded**	20

Sign Here

Under penalties of perjury, I declare that I have examined this return, including any accompanying schedules and statements, and to the best of my knowledge and belief, it is true, correct, and complete. Declaration of preparer (other than donor) is based on all information of which preparer has any knowledge.

May the IRS discuss this return with the preparer shown below? See instructions. ☐ Yes ☐ No

Signature of donor _____ Date _____

Paid Preparer Use Only

Print/Type preparer's name	Preparer's signature	Date	Check ☐ if self-employed	PTIN
Firm's name ▶			Firm's EIN ▶	
Firm's address ▶			Phone no.	

For Disclosure, Privacy Act, and Paperwork Reduction Act Notice, see the instructions for this form. Cat. No. 16783M Form **709** (2019)

Form 709 (2019)   Page **2**

SCHEDULE A   **Computation of Taxable Gifts** (Including transfers in trust) (see instructions)

A   Does the value of any item listed on Schedule A reflect any valuation discount? If "Yes," attach explanation . . . . . . Yes ☐   No ☐

B   ☐ ◄ Check here if you elect under section 529(c)(2)(B) to treat any transfers made this year to a qualified tuition program as made ratably over a 5-year period beginning this year. See instructions. Attach explanation.

Part 1—Gifts Subject Only to Gift Tax. Gifts less political organization, medical, and educational exclusions. See instructions.

A Item number	B • Donee's name and address • Relationship to donor (if any) • Description of gift • If the gift was of securities, give CUSIP no. • If closely held entity, give EIN	C	D Donor's adjusted basis of gift	E Date of gift	F Value at date of gift	G For split gifts, enter ½ of column F	H Net transfer (subtract col. G from col. F)
1							

Gifts made by spouse—*complete only if you are splitting gifts with your spouse and he/she also made gifts.*

Total of Part 1. Add amounts from Part 1, column H . . . . ▶

Part 2—Direct Skips. Gifts that are direct skips and are subject to both gift tax and generation-skipping transfer tax. You must list the gifts in chronological order.

A Item number	B • Donee's name and address • Relationship to donor (if any) • Description of gift • If the gift was of securities, give CUSIP no. • If closely held entity, give EIN	C 2632(b) election out	D Donor's adjusted basis of gift	E Date of gift	F Value at date of gift	G For split gifts, enter ½ of column F	H Net transfer (subtract col. G from col. F)
1							

Gifts made by spouse—*complete only if you are splitting gifts with your spouse and he/she also made gifts.*

Total of Part 2. Add amounts from Part 2, column H . . . . ▶

Part 3—Indirect Skips and Other Transfers in Trust. Gifts to trusts that are indirect skips as defined under section 2632(c) or to trusts that are currently subject to gift tax and may later be subject to generation-skipping transfer tax. You must list these gifts in chronological order.

A Item number	B • Donee's name and address • Relationship to donor (if any) • Description of gift • If the gift was of securities, give CUSIP no. • If closely held entity, give EIN	C 2632(c) election	D Donor's adjusted basis of gift	E Date of gift	F Value at date of gift	G For split gifts, enter ½ of column F	H Net transfer (subtract col. G from col. F)
1							

Gifts made by spouse—*complete only if you are splitting gifts with your spouse and he/she also made gifts.*

Total of Part 3. Add amounts from Part 3, column H . . . . ▶

(If more space is needed, attach additional statements.)   Form **709** (2019)

Form 709 (2019) Page **3**

Part 4—Taxable Gift Reconciliation

1	Total value of gifts of donor. Add totals from column H of Parts 1, 2, and 3	1
2	Total annual exclusions for gifts listed on line 1 (see instructions)	2
3	Total included amount of gifts. Subtract line 2 from line 1	3

Deductions (see instructions)

4	Gifts of interests to spouse for which a marital deduction will be claimed, based on item numbers _____ of Schedule A	4	
5	Exclusions attributable to gifts on line 4	5	
6	Marital deduction. Subtract line 5 from line 4	6	
7	Charitable deduction, based on item numbers _____ less exclusions	7	
8	Total deductions. Add lines 6 and 7		8
9	Subtract line 8 from line 3		9
10	Generation-skipping transfer taxes payable with this Form 709 (from Schedule D, Part 3, col. G, total) . . .		10
11	**Taxable gifts.** Add lines 9 and 10. Enter here and on page 1, Part 2—Tax Computation, line 1		11

Terminable Interest (QTIP) Marital Deduction. (See instructions for Schedule A, Part 4, line 4.)

If a trust (or other property) meets the requirements of qualified terminable interest property under section 2523(f), and:

    a. The trust (or other property) is listed on Schedule A; and

    b. The value of the trust (or other property) is entered in whole or in part as a deduction on Schedule A, Part 4, line 4, then the donor shall be deemed to have made an election to have such trust (or other property) treated as qualified terminable interest property under section 2523(f).

If less than the entire value of the trust (or other property) that the donor has included in Parts 1 and 3 of Schedule A is entered as a deduction on line 4, the donor shall be considered to have made an election only as to a fraction of the trust (or other property). The numerator of this fraction is equal to the amount of the trust (or other property) deducted on Schedule A, Part 4, line 6. The denominator is equal to the total value of the trust (or other property) listed in Parts 1 and 3 of Schedule A.

If you make the QTIP election, the terminable interest property involved will be included in your spouse's gross estate upon his or her death (section 2044). See instructions for line 4 of Schedule A. If your spouse disposes (by gift or otherwise) of all or part of the qualifying life income interest, he or she will be considered to have made a transfer of the entire property that is subject to the gift tax. See *Transfer of Certain Life Estates Received From Spouse* in the instructions.

12   **Election Out of QTIP Treatment of Annuities**

    ☐ ◀ Check here if you elect under section 2523(f)(6) **not** to treat as qualified terminable interest property any joint and survivor annuities that are reported on Schedule A and would otherwise be treated as qualified terminable interest property under section 2523(f). See instructions. Enter the item numbers from Schedule A for the annuities for which you are making this election ▶

SCHEDULE B	**Gifts From Prior Periods**

If you answered "Yes" on line 11a of page 1, Part 1, see the instructions for completing Schedule B. If you answered "No," skip to the Tax Computation on page 1 (or Schedule C or D, if applicable). Complete Schedule A before beginning Schedule B. See instructions for recalculation of the column C amounts. Attach calculations.

A Calendar year or calendar quarter (see instructions)	B Internal Revenue office where prior return was filed	C Amount of applicable credit (unified credit) against gift tax for periods after December 31, 1976	D Amount of specific exemption for prior periods ending before January 1, 1977	E Amount of taxable gifts

1	Totals for prior periods	1	
2	Amount, if any, by which total specific exemption, line 1, column D, is more than $30,000		2
3	Total amount of taxable gifts for prior periods. Add amount on line 1, column E, and amount, if any, on line 2. Enter here and on page 1, Part 2—Tax Computation, line 2		3

(If more space is needed, attach additional statements.)   Form **709** (2019)

INCOME TAX ISSUES RELATED TO GIFTS

Donee's Adjusted Basis of Gifted Property

When a donor makes a gift of property other than cash to a donee, the donee's basis in the property generally equals the donor's adjusted basis. The holding period of the donee will include the holding period of the donor for purposes of subsequent transfers and the determination of long or short-term capital gains.

> **Example 5.40**
> On April 13, 2020, Roman gifts a painting to Leroy with a fair market value of $35,000. Roman's adjusted basis in the painting was $4,000 and Roman had purchased the painting on January 1, 1987. Leroy's adjusted basis in the painting is $4,000 and his holding period began on January 1, 1987.

> **Example 5.41**
> Assume, in the above example, Leroy sold the painting on May 12, 2020 for $31,000. Because Leroy receives a carryover basis from Roman, his basis in the property would be $4,000 and his holding period would include Roman's holding period. As such, Leroy would have a long-term capital gain of $27,000 ($31,000 - $4,000).

Exceptions

Certain exceptions apply to the general basis rule stated above. The first exception occurs when the fair market value of the property at the date of the gift is less than the donor's adjusted basis. In this case, the donee will have one basis for gains and one basis for losses, sometimes referred to as the **double-basis (or bifurcated basis) rule**. The basis for losses is the fair market value as of the date of the gift (the lower value) and the basis for gains is the donor's adjusted basis (the higher value). If the donee subsequently sells the property for an amount between the two bases there is no gain or loss. Due to the application of the double-basis rule, if a donor gives away property that has a loss attached to it, he/she would have been better off selling the property, taking the capital loss against taxable income, and gifting the cash proceeds from the sale to the donee. When loss property is gifted, and is sold by the donee at a price less than the donor's basis, the difference between the donor's basis and the sale price will never be recovered in the form of a capital loss. When a donee must use the double-basis rule to determine his adjusted basis in gifted property, the holding period for the determination of long or short-term capital gains is determined as follows: (1) if the gain basis is used, the holding period of the donor is included with the holding period of the donee, but (2) if the loss basis is used, the holding period of the donee begins at the date of the gift. Stated simply, in a gift scenario, the holding period follows the basis used in disposition.

> **Key Concepts**
> 1. Generally, what is a donee's adjusted basis in property?
> 2. What are the exceptions to the general basis rules?

Example 5.42

TJ transfers stock to Angela with a fair market value at the date of the gift of $250,000. TJ's adjusted basis in the stock was $400,000 and he had held the stock for seven months. Because TJ has gifted Angela stock with a fair market value lower than his adjusted basis, Angela must follow the double-basis rule for the stock. If Angela subsequently sells the stock six months after the gift for $440,000, she will have a long-term capital gain of $40,000. If she were to subsequently sell the stock for $300,000, Angela would not recognize a gain or loss. If Angela were to subsequently sell the stock six months after the date of the gift for $200,000, she would recognize a short-term capital loss of $50,000.

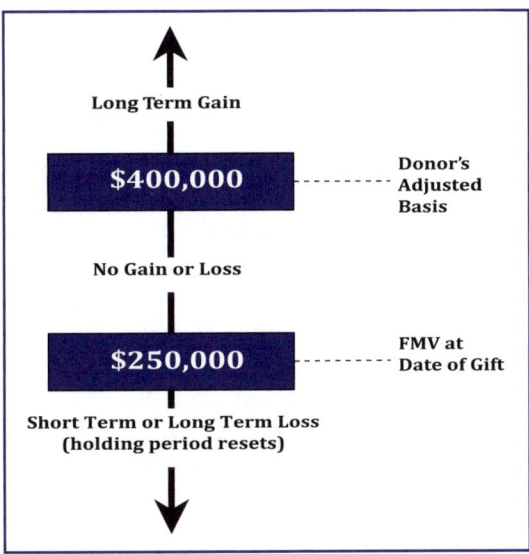

The second exception to the general basis rule occurs when the donor gives property with a fair market value in excess of his adjusted basis and the donor pays gift tax. (If gift tax has been paid, realize that the entire applicable gift tax credit of $4,577,800 has already been used, implying that the donor has made cumulative taxable gifts of at least $11,580,000 over his/her lifetime.) The gift tax associated with the appreciation is added to the donor's original adjusted basis to determine the donee's basis. The holding period for the donee in this case will always include the holding period of the donor.

$$\text{Donor's Adjusted Basis} + \left(\frac{\text{Appreciation}}{\text{FMV}} \times \text{Gift Tax Paid}\right) = \text{Donee's Adjusted Basis}$$

If the annual exclusion applied to the gift, the denominator for the gift tax paid adjustment is the fair market value less the annual exclusion used.

$$\text{Donor's Adjusted Basis} + \left(\frac{\text{Appreciation}}{\text{FMV} - \text{Annual Exclusion}} \times \text{Gift Tax Paid}\right) = \text{Donee's Adjusted Basis}$$

Example 5.43

Jimmy gave Lou 400 shares of ABC Corporation stock with a fair market value of $100,000 and Jimmy did not use his annual exclusion for this transfer. Jimmy's adjusted basis in the stock was $40,000, and he paid $5,000 of gift tax on the transfer. Lou's adjusted basis will be a carryover basis from Jimmy plus an allocation of the gift tax paid on the appreciation of the stock calculated as follows:

$$\left(\$40,000 + \left(\frac{\$60,000}{\$100,000} \times \$5,000\right) = \$43,000\right)$$

Example 5.44

On March 3, 2020, Mr. Hawk gifted rare art with a fair market value of $25,000 to his son, Derek. Mr. Hawk's adjusted basis in the rare art was $38,000 and he paid $5,000 of gift tax on the transfer. Derek's basis in the rare art is subject to the double-basis rule. If he sells the rare art for an amount greater than $38,000, Mr. Hawk's adjusted basis carries over to Derek and Derek's adjusted basis is $38,000. If he sells the rare art for an amount less than $25,000, the fair market value at the date of the transfer, Derek's adjusted basis is $25,000. Finally, if Derek sells the rare art at a price between $25,000 and $38,000, he will not have a gain or loss. In this case, when the fair market value is less than the donor's adjusted basis, gift tax paid is not allocated to the donee's adjusted basis since none of the gift tax paid was associated with appreciation in the value of the gift.

> **Quick Quiz 5.6**
>
> 1. If at the date of a gift, the fair market value of the gifted property is greater than the donor's adjusted basis in the gifted property, the donee's basis in the property received will be the fair market value at the date of the gift.
>   a. True
>   b. False
>
> 2. If at the date of a gift, the fair market value of the gifted property is less than the donor's adjusted basis in the gifted property, the donee will be subject to the double-basis rule.
>   a. True
>   b. False
>
> False, True.

Example 5.45

Prior to 2020, Santiago has made taxable gifts of $11,580,000. In 2020, Santiago gave a piece of real estate with a fair market value of $515,000 to Bella. He allocated his 2020 annual exclusion of $15,000 to the transfer. Santiago's adjusted basis was $225,000 and he paid gift tax of $200,000 at the time of the gift ($12,080,000 total taxable gifts = $4,777,800 - $4,577,800 credit = $200,000 gift tax paid).[1] Bella's adjusted basis in the real estate is:

$$\$225,000 + \left(\frac{\$515,000 - \$225,000}{\$515,000 - \$15,000} \times \$200,000\right) = \$341,000$$

---

1. All taxable gifts above the lifetime limit are taxed at 40% = > $500,000 x 40% = $200,000.

Exhibit 5.10 | Summary of Basis of a Gift

- The general rule applies when the fair market value (FMV) of the gift is greater than or equal to the donor's basis. The basis to a donee is the basis of the donor.
- The first exception to the general rule is when the fair market value of the gift is less than the donor's basis. The basis to a donee is the donor's basis for gains and the fair market value for losses.
- The second exception to the general rule is when the donor has paid gift tax on appreciation of the gifted asset. The donee's basis is the donor's basis plus an adjustment for the allocated portion of gift tax the donor paid associated with the appreciation of the asset that occurred while in the hands of the donor.

GIFT STRATEGIES

Achieving Client Goals with Direct Gifts

Recall that one of the estate planning objectives mentioned earlier in the text was the effective and efficient transfer of property. Nothing could be more effective or efficient than a direct gift during life from the client to a loved one. With a direct gift, the transferor can assure the completion of the gift, see the beneficial effect and joy the gift brings to the donee, and enjoy the pleasure of making the gift. Furthermore, a direct gift has low transaction costs, (usually only a fee to change the title to the asset, such as a state fee charged to re-title a car to the name of the donee). Unfortunately, whenever a donor makes a direct gift, the client loses control of the gifted asset, and any future income and/or appreciation derived from the gifted asset, because the asset becomes the property of the donee at the date of the gift. Also, there is some risk that the donee may not act or use the gift in the manner intended by the transferor. The donor can do little, if anything, to change any outcome after the gift has been completed. Even with these noted disadvantages, lifetime direct gifts remain a cornerstone of estate planning.

> **Key Concepts**
>
> 1. Which types of property are most likely to experience significant appreciation?
> 2. What are the characteristics of the ideal property to gift to charity?

Gifts of Appreciating Property

If the overall objective of the client is federal gross estate reduction, the client should gift property that has the greatest potential for future appreciation, rather than transferring cash or fully-appreciated property. A gift of property is valued for gift tax purposes at the fair market value as of the date of the gift. Therefore, any future appreciation on the transferred property will belong to the transferee (donee) and, thus, is excluded from the transferor's federal gross estate. Property, which commonly experiences substantial future appreciation includes but is not limited to:

1. business interests
2. real estate
3. art or other collections
4. investment securities (stocks and bonds)
5. other intangible rights (patents, copyrights, royalties)

Thus, the selection of property for gifting requires careful financial and estate planning consideration. Usually, if the donor's objective is restricting or decreasing the growth of the federal gross estate, cash is not necessarily the most appropriate gift.

Gifts to Spouses

Gifts to citizen spouses are not subject to gift tax and may be in any amount. Frequently, large gifts are made to a spouse so that the spouse will have an amount equal to the applicable exemption amount for estates ($11,580,000 for 2020). While TRA 2010 introduced portability of a deceased spouse's unused exemption, this provision was to sunset on December 31, 2012 however it was made permanent by ATRA 2013. In many planning situations, equalization of the estates of spouses (covered in more detail later) still makes sense. Spousal gifts can be made outright or in a qualified trust. If the wealthier spouse simply wants to use the lifetime exemption of the non-wealthy spouse he or she can make use of the split gift election to gift assets to a junior generation and thus use the spouse's credit equivalency. Recall that gifts to non-citizen spouses are limited to an annual exclusion amount of $157,000 (2020) and there is no unlimited marital deduction for transfers at death unless certain requirements (discussed in the marital deduction chapter) are met.

Gifts to Minors

Gifts to minors, excepting small amounts, are usually made either in trust or through a custodian type account. The Uniform Gifts to Minors Act (UGMA) provides that gifted property is transferred to a named custodian under the state UGMA. Permissible gifts include cash, securities, life insurance, and annuities. The custodian is permitted to spend money on behalf of the minor and serves without posting a bond and normally without the need to file accountings with the probate court. The Uniform Transfers to Minors Act (UTMA) was designed to replace UGMA. The UTMA expands the kind of property that can be transferred to minors to almost any type of asset including real estate and partnership interests. UGMAs and UTMAs are less expensive than establishing trusts and transfers to either are considered gifts of a present interest. The only caution is that UGMAs and UTMAs cannot be used to provide what would otherwise be legal support. There could also be estate tax consequences for the donor if the donor serves as guardian of the UGMA/UTMA account (discussed in more detail in Chapter 6). Gifts in trust to minors under 2503(b) and 2503(c) of the Internal Revenue Code will be covered in Chapter 8.

Single Party Gift Strategies

One of the most common donor objectives in establishing a gifting program is to reduce the overall gross estate of the donor. To achieve this goal, it is generally never wise to gift cash. Rather, the donor should prepare a current balance sheet with a forecast of which property is likely to experience the greatest appreciation. Once this is determined, the donor should select from those assets that are expected to appreciate the most. This strategy will remove highly appreciating assets from the donor's gross estate and future appreciation will occur in the hands of the donee. Unless the donor is very close to death, this strategy will be superior to receiving a step-up in basis for transfers at death (since the highest marginal gift and estate tax rates are 40 percent and the long-term capital gain rate for income tax purposes, including the Affordable Care Act surtaxes, can be as high as 23.8 percent).

Example 5.46

If the objective is to reduce the gross estate, which of the following assets would be the most appropriate to transfer?

	Assets	FMV	Adjusted Basis	Expected Appreciation
Public Stock	A	$100,000	$20,000	5%
Cash	B	$100,000	$100,000	3%
Public Stock	C	$100,000	$50,000	12%
Public Stock	D	$100,000	$75,000	11%
Public Stock	E	$100,000	$125,000	3%
Closely-Held Company Stock	F	$100,000	$0	15%

The intent is to determine the best asset to transfer considering current earnings, potential gains and losses, and future appreciation. The most appropriate assets to transfer (in order) are closely held company Stock F, then Stock C, and then Stock D (because assets that are expected to appreciate the most should be transferred first). One should not transfer Stock E by sale to a related party or gift the asset because the income tax loss would be disallowed. Stock E should be sold so the donor may recognize the capital loss (only the donor can recognize the economic value of the loss).

Multiparty Gift Strategies

If one of the purposes of gifting is to minimize future income and transfer taxes for the donor, and if there are multiple donees, it is wise to consider which assets to give to which donee. Here is a general set of guidelines:

1. Rarely gift property when the fair market value is less than the adjusted basis. Rather, sell the property and let the donor recognize a capital loss for income tax. The donor can then gift the cash proceeds to the donee who can then purchase the property with the proceeds. In cases where there is a temporary decline in value and the donee will hold the property at least until the value of the property appreciates to the donor's basis, it may be appropriate to gift property where the fair market value is lower than the basis.
2. Consider gifting property with the greatest appreciation potential to the youngest donee available who has the most time for the asset to appreciate.
3. When making gifts to charities, always gift appreciated property to avoid the capital gain taxes on the difference between the fair market value and the donor's adjustable taxable basis. For such property, the donor may able to deduct the fair market value as a charitable deduction, subject to the income tax limitations.
4. Gift income-producing property to the donee in the lowest marginal income tax bracket so that the income is subject to the lowest possible income tax.

> **Quick Quiz 5.7**
>
> 1. If the overall objective of a client is federal gross estate reduction, the client should make cash gifts.
>   a. True
>   b. False
>
> False.

Example 5.47

Assume that Arthur wants to make equal dollar value gifts to four parties: his mother, his son, his favorite charity, and a lifelong friend who is about the same age as Arthur. In determining what assets he should give to these various donees, Arthur should consider income tax issues, income needs of the recipient, and the actual and potential appreciation of the property. Specifically, Arthur should consider his basis in each piece of property, the potential for a charitable income tax deduction, the potential for avoidance of capital gains tax on appreciated property, and future income tax.

Donor	Arthur, age 65
Donee 1	Mother, age 85, (Low Marginal Rate Taxpayer)
Donee 2	Son, age 40
Donee 3	Charity
Donee 4	Lifelong friend, age 60

Assume Arthur has the following assets:

Assets	FMV	Adjusted Basis	Yield	Future Appreciation
Stock A	$35,000	$5,000	1%	3%
Stock B	$35,000	$26,000	0	11%
Stock C	$35,000	$35,000	2%	5%
Bond D	$35,000	$35,000	6%	+/- 1%
Bond E	$35,000	$50,000	4%	0

Who should receive which asset?

Asset with Loss	Highly Appreciated Assets	Highly Appreciated Assets	Highest Income Property	Other
Bond E	Stock A	Stock B	Bond D	Stock C
Arthur should retain or sell for capital loss	To charity to avoid capital gain and receive charitable income tax deduction	To youngest, non-charitable party to receive greatest compounding	To oldest party, Mom	By default to similar age friend

Summary Solution:
- Arthur should keep the loss property, Bond E. He should sell it and recognize the capital loss.
- Gift the most appreciated property to the charity to get the charitable contribution deduction.
- Gift the property with the highest potential for appreciation to the son who is the youngest donee.
- Gift income producing property to Mom who is in the lowest marginal income tax bracket.
- By default, Arthur's friend should get Stock C.

Exhibit 5.11 | Basic Strategies for Transferring Wealth Through Gifts

Generally, if the objective of the transferor is to reduce the size of the transferor's gross estate, the transferor can use the following lifetime gifting techniques to achieve a lower gross estate at death:

1. Make optimal use of qualified educational transfers (pay tuition for children and grandchildren from private school through professional education).
2. Pay medical costs for children, grandchildren, and heirs directly to provider institutions.
3. Make optimal use of the $15,000 annual gift exclusion ($30,000 if the gift is made jointly with the spouse). Example: Barry is married to Joan and has 3 adult children who all have stable marriages and there are 7 grandchildren. Barry and Joan can gift $390,000 per year without coming into the gift tax system. ($30,000 x 13 transferees, including 3 children, 3 spouses, 7 grandchildren)
4. A spouse may make unlimited lifetime gifts to their spouse who is a U.S. citizen.
5. Steps 1 - 3 above are completely exhausted, the transferor can begin using his/her lifetime applicable gift tax credit equivalency amount ($11,580,000 for year 2020) while still paying no gift tax until the summation of lifetime taxable gifts exceeds the applicable exclusion amount.
6. Any gift tax paid on gifts prior to three years of death will also reduce the estate of the transferor. This is discussed below.

Exhibit 5.12 | Multi-Party Gift Strategies

ADVANTAGES OF LIFETIME GIFTS VS. BEQUESTS

While at first glance it may appear that transfers during life or at death are subject to the same transfer taxes because the gift and estate tax system use the same tax rate schedules, there is a big difference between lifetime and testamentary gifts. Lifetime gifts have significant advantages from a transfer tax point of view compared to testamentary, or at death, transfers (bequests).

First, any appreciation on a gifted asset occurring after the date of the gift is excluded from the donor's gross estate. Second, any gift tax paid on a taxable gift is excluded from the donor's gross estate if the gift was made more than three years prior to the donor's death. Third, the cash used to pay the estate tax is included in the decedent's federal gross estate. Fourth, gifts during life, unlike bequests at death, qualify for the annual exclusion which transfers $15,000 (2020) free of transfer taxes. Fifth, any gift of income producing property transfers the income from the donor to the donee after the date of the gift and reduces the donor's gross estate. Finally, payments of support obligations and the expenses that would be considered qualified transfers during life are excluded from the calculation of gift tax. The estate tax calculation includes the transfers for future support and future qualified transfers. The following chart provides a summary of the advantages listed above.

> **Key Concepts**
> 1. List the advantages of making lifetime gifts.

> **Quick Quiz 5.8**
> 1. The donor of income producing property will include the post-gift income on his income tax return.
>   a. True
>   b. False
>
> *False.*

Exhibit 5.13 | Advantages of Lifetime Gifts vs. Bequests to Transferor

Transfers	Gifts and Lifetime Transfers effect on Gross Estate	Bequests at Death effect on Gross Estate
Support payments	Excluded from gross estate	Not Applicable
Qualified transfers	Excluded from gross estate	Not Applicable
Annual exclusion	Applicable	Not Applicable
Future appreciation on assets transferred	Excluded from gross estate	Included in gross estate
Future income on transferred assets	Excluded from gross estate	Not Applicable
Transfer tax paid for gifts made more than three years before death	Excluded from gross estate	Not in gross estate
Cash used to pay estate taxes	N/A	Included in gross estate

KEY TERMS

American Taxpayer Relief Act (ATRA 2012) - Tax act signed by President Barack Obama in January of 2013. The act reunified the estate and gift tax and set the transfer tax exemption at $5,000,000 (indexed for inflation) and a 40 percent marginal transfer tax rate.

Annual Exclusion - An exclusion from gift taxes for present interest transfers less than or equal to $15,000 per year per donee.

Consideration - Payment or transfer of property in return for other property.

Crummey Provision - The right of a trust beneficiary to withdraw some or all of any contribution to a trust for a limited period of time after the contribution. A Crummey provision converts what otherwise would have been a gift of a future interest (not eligible for the annual exclusion) to a gift of a present interest, eligible for the annual exclusion.

Direct Gift - A direct payment of cash or transfer of property to a donee.

Donee - The person who receives the gift.

Donor - The person who gives the gift.

Double-Basis (or Bifurcated Basis) Rule - When the fair market value of the property at the date of the gift is less than the donor's adjusted basis. In this case, the donee will have one basis for gains and one basis for losses.

Economic Growth and Tax Relief Reconciliation Act of 2001 (EGTRRA 2001) - Tax act signed by President George W. Bush in June of 2001. The act phased in a repeal of the estate and generation-skipping transfer tax. It also created separate applicable credits for gift tax and estate tax until 2011.

Five-and-Five Lapse Rule – The lapse of a general power of appointment, like the release of such a power, results in a transfer for gift tax purposes. This rule applies only to the extent the value of the property subject to the lapsed powers exceeds the greater of $5,000 or 5 percent of the aggregate value of the assets out of which the powers could have been satisfied.

529 Plan - A tax-advantaged savings plan designed to encourage saving for future college costs.

Future Interest - An interest which is limited in some way by a future date or time. A gift of a future interest does not qualify for the annual exclusion.

Gift - A voluntary transfer, without full consideration, of property from one person (a donor) to another person (a donee) or entity.

Incomplete Transfer - Any transfers that include a revocable beneficiary designation or a transfer to a revocable trust. Incomplete transfers are not considered gifts for gift tax purposes.

Indirect Gift - A payment, or transfer, to a third party on behalf of a donor for the benefit of the donee.

Net Gift - A gift that requires the donee to pay the gift tax. The gift tax is based on the value of the transfer less the gift tax.

Present Interest - An unrestricted right to the immediate use of property. A present interest gift qualifies for the annual exclusion.

Qualified Transfers - A payment made directly to a qualified educational institution for tuition, excluding room and board, or a payment made directly to a medical institution for the qualified medical expenses of someone else. Qualified transfers are excluded from gift tax.

Reversionary Interest - Interests that have been transferred and subsequently revert back to the transferor. Also includes a possibility that the property transferred by the decedent may return to him or his estate and a possibility that property transferred by the decedent may become subject to a power of disposition by him.

Split Gift Election - An election available to a donor of separate property which allows him to utilize his spouse's annual exclusion and transfer up $30,000 per year per donee without incurring gift tax.

Statute of Limitations - The period of time allowed for the IRS to assess any additional gift tax, generally three years, unless the gift is not adequately disclosed on a filed gift tax return. If the gift is not adequately disclosed, the statute of limitations will never expire.

Tax Cuts and Jobs Act of 2017 (TCJA) - Tax act signed in December 2017 by President Donald Trump that increased the transfer tax exemption to $11,580,000 for 2020 (and increased that exemption for inflation after 2018).

Tax Relief, Unemployment Insurance Authorization, & Job Creation Act of 2010 (TRA 2010) - Tax act signed December 2010 that extended various income and estate tax provisions of EGTRRA and introduced exemption portability. The provisions of TRA 2010 were made permanent by ATRA.

Taxable Gift - A gift in excess of the annual exclusion. Does not create a tax liability until the lifetime exemption for taxable gifts is exhausted. A taxable gift does not include any qualified transfers.

DISCUSSION QUESTIONS

SOLUTIONS to the discussion questions can be found exclusively within the chapter. Once you have completed an initial reading of the chapter, go back and highlight the answers to these questions.

1. Explain the gift and estate tax reforms created by ATRA 2012 and TCJA 2017.

2. List the elements of a gift.

3. List and define the various types of gifts.

4. List the imputed interest rules for no-interest loans and below-market loans.

5. How is the creation of a joint bank account where one party contributes the entire amount treated for gift tax purposes?

6. Discuss the requirements and limitations of the annual exclusion.

7. Explain the advantage of using the election to split gifts.

8. Explain the use of the Crummey provision.

9. Qualified transfers allow certain indirect gifts to be excluded from gift taxation. Explain these gifts and the requirements to exclude them from gift taxation.

10. How are gifts to spouses treated for gift tax purposes?

11. What is the due date to file Form 709, the United States Gift (and Generation-Skipping Transfer) Tax Return?

12. Who must file Form 709, the United States Gift (and Generation-Skipping Transfer) Tax Return?

13. List the steps in calculating the gift tax.

14. A donee's adjusted basis of gifted property is generally the donor's basis. List the two circumstances when this is not true.

15. List three advantages of making lifetime gifts as compared to transfers at death.

chapter 5

MULTIPLE-CHOICE PROBLEMS

A sample of multiple choice problems is provided below. Additional multiple choice problems are available at money-education.com by accessing the Student Practice Portal.

1. Grandmother Jones contributed $2,500,000 to a revocable trust. She has a life expectancy of 24 years and she will receive an 8% per year annuity from the trust. At her death, the corpus will be paid to her granddaughter, Lisa. What is Grandmother Jones's taxable gift?
    a. $0.
    b. $2,094,752.
    c. $2,485,000.
    d. $2,500,000.

2. In the current year, Jerry loaned his daughter, Charisse, $15,000 to purchase a new car. The loan was payable on demand, but there was no stated interest rate. The applicable federal rate for the current year was 10%, and Charisse had $900 of net investment income for the year. For gift tax purposes with regards to this loan, how much has Jerry gifted Charisse during the current year?
    a. $0.
    b. $900.
    c. $1,500.
    d. $15,000.

3. Mary and Emile would like to give the maximum possible gift that they can to their son without having to pay gift tax. Mary and Emile have never filed a gift tax return and live in a community-property state. How much can they transfer in 2020 to their son free of gift tax?
    a. $30,000.
    b. $4,577,800.
    c. $11,580,000.
    d. $23,190,000.

4. During the year, Sean made the following gifts to his daughter:
    1. An interest-free loan of $6,000 to purchase an SUV. The applicable federal rate was 6%. The loan has been outstanding for two years.
    2. A corporate bond with an adjusted basis of $15,000 and a fair market value of $16,000.
    3. A portfolio of stock with an adjusted basis of $10,000 and a fair market value of $25,000.

    Sean's wife agrees to elect gift-splitting for the year, but she did not make any gifts of her own. What is the amount of total taxable gifts made by Sean during the year?
    a. $5,500.
    b. $7,500.
    c. $7,680.
    d. $20,680.

5. Donna and Daniel have lived in Louisiana their entire marriage. Currently, their combined net worth is $4,000,000 and all of their assets are community property. After meeting with their financial advisor, Donna and Daniel begin a plan of lifetime gifting to reduce their gross estates. During 2020, they made the following cash gifts:

Son $80,000
Daughter $160,000
Republican National Committee $75,000
Granddaughter $15,000

What is the amount of the taxable gifts to be reported by Donna?

   a. $35,500.
   b. $90,000.
   c. $127,500.
   d. $255,000.

QUICK QUIZ EXPLANATIONS

Quick Quiz 5.1
1. True.
2. True.
3. False. The donor of a gift is primarily liable for any gift tax due.
4. True.

Quick Quiz 5.2
1. True.
2. True.
3. False. Community property is deemed to be owned equally by both spouses. Since a total of $15,000 was gifted, each spouse is deemed to make a gift of $7,500, which is below the annual exclusion.
4. True.
5. True.

Quick Quiz 5.3
1. False. Gifts of remainder interests in trusts are gifts of future interests, and therefore, do not qualify for the annual exclusion. A gift of a mandatory income interest in a trust is a present interest gift, and would qualify for the annual exclusion.
2. True.

Quick Quiz 5.4
1. False. Qualified transfers are available in addition to the annual exclusion, and there is no limit on the amount of the transfer.
2. True.
3. False. Qualified transfers must be made directly to the provider of the services, reimbursement of expenses will not qualify.
4. True.

Quick Quiz 5.5
1. False. The donor must file a gift tax return by April 15th of the year following the gift.

Quick Quiz 5.6
1. False. This statement is not always true. In some cases, when gift tax has been paid by the donor, the donee's basis will equal the donor's basis plus the portion of the gift tax paid attributable to appreciation in the property.
2. True.

Quick Quiz 5.7
1. False. When the overall objective is a reduction in the gross estate, gifts of appreciating property, as opposed to cash, would be more appropriate.

Quick Quiz 5.8
1. False. Once a completed gift is made, income generated by the property that was the subject of the gift will be reported by the donee, not the donor.

6
ESTATE TAX

LEARNING OBJECTIVES

1. Identify each line of the abbreviated estate tax formula.
2. Define the gross estate.
3. Clarify what happens to gifts made within three years of death.
4. Clarify what happens to retained and reversionary interests.
5. Clarify what happens to revocable interests.
6. Clarify what happens to the proceeds of life insurance where there is incidence of ownership.
7. Determine the valuation of assets at death and the associated valuation method.
8. Identify discounts such as minority discounts, marketability discount, blockage discount, and key person discount.
9. Calculate the value of an equity security for a decedent.
10. Describe the alternate valuation date and its requirements.
11. Identify the exceptions to the alternate valuation date.
12. Identify the deductions to the gross estate in determining the adjusted gross estate.
13. Describe the unlimited marital and charitable deductions.
14. Calculate the estate tax liability.
15. Describe exemption portability.
16. Describe the filing requirements for Form 706 and its associated penalties.
17. Calculate the adjusted basis to heirs and legatees of property acquired from a decedent.

CFP Board Resource Document - Student-Centered Learning Objectives based upon CFP Board Principal Topics.

This chapter provides an overview of the Federal Estate Tax System with specific focus on the formula used to calculate the estate tax. The chapter begins by looking at how property is included in a decedent's gross estate, followed by the various deductions available in planning to reduce the gross estate. Many of these deductions will be explored in detail in later chapters, including deductions to determine the adjusted gross estate (covered in Chapter 12 – Special Elections & Post Mortem Planning), the charitable deduction (covered in Chapter 9) and the marital deduction (covered in Chapter 10). Having a basic understanding of how the estate tax system works is necessary before looking at the planning details of these deductions so that planners – and clients – don't get lost in the details and lose sight of the big picture – crafting a plan to meet the client's goals and objectives. This chapter also reviews some of the income tax rules that you have seen in prior courses that have an impact on the estate planning process.

chapter 6

INTRODUCTION

When a citizen or resident of the United States dies, an estate tax is imposed on the decedent's transfer of property to his heirs. The gift tax system imposes a transfer tax on transfers during life. The generation-skipping transfer tax system (discussed in Chapter 13) taxes transfers made during life, or at death, to skip persons, who are generally two or more generations below the decedent.

The estate tax applies to all transfers at death of property owned by the decedent and property over which the decedent had a sufficient interest to require inclusion in the gross estate.

The Federal transfer tax system is designed to tax all transfers of wealth, during lifetime or at death, using a common progressive rate structure. As a consequence, the estate tax is coordinated with the gift tax by including taxable gifts (at the fair market value on the date of the gift) in the estate tax calculation.

All property owned directly or indirectly by the decedent, in whole or in part, at the time of death is included in the decedent's estate at the fair market value as of the date of death (or the alternative valuation date, if elected). Several questions arise when considering what property should be included in a decedent's estate, including:
1. whether the decedent had a sufficient ownership interest to require inclusion; and
2. whether or not property can be transferred at the decedent's death.

In some cases, the decedent's rights to the property may be limited, and will therefore not require inclusion in the estate (for example, property transferred in trust to the decedent that imposes specific limitations on the beneficiary's right to access the property, and property interests that expire at the death of the decedent, such as a single life annuity on the decedent's life, may be excluded from the estate, as well). In other cases, property that is not titled in the decedent's name may be included in the decedent's estate, such as property owned by others over which the decedent held a general power of appointment.

The federal estate tax is applied to the estate tax base, and the decedent's estate is liable for the payment of estate taxes. The manner in which property is transferred (e.g., by probate, intestacy, joint titling, trust, contract, TOD, POD) is generally irrelevant to the calculation of estate tax provided that the decedent's property is being transferred at death.

The estate tax applies to both citizens and residents of the United States and to nonresidents of the United States. For U.S. citizens and residents, estate tax is imposed on worldwide assets. Non-U.S. citizens and non-U.S. residents only pay estate tax on assets located within the United States.

It is particularly important when studying the estate tax to understand the differences between gross estate, taxable estate, and tentative tax base. Exhibit 6.1 is the first page of the estate tax return, Form 706, which should help to gain a perspective of each of these terms. Much of this chapter deals with the gross estate. However, most of what is on the first page of Form 706 is also discussed in this chapter.

Exhibit 6.1 | Form 706

Form 706 (Rev. August 2019)
Department of the Treasury
Internal Revenue Service

United States Estate (and Generation-Skipping Transfer) Tax Return

▶ Estate of a citizen or resident of the United States (see instructions). To be filed for decedents dying after December 31, 2018.
▶ Go to www.irs.gov/Form706 for instructions and the latest information.

OMB No. 1545-0015

Part 1—Decedent and Executor

1a Decedent's first name and middle initial (and maiden name, if any)	1b Decedent's last name
	2 Decedent's social security no.
3a City, town, or post office; county; state or province; country; and ZIP or foreign postal code	3b Year domicile established
	4 Date of birth
	5 Date of death
6a Name of executor (see instructions)	6b Executor's address (number and street including apartment or suite no.; city, town, or post office; state or province; country; and ZIP or foreign postal code) and phone no.
6c Executor's social security number (see instructions)	
	Phone no.

6d If there are multiple executors, check here ☐ and attach a list showing the names, addresses, telephone numbers, and SSNs of the additional executors.

7a Name and location of court where will was probated or estate administered | 7b Case number

8 If decedent died testate, check here ▶ ☐ and attach a certified copy of the will. 9 If you extended the time to file this Form 706, check here ▶ ☐

10 If Schedule R-1 is attached, check here ▶ ☐ 11 If you are estimating the value of assets included in the gross estate on line 1 pursuant to the special rule of Reg. section 20.2010-2(a)(7)(ii), check here ▶ ☐

Part 2—Tax Computation

1	Total gross estate less exclusion (from Part 5—Recapitulation, item 13)	1
2	Tentative total allowable deductions (from Part 5—Recapitulation, item 24)	2
3a	Tentative taxable estate (subtract line 2 from line 1)	3a
b	State death tax deduction	3b
c	Taxable estate (subtract line 3b from line 3a)	3c
4	Adjusted taxable gifts (see instructions)	4
5	Add lines 3c and 4	5
6	Tentative tax on the amount on line 5 from Table A in the instructions	6
7	Total gift tax paid or payable (see instructions)	7
8	Gross estate tax (subtract line 7 from line 6)	8
9a	Basic exclusion amount 9a	
b	Deceased spousal unused exclusion (DSUE) amount from predeceased spouse(s), if any (from Section D, Part 6—Portability of Deceased Spousal Unused Exclusion) 9b	
c	Restored exclusion amount (see instructions) . . . 9c	
d	Applicable exclusion amount (add lines 9a, 9b, and 9c) 9d	
e	Applicable credit amount (tentative tax on the amount in line 9d from Table A in the instructions) 9e	
10	Adjustment to applicable credit amount (May not exceed $6,000. See instructions.) 10	
11	Allowable applicable credit amount (subtract line 10 from line 9e)	11
12	Subtract line 11 from line 8 (but do not enter less than zero)	12
13	Credit for foreign death taxes (from Schedule P). (Attach Form(s) 706-CE.) 13	
14	Credit for tax on prior transfers (from Schedule Q) . . 14	
15	Total credits (add lines 13 and 14)	15
16	Net estate tax (subtract line 15 from line 12)	16
17	Generation-skipping transfer (GST) taxes payable (from Schedule R, Part 2, line 10)	17
18	Total transfer taxes (add lines 16 and 17)	18
19	Prior payments (explain in an attached statement)	19
20	Balance due (or overpayment) (subtract line 19 from line 18)	20

Under penalties of perjury, I declare that I have examined this return, including accompanying schedules and statements, and to the best of my knowledge and belief, it is true, correct, and complete. Declaration of preparer (other than the executor) is based on all information of which preparer has any knowledge.

Sign Here
Signature of executor   Date
Signature of executor   Date

Paid Preparer Use Only

Print/Type preparer's name	Preparer's signature	Date	Check ☐ if self-employed	PTIN
Firm's name ▶			Firm's EIN ▶	
Firm's address ▶			Phone no.	

For Privacy Act and Paperwork Reduction Act Notice, see instructions.   Cat. No. 20548R   Form **706** (Rev. 8-2019)

chapter 6

THE GROSS ESTATE

The starting point for determining the estate tax due is to calculate the value of a decedent's gross estate. The decedent's **gross estate** is defined as the fair market value of all interests owned by the decedent at the time of death. A decedent's gross estate may also include certain property interests the decedent transferred during his lifetime as well as the decedent's interest in any jointly held property and, in some cases, the proceeds of life insurance on the decedent's life.

> **Key Concepts**
>
> 1. Identify the types of property that are included in the gross estate.
> 2. Describe the applicable code sections related to the gross estate and the inclusion rules associated with these sections.

An estate planner must have a clear understanding of the current and projected value of the client's gross estate in order to develop a meaningful estate plan. The value and types of interests included in the gross estate will directly determine which planning techniques should be considered for use with the client.

Exhibit 6.2 | The Abbreviated Estate Tax Formula - Gross Estate

Total Gross Estate Less Exclusions		$ _____	Gross Estate
Less: Tentative Total Allowable Deductions		$ _____	
Equals: Tentative Taxable Estate	$ _____		
Less: State Death Tax Deduction	$ _____		
Equals: Taxable Estate (subtract 3b from 3a)		$ _____	
Plus: Adjusted Taxable Gifts		$ _____	
Equals: Tentative Tax Base		$ _____	
Equals: Tentative Tax on the Amount from Table A in the Instructions		$ _____	
Less: Total Gift Tax Paid or Payable		$ _____	
Gross Estate Tax		$ _____	

Property interests included in a decedent's gross estate are defined in Sections 2033-2044 of the Internal Revenue Code. Each of these code sections are discussed below to explain the full scope and the many nuances of asset inclusion in the decedent's gross estate.

Furthermore, additional rules may be applicable to transactions before 1947, thus subsequent research is needed for client transactions before this date. **Exhibit 6.3** outlines the major sections of the Internal Revenue Code related to the calculation of a client's gross estate and the topics detailed in each section.

Exhibit 6.3 | Federal Estate Tax Sections of the IRC

IRC Section	Property Description
2033	Property owned by the decedent or in which the decedent had an interest at his date of death.
2034	Dower and curtesy interests.
2035	Gift tax paid on gifts made within three years of the decedent's date of death. Gifts of an interest described under 2036, 2037, 2038, 2042, made within three years of the decedent's date of death.
2036	Property transferred prior to the decedent's date of death in which the decedent retained a life interest.
2037	Property transferred prior to the decedent's date of death in which the decedent retained a reversionary interest.
2038	Property transferred prior to the decedent's date of death in which the decedent retained the right to amend, revoke, or alter the transfer.
2039	Annuities.
2040	Jointly owned property.
2041	Powers of appointment.
2042	Proceeds of life insurance receivable by the decedent's estate, or in which the decedent possessed any incidents of ownership at his death.
2044	Property for which a QTIP marital deduction was previously allowed.

Property Owned by the Decedent (IRC Section 2033)

IRC Section 2033 requires the value of all property in which the decedent held an interest at his death to be included in the gross estate. Examples of the types of assets included in the decedent's gross estate by this section include: cash, stocks, bonds, retirement accounts, notes receivables, residences, automobiles, clothes, household furnishings, art collections, and income tax refunds due. In many estates, most of the assets included in a decedent's gross estate will consist of Section 2033 assets.

Some property owned by a decedent and included in the estate under Section 2033 may not be immediately apparent. For example, rental payments that have accrued and are receivable before the decedent's death on rental property will be included in the decedent's gross estate. Also, the interpolated terminal reserve (which is approximately the cash surrender value) or the policy's replacement cost (if the policy was paid up) of a permanent life insurance policy owned by the decedent on the life of someone else is included in a decedent's gross estate under Section 2033. Additionally, state income tax refunds due at the decedent's date of death are included in the decedent's gross estate. Medical insurance reimbursements due to a decedent are also included in the gross estate. These reimbursements usually occur when a decedent has paid hospital, doctor, or other medical bills and, subsequently, an insurance company reimburses the expenses.

A court award for pain and suffering, which the decedent experienced as the result of a fatal automobile accident caused by another person, would also be included in the decedent's gross estate. Even though the court award may be paid to the decedent's surviving spouse or heirs, its value is included in the decedent's gross estate because the cause of action was personal to the decedent. In contrast, a court award for wrongful death paid to the decedent's family will be excluded from the decedent's gross estate. Since a wrongful death suit is based on the family's loss of the decedent's future earnings, it is not considered an asset owned the decedent and is therefore not included in the decedent's gross estate. **Exhibit 6.4** lists most of the asset types that are included in a decedent's gross estate under Section 2033.

Exhibit 6.4 | Abbreviated List of Assets Included in the Gross Estate Under IRC Section 2033

Cash
Stocks and bonds
Retirement accounts
Notes receivable
Personal residences
Other real estate
Household goods
Automobiles
Business interests
Life insurance on someone else's life
Collectibles (art, wine, jewelry)
Vested future rights
Outstanding loans due from others
Income tax refunds owed to the decedent
Patents/copyrights
Pain and suffering award
Damages owed to the decedent
Dividends declared and payable
Income in respect of decedent (Wages receivable)
Any other tangible personal property

Dower and Curtesy Interest (IRC Section 2034)

The common law concepts of dower and curtesy were developed to require that a surviving spouse receive a statutory share of their deceased spouse's estate. The curtesy right is a husband's right to receive a life estate, at his wife's death, in the land she owned in fee simple if the couple had at least one child. The dower right was traditionally a wife's right to a life estate in one third of the land her husband owned in fee simple at his death. Dower rights later evolved to be more consistent with curtesy rights by giving the wife a life estate in all property owned at death, not just one third. In the United States, dower and curtesy rights have been replaced in many states with a statutory right of election in favor of the surviving spouse. A statutory right of election prevents a decedent from disinheriting a spouse, by allowing a surviving spouse to elect against the deceased spouse's testamentary estate plan and take between 1/3 and 1/2 of the deceased spouse's assets (depending on state law). IRC Section 2034 includes the fair market value of any property subject to dower, curtesy, or elective share rights in a decedent's gross estate.

Example 6.1

Marguerite's will bequeaths all of her property to her son, Jeff. However, Marguerite's state of residence allows her surviving husband to take 1/2 of Marguerite's assets (elective share right) regardless of the will provision. In either case, Marguerite's estate will include the full fair market value of her assets. Her husband's elective share right does not alter the inclusion of the assets in her gross estate. As will be discussed below, the property passing to her husband may be eligible for the unlimited marital deduction.

Gifts Made Within Three Years of Death (IRC Section 2035)

Section 2035 of the IRC includes a lookback provision that requires the value of certain lifetime transactions to be included in a decedent's gross estate. Specifically, IRC Section 2035 requires a decedent's gross estate to include (1) any gift tax paid on gifts made within three years of the decedent's date of death, (2) the value of any property gifted within three years of the decedent's date of death if the property would have been included in the decedent's gross estate under IRC Sections 2036, 2037, or 2038, and (3) the death proceeds of any life insurance policy insuring the decedent's life that was gifted within three years of the decedent's date of death.

Gift Tax Paid Within Three Years of Death

Any gift tax paid on gifts made within three years of a decedent's date of death must be added to the gross estate. This is called the gross-up rule and is designed to prevent the amount of the gift tax paid from escaping the gross estate and ultimately transfer tax. The actual value of the gifts made within three years of the decedent's date of death are NOT included in the decedent's gross estate; only the gift tax paid is included in the gross estate. The value of the gifts themselves are added to the taxable estate just like any other post-1976 taxable gifts. The effect of the gross-up rule is to require the decedent to pay estate tax on amounts used to pay gift tax for lifetime transfers made within three years of the transferor's death.

Example 6.2

On March 13th of the current year, Travis gave his brother a tract of land valued at $1,000,000. Travis had already used his applicable gift tax credit and accordingly paid gift tax of $400,000 on this transfer to his brother. Fifteen months after the gift to his brother, Travis died. Consequently, Travis's gross estate will include $400,000 relating to the gift tax paid on the transfer to his brother within three years of his death.

The inclusion required by IRC Section 2035 only applies to actual gift tax paid (i.e., cash paid by the decedent). Gifts shielded from gift tax by the applicable gift tax credit, marital deduction, or annual exclusion will not trigger the application of the gross-up rule.

Example 6.3

On February 2nd of the current year, Richard gave his three daughters taxable gifts of $60,000 each. Richard has not made any previous gifts during his lifetime, and as such no gift tax was due on the transaction because of the application of his applicable gift tax credit. Six months after the gifts, Richard died. Richard's gross estate will not include any amounts related to these gifts to his daughters because taxable gifts are not included in the gross estate and there was no gift tax paid.

Property Gifted Within Three Years of Death

IRC Section 2035 also requires inclusion of the value of property gifted by the decedent within three years of his death, which would otherwise have been included in the decedent's gross estate under Sections 2036 (transfers with a life estate), 2037 (transfers taking effect at death), or 2038 (revocable transfers). These IRC sections are referred to as the retained interest provisions of the Code. They include partial transfers of property, and are premised on the notion that since the decedent made a gift of property but retained a certain degree of control and enjoyment over the property, the fair market value of the property at the date of the decedent's death should be included in the decedent's gross estate if he dies within three years of the transfer. Each of these sections is discussed in detail below.

Transfer of a Life Insurance Policy Within Three Years of Death

Under Section 2035, the proceeds of a life insurance policy on the life of the decedent will be included in the decedent's gross estate if, within three years of the decedent's death, the decedent made a gratuitous completed transfer of the policy.

Example 6.4

Gianni was the sole owner of a paid-up whole life insurance policy on his own life with a death benefit of $3,000,000. On April 3, 2018, the policy had a replacement cost of $232,000 and Gianni gave the policy to his son, Oscar. Since Gianni had already used his applicable gift tax credit and his annual exclusion for his son, Oscar, he paid $92,800 of gift tax on the transfer. Unexpectedly, Gianni died on May 30, 2020. Because Gianni gratuitously transferred the life insurance policy to Oscar within three years of his death, Gianni's gross estate will include the death benefit of the policy transferred of $3,000,000. Gianni's estate will get credit for the gift tax paid.

If the decedent continued to pay premiums on a policy gifted within three years of death, the premiums payments would be a gift eligible for the annual exclusion (if they are considered a present interest transfer); and any gift tax paid on the gift may be included in the decedent's gross estate under Section 2035.

Example 6.5

If, in the above example, Gianni's whole life insurance policy had not been paid up, and Gianni gave money to Oscar to pay policy premiums, the additional premiums would be treated as gifts eligible for the annual exclusion. Any gift tax paid within three years of his death on the premium payments would also be included in Gianni's gross estate.

Chapter 11 of this text is devoted to estate planning with life insurance and its gift and estate tax consequences. See Chapter 11 for additional discussion of life insurance.

Transfers with a Retained Life Estate (IRC Section 2036)

A decedent's gross estate includes the value of any interest in property transferred by the decedent, in which he retained some interest in the property during his life. A transferred interest is treated as having been retained if, at the time of the transfer, there was an understanding, expressed or implied, that the interest or right would later be conferred. Three basic situations cause the fair market value of the property at the decedent's date of death to be included in the decedent's gross estate: an interest retained for life, an interest retained for a period only ascertainable by death, and a retained interest held at death.

Interest Retained for Life

A decedent who retains or reserves an interest in transferred property for his life must include the value of that property in his gross estate under IRC Section 2036. An example of this situation is when the decedent transfers property but retains the income, use or enjoyment, or the right to exercise voting rights over that property for a period not ascertainable without reference to his death.

Example 6.6

Clara conveys her home to her three children and relinquishes any legal ownership in the home. At the time of the transfer, the value of the home was $200,000. The titling document indicates that Clara retained the right to live in the home for the remainder of her life. Because Clara retained the right to live in the home, the full fair market value of the home at her date of death will be included in her gross estate.

Interest Retained for a Period Only Ascertainable by Death

A decedent who retains an interest in property for any period not ascertainable without reference to the decedent's death must include the fair market value, determined at the decedent's date of death, of the property in his gross estate under IRC Section 2036.

Example 6.7

Sawyer transferred his bond portfolio to his favorite son, Jackson, but reserved the right to receive quarterly bond income payments. The transfer agreement also stated that the income payable for the period between the last quarterly payment and Sawyer's date of death was to be payable to Jackson. Even though Sawyer's right to the interest terminated before his death, the fact that the termination of his interest was not determinable without reference to Sawyer's death requires inclusion of the fair market value, at Sawyer's date of death, of the bond portfolio in Sawyer's gross estate.

Retained Interest Held at Death

When a decedent transfers property and retains or reserves an interest for any period of time, and that interest does not in fact end before the decedent's death, the fair market value of the property at the decedent's date of death must be included in his gross estate. The inclusion also applies when the decedent retains the use, possession, right to the income, other enjoyment of the transferred property, or the right, either alone or with another person, to designate the person, or persons, who shall possess or enjoy the transferred property or its income.

Example 6.8

Haley transferred the ownership interest in her home to her son, but retains the right to live in the home for the following 10 years. Haley died 5 years after the transfer. Since Haley died during the 10-year period in which she retained the interest, the fair market value of the property at Haley's date of death is included in her gross estate under IRC Section 2036.

If a decedent retained an interest in property transferred by him, the amount to be included in his gross estate under Section 2036 is only a corresponding proportion of the property less the value of any outstanding income interest, which is not subject to the decedent's interest or right and which is actually being enjoyed by another person at the time of the decedent's death.

Transfers Taking Effect at Death (IRC Section 2037)

A decedent's gross estate also includes the fair market value at the decedent's date of death of any interest in property transferred by the decedent if the transfer was conditioned on all of the following:
- possession or enjoyment of the property can be obtained only by surviving the decedent, and
- the decedent has retained a reversionary interest in the property, and
- the value of such reversionary interest immediately before the death of the decedent exceeds five percent of the value of such property.

IRC Section 2037 applies whether the interest is held in a trust or is held outright, but it will not apply to property transferred for full and adequate consideration.

Example 6.9
Jon transferred $1,000,000 to a trust with the income payable to his wife, Wanda, for her life, with the remainder payable to himself; but if he is not living at his wife's death, then to his daughter, Kayla, or her estate. Jon died while Wanda was still living, and the value of his reversionary interest immediately before death was greater than 5% of the value of the trust. Since Kayla cannot obtain possession or enjoyment of the property without surviving Jon, the value of the property, less the value of Wanda's outstanding life estate, is included in Jon's gross estate.

Reversionary Interest
A **reversionary interest** is any interest that includes a possibility that the property transferred by the decedent may return to him or his estate, or the possibility that property transferred by the decedent may become subject to a power of disposition by him. A reversionary interest does not include any of the following interests:
- A transferor's right to income only, such as the right to receive the income from a trust after the death of another person; however, this right may cause inclusion in the gross estate under Section 2036.
- The possibility that the decedent, during his lifetime, might have received in return an interest in transferred property by inheritance through the estate of another person. Similarly, a statutory right of a spouse to receive a portion of whatever estate a decedent may leave at the time of his death is not a reversionary interest.

Example 6.10
Lucas transferred $100,000 to a trust which will pay the income interest to Lucas for the following ten years and the remainder to Lucas's daughter Rebecca. Lucas does not retain any other rights to the transferred property. If Lucas died twelve years after making the transfer, his gross estate will not include any amount related to the transfer because he had only retained an income interest payable for a period that ended before his death. Had Lucas died within the 10-year income payment period, the full fair market value of the transferred property at his date of death would be included in his gross estate, under IRC Section 2036.

The fair market value of a decedent's reversionary interest is calculated as of the moment immediately before his death, and election of the alternate valuation date (discussed below) is not available. The fair market value is determined using recognized valuation principles for determining the fair market value for estate tax purposes of future or conditional interests in property. These valuation principles are beyond the scope of this text.

Valuation Rule for Reversionary Interests

To determine whether or not the decedent retained a reversionary interest in transferred property of a value in excess of five percent, the fair market value of the reversionary interest in the property is compared with the fair market value of the transferred property, including interests in the property that are not dependent upon survivorship of the decedent.

Example 6.11

Keith transferred stocks into a trust with the income payable to Austin for life, with the remainder payable to Channing. If Austin predeceases Keith, then the property will revert back to Keith. If Keith dies before Austin, then the value of the reversionary interest immediately before his death is compared with the value of the trust corpus. If Keith had retained a reversionary interest in only one-half of the trust corpus, the value of his reversionary interest would be compared with the value of one-half of the trust corpus.

Revocable Transfers (IRC Section 2038)

A decedent's gross estate includes the fair market value at the decedent's date of death of any interest in property transferred by the decedent if the enjoyment of the interest was subject, at the date of the decedent's death, to any change through the exercise of a power by the decedent to alter, amend, revoke, or terminate the gift, or if the decedent relinquished these powers in contemplation of death.

It is immaterial in what capacity the power was exercisable by the decedent or by another person or persons in conjunction with the decedent. Whether the power was exercisable alone or only in conjunction with another person or persons, whether or not the power can only be exercised in conjunction with a person having an adverse interest, and at what time or from what source the decedent acquired his power does not affect the property's inclusion in the gross estate. Section 2038 is applicable to any power affecting the time or manner of enjoyment of property or its income, even though the identity of the beneficiary is not affected.

Example 6.12

Nellie places property in a trust for Jesse. The trust is an irrevocable trust, and both the income and remainder are payable to Jesse. Nellie retains the right to accumulate or distribute earnings, and the right to change the income beneficiary. Even though Jesse will receive the property at termination of the trust, Nellie's right to change the income beneficiary causes inclusion of the fair market value of the trust assets in Nellie's gross estate.

Section 2038 does not apply:
1. To the extent that the transfer was for full and adequate consideration in money or money's worth, or
2. If the decedent's power could be exercised only with the consent of all parties having an interest (vested or contingent) in the transferred property, and if the power adds nothing to the rights of the parties under local law, or
3. To a power held solely by a person other than the decedent. But, for example, if the decedent had the unrestricted power to remove or discharge a trustee at any time and appoint himself trustee, the decedent is considered as having the powers of the trustee. However, this result would not follow if he only had the power to appoint himself trustee under limited conditions, which did not exist at the time of his death.

Annuities (IRC Section 2039)

A **straight single life annuity** is an annuity paid to the annuitant until his death. A decedent who owned a straight life annuity before his death will not include any amount related to the annuity in his gross estate since the annuitant's interest in the contract terminated at his death. A **survivorship annuity** is an annuity that provides payments to one person, and then provides payments to a second person upon the death of the first. When the first annuitant dies, the value of a comparable policy on the second annuitant is included in the first annuitant's gross estate. If the second to die has contributed to the purchase of the policy, then only the proportionate value of the annuity is included in the gross estate of the first to die.

Example 6.13
Steve purchases a straight single life annuity. When he dies, the annuity is not included in his gross estate because the annuity extinguishes upon Steve's death.

Example 6.14
Steve purchases a survivorship annuity. Steve dies and his companion, Erin, becomes the annuitant. The value of a comparable annuity, based on Erin's age, is included in Steve's gross estate.

Example 6.15
Steve and Erin purchase a survivorship annuity together. They each pay half of the premiums. When Steve dies, only one half of the value of Erin's survivorship annuity will be included in his gross estate, since he contributed only one-half of the premiums.

Under Section 2039, the value of the survivorship annuity included in a decedent's gross estate is based on the ratio of the decedent's contributions to the survivorship annuity's total cost to the total cost of the survivorship annuity. This ratio is then multiplied by the value of the annuity at the decedent's date of death.

$$\text{Gross Estate Inclusion} = \left(\text{Value of annuity at decedent's death} \times \frac{\text{Decedent's cost basis}}{\text{Total annuity cost basis}}\right)$$

> **Example 6.16**
> Louis and Margie each contributed $15,000 to the purchase price of a survivorship annuity contract. The annuity will pay an annuity over their joint lives and will continue the annuity for the survivor's life. Assume that the value of the survivorship annuity at the first death is $20,000. Since the decedent contributed one-half of the cost of the annuity contract, the amount to be included in his gross estate under Section 2039 is $10,000. ($20,000 x ($15,000 ÷ $30,000) = $10,000.

Recall that this will not apply to a single life annuity, as the value of single life annuity will not be included in a decedent's gross estate.

Joint Interests (IRC Section 2040)

Section 2040 requires the following jointly held interests to be included in a decedent's estate:

- Property held by the decedent and any other person as joint tenants with rights of survivorship.
- Property held by the decedent and spouse as tenants by the entirety.
- A deposit of money, or a bond or other instrument owned by the decedent, but held in the name of the decedent and any other person, which is payable to either the decedent or a survivor.

A decedent's gross estate includes the fair market value at a decedent's date of death of any property jointly held by the decedent and another person with a right of survivorship. To the extent that the property was acquired by the decedent and the other joint owner or owners by gift, devise, bequest, or inheritance, the value of the decedent's fractional share of the property is included in his gross estate. In all other cases, the value of the property is included based on the actual contribution rule as discussed in Chapter 3. The actual contribution rule requires the full fair market value of the property less any amount attributable to, and actually paid for by another joint owner or owners, to be included in the decedent's gross estate.

The value attributable to the other joint owner or owners only considers the portion of their ownership that is not attributable to money or other property acquired by the other joint owner from the decedent for less than a full and adequate consideration. For example, a surviving joint owner would not be credited with any value for any portion of the property acquired as a gift from the decedent. In such a case, the decedent would include the full fair market value of the property, even though he may own less than 100 percent of the property. Recall from Chapter 3, the actual contribution rule does not apply to spouses who are named as joint tenants. In such cases, each spouse is deemed to have contributed exactly fifty percent of the financial consideration for the property.

To prove that the entire value of jointly held property does not have to be included in a decedent's gross estate, the executor must submit facts sufficient to show that property was not acquired entirely with consideration furnished by the decedent, or was acquired by the decedent and the other joint owner or owners by gift, bequest, devise, or inheritance.

The application of this section may be explained in the following examples, each of which assumes that the other joint owner or owners survived the decedent.

Example 6.17

At Mario's death, he was the joint owner with his son, Richard, of a building that had a fair market value of $130,000. Six years ago at the time the building was purchased, Mario paid the full purchase price of $60,000 to the seller. Richard received his interest in the property as a gift from his father four years prior to Mario's death. Because Mario contributed the full amount towards the purchase price of the building, the full fair market value of the building as of his date of death is included in his gross estate. As such, Mario's gross estate will include $130,000, with regard to the jointly owned building.

Example 6.18

Assume the same facts as above except that at the purchase of the building, Mario and Richard each contributed $30,000 towards its purchase price. Because Richard actually contributed 50% of the purchase price of the building, 50% of the value at Mario's date of death is attributable to Richard. Accordingly, Mario's gross estate will include 50% of the fair market value of the building or, $65,000, in relation to the jointly owned building.

Example 6.19

Assuming the same facts as above except that Mario and Richard had both received their ownership interested as gifts from Mario's father, Mario would only include the fair market value attributable to his ownership interest of 50%, or $65,000, in his gross estate.

Example 6.20

Don and his wife, Diane, own a tract of land joint tenancy with rights of survivorship. The tract of land has a fair market value of $600,000 at Diane's date of death. At the time the tract of land was purchased, Don paid the full purchase price of $120,000. Diane's gross estate will include 50%, or $300,000, related to the tract of land because the actual contribution rule does not apply to property owned jointly between spouses.

Powers of Appointment (IRC Sections 2041 and 2514)

A decedent's gross estate includes the value of property over which the decedent possessed, exercised, or released certain powers of appointment. As discussed in Chapter 3, a **Power of Appointment** is the power to decide who will enjoy or own property.

The parties to a grant of a power of appointment are the donor, the holder, and the appointee. The donor grants the power. The holder receives the power. The appointee is the person whom the holder appoints to enjoy the property.

Powers of appointment can be general or limited. A general power of appointment is a power in which the holder can appoint the property to any one of the following:
1. to the holder,
2. to the holder's estate,
3. to the holder's creditors, or
4. to the creditors of the holder's estate.

When the holder of the power can exercise the power in any of these ways, he has the right to enjoy the property if he should choose to appoint the property to himself, his creditors, his estate, or his estate's creditors. A general power of appointment should usually only be given to a spouse because of the potential for estate tax consequences for the holder of the power (discussed below). A limited power of appointment is any power that is not a general power. A limited power is also called a "special" power.

The gross estate of a decedent includes any assets over which the decedent held a general power of appointment at the time of his death. Exercise or non-exercise of the power does not change the estate tax result, but there are several exceptions. If the right to exercise a general power of appointment is subject to an ascertainable standard (health, education, maintenance, or support), then the power is not a general power of appointment and the property is not included in the decedent's gross estate. If the right to exercise requires approval of the holder and someone else (who is termed an adverse party – someone who has an interest in the property), then the power of appointment is not included in the decedent's gross estate.

Example 6.21
Jill is the beneficiary of a trust established by her husband, Jeff. The trust is funded with assets valued at $100,000. The trust includes a power of appointment clause allowing Jill to appoint up to $20,000 to herself each year. Jill dies before exercising her power in the current year. $20,000 will be included in Jill's gross estate under Section 2041, regardless of the fact that she did not exercise the power.

Example 6.22
Jill is the beneficiary of a trust established by her husband, Jeff. The trust is funded with assets valued at $100,000. The trust includes a power of appointment clause allowing Jill to appoint up to $20,000 to herself each year for educational expenses. Jill dies in the current year. Nothing is included in Jill's gross estate under Section 2041 because her power of appointment was limited by an ascertainable standard.

If the right to exercise is limited to the greater of $5,000 or five percent of the aggregate value of the property each year, referred to as a five-and-five" power, and the power lapses before the decedent's death, then the power of appointment is not included in the decedent's gross estate. The five-and-five power is designed to limit the withdrawal right to a de minimis amount and penalize those withdrawals that exceed the de minimis amount.

Example 6.23
Mary Sue is the beneficiary of a trust established by her deceased husband, Dan. The trust includes a power of appointment clause allowing Mary Sue to appoint to herself the greater of $5,000 or 5% of the trust principal each year. If Mary Sue does not exercise her right to withdraw this year, she cannot take an extra $5,000 or 5% out of the trust principal next year, and the power is said to have lapsed.

Example 6.24

Mary Sue is the beneficiary of a trust established by her deceased husband, Dan. The trust includes a power of appointment clause, allowing Mary Sue to appoint to herself the greater of $5,000 or 5% of the trust principal each year. Before exercising the five-and-five power for the current year, Mary Sue died before her right to withdraw expired. The trust balance at the time of her death was $500,000. Mary Sue will include the value of her power of appointment in her gross estate (which, in this case, is $25,000, or 5% of $500,000).

Assets subject to a limited power of appointment are not included in the power holder's gross estate at death.

Proceeds of Life Insurance (IRC Section 2042)

As will be discussed in Chapter 11, IRC Section 2042 includes the death benefit proceeds of a life insurance policy on the life of the decedent in the decedent's gross estate if, at the decedent's death, either the proceeds were receivable by the decedent's estate or the decedent possessed any incident of ownership in the policy (discussed below). Section 2042 also requires inclusion of the death benefit of a split-dollar life insurance policy on the life of the decedent where the insured possessed an incident of ownership in the policy even though a part of the proceeds may be payable to a third party, usually the employer.

Inclusion Under Other Sections of the IRC

Generally, the amount to be included in a decedent's gross estate under Section 2042 is the full death benefit payable from the life insurance policy. If the proceeds of the life insurance policy are made payable to a beneficiary in the form of an annuity for life, or for a term of years, the amount to be included in the decedent's gross estate is the value of the available lump-sum payment at the decedent's death, or if no lump-sum option was available, the amount used by the insurance company to determine the annuity payment.

If under the terms of the life insurance policy, the proceeds payable to a beneficiary are subject to the beneficiary's obligation to pay taxes, debts, or other charges enforceable against the estate from the life insurance policy proceeds; then the amount of such proceeds required for the payment of the beneficiary's obligation is includible in the decedent's gross estate. Similarly, if the decedent purchased a life insurance policy in favor of another person or a corporation, as collateral security for a loan or other accommodation, its proceeds are considered to be received by the estate and are, therefore, included in the decedent's gross estate. In such a case, any related loan outstanding at the decedent's date of the death, plus interest accrued to that date, will be deducted in determining the decedent's taxable estate (discussed below).

Quick Quiz 6.1

1. A court award for wrongful death paid to the decedent's family will be included in the decedent's gross estate.
   a. True
   b. False

2. The value of the decedent's reversionary interest is calculated as of the moment immediately before his death or the alternate valuation date.
   a. True
   b. False

3. Proceeds of a life insurance policy on the life of the decedent will be included in the decedent's gross estate if, at the decedent's death, the decedent possessed any incidents of ownership in the policy.
   a. True
   b. False

4. A straight life annuity is included in a decedent's gross estate since the annuitant's interest terminates at his death.
   a. True
   b. False

False, False, True, False.

> **Example 6.25**
> At his date of death, Scott was the owner of a whole life insurance policy on his own life. His daughter, Rebecca, was the listed beneficiary at the time of his death, and the full policy proceeds of $300,000 were paid to Rebecca after Scott's death. Scott's gross estate will include the full death proceeds of $300,000 because Scott was the owner of the life insurance policy at the time of his death.

If the proceeds of a life insurance policy made payable to the decedent's estate is considered community property under the local community property law and, as a result, one-half of the proceeds belongs to the decedent's spouse, then only one-half of the proceeds is included in the decedent's gross estate.

Incidents of Ownership

"Incidents of ownership" are not limited to the direct ownership of the life insurance policy in the technical legal sense. An incident of ownership is the right of the insured, or his estate, to enjoy any of the economic benefits of the policy. Thus, it includes, among others, the powers to change the beneficiary, surrender or cancel the life insurance policy, assign the life insurance policy, revoke an assignment, pledge the life insurance policy for a loan, or obtain from the insurer a loan against the surrender value of the policy.

A decedent is considered to have an incident of ownership in a life insurance policy on his life held in trust if the decedent has the power to change the beneficial ownership in the policy or its proceeds, or has the power to change the time or manner of enjoyment of the property for the trust beneficiaries even though the decedent may not have a beneficial interest in the trust.

> **Example 6.26**
> Six years before her death, Roxanne transferred a paid-up whole life insurance policy on her life to her son, Daniel. At the time of the gift, Roxanne retained the right to change the beneficiary of the life insurance policy and, as such, was deemed to have an incident of ownership in the policy at her date of death. Accordingly, the full death benefit would be included in Roxanne's gross estate.

Recall that in some instances, the proceeds of a life insurance policy are included in a decedent's gross estate under a different section of the Internal Revenue Code. For example, if the decedent possessed incidents of ownership in a life insurance policy on his life but gratuitously transferred all rights in the life insurance policy within three years of his date of death, the proceeds would be included in his gross estate under Section 2035. Also, a decedent must include in his gross estate the value of rights in a life insurance policy on the life of another person.

chapter 6

Property for which Marital Deduction was Previously Allowed (IRC Section 2044)

A marital deduction will be allowed for property included in the gross estate of the first spouse to die and transferred to the surviving spouse if a QTIP election is properly made at the death of the first spouse. When a QTIP election is made, any property remaining at the death of the surviving spouse must be included in the surviving spouse's gross estate. This topic will be discussed in detail in Chapter 10.

VALUATION OF ASSETS AT DEATH

The valuation of property included in a decedent's gross estate is either the fair market value at the decedent's date of death, or if properly elected by the executor, the fair market value at the alternate valuation date (discussed below). Fair market value is the value that would be paid for the property in a transaction where there is a willing buyer and willing seller, where neither party is acting under compulsion, and where both parties have full knowledge of the facts. "Fair market value" is the value that the assets would trade at in a perfect world. Unfortunately, a perfect world does not exist. Sometimes it is difficult to ascertain the fair market value of property due to a lack of an established market or the lack of factual knowledge about the property.

> **Key Concepts**
>
> 1. Describe the valuation issues related to real estate, stocks, life insurance, and closely held businesses.
> 2. What is the alternate valuation date and why is it used?

Hard-to-Value Assets

Hard-to-value assets such as real estate, art, jewelry, antiques, collectibles, and closely held business interests usually require an appraisal. Appraising the value of property is as much of an art as it is a science, and appraisers tend to specialize in valuing specific types of property. When closely held businesses are being appraised (discussed in detail below), the extent of the decedent's ownership interest is important, since minority and marketability discounts may apply.

CASE STUDY 6.1

In the *Estate of Elkins v. Commissioners,* the Fifth Circuit Court of Appeals allowed a 44.75 percent discount for a decedent's fractional share of valuable works of art. However, it should be noted that the IRS presented no evidence to refute the estate's expert. The court found that a fractional interest in art was worth less than the fraction owned times the total fair value because a fractional interest had liquidity and marketability restrictions.

Closely Held Businesses
Closely held businesses are difficult to value because of the unique characteristics they possess. Factors to be considered in valuing a closely held business include the following:
- Nature of the business
- Economic outlook
- Book value of stock
- Financial condition of the business
- Goodwill
- Shares that have been sold previously
- Earnings capacity and the ability to pay dividends

The value of closely held businesses may be significantly reduced using various valuation discounts. These discounts are commonly associated with use of a family limited partnership, a family limited liability company, or some other closely held business.

Minority Discount
A **minority discount** is a reduction in the value of an asset caused by the transfer of a minority interest in a business. A minority interest is any interest that is not a controlling interest. Minority owners cannot manage the business or compel its sale or liquidation. Therefore, outside buyers would not be willing to pay the same proportional amount for a minority interest as they would for a majority or controlling interest. For transfer tax purposes, minority discounts (when available) often range between 15 percent to 50 percent.

Lack of Marketability Discount
A **lack of marketability discount** is a reduction in the value caused by the transfer of an asset that has an inherent lack of marketability. Interests in a closely held business and partnership interests are more difficult to sell than interests in more marketable assets such as publicly traded stock. Therefore, a discount is often allowed for the lack of marketability. Lack of marketability discounts typically range between 15 percent to 50 percent, and can be applied to both minority and majority interests. A lack of marketability discount can be used in combination with a minority discount to produce an even larger overall discount.

> **Example 6.27**
> Tom died owning a 3% interest in a closely held business. The business is valued at $500,000, and an appraiser applied a lack of marketability discount and a minority discount that totaled 40%. The value of the 3% interest included in Tom's gross estate is only $9,000 [$500,000 x 3% x (100% - 40%)].

Blockage Discount
A **blockage discount** is attributable to the value of large blocks of corporate stock that are listed on a public exchange. A discount may be available because a large block of stock is often less marketable than smaller amounts of stock. In theory, a large amount of stock included in the decedent's gross estate cannot be liquidated at one time without causing a decrease in the stock's market price. The actual amount of the discount would be based on the decrease in the realizable price below the current market price of the stock.

Key Person Discount

A discount may be allowed for a business in which a key person has died or becomes disabled, called a **key person discount**. The discount is based on the economic reality that the value of the stock of a closely held business will decline if a key person, such as the founder, dies or becomes disabled. The discount may be reduced by the value of key person life insurance proceeds payable to the corporation on the death of the key person.

Financial Securities

Financial securities are priced by the market and appear to be easily valued. The fair market value of a financial security is not, however, its closing price on the date of the decedent's death. Rather, it is the average of the high and low trading price for the decedent's date of death or the alternate valuation date (discussed below). If the valuation date is a weekend, the valuation of the financial security is the average of the applicable values for the trading day before and the trading day after.

Example 6.28

Rex died on Friday, June 11. His gross estate included 100 shares of XCD Corporation stock. On the date of Rex's death, the XCD Corporation stock closed at a price of $10, but had traded at a high price during the day of $11 and a low price of $8. The value of the 100 shares of XCD Corporation stock in Rex's gross estate is $950 [(($11 + $8) ÷ 2) x 100], the average of the high and low price for the date of death.

Example 6.29

Diane died on Saturday, June 12. Her gross estate included 200 shares of Tel Corporation stock. Because Diane died on a Saturday and the stock is not traded on a Saturday, the average of the values as determined on the previous Friday and the subsequent Monday are used to value the stock. The following per share information was determined.

	High	Low	Average
Friday, June 11	$62.00	$61.00	$61.50
Monday, June 14	$63.00	$61.00	$62.00

The 200 shares of Tel Corporation stock will be included in Diane's gross estate at $12,350 [(($61.50 + $62.00) ÷ 2) x 200].

Accrued Interest

If the financial security included in the decedent's gross estate is a bond or any other type of interest bearing instrument, any interest accrued, but not paid to the decedent at the decedent's date of death, is added to the value of the instrument.

Example 6.30
Rosie's gross estate included a semi-annual coupon bond. On the date of her death, the bond traded at a high price of $980 and a low price of $976. A coupon interest payment of $60 was also due to be paid six days after Rosie's death. $59 of the interest payment had accrued at the time of Rosie's death. The bond will be included in Rosie's gross estate at a value of $978 [($980 + $976) ÷ 2] plus the accrued interest of $59, for a total value related to the bond of $1,037 ($978 + $59).

Accrued Dividends
If the financial security included in a decedent's gross estate is a dividend paying stock, the value of any declared dividends at the decedent's date of death may also be included in the decedent's gross estate. The inclusion of the dividend, and its presentation in the gross estate, depends upon the decedent's date of death in relation to the dividend date of declaration, the X dividend date, the date of record, and the date of payment, as discussed below.

Dividend Payment Dates
Four dates are important when discussing the payment of a dividend. These dates are:
1. **The dividend declaration date** - the date when the board of directors declares a dividend payment. This action creates an obligation for the company to make a dividend payment.
2. **The ex-dividend date** - The ex-dividend date is generally set one business day before the date of record. Ex-dividend means that the stock trades "ex" or without the dividend distribution. If a stock is currently valued at $100 and the company declares a $5 dividend, then the stock should theoretically decline in value by $5 to a price of $95 on the ex-dividend date. From an economic standpoint, the shareholder is in the same position after the ex-dividend date as before. Prior to the dividend, the shareholders owned stock worth $100. After the dividend payment, the shareholders own shares of stock worth $95 and has a right to $5 in cash per share of stock owned. The day before the ex-dividend date is the last day the stock can be purchased in order to receive the dividend payment. Investors who purchase stock on the ex-dividend date or after will not receive the dividend payment. Instead, the seller of those shares will receive the dividend.
3. **The record date** - When a company declares a dividend, it sets a date of record. The date of record is the date the company determines who owns the company stock for the purpose of receiving the dividend. If an investor bought the stock prior to the ex-dividend date, the he or she will be reflected as a common stock holder. The difference in time is due to the time it takes to settle stock trades. Generally, it takes three days after the execution of the purchase of a share of stock for the trade to settle.
4. **The payment date** - The date of payment is the date on which the dividend will actually be paid. Remember that the dividend will be paid to those who owned the shares as of the date of record. Anyone who sells his or her shares on or after the ex-dividend date, will receive the dividend payment.

Example 6.31

XYZ declares a dividend on May 28th and sets the date of record as June 8th. The ex-dividend date is one business day before the date of record, which is June 7th. The date of payment is set as June 14th.

Date of Declaration May 28th	Ex-Dividend Date June 7th	Date of Record June 8th	Date of Payment June 14th

An investor who purchases the stock by June 6th will be entitled to receive the dividend scheduled for payment on June 14th. An investor of XYZ stock who sells the stock on the ex-dividend date or after will also receive the dividend.

Exhibit 6.5 | Accrued Dividends

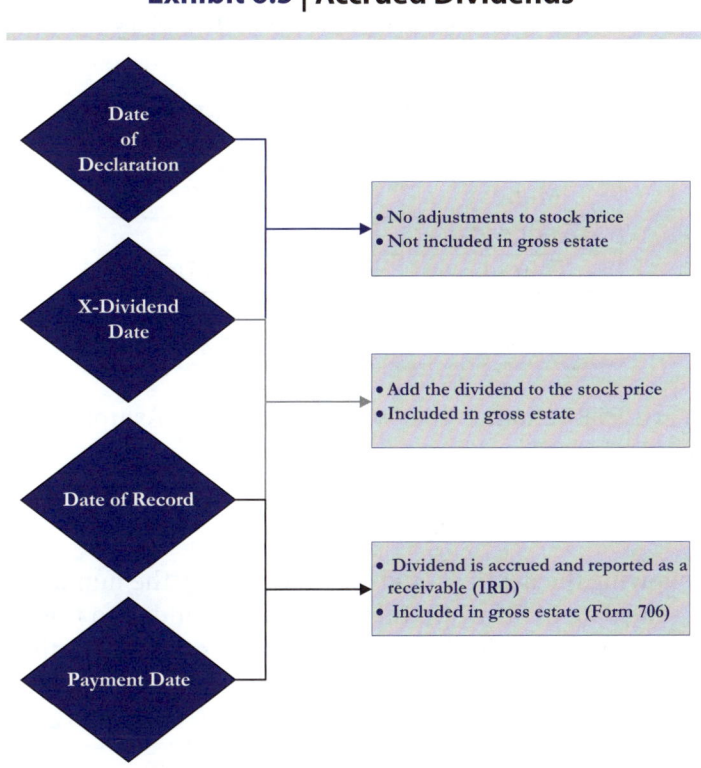

Financial Securities Not Traded on Valuation Date

If the stock is not traded on the decedent's date of death, the value of the stock according to the IRS Regulations should be the stock price following the decedent's date of death multiplied by the number of days from the stock trade before the date of death. Added to this is the stock price directly preceding the death multiplied by the number of days (trading days) between the death and the next trading day. This sum should be divided by the sum of the days before and after the death. Weekends, holidays, or other days that the market is closed are not included in the calculation.

$$\text{Valuation included in decedent's gross estate} = \frac{\begin{pmatrix}\text{Trading price after decedent's date of death}\end{pmatrix} \times \begin{pmatrix}\text{Number of days between decedent's date of death and the first preceding trade}\end{pmatrix} + \begin{pmatrix}\text{Trading price before decedent's date of death}\end{pmatrix} \times \begin{pmatrix}\text{Number of days between decedent's date of death and the next subsequent trade}\end{pmatrix}}{\text{The sum of the days before and after the date of death}}$$

Example 6.32

Unpopular Inc. stock does not trade on a regular basis. If Ashton dies, owning infrequently traded stock, on Thursday, May 6 and the most recent trades for Unpopular stock are:

Day of the week	Date	Price
Monday	5/3	$27
Wednesday	5/5	$25
Thursday	5/6	Date of Death
Monday	5/10	$28
Tuesday	5/11	$29

The date of death artificial valuation that will be included in Ashton's gross estate is $26, as calculated below.

$$\frac{(28 \times 1) + (25 \times 2)}{3 \text{ days}} = \frac{78}{3} = \$26$$

The stock price following the death should be multiplied by the number of days from the stock trade before the date of death (in this case, 1 day). Added to this is the stock price directly preceding the death, multiplied by the number of days (trading days) between the death and the next trading day (in this case, 2 days, Friday and Monday). This sum should be divided by the sum of the days before and after the death (2 + 1 = 3 days).

Life Insurance

The value of life insurance for gift tax purposes is the interpolated terminal reserve (which approximates the cash value of the policy) if the policy is in pay status, or the replacement cost of the policy if it is paid up. Alternatively, the value of life insurance included in the gross estate of an insured who owned or possessed incidents of ownership in a policy will be its face value (the death proceeds). If an annuity settlement option is chosen by the beneficiary, the amount includible in the decedent's gross estate will be the amount that would have been payable as a lump sum (generally the death proceeds).

chapter 6

The Alternate Valuation Date

Because death is presumed to be involuntary, the **alternate valuation date** is provided to give relief to a decedent who happened to die on a date where his gross estate had a high value due to temporary market conditions. The executor can make an election to value the estate on the date six months after the decedent's date of death, if such election will decrease both the value of the gross estate and the estate tax liability. Under this election, all assets are valued at the date six months after the decedent's date of death or the asset's date of disposition, if earlier than six months. The alternate valuation date initially applies to all assets in the gross estate, not just to specific assets.

Exhibit 6.6 | Alternate Valuation Date Summary

To Qualify for the Alternate Valuation Date (AVD)
1. The total value of the gross estate must decline after the date of death, AND
2. The total estate tax must be less than the estate tax calculated using the date of death values.
Valuation if AVD is Properly Elected
1. All assets valued at the alternate valuation date
2. Except: <ul><li>Assets distributed or sold after death but before the alternative valuation date, which are valued at the date of distribution or sale, and</li><li>Wasting assets (annutized annuities, patents, royalties, installment notes, lease income, value of the reversionary interest), which must be valued at the date of death.</li></ul>

There are several exceptions to using the alternate valuation date to value assets. Wasting assets are always valued at the decedent's date of death. Wasting assets include those assets whose value changes merely due to the passage of time, rather than market conditions. Annuities, patents, copyrights, and installment notes are examples of wasting assets which must be valued at the decedent's date of death. Additionally, assets disposed of between the decedent's date of death and the alternate valuation date will be valued as of their date of disposition.

Since the election to use the alternate valuation date creates a lower valuation in the decedent's gross estate, it also results in a lower income tax basis to the heirs of the estate. Consideration should be given to the marginal estate tax rate versus the heir's marginal income tax rate to determine the overall lowest tax cost. An assessment should also be made as to whether the beneficiary intends to sell or otherwise dispose of the asset some time in the near future so that the most appropriate income tax basis will be used.

Quick Quiz 6.2

1. A minority interest is any interest that, in terms of voting, is not a controlling interest.
   a. True
   b. False

2. The executor can make an election to value the estate nine months after the date of death.
   a. True
   b. False

3. Assets disposed of between the date of death and the alternate valuation date are valued on the date of disposition if the alternate valuation date is properly elected.
   a. True
   b. False

True, False, True.

To elect the alternate valuation date, an estate tax return must be filed, and both the value of the gross estate and the total estate tax liability must be lower than what the primary date of death valuation date would have yielded. The election to utilize the alternate valuation date is made on Form 706, but will not be valid if the return is filed more than one year after the time prescribed by law (including extensions) for filing the Form 706.

Example 6.33

Riley died recently and left the assets shown below at their fair market value at his date of death (DOD) and at six months after his DOD:

Item	Value at DOD	Value Six Months after DOD
Land	$5,000,000	$4,500,000
Stock	$300,000	$310,000
Annuity	$100,000	$95,000
Condominium	$300,000	Sold 2 months after DOD for $295,000
Total	$5,700,000	$5,200,000

If Riley's executor properly elects the alternate valuation date, Riley's total estate will be $4,500,000 + $310,000 + $100,000 + $295,000 = $5,205,000. The land and stock are valued at the alternate valuation date, the annuity (a wasting asset) must be valued at Riley's DOD ($100,000), and the condominium will be valued as of the sale (disposition) date ($295,000).

One final point is worth making. Since most individuals will not incur an estate tax when they die, the election to use the alternative valuation date is not available to them. This is because the value of each asset in the estate is also the basis for heirs for income tax (capital gains) purposes, going forward.

DEDUCTIONS TO DETERMINE THE ADJUSTED GROSS ESTATE

To determine the **adjusted gross estate**, certain deductions are taken from the gross estate in recognition that the entire value of the gross estate will not be transferred to the heirs due to the presence of these costs. Under our transfer tax system, the estate will be subject to tax on the value of the property transferred to the surviving heirs.

The adjusted gross estate is determined by deducting the following items from the gross estate:
- funeral expenses
- last medical expenses
- administrative expenses
- debts of the decedent
- losses during estate administration

> **Key Concepts**
> 1. Describe the deductions available from the gross estate.
> 2. What expenses are deductible from the adjusted gross estate to determine the taxable estate?

The application of the Qualified Family owned business deduction (which was repealed for tax years after 2003 but may still impact certain estates), Section 6166 Installment Payments of Estate Tax, and Section 2032A Special Use Valuation all depend upon the size of the adjusted gross estate. These provisions will be discussed at length later in the textbook.

Exhibit 6.7 | The Abbreviated Estate Tax Formula - Deductions from the Gross Estate

Gross Estate		$_____	Gross Estate
Less Deductions:			
Last Medical Expense	$_____		
Administrative Expenses	$_____		
Funeral Expenses	$_____		
Debts of Decedent	$_____		
Losses During Estate Administration	$_____	$_____	Deductions
Equals: Adjusted Gross Estate		$_____	Adjusted Gross Estate

Funeral Expenses

Reasonable expenses for the decedent's funeral, such as interment costs, the cost of the burial plot, grave marker, and transportation of the body to the place of burial are deductible from the gross estate to determine the adjusted gross estate. A reasonable expenditure for a tombstone, monument, or mausoleum, or for a burial lot, either for the decedent or his family, including an estimate of reasonable future care, may also be deductible from the gross estate. These funeral expenses must actually be incurred by the estate to be deducted.

Last Medical Expenses

Medical expenses related to the decedent's last illness are deductible from the decedent's gross estate provided the expenses are not included as a deduction on the decedent's final federal income tax return.

Administrative Expenses

Any expenses related to the administration of the estate are deductible from either the estate tax return (Form 706) or the estate's income tax return (Form 1041). The amounts deductible as administrative expenses are limited to expenses that are actually and necessarily incurred in the administration of the decedent's estate. Examples of these expenses include expenses related to the collection of the assets, payment of the debts, and the distribution of property to the heirs. More specifically, these expenses often include attorney and accountant fees for preparing the decedent's estate tax return and the estate's income tax return, the expenses related to retitling the assets through the probate process, and the executor's fee (often limited by state law). The costs of appraisals, any fees related to valuing the assets included in the gross estate, and the debts deducted from the gross estate are also considered administrative expenses that are deductible from the gross estate in arriving at the adjusted gross estate. Any expenditures not essential to the proper settlement of the decedent's estate, but incurred for the individual benefit of any heirs or legatees, are not deductible.

Because the decedent's estate tax return is usually filed before the administration of the estate has been completed, executors may deduct an estimate of the future administrative expenses.

Debts

The value of the decedent's debts at his date of death are deductible from the decedent's gross estate in calculating the adjusted gross estate. Debts are any amount the decedent was obligated to pay the moment before his death, including any interest accrued up to the decedent's date of death. Debts generally include items such as outstanding mortgages, income tax due, gift tax payable, credit card balances, and other miscellaneous outstanding debts such as amounts due to retailers and other monthly service type providers (gas bills, electric bills, etc.). Liabilities imposed by law or arising out of torts are also deductible. Only those claims which are enforceable against the decedent's estate may be deducted. Only interest accrued to the date of the decedent's death is allowable even if the executor elects the alternate valuation date.

Losses During Estate Administration

Any losses to the estate during the period of administration, including casualty and theft losses, are deductible expenses. Losses can arise during the administration of an estate just as they can arise during an individual's life. For example, an estate can suffer a loss due to a fire, storm, shipwreck, casualty, or theft. The value of the loss is only deductible if the loss is not reimbursed by the decedent's insurance provider. If the loss is partially reimbursed, the excess of the loss over the reimbursement is a deduction from the gross estate to arrive at the adjusted gross estate.

> ### Quick Quiz 6.3
>
> 1. Funeral expenses are allowed as funeral expense deductions even if they have not been incurred.
>   a. True
>   b. False
> 2. Administration expenses include appraisal and valuation fees necessary to determine the value of assets included in the gross estate for estate tax purposes.
>   a. True
>   b. False
> 3. Liabilities imposed by law or arising out of torts are not deductible.
>   a. True
>   b. False
> 4. The taxable estate of a decedent is the gross estate less the marital and charitable deductions.
>   a. True
>   b. False
>
> *False, True, False, False.*

To be deductible, the loss must occur during the administration of the estate. Any loss before the death of the decedent is accounted for on the decedent's final income tax return. Any loss with respect to an asset after its distribution to the heir is not deductible by the decedent's estate, but on the heir's income tax return.

No deduction is allowed under this section if the estate has waived its right to take the deduction on the estate tax return in order to permit its allowance on the estate's income tax return.

chapter 6

DEDUCTIONS TO DETERMINE THE TAXABLE ESTATE

Exhibit 6.8 | The Abbreviated Estate Tax Formula - Adjusted Gross Estate Through Taxable Estate

Adjusted Gross Estate		$ _____	Adjusted Gross Estate
Less: Unlimited Charitable Deduction	$ _____		
Less: Unlimited Marital Deduction	$ _____		
Less: State Death Tax Deduction	$ _____	$ _____	
Equals: Taxable Estate		$ _____	Taxable Estate

The Charitable Deduction

An unlimited charitable deduction is allowed for the value of assets included in the decedent's gross estate which are transferred to a charitable organization at the decedent's date of death. Chapter 9 is devoted to charitable deductions from the adjusted gross estate used to determine the taxable estate.

The Unlimited Marital Deduction

An unlimited marital deduction is allowed for the value of assets included in the decedent's gross estate, which are transferred to the decedent's surviving spouse. Chapter 10 is devoted to the unlimited marital deduction, which is a deduction from the adjusted gross estate to determine the taxable estate.

State Death Tax Deduction

A deduction for estate, inheritance, legacy, or succession taxes paid to any state, territory, or the District of Columbia is allowed for decedents dying after 2004. Prior to 2005, a credit against the estate tax was allowed. The credit for state death taxes reduced the total estate tax dollar-for-dollar for the state death tax paid. In contrast, the deduction for state death taxes only reduces the total taxable estate by the amount of the state death taxes paid, which reduces the total estate tax by an amount equal to the state death taxes multiplied by the estate's marginal estate tax rate. As such, the replacement of the credit for state death taxes with the deduction for state death taxes will increase the overall estate taxes due at the decedent's death.

The deduction can be claimed for payments that are anticipated, but not yet paid; however, the payments must be made within four years after the return is filed. Certain exceptions may apply if a section 6166 election is made (discussed in Chapter 13) to pay the federal estate tax in installments. The deduction is not subject to any dollar limits. If property is transferred to the state in lieu of cash the deduction is the lesser of the state inheritance tax liability discharged or the fair market value of the property on the date of transfer.

Example 6.34

Mary recently died in a state with an estate tax. Her CPA estimated that her estate will pay $450,000 in state death taxes. Her executor will be able to deduct the $450,000 from her adjusted gross estate in determining her taxable estate on the Federal Form 706.

The Taxable Estate

The **taxable estate** is the adjusted gross estate less the unlimited charitable and marital deductions discussed above and in detail in Chapters 9 and 10 respectively. The taxable estate is not the final calculation in the calculation of the total estate tax. The total of all post-1976 taxable gifts are added to the taxable estate to determine the tentative tax base. Any state death taxes paid are deducted from this.

DETERMINING THE TENTATIVE TAX

Thus far in the estate tax calculation, most values have been based upon the fair market value of assets the decedent had an interest in at his death. However, the estate tax calculation and the gift tax calculation are based on a unified transfer schedule which taxes all transfers made over a decedent's lifetime and at death at the same tax rates. Accordingly, the total value of all post-1976 taxable gifts (valued as of the date of the gifts) must be added to the decedent's taxable estate.

Exhibit 6.9 | The Abbreviated Estate Tax Formula (Taxable Estate Through Tentative Tax Base)

Taxable Estate		$ _____	Taxable Estate
Add: Previous (post 1976) Taxable Gifts	$ _____	$ _____	
Equals: Tentative Tax Base	$ _____	$ _____	Tentative Tax Base

Post-1976 Taxable Gifts

All taxable gifts after 1976 must be added to a decedent's taxable estate. These gifts are added back at the fair market value as of the date of the gift. These values can be directly determined from an individual's previously filed gift tax returns.

The Tentative Tax Base

The tentative tax base is the amount used to determine the tentative tax, the total transfer (estate and gift) tax on all transfers during an individual's life and at the individual's death. The **tentative tax base** equals the sum of taxable estate plus the post-1976 taxable gifts.

The Tentative Tax

The **tentative tax** is the total transfer taxes, estate and gift, on all property transferred by the decedent during his life and at his death. It is determined by applying the tax rate from the unified tax rate schedule to the tentative tax base (the combined value of the taxable estate and post-1976 taxable gifts).

The tentative tax is then reduced by the total gift tax paid during the individual's life, or payable on gifts included in the tax base to give the decedent credit for the tax paid on the post-1976 taxable gifts added when determining the tentative tax base. The estate tax remaining after the reduction for the gift tax paid may be further reduced by certain available credits as discussed below.

Exhibit 6.10 | Tax Rate Schedule for Gifts and Estates (2020)

Over $0 but not over $10,000	**18%** of such amount.
Over $10,000 but not over $20,000	$1,800 plus **20%** of the excess of such amount over $10,000
Over $20,000 but not over $40,000	$3,800 plus **22%** of the excess of such amount over $20,000
Over $40,000 but not over $60,000	$8,200 plus **24%** of the excess of such amount over $40,000
Over $60,000 but not over $80,000	$13,000 plus **26%** of the excess of such amount over $60,000
Over $80,000 but not over $100,000	$18,200 plus **28%** of the excess of such amount over $80,000
Over $100,000 but not over $150,000	$23,800 plus **30%** of the excess of such amount over $100,000
Over $150,000 but not over $250,000	$38,800 plus **32%** of the excess of such amount over $150,000
Over $250,000 but not over $500,000	$70,800 plus **34%** of the excess of such amount over $250,000
Over $500,000 but not over $750,000	$155,800 plus **37%** of the excess of such amount over $500,000
Over $750,000 but not over $1,000,000	$248,300 plus **39%** of the excess of such amount over $750,000
Over $1,000,000	$345,800 plus **40%** of the excess of such amount over $1,000,000

CREDITS FROM THE TENTATIVE TAX

The tentative tax less the gift tax paid during a decedent's life is further reduced by certain available credits such as the applicable estate tax credit (unified credit), the credit for tax on prior transfers, and the foreign death tax credit.

Exhibit 6.11 | The Abbreviated Estate Tax Formula - Credits

Tentative Tax		$ _____	Tentative Tax
Less: Credits			
Previous Gift Tax Paid or Payable	$ _____		
Applicable Estate Tax Credit	$ _____		
Credit for Tax Paid on Prior Transfers	$ _____		
Foreign Death Tax Credit	$ _____	$ _____	Total Credits
Equals: Federal Estate Tax Liability		$ _____	Federal Estate Tax Liability

Applicable Estate Tax Credit

As discussed in Chapter 5, the applicable estate tax credit equivalency amount will exclude up to $11,580,000 (for 2020) of cumulative taxable transfers during an individual's lifetime or at death from estate transfer tax. The applicable estate tax credit equivalency can be defined as the taxable fair market value of the property that can be transferred without creating an estate tax greater than the applicable estate tax credit. The applicable estate tax credit for 2020 is $4,577,800.

For tax years beginning before December 31, 2003 and after December 31, 2010, the credit available against lifetime transfers and the credit available against transfers at death is unified. An individual could transfer a statutorily determined amount without incurring transfer taxes either during life or at death. Accordingly, the credit was known as the unified credit. However, between 2001 and 2010, EGTRRA 2001 created different credit amounts applicable to transfers during life and transfers at death, thus the credit was no longer unified. EGTRRA 2001 increased the unified credit against estate taxes for years after 2003, while the unified credit against gift taxes for years after 2003 remains at the same amount. When the credit amounts were not unified, the credit against gift taxes was referred to as the "applicable gift tax credit" and the credit against the estate tax was referred to as the "applicable estate tax credit." The following exhibit illustrates the differences in the applicable gift and estate tax credits.

Exhibit 6.12 | Applicable Gift and Estate Tax Credits and Exclusion Amounts

Year of Death	Applicable Estate Tax Credit	Applicable Estate Tax Credit Equivalency	Applicable Gift Tax Credit	Applicable Gift Tax Credit Equivalency
1997	$192,800	$600,000	$192,800	$600,000
1998	$202,050	$625,000	$202,050	$625,000
1999	$211,300	$650,000	$211,300	$650,000
2000	$220,550	$675,000	$220,550	$675,000
2001	$220,550	$675,000	$220,550	$675,000
2002	$345,800	$1,000,000	$345,800	$1,000,000
2003	$345,800	$1,000,000	$345,800	$1,000,000
2004	$555,800	$1,500,000	$345,800	$1,000,000
2005	$555,800	$1,500,000	$345,800	$1,000,000
2006 - 2008	$780,800	$2,000,000	$345,800	$1,000,000
2009	**$1,455,800**	**$3,500,000**	**$345,800**	**$1,000,000**
2010	REPEALED*	REPEALED*	$330,800	$1,000,000
2011	$1,730,800	$5,000,000	$1,730,800	$5,000,000
2012	$1,772,800	$5,120,000	$1,772,800	$5,120,000
2013	$2,045,800	$5,250,000	$2,045,800	$5,250,000
2014	$2,081,800	$5,340,000	$2,081,800	$5,340,000
2015	$2,117,800	$5,430,000	$2,117,800	$5,430,000
2016	$2,125,800	$5,450,000	$2,125,800	$5,450,000
2017	$2,141,800	$5,490,000	$2,141,800	$5,490,000
2018	$4,417,800	$11,180,000	$4,417,800	$11,180,000
2019	$4,505,800	$11,400,000	$4,505,800	$11,400,000
2020	$4,577,800	$11,580,000	$4,577,800	$11,580,000

Exemption Portability

TRA 2010 created the **deceased spouse's unused exclusion amount (DSUEA)**, otherwise known as "exemption **portability**" for tax years 2011 and 2012 by permitting the executor of a deceased spouse's estate to elect (on a timely filed estate tax return) to transfer the "deceased spousal unused exclusion amount" to the surviving spouse. ATRA 2012 made portability permanent. The deceased spousal unused exclusion amount (DSUEA) is the lesser of:

1. the basic exclusion amount (as adjusted for inflation), or
2. the excess of:
   - the applicable exclusion amount of the last such deceased spouse of such surviving spouse, over
   - the amount of the exemption previously used on the estate tax return of such deceased spouse.

Example 6.35
When Dan died in 2020, he had a taxable estate of $2,000,000. During his lifetime, Dan had not made any gifts of property in excess of the gift tax annual exclusion. When filing Dan's estate tax return, his executor, Gabriel, elects to transfer Dan's "deceased spousal unused exclusion amount" (DSUEA) to Dan's wife, Cheryl. Dan's DSUEA is $9,580,000 (the lesser of (1) the standard exclusion amount of $11,580,000, or (2) the standard exclusion amount of $11,580,000 less Dan's taxable estate of $2,000,000 less Dan's adjusted taxable gifts ($0) = $9,580,000).

Several safeguards to avoid abuse of exemption portability were imposed by the legislation, including a change to the normal statute of limitations, a filing requirement, and an anti-stacking provision.

First, as discussed in our review of gift taxes, the statute of limitations is suspended, permitting the IRS to examine the estate tax return of any predeceased spouse at any time to determine the appropriate deceased spousal unused exemption amount. While the statute of limitations does not permit the IRS to impose additional taxes on the decedent's estate if the examination is opened after the normal statute of limitations expires, it does permit the service to adjust the amount of the deceased spousal unused exemption amount. This may be of particular concern for estates where valuation discounting is used to manage the value of assets included in the gross estate.

Second, in order to permit a surviving spouse to use the deceased spouse's unused exemption amount, an election must be made, requiring the timely filing of an estate tax return (Form 706). Estates with no tax liability, and those who would otherwise not be required to file may nevertheless wish to file an estate tax return to make this election preserving the deceased spouse's unused exemption amount.

Example 6.36
Continuing with our last example, Dan's estate would not be required to file an estate tax return, since his gross estate is less than the applicable credit amount of $11,580,000. Nevertheless, the executor must file the estate tax return on a timely basis if he would like to transfer Dan's DSUEA of $9,580,000 to Cheryl.

Finally, the legislation makes it quite clear that portability applies only to the last deceased spouse's unused exemption amount. If a surviving spouse remarries, and dies prior to the new spouse, any exemption obtained from the first deceased spouse's estate that remains unused will be lost. The surviving spouse's own unused exemption could be transferred to the new husband, but the first husband's unused exemption that was transferred to the spouse will not be eligible for transfer to the new husband.

Example 6.37

Using the same facts as the prior example, assume that a year after Dan's death, Cheryl marries Armando, and Cheryl dies on the first anniversary of their wedding. Cheryl has a taxable estate of $1 million, and had not made any gifts during her lifetime in excess of the gift tax annual exclusion. Cheryl's executor may elect to transfer Cheryl's DSUEA of $10,180,000 $10,580,000 to Armando, but none of Dan's DSUEA of $9,580,000 can be transferred to Armando. Dan's DSUEA is lost.

Alternatively, if the new spouse dies prior to the surviving spouse, the surviving spouse will be able to use the second spouse's (the "last deceased spouse's") unused exemption, but will lose any remaining unused exemption of the first spouse.

Example 6.38

Continuing with our example, assume that Armando, not Cheryl, dies on the first anniversary of their wedding. Armando had a taxable estate of $7 million, and his DSUEA is 0$4,580,000. Since Armando is Cheryl's last deceased spouse, she will not be able to use Dan's DSUEA of $9,580,000 when she dies.

As might be anticipated, this tax provision may have a non-tax impact, and may encourage individuals who have received a large unused exemption from a predeceased spouse not to remarry. See Chapter 10 for a discussion of DSUEA for gifts and non-citizen spouses.

> **Key Concepts**
>
> 1. Describe the credits available against the tentative estate tax.
> 2. Identify the payment and reporting requirements of the Form 706.
> 3. What penalties are imposed with regard to filing the Form 706 late?

Credit for Tax Paid on Prior Transfers

If property included in a decedent's gross estate was inherited from someone else within the recent past and estate tax was paid at that transfer, a credit is available for the estate taxes paid at that time. The credit is calculated using a percentage limitation based upon the length of time the decedent survived the transferor. The calculation of this credit is beyond the scope of this text, but generally the credit is calculated by multiplying the appropriate percentage from the following table by the attributable estate tax paid at the transferor's death.

Exhibit 6.13 | Credit For Tax Paid on Prior Transfers

Years Between Deaths	Credit Percentage
More than 2, not more than 4	80%
More than 4, not more than 6	60%
More than 6, not more than 8	40%
More than 8, not more than 10	20%
More than 10	0%

Example 6.39

George died in 2020, and had a taxable estate of $15 million. In 2015, George inherited $5 million from his mother, Victoria. Victoria's estate paid $2 million in estate taxes (40% of $5 million) on George's inheritance. Since George died five years after his mother, and $2 million of estate taxes were paid on his inheritance, George's estate is entitled to a $1.2 million prior transfers credit ($2 million x 60%) when calculating his estate tax.

Foreign Death Tax Credit

A credit is allowed against the calculation of the federal estate tax for any estate, inheritance, legacy, or succession taxes paid to a foreign country. The credit is allowed only for foreign death taxes paid:
1. with respect to property situated within the country to which the tax is paid,
2. with respect to property included in the decedent's gross estate, and
3. on behalf of a decedent who was a citizen or resident of the United States at the time of his death.

No credit is allowed for interest or penalties paid in connection with the payment of foreign death taxes.

ESTATE TAX LIABILITY

The federal **estate tax liability** is equal to the tentative tax less any applicable credits available to a decedent's estate.

Exhibit 6.14 | The Abbreviated Estate Tax Formula - Credits

Tentative Tax	$ _____	Tentative Tax
Less: Credits	$ _____	
Equals: Federal Estate Tax Liability	$ _____	Federal Estate Tax Liability

The federal estate tax must be paid by the executor or administrator of a decedent's estate. The entire tax is payable by the estate, regardless of the fact that the gross estate may consist, in part, of property which does not come within the possession of the executor or the administrator. If there is no executor or administrator, any person in actual or constructive possession of any property of the decedent is required to pay the entire tax to the extent of the value of the property in his possession. The executor or administrator will become personally liable to the United States if he pays any other estate debts before paying the debts due to the United States.

If the estate tax is not paid by the due date, then the spouse, transferee, trustee, surviving tenant, person in possession of the property by reason of the exercise, nonexercise, or release of a power of appointment, or beneficiary who receives or possesses on the date of the decedent's death, property included in the gross estate under Sections 2034 through 2042, is personally liable for the tax to the extent of the value, at the time of the decedent's death, of such property.

PAYING AND REPORTING ESTATE TAXES

Filing Requirements

The federal estate tax return, Form 706, must be filed if a decedent's gross estate, plus adjusted taxable gifts, is greater than the applicable estate tax credit equivalency (also called the applicable estate tax exclusion amount) for the year of death. When required, Form 706 and the payment of any estate tax owed is due nine months after the decedent's date of death. The executor may request an extension to file the return for an additional six months by filing IRS Form 4768 within nine months after the decedent's date of death. The executor may also request an extension of time, up to 12 months, to pay the estate tax due if the request is based upon reasonable cause. Form 4768 can also be filed for estates with closely held business interests that exceed 35 percent of the decedent's gross estate, which could allow for installment payments of the estate tax over 14 years (See Section 6166). Any estate tax that cannot be paid at the original due date of the estate tax return will begin to accrue interest, and if an extension has not been granted, penalties will also accrue (as discussed below). Some examples follow that illustrate cases involving reasonable cause for granting an extension of time to pay.

Example 6.40
An estate includes sufficient liquid assets to pay the estate tax when otherwise due. The liquid assets, however, are located in several jurisdictions and are not immediately subject to the control of the executor. Consequently, the assets cannot be readily marshalled by the executor, even with the exercise of due diligence so the executor does not have the funds necessary to pay the estate tax due.

Example 6.41
An estate is primarily comprised of assets consisting of rights to receive payments in the future (i.e., annuities, royalties, contingent fees, or accounts receivable). These assets provide the executor with insufficient present cash to pay the estate tax when due and the estate cannot borrow against these assets except upon terms which would inflict loss upon the estate.

Example 6.42
An estate includes a claim to substantial assets, which cannot be collected without litigation. Consequently, the size of the gross estate is unascertainable as of the time the tax is otherwise due.

Exhibit 6.15 | Form 4768

Form 4768
(Rev. February 2020)
Department of the Treasury
Internal Revenue Service

Application for Extension of Time To File a Return and/or Pay U.S. Estate (and Generation-Skipping Transfer) Taxes

▶ Go to *www.irs.gov/Form4768* for instructions and the latest information.

OMB No. 1545-0181

Part I — Identification

Decedent's first name and middle initial	Decedent's last name	Date of death
Name of executor	Name of application filer (if other than the executor)	**Decedent's social security number**
Address of executor (number, street, and room or suite no.)		Estate tax return due date
City, state, and ZIP code	Domicile of decedent (county, state, and ZIP code)	Daytime telephone number of executor

Part II — Extension of Time To File Form 706, 706-A, 706-NA, or 706-QDT (Section 6081)

Form for which extension of time to file is being requested:
☐ Form 706   ☐ Form 706-A   ☐ Form 706-NA   ☐ Form 706-QDT

Automatic Extension

☐ Check here if you are applying for an automatic 6-month extension of time to file, and the time for filing has not passed.

Extension For Cause/Form 4768 Not Filed In Time For Automatic Extension

☐ Check here if you are applying for an extension of time to file, based on good and sufficient cause, and the time for filing has passed. Also you **must** attach a statement explaining in detail why a request for automatic extension was not timely made, why it was impossible or impractical to file the return by the due date, and the specific reasons why you have good and sufficient cause for not requesting the automatic extension. If granted, the 6-month extension for cause runs from the original due date of the return. See instructions.

Additional Extension

☐ Check here if you are an executor out of the country applying for an extension of time beyond the 6-month automatic extension to file. Also you **must** attach a statement explaining in detail why it was impossible or impractical to file the return by the due date. See instructions.

Enter extension date requested

Part III — Extension of Time To Pay (Section 6161)

You must attach your written statement to explain in detail why it is impossible or impractical to pay the full amount of the estate (or GST) tax by the return due date. If the taxes cannot be determined because the size of the gross estate is unascertainable, check here ▶ ☐ and enter "-0-" or other appropriate amount on Part IV, line 3. You must attach an explanation.

Enter extension date requested (Not more than 12 months)

- If this request is for the tax that will be or was due with the filing of the return, check here . . . . ▶ ☐
- If this request is for the tax that will be due as a result of an amended or supplemental return, check here . . . . ▶ ☐
- If this request is for additional tax due as a result of an examination of your return, check here . . . . ▶ ☐
- If this request is for a section 6166 installment payment, check here . . . . ▶ ☐

Part IV — Payment To Accompany Extension Request

1	Amount of estate and GST taxes estimated to be due	1
2	Amount of cash shortage (complete Part III)	2
3	**Balance due** (subtract line 2 from line 1) (see instructions)	3

Signature and Verification

If filed by executor—Under penalties of perjury, I declare that I am an executor of the estate of the above-named decedent and that to the best of my knowledge and belief, the statements made herein and attached are true and correct.

_____ _____ _____
Executor's signature   Title   Date

If filed by someone other than the executor—Under penalties of perjury, I declare that to the best of my knowledge and belief, the statements made herein and attached are true and correct, that I am authorized by an executor to file this application, and that I am (check applicable boxes):

☐ A member in good standing of the bar of the highest court of (specify jurisdiction) ▶ _____
☐ A certified public accountant duly qualified to practice in (specify jurisdiction) ▶ _____
☐ A person enrolled to practice before the Internal Revenue Service.
☐ A duly authorized agent holding a power of attorney. (The power of attorney need not be submitted unless requested.)

_____ _____
Filer's signature (other than the executor)   Date

Mail to: Internal Revenue Service Center, Attn: Estate & Gift, Stop 824G
7940 Kentucky Drive, Florence, KY 41042-2915

Penalties

If an executor does not request an extension of time to file, or an extension of time to pay, the estate may be subject to penalties. The penalty is a function of the estate tax due times a percentage based on the delay. The failure-to-file penalty is five percent per month up to a maximum penalty of 25 percent. If the failure-to-file is determined to be fraudulent, the penalty is increased to 15 percent per month up to a maximum of 75 percent. The failure-to-pay penalty is 0.5 percent per month up to a maximum penalty of 25 percent. If, in one month, both the failure-to-file penalty and the failure-to-pay penalty apply, the failure-to-file penalty is reduced by the failure-to-pay penalty. For purposes of this calculation, any fraction of a month counts as a full month. Note that the failure to pay and failure to file penalties for estate tax purposes match the rules imposed for income tax purposes.

Example 6.43

The executor files the estate tax return 45 days after the due date and the executor had not requested an extension of time to file or pay. Along with the return she remits a check for $10,000, the balance of the estate tax due. Disregarding any interest which may be assessed, the combined total failure-to-file and failure-to-pay penalties equal $1,000.

The calculation is as follows:

Failure-to-pay penalty:		
[0.5% x $10,000 x 2 (two months, any fraction counts as a full month)]		$100
Plus: Failure-to-file penalty [5% x $10,000 x 2 months]	$1,000	
Less: Failure-to-pay penalty (they run concurrently)	($100)	$900
Total penalties (failure-to-file and failure-to-pay)		$1,000

As illustrated, the failure-to-file penalty of $1,000 is reduced by the failure-to-pay penalty of $100 creating a total failure-to-file penalty of $900. Adding the failure-to-pay penalty of $100 to the failure to file penalty creates a total penalty of $1,000 ($100 + $900).

ADJUSTED BASIS TO HEIRS AND LEGATEES

Generally when an heir receives property from a decedent, the adjusted basis of the property for income tax purposes is the property's fair market value as reported on the decedent's estate tax return. This can be either the fair market value at the decedent's date of death or the alternate valuation date (six months after the date of death) if it was selected. The new adjusted basis is referred to as a "step-to" fair market value basis for the heir because the heir "steps to" the new basis at the date of death or alternate valuation date, if applicable. There are several exceptions to the general rule which are discussed individually below.

The holding period of property acquired from a decedent is always deemed to be long-term (i.e., held for the required long-term holding period). This provision applies regardless of whether the property is disposed of at a gain or loss and regardless of decedent's holding period.

chapter 6

Basis of Property Acquired from a Decedent

The Surface Transportation and Veterans Health Care Choice Improvement Act of 2015 was signed into law in 2015 and added subsection (f) to IRC Section 1014 and added IRC Section 6035. The purpose of these laws is to provide consistency in basis reporting between an estate and anyone acquiring property from the estate. The law provides new reporting requirements, which are effective as of July 31, 2015.

IRC Section 1014 deals with the basis of property acquired from a decedent. Section 1014(f) requires that the basis of property in the hands of the heir be consistent with the value of the property reported on the estate tax return (Form 706) of the decedent. The reason for this rule and the required reporting under IRC Section 6035 is to prevent taxpayers from overstating basis of inherited property. Effective with this change in the law is that overstating basis may be subject to accuracy-related penalties under IRC Section 6662.

The executor of any estate required to file a return (Form 706) shall furnish to the IRS and to each person acquiring any interest in property included in the decedent's gross estate for Federal estate tax purposes a statement identifying the value of each interest in such property as reported on the estate tax return. This requirement allows the IRS to match the basis of inherited assets to the value reported on Form 706 (the estate tax return).

> ### Quick Quiz 6.4
>
> 1. The lifetime applicable estate tax credit amount excludes up to $4,577,800 (for 2020) of cumulative taxable transfers.
>   a. True
>   b. False
>
> 2. A foreign death tax credit is allowable for interest or penalties paid in connection with foreign death taxes.
>   a. True
>   b. False
>
> 3. An extension of time to pay tax at the request of the executor may be granted for a reasonable period of time, not to exceed 12 months.
>   a. True
>   b. False
>
> 4. The failure-to-pay penalty is reduced by the failure-to-file penalty giving the adjusted failure-to-pay penalty.
>   a. True
>   b. False.
>
> False, False, True, False.

IRD Assets

Assets classified as **income in respect of a decedent (IRD)** assets do not qualify for the Section 1014 "step-to" basis adjustment. IRD assets are those resulting from income-tax deferral planning. When a taxpayer has the choice of either recognizing income or deferring that income into the future, an IRD asset is created. Common examples of IRD assets include qualified retirement plans, 401(k) and 403(b) plans, IRAs, annuities, savings bonds, and installment notes. The beneficiary of these assets will have an adjusted basis equal to the decedent's adjusted basis, if any, in the asset. Denying IRD assets a Section 1014 "step-to" basis adjustment ensures that the government will be able to collect the income tax due on the deferred income.

Example 6.44

Over his lifetime, Reginald made regular contributions to his IRA, and always claimed an income tax deduction for the contributions. Reginald died this year when the IRA was worth $400,000, and the total value of his gross estate, including the IRA was $800,000. Since Reginald has an estate under the applicable exemption amount of $11,580,000 (2020), there will be no estate tax due. However, his heirs will have a basis in the IRA equal to Reginald's basis, since the IRA is an IRD asset. When they take distributions from the IRA, the heirs will have to pay income tax on these distributions. Had the step-to basis adjustment of Section 1014 applied, Reginald's heirs would not have had to pay income tax on the IRA accumulation, even though Reginald had constructive receipt over the contributions to the account, but chose to defer the taxes on that income.

Basis in the Hands of an Heir/Donor

If an heir receives property from a decedent that was acquired by the decedent through a gift from the same heir within one year of the decedent's death, the heir/donor takes the decedent's basis (which will be the donor's basis). The heir/donor does not receive a step-to fair market value in the adjusted basis of the property.

Example 6.45

Joey gives property to his son that at the date of gift has a fair market value of $7,000. No gift taxes were paid. Joey has an adjusted basis in the property of $2,300. Joey's son dies within one year of the date of the gift. Joey's son bequeathed the property back to Joey. Because Joey had gifted the property to his son and received it back as an inheritance within one year, Joey's adjusted basis in the property is $2,300 (his original adjusted basis).

Surviving Owner

A decedent's share of property titled as joint tenancy with rights of survivorship will pass to the surviving property owners. After the decedent's death, the survivor determines his basis in the property by adding the value of the property included in the decedent's gross estate to his (the survivor's) original adjusted basis.

Example 6.46

Michael and Jeff owned, as joint tenants with rights of survivorship, land that they purchased for $60,000. Jeff furnished two-thirds of the purchase price and Michael one-third. At the date of Jeff's death, the property had a fair market value of $100,000. Michael figures his new adjusted basis in the property as follows:

Interest Michael bought initially	$20,000
Interest Michael received @ Jeff's death (2/3 of $100,000)(Step-to fair market value)	$66,667
Michael's adjusted basis after Jeff's death	$86,667

chapter 6

Community Property

As discussed in Chapter 3, community property is a form of property ownership between spouses in which each spouse is deemed to own a one-half interest in all of the property acquired during their marriage. Community property does not have an automatic right of survivorship at the death of one spouse. For a decedent who owns community property with his spouse, only one-half of the fair market value of the property is included in the decedent's gross estate.

An heir who receives a decedent's half of community property will receive the one-half interest with an adjusted basis equal to the fair market value at the decedent's date of death or the alternate valuation date, whichever is used on the decedent's estate tax return. The surviving spouse's one-half interest in community property will also receive a step-to fair market value at the decedent's date of death even though it was not included in the decedent's gross estate. This special treatment which gives a step-to fair market value adjusted basis to both halves of the property interest at the death of one spouse is only applicable to community property.

Community property receives an adjustment in adjusted basis to the fair market value on both spouses' shares at the death of the first spouse.

Example 6.47

Ted and his wife, Alice, own a mountain retreat. Ted dies and leaves the property, which has a basis of $200,000 and a fair market value at Ted's date of death of $1,000,000, to Alice. If the property is community property, Alice's new adjusted basis in the property is $1,000,000. If the property is not community-property, Alice's new adjusted basis is $600,000 (her original adjusted basis of $100,000 plus his one-half at the fair market value at his date of death of $500,000).

CUMULATIVE EXAMPLE

The cumulative example in Chapter 4 detailed the calculation of the probate estate. Continuing with that example, we calculate the gross estate and the estate tax due after presenting some additional facts that have been modified for use in this example.

Cody and Reese were married years ago and had one child, Amber. Cody and his longtime friend, Kandi, were recently flying in Kandi's new plane. For a brief period, Kandi was distracted and lost control of the plane. Unfortunately, the plane crashed and Kandi died instantly and Cody died a few days later as a result of the injuries sustained during the crash. When Cody died, he and Reese owned the following property:

- Personal residence valued at $500,000 held tenancy by the entirety. The home had an outstanding mortgage of $200,000.
- Car 1 valued at $10,000 held fee simple by Cody.
- Car 2 valued at $15,000 held joint tenancy with rights of survivorship by Cody and Amber.
- Diamond ring valued at $50,000 held fee simple by Reese.
- Boat valued at $20,000 held tenancy in common by Cody and Amber (equal contribution).
- Life Insurance Policy 1 on Reese's life owned by Cody. The fair market value of the policy was $100,000 and the death benefit was $200,000. The beneficiary is Amber.
- Life Insurance Policy 2 on Cody's life, owned by Cody. The fair market value of the policy was $85,000 and the death benefit was $500,000. The only beneficiary is Kandi.
- IRA account valued at $4,500,000 owned by Cody with Amber as the beneficiary.
- Irrevocable Trust by Cody for the benefit of Amber created five years ago. The trust is valued at $500,000, and Amber is the beneficiary at Cody's death. There were no taxable gifts on the initial or subsequent transfers to the trust.

Note: Unless otherwise stated, assume equal contributions were made by all parties for jointly owned property.

The accident was found to be the fault of the plane manufacturer; therefore, Cody's heirs received $100,000 for wrongful death and $500,000 for his pain and suffering. Cody's last medical expenses were $40,000, his funeral expenses were $30,000, the administrative fees for the estate were $100,000, and he had existing debts of $100,000. Cody's will left $100,000 to a qualifying charity and the remaining probate assets to Reese. His will states that debts and expenses will reduce the assets that will transfer to Reese. The following charts are provided to assist in answering this problem. The solution follows.

chapter 6

Exhibit 6.16 | Gross Estate Calculation (complete the last column)

Asset	Full Value	Cody's Interest	Probate Estate	Gross Estate
Home	$500,000	$250,000	$0	
Car 1	$10,000	$10,000	$10,000	
Car 2	$15,000	$7,500	$0	
Diamond Ring	$50,000	$0	$0	
Boat	$20,000	$10,000	$10,000	
Life Insurance 1	$100,000	$100,000	$100,000	
Life Insurance 2	$500,000	$500,000	$500,000	
IRA	$4,500,000	$4,500,000	$0	
Trust	$500,000	$0	$0	
Wrongful Death	$100,000	$0	$0	
Pain and Suffering	$500,000	$500,000	$500,000	
Total	$6,795,000	$5,877,500	$1,120,000	

Exhibit 6.17 | The Abbreviated Estate Tax Formula (fill in the appropriate amounts)

Gross Estate		_____
Less Deductions:		
Last Medical Expenses	_____	
Administrative Costs	_____	
Funeral Expenses	_____	
Debts of the Decedent	_____	
Losses During the Administration of the Estate	_____	_____
Equals: Adjusted Gross Estate		_____
Less: Unlimited Charitable Deduction	_____	
Less: Unlimited Marital Deduction	_____	
Less: State Death Tax Deduction	_____	_____
Equals: Taxable Estate		_____
Add: Previous Taxable Gifts (post 1976)		_____
Equals: Tentative Tax Base		_____
Tentative Tax		_____
Less: Allowable Credits		
Credit for Previous Gift Tax Paid	_____	
Applicable Estate Tax Credit (Unified Credit)	_____	
Credit for Tax Paid on Prior Transfers	_____	
Foreign Death Tax Credit	_____	
Equals: Federal Estate Tax Liability	_____	_____

Cumulative Example

Example Solutions

Gross Estate Calculation

Note that the pain and suffering award is included in Cody's gross estate because it is personal to Cody, while the proceeds of wrongful death award are not included in Cody's gross estate because it is not personal to Cody.

Asset	Full Value	Cody's Interest	Probate Estate	Gross Estate
Home	$500,000	$250,000	$0	$250,000
Car 1	$10,000	$10,000	$10,000	$10,000
Car 2	$15,000	$7,500	$0	$7,500
Diamond Ring	$50,000	$0	$0	$0
Boat	$20,000	$10,000	$10,000	$10,000
Life Insurance 1	$100,000	$100,000	$100,000	$100,000
Life Insurance 2	$500,000	$500,000	$500,000	$500,000
IRA	$4,500,000	$4,500,000	$0	$4,500,000
Trust	$500,000	$0	$0	$0
Wrongful Death	$100,000	$0	$0	$0
Pain and Suffering	$500,000	$500,000	$500,000	$500,000
Total	**$6,795,000**	**$5,877,500**	**$1,120,000**	**$5,877,500**

Estate Tax Calculation

Gross Estate		$5,877,500	Gross Estate
Less Deductions:			
Last Medical Expenses	$40,000		
Administrative Expenses	$100,000		
Funeral Expenses	$30,000		
Debts of the Decedent	$100,000		
Losses During the Administration of the Estate	$0	$270,000	Deductions
Equals: Adjusted Gross Estate		$5,607,500	Adjusted Gross Estate
Less: Charitable Deduction	$100,000		
Less: Marital Deduction	$1,000,000		
Less: State Death Tax Deduction		$1,100,000	
Equals: Taxable Estate		$4,507,500	Taxable Estate
Add: Previous Taxable Gifts (post 1976)		$0	Post-1976 Gifts
Equals: Tentative Tax Base		$4,507,500	Tentative Tax Base
Tentative Tax		$1,748,800	[1] Tentative Tax
Less: Allowable Credits			
Credit for Previous Gift Tax Paid	$0		
Applicable Estate Tax Credit (Unified Credit)	$1,748,800		
Credit for Tax Paid on Prior Transfers	$0		
Foreign Death Tax Credit	$0	($1,748,800) [2]	
Equals: Federal Estate Tax Liability		$0	Federal Estate Tax Liability

1. Tentative tax on $4,507,500 = $345,800 + (40% x $3,507,500) = $1,748,800
2. Cody has an unused estate transfer credit of $2,829,000 ($4,577,800 - $1,748,800) or the equivalent exclusion of $7,072,500 ($11,580,000 - $4,507,500 x 40%), which his executor filing a timely Form 706 can and should transfer to Reese, his surviving spouse.

Marital Deduction Summary

Asset	Gross Estate	Available for Spouse	Available for Marital Deduction
Home	$250,000	Yes	$250,000
Car 1	$10,000	Yes	$10,000
Car 2	$7,500	No	$0
Diamond Ring	$0	-	$0
Boat	$10,000	Yes	$10,000
Life Insurance 1	$100,000	Yes	$100,000
Life Insurance 2	$500,000	Yes	$500,000
IRA	$4,500,000	No	$0
Trust	$0	-	$0
Pain & Suffering	$500,000	Yes	$500,000
Wrongful Death	$0	-	$0
Total	**$5,877,500**		**$1,370,000**

The marital deduction is determined by adding the assets that transfer to the spouse and subtracting from that amount the amounts that must be paid from the probate estate. The estate can only receive a marital deduction for the amount of assets the surviving spouse actually receives.

Amount available for marital deduction	$1,370,000
Less expenses paid from the amount available for the marital deduction:	
• Medical Expenses	$40,000
• Administrative Expenses	$100,000
• Funeral Expenses	$30,000
• Debts (1/2 of mortgage)	$100,000
• Charitable contribution	$100,000
Total Net Marital Deduction	**$1,000,000**

KEY TERMS

Adjusted Gross Estate - The adjusted gross estate is equal to the gross estate less any deductions for funeral expenses, last medical expenses, administrative expenses, debts, and losses during the administration of the estate.

Alternate Valuation Date - An alternate date, other than the date of death, to value a decedent's gross estate. The alternate valuation date is either six months after the date of death, or if the asset is disposed of within six months of the date of death, the asset's disposition date. Wasting assets do not qualify to use the alternative valuation date.

Blockage Discount - A reduction in the fair market value of a large block of publicly-traded stock because the transfer of a large block of stock is less marketable than other transfers of smaller amounts of stock.

Date of Declaration - The date a board of directors approves and declares a dividend to be paid to its shareholders.

Date of Record - The date that a dividend paying company determines the owners of its stock who are entitled to a dividend (regardless of whether or not the individual owns the stock as of the payment date).

Deceased Spouse's Unused Exclusion (DSUE) -The portion of the $11,180,000 (2018) transfer tax exemption that is not used by a deceased spouse to shield transfers from estate tax that is transferred to the surviving spouse pursuant to an election made by the deceased spouse's executor on a timely filed estate tax return.

Estate Tax Liability - The amount equal to the tentative tax less any applicable credits available to a decedent's estate.

Gross Estate - The gross estate consists of the fair market value of all of a decedent's interests owned at the decedent's date of death plus the fair market value of certain property interests the decedent transferred during his life, in which he retained some rights, powers, use, or possession.

Income in Respect of Decedent (IRD) Assets - Assets that, as a result of income deferral, have built in income that must be recognized by the beneficiary of the asset.

Key Person Discount - A reduction in the fair market value of transferred stock due to an economic reality that the value of the stock will decline if a key person, such as the founder, dies or becomes disabled.

Lack of Marketability Discount - A reduction in the fair market value of a transferred asset because the interest is more difficult to sell to the public.

Minority Discount - A reduction in the fair market value of a transferred interest in property because the interest is not a controlling interest.

Portability - The ability of the executor of an estate to timely file Form 706 to transfer the decedent's unused credit exclusion to the surviving spouse.

Power of Appointment - The power to name who will enjoy or own property.

Reversionary Interest - Interests that have been transferred and subsequently revert back to the transferor. Also, includes a possibility that the property transferred by the decedent may return to him or his estate and a possibility that property transferred by the decedent may become subject to a power of disposition by him.

Straight Single Life Annuity - An annuity for a term equal to the annuitant's life.

Survivorship Annuity - An annuity that provides payments to one person, and then provides payments to a second person upon the death of the first.

Taxable Estate - The adjusted gross estate less the available unlimited marital and unlimited charitable deductions.

Tentative Tax - The estate tax calculated on the tentative tax base.

Tentative Tax Base - The tentative tax base equals the taxable estate plus all post-1976 taxable gifts.

X Dividend Date - The date the market price of a stock adjusts for a declared dividend (i.e., the market price of the stock is reduced approximately by the amount of the dividend).

DISCUSSION QUESTIONS

SOLUTIONS to the discussion questions can be found exclusively within the chapter. Once you have completed an initial reading of the chapter, go back and highlight the answers to these questions.

1. List six assets included in a decedent's gross estate.

2. What is a revocable transfer?

3. If a decedent owns a life insurance policy on his own life, at what value is it included in his gross estate?

4. What is meant by "incidents of ownership" in a life insurance policy?

5. What is a straight single life annuity, and to what extent is its value included in a decedent annuitant's gross estate?

6. What is a general power of appointment?

7. How is real estate valued for purposes of inclusion in a decedent's gross estate?

8. How are publicly traded common stocks valued in a decedent's gross estate?

9. List three valuation discounts.

10. What are the requirements for an estate to elect the alternate valuation date?

11. List three available deductions from a decedent's gross estate.

12. How is the applicable estate tax credit related to the applicable estate tax credit equivalency?

13. Explain the availability of the credit for tax on prior transfers.

14. Under what circumstances may an estate take a credit for foreign death taxes paid?

15. When is a decedent's federal estate tax return due?

16. What is an heir's adjusted basis in property inherited?

17. How is the holding period of inherited property in the hands of the heir calculated?

chapter 6

MULTIPLE-CHOICE PROBLEMS

A sample of multiple choice problems is provided below. Additional multiple choice problems are available at money-education.com by accessing the Student Practice Portal.

1. Jack had been working with an estate planner for several years prior to his death. Accordingly, Jack made many transfers during his life in an attempt to reduce his potential estate tax burden, and Jack's executor, Tom, is thoroughly confused. Tom comes to you for clarification of which assets to include in Jack's gross estate. Which of the following transactions will not be included in Jack's gross estate?
    a. Jack gave $40,000 to each of his three grandchildren two years ago. No gift tax was due on the gifts.
    b. Jack purchased a life insurance policy on his life with a face value of $300,000. Jack transferred the policy to his son two years ago.
    c. Jack and his wife owned their personal residence valued at $250,000 as tenants by the entirety.
    d. After inheriting a mountain vacation home from his mother, Jack gifted the vacation home to his daughter to remove it from his gross estate. Jack continued to use the property as a weekend getaway and continued all maintenance on the property.

2. The gross estate of a decedent who died in the current year would not include which of the following items?
    a. A luxury sedan, valued at $60,000, driven every day by the decedent.
    b. Cash of $1,000,000 given to decedent's daughter two years ago. No gift tax was paid on the transfer.
    c. A bond given to decedent's cousin last year. Gift tax of $4,000 was paid on the transfer.
    d. A home which the decedent owned as tenants by the entirety with his wife.

3. Gus dies owning several shares of an infrequently traded stock. If Gus dies on Wednesday, November 7th, and the stock has the following trading information:
    Monday, 11/5 $31
    Thursday, 11/8 $36
    Monday, 11/12 $28

    What is the per share value (rounded to the nearest dollar) of the stock on the federal estate tax return?
    a. $31.
    b. $33.
    c. $34.
    d. $36.

4. Johnny died eight months ago and his executor is finalizing his estate tax return. The executor has determined that Johnny's gross estate includes $400,000 of real estate, $750,000 of cash and cash equivalents, and $300,000 of qualified retirement plans. The total gross estate is $1,450,000. As the executor reviews the deductions, which of the following will he deduct from the total gross estate to arrive at the adjusted gross estate on his Form 706?
    a. Income in Respect of Decedent (IRD).
    b. Unlimited charitable deduction.
    c. Unlimited marital deduction.
    d. Executor's fee.

5. Jude has begun some estate planning. What is the maximum amount of estate tax Jude can avoid by using the applicable estate tax credit during 2020?
    a. $780,800.
    b. $3,500,000.
    c. $4,577,800.
    d. $11,580,000.

chapter 6

QUICK QUIZ EXPLANATIONS

Quick Quiz 6.1
1. False. Wrongful death actions belong to the survivors, not the decedents and are not included in the decedent's gross estate.
2. False. The alternative valuation date is not available for reversionary interests.
3. True.
4. False. Since there is nothing left to transfer, a straight life annuity is excluded from the decedent's gross estate.

Quick Quiz 6.2
1. True.
2. False. If the alternative valuation date is selected, the assets must be valued six months (not 9 months) after death.
3. True.

Quick Quiz 6.3
1. False. To be deductible for estate tax purposes, funeral expenses must have actually been incurred and, if paid, are under funeral expenses. If unpaid, they are deductible as an estate debt.
2. True.
3. False. Debts, including liabilities arising out of tort litigation, are deductible from the gross estate.
4. False. The taxable estate also includes deductions for funeral expenses, final medical expenses, administrative expenses, debts, and losses during estate administration.

Quick Quiz 6.4
1. False. The lifetime applicable estate tax credit amount excludes up to $11,580,000 (2020) of cumulative taxable transfers.
2. False. A foreign death tax credit is allowed for foreign death taxes paid; it is not permitted for interest and penalties assessed on foreign death taxes.
3. True.
4. False. The failure to file penalty is reduced by the failure to pay penalty giving the adjusted failure-to-file penalty.

7
TRANSFERS DURING LIFE & AT DEATH

LEARNING OBJECTIVES

1. Understand arm's length transactions.
2. Identify transfers to loved ones not subject to gift tax.
3. Describe partial sale/partial gift transactions.
4. Describe full consideration transfers including private annuities and self-canceling installment notes.
5. Describe a GRIT, a GRAT, a GRUT, and a QPRT.
6. Understand the meaning of AFR.
7. Identify the Section 7520 rate.
8. Describe an intentionally defective grantor trust (IDGT).
9. Describe the advantages and disadvantages of a family limited partnership and its usual objectives.
10. Describe transfers at death by will, by contract, and by operation of law.

CFP Board Resource Document - Student-Centered Learning Objectives based upon CFP Board Principal Topics.

INTRODUCTION

Individuals engage in many types of asset transfers throughout their lives. These transfers include transfers to strangers, which are usually arm's-length transactions with each transacting party having the expectation of receiving consideration in terms of fair value in return for whatever was transferred. Lifetime transfers also include transfers to related parties and loved ones. These transfers are often designed to benefit loved ones by transferring property to them gratuitously or at below fair market value (e.g., gift, bargain sale, sales with death options).

Key Concepts

1. Understand why lifetime transfers are more beneficial than those made at death.
2. Define an arm's-length transaction.
3. Define an installment sale.
4. Explain when an installment sale is an arm's-length transaction.

Lifetime Transfers

Chapter 5 identified some of the advantages of gifting property during life versus making bequests at death (see **Exhibit 5.13**). Unlike the discussion of gifts in Chapter 5, this chapter describes many transfers that do not involve gifts, but instead involve sales and other transfers (even between related parties and loved ones). When property is gifted, the fair market value of the property is removed from an individual's gross estate. The value of the property is also removed from the individual's gross estate when it is sold, but the sale does not usually reduce an individual's overall gross estate since the consideration received replaces the fair market value of the property transferred. While there is no immediate impact on the transferor's taxable estate when property is sold for full and adequate consideration, a significant estate planning benefit can be realized over time if the asset sold has significant potential for appreciation and was replaced with an asset with a lower or no growth potential (this is referred to as an asset or estate freeze). This type of planning allows senior family members to transfer the future appreciation on assets out of their estates to junior family members. The result of this type of transfer is that the future appreciation escapes transfer taxes.

Although a sale of property does not qualify for many of the advantages identified in Exhibit 7.1 (such as the annual exclusion, the support exclusion, and the qualified transfers exclusion), the sale of any asset may be advantageous for several reasons. First, when an asset is sold, it is removed from the transferor's gross estate and often replaced with cash or a receivable. Even though the gross estate is not immediately reduced by the sale of the asset, any future appreciation of the value of the sold asset will be excluded from the transferor's gross estate. Second, any future income from the asset after the sale may be excluded from the transferor's income tax and gross estate. Finally, when an individual sells an asset during life, he is subject to capital gains tax on the appreciation above his adjusted basis. The capital gain income tax, when paid, also reduces the transferor's gross estate. The following chart summarizes the similarities and differences between all three techniques.

Exhibit 7.1 | Comparison of Gifts/Bequests and Sales on Gross Estate of Transferor

Transfer Type	Gifts and Lifetime Transfers	Bequests at Death	Sales During Life
Support	Excluded from Gross Estate	N/A	N/A
Qualified Transfers	Excluded from Gross Estate	N/A	N/A
Annual Exclusion	Excluded from Gross Estate	N/A	N/A
Future Appreciation	Excluded from Gross Estate*	Included in Gross Estate	Excluded from Gross Estate
Income on Transferred Assets	Excluded from Gross Estate	Included in Gross Estate	Excluded from Gross Estate
Gift Tax Paid	Excluded from Gross Estate**	N/A	N/A
Income (Capital Gains) Tax Paid	N/A	N/A	Excluded from Gross Estate

* Provided that the grantor does not retain an interest in the property under Sections 2036 - 2038.
** Unless the gift tax is paid on gifts made within three years of death, in which case the gift tax is included in the gross estate under the gross-up rule.

ARM'S-LENGTH TRANSACTIONS

An **arm's-length transaction** is typically a transfer between unrelated parties in the form of a sale, an installment sale, or an exchange. Each of these transactions involves a transfer of property between individuals for valuable consideration based on the fair market value of the transferred property. These types of transfers usually have no impact on the transferor's gross estate or on the transferor's balance sheet until income tax is paid (since the seller may have to recognize gain on the transaction and pay income tax on the gain, the cash outflow for any tax payment reduces the seller's gross estate). While the relative liquidity of a transferor's total assets may change after the transfer, the total value of assets is theoretically equal to what it was prior to the transfer. Arm's-length transactions generally do not attempt to reduce the transferor's gross estate or to economically benefit the transferee. The buyer and the seller enter the transaction with no intent to transfer property to the other at a cost less than fair market value.

Sale

A **sale** is the direct transfer of property to another for money or property of equal fair market value. A sale does not directly affect the gross estate of the seller or the buyer, as each party to the sale has transferred one asset for another asset of equal value.

Example 7.1

Jerry agrees to sell Claude his 47' yacht for $180,000 cash. Before the sale, Jerry's gross estate totaled $980,000, comprised of $800,000 of cash and the yacht with a fair market value of $180,000. Before the sale, Claude's gross estate totaled $1,400,000 of cash. After the sale, Jerry would have a gross estate with the same total of $980,000, but now it would be completely comprised of cash. Claude would have a gross estate with the same total of $1,400,000, but it would be comprised of $1,220,000 of cash and the 47' yacht with a fair market value of $180,000.

Estate planners can consider selling assets with high appreciation potential to younger family members. This type of sale shifts the future appreciation to the younger generation and replaces the transferred property with an asset that will have lower appreciation potential. This type of planning may be particularly appropriate for individuals who have already used their lifetime gift exemption, and wish to make a transfer that does not trigger the imposition of a gift tax.

Installment Sale

An **installment sale** is a sale of property in which the buyer makes a series of installment payments to the seller. The effect of this transaction is that the buyer pays the seller the purchase price of the property over a specified term plus interest at the current market rate. The installment payments are paid in cash over the term of the note, and at the seller's death any outstanding principal of the installment note, including any accrued interest, is included in the seller's gross estate. An installment sale, therefore, does not immediately reduce the fair market value of the seller's gross estate.

> **Quick Quiz 7.1**
>
> 1. A sale is a mutual transfer between individuals of assets with equal fair market values.
>   a. True
>   b. False
> 2. A sale qualifies for the annual exclusion.
>   a. True
>   b. False
> 3. Individuals may enter into arm's-length transactions with loved ones.
>   a. True
>   b. False
>
> *True, False, True.*

Example 7.2

Jackson agreed to sell his vacation property to Barry for $250,000 payable over 10 years at $25,000 per year. Before the sale, Jackson's gross estate totaled $1,250,000 including cash of $1,000,000 and the value of the vacation home. Barry paid Jackson four installment payments, totaling $100,000, but still owed Jackson $150,000 of principal when Jackson died. Jackson consumed the interest payment received on the note, but saved the principal payments. Jackson's gross estate totals $1,250,000, but will be comprised of $1,100,000 of cash and $150,000 of a note receivable from Barry.

An installment sale may be entered into by a related buyer and seller with the intention of accomplishing a planning objective. The agreed upon sales price of the property in the installment sale may be the property's fair market value, but the interest rate charged on the note may not be commensurate with the true level of risk the seller is assuming with the note. The interest rate may be lower than the current market rate of interest or may even be equal to zero. In either case, the buyer benefits because of the lower interest payment required and the seller benefits because he will receive less interest income and will therefore reduce his gross estate by the interest income reduction.

Example 7.3

Carolyn owns a business with a fair market value of $200,000. Carolyn agrees to sell the business to her daughter, Janice, at the fair market value using an installment sale. Since Janice does not have a job, does not have a steady income, and recently filed for bankruptcy, the appropriate interest rate that should be charged on the note is 18 percent. However, Carolyn agrees to set the interest rate at four percent. Because the offered interest rate is lower than the fair market value interest rate, Janice will have a smaller periodic note payment and Carolyn will have less taxable interest income and thus a lower gross estate. Note: the IRS may challenge the transaction, however, and attempt to treat it as a gift/sale transaction or bargain sale.

There is a practical limitation on this planning technique. The interest rate charged on the note may be below the prevailing market rate when considering the risk characteristics of the borrower, but must be at least equal to the **applicable federal rate (AFR)** in order to avoid gift loan treatment. **Exhibit 7.2** shows the annual short-term, mid-term, and long-term rates for May 2020. These rates would be applicable to transactions, for the appropriate term, for May 2020 and up to two months after May 2020.

Exhibit 7.2 | Applicable Federal Rates (AFR)(May 2020)

Short-Term Rate	Mid-Term Rate	Long-Term Rate
≤ 3 Years	> 3 Years - ≤ 9 Years	> 9 Years
0.25%	0.58%	1.15%

An installment sale to a family member structured with a final balloon payment and with only interest paid annually and at the AFR in a low interest rate environment may well benefit the transferee while freezing the value of the transferred property for the transferor. Once the asset is sold to the family member any appreciation will be in the estate of the transferee. Subsequent to the sale, the transferor has a fixed income investment.

If the seller (transferor) dies before the completion of the payments, the balance due plus any accrued interest is included in the seller's gross estate. If the installment sale provides for interest only with a final balloon payment, the installment payments received by the seller are all ordinary income. If the seller has unused losses from other transactions, he can avail himself of installment sale rules permitting him to recognize all capital gains in the year of the sale. If the installment note is structured with both principal and interest payments, the seller will recognize ordinary income to the extent of interest and the remainder of each payment will be divided between capital gain and return of basis.

Example 7.4

Ari, age 55, sells his son Elijah, age 30, an asset with an adjusted taxable basis of $1,000,000 for its fair market value of $2,500,000 over a term of 9 years with an assumed annual interest rate of 0.58% (the mid-term AFR for 9 years). The annual payment for the installment sale is $285,895.45 (calculated below):

>   N   = 9
>   i   = 0.58% (assumed midterm rate)
>   PV = $2,500,000
>   FV = $0
>   PMT = $285,895.45

The first payment Ari receives consists of:

Interest (ordinary income): $2,500,000 x 0.58%	$14,500.00
Capital gain: 60% ($285,895.45 - $14,500.00)	$162,837.27
Return of basis: 40% ($285,895.45 - $14,500.00)	$108,558.18
	$285,895.45

Notice that Ari has now frozen his transferred property at $2,500,000 (the value of the notes). He plans to consume the $285,895.45 during retirement, thus leaving a value on these transferred assets of zero after 9 years.

Meanwhile, suppose that Elijah, his son, achieves an annual 10% return on these same assets. At the end of the 9 years Elijah has $5,894,869.23 (calculated below) less what he paid to Ari $2,573,059.02 ($285,895.45 x 9 payments).

>   N   = 9
>   i   = 10%
>   PV = $2,500,000
>   PMT = $0
>   FV = $5,894,869.23

Ari has managed to transfer $3,321,810.21 ($5,894,869.23 - $2,573,059.02) to Elijah without any transfer taxes and Ari will have zero assets in 9 years from this transfer, if he consumes all of the payments.

Assume Ari had retained ownership of the asset, it appreciated the same way, he consumed the same amount annually ($285,895.45), he died in exactly 9 years, and paid 40% transfer tax, and Elijah was his only heir. Ignoring any consumption, Elijah would have received $1,207,535.17, so the family is better off by approximately $2.1 million, by using the installment sale.

>   N   = 9
>   i   = 10%
>   PV = $2,500,000
>   PMT = <$285,895.45>
>   FV = $2,012,558.61
>   x 0.60 (1 - 0.40)
>   Net = $1,207,535.17

Note: Elijah cannot sell the asset within two years without triggering the entire capital gain to Ari because of related party rules as they are applied to installment sales. Also, while Ari may forgive the indebtedness as it comes due under the notes there can be no pre-existing plan to do so. Otherwise, the asset will be included in his gross estate.

Exchange

An **exchange** is a mutual transfer of assets of equal fair market values between individuals. Like the installment sale and the outright sale, an exchange will not immediately impact a transferor's gross estate.

Example 7.5
Martin and Jesse each owned a car with a fair market value of $36,000, and the two agreed to an even exchange for each other's car. After the exchange of the cars, both Jesse and Martin would have gross estates equal to their gross estates before the exchange, only now their estates are comprised of different assets.

Similar to an outright sale or an installment sale, an exchange can be used to accomplish a similar outcome of removing future appreciation from an estate. However, exchanges are not used as frequently as sales and other estate planning techniques.

TRANSFERS TO LOVED ONES

As used in this text, the term "loved ones" denotes both related parties (family members) and other intended beneficiaries who are not technically related parties. Transfers of assets to loved ones can be structured as an arm's-length transaction in the same way as transfers to strangers (through sale, installment sale, or exchange). However, there are additional transfer methods that are designed to benefit a transferee loved one that would not be used with any unrelated or non-loved-one party. These include an installment sale with a low AFR or interest rate, partial sale-gift transactions, outright gifts, gifts in trusts, transactions that use minority and liquidity discounts (usually gifts), and transfers that are not subject to the gift tax rules. Each one of these transfers, other than the installment sale at low AFR, is examined separately below.

> ### Key Concepts
> 1. List three common examples of transfers not subject to gift tax.
> 2. What is the term of a private annuity?
> 3. What are the income tax consequences of a SCIN to the seller?
> 4. How is the buyer's adjusted basis determined in property acquired in a private annuity?

Transfers Not Subject to Gift Tax

Chapter 5 covers transfers to loved ones that are not subject to gift tax. These transfer techniques include those used to satisfy legal support obligations, qualified transfers, and below-market rate loans. As you may recall from Chapter 5, transfers not subject to gift tax reduce an individual's gross estate without using the annual exclusion or the individual's lifetime gift exemption.

Example 7.6
A grandparent pays medical school or law school tuition for a grandchild. The payments are made directly to the institutions and are treated as qualified transfers not subject to gift tax. These tuition payments immediately reduce the grandparent's gross estate without using any of the grandparent's annual exclusion or applicable estate tax credit.

Example 7.7
Dave's wife has a gross estate that falls below the applicable gift and estate tax exemption of $11,580,000 for 2020. Dave can give his wife an amount equal to the difference between his wife's gross estate and the applicable gift and estate tax exemption without incurring gift taxes, thus lowering Dave's gross estate without using any of his applicable gift and estate tax credit amount. Dave's wife will be able to fully use her applicable estate tax credit amount in the event that she dies before Dave. Dave is able to make this transfer because of the unlimited marital deduction.

Gifts Outright and in Trust

When an individual makes a gift, either outright or in trust, the gifted property is transferred to the donee or to the trustee of the trust. As discussed in Chapter 5, the donor of the property may be required to file a gift tax return, depending upon the value of the gifted property, and must also determine whether the gift qualifies as a present or future interest gift. Recall that the annual exclusion is available to offset the gift tax consequences of the transfer only if the gift is a gift of a present interest.

Usually, outright gifts and gifts in trust are reserved for transfers to loved ones. Ideally these gifts are gifts of a present interest and qualify for the annual exclusion, reduce the transferor's gross estate (since the donor relinquishes all control), and remove future appreciation of the gifted property from the transferor's gross estate. Also, if gift tax is paid after full use of the applicable lifetime gift tax credit, the gift tax paid from the transferor's gross estate is also removed from the transferor's gross estate if the transferor lives at least three years following the date of such gift.

Example 7.8
In 2020, Felix started a company with 1,000 shares of stock. Felix's capital contribution was $1,000 or $1 per share. After his contribution, Felix immediately gifted 100 shares of the stock to his daughter, and filed a gift tax return showing the fair market value of the gift to be $100 (100 shares x $1). This gift is exempt from gift tax because it is a gift of a present interest and Felix can use his annual exclusion. (Note that if this was Felix's only gift this year, he would not be required to file a gift tax return, but he may choose to file return for the purpose of starting the statute of limitations on the transaction.) Two years later, in 2022, when Felix's company was worth $200,000 ($200 per share) Felix transferred 100 shares to his daughter, and filed a gift tax return valuing the transfer at $15,000 which is equal to the annual exclusion of $15,000 ((100 x $200) = $20,000 less minority and marketability discounts of 25%). Felix attached an appraisal done by a competent independent appraiser to his tax return. In 2023, after the three-year statute of limitations expired on both gifts, the company was sold for $5,000,000, or $5,000 per share. Felix has successfully transferred approximately $1,000,000 (200 shares x $5,000) to his daughter while only using his annual exclusions to make the gifts. (This example

assumes that the valuation was proper in 2020, that the combined minority and marketability discounts of 25% were appropriate, and that the annual exclusion in 2022 remains at $15,000.)

As discussed in Chapter 5, when direct outright gifts are made, the value of the gifted property for gift tax purposes should be documented with a proper appraisal report if the gifted property is not cash, marketable securities, or if a valuation discount is claimed when valuing the property. Because the reported value on the gift tax return may be challenged by the IRS, the transferor should file a gift tax return to begin the running of the statute of limitations (generally 3 years). Any increase in the fair market value of the property under audit by the IRS will subject the transferor to additional gift tax, potential tax penalties, and interest. Under IRC Section 6501(c)(9), the IRS can challenge, at any time in the future, any gifts that are not properly disclosed on a gift tax return.

Partial Sale-Gift Transactions

When an individual sells an asset for an amount less than the asset's fair market value, the seller is deemed to have made a gift to the buyer equal to the difference between the fair market value of the property and the actual sales price. These combination sale-gift transactions, also known as bargain sales, generally occur between family members since the seller will only realize a discounted price from the sale in an effort to transfer the property to a family member at a reduced cost. Usually the gift amount (the discount from fair market value) would not exceed the seller's (donor's) annual exclusion or remaining applicable lifetime gift tax credit equivalency amount.

With a bargain sale, the property is removed from the transferor's gross estate and is replaced by a reduced amount equal to the consideration paid by the buyer. Any appreciation or income on the property after the transaction is completed is attributable to the buyer/donee.

Example 7.9
Larry owned an office building with a fair market value of $12,595,000. He wants to transfer the property to his son, Greg, but does not want to pay any gift tax on the transfer and wants to benefit Greg in the transfer. Larry agrees to sell the building to Greg for $1,000,000 (a $11,595,000 discount from the fair market value). The discount of $11,595,000 is treated as a present interest gift eligible for the annual exclusion ($15,000), and a taxable gift of $11,580,000. Since Larry has not made any prior taxable transfers, the $11,580,000 taxable gift will be offset by Larry's applicable lifetime gift tax exclusion and no gift tax will be due. Greg will have purchased the building at a discount and all future appreciation and income from the property will be his.

Full Consideration Transfers/Sales

There are some transfers for full and adequate consideration (typically structured as a sale of property), intended to benefit transferee loved ones, that a transferor would not typically consider with an arm's-length transferee. These transfers include private annuities and self-canceling installment notes (SCIN).

Private Annuities

A **private annuity**, unlike a commercial annuity, is a transaction between two (usually related) private parties. The seller/annuitant sells an asset to a buyer generally in exchange for an unsecured promise from the buyer to make fixed payments to the annuitant for the remainder of the annuitant's life. A common age for a transferor to consider using a private annuity is at retirement to produce retirement income for the transferor and transfer an appreciating asset to the next or later generation. The annuity term is equal to the life expectancy of the seller/annuitant based on the annuitant's age at the date of sale. The interest rate used for determining the interest portion of each payment and the present value of the private annuity is the **Section 7520 rate**. (The Section 7520 rate equals 120% of the Federal Midterm Rate.) While the life expectancy of the annuitant (as determined by the IRS mortality tables) is used for income tax and financial calculations, a private annuity requires payments to be made over the lifetime of the seller/annuitant which may fall short of or exceed the life expectancy found in the IRS mortality tables. By selling the asset as a private annuity, the annuitant receives a constant stream of income for the remainder of his life, and removes the asset transferred and any of its subsequent appreciation from his gross estate.[1] Following the proposed regulations, the entire capital gain would be recognized in the year of the sale. If the entire capital gain is recognized then the sale could be secured.

Exhibit 7.3 illustrates the application of a private annuity with an individual whose life expectancy is 16 years as of the date of the sale. The annuity payment is calculated using a term of 16 years. If the seller outlives his life expectancy, the annuity payments continue until the seller's death (21 years after the sale is assumed in the exhibit). On the other hand, if the seller dies prior to the term of 16 years, the annuity payments terminate at the seller's death (seven years after the sale is assumed in the exhibit).

---

1. In October of 2006, the IRS promulgated a set of proposed regulations that taxes the annuitant in the year when the private annuity is made. As of this writing, the IRS has not made final regulations. Therefore, an annuitant should still be able to defer any gain over his or her life expectancy.

Exhibit 7.3 | Private Annuity Graphical Illustration

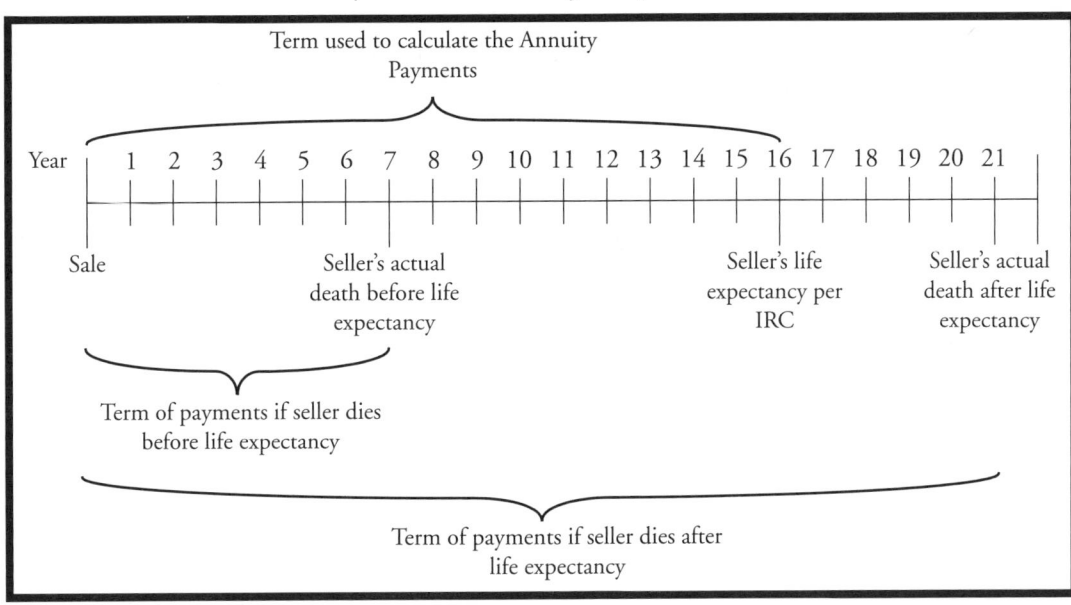

Gift and Estate Tax Consequences of Private Annuities

Provided the fair market value of the property transferred is equal to the present value of the life annuity, there is no taxable gift upon the sale of the property in exchange for the private annuity. Since the annuitant does not have any right to annuity payments after his death, the value of the private annuity is zero at the death of the annuitant and is not included in the seller/annuitant's gross estate. Any annuity payments received before the seller's death will be included in the seller's gross estate to the extent the funds are not consumed. This technique of transferring assets without triggering transfer tax is particularly effective when the actual life expectancy of the annuitant is substantially less than the table life expectancy. In such a case, the annuitant is not expected to reach his life expectancy and the asset transferred in exchange for the private annuity plus its future appreciation is transferred to the buyer without the imposition of transfer taxes and without use of the applicable estate or gift tax credit amount. To prevent abuse in this planning area, Treasury Regulations prohibit the use of private annuities if the seller/annuitant is terminally ill. If, however, the annuitant survives for at least eighteen months after the date of the sale, it is presumed that he was not terminally ill as of the date of the sale.

Risks

A private annuity involves investment risks for both the seller/annuitant and the buyer. The annuitant is selling an asset in return for an unsecured promise to receive payments from the buyer. The seller bears the risk that the buyer will not make the required payments (default risk). Additionally, the annuitant has purchasing power risk, interest rate risk, and reinvestment risk due to the receipt of serial payments over a period of time. The buyer, on the other hand, bears the risk that the annuitant will substantially outlive his life expectancy, thus requiring the buyer to continue paying the annuitant until the annuitant's death. If this happens, the buyer will pay significantly more than he would have paid if he bought the property in an outright sale or for an installment note. The buyer also has business risk; the risk that the asset is not worth the value of the annuity or the risk that the value of the business declines significantly after the transaction.

Income Tax Issues
Annuitant

If the 2006 proposed regulations are not followed, each private annuity payment is split into three components: (1) interest (at the Section 7520 interest rate in effect at the date of the sale), (2) capital gain, and (3) income-tax free return of capital (adjusted basis).

Example 7.10

Father, age 70, sells his business to his son. The fair market value of the business is $2,000,000 and father's adjusted basis is $1,200,000. The assumed Section 7520 rate for the month of the sale is 6% and father's life expectancy according to the IRS life expectancy table is 16 years. What is the yearly payment from son to father? What amount of each payment is capital gain, ordinary income and return of capital?

To calculate the answer, follow these steps:

1. Calculate the yearly payment using simple time value of money.
   N = 16
   PV = $2,000,000
   i = 6%
   FV = 0
   PMT_{OA} = $197,904.29

2. Multiply the yearly payment by the number of years the payments are expected to be made. This is the total payment expected to be made.
   $197,904.29 x 16 payments = $3,166,468.64, or

3. Divide the adjusted basis by the total expected payments. This is the exclusion ratio.
   $$\frac{\text{Adjusted Basis}}{\text{Total Expected Payment}} = \text{Exclusion Ratio}$$
   $$\frac{\$1,200,000}{\$3,166,468.64} = 37.9\%$$

4. Multiply the yearly payment by the exclusion ratio. This is the return of adjusted basis.
   Annual Payment x Exclusion Ratio = Return of Adjusted Basis
   $197,904.29 x 37.9% = $75,005.73

5. Subtract the adjusted basis from the current fair market value and divide by the number of expected payments. This is the yearly capital gain portion.

   $2,000,000 Fair Market Value
   - $1,200,000 Adjusted Basis
   $800,000 Total Capital Gain
   ÷16
   $50,000 Annual Capital Gain Recognized

---

6. Subtract both the return of adjusted basis and the capital gain from the yearly annuity payment. This determines the interest portion.

$197,904.29 Yearly Annuity Payment
- $75,005.73 Return Basis Component
- $50,000.00 Capital Gain Component
$72,898.56 Interest and Ordinary Income Component

In this example, if the father died unexpectedly from a heart attack two years after the sale, he was able to transfer $2,000,000 of property out of his gross estate while only receiving payments of $395,808.58 ($197,904.29 x 2) from his son. If the property appreciated at a rate of 10% per year, the father transferred $2,420,000 in value ($2,000,000 at 10% appreciation per year for two years), received $395,808.58 in return and did not pay any transfer (gift or estate) taxes.

If the 2006 proposed regulations are followed, the entire $800,000 gain must be recognized in the year of transfer. However, any future appreciation would not be in the transferor's gross estate. Most experts think that the proposed regulations seriously diminish the usefulness of private annuities as an estate transfer technique.

Financial Impact on the Buyer

The buyer makes the serial payment consisting of the interest and principal. The interest payments are nondeductible for income tax purposes, and the buyer's adjusted basis in the property that is exchanged for the private annuity is equal to the total of all annuity payments actually paid. If the seller/annuitant dies shortly after the transfer, the buyer will have a low basis in the asset, which will require payment of capital gains tax if the asset is later sold. The increase in capital gains tax, however, will likely be more than offset by the estate tax savings.

Self-Canceling Installment Notes (SCIN)

Another transfer device that can be used when the transferor is in poor health is the **self-canceling installment note (SCIN)**. The SCIN transaction involves a sale for the full fair market value of the property transferred over a term defined by the seller. The unique feature of a SCIN is that if the seller dies before all of the installment payments have been made, the note is canceled and the buyer has no further obligations. In this instance, the seller is taking the risk that he will die before receiving all payments under the SCIN and as a result must be compensated for this risk. The buyer will pay a premium, called a SCIN premium, to compensate the seller for this risk. All else equal, therefore, the buyer will pay more for property sold by a SCIN than he would pay in a straight installment sale. Unlike the private annuity, where the seller usually cannot take a security interest in the underlying property, a SCIN can be secured.

Exhibit 7.4 illustrates the application of a SCIN with an individual whose life expectancy is 16 years from the date of the sale. The SCIN payment is determined using the IRC life expectancy factor, which is the maximum term of the SCIN. However, if the seller dies prior to his life expectancy (seven years as illustrated in the exhibit) the SCIN payments terminate at that point.

Exhibit 7.4 | SCIN Graphical Illustration

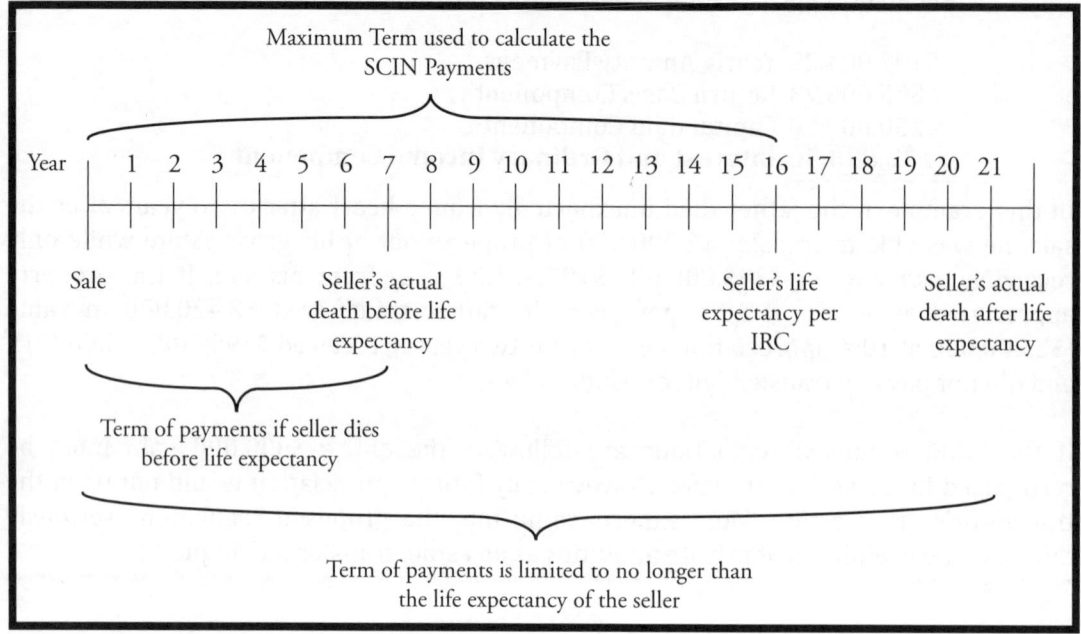

Gift and Estate Tax Consequences

The property transferred by a SCIN is removed from the seller's gross estate, but the payments received will, if not consumed, be included in the seller's gross estate. There is no gift involved in a SCIN provided the present value of the note less the SCIN premium is equal to the fair market value of the asset transferred, and the SCIN premium is appropriate for the mortality risk of the transferor and the value transferred. Like the private annuity, the SCIN is typically used when the transferor is in poor health and expected to die before the end of the defined SCIN term. The SCIN term cannot exceed the life expectancy as determined by the IRS tables or there will be a retained interest subjecting the entire asset to inclusion in the gross estate of the transferor.

Income Tax Consequences - Buyer/Seller

A SCIN is classified for tax purposes as an installment sale. The buyer will make serial payments of interest and principal. Unlike the tax treatment that applies to private annuities, the interest paid by the buyer for a SCIN is deductible if permitted by the Code (for example, business interest, qualified residence interest, or investment interest). In addition, the buyer's adjusted basis in the property, regardless of the number of installment payments made, is the agreed upon purchase price of the property which includes the full face value of the remaining note payments.

The seller receives the installment payments in three components:
1. interest income,
2. capital gain,
3. return of adjusted basis, and also receives the SCIN premium as either additional interest income or capital gain depending upon how the SCIN premium was calculated.

Risks

The seller of property under a SCIN undertakes default risk, interest rate risk, purchasing power risk, and reinvestment risk. The buyer's risk is that the transferor outlives the SCIN term, and thus the buyer pays more for the property, by an amount equal to the SCIN premium, than he would have paid under a normal installment sale. The buyer also has business risk (the risk the asset is not worth the value of the note). One unfavorable consequence of a SCIN is that at the seller's death, the remaining capital gain that would have been due from future payments is deemed transferred. The difference between the seller/decedent's adjusted basis and the original sales price will be recaptured on the estate's income tax return (Form 1041). The upside of this is that the buyer will set the original sales price as his cost basis, despite the reality of how much he actually paid.

Calculating the Annual Payment (the SCIN Premium)

There are two ways to calculate the value of the self-canceling feature (the SCIN premium):
1. Add a value to the asset transferred to reflect the value of the right to cancel and the risk to the seller that the remaining notes may be canceled.
2. Increase the interest rate to reflect a SCIN premium interest rate that reflects the mortality risk.

It would be unusual to attempt to value an asset including the mortality risk, as most valuation experts are not equipped to value the mortality risk. Therefore, it is common that the risk premium (SCIN premiums) is reflected in the interest rate.

To calculate the payments on a note for $1 million, the payments must be adjusted for the probability that the transferor is alive to receive the payments. Multiplying the future payments by a probability of being alive requires higher payments to equal the same FMV today.

Exhibit 7.5 | Determining the Probability of Living One Additional Year

Excerpt from Table 2000CM: Table 2000CM provides the probability of living to the stated age. The probability at birth of living to age 30 is almost 98 percent.

Age x	l_x
25	98202
26	98111
27	98022
28	97934
29	97844
30	97750
31	97652
32	97549
33	97441
34	97324
35	97199
36	97065

Age x	l_x
62	85691
63	84620
64	83465
65	82224
66	80916
67	79530
68	78054
69	76478
70	74794
71	73001
72	71092
73	69056

Age Range	Probability of living one year for the age range indicated
62 to 63	0.98750
63 to 64	0.98635
64 to 65	0.98513
65 to 66	0.98409
66 to 67	0.98287

The probability of living from one year to another is determined by dividing the factor value for the older year by the factor value for the younger year. The result is the probability of surviving that one year. For example, the probability of living from age 62 to age 63 is determined by dividing 84620 by 85691, which results in a probability of 0.98750.

Example 7.11

A five-year note of $1 million to a 62-year-old using Table 2000 CM tables and an assumed Section 7520 rate of 1.2% would be:

$$\text{Age } 62 - 63 = P_1 = 0.98750$$
$$\text{Age } 63 - 64 = P_2 = 0.98635$$
$$\text{Age } 64 - 65 = P_3 = 0.98513$$
$$\text{Age } 65 - 66 = P_4 = 0.98409$$
$$\text{Age } 66 - 67 = P_5 = 0.98287$$

$$PV = \frac{P_1 PMT}{1.012^1} + \frac{P_2 PMT}{1.012^2} + \frac{P_3 PMT}{1.012^3} + \frac{P_4 PMT}{1.012^4} + \frac{P_5 PMT}{1.012^5}$$

$$PMT = \frac{\$1,000,000}{\sum_{N=1}^{5}\left(\frac{P_N}{1.012^N}\right)} = \frac{\$1,000,000}{4.753590} = \$210,367.32$$

The calculation requires adjustments for the probability of the transferor living through the year (e.g., 62-63=0.98850). The annual payment necessary using the Section 7520 rate is $210,367.43. Recalculating the i for this payment yields an i of 1.708592 (rounded). Note that if the five-year annual AFR was 0.95 percent, it and would be used for an installment sale. For example, the payment for a $1,000,000 installment sale over five years would be $205,735.93. Therefore, the SCIN premium in dollars is $22,511.33 ($1,022,511.33 - $1,000,000) at 0.95%. The SCIN premium interest rate is 0.758592% or (1.708592 - 0.95), the excess of the Section 7520 rate over the AFR and combined with the mortality risk (P_1-P_5).

In a low-interest rate environment, a SCIN from a transferor in ill health may be an especially attractive transfer technique. Imagine that the asset appreciates at 10 percent annually and the transferor only lives two years.

Generally, the life expectancy will be determined by mortality tables 2000 CM even when ill health is a factor. However, the IRS requires disclosure of terminal illness or poor health, but defines terminal illness as "incurable illness or other deteriorating physical condition that would substantially reduce a persons life expectancy to the extent that there is a 50 percent or greater probability that the individual will not survive for more than one year from the date of valuation."

SCIN vs. Private Annuity

Both the SCIN and the private annuity are full consideration sales between related parties entered into for the purpose of transferring property at a reduced cost to the buyer and reducing the seller's gross estate. As discussed above, each has its own advantages and disadvantages which may fit particular situations. For example, SCIN payments only continue until the death of the seller or the end of the SCIN term, whereas private annuity payments continue for the life of the seller.

Additionally, a SCIN permits the seller to keep a security interest in the property sold. For a seller who is concerned about the default risk of the buyer, the use of a SCIN provides security because the seller could reclaim the property sold in the event the buyer defaults.

From the buyer's perspective, a SCIN allows the buyer to deduct the portion of the SCIN payment attributable to interest if the property purchased is business, investment property, or a personal residence, whereas interest associated with a private annuity payments is nondeductible. A SCIN also provides the buyer an adjusted basis in the property purchased equal to the agreed upon purchase price of the property, but the adjusted basis for property acquired by private annuity is the sum of the annuity payments actually paid to the seller. Both of these differences will substantially affect the buyer's tax liability during the term of the payments and after the seller's death. Each individual situation, as well as the buyer's intentions, should be considered when arranging a transfer as either a private annuity or a SCIN.

> **Quick Quiz 7.2**
>
> 1. The private annuity can be secured?
>   a. True
>   b. False
> 2. The SCIN is the same as an installment sale.
>   a. True
>   b. False
> 3. The SCIN level premium is like a term insurance premium over a declining value.
>   a. True
>   b. False
>
> *False, False, True.*

Exhibit 7.6 | SCIN vs. Private Annuity

	SCIN	Private Annuity
Term of Payment	Determined by Seller (not to exceed life expectancy)	Life of Annuitant
Deductibility of Interest	Depends on Property	None
Buyer's Adjusted Basis	Purchase Price of Property	Sum of Annuity Payments Actually Paid
Seller May Retain Security Interest	Yes	Not Generally

Grantor Retained Trusts

Grantor retained trusts include Grantor Retained Income Trusts (GRITs), Grantor Retained Annuity Trusts (GRATs), and Grantor Retained Unitrusts (GRUTs). These trusts are irrevocable and are used to transfer assets from one family member to another (or some other loved one) over time while retaining an income stream for the grantor during the trust term. The value of the gift to the beneficiary is determined by reducing the FMV of the donated property by the value of the retained interest or income stream. This income stream can be in the form of an income interest, an annuity payment or a unitrust payment.

> **Key Concepts**
> 1. Discuss the risks of creating a GRAT.
> 2. Who receives the annuity payment in a typical GRAT?
> 3. What is the value of a gift in a GRIT where the remainderman is a family member?

This technique allows for the transfer of an asset at a discounted gift tax value, since the beneficiary does not receive the property until the end of the trust term and the technique removes the future appreciation of the asset from the grantor's estate. A GRAT is successful in removing appreciating property from the estate as long as the grantor lives beyond the trust term. To be successful, the growth rate of the asset contributed to the trust must exceed the required interest rate, known as the 7520 rate.

Grantor Retained Income Trusts (GRIT)

Grantor retained income trusts are irrevocable trusts in which the grantor retains an income interest in the trust for the term of the trust. Thus, the grantor will donate property to the trust and the income from the asset will be distributed to the grantor during the term of the trust. At the end of the trust term, the remaining property is distributed to the beneficiary (remainderman).

These types of trusts are used to transfer property at a lower gift tax value to beneficiaries. The value of the gift equals the FMV of the property transferred minus the value of the retained annuity interest. The value of the income interest that is retained by the grantor equals the present value of the income stream based on the 7520 rate.

Notice that the valuation of the income stream does not have anything to do with the true income in the trust. The value of the retained interest is the same whether the contributed asset produces a lot of income or a minimal amount of income. As a result, non-income producing assets were often contributed to GRITs so that more appreciation could be transferred at a lower gift tax.

However, Chapter 14 of the Internal Revenue Code, which was added by the Revenue Reconciliation Act of 1990, severely limited the use of GRITS. Specifically, IRC Section 2702 values the retained interest at zero when the transfer is to a family member. The result of this is that a transfer (the gift) to a family member in a GRIT will be valued at 100 percent of the FMV. There is no offset for the retained income interest. While this code section greatly limits the benefits of the GRIT for inter-family transfers, the definition of family creates an opportunity that is discussed below. Family is defined as a spouse, lineal descendants of the grantor or the spouse, any siblings or a spouse of a sibling.

IRC Section 2702 provides for exceptions to the zero valuation of the retained interest for a retained interest of a personal residence (see discussion of QPRT), or an annual annuity or unitrust payment (see GRAT and GRUT). The limitations under this code section are one of the primary reasons that GRATs are popular today, instead of GRITs.

As mentioned above, the definition of family for this code section allows for GRITs to be used when transfers are to be made to "non-family" members. This type of transfer could benefit couples who are not married, since the partners would not be considered family members of each other. In these situations, the GRIT continues to be feasible. With the Supreme Court striking down DOMA (Defense of Marriage Act), GRITs are no longer an effective planning technique for spouses of same-sex marriage. However, they remain viable for unmarried couples.

Grantor Retained Annuity Trust (GRAT)

A **grantor retained annuity trust (GRAT)** is an irrevocable trust that pays a fixed annuity to the grantor for a defined term and pays the remainder interest of the trust to a non-charitable beneficiary at the end of the GRAT term. The GRAT is funded by the grantor with a transfer of property, and the annuity can be a stated dollar amount, fixed fraction, or a percent of the initial fair market value of the property transferred to the GRAT. The following exhibit illustrates the formation and application of a GRAT and provides a comparison to a GRIT.

Exhibit 7.7 | Formation of a GRAT v. GRIT

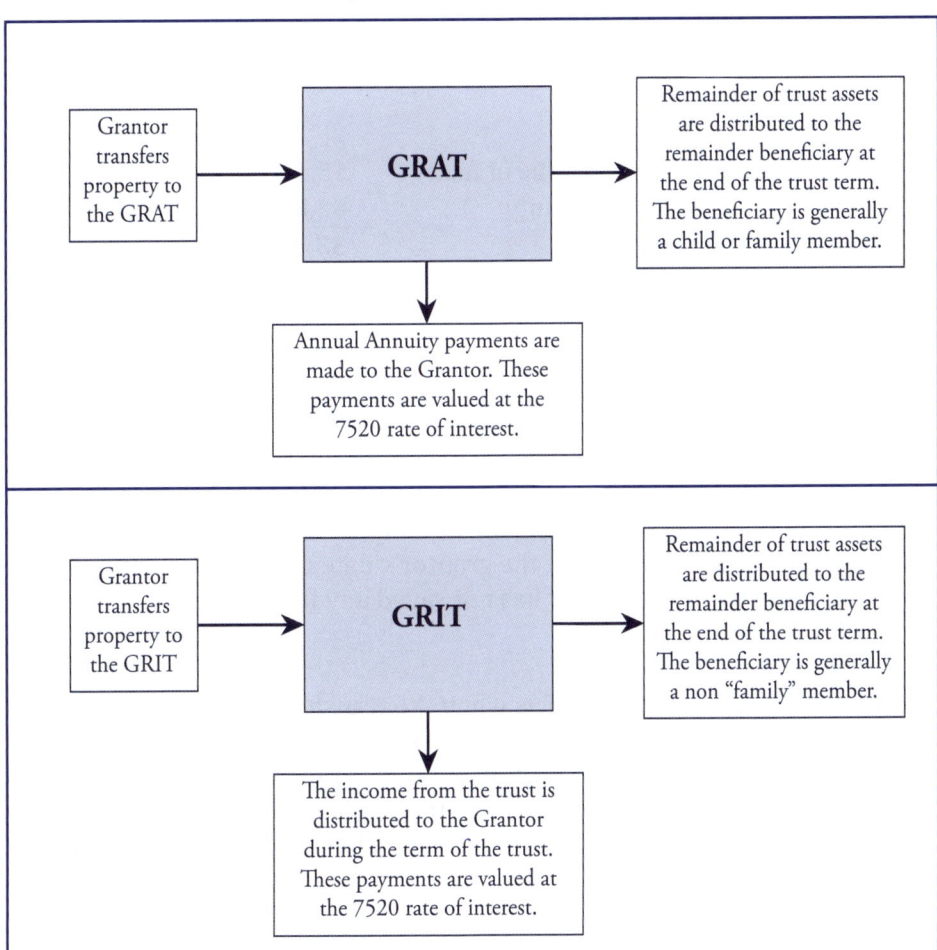

Gift and Estate Tax Consequences

At the creation of a GRAT, assuming the retained annuity interest is payable to the grantor, the annuity portion is not subject to gift tax. However, the present value of the expected future remainder interest is a gift of a future interest subject to gift tax. The value of the remainder interest is determined by subtracting the present value of the expected future annuity payments from the fair market value of the original transfer to the GRAT. If the investment rate of return exceeds the Section 7520 rate, the GRAT will successfully pass wealth to the remainder beneficiaries.

Example 7.12

Rowan, age 55, transfers a business with a fair market value of $5,450,000 to a GRAT with a term of 10 years. Assume the Section 7520 interest rate at the date of transfer is 1.2% and Rowan retains an annual annuity payment of $213,436 from the trust. The remainder beneficiary is Rowan's son Remy. What is the taxable gift at the date of transfer?

N = 10 Years
PMT = $213,436
i = 1.2%
PV = $2,000,000

Fair Market Value of Asset	$5,450,000
Less PV of Annuity	$2,000,000
Taxable Gift	**$3,450,000**

Rowan can use a portion of his applicable lifetime gift tax exclusion to transfer the asset to Remy, and if Rowan outlives the GRAT term, the entire asset has transferred to Remy without being subject to any transfer tax.

The term of the annuity is defined by the grantor. The longer the term, the higher the present value of the annuity payments and thus the lower the value of the remainder interest for gift tax purposes. However, if the grantor of the GRAT dies during the annuity term, the amount necessary to replace the annuity payments specified in the GRAT, as of the grantor's date of death, is included in his gross estate under Section 2036. If this occurs, the grantor has not saved any transfer tax.

Appreciating Property

An appropriate time to consider using a GRAT is when the transferor holds property that is expected to appreciate at a rate greater than the Section 7520 interest rate applicable to the GRAT. At the end of the GRAT term, (provided the grantor survives the annuity term) the property will transfer to the remaindermen. In this situation, the grantor will have transferred the appreciated remainder interest in the property at a gift tax cost calculated using the present value of the remainder interest at the date of transfer.

Example 7.13

In 2020, Eric, age 55, transfers $12,580,000 to a 10-year GRAT. The remainderman is Eric's only child, Andrew. Assume the Section 7520 rate is 1.2%. Eric retains an annual annuity payment of $106,718 yielding a present value of the retained interest of $1,000,000 and a future interest taxable gift of $11,580,000, against which Eric can use his applicable gift tax exclusion, and thus pay no gift tax.

PMT = $106,718
N = 10
i = 1.2%
PV = $1,000,000 (Present Value of Retained Annuity Interest)
Gift = $11,580,000
Value of Property Contributed to GRAT ($12,580,000) less Value of Retained Annuity Interest ($1,000,000) = Value of Remainder Interest ($11,580,000)

If the property transferred to the GRAT actually appreciates at 10% annually, the growth in excess of the assumed Section 7520 rate, 1.2%, will be transferred to the remaindermen transfer tax free. The following chart illustrates the growth of the property and the amount that will transfer to the remainder beneficiary using assumptions.

Assuming that all works as planned, (Eric lives through the 10 years and annually consumes the $106,718 annuity) Eric will transfer to Andrew $30,928,469, the value of the asset at the end of the GRAT term, by simply using his applicable gift tax exclusion in 2020.

Year	Beginning Balance	10% Growth	Annuity Payment	Ending Balance
1	$12,580,000	$1,258,000	($106,718)	$13,731,282
2	$13,731,282	$1,373,128	($106,718)	$14,977,692
3	$14,997,692	$1,499,769	($106,718)	$16,390,743
4	$16,390,743	$1,639,074	($106,718)	$17,923,099
5	$17,923,099	$1,792,310	($106,718)	$19,608,691
6	$19,608,691	$1,960,869	($106,718)	$21,462,842
7	$21,462842	$2,146,284	($106,718)	$23,502,409
8	$23,502,409	$2,350,241	($106,718)	$25,745,931
9	$25,745,931	$2,574,593	($106,718)	$28,213,806
10	$28,213,806	$2,821,381	($106,718)	$30,928,469

Note that Eric could have only transferred $1,000,000 to the GRAT with the same annuity payment of $106,718, thus creating a zero value gift (the value of the annuity is $1,000,000, creating a remainder interest with a value of $0). At the end of the 10 year GRAT term the remainder interest would be $892,932. This amount will be transferred with no transfer tax and without any use of the applicable gift tax exclusion.

Risk

Upon creation of the GRAT, the greatest risk is the grantor's failure to survive the GRAT term, causing the value of the annuity payments specified in the GRAT to be included in the grantor's gross estate. However, this risk is minimal because if this occurs (ignoring transactional costs) the grantor is no worse off than if he had not created the GRAT. Without the GRAT, the property would also have been included in his gross estate.

Income Tax Consequences

A GRAT is subject to the grantor trust rules for income tax purposes. There are no income tax consequences on the initial transfer to the GRAT because for income tax purposes, the grantor is still deemed to own all of the assets in the GRAT. However, all trust income flows through to the grantor annually, and is included in the grantor's income, without regard to the amount of the distributions made to the grantor. The grantor's usual objective in establishing a GRAT is to remove appreciation potential of the assets from his gross estate while minimizing transfer taxes. Income tax savings is not the primary motivation to establish a GRAT, but is a nice feature for the transferee.

Grantor Retained Unitrust (GRUT)

Another device similar to the GRAT is a **grantor retained unitrust (GRUT)**. Instead of paying a fixed annuity, a GRUT pays a fixed percentage of the trust's assets each year as revalued on an annual basis. For example a 15 percent GRUT pays out 15 percent of the value of the assets in the GRUT every year. Since the value of the assets will change, the annual payment will fluctuate each year. The GRUT is less suitable for hard to value assets (e.g., real estate, businesses) because the annual revaluation requirement is cumbersome. Also, if the asset is appreciating faster than the Section 7520 interest rate it causes the annual payment to the grantor to increase each year, which defeats the objective of lowering the grantor's gross estate. For these reasons, GRUTs are used less frequently than GRATs in estate plans.

> ### Quick Quiz 7.3
>
> 1. A SCIN payment terminates at the death of the buyer.
>   a. True
>   b. False
> 2. The value of a GRIT is calculated by using the FMV less the present value of the retained interest.
>   a. True
>   b. False
> 3. At the date a GRAT is funded, the value of the remainder interest is the excess of the value of the contribution to the trust over the present value of the annuity stream.
>   a. True
>   b. False
>
> False, True, True.

Short-Term GRATs or Rolling GRATs

The major risk of a long-term GRAT is that the transferor does not outlive the GRAT term. To mitigate against this risk, a transferor could use a series of short-term GRATS or rolling GRATS where the excess of the GRAT payment over the needed amount for consumption is transferred to a new GRAT. While such a technique is possible, one risk is the potential change in the Section 7520 rate. Such a technique is much more complicated than a single, long-term GRAT. As you will discover in Chapter 13, the GST exemption can only be allocated to a GRAT at the end of the GRAT term, making a GRAT ineffective for leveraging the generation skipping exemption.

Transfer to an Intentionally Defective Grantor Trust (IDGT)

An **intentionally defective grantor trust (IDGT)** is an irrevocable trust that is used to freeze the value of assets transferred to family members or loved ones for estate tax purposes. A gift to an IDGT is a completed gift for estate and gift tax purposes, but the IDGT is treated as a grantor trust for income tax purposes. The trust is intentionally established as a grantor trust. The purpose of this structure is to transfer an appreciating asset to a family member while the trust income remains taxable to the grantor. This tax treatment of the trust income is an additional benefit to the transferee since the payment of income tax will reduce the grantor's gross estate. If the trust had to pay the income tax, it would reduce the value of the gift and the rate of income tax may be higher due to the narrow trust income tax brackets. Thus, the tax treatment is a additional "tax-free" transfer to the beneficiary.

There are several ways that a trust can "qualify" as an IDGT. This grantor trust treatment is caused by retaining one of the powers found in IRC Sections 673 through 677. It is important that the trust document be drafted in such a way as to include a power that results in grantor income tax treatment but avoids estate tax inclusion. Some of the grantor retained powers that can cause grantor income tax treatment are listed below:

- The power to exchange property of equal value with the trust or by controlling the trust investments.[1]
- To the extent that the grantor has a reversionary interest in the trust that is greater than 5 percent of the value of the trust.
- To the extent that the grantor can benefit from trust income or can distribute income to the grantor's spouse.[2]
- The power to borrow from the trust without adequate interest or adequate security.[3]

Example 7.14

Anthony transfers a $5 million LLC interest to a trust for Donna and her children.[4] There is no gift tax because the gift is less than the current lifetime exemption amount. The LLC is taxed as a partnership and has annual income of approximately $500,000. The trust document gives Anthony certain powers, including the power to substitute assets. Because the trust is treated as a grantor trust for income tax purposes, Anthony must report the trust income on his personal income tax return. Assuming that he is in the 45% income tax bracket for federal and state income tax and the trust would pay the same amount, he is effectively shifting an additional $225,000 annually by paying the tax.

Installment Sale to an IDGT

A fairly common estate planning technique is for a transferor to sell an appreciating asset to a IDGT in exchange for a promissory note. This technique effectively freezes the value of the asset (note) in the transferor's estate. An IDGT can also be used to sell assets or partial interests in assets, whose value can be discounted due to a minority discount or a discount for lack of marketability, thus magnifying the benefit to the transferees.

This technique is accomplished by first establishing the IDGT so that any gifts are complete for estate and gift tax purposes, but the IDGT is treated as a grantor trust for income tax purposes. Once the trust is formed, the grantor will generally donate money worth at least 10 percent of the asset that will be sold to the trust. These donated funds are what is often referred to as seed money and as such are a gift. Once the trust is

---

1. IRC Section 675(4).
2. IRC Section 677(a).
3. IRC Section 673(a).
4. IRC Section 675(2).

funded, it enters into a purchase agreement to buy an asset from the grantor in exchange for a promissory note. The note will have an interest rate equal to the AFR and the trust will make payments to the grantor at least annually. The structure of the note can be interest only with a final balloon payment.

When the grantor sells the asset to the trust, it is not a taxable transaction because the grantor is effectively selling the asset to himself for income tax purposes. In addition, the interest payments from the trust to the grantor are not taxable income because the grantor is deemed the owner of the trust assets for income tax purposes.

There are many benefits of this transaction including:
- The value of the assets sold freezes upon the sale.
- The remaining value of the note is the only asset included in the estate if the grantor dies during the term of the note. Unlike a GRAT, the grantor does not have to outlive the note term. However, some practitioners believe that the remaining installment sale gain is deferred and taxed as income in respect of a dependent (IRD) in the event that the grantor dies during the term of the note.
- Any future appreciation of the asset sold to the IDGT escapes transfer tax.
- The valuation discount and the income tax paid by the grantor are additional benefits to the transferees that escape transfer taxation.
- The grantor can allocate GST to the "seed money" and thus leverage the asset purchase.

Exhibit 7.8 | Installment Sale to an IDGT

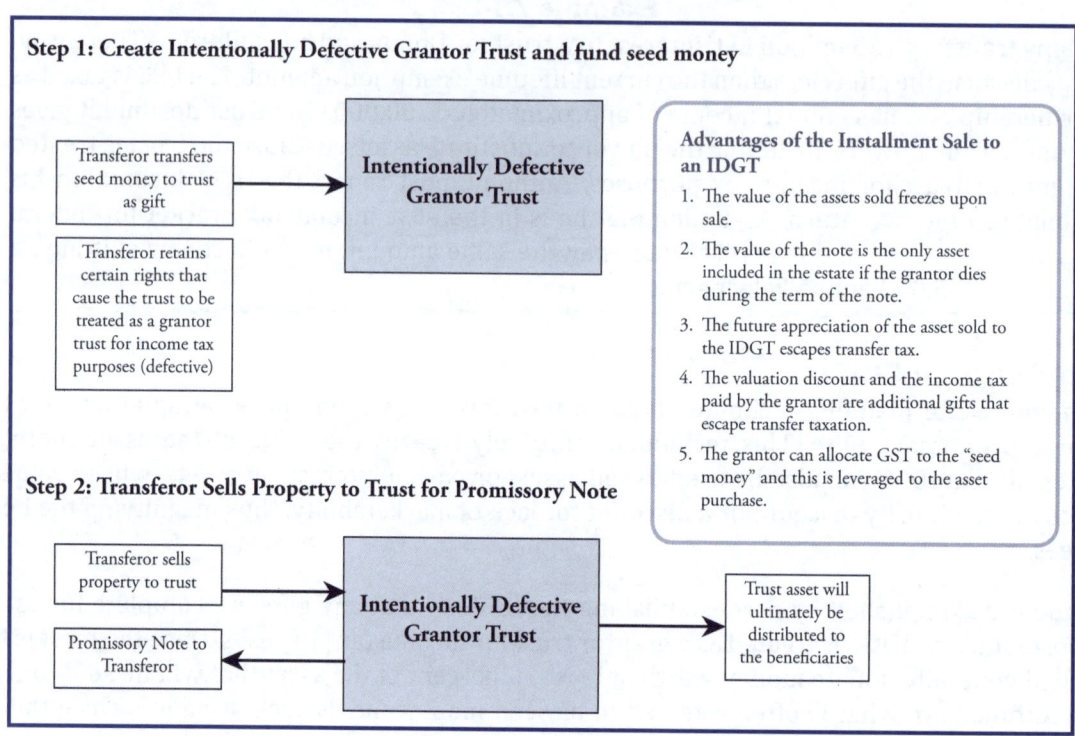

Exhibit 7.9 | GRAT and Installment Sale to an IDGT Comparison

	GRAT	Installment Sale to IDGT
Trustee	Grantor can serve as trustee	Independent trustee
Payments	Annually Can be delayed up to 105 days after anniversary date	Annually Can be interest only with balloon balance paid at term end
Interest Rate	Section 7520 rate	AFR
Gift *(Tax: Gift Tax)*	Remainder interest is taxable gift, but can be zeroed out	Seed money is a gift of a present interest
Can Terminate	No	Yes, note can be prepaid if asset is not performing
Must Grantor Survive to Avoid Estate Inclusion *(Tax: Estate Tax)*	Yes	No
GST Exemption *(Tax: GST Tax)*	No Can only be allocated at end of term	Yes Allocate sufficient exemption to seed money
Income *(Tax: Income Tax)*	3 tiers for each payment	Taxed to grantor

Qualified Personal Residence Trust (QPRT)

A **qualified personal residence trust** (QPRT) is a special form of a GRIT. The grantor contributes a personal residence to a trust and instead of receiving the trust income, the grantor of the QPRT receives use of the personal residence as the income component.

At the end of the trust term, the residence passes to the remaindermen. If the grantor is still living, he may then lease, at a fair market value rent, the property from the remaindermen and continue to use it as his personal residence. If the grantor dies before the expiration of the trust term, the fair market value of the residence is included in the grantor's gross estate.

> ### Key Concepts
> 1. How is the value of the annuity in a QPRT calculated?
> 2. Typically, who controls a family limited partnership?

A QPRT may only be established with a personal residence (which can include the primary residence or a vacation home) of the grantor. No more than two QPRTs established by a single grantor may be in existence at any one time. In the case of spouses who have a joint interest in a personal residence, they can transfer the property to the same or separate QPRTs. The use of separate trusts may be more appropriate if the life expectancy of each spouse is substantially different. If a residence transferred to a QPRT is sold, it can be replaced using the proceeds in the QPRT. The capital gain exclusion rules ($250,000 for single, $500,000 for married filing jointly) are applicable with regard to any income tax consequences. In states that offer homestead exemptions, the trust should be carefully worded to allow the taxpayer to continue to claim the homestead exemption after the residence is transferred to the QPRT.

Gift and Estate Tax Consequences (QPRTs)
The original transfer of the residence is treated as a gift to the extent that the fair market value of the residence exceeds the present value of the grantor's retained interest (the use) as determined under Section 7520. This is an excellent transfer device when the personal residence is appreciating at a much greater rate than the Section 7520 interest rate and there is an intent to keep the property in the family for the long-term. The benefit of a QPRT is that it freezes the value of the personal residence for estate tax purposes. The residence is transferred at a lower transfer tax and all future appreciation will escape transfer tax assuming the grantor lives throughout the trust term.

As in the case of the GRAT, if the grantor dies during the term of the QPRT, the full fair market value of the home will be included in the grantor's gross estate. However, if the grantor outlives the QPRT term, the personal residences will not be included in the decedent's gross estate.

Tangible Personal Property Trust (TPPT)
Tangible personal property trusts (TPPTs) are very similar to QPRTs, with one exception – a TPPT is funded with personal property, not real property. TPPTs usually transfer artwork, antiques, and other items of personal property that have the potential to appreciate in value. The grantor retains the right to use the personal property as the "annuity" interest component of the trust. At the end of the trust term, the personal property transfers to the remainder beneficiary.

Gift and Estate Tax Consequences
The original transfer of the personal property to the trust is treated as a gift to the extent that the fair market value of the personal property exceeds the present value of the grantor's retained interest. Valuation of the retained interest, however, is difficult, and the IRS will scrutinize the transfer to a TPPT due to the difficulty of valuing the right to use a piece of tangible personal property.

As in the case of the QPRT, if the grantor dies during the term of the TPPT, the full fair market value of the trust property will be included in the grantor's gross estate. However, if the grantor outlives the trust term, the property will not be included in the grantor's gross estate.

Family Limited Partnerships (FLP)
A **family limited partnership** (FLP) is a limited partnership created under state law with the primary purpose of transferring assets to younger generations using valuation discounts.

Usually, one or more family members transfer highly appreciating property to a limited partnership in return for both the one percent general and the 99 percent limited partnership interests. In a limited partnership, the general partner has unlimited liability and the sole management rights of the partnership, while the limited partners are passive investors with limited liability and no management rights.

Gift and Estate Tax Consequences
Upon creation of the partnership, there are neither income nor gift tax consequences because the entity created (the limited partnership and all of its interests, both general and limited) is owned by the same person, or persons, who owned the assets before the transfer.

chapter 7

Once the FLP is created, the owner of the general and limited partnership interests values the limited partnership interests. Since there are usually transfer restrictions on the limited partnership interests (limiting the marketability), and the limited partners have little control of the management of the partnership (lack of control), limited partnership interests are usually valued with a substantial discount. It is not uncommon for the value of such discounted interests to range between 20-40 percent less than similar proportional interests. The original transferor (grantor) then begins an annual gifting program using the discounts, the gift tax annual exclusion, and gift-splitting (where applicable) to transfer limited partnership interests to younger generation family members at reduced transfer costs.

Example 7.15

In 2020, Adam, age 52, is married to Barb and they have three children and nine grandchildren. The three children are happily married and Adam and Barb think of their children's spouses as their own children. Adam transfers a 100% interest in a business with a fair market value of $3,200,000 to a family limited partnership. Adam receives back a general partnership interest of one percent and 150 units of limited partnership interests representing 99 percent, at $21,120 (($3,200,000 x 99%) / 150) per unit. Adam then transfers two limited partnership units to each child, spouse of child, and grandchild using a 28.977% percent discount, the annual exclusion, and the split gift election.

Applying the discount of 28.977% to the $21,120 unit value equals $15,000, the amount of the annual exclusion.

Donees: 3 children + 3 spouses + 9 grandchildren = 15 donees.

Gifts: 15 donees x 2 units x $15,000 = $420,000 (valued at $633,600 before the discount).

In this scenario, Adam does not pay any transfer tax. It will take six years with this level of distribution for Adam to transfer his entire limited partnership interest under the annual exclusion to his children, their spouses, and his grandchildren. While this may take six years, it has the potential of saving 40 percent of the value transferred in addition to the tax saved on the future appreciation.

Asset Control

One of the unique features of the FLP, and perhaps its most important non-tax benefit, is that the original owner/transferor can maintain control of the property transferred to the limited partnership by only retaining a small general partnership interest. If the FLP is funded with a business interest, the general partner could remain president of the business, direct the company's strategic plan, receive reasonable compensation and fringe benefits, hire and fire employees, receive executive perks, and generally control the limited partners' interests. As with all limited partnerships, the limited partners have no control over any of these enumerated management decisions.

The FLP is often undertaken as a series of transfers, including an initial nontaxable contribution of property to the partnership followed by annual exclusion gifts of limited partnership interests. While a general partner has control over partnership affairs, an individual who transfers his property to an FLP needs to be financially secure without the transferred property, both from a net worth and cash flow perspective.

Exhibit 7.10 | Family Limited Partnership

FLP Technique:

1. Partnership is created under state law with a partnership agreement.
2. A 1% general partnership (GP) interest is created along with a 99% limited partnership (LP) interest.
3. Transferor transfers property to the FLP in exchange for the GP and LP interests.
4. The general partner is responsible for managing the FLP and maintains control over the FLP assets.
5. Over time, the GP will generally donate LP interests to family members taking advantage of valuation discounts due to lack of marketability and lack of liquidity. These donations will make use of the annual exclusion.
6. The FLP owns the assets donated, which creates a layer of asset protection for the limited partners.

What to Avoid:

1. Creating the FLP near the death of the transferor.
2. Only transferring marketable securities, while attempting to claim a high valuation discount.
3. Contributing personal use assets in the FLP.
4. Not having a professional valuation completed as part of a discount.
5. Using FLP assets to pay for personal expenses of the general partner.
6. Making distributions that fail to follow the terms of the partnership agreement.
7. Not changing the title of assets contributed to the partnership.
8. Making too many distributions from the FLP. The FLP needs to have a valid business purpose.

Asset Protection

The use of the FLP structure can also help protect family assets. By placing the assets in the FLP and only making gifts of limited partnership interests to heirs, judgments or liens entered against a donee (limited partner) will not jeopardize the assets of the partnership. A donee's creditor would not be able to force the donee to liquidate his interest, since the donee does not have the right to force the liquidation of a limited partnership interest.

Transferring limited partnership interests to children and children's spouses can also help protect assets from divorce claims. If the child and his spouse divorce, even if the divorced spouse received a limited partnership interest, he or she could not force distributions from the partnership, participate in management, require his or her interest to be redeemed, or force a liquidation of the partnership.

Design and Implementation

The creation of family limited partnerships and the use of discounts to transfer value at a lower gift tax cost has been regularly contested by the IRS. However, in several cases, the courts have ruled in favor of the taxpayer and upheld discounts on the valuation of limited partnership interests in the range of 10 percent to 40 percent as long as the FLP was operated like a separate business. The IRS has won and the valuation discounts have not been allowed in cases where the family withdrew money from the business at leisure, shared checking accounts with the business, had the FLP pay medical or other ordinary living expenses for the family, and when other non-business transactions were prevalent within the FLP.

The estate planning benefits of the FLP are lost and expenses are increased (as the result of legal fees) when the IRS successfully contests the use of the FLP arrangement. To mitigate against this risk and to ensure the use of the favorable discounts, the FLP should possess economic substance by having its own checking accounts, tax identification number, payroll (including payment of reasonable compensation to the general partner if he is managing the business), and should not allow family members to withdraw funds at will, nor should the FLP pay for personal expenses of its owners.

> **Quick Quiz 7.4**
>
> 1. At the end of the QPRT term, the annuitant must sell the home.
>   a. True
>   b. False
>
> 2. A family limited partnership utilizes lack of control and marketability discounts to transfer the partnership interests at a reduced transfer tax cost.
>   a. True
>   b. False
>
> *False, True.*

Challenges by the IRS

The IRS has challenged that gifts of LLC membership interest were not gifts of a present interest, and therefore, did not qualify for the annual exclusion. The tax court in Hackl used a two-part test requiring the donee to have an unrestricted and non-contingent right to the immediate use, possession, and enjoyment of either:
1. the property, or
2. the income from the property.

In this case, a member could not withdraw from or dissolve the company. Regarding income, none was expected for three years and the grantor, manager had discretion to distribute that income making the amount flowing to the beneficiary not ascertainable. To mitigate against this risk, it would be wise to consider a put option to the donee for 30 days, similar to a Crummey power, permit the donee to withdraw his value for a limited period of time, or all transfer interest with a right of first refusal by the entity.

> **Quick Quiz 7.5**
>
> 1. Only a limited partner can manage a family limited partnership.
>   a. True
>   b. False
>
> 2. At formation of a family limited partnership, the founder is subject to gift tax on the transfer of the property interest to the family limited partnership.
>   a. True
>   b. False
>
> *False, False.*

The IRS has also claimed that the estate of the decedent grantor should include the assets transferred from the decedent under Section 2036(a)(1) and Section 2036(a)(2) (retained interest).

The tax court in Strangi found that the grantor had the right to make distribution decisions, and was therefore, a retained interest under Treasury Regulation 20.2036-1(a). The court also found that there was an implied agreement among partners that Strangi (the grantor) retained possession and enjoyment of the transferred assets.

Exhibit 7.11 | Summary Steps to Avoid IRS Challenges to FLPs

1. Establish a legitimate non-tax reason for forming the FLP.
2. Strictly abide by formalities required of a partnership and the right to vote on liquidation.
3. Distribution decisions should be eliminated for the grantor.
4. Do not transfer all of the grantor's assets (leave enough to meet living needs).
5. Have other family members contribute to the partnership and actively participate in the negotiations for formation.
6. Document the business rationale for formation and all material decisions.
7. Do not transfer personal use assets.
8. Use qualified appraisers.

Exhibit 7.12 | Summary Characteristics of Family Limited Partnerships (FLPs)

Advantages	Disadvantages
• Control retained by senior family member	• Attorney setup fees
• Valuation discounts	• Appraisal fees
• Annual exclusion gifts	• Operational requirements
• Some creditor protection	
• Restrictions can be placed on transferability of limited partnership interests of junior family members	

Summary

Whereas the SCIN and the private annuity are both sales transactions for adequate consideration and the retained interest trusts (GRAT/QPRT/TPPT) are partial gift/partial sale transactions, the FLP is often used to engage in a series of gifts. With each of the private annuity, SCIN, GRAT, or QPRT, the senior family member either needs or desires the income from or use of the transferred property. With the FLP, the transferor wants to retain control of the property temporarily and ultimately transfer the property under the annual exclusion gifting regime. In all cases, the transferor's intent is to reduce his gross estate and avoid or minimize transfer taxes. However, when transferring assets during life in order to reduce the gross estate, individuals must be aware of the impact that such transfers may have on certain government programs.

chapter 7

Medicare/Medicaid

Medicare is a federally funded health insurance program primarily designed for individuals over the age of 65. Under certain circumstances, Medicare provides limited long-term care benefits. Traditional Medicare will generally pay the full cost of nursing home stays for the first 20 days and can continue to pay the cost of the nursing home stay for the next 80 days, subject to a daily deductible of approximately $176.00 (as of 2020).[1] For individuals covered by a Medicare Managed Care plan, there is no deductible for days 21 through 100, but there are strict qualifying rules. Therefore, even under the best of circumstances, the maximum benefit will only be for 100 days.

Medicaid is also a health insurance program sponsored by the federal government and administered by the states, but it is primarily intended to benefit certain low-income individuals and families. One of the primary benefits of Medicaid is that, unlike Medicare, the Medicaid program will pay for long-term care in a nursing home for qualifying individuals. Medicare does not cover "custodial" stays in a nursing home, which often occur with diseases such as Alzheimer's or Parkinson's. Eligibility for Medicaid is subject to certain requirements, such as age; whether the applicant is pregnant, disabled, blind, or aged; the applicant's income and resources; and whether the applicant is a U.S. citizen or a lawfully admitted immigrant. The rules for counting income and resources vary from state to state and from group to group.

Key Concepts

1. Understand the basic differences between Medicare and Medicaid.
2. Explain the basic qualifications for Medicaid benefits.
3. Differentiate between assets that are counted and those that are not counted for Medicaid eligibility.
4. Discuss the advantages of long-term care insurance in estate planning.

Because the Medicaid eligibility requirements are strict, particularly with respect to the applicant's income and resources, individuals often seek to plan for their Medicaid eligibility long before they need it. For example, in most states there is a Medicaid monthly income limit for an individual (although the states vary in amount). In addition, a Medicaid recipient cannot have countable resources in excess of the state mandated amount. (To determine the limits for any particular state, go to the state's website.) Countable resources include any assets that are available to the Medicaid recipient other than certain exempt assets. Thus, many individuals find themselves in the position of not having enough assets to pay for nursing home care, but also having too many assets to qualify for Medicaid.

In determining an individual's eligibility for Medicaid, certain assets are counted, while others are excluded. When applying for Medicaid assistance, applicants must provide documentation of the assets that they own.

While each state sets its own threshold for the amount of countable assets a person can have and still qualify for Medicaid, most states permit a single person to retain $2,000 in countable assets, and married couples living in the same household are permitted $3,000 in countable assets.

Assets that are counted for Medicaid eligibility include:
- checking and savings accounts
- stocks and bonds
- certificates of deposit
- real property other than your primary residence
- additional motor vehicles if you have more than one

---

1. Latest information as of publication date.

Assets that do not count for eligibility include:
- primary residence
- personal property and household belongings
- one motor vehicle
- life insurance with a face value under $1,500
- Up to $1,500 in funds set aside for burial
- certain burial arrangements such as pre-need burial agreements
- assets held in specific types of trusts

A personal residence is often an individual's largest and most valuable asset, and is not considered for Medicaid eligibility purposes. There are, however, limits as to the amount of equity that a person can maintain and still qualify for Medicaid. For 2020, the minimum equity limit is $595,000. States have the option of using a higher limit.[1]

Middle-income individuals typically do not qualify for Medicaid, and often do not have enough resources to self-insure against the need for nursing home coverage. The Deficit Reduction Act of 2005 (DRA) created the Qualified State Long Term Care Partnership program to encourage more people to purchase long-term care insurance. Residents of some states may be eligible to find long-term care coverage through a State Partnership Program that links special Partnership-qualified (PQ) long-term policies provided by private insurance companies with Medicaid. These PQ policies:
- Help people purchase shorter term, more complete long-term care insurance
- include inflation protection, so the dollar amount of benefits received can be higher than the amount of insurance coverage purchased
- allow people to apply for Medicaid under modified eligibility rules if there is continued need for long-term care after the policy maximum is reached
- Include a special "asset disregard" feature that allows individuals to keep assets like personal savings above the usual $2,000 Medicaid limit.

Example 7.16

Marge, a single lady, purchases a partnership policy with a value of $100,000. Several years later she receives benefits under that policy up to the policy's lifetime maximum coverage (adjusted for inflation) equaling $150,000.

Marge eventually requires more long-term care services, and applies for Medicaid. If Marge's policy was not a Partnership-qualified policy, in order to qualify for Medicaid, she would be entitled to keep only $2,000 in assets. She would have to spend down any assets over and above that amount.

Since Marge purchased a partnership-qualified policy, however, she can keep $152,000 in assets and the state will not recover those funds after her death. Marge would only have to spend down her assets over and above the $152,000 amount in order to be eligible for Medicaid.

As the example above implies, since partnership-qualified policies must include inflation protection, the amount of the benefits received can be higher than the amount of insurance protection purchased. For

---

1. The maximum equity limit is $893,000 for 2020.

example, if an individual purchases a partnership-qualified long term care insurance policy and receives $100,000 in benefits from it, he or she can apply for Medicaid and, if eligible, retain $100,000 worth of assets over and above the state's Medicaid asset threshold. States must certify that partnership policies meet the specific requirements for their partnership program, including that those who sell partnership policies are trained and understand how these policies relate to public and private coverage points.

The Medicaid program is intended to provide coverage for long-term care services for individuals who are unable to afford it. Some individuals, with assistance from financial planners and attorneys, have found ways of arranging assets so that the assets are preserved for the individual and/or family members, but are not countable when Medicaid eligibility is determined. The Deficit Reduction Act of 2005 (DRA) addresses key areas related to transfers of assets for less than fair market value and makes it more difficult for individuals with resources to qualify for Medicaid.

When a Medicaid application is received, States conduct a review, or "look-back," to determine whether the individual (or his or her spouse) transferred assets (e.g., cash gifts to children, transfers of real estate, and the like) to another person or party for less than fair market value (FMV). The DRA lengthened the "look-back" period to 60 months (five years) prior to the date the individual applied for Medicaid.

The consequence of transferring assets during the look-back period is a delay in the date an individual will qualify to receive long-term care services under Medicaid. Under the DRA, the penalty period for transfers made on or after February 8, 2006 begins on the later of: (1) the date of the transfer; or (2) the date the individual enters a nursing home and is found eligible for coverage of institutional level services that Medicaid would pay for were it not for the imposition of the transfer penalty.

The length of the penalty period is determined by dividing the value of the transferred asset by the average monthly private-pay rate for nursing facility care in the State. For example, if an individual gave away assets worth $90,000 and the average monthly private pay rate in their state is $3,000, the individual would be ineligible to receive Medicare benefits for the first 30 months (90,000 / 3 = 30) of their nursing home stay. There is no limit to the length of the penalty period.

> **Key Concepts**
>
> 1. How is the value of the annuity in a QPRT calculated?
> 2. Typically, who controls a family limited partnership?

For certain types of transfers, these penalties are not applied. The principal exceptions include transfers to a spouse, or to a third party for the sole benefit of the spouse; transfers by a spouse to a third party for the sole benefit of the spouse; transfers to certain disabled individuals, or to trusts established for those individuals; transfers for a purpose other than to qualify for Medicaid; and transfers where imposing a penalty would cause an undue hardship.

Medicaid planning is often undertaken to preserve assets for children or relatives, or to preserve assets for a spouse. It is also done to preserve assets that could be used to enhance care above what is provided for under Medicaid. Some question whether Medicaid planning is ethical and/or moral. There are many advisors and attorneys who assist people in transferring assets to qualify for Medicaid benefits, and there are many who believe it is unethical and will not engage in this type of planning. Consider the following two examples.

Example 7.17

Barry worked as a plumber since he was 18-years-old. He worked hard his entire life and has saved a fair amount of money by not going on vacations, eating at home, and living modestly. He just turned age 65 and has been diagnosed with Alzheimer's disease. He had hoped that he would be able to leave some of his money to his daughter for his grandson's college education. However, he is concerned that he will spend his life's savings on long-term care. He is also concerned that his wife will be without the necessary funds to care for her needs.

Example 7.18

Larry worked as a plumber since he was 18-years-old. He worked hard his entire life, but also enjoyed his life by buying expensive cars, vacationing several times a year, and always purchased the latest in fashion trends. While he has earned a significant amount of money over his career, he has almost nothing saved and lives in an apartment. He just turned age 65 and has been diagnosed with Alzheimer's disease. He is very concerned about the progressiveness of the disease and the prospect of needing long-term care and not being able to afford it.

Despite the fact that Larry has been at least somewhat irresponsible in terms of spending, he is entitled to Medicaid. From an ethical perspective, the case can be made that Medicaid is designed for the poor and therefore Larry should receive it and Barry should not. This outcome may or may not be palatable. Barry, on the other hand, is left with the choice of spending down his assets (using them for long-term care needs) and then applying for Medicaid or engaging in Medicaid planning.

In Helvering v. Gregory, Judge Learned Hand famously wrote about tax planning: "Any one may so arrange his affairs that his taxes shall be as low as possible; he is not bound to choose that pattern which will best pay the Treasury; there is not even a patriotic duty to increase one's taxes." Considering this quote and the idea of preserving assets for a spouse, one might conclude that Medicaid planning is not unethical. Some might even conclude that Medicaid planning is not only ethical, but prudent. However, what is certain is that there is an ethical question that must be answered before undertaking this type of planning.

There is a product available that will permit individuals to avoid the ethical and moral consequences of Medicaid planning and provide for their long-term care needs if needed, while at the same time preserving assets for lifetime consumption or transfer to family members - Long Term Care Insurance. The alternatives to long-term care insurance are self-financing nursing home costs. or engaging in Medicare planning. Self-insuring requires that an individual keep a significant amount of assets until death just in case those assets are needed to pay for long-term care, and Medicaid planning effectively renders the individual a pauper. If long-term care insurance is employed in planning, an individual can keep the amount of wealth he or she

> **Quick Quiz 7.6**
>
> 1. Philip owns a home worth $250,000, which has a $50,000 mortgage. Philip could still qualify for Medicaid.
>   a. True
>   b. False
> 2. The Medicaid look-back period is six years.
>   a. True
>   b. False
>
> True, False.

is comfortable with, and can transfer, long before death, excess wealth to facilitate the estate planning process. Long term care insurance provides a hedge that opens up new planning opportunities for the purchaser, and should be considered as part of a comprehensive financial plan and estate plan.

TRANSFERS TO CHARITIES

Many of the transfers that can be made during life to non-family members (arm's-length) and to loved ones (arm's-length, full sales, partial sales, partial gifts, and full gifts) are presented above. Chapter 9 discusses another type of transfer during our lives - transfers to charitable organizations.

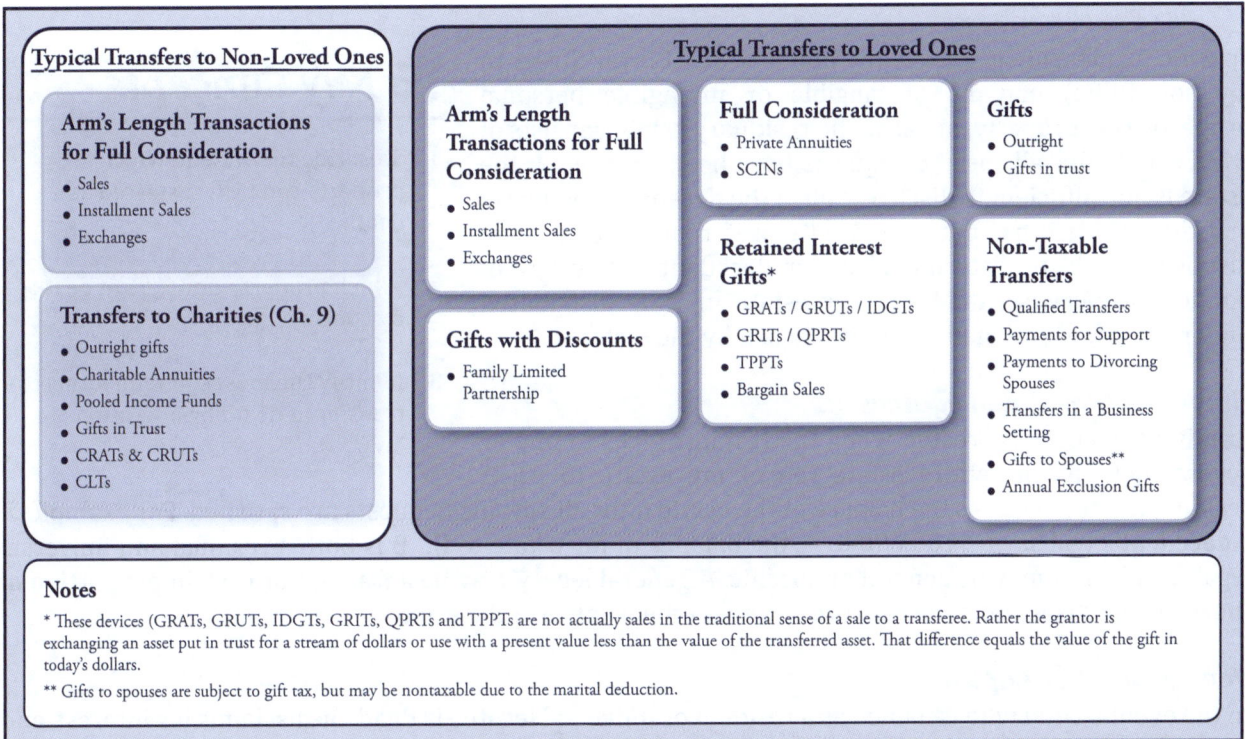

Exhibit 7.13 | Summary of Transfers During Life

TRANSFERS AT DEATH

Property can be transferred at death in one of three ways:
1. by will
2. by contract (beneficiary designation)
3. by operation of law (e.g., titling of property, use of trusts, intestacy)

When an individual dies, all of his or her property must be transferred in some combination either to heirs, charities, or the government (taxes).

Transfers by Will

A will is a legally enforceable document that transfers property to designated beneficiaries at death. To be effective, a will should meet the minimum requirements set forth under state law. A person who dies with a will is said to have died testate and is referred to as a testator. The will should direct the payment of expenses, debts, and taxes, but if such a determination is not made in the will, the decedent's state law of domicile will control. After the debts, expenses, and taxes have been paid, the remaining property is transferred to the beneficiaries, generally in the following order:

1. Personal property is transferred to legatees.
2. Real property is transferred to devisees.
3. Residuary legatees take anything remaining in the estate that has not been specifically disposed of by will.

Specific bequests (e.g., I leave my home at 321 Clover Street to my son Billie) may be of tangible or intangible personal property, real property, or cash. The residuary estate consists of what is left after all specific bequests have been satisfied. If the estate is not sufficient to discharge all of the decedent's bequests and the decedent has not expressed a preference, the order of disposition will be determined under decedent's state law of domicile. Otherwise, the residuary estate may be distributed under one of several methods to be chosen by the testator.

> **Key Concepts**
>
> 1. Describe the ways in which property can be transferred at death.
> 2. Which property transfers at death by contract law?
> 3. Identify the most common forms of transfer at death by operation of law?

Universal/Residual Legatees

A universal legacy is created when the testator gives to one or several persons his entire estate (all of my estate to A). A residual legatee receives the balance of the estate after all specific bequests are satisfied. For example, if a decedent's will says "$100,000 to A, the balance of my estate to B," B is both a residual and universal legatee. A legacy may be general or specific. A general legacy may be a fraction or certain proportion of the estate or a fraction or certain proportion of the balance of the estate.

Per Stirpes/Per Capita

In the event a child who is named as a residual or universal legatee is dead, or disclaims his interest, and such pre-deceased child has children, those children may take by representation per stirpes (the children share their pre-deceased parent's interest) or per capita (the children become equal beneficiaries in the estate with no relation to the deceased child's interest).

Example 7.19

Brandy has three children - Amber, Britney, and Charley. Each child has two children of their own. Assume Brandy dies and is survived only by Britney and Charley. If Amber's children inherit per stirpes then each of them will share Amber's 1/3 interest (i.e., 1/6 to each of Amber's children). If instead the children inherit per capita, then Amber's two children move into the same generation as Britney and Charley and each of them will receive 1/4 of Brandy's assets.

Disinheritance

A testator may attempt to disinherit specific people, or a class of people, by not listing them as legatees in the will. Simply not listing an heir in a will may not be sufficient to disinherit them if it appears to the court to be an oversight.

In the United States, it is not possible to completely disinherit a surviving spouse, since he or she could exercise his or her right of election against the estate, and receive between one-third and one-half of the property under state law, unless the couple entered into a legally enforceable prenuptial agreement.

Property Transferred at Death by Contract

There are several ways to transfer property at death by contract. These include use of life insurance, annuities, qualified plans, individual retirement plans (IRAs), transfer-on-death accounts (TODs), Totten Trusts, and payable on death bank accounts (PODs). The distinguishing feature in all of these types of transfers is that an agent (for example, a life insurance company) is directed to transfer or pay a named beneficiary upon the death of the principal. Quite commonly all that is necessary to have the agent pay the named beneficiary is for the beneficiary to present a certified death certificate to the agent.

Transfers at Death by Operation of Law

The most common forms of transfer at death by operation of law include joint titling of property with a survivorship feature, intestacy, revocable trusts becoming irrevocable, and other trusts created under the trust law.

Titling

Two forms of titling that have survivorship features are joint tenancy with right of survivorship and tenancy by the entirety. The surviving joint owners of the property take the property outright after presenting a certified death certificate. The property is not transferred through the probate process, but is transferred to the joint owners by operation of law.

Trusts

An irrevocable trust will operate in accordance with the terms of its governing instrument and is not subject to the probate process. Some trusts are created by will (testamentary trusts), or are created (but not funded) prior to the grantor's death waiting for assets to be transferred to them pursuant to the terms of the grantor's will (standby trusts).

Care must be taken if assets under the will are to pour over to a preexisting trust or if non-will assets (e.g., those under contract) are to pour over to a testamentary trust (beneficiary of life insurance is the XYZ trust, a testamentary trust).

All assets transferred to a testamentary trust pursuant to the decedent's will are included in the decedent's probate estate. If the beneficiary of any assets that would normally pass by contract is the decedent's estate, then those assets will also be included in the probate estate.

Probate

As discussed in Chapter 4, transfers through probate are governed by either the intestacy laws (when the decedent dies without a will) or the decedent's will (in which case the decedent is said to have died testate). The intestacy rules apply when there is no will, the will is invalid in whole or in part, or the will does not dispose of all of the decedent's probate property. Intestate successors are commonly called heirs, testate successors are called legatees (for personal property transfers), and devisees (for real property transfers).

If intestacy rules apply, the state will commonly classify and prioritize heirs. The most common prioritization is (note that different states may have differing orders):
1. Surviving spouse
2. Descendants
3. Parents, siblings, and descendants of siblings
4. More remote ascendants (grandparents, aunts, uncles)
5. More remote collaterals (cousins, nieces, nephews)
6. Decedent's domiciliary state

Usually the most favored class takes to the exclusion of other classes and the nearest relative in the class takes to the exclusion of other more distant relatives in that same class. Persons of the same degree of distance share equally. Descendants of relatives who would take, but have predeceased the descendant, take according to state law. A renunciation or disclaimer by an heir may also lead to representation per stirpes.

Charitable Transfers at Death

All property of the decedent at death must be included in the gross estate. However, there is an unlimited charitable estate tax deduction. There is no income tax deduction for assets left to a charity at death. Property can be left to charities by contract, through use of state titling laws, in trust laws, and by will. Property generally does not pass to charities by virtue of intestate laws except where there are no living relatives, and at that point the assets escheat (transfer) to the state (these rules may vary by state).

In the event a split interest charitable remainder trust (CRT) is established at death, the charitable estate tax deduction is equal to the fair market value of the property transferred to the CRT less the discounted present value of the retained interest (the annuity or unitrust). The annuitant could be the surviving spouse or some other person. If such property should also qualify for the unlimited marital deduction the surviving spouse must be the only non-charitable beneficiary (see Chapter 9 for full discussion on charitable transfers).

> **Quick Quiz 7.7**
> 1. A testamentary transfer is a transfer in a will.
>   a. True
>   b. False
> 2. A transfer-on-death account (TOD) transfers property through the probate process.
>   a. True
>   b. False
>
> True, False.

ESTATE PLANNING FOR SMALL ESTATES

After the enactment of ATRA 2012, which increased the transfer tax exemption to $5 million and subjected it to inflation adjustments in subsequent years, and TCJA 2017, which raised the exemption to $11,580,000 for 2020 with adjustments for inflation thereafter, most individuals will find that they will not be subject to transfer taxes. Based on data from the 2016 Survey of Consumer Finances, a household with a net worth of $23,160,000 (two times the transfer tax exemption amount) would be in the 99.5 percent wealth percentile, meaning only 0.5 percent of American households are potentially subject to transfer taxes after the enactment of TCJA 2017. Individuals and households with small estates (a small estate, for our discussion here, means an estate equal to or less than the exemption amount for an individual, or two times the exemption amount for a household), therefore, will not have to worry about the planning complexity that comes with gift tax, estate tax, and generation skipping transfer tax planning.

While the complexity of tax planning is not an issue for small estates, individuals with small estates still need to do estate planning. The effective transfer of assets during lifetime or at death, and the protection of those assets against outside attacks still needs to be addressed. Planning for incapacity through the use of general powers of attorney, health care powers of attorney and living wills is just as important in an estate with no transfer tax liability as it is in an estate that will trigger transfer taxes. The purpose of this section is to review the concerns that will be faced by individuals and households with small estates, and how an advisor can address those concerns.

Estate Equalization

Prior to the enactment of TRA 2010, equalization of the estates of spouses was a concern for any married couple with assets above the transfer tax exemption amount. By equalizing their estates, a married couple could avoid transfer tax on a larger portion of their wealth passing to their heirs.

Example 7.20
Zeke and Sarah have been married for 40 years, and have three children. Assume that the transfer tax exemption is $5,000,000 (the threshold set in 2012 without inflation adjustments) and that Zeke has a net worth of $8 million and Sarah has a net worth of $1 million. If Zeke died and left all of his estate to his children, Zeke would incur an estate tax on that transfer. To avoid this result, through the use of various planning devices (such as lifetime gifting, or the use of the marital deduction at death), Zeke would want to make sure that $3 million of his net worth is transferred to Sarah so that his estate would equal the exemption amount of $5 million and not be subject to tax. If Sarah received $3 million from Zeke, her total estate would be $4 million, which would be below the exemption amount and would not be subject to tax. If it was unclear whether Zeke or Sara would die first, the most prudent approach would be for Zeke to make a gift to Sarah of $3 million in assets (which would not trigger a gift tax, since all gifts to spouses are exempt from gift tax) so that if Sarah died first, both of their estates would be shielded by the exemption amount.

For couples with combined estates below the exemption amount, there was no need to equalize estates, since each would have an estate below the exemption and it would not be subject to tax.

TRA 2010 temporarily fixed this equalization problem by introducing portability of the estate tax exemption. Portability permitted one spouse to transfer their unused exemption to the other spouse by making an election on a timely filed estate tax return. The portability of a spouse's unused exemption was made permanent in ATRA 2012. With portability of the exemption, individuals who did not equalize estates could fix that situation upon the death of the first spouse by transferring the exemption of the deceased spouse to the surviving spouse.

> **Example 7.21**
> Assume the same facts above (Zeke and Sarah example), but that Sarah dies first. With portability of the estate tax exemption, Sara's could leave her $1 million in assets to her children, and then transfer her remaining $4 million exemption to Zeke. When Zeke died at a later time, Zeke would have an $8 million estate and a $9 million exemption ($5 million for himself and $4 million from Sarah's estate), so he would not have to pay any tax. In the event that Zeke died first, he would still want to leave $3 million in assets to Sarah to avoid tax on his estate, with the rest passing to his children.

While portability of the estate exemption provided more flexibility in planning, there are still problems with portability. For example, a spouse could only use the most recent deceased spouse's exemption, so if a widow/er remarries, and their new spouse dies before the exemption of the first spouse was used, that exemption is lost. Furthermore, while portability permits transfer of the exemption for gift and estate tax purposes, it does not permit transfer of the generation skipping transfer tax exemption.

With the expansion of the exemption under TCJA 2017 to $11,580,000, fewer people will need to concern themselves with estate equalization and portability. For households (married couples) with a combined net worth safely below the single exemption amount, it is unlikely that transfer taxes will be due even if the couple does not equalize estates or directly take advantage of the portability provisions of the code.

Couples with combined estates over the single exemption amount of $11,580,000 however will still need to consider equalization of estates in their estate plans to minimize potential exposure to estate tax, and how the use of portability of the estate and gift tax exemption can be incorporated into that plan. Traditional planning techniques, such as equalization of the estates of married couples through gifting, or the use of testamentary trusts for the surviving spouse combined with the exemption portability provisions of the code may be more appropriate than simply relying on the portability rules.

Gifting Strategies

Individuals with small estates may also wish to change their gifting strategies to maximize the tax benefits for their families.

When the exemption amount was modest, planners frequently recommended gifting assets, particularly highly appreciating assets, to remove appreciation in property values from the transfer tax system. Gifts, of course, typically result in a carry-over basis in the hands of the beneficiary, which will subject the beneficiary to income tax on any gain when the gifted asset is sold. When transfer tax rates are high (currently they are 40%) and capital gains tax rates are low (currently they can be as high as 23.8 percent), this tradeoff made sense. Avoiding an estate tax on appreciation at 40 percent but replacing that with a tax of 23.8 percent on the gain resulted in 16.2 percent more for the beneficiary.

Individuals with small estates, however, should avoid making gifts of appreciated property during lifetime. Provided that the individual's gross estate will not exceed the exemption amount at death (which would include the value of their assets currently plus additions and appreciation on that property up to the date of their death), a death-time transfer of the property would maximize the inheritance, and minimize taxes, for the heirs. Assets that transfer through a decedent's estate qualify for a step-to basis under IRC Section 1014, which means that a beneficiary who receives an asset from the estate of a decedent will have a basis in that asset equal to the fair market value on the date of the decedent's death. Provided that an asset will appreciate during an individual's lifetime, and the individual's estate will not exceed the estate tax exemption amount, there will be no transfer tax due on the transfer at death, and the family members will escape the capital gains tax that would have resulted from the carry-over basis had the asset been transferred to them as a gift.

If an individual with a small estate would like to make a gift, it would be best to make gifts of cash or assets that have low appreciation potential. Lifetime transfers up to the exemption amount will be exempt from gift tax, and the potential capital gains tax that must be paid by the beneficiary will be limited.

Retained Interest Transfers

Transfers of property in which a decedent had retained an interest (such as the right to receive income, the right to use the property, the right to vote the shares of transferred stock, or the right to terminate, alter, revoke or amend a gift) are included in the estate of a decedent at the fair market value of the property on the date of death (IRC Sections 2036-2038). Unlike an outright gift, which transfers appreciation to the recipient and out of the estate of the donor, a retained interest gift subjects all appreciation occurring during the life of the donor to be subject to estate tax. When an individual has an estate over the transfer tax exemption amount, these types of transfers can be problematic because they will increase the size of the taxable estate and require the payment of additional estate taxes.

Retained interest transfers can be particularly valuable for individuals with small estates, however.

With high estate tax exemptions, those who expect their estates to remain below the exemption amount can make use of retained interest transfers to achieve asset protection while permitting their heirs to receive the property and have a basis in that property equal to the fair market value of the property on the date of the transferor's death.

The asset protection benefits are attained by splitting the property into various interests, making it difficult for a creditor to be able to access the property to satisfy debts of the owner. The appreciation in the asset during the life of the original owner escapes capital gains tax in the hands of the beneficiary since the asset will be included in the original owner's estate, and will therefore qualify for a IRC Section 1014 step-up in basis at the death of the original owner.

Example 7.22

Sal is getting up in years, and would like to preserve his assets for his wife, Norma, and his children should he die before them. Ten years ago, Sal's widowed mother, Maria, who had an advanced case of Alzheimer's disease, had to go into a nursing home. Maria died five years after entering the nursing home, but not before all of her assets were consumed to pay for her care. Sal does not want this to happen to his assets, which consist primarily of his home and his retirement accounts. Sal transfers his home to his children while retaining for himself and his wife the right to live in the home for the rest of their joint lives. Provided that Sal does not enter a nursing home for at least five years after the transfer, a majority of the value of the home will be protected from the claims of Medicare (which will pay for his care after all of his other assets are exhausted). Medicare could consider the life use of the home as an asset and attempt to receive value from that, but that would be relatively small in comparison to the value of the house, and will decline in value each year as Sal gets older. Provided that the 5-year window has passed, the majority of the home will be protected from Medicare claims, and will go to his children. When Sal dies, the full fair market value of the house will be included in his gross estate because Sal had the right to use the house for life, but since the value of his estate (including that value) does not exceed the exemption amount of $11,580,000 (2020), Sal will not have to pay any federal estate tax. The house, nevertheless, was included in the Sal's gross estate, and ultimately was distributed to his children, so his children will receive a basis in the house equal to the fair market value of the house on the date of Sal's death. All of the appreciation in the home during Sal's life will escape capital gains tax in the hands of Sal's children.

As the example above illustrates, judicious use of retained interest transfers can achieve asset protection while at the same time minimizing exposure to taxes for the heirs of an individual with a small estate.

Incapacity Planning

Regardless of the size of the estate, incapacity planning is an important part of the estate planning process. If an individual can no longer make financial or health decisions for him/herself, it is best to address what will happen through the use of various estate planning documents than permit a court to appoint a guardian and take control of that process, increasing the time and expense associated with making those decisions.

Everyone, whether their estate is large or small, should consider using a general power of attorney or a revocable trust (or both) to provide for the management of their financial assets when they can no longer manage them themselves. Failure to do this may result in a court appointed guardian who may not know the goals and objectives of the client, as well as the filing of accountings with the court, increasing the expense and complexity of managing the assets. It would be far better for an individual to choose the person who will serve in that capacity, and execute the documents (power of attorney or revocable trust) to appoint that person and specify how assets should be managed in the event the individual becomes incapacitated.

Health decisions must also be made for incapacitated persons. Like the situation with financial matters, it is best for an individual to address how this will be done, and who will be making those decisions, before becoming incapacitated. A health care power of attorney can name an individual who is allowed to make health decisions for the grantor of the power, and a living will can be executed if the individual would not like to have extraordinary measures taken to keep him or her alive when physicians determine that therapeutic treatment is not an option. Failure to execute these documents will permit a probate court to appoint a guardian for making health care decisions (who may or may not make decisions in accordance with the wishes of the incapacitated person). Failure to execute a living will can result in prolonged litigation over the best course of action to take in dire circumstances, which can cost a significant amount of money and deprive those funds from being used for the individual's care, or, after the individual's death, being transferred to his or her heirs.

Individuals with Small Estates Still Need to Plan

As the discussion above illustrates, all individuals should carefully consider their situation and make appropriate estate plans to protect their assets and their health. While the complexity of sophisticated tax planning will not be a concern for 99.5 percent of Americans in a post TCJA world, failing to engage in appropriate estate planning could have a big impact on an individual while he or she is alive, and on his or her heirs after death.

KEY TERMS

Applicable Federal Rate (AFR) - Rates published monthly by the IRS for federal income tax purposes, in accordance with section 1274(d) of the Internal Revenue Code. Interest rates on loans should not be less than the AFR for the loan to be considered a taxable event and not a gift by the IRS.

Arm's-Length Transaction - A transfer generally between unrelated parties in the form of a sale, an installment sale, or an exchange.

Exchange - A mutual transfer of assets with equal fair market values between individuals.

Family Limited Partnership (FLP) - A limited partnership created under state law with the primary purpose of transferring assets to younger generations using minority and marketability discounts to create reduced gift tax valuations.

Grantor Retained Annuity Trust (GRAT) - An irrevocable trust that pays a fixed annuity to the grantor (settlor) for some defined term, and pays the remainder interest of the trust to a non-charitable beneficiary.

Grantor Retained Income Trust (GRIT) - An irrevocable trust in which the grantor retains an income interest in the trust for the term of the trust. Thus, the grantor will donate property to the trust and the income from the asset will be distributed to the grantor during the term of the trust. At the end of the trust term, the remaining property is distributed to the beneficiary (remainderman).

Grantor Retained Unitrust (GRUT) - An irrevocable trust that annually pays a fixed percentage of the value of its assets (as revalued on an annual basis) to the grantor or (settlor) for some defined term, and pays the remainder interest of the trust to a non-charitable beneficiary.

Installment Sale - A sale of property that includes a note from the buyer to the seller. The buyer pays the seller the full valuable consideration of the property over a specified set of terms.

Intentionally Defective Grantor Trust (IDGT) - An intentionally defective grantor trust (IDGT) is an irrevocable trust that is used to freeze the value of assets transferred to family members or loved ones for estate tax purposes. A gift to an IDGT is a completed gift for estate and gift tax purposes, but is treated as a grantor trust for income tax purposes. It should be noted that the trust is intentionally established as a grantor trust.

Medicaid - A state and federal assistance program that pays for medical care and most long-term care expenses for eligible persons with low incomes and limited assets.

Medicare - A federal program that pays for healthcare for persons over age 65 and for people under age 65 with disabilities.

Private Annuity - The annuitant sells an asset to a buyer in exchange for an unsecured promise from the buyer to make fixed annual payments to the annuitant for the remainder of the annuitant's life.

Qualified Personal Residence Trust (QPRT) - A special form of a GRIT in which the grantor transfers his home to the QPRT and receives "use" of the personal residence as the annuity. The remainder interest of the trust passes to a non-charitable beneficiary.

Sale - The direct transfer of property to another for a note, money, or property of equal fair market value.

Section 7520 Rate - To be used to value certain charitable interests in trusts. Pursuant to IRC 7520, the interest rate for a particular month is the rate that is 120 percent of the applicable federal midterm rate (compounded annually) for the month in which the valuation date falls. That rate is then rounded to the nearest two-tenths of one percent. For example, if the rate that is 120 percent of the applicable federal rate (compounded annually) for specific month is 1.28 percent. That rate is then rounded to the nearest two-tenths of one percent or 1.2 percent for purposes of IRC 7520.

Self-Cancelling Installment Note (SCIN) - An installment sale that terminates at the earlier of the (1) death of the seller or (2) the term set forth in the installment note.

Tangible Personal Property Trusts (TPPT) - A special form of a GRAT in which the grantor transfers tangible personal property to the TPPT and receives "use" of the property as the annuity. The remainder interest transfers to a non-charitable beneficiary.

chapter 7

DISCUSSION QUESTIONS

SOLUTIONS to the discussion questions can be found exclusively within the chapter. Once you have completed an initial reading of the chapter, go back and highlight the answers to these questions.

1. Explain how an intra-family sale of property can be an advantageous strategy for reducing an individual's gross estate.

2. List three of the major differences in the gross estate treatment of transfers during life and bequests at death.

3. List the transfer techniques most commonly used with loved ones.

4. What is the term of a private annuity?

5. What is the buyer's adjusted basis in property purchased through a private annuity?

6. What is the SCIN premium?

7. If the seller outlives the term of a SCIN, how is the buyer affected?

8. What is the buyer's adjusted basis in property purchased through a SCIN?

9. Explain the gift tax consequences of a SCIN and a private annuity.

10. What is a GRIT?

11. What is a Grantor Retained Annuity Trust (GRAT)?

12. Explain the gift tax consequences of a GRAT.

13. What are the tax consequences if the grantor of a GRAT dies before the trust term ends?

14. How does a Grantor Retained Unitrust (GRUT) differ from a GRAT?

15. What is a Qualified Personal Residence Trust (QPRT)?

16. Explain the gift tax consequences of a QPRT.

17. What is the usual primary purpose of establishing a family limited partnership?

18. Discuss the discounts available when valuing the interests of a family limited partnership.

19. List the disadvantages of using a family limited partnership to transfer interest in property.

20. Which property transfers at death by contract?

21. In determining an individual's eligibility for Medicaid, what assets are counted and what assets are excluded?

22. Is Medicaid planning ethical?

23. Discuss why most small estates do not have to be concerned about estate tax following TCJA 2017.

24. Discuss why small estates continue to have a need for estate planning following TCJA 2017.

25. Explain why estate equalization in small estates is no longer necessary under TCJA 2017.

26. Explain how the increase in the estate and gift exemption affects the strategies of lifetime transfers for small estates.

chapter 7

MULTIPLE-CHOICE PROBLEMS

A sample of multiple choice problems is provided below. Additional multiple choice problems are available at money-education.com by accessing the Student Practice Portal.

1. Which of the following statements regarding installment sales is correct?
    a. All payments received by the seller in an installment sale are considered interest income.
    b. At the death of the seller, the principal balance of the installment sale is included in the seller's gross estate.
    c. The present value of the expected remainder value of the property sold in an installment sale is subject to gift tax at the date of the transfer.
    d. An installment sale would never be used with a related party.

2. In 2020, Roxanne paid Badlaw University $12,000 for her nephew's tuition and gave her nephew $25,000 in cash. Roxanne is single and did not make any other gifts during the year. What is the amount of Roxanne's taxable gifts for the year?
    a. $0.
    b. $2,000.
    c. $10,000.
    d. $24,000.

3. Todd purchased his mother's home through use of a SCIN. Under the terms of the SCIN, Todd was to pay his mother $20,000, plus interest, and a SCIN premium, per year for 10 years. If Todd's mother died after 4 payments were made, what would be Todd's adjusted basis in the home?
    a. $0.
    b. $80,000.
    c. $160,000.
    d. $200,000.

4. Harry, age 60, owns 400 shares of ABC Corporation, which he expects to increase 300% over the next four years. Harry eventually wants to transfer the stock in ABC Corporation to his son, Billy, but Billy is currently incapable of managing the stock or the income from the stock. Harry expects Billy to be responsible in five years. Of the following, which transfer method would work best to remove the expected appreciation of the stock from Harry's gross estate and protect the property for Billy?
    a. Private annuity.
    b. SCIN.
    c. GRAT.
    d. QPRT.

5. Of the following statements regarding a Qualified Personal Residence Trust (QPRT), which is true?
    a. At the end of the QPRT term, the residence reverts to the grantor.
    b. At creation of the QPRT, the grantor has a taxable gift to the remainder beneficiary eligible for the annual exclusion.
    c. At the end of the QPRT term, the grantor must begin paying rent to the remainder beneficiaries of the QPRT if he continues to live in the residence.
    d. A QPRT is ideal for a personal residence that is expected to appreciate at a lower rate than the Section 7520 rate.

chapter 7

QUICK QUIZ EXPLANATIONS

Quick Quiz 7.1
1. True.
2. False. A sale is not a taxable gift and does not qualify for the gift tax annual exclusion.
3. True.

Quick Quiz 7.2
1. False. A SCIN cannot be secured.
2. False. A SCIN is different than an installment sale because of the SCIN premium.
3. True.

Quick Quiz 7.3
1. False. A SCIN payment terminates at the death of the seller, not at the death of the buyer.
2. True.
3. True.

Quick Quiz 7.4
1. False. At the end of the QPRT term, the remainder beneficiary of the QPRT owns the home. There is no legal requirement that forces the sale of the home.
2. True.

Quick Quiz 7.5
1. False. Only a general partner can manage a family limited partnership.
2. False. There are no gift tax consequences on the formation of a family limited partnership. Gift tax consequences do result upon transfer of family limited partnership units to other individuals.

Quick Quiz 7.6
1. True.
2. False. The look-back period is 60 months.

Quick Quiz 7.7
1. True.
2. False. A transfer on death account (TOD) is a probate avoidance device.

8
TRUSTS

LEARNING OBJECTIVES

1. Define the structure of a trust.
2. Identify the parties to a trust agreement including the grantor, the trustee, and the beneficiaries.
3. Describe the benefits of a trust.
4. Describe split interests in property.
5. Describe the advantages of a living trust including avoiding probate.
6. Discuss trust duration and the rule against perpetuities.
7. Describe the accounting and income taxation of trusts.
8. Describe the gift tax treatment as applied to trusts.
9. Describe whether or not trust assets are included or excluded from the gross estate.
10. Identify and classify the different trust arrangements.
11. Identify and discuss the Crummey provision associated with trusts.
12. Describe the 5/5 lapse rule and the creation of a hanging power.
13. Describe the benefits of irrevocable life insurance trusts, bypass (credit shelter) trusts, power of appointment trusts, and qualified terminable interest property (QTIP) trusts.
14. Describe trust for minors.
15. Describe Totten trusts and blind trusts.
16. Describe special needs trusts.
17. Describe trusteed IRAs.
18. Describe "see-through" trusts.

CFP Board Resource Document - Student-Centered Learning Objectives based upon CFP Board Principal Topics.

INTRODUCTION

Trusts are used in estate planning to provide for the management of assets and flexibility in the operation of the plan. Most trusts, other than charitable trusts, provide great flexibility by allowing the trustee to make decisions based on the criteria set forth in the trust document by the grantor. This flexibility can be particularly important when the trust arrangement will last for an extended period of time. Charitable trusts are often used in estate planning, but are relatively inflexible both in their creation and in their operation because the government mandates the inclusion of specific provisions in the trust document to achieve income tax benefits for the donor. Charitable trusts generate tax benefits for the grantor and are often used for both lifetime and testamentary planning purposes. The purpose of this chapter is to introduce the reader to trust concepts, describe how trusts work, and review the advantages, disadvantages, and uses of specific types of trusts commonly used in the estate planning process.

The basic structure of a trust is depicted by the following diagram:

chapter 8

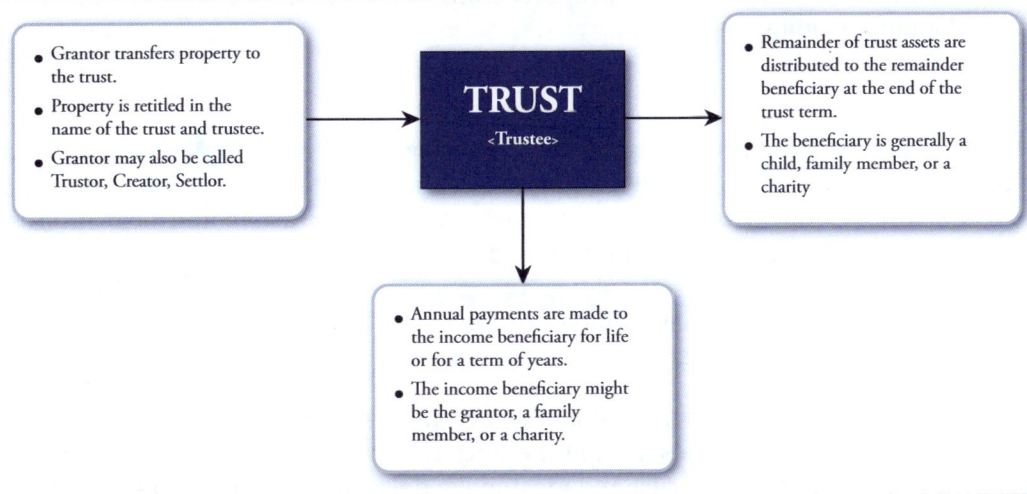

Exhibit 8.1 | Basic Structure of a Trust

DEFINITIONS

A **trust** is a structure that vests legal title to assets in one party, the trustee, who manages those assets for the benefit of others, who are referred to as the beneficiaries of the trust. While the trustee holds legal title to the assets, the beneficiaries hold the beneficial, or equitable, interest in the trust. By splitting the title to trust properly into legal and equitable interests, a trust can be a used to manage the property and the tax consequences attached to the transfer of property.

To form a trust, a grantor of a trust transfers (retitles) money or other property to the trustee. The money or property transferred is referred to as the trust principal, corpus, res, or fund. The trust principal will be managed by the trustee to accomplish the grantor's objectives as expressed in the detailed provisions of the trust document.

PARTIES

The three parties to a trust agreement are the grantor, the trustee, and the beneficiaries.

Grantor (Settlor, Creator, Trustor)

The **grantor** is the person who creates and initially funds the trust. In some instances, a grantor is referred to as a **settlor, trustor, or creator**. These names all have the same meaning. As the individual who creates the trust arrangement, the grantor establishes the terms and conditions of the trust and determines the scope and limit of the trustee's discretion in managing the trust assets.

> ### Key Concepts
> 1. Identify the parties to a trust.
> 2. List the duties of a fiduciary.
> 3. Differentiate between an income beneficiary and a remainder beneficiary.

In sophisticated estate planning situations, a single trust may have multiple grantors. For example, many family members, and possibly many generations of family members, may contribute property to a dynasty trust (discussed in Chapter 13). While those individuals who become grantors of a trust after its creation are not usually permitted to change the terms of the trust, making transfers to an existing trust may be a cost effective way of arranging for property transfers if the existing trust arrangement satisfies the objectives of multiple family members.

Trustee

The **trustee** is the individual or entity responsible for managing the trust assets and carrying out the directions of the grantor that are formally expressed in the trust instrument. A trustee is said to be vested with legal title to the trust assets, but must, at all times, act in the best interest of trust beneficiaries. As such, the trustee is considered to be a **fiduciary**, a person who has a legal duty to act in the best interest of another as a result of holding a position of trust and confidence. Other individuals and entities considered to be fiduciaries include executors and administrators of decedents' estates, as well as guardians of minors and incapacitated individuals.

The law imposes several duties to ensure that a fiduciary always acts in the best interests of those he is charged to protect. Among these duties are (1) the duty of loyalty and (2) the duty of care. A trustee must be loyal to the beneficiaries of a trust and must make decisions that are in the best interests of the beneficiaries (and consistent with the terms of the trust) even if those decisions result in a loss to the fiduciary. Furthermore, a trustee owes a duty of care to all beneficiaries, and therefore should make decisions only after engaging in a diligent investigation of the facts and thoughtful consideration of the impact on all of the beneficiaries.

These duties of loyalty and care can be summarized in a concept referred to as the Prudent Man Rule. The **Prudent Man Rule** states that the trustee, as a fiduciary, must act in the same manner that a prudent person would act if the prudent person was acting for his own benefit after considering all of the facts and circumstances surrounding the decision. Simply stated, the standard is a codification of the golden rule – do unto others as you would have them do unto you. Most states have adopted the Prudent Man Rule as a way of assessing trustee performance, and have codified this standard in the Prudent Investor Act. The Prudent Investor Act sets some practical limits on the nature and type of investments that trustees can purchase under the Prudent Man Rule.

One of the most important decisions a grantor makes when creating a trust is the appointment of the trustee. The grantor should appoint an individual or entity who will carry out the grantor's intent as expressed in the trust instrument. Sometimes, more than one trustee is appointed to create a system of checks and balances over trust operations. When only one trustee is in charge, it is difficult to challenge the decisions of the trustee when the trustee fails to act in accordance with the terms of the trust document and the Prudent Man Rule. Furthermore, care must be exercised when appointing a trustee who is either a current or potential beneficiary of the trust, or a person who can make discretionary distributions from the trust to benefit a person for whom he has a legal support obligation. In such cases, the trustee may be deemed to have a general power of appointment over the trust, requiring an inclusion of the fair market value of the trust assets in the trustee's gross estate should the trustee die while holding such power.

Beneficiary

The **beneficiary** is the person (or persons) who holds the beneficial title to the trust assets. While the beneficiary's name does not appear on the deed to the trust assets, the trustee must manage the assets in the best interests of the beneficiary.

A trust may have more than one type of beneficiary. Since most trusts are designed to terminate at some point in the future, the two most common types of beneficiaries are income and remainder beneficiaries.

The **income beneficiary** is the person or entity who has the right to current income or distributions from the trust or the current right to use the trust assets. When distributions are made during the term of the trust, the income beneficiary is generally the person who receives those distributions.

The **remainder beneficiary** is the individual or entity who is entitled to receive the assets that remain in the trust on the date of its termination.

Sometimes, the income and remainder beneficiaries of a trust are the same person (or persons).

Example 8.1
Christopher is concerned about the ability of his son, Sampson, to manage money. Nevertheless, Christopher would like to begin to transfer assets to Sampson now to help minimize the value of Christopher's future estate and the resulting estate tax liability. Christopher believes that as Sampson matures, he will become more responsible and therefore should be entitled to have access to the assets. To accomplish his goal, Christopher creates a trust, and begins to make annual transfers of property to the trust. The trust names Sampson as the income beneficiary and states that fifteen years from now, the trust will terminate and Sampson (or his issue, per stirpes) will receive the assets remaining in the trust at that time. Provided Sampson lives for the next 15 years, he is both the income and the remainder beneficiary of the trust.

In other situations, the income and remainder beneficiaries of the trust are different persons.

Example 8.2
Henry and his wife, Sandra, have two children, Jennifer and Jackie. Jackie is a special needs child. Because Jackie is unable to completely support herself, Henry would like to ensure that she is provided for, but wants to protect his assets for the benefit of Jennifer and her children. Henry created a trust naming Jackie as the discretionary income beneficiary for her lifetime. The trustee, therefore, can make distributions for the benefit of Jackie or purchase assets for her use. At Jackie's death, any remaining assets of the trust will be distributed to Jennifer outright, or if Jennifer does not survive Jackie, to Jennifer's children in equal shares, per stirpes. The trust that Henry created names Jackie as the discretionary income beneficiary and Jennifer (or her issue) as the remainder beneficiary. Note that if the trust income exceeds Jackie's needs, as determined by the trustee, the excess may be retained by the trustee for the benefit of Jennifer, the remainder beneficiary.

It is also possible for a trust to have only income beneficiaries and no remainder beneficiaries.

Example 8.3

Thomas has been working on his estate plan and has expressed an interest in establishing a dynasty trust for the benefit of his family. If the trust is created in a state that has abolished the rule against perpetuities (discussed below), or in an offshore jurisdiction, the trust will not terminate. Thomas creates a dynasty trust for the benefit of his descendants, or for the benefit of his family based on degrees of consanguinity in the event of an indefinite failure of issue. Because the trust will never terminate, there are no remainder beneficiaries of the trust. All of the individuals who are entitled to benefit from the trust are considered income beneficiaries.

Traditionally, income beneficiaries are entitled to receive all of the income from the trust and the remainder beneficiaries are entitled to receive the principal of the trust. Each state defines income and principal for trusts established in that state, but generally the term "income" includes dividends and interest earned on trust investments, and "principal" includes the original trust principal plus all capital gains. Capital gains, or gains derived from the appreciation in value of trust property, are considered corpus of the trust and are retained in the trust for the benefit of the remainder beneficiaries. In most states, absent instructions contained in the trust document to the contrary, the income beneficiary will receive income and dividends and the trust will retain the capital gains for the benefit of the remaindermen.

When long-term trusts (such as dynasty trusts) are created, the income beneficiaries are not always permitted to receive a distribution of the trust income. It is more common for long-term trusts to give the trustee discretion as to the timing and amount of income distributions, and to include specific language in the trust instrument authorizing the trustee to purchase assets for the use of the beneficiaries of the trust. Allowing beneficiaries to use trust assets, instead of requiring distributions from the trust, often results in better estate planning from a multi-generational perspective.

> ### Quick Quiz 8.1
> 1. A trust must always have at least two beneficiaries.
>   a. True
>   b. False
> 2. The grantor is the individual who contributes property to a trust.
>   a. True
>   b. False
> 3. The income beneficiary of a trust will receive the corpus of the trust at the end of the trust's term.
>   a. True
>   b. False
>
> False, True, False.

Example 8.4

At his death, Gerald created a dynasty trust for the benefit of his family. The trust requires the trustee to distribute the income to his children, and when each child dies, to split up that child's share and distribute the income to the child's children. All of Gerald's children are independently wealthy and are renowned art collectors. When they receive the income distributions from the trust, they use the money to purchase art that is displayed in their homes and offices. When each of the children die, the fair market value of the art that they purchased will be included in their gross estates, and will be subject to estate tax.

Example 8.5

Assume the same facts as above, except that Gerald's trust did not mandate the distribution of income to the children. Instead, the trustee used the income of the trust to purchase artwork that is displayed in the homes and offices of the children. When the children die, the fair market value of the artwork will not be included in their gross estates and will not be subject to estate tax, since the children did not own the artwork, and therefore have nothing to transfer through their estate at death. Gerald's grandchildren can now enjoy the art owned by the trust and exclude the value of the art from their gross estates as well. In such a case, the income earned by the trust is subject to income tax at the trust level.

As the above examples demonstrate, the ability to separate the ownership of assets (vested in the trustee) from the use of assets (vested in the trust beneficiaries) can, over time, save a significant amount of money for the family by avoiding the transfer tax over multiple generations. Trust beneficiaries do not have to own assets outright; it is better to give them the right to use trust assets as if they owned them.

WHY USE A TRUST

Management

A principal reason for establishing a trust is to provide for the management of the trust property. Not everyone is adept at managing assets. A person not experienced in handling wealth may squander it or invest imprudently. A trust can be used to provide professional management of assets for individuals who are not suited, by training or experience, to manage assets for themselves.

Example 8.6

Suzanne thinks of herself as the world's foremost expert in the fields of personal finance and money management. Her husband and children have relied on her to manage all of the family finances. Instead of leaving her property outright to her family when she dies, Suzanne can transfer the property into a trust, name professional money managers as trustees, and they will manage the money for her husband and children.

Creditor Protection

When asked, most individuals would say they would rather receive an outright transfer of money than a transfer in trust. This is often based on the belief that with an outright transfer, they will have complete control over the assets and can use the assets in a way that will maximize their utility. If an outright transfer of assets is made, however the creditors of the recipient (judgment creditors or otherwise) will have access to those funds to satisfy outstanding obligations.

Key Concepts

1. Identify at least three reasons to use a trust.
2. What is a temporal discount?
3. Who is subject to the income tax on the income of a grantor trust?

If property is placed in a trust with appropriate spendthrift protection provisions instead of being transferred outright, the creditors of the beneficiary will not be able to access the funds in the trust to satisfy outstanding creditor claims. A spendthrift clause, coupled with a provision that allows the trustee to make distributions solely on a discretionary basis, is a very strong and effective asset protection tool. The **spendthrift clause** simply states that the beneficiary may not anticipate distributions from the trust, and may not assign, pledge, hypothecate, or otherwise promise to give distributions from the trust to anyone and, if such a promise is made, that promise is considered to be void and may not be enforced against the trust. Most states enforce spendthrift clauses, since the property in trust never belonged to the beneficiary and the beneficiary cannot be sure that he will ever receive discretionary distributions from the trustee. In some states, claims for spousal or child support can be obtained from a trust despite the presence of a spendthrift clause.

Example 8.7
Pat, a registered nurse, always wanted her children to enter the medical profession. None of her children became physicians, but her grandson, Luca, decided to go to medical school. Understanding the malpractice dilemma faced by physicians, Pat decided she wanted to protect any property that would pass during her lifetime, or at her death, to Luca from Luca's creditors. She created a trust that named Luca as the discretionary income beneficiary for life and upon Luca's death, would distribute the trust corpus to Luca's children in equal shares, per stirpes. The trust included a spendthrift clause. If a malpractice claim is filed against Luca, the assets in the trust will not be available to satisfy those claims. If the trust purchases assets for Luca's use instead of making distributions to Luca, those assets will also be protected. Note that if Pat had not used a trust, any assets that she transferred to Luca directly would be subject to malpractice claims.

A spendthrift clause protects the trust assets from the claims of the beneficiary's creditors provided that the beneficiary did not create the trust for his own benefit. If the beneficiary is also the grantor of the trust, the trust is referred to as a **self-settled trust** and, as a general rule, spendthrift protection will not apply. While states allow protection when an individual creates a trust for another person, the assets of a self-settled trust are not protected. A few states, such as Alaska and Delaware, have changed their laws to allow the creation of a self-settled asset protection trust, but this protection is far from being the majority rule in the United States.

Example 8.8
Jonathan decided that he needed to protect his assets from his potential creditors, and created a trust in the state of Texas. He transferred all of his assets to the trust and named himself as the discretionary beneficiary of the trust. The trust included a spendthrift clause. Despite the presence of a spendthrift clause, Jonathan's creditors will be able to gain access to the trust assets to settle any debts since the trust is a self-settled trust.

Split Interests in Property

A trust is often used to take a single asset or property interest and divide it into different interests to achieve a client's estate planning and wealth transfer objectives. As already illustrated in this chapter, a trust can create two or more separate property interests – an income interest and a remainder interest. This may be particularly important for clients who have most of their estate tied up in a very valuable asset that they do not want to sell and do not want to divide amongst their children.

Example 8.9

William owns a farm that has been in his family for over 100 years. The farm is the primary asset in his estate and generates substantial income for William and his family. Some of William's children are interested in continuing the farming business, while others are pursuing different careers. William and his wife, Marge, want to treat all of their children equally, meaning that they want each of their children to receive the same amount of money or property from their estate. If the children who want to run the farm receive the farmland, there will be no other assets to give to the other children. William can put the land into a trust that allows the trustee to lease the land to the children who will run the farm. He can name his other children as the income beneficiaries of the trust, so that they derive some value from William and Marge's estate for a period of time, after which the land will be distributed to the children running the farming operation. In this case, the single piece of farmland has been split into two separate pieces – an income interest and a remainder interest. The children who wish to continue the farming can do so, provided that they "pay" for the other children's interest in the land through the income of the farming operation. The children pursuing other opportunities will "cash-out" over time and will therefore be treated fairly in the eyes of William and Marge.

From a more sophisticated planning perspective, a split interest arrangement (i.e., a trust) can be used to create temporal discounts on the transfer of property. A temporal discount is a discount generated by the passage of time. By delaying a beneficiary's enjoyment of the property, it is possible to lower the value of a gift or estate transfer for tax purposes.

Example 8.10

Denzel recently transferred $1,000,000 to a trust. Denzel retained the right to receive an annuity of $50,000 each year for 10 years. Upon termination of Denzel's annuity income interest, the trust will terminate and the assets will be transferred to Malcolm and Olivia. When Denzel created the trust, he made a completed gift of the remainder interest in the trust to Malcolm and Olivia. The present value of the $50,000 per year income stream that Denzel will receive is $350,000, and therefore the remainder interest in the trust is $650,000 ($1,000,000 initial funding - $350,000 income interest retained). Since Malcolm and Olivia had to wait to receive the gift (in this case, they had to wait 10 years), Denzel was able to generate a $350,000 temporal discount on the transfer for gift tax purposes. Denzel will have a taxable gift of $650,000 against which he could use some of his applicable gift tax credit.

Avoiding Probate (Living Trust)

Perhaps one of the most popular uses of a trust is to avoid probate. Probate is the process of collecting a decedent's property, paying off the decedent's debts and any taxes that may be due, and transferring (retitling) what is left to the decedent's heirs. In some states, probate is an expensive process, sometimes costing five to six percent of the value of the decedent's probate estate.

An alternative to the probate process is the use of a **revocable living trust**. All of an individual's property is transferred (retitled) to a revocable trust (a trust that the grantor can terminate at anytime) that is managed by the grantor and is for the benefit of the grantor during his lifetime. Upon the grantor's death, the trust becomes irrevocable and the property passes to the grantor's heirs under the terms of the trust. Since the probate court does not need to intervene and transfer the property (the property will transfer according to the trust document), probate costs and expenses are avoided on the trust property. It is important to remember, however, that a revocable trust does not avoid estate taxes – it only avoids the probate process and the resulting probate fees and expenses. Because the grantor retains an interest in a revocable trust, the full fair market value of the assets is included in his gross estate for estate tax purposes.

Minimizing Taxes

When used appropriately in the estate planning process, trusts can generate transfer and income tax savings. The tax savings result from:
1. the transfer of future appreciation to the grantor's heir,
2. the minimization of transfer taxes on subsequent generations,
3. the reduction in the size of the grantor's gross estate, and
4. the reduction of income taxes for the donor of income produced on the transferred asset.

Once an irrevocable trust is established and funded, all future appreciation in the trust assets belongs to the beneficiaries of the trust. The appreciation and income occurring after the gift was made is not taxable to the grantor. Contrast this with a situation where the grantor retains the property throughout his lifetime and bequeaths the property to his heirs at death. In this case, all of the appreciation on the property is subject to estate tax because the appreciation occurred before the transfer of the property.

When a trust is established to last for multiple generations, transfer tax is minimized by preventing the property from being included in each beneficiary's gross estate. Since the gift and estate taxes are transfer taxes, not property taxes, and the property is not transferred, no transfer tax can result.

> ### Quick Quiz 8.2
>
> 1. A trust cannot provide for creditor protection.
>   a. True
>   b. False
> 2. Including a spendthrift clause in a trust allows a trustee to use trust assets for administration expenses.
>   a. True
>   b. False
> 3. Property in a revocable living trust with a living beneficiary avoids probate.
>   a. True
>   b. False
> 4. Property in a revocable living trust avoids federal estate taxes.
>   a. True
>   b. False
>
> False, False, True, False.

chapter 8

> **Example 8.11**
> Brian created a trust thirty years ago (in a state that has abolished the rule against perpetuities) that provided income to his only child, Michael, who died this year. Despite the fact that Michael was the primary beneficiary of the trust and was permitted to use the trust's assets, none of the assets in the trust will be included in Michael's gross estate, since he did not own the assets. Michael's children will now be able to receive trust benefits and use the trust's assets. If, in contrast, Brian gave the assets transferred in trust directly to Michael, those assets would have been subject to estate tax, perhaps leaving only about half of the assets for Michael's children.

Finally, when a grantor trust is created (discussed below), the grantor is required to pay the income tax liability on the trust income. By paying the income tax liability, the grantor of the trust reduces his gross estate by the amount of the income taxes paid. In addition to reducing the size of the grantor's gross estate, the payment of the trust's income tax liability is not considered to be a taxable gift, since the payment requirement is imposed by tax law. Contrast this with a situation where an individual, without legal compulsion, agrees to pay the income tax liability of another. In this instance, the payment of the income tax liability would be considered a gift for gift tax purposes.

TRUST DURATION – THE RULE AGAINST PERPETUITIES

A potential problem with the use of trusts is that the property placed in trust may be removed from the stream of commerce for a very long period of time, and would therefore violate a common law dictate stating that any restraint on the alienation of property is void as a matter of law.

> **Key Concepts**
> 1. Which states have abolished the rule against perpetuities?
> 2. Identify the situations in which the grantor of an irrevocable trust must include the trust assets in his gross estate.

In the late 1500's, the Duke of Norfolk, whose oldest son and heir was non compos mentis (not competent), created a trust to protect the family property for his son. The Duke transferred all of his property to the trust, and prohibited the trustee from selling any of the property, thereby removing the property from commerce. This trust provision created controversy amongst many who did not believe that property should be encumbered with such restrictions. After many years of litigation, the Duke of Norfolk's case was resolved when Lord Chancellor Nottingham decided the case and issued what is now known as the **rule against perpetuities** (RAP). The RAP states that all interests in trust must vest, if at all, within lives in being, plus 21 years.

The RAP appears to be a simple rule, but it's interpretation has been far from easy. Since the Duke of Norfolk's case, numerous court decisions have further interpreted the rule. In addition, there are many treatises that have been written attempting to explain the purpose and application of the rule. From a practical perspective, the effect of the RAP was to place a limit on the amount of time that property could be held in trust. As the rule states, all interests in trust must vest, if at all, within lives in being (persons alive at the inception of the trust) plus 21 years. Note that it is possible to have a trust last longer than the RAP period, provided that all interests in the trust vest within the RAP period. For example, if all of the beneficiaries of the trust are given a testamentary general power of appointment over their portion of the trust assets during the perpetuities period, the trust will not have to terminate until 21 years after the last beneficiary holding the testamentary general power of appointment dies. The general power of appointment will cause the trust interest to vest in each beneficiary holding such power and will therefore meet the requirements of the RAP.

Due to the uncertainties associated with the length of the perpetuities period under the RAP, some states have adopted the **uniform statutory rule against perpetuities**. The uniform statutory rule against perpetuities sets the perpetuities period at 90 years, and creates a presumption that all interests that vest within that 90-year period are valid interests. The IRS recognizes the perpetuities period contained in the uniform statutory rule against perpetuities, provided that the perpetuities period is not defined in the governing instrument as the longer of the 90-year period or the Common Law RAP period.

Some states have taken a completely different approach, such as Alaska, Delaware, and South Dakota, and have abolished the RAP. In these states it is possible to create a trust that will have a perpetual duration. To address a common law issue concerning the alienation of property, however, most states that have abolished the RAP have also adopted legislation stating that the grantor of a perpetual trust may not include language in the trust prohibiting the trustee from selling the property. These laws are known as anti-alienation statutes. The replacement of the RAP with anti-alienation statutes seems to address the original issue brought forth in the Duke of Norfolk's case more appropriately. If alienation of property is the issue, the fatal flaw in the Duke's plan was not that he placed the property in trust, but rather that he prohibited the trustee from selling the property. As long as the trustee can freely dispose of the property (thereby keeping the property in the stream of commerce), it should not matter how long the trust holding the property can be in existence. The repeal of the RAP presents several attractive estate planning opportunities for clients with long-term wealth transfer goals.

> **Quick Quiz 8.3**
>
> 1. The uniform statutory rule against perpetuities set the perpetuities period at 90 years.
>   a. True
>   b. False
> 2. If a grantor retains the right to receive income from a trust, the value of the trust will be included in his gross estate.
>   a. True
>   b. False
> 3. If gift tax is paid on a transfer to a trust within three years of the decedent's date of death, the gift tax is included in the decedent's gross estate.
>   a. True
>   b. False
>
> True, True, True.

ACCOUNTING AND INCOME TAXATION OF TRUSTS

Income Taxation of Trusts

Trusts are treated for income tax purposes as hybrid entities. All income a trust receives, whether from foreign or domestic sources, is taxable to the trust, to the beneficiary, or to the grantor of the trust unless specifically exempted by the Internal Revenue Code (IRC). To the extent that the income of the trust is distributed to the beneficiaries, the beneficiaries who receive the distributions will be subject to income tax on the income. In the absence of provisions to the contrary in the trust instrument, the trust is allowed to deduct distributions to beneficiaries from its taxable income, with a few modifications. Therefore, trusts can eliminate income tax at the trust level by making distributions to beneficiaries.

The income taxation of trusts and estates is governed by Subchapter J of the Code, which creates a model whereby income tax liability is shared by the trust or estate and its beneficiaries. Under Subchapter J, a trust or estate pays income tax on the amount of income it retains, and the beneficiaries pay income tax on the distributions of trust income that they receive. This approach ensures that trust income will not be subject to double taxation and places the burden of paying the income tax on the party receiving the income. Since trustees of a trust (or the executors/administrators of an estate) are often given the discretionary right to distribute income to the beneficiaries, the trustee or executor can avoid taxation at the trust level by passing all income through to the beneficiaries.

A special rule may apply to certain gains earned by a trust if the grantor makes a contribution of appreciated property to the trust. If the appreciated property is sold within two years of the date of transfer, an income tax is imposed on the trust equal to what the grantor would have paid if the gain had been included in his or her income for the year the sale occurred.

> ## Key Concepts
>
> 1. Describe how trusts, and their beneficiaries, are taxed for federal income tax purposes.
> 2. Describe the tax motivation for distributing trust income to the beneficiaries of the trust.
> 3. Identify the difference between simple and complex trusts.
> 4. Identify the purposes of distributable net income.

The income tax rate schedule that applies to estates and trusts is compressed when compared to individual tax rates. Once a trust or estate has $12,950 in 2020 taxable income it is subject to income tax at the highest marginal income tax rate for trusts and estates (See Exhibit 8.2). Investment income over $12,950 in 2020 will also be subject to the 3.8 percent Medicare surtax imposed by the Affordable Care Act, raising the effective tax rate for income over $12,950 (in 2020) to 40.8 percent for ordinary income and 23.8 percent for qualified dividends and long-term capital gains. If trust beneficiaries find themselves in income tax brackets below 37 percent, income tax minimization can be achieved by distributing the trust income to the beneficiaries, who will then pay tax on the trust income at their marginal income tax rate (plus the 3.8 percent Medicare surtax if their adjusted gross income exceeds $200,000 for single individuals and $250,000 for those who are married filing jointly).

In the past, some planners have tried to avoid the imposition of the harsh marginal income tax rate table for trusts by establishing a series of trusts, all of which will have income that is expected to remain in the lowest marginal tax bracket. To prevent this type of planning, the Internal Revenue Code treats a set of substantially similar trusts, created for the purpose of avoiding income tax at higher marginal rates, to be taxed as a single trust.

Exhibit 8.2 | Income Tax Rate Schedule for Estates and Trusts (2019)

If taxable income is:	The tax is:
Not over $2,600	**10%** of taxable income
Over $2,600 but not over $9,450	$260 plus **24%** of the amount over $2,600
Over $9,450 but not over $12,950	$1,904 plus **35%** of the amount over $9,450
Over $12,950	$3,129 plus **37%** of the amount over $12,950

Simple and Complex Trusts

Simple trusts are trusts that mandate the annual distribution of all trust income. The beneficiaries of a simple trust pay all of the income tax on the income of the trust. The trust does not incur any income tax liability because it is able to fully deduct the amount distributed to the beneficiaries from the amount of income earned. If the trust incurred any capital gains, however, the trust would have tax liability if those gains are set aside for the remainder beneficiaries of the trust.

A simple trust has all of its income (but not necessarily any of its principal) distributed on an annual basis to its beneficiaries. The definition of income for this purpose is limited to interest and dividends earned on trust assets. To be classified as a simple trust, there cannot be any principal distributions or charitable gifts made during the year. Any trust that has a distribution of principal or makes charitable gifts will be treated as a complex trust for that year.

A complex trust, on the other hand, is a trust that is permitted to accumulate income, benefit a charity, or distribute principal. A simple trust becomes a complex trust in any year in which it distributes principal or benefits a charity. It then reverts back to a simple trust in subsequent years. If the complex trust accumulates income, it is taxed on that income at the trust income tax rates (see Exhibit 8.2). Each beneficiary of a complex trust is taxed on his pro rata share of the distribution deduction taken by the trust. The distribution deduction is the lesser of the amount actually distributed to the beneficiaries of the trust or distributable net income. Distributable net income, as calculated under Section 643(a), is an approximation of the actual economic benefit available to the income beneficiaries of the trust and is the maximum amount that can be taxed to the beneficiaries. Income distributed to the beneficiaries has the same character in the hands of the beneficiaries as it does in the hands of the trust (e.g., ordinary income, capital gain, etc.). Distributions in excess of distributable net income are generally treated as tax-free distributions of principal.

Simple and complex trusts are treated as separate taxable entities for income tax reporting purposes. Trusts are permitted to take many of the same deductions available to individuals, such as deductions for investment or business interest paid, taxes paid, depreciation and depletion, charitable contributions, and administration expenses necessary to maintain, preserve, and increase the income or principal of the trust. Due to their nature as pass-through entities, trusts are also permitted to deduct income distributed to the beneficiaries, which is referred to as the distribution deduction. Note that a simple trust that has only interest and dividend income and distributes all of that income to the beneficiaries will not be subject to income tax due to the presence of the distribution deduction. Simple trusts that have realized capital gains, and complex trusts, are typically subject to income taxation at the trust level. A simple trust is entitled to a personal exemption of $300, complex trusts are entitled to a personal exemption of $100, and estates are entitled to a personal exemption of $600. This means that the first $300 or $100 of trust income, or the first $600 of income for an estate is exempt from income taxation after the appropriate deductions are claimed.

Distributable Net Income
The determination of what constitutes income for trusts and estates as set forth in the Internal Revenue Code is complex. The concept of **distributable net income** (DNI) is used by the Code to ensure that income earned by a trust is subject to only one level of tax. DNI equals the total income of a trust *or* estate for the taxable year, after making the following adjustments:
1. Adding back the allowable deduction for income distributed to trust beneficiaries and the trust's personal exemption.
2. Excluding capital gains if they are not either,
   - paid, credited, or required to be distributed to a beneficiary in the taxable year, or
   - paid, permanently set aside, or used for charitable purposes.
3. Adding tax exempt interest, and, in the case of a foreign trust, foreign income reduced by the deductions allowed against that income, with a proportionate amount of tax-exempt or foreign income allocated to the charitable deduction if claimed by the trust.

Extraordinary dividends and taxable stock dividends are excluded from the DNI of a simple trust if the trustee allocates them in good faith to the corpus of the trust in accordance with the requirements of the governing instrument or state law, and does not distribute them to the beneficiaries.

As indicated above, capital gains are excluded from DNI unless they are distributed or required to be distributed to a beneficiary, or are paid or permanently set aside for the benefit of a charity. Unless the trust instrument or state law specifies otherwise, capital gains are usually considered to be a return to principal and are typically not available for distribution to the income beneficiaries. If a trust has capital gains and does not distribute those gains to the beneficiaries, however, the trust will be subject to some income tax for the year. If a trust distributes capital gains, then the beneficiary will pay income tax on the capital gains. In this scenario, the trust will not be liable for capital gains income taxation (capital gains will be included in DNI) since the gains are passed through to the beneficiary.

DNI is used in the income tax system for three purposes in income taxation:
1. to ensure that a trust or estate receives a deduction for income that it actually distributes to its beneficiaries,
2. to limit the beneficiary's exposure to income taxation on trust distributions, and
3. to maintain the character of the income that is distributed to the beneficiaries.

The trust's DNI (calculated in accordance with the rules set forth above) represents the maximum distribution deduction the trust may take for distributions of income to trust beneficiaries. The calculation of DNI ensures that the trust is not able to receive a distribution deduction for distributions of principal to the beneficiaries. Since DNI essentially equals trust income, the distribution deduction should be, and is, limited to this amount.

Example 8.12
The Jarvis Family Trust received $4,000 in taxable interest, $4,000 in tax-exempt interest, $12,000 in dividends, and $60,000 in capital gains during the current tax year. The trust is not required to distribute its income to its beneficiaries on an annual basis, and will therefore be considered a complex trust for income tax purposes. DNI for the year equals $20,000 ($4,000 in taxable interest, $4,000 in tax exempt interest, and $12,000 in dividends). Capital gains are not included in DNI since the trustee is not permitted to distribute principal to the beneficiaries, and there are no charitable beneficiaries of the trust. The maximum distribution deduction the trust is entitled to this year equals its DNI of $20,000.

Example 8.13
Continuing with the example, assume that the Jarvis Family Trust distributes all of its income to its beneficiaries. Ignoring other deductions and exemptions, the trust will have a total of $80,000 in income for the year (including capital gains). When the trust distributes $20,000 to the beneficiaries, it receives a distribution deduction of a like amount. The difference of $60,000 (representing capital gains in this example that are allocated to principal and retained by the trust) will be subject to tax at the trust level.

In the event that the trust document permits the trustee to distribute both income and principal to the beneficiaries, the trust's distribution deduction is limited to its DNI. Since principal is not included in income or DNI, it should not qualify the trust for a deduction for income tax purposes.

Example 8.14

Continuing with the previous example, assume that the Jarvis Family Trust gives the trustee the power to make both principal and income distributions, and the trustee distributes $100,000 to the beneficiaries in the current tax year. The beneficiaries will have a total of $80,000 of income potentially subject to tax, and the trust will receive a distribution deduction of $80,000. The remaining portion of the distribution, or $20,000 will be treated as a tax-free distribution of capital. Generally, capital gains are not included in DNI unless they are paid, credited, or required to be distributed to a beneficiary in the taxable year. Since the capital gains, as well as the interest and dividend income, are distributed to the beneficiaries, they are included in DNI. In this case, the beneficiaries will pay tax on all trust income for the current year, and the trust will not be liable for any tax because the trust is funneling the income through to the beneficiaries.

Another purpose of DNI is to ensure that the income distributed to the beneficiaries retains its character for income tax purposes. From the beneficiary's standpoint, this is important since different forms of income are subject to different levels of tax. For example, tax-exempt income and stock dividends are tax exempt when received by the beneficiaries, interest and non-qualified dividends are taxed at ordinary tax rates, and capital gains and qualified dividends are taxed at capital gains tax rates.

Example 8.15

Continuing with the previous example, when the Jarvis Family Trust distributes $100,000 to its beneficiaries this year, only $80,000 is potentially subject to taxation (which equals the trust's DNI for the current tax year). Of that $80,000, $4,000 is tax-exempt interest, which will not be subject to tax. Interest and dividends make up $12,000 of the DNI, which will be taxed according to the taxpayers rate, and the remaining $60,000 of DNI represents capital gain, which will be taxed at capital gains rates (ordinary tax rate if the gain is a short-term gain, and a maximum of 20 percent if the gain is a long-term capital gain provided. The additional $20,000 distributed to the beneficiaries is a distribution of principal, and is therefore treated as a nontaxable return of capital.

Gift Tax as Applied to Trusts

Whether or not a transfer to a trust will be taxable for gift tax purposes depends on the characteristics of the trust. If the trust is a revocable trust, a transfer to the trust will not be considered a completed gift for gift tax purposes, and therefore will not be subject to gift tax. If the trust is an irrevocable trust, any transfer to the trust will be considered a taxable gift (unless the grantor retains some interest in the trust) subject to gift tax. When irrevocable trusts are created for charities, however, the unlimited gift tax charitable deduction is available to avoid gift tax on the portion of any transfer that is determined to be for the charity.

chapter 8

Inclusion/Exclusion from Gross Estate of Trust Assets

For estate tax purposes, the assets held by an irrevocable trust funded during a grantor's lifetime are generally excluded from the gross estate of the grantor. When a grantor funds an irrevocable trust for a non-charitable beneficiary, gift tax rules apply because the transfer is treated as a completed gift at that time. Therefore, the gift tax liability must be calculated, and to the extent that the gift liability exceeds the grantor's remaining applicable gift tax credit, gift tax must be paid. Since the taxable transfer occurs during the life of the grantor, the grantor no longer owns the property and therefore it is not included in the grantor's gross estate at his death.

There are some situations, however, where the value of the assets of an irrevocable trust funded during the grantor's life are included in the grantor's gross estate. The assets of an irrevocable trust are included in the grantor's gross estate if a grantor makes a transfer to an irrevocable trust, but retains:
1. the right to receive income from the trust;
2. the right to use the trust assets;
3. the ability to exercise voting rights on stock transferred to the trust;
4. a reversionary interest with a value greater than five percent of the trust;
5. the right to terminate, alter, amend, or revoke the trust; or
6. the right to control beneficial enjoyment of the trust.

> **Quick Quiz 8.4**
>
> 1. Distributable net income (DNI) of a trust is the amount that must be distributed to the trust beneficiaries on an annual basis.
>   a. True
>   b. False
>
> 2. Assets transferred to a trust are excluded from the gross estate of the trust's grantor.
>   a. True
>   b. False
>
> 3. Gift tax paid on transfers to a trust within 3 years of the grantor's date of death will be included in the grantor's gross estate.
>   a. True
>   b. False
>
> *False, False, True.*

To the extent that the grantor paid gift tax on the transfers made to the trust, and the value of the trust assets are included in his gross estate, the grantor's estate will receive a tax credit for the gift taxes actually paid.

Example 8.16

Forty years ago, Shay purchased a tract of raw land several miles outside of a major city. Over the years, the city has expanded, and the land that Shay owns has appreciated in value. Shay transferred the land to a Charitable Remainder Unitrust (CRUT - discussed in Chapter 9), and retained the right to receive a 5% unitrust payout each year for life, and named the local library (a qualified charity) as the remainder beneficiary of the trust. When Shay dies, the full value of the assets inside the CRUT will be included in his gross estate, since at the date of his death, he had a right to receive income from the trust. His estate will also be entitled to a charitable deduction for the same amount, since the trust terminates at Shay's death and all of the trust assets are transferred to charity. Note that the inclusion of the CRUT assets in his gross estate will not increase his estate tax liability due to the availability of the charitable deduction, but may have an impact on his ability to qualify for a Section 303 redemption, a Section 6166 deferral of estate tax, or a Section 2032A special use valuation (discussed in Chapter 12).

Example 8.17

Thirty five years ago, Don purchased a beach house in Stone Harbor, NJ. Ten years ago, Don transferred the beach house to a qualified personal residence trust (QPRT), retaining the right to use the property for 20 years, with the remainder interest passing to his only daughter, Beth. Don passed away last month. The full fair market value of the beach house (the only asset of the QPRT) will be included in Don's gross estate, since at the time of his death, he had a retained right to use the property that had been transferred to the trust. To the extent that Don paid gift tax on the value of the remainder interest that was given to Beth, his estate will receive a credit for the deemed gift taxes paid (to avoid double transfer taxation as discussed in Chapter 6).

In the event a grantor makes a transfer to an irrevocable trust in which the grantor retains an interest, and the grantor releases his interest in the trust within three years of death, the three-year rule (IRC Section 2035) requires the full fair market value of the trust to be included in the grantor's gross estate.

Example 8.18

Ellen created and funded an irrevocable trust five years ago for the benefit of her daughter, Marguerite. The purpose of the trust was to hold Ellen's extensive jewelry collection, and to avoid transfer tax on the subsequent appreciation of the jewelry. Upon funding the trust, Ellen paid a gift tax on the transfer. Ellen also reserved the right to occasionally use some of the jewelry that she had irrevocably transferred to the trust. When she attended an estate planning seminar last week, Ellen realized that her retained right to use the jewelry held in the trust would cause the fair market value of the trust assets to be included in her gross estate. Consequently, Ellen released her retained right to use any of the jewelry currently owned by the trust. If Ellen dies within three years of releasing her right to use the jewelry, the full fair market value of the trust assets will be included in her gross estate, and her estate will receive a credit for the gift taxes deemed paid on the transfer of the jewelry to the trust. If Ellen dies more than three years after the release of her right to use the jewelry, the fair market value of the trust assets will not be included in her gross estate.

Example 8.19

Thirty five years ago, Don purchased a beach house in Stone Harbor, NJ. Ten years ago, Don transferred the beach house to a qualified personal residence trust (QPRT), retaining the right to use the property for 20 years, with the remainder passing to his only daughter, Beth. Assuming that Don is alive upon the expiration of his retained interest in the trust, the value of the trust assets will not be included in his gross estate. In this case, Don did not release his right to use the property; rather, his retained right expired due to the passage of time. Don does not have to satisfy the three-year rule, since he did not take any action to terminate his retained interest.

As noted earlier, if a grantor makes a transfer to an irrevocable trust in which he does not retain an interest, there is no inclusion in the gross estate of the grantor. The lifetime gift to the trust will, however, be an adjusted taxable gift to the extent that the value of the transfer exceeds the allowable annual exclusion amount. As detailed in Chapter 6, if the gift to the trust was made within three years of the grantor's death, any gift taxes actually paid on the transfer will also be included in the grantor's gross estate.

Example 8.20

Five years ago, Adam created and funded the Luckhardt Dynasty Trust, a perpetual trust for the benefit of his heirs. At the time the trust was created, Adam transferred $1,000,000 to the trust and allocated a portion of his generation-skipping transfer tax exemption (see Chapter 13) to the transfer. Since Adam had used his applicable gift tax credit and applicable annual exclusions in prior transfers to family members, the funding of the dynasty trust was a fully taxable event for gift tax purposes, and Adam paid $400,000 in gift taxes on the transfer. If Adam dies this year, there will not be anything included in his gross estate related to this transaction, since he died more than three years after the transfer. In funding the trust, however, Adam made an adjusted taxable gift of $1,000,000 (recall that no annual exclusions were used in making the transfer), which will be added back to his tentative taxable estate for purposes of calculating his estate tax, and his estate will be given a credit for the gift taxes deemed paid.

Example 8.21

Assume the same facts as above, except that Adam created the Luckhardt Dynasty Trust two years before his death. Since Adam died within three years of making the transfer, the $400,000 in gift taxes paid will be included in his gross estate under the three-year rule and the $1,000,000 adjusted taxable gift will be added to his tentative taxable estate for purposes of calculating the estate tax. Adam's estate will also receive a credit for the gift taxes actually paid on all prior transfers, including this transfer to the Luckhardt Dynasty Trust.

In addition to income, gift, and estate taxes, a trust may be subject to generation-skipping transfer taxes (GSTT). Whenever a trust will include a skip person as a beneficiary, it is important to consider the GSTT ramifications, and, if appropriate, allocate a portion of the GST exemption to the trust to avoid a current or future GSTT. Refer to Chapter 13 on Generation-Skipping Transfer Taxes for more information on this subject.

Exhibit 8.3 | Summary of Tax Issues Related To Trusts

	Revocable Trusts	Irrevocable Trusts
Income Tax	Income is taxed to grantor.	• Income is taxed to beneficiaries if distributed. • Income is taxed to trust if retained (unless the trust is a grantor trust, in which case all income is taxed to the grantor).
Gift Tax	No gift tax consequences, since the grantor can take the property back.	• Treated as a completed gift and is subject to gift tax.
Estate Tax – Gross Estate	Full fair market value of trust assets included in the grantor's gross estate.	Not included in the gross estate of the grantor unless: • The grantor retained an interest as of the date of his death; • The grantor released an interest in the trust within 3 years of his death; or • The grantor did not retain an interest in the trust but funding the trust generated a gift tax within 3 years of the grantor's death.
Estate Tax – Adjusted Taxable Gift	No adjusted taxable gift.	• To the extent the gift to the trust exceeds the annual exclusion (if applicable), the adjusted taxable gift is added back to the tentative tax base for purposes of calculating the estate tax due.
Generation-Skipping Transfer Tax	GSTT is not an issue, since the trust assets are included in the grantor's estate.	• GSTT may be an issue, depending on the identification of the beneficiaries of the trust.

CLASSIFICATION OF TRUST ARRANGEMENTS

Revocable Trusts

The grantor of a **revocable trust** retains the right to revoke the trust at any time prior to his incapacity or death. Revocable trusts are commonly used to avoid probate and to provide for management of the grantor's assets should he become incapacitated.

> **Key Concepts**
>
> 1. What is a funded trust?
> 2. Which type of trust can accumulate income?

Irrevocable Trusts

In contrast to the revocable trust, the grantor of an **irrevocable trust** cannot take back the property that was transferred to the trust. To achieve estate and gift tax planning objectives, a trust must be irrevocable. Not all irrevocable trusts are effective for estate tax purposes, however if, for example, the grantor retains some right over the property transferred to the trust, the value of the trust assets may be included in his gross estate for estate tax purposes.

Inter Vivos Trust

Any trust that is created during the lifetime of the grantor is referred to as an **inter vivos trust**. All revocable trusts are also inter vivos trusts. Irrevocable trusts can be either inter vivos trusts (if created during the grantor's lifetime) or testamentary trusts (if created by the grantor's will).

Testamentary Trusts

A trust created after the death of the grantor is referred to as a **testamentary trust**. Generally, the grantor leaves instructions in his will for the executor of the estate to create and fund a trust after the grantor's death. Two of the most common types of testamentary trusts are credit shelter (or bypass) trusts and marital deduction trusts (QTIP Trusts, General Power of Appointment Trusts, or Estate Trusts).

Standby Trust

A **standby trust**, also known as a contingent trust, is a trust created during the grantor's lifetime that is either unfunded or minimally funded. The trust simply stands by and waits for a triggering event to activate it. The trust may be used during life, during times of incapacity, or at death to assist with estate administration.

Pourover Trust

A **pourover trust** is a trust that receives assets from another source, generally the grantor's estate at the grantor's death. The trust is generally unfunded or minimally funded until the assets pour into the trust.

Grantor Trust

Grantor trusts can be revocable or irrevocable trusts. To qualify for grantor trust status, the trust must be an inter vivos trust. When a trust is characterized as a grantor trust, the grantor of the trust, not the trust itself or the trust beneficiaries, is responsible for paying the income tax attributable to the trust's income. Grantor trusts, particularly when combined with other planning tools, are very powerful estate planning vehicles.

Funded or Unfunded

A trust can be either funded or unfunded. A funded trust is a trust that has received a transfer of property from the grantor. Technically, a trust is not considered to be in existence until it is funded. A properly drafted trust document is not enough – to come alive, the trust must have property transferred into it.

An unfunded trust is a trust that has been drafted, but not funded. In some instances, individuals wish to have a trust created so that it is available to receive money or property in the future. As discussed above, a standby trust can be used for this purpose.

> ### Quick Quiz 8.5
>
> 1. The grantor of a revocable trust cannot take back the property that was transferred to the trust.
>   a. True
>   b. False
>
> 2. A trust created by the will of a decedent is known as a testamentary trust.
>   a. True
>   b. False
>
> 3. Any trust that requires all of its income to be distributed on an annual basis is a complex trust.
>   a. True
>   b. False
>
> False, True, False.

Simple or Complex

For income tax purposes, a trust can be either a simple trust or a complex trust. A **simple trust** is any trust that requires all of the trust income to be distributed on an annual basis to the beneficiaries, and does not have a charitable organization as one of its beneficiaries. A **complex trust** is any trust that does not meet the definition of a simple trust. That is, a complex trust is a trust that is either permitted to accumulate income, or a trust that may make distributions to a charitable organization.

SPECIFIC TRUSTS USED IN ESTATE PLANNING

Inter Vivos Revocable Trusts

Perhaps the most common type of trust created today is the revocable trust. A revocable trust must be created during the grantor's lifetime (once the grantor dies, he can no longer take action to revoke a trust), and is therefore a form of inter vivos trust. All revocable trusts are grantor trusts for federal income tax purposes, requiring the grantor of the trust to pay income tax on all of the trust income.

Probate Avoidance

Revocable trusts are effective probate avoidance devices. When an individual creates a revocable trust and transfers all of his property to the trust, the disposition of the trust property at the death of the grantor will be governed by the trust and will not become part of the grantor's probate estate. The grantor's will does not control the disposition of the property because the property is not included in the probate estate. A revocable trust becomes irrevocable upon the grantor's death.

The use of revocable trusts is important in states that have high probate costs. In some states, the cost of probating a decedent's will could range from five to six percent of the value of the probate estate. For individuals with large estates residing in a state where probate costs are high, the use of a revocable trust may be prudent. In other states, probate costs are more reasonable, and therefore, a revocable trust may not be necessary as probate is not costly and perhaps not worth avoiding.

Privacy

Regardless of the costs associated with probating a decedent's will, the use of a revocable trust can provide a degree of privacy for the decedent and his family. To probate a will, the will must be submitted to the probate court (in some states, the probate court is referred to as the Surrogates Court or the Orphans Court), and the will is open for public inspection. The activities of the executor are supervised by the court, and a record of the decedent's property and debts is placed on file, along with the names of the individuals who will receive the property. As an alternative to this public airing of the decedent's assets and affairs, a revocable trust could be created in conjunction with the will. Any assets the grantor places into the revocable trust during his lifetime will pass according to the terms of the trust, and assets outside of the trust that are subject to probate at his death are transferred to the revocable trust in accordance with the directions contained in the decedent's will. While the will is a public document, the disposition of the assets under the terms of the trust document is a private matter. A good example of a will that pours over to a revocable trust is the will of John F. Kennedy, Jr. (see **Exhibit 8.4**). While John F. Kennedy, Jr. included a few specific bequests in his will, the majority of his assets passed to a trust that governed the ultimate disposition of the property.

Discourages Will Contests

Another benefit associated with the use of a revocable trust is that will contests are discouraged. While state law differs in this area, it is more difficult for a decedent's beneficiaries and the heirs-at-law to contest the disposition of property through a revocable trust than through a will. As discussed in Chapter 4, the Uniform Probate Code gives any individual who can potentially benefit from a will contest the right to contest the will. This means that anyone whose share of the estate would be larger in the event that a will contest was successful can contest the will. Note that any heir-at-law who was not specifically provided for may be inclined to contest the will, since he has nothing to lose by doing so. Furthermore, all beneficiaries and heirs-at-law must be notified of the death of the decedent and the submission of the will for probate so that they have the opportunity to bring a will contest if desired. A revocable trust, in contrast, does not have any notice requirements, and the terms of the trust generally remain confidential and are not subject to public inspection. Heirs-at-law who are not named as beneficiaries of the revocable trust are generally not entitled to see the trust document, and if a will contest is brought, a higher standard must be met to break the trust as compared with setting aside a will in a probate court. While a revocable trust does not provide complete protection against contests, it creates more obstacles for a potential claimant than a will contest.

> **Key Concepts**
> 1. Identify the name of the trust in John F. Kennedy, Jr.'s will.
> 2. Indicate at least three benefits of using a revocable living trust.
> 3. What is the main goal of utilizing a testamentary bypass trust?

Estate Taxes

Revocable trusts provide significant probate avoidance and privacy benefits, but are not effective for reducing taxes for estate planning purposes. Because the trust is revocable by the grantor, the grantor has not made a completed gift to the revocable trust for gift tax purposes. Therefore, no gift tax is due upon creation of the trust, but the entire value of the trust is included in the grantor's gross estate for estate tax purposes. Revocable trusts are probate-efficient but not estate tax-efficient devices. Many people mistakenly believe that once the trust is created and they have transferred their assets to the trust, they will avoid state and federal estate and inheritance taxes at their death. As stated, the establishment of the revocable trust will only shelter the assets from inclusion in the probate estate.

Exhibit 8.4 | John F. Kennedy Jr.'s Will

THE LAST WILL AND TESTAMENT OF JOHN F. KENNEDY, JR.

John F. Kennedy, Jr. planned to leave the bulk of his holdings to his wife, Caroline Bessette-Kennedy, or their children. But John and Caroline died together in a plane crash in July of 1999 without leaving any issue (children). Therefore, his property will go to the children of his sister, Caroline Kennedy Schlossberg. The bulk of his estate is left to the beneficiaries of a trust he established in 1983. Kennedy also left the scrimshaw set, or carved whale ivory set, once owned by his father to nephew John B.K. Schlossberg. Kennedy's cousin Timothy P. Shriver was named executor of the will. Kennedy's estate is reportedly worth $100 million.

I, JOHN F. KENNEDY, JR., of New York, New York, make this my last will, hereby revoking all earlier wills and codicils. I do not by this will exercise any power of appointment.

<u>FIRST</u>: I give all my tangible property (as distinguished from money, securities and the like), wherever located, other than my scrimshaw set previously owned by my father, to my wife, Carolyn Bessette-Kennedy, if she is living on the thirtieth day after my death, or if not, by right of representation to my then living issue, or if none, by right of representation to the then living issue of my sister, Caroline Kennedy Schlossberg, or if none, to my said sister, Caroline, if she is then living. If I am survived by issue, I leave this scrimshaw set to said wife, Carolyn, if she is then living, or if not, by right of representation, to my then living issue. If I am not survived by issue, I give said scrimshaw set to my nephew John B.K. Schlossberg, if he is then living, or if not, by right of representation to the then living issue of my said sister, Caroline, or if none, to my said sister Caroline, if she is then living. I hope that whoever receives my tangible personal property will dispose of certain items of it in accordance with my wishes, however made known, but I impose no trust, condition or enforceable obligation of any kind in this regard. <u>SECOND</u>: I give and devise all my interest in my cooperative apartment located at 20-26 Moore Street, Apartment 9E, in said New York, including all my shares therein and any proprietary leases with respect thereto, to my said wife, Carolyn, if she is living on the thirtieth day after my death.

<u>THIRD:</u> If no issue of mine survive me, I give and devise all my interests in real estate, wherever located, that I own as tenants in common with my said sister, Caroline, or as tenants in common with any of her issue, by right of representation to Caroline's issue who are living on the thirtieth day after my death, or if none, to my said sister Caroline, if she is then living. References in this Article THIRD to "real estate" include shares in cooperative apartments and proprietary leases with respect thereto.

<u>FOURTH:</u> I give and devise the residue of all the property, of whatever kind and wherever located, that I own at my death to the then trustees of the John F. Kennedy Jr. 1983 Trust established October 13, 1983 by me, as Donor, of which John T. Fallon, of Weston, Massachusetts, and I are currently the trustees (the "1983 Trust"), to be added to the principal of the 1983 Trust and administered in accordance with the provisions thereof, as amended by a First Amendment dated April 9, 1987 and by a Second Amendment and Complete Restatement dated earlier this day, and as from time to hereafter further amended whether before or after my death. I have provided in the 1983 Trust for my children and more remote issue and for the method of paying all federal and state taxes in the nature of estate, inheritance, succession and like taxes occasioned by my death.

<u>FIFTH:</u> I appoint my wife, Carolyn Bessette-Kennedy, as guardian of each child of our marriage during minority. No guardian appointed in this will or a codicil need furnish any surety on any official bond.

<u>SIXTH</u>: I name my cousin Anthony Stanislaus Radziwill as my executor; and if for any reason, he fails to qualify or ceases to serve in that capacity, I name my cousin Timothy P. Shriver as my executor in his place. References in this will or a codicil to my "executor" mean the one or more executors (or administrators with this will annexed) for the time being in office. No executor or a codicil need furnish any surety on any official bond. In any proceeding for the allowance of an account of my executor, I request the Court to dispense with the appointment of a guardian ad litem to represent any person or interest. I direct that in any proceeding relating to my estate, service of process upon any person under a disability shall not made when another person not under a disability is a party to the proceeding and has the same interest as the person under the disability.

<u>SEVENTH</u>: In addition to other powers, my executor shall have power from time to time at discretion and without license of court: To retain, and to invest and reinvest in, any kind or amount of property; to vote and exercise other rights of security holders; to make such elections for federal and state estate, gift, income and generation-skipping transfer tax purposes as my executor may deem advisable; to compromise or admit to arbitration any matters in dispute; to borrow money, and to sell, mortgage, pledge, exchange, lease and contract with respect to any real or personal property, all without notice to any beneficiary and in such manner, for such consideration and on such terms as to credit or otherwise as my executor may deem advisable, whether or not the effect thereof extends beyond the period settling my estate; and in distributing my estate, to allot property, whether real or personal, at then current values, in lieu of cash.

Inter Vivos Irrevocable Trusts

To achieve estate and gift tax benefits, a trust created during the grantor's lifetime must be irrevocable. When an inter vivos irrevocable trust is created, the grantor cannot take the property back after it has been transferred to the trustee. Consequently, a transfer of money or property to the trust is considered a completed gift to the beneficiaries of the trust, and gift tax may be due at that time.

Gift Tax

Most transfers to trusts are transfers of a future interest and are therefore not eligible for the annual gift tax exclusion. However, a transfer to a trust which requires the income of the trust to be paid to the income beneficiary each year will qualify as a gift of a present interest eligible for the annual exclusion to the extent of the present value of the income interest. Also, a transfer to a trust which includes a Crummey power will qualify as a present interest and will be eligible for the annual exclusion (discussed in detail below).

After the application of the annual exclusion, an individual's applicable gift tax credit will offset any gift tax liability, but once the credit has been exhausted, the individual will be required to pay gift tax on the transfer.

Example 8.22

Jennifer created an irrevocable trust for the benefit of her son, Patrick, and funded it with a gift of $15,000. The trust requires the Trustee to distribute the income of the trust to Patrick on an annual basis. Upon Patrick's death, the principal of the trust will be distributed as directed by Patrick (Patrick has a testamentary general power of appointment). The value of Patrick's income interest, determined in accordance with IRS valuation requirements (see Chapter 7 for more information on using the Section 7520 interest rate) is $10,500. Therefore, $10,500 (a gift of a present interest) of the $15,000 gift will qualify for the gift tax annual exclusion, and the gift tax on the remaining $4,500 will first be offset by Jennifer's remaining applicable gift tax credit amount. To the extent that Jennifer has already used her applicable gift tax credit amount, the $4,500 future interest gift will result in the current requirement to pay gift tax.

Crummey Power

A Crummey power makes it possible to qualify a transfer to an irrevocable trust for the gift tax annual exclusion. A Crummey power (named for the taxpayer who first used the technique) allows the beneficiaries of the trust to withdraw any contribution made to the trust within a certain period of time (typically 30 days). Since this gives the beneficiary a general power of appointment over the property transferred to the trust (the general power is the right to reduce the contribution to the trust to the beneficiary's possession), the transfer to the trust is treated as a present interest transfer for gift tax purposes, and therefore qualifies for the gift tax annual exclusion.

Example 8.23

Judy created a trust for the benefit of her son, Chris. Each year, Judy contributes $5,000 to the trust, and Chris has a right to withdraw the contribution for 30 days. The trust allows the trustee to accumulate income and principal, and make discretionary distributions to Chris. Since Chris has the right to withdraw the $5,000 contribution each year, the gift is a gift of a present interest and qualifies for the gift tax annual exclusion.

Qualifying a transfer to an irrevocable trust for the gift tax annual exclusion through the use of a Crummey power can create an estate tax problem for the beneficiary who has the Crummey demand right. Recall that the Crummey power is a general power of appointment, and the IRC requires property subject to a general power of appointment to be included in the power-holder's gross estate if the power holder dies while holding the power. Therefore, the grantor can qualify for the gift tax annual exclusion only if the beneficiary will be subject to estate tax on the property over which he held a withdrawal power.

In addition, if there are multiple beneficiaries of the trust and the power holder allows the right to appoint the assets to lapse, then a taxable gift has occurred. The Code does, however, provide one exception known as the de minimis rule, or Five-and-Five power, which states that the only portion of the transfer considered to be a taxable gift will be the lapsed general power of appointment which exceeds the greater of (1) $5,000 or (2) five percent of the trust corpus. When the annual exclusion was first granted, it was less than $5,000. Over time, the annual exclusion has increased because it is adjusted for inflation. The $5,000 associated with the five-and-five power, however, is not adjusted for inflation. As a result, the five-and-five power no longer necessarily shelters 100 percent of an annual exclusion contribution from gift tax. Therefore, whenever a trust that gives the beneficiaries the right to demand distribution of the grantor's contribution to the trust is created, the five-and-five power must be considered.

Example 8.24

William created a Crummey trust this year for the benefit of his son, Gerald. Recently, William attended a seminar on financial planning and learned that he can give $15,000 a year to Gerald without gift tax consequences. When he created the trust, he made a gift of $15,000 to the trust, and Gerald had the right to withdraw the entire contribution so that it would qualify as an annual exclusion gift. Since the trust had no value until William transferred the $15,000 to the trustee, $5,000 (the greater of $5,000 or 5% of the trust assets) worth of Gerald's demand right (a general power of appointment) will lapse if Gerald does not make a withdrawal. This is the de minimis amount. The remaining $10,000 ($15,000 - $5,000) of the withdrawal right exceeds the de minimis amount, and although there are no gift tax consequences (because Gerald is the only beneficiary of the trust), estate tax consequences for Gerald may result if he dies holding the power.

Example 8.25

Assume the same facts as above, except that William created the trust for Gerald's benefit 30 years ago. The current value of the trust is $650,000. This year, William transfers $15,000 to the trust and Gerald has the right to demand a distribution of that amount pursuant to the Crummey power. The entire $15,000 gift made to the trust is subject to a general power of appointment, but it will be ignored and lapse, since $15,000 is less than 5% of the value of the trust $32,500 ($650,000 x 5%). Therefore, there will be neither estate nor gift tax consequences to Gerald.

Example 8.26

Patrick created a Crummey trust for the benefit of his daughters, Ellen, Anna, and Margaret. Each of the children has the right to withdraw, pursuant to the Crummey power, a proportionate share of the annual contribution. Patrick transferred $15,000 to the trust this year. Consequently, each of his children can withdraw $5,000 ($15,000 ÷ 3). Since the amount each daughter can withdraw is equal to or less than the greater of $5,000 or 5% of the trust corpus, the withdrawal rights will lapse and the children will not suffer any estate tax consequences as a result of holding the withdrawal right.

In addition, it is important that the beneficiary refrain from taking any action with respect to the lapsing power. If the beneficiary releases the power by telling the trustee that he will not exercise the right during the lapse period, it is possible for the IRS to argue that a lapse of the right never occurred, and consequently, there should be inclusion in the beneficiary's gross estate since the beneficiary held a general power of appointment and took action by releasing the right. Recall that the gross estate includes property over which the decedent exercised a power of appointment. Beneficiaries of Crummey trusts should not make an affirmative election to forgo the right to withdraw; the right to withdraw should be terminated by the passage of time, as set forth in the trust document, without the beneficiary's affirmative action.

While the five-and-five lapsing amount places a de minimis limitation on the amount that a beneficiary can appoint without being subject to tax, the gift tax annual exclusion also imposes a limitation. Only the first $15,000 in gifts to an individual will qualify for the gift tax annual exclusion. Any amount over the $15,000 threshold will create a taxable gift and will result in either (1) a reduction in the grantor's applicable gift tax credit or (2) a requirement to pay gift taxes. Most individuals who create Crummey trusts limit the beneficiary's withdrawal right by stating that the beneficiary is not permitted to withdraw more than the annual exclusion amount.

Example 8.27

David created a trust this year for the benefit of his son, Lewis. The trust gives Lewis an unlimited Crummey withdrawal right over the entire contribution made by David. This year, David makes a gift of $100,000 to the trust. Despite the fact that Lewis can withdraw the entire amount, only $15,000 of the gift will qualify for the gift tax annual exclusion. The remaining $85,000 will be considered a taxable gift and will either deplete David's applicable gift tax credit or require him to pay gift tax. Furthermore, since the lapsing amount (as discussed above) this year is $5,000 (the trust had no other assets at the time the contribution was made), Lewis is deemed to have a general power of appointment over $95,000, which may result in estate tax consequences for Lewis. If David had limited Lewis' withdrawal right to the gift tax annual exclusion amount, the consequences would be exactly the same for David, but Lewis would be deemed to have a general power of appointment over only $10,000 as opposed to $95,000. This may have assisted in saving transfer taxes for the family over time.

There are three primary ways of dealing with the lapsing issue from an estate planning perspective. Some grantors will state that the withdrawal right of each of the beneficiaries may be no more than the lesser of (1) the gift tax annual exclusion amount or (2) the greater of $5,000 or five percent of the trust corpus. When this approach is taken, the general power of appointment held by the beneficiary will never exceed the lapsing amount, and therefore the beneficiary will not be subject to any estate tax consequences. Provided that he allows the general power of appointment to lapse, this is the simplest way of dealing with the lapsing issue, but may not be practical in some situations.

The second method of dealing with the lapsing issue is to create a hanging power. A hanging power states that, to the extent that a demand beneficiary has a right to withdraw that does not lapse (the portion of the gift tax annual exclusion amount over the five-and-five amount), the non-lapsing portion will hang over to a subsequent year, when it can lapse under the five-and-five standard.

Example 8.28

Randy created a Crummey trust for the benefit of his son, Keegan. Randy contributes $15,000 annually at the beginning of each year. Keegan has a cumulative annual right of withdrawal over any property transferred to the trust during the year. The withdrawal right lapses at the end of each year to the extent of the greater of $5,000 or 5% of the trust property. Keegan does not make any withdrawals. Contributions to the trust and the hanging power are illustrated in the following table.

Year	Value of Trust at Beginning of Year	Contribution	Lapsing Amount (5/5 Lapse Rule)	Amount that "Hangs"	Cumulative Total Hanging Amount
1	$0.00	$15,000.00	$5,000.00	$10,000.00	$10,000.00
2	$16,500.00	$15,000.00	$5,000.00	$10,000.00	$20,000.00
3	$34,650.00	$15,000.00	$5,000.00	$10,000.00	$30,000.00
4	$54,615.00	$15,000.00	$5,000.00	$10,000.00	$40,000.00
5	$76,576.50	$15,000.00	$5,000.00	$10,000.00	$50,000.00
6	$100,734.15	-	$5,036.71	-	$44,963.29
7	$110,807.57	-	$5,540.38	-	$39,422.91
8	$121,888.32	-	$6,094.42	-	$33,328.50
9	$134,077.15	-	$6,703.86	-	$26,624.64
10	$147,484.87	-	$7,374.24	-	$19,250.39
11	$162,233.36	-	$8,111.67	-	$11,138.73
12	$178,456.69	-	$8,922.83	-	$2,215.89
13	$196,302.36	-	$9,815.12	-	$0.00

Assume that the trust balance grows at a rate of 10% annually.

In this example, Randy makes contributions to the trust in Years 1 through 5. In Years 1 through 5, the contribution that Randy makes exceeds the de minimis amount, and therefore Keegan has a general power of appointment (withdrawal right) that "hangs over." During the funding period, the total amount that hangs over increases each year. Note that in Year 6, when the value of the trust exceeds $100,000, the amount that lapses moves from the $5,000 minimum amount to 5% of the value of the trust assets. After Year 5, Randy does not make any additional contributions to the trust, but the value of the trust continues to grow at a rate of 10% per year.

Since there is a "hanging amount" from prior years, Keegan continues to have a withdrawal right each year equal to the lapsing amount. In Years 6 through 13, the lapsing amounts reduce the hanging withdrawal right until Year 13, when Keegan no longer has a right to withdraw any money from the trust.

Provided Keegan lives until the hanging amount has been extinguished, he will not have to worry about estate tax consequences as a result of holding a withdrawal right over the annual contribution that Randy made to the trust. If Keegan dies before the hanging amount is used up, there will be an inclusion in his gross estate, since he held a general power of appointment over the property and not all of the general power lapsed prior to his death.

A third way of dealing with the lapsing issue is to give the demand beneficiary a continuing right to appoint a portion of the trust equal to the non-lapsing amount. This is a simpler solution than the hanging power, but will result in a small inclusion in the beneficiary's gross estate.

Example 8.29
Assume the same facts as above. Instead of including a hanging power provision in the trust document, Randy gives Keegan a continuing power to appoint the amount in excess of the lapsing amount. In year 5, the last year that Randy made a contribution to the trust, the total withdrawal right that did not lapse was $50,000. This represents the amount of the general power of appointment that Keegan possessed that did not lapse under the five-and-five rule. When Keegan dies, his gross estate will include $50,000 since he had the continuing right to appoint that property. Note that the fair market value of the assets in the trust will not be included in his estate (assuming there were no other retained rights involved that would cause inclusion).

Life Insurance Trusts

A life insurance trust is an irrevocable inter vivos trust often referred to as an **irrevocable life insurance trust** (ILIT) or **wealth replacement trust** (WRT). Life insurance is often used to replace the wealth for a decedent's family that was lost through estate and inheritance taxation or charitable contributions at the decedent's death, and therefore may be referred to as a wealth replacement trust.

The purpose of an ILIT is to prevent an insured party from having incidents of ownership in the life insurance policy on his life. When a person owns a policy on his own life, the death benefit of that policy is included in his gross estate under IRC Section 2042. Provided that an insured person did not own the policy or any incident of ownership over the policy within three years of his death, the death benefit of the policy is not subject to estate taxation.

When an ILIT is created, the grantor often wants to qualify the gifts to the ILIT for the gift tax annual exclusion so that his applicable gift tax credit amount will be available for other planning either during lifetime or at death. Since an ILIT is irrevocable, transfers to the ILIT are usually made subject to a Crummey withdrawal right on behalf of the beneficiaries. ILITs are discussed in depth in Chapter 11.

Bypass (Credit Shelter) Trusts

A **bypass (or credit shelter) trust**, also known as a "B Trust," is commonly used in estate planning. A bypass trust can be either an inter vivos (during lifetime) or a testamentary (at death) trust.

Testamentary Bypass Trust

The most common approach to using a bypass trust calls for the creation of the trust at the individual's death. Most couples who have over $11,580,000 and equal to or less than $23,160,000 in joint assets (in 2020) can completely avoid federal estate taxation by transferring $11,580,000 in property to a bypass trust at the death of the first spouse or possibly by electing to transfer the first spouse's exemption to the surviving spouse under the portability provisions of the code (discussed in Chapter 6). While the $11,580,000 will be subject to estate tax if a bypass trust is used (since it will not qualify for the marital deduction), the decedent's applicable estate tax credit will be available to completely offset estate tax up to $4,577,800 (the credit equivalency amount of in $11,580,000 taxable transfers).

> **Quick Quiz 8.6**
>
> 1. The most common use for an inter vivos revocable trust is to avoid federal estate taxes.
>   a. True
>   b. False
>
> 2. An ILIT is created to own the life insurance policy on the grantor's life and ensure inclusion in the decedent's gross estate.
>   a. True
>   b. False
>
> *False, False.*

It should be noted that bypass trusts are not as useful as in the past with the introduction of a surviving spouse's ability to use a deceased spousal unused exclusion amount. This provision was made permanent by the ATRA 2012 and allows a surviving spouse to exclude up to $23,160,000 assuming that the deceased spouse did not make use of the lifetime exemption. The Deceased Spouse's Unused Exemption (DSUE), however, is not indexed for inflation in years after the first spouse's death. In circumstances where assets are expected to appreciate rapidly and the surviving spouse will not use the DSUE to transfer those assets quickly to intended recipients, use of a bypass trust may be preferable to invoking the portability provisions since subsequent appreciation in the value of assets inside of a properly structured bypass trust will not be subject to transfer tax at the surviving spouse's death.

Transferring property to a bypass trust does not deprive the surviving spouse from using the property. The bypass trust can be structured so that all of the income of the trust is payable to the surviving spouse. In addition, the trustee can be given the right to make discretionary distributions of principal for the surviving spouse's health, education, maintenance, and support (an ascertainable standard). Furthermore, the surviving spouse can be given the right to demand, on an annual basis, the greater of $5,000 or five percent of the trust corpus. While the surviving spouse will not have title to the property in the bypass trust, all of the property can be made available to the surviving spouse so that the surviving spouse can maintain his standard of living. Upon the surviving spouse's death, the assets in the bypass trust usually pass to the children (or some other non-charitable beneficiary), and are not included in the surviving spouse's gross estate for federal estate tax purposes (even with the powers given to the surviving spouse).

Inter Vivos Bypass Trust

While most individuals create a bypass trust at death, creating an inter vivos bypass trust can yield even bigger benefits. When all property transfers occur at the death of an individual, everything is potentially included in the gross estate and subject to estate tax. Instead of waiting until death to create the trust, an individual can transfer $11,580,000 in assets (2020) to an inter vivos bypass trust and shield the transfer with the applicable gift tax credit amount. Once this is accomplished, all future growth and appreciation in the property that is transferred to the bypass trust escapes federal estate taxation at the decedent's death. While most people will not be interested in using this technique due to a loss of control over the assets transferred to the trust, very high net worth individuals should consider using their applicable gift tax credit amount during their lifetime to avoid subjecting the appreciation of the property to transfer tax.

Example 8.30

Elizabeth is a very wealthy individual. She is 54-years-old, is married to Philip, and has four children. She has never used any of her applicable gift tax credit amount for planning purposes. Elizabeth owns an asset that she believes will appreciate substantially in the future. The current value of the asset is $11,580,000, and she decides to transfer the asset to an inter vivos bypass trust. Once the asset is transferred, she will have used her applicable gift tax credit, and all future lifetime transfers will be subject to transfer tax (with the exception of annual exclusion gifts and qualified transfers). Elizabeth died at the age of 84. As she had expected, the asset she transferred to the bypass trust appreciated in value at an after-tax rate of return of 6%. The $11,580,000 transferred to the trust when she was 54-years-old grew to $66,509,628 by the date of her death. By creating the bypass trust during her lifetime, $54,929,628 ($66,509,628 - $11,580,000) was transferred to Elizabeth's heirs without transfer tax consequences. Had Elizabeth continued to own the asset and created a bypass trust at her death, her estate would have included the $66,509,628, and the estate would have paid estate tax (at the 40% 2020 rates) of approximately $22,026,051 presuming she had no other assets, her husband predeceased her, and she had no additional exemption resulting from portability.[1]

Power of Appointment Trusts

Power of appointment trusts are inter vivos or testamentary irrevocable trusts. As the name implies, the trust grants the beneficiary a power of appointment over the trust assets. The power of appointment can be a general power of appointment or a limited (special) power of appointment. However, the power must be a general power of appointment to qualify for the marital deduction.

Power of appointment trusts are frequently used in planning to take advantage of the unlimited estate tax marital deduction. A trust that grants a surviving spouse a power of appointment over the assets during lifetime may qualify for the marital deduction in the estate of the first spouse to die. A special type of power of appointment trust, called an **estate trust**, grants the surviving spouse a testamentary general power of appointment over the trust assets. More information on the requirements and uses of power of appointment trusts for marital deduction purposes can be found in Chapter 10.

---

1. $26,603,851 - $4,577,800 = $22,026,051

Power of appointment trusts may also be used to avoid the generation-skipping transfer tax. By granting a non-skip person a general power of appointment over a trust that will distribute assets to a skip person, it is possible to change the identity of the transferor for tax purposes. Since the non-skip person will be required to include the value of the trust assets in his gross estate because of the general power of appointment, he will be considered the transferor for generation-skipping transfer tax purposes. This technique is useful for individuals who have already used their generation-skipping transfer exemption and desire to transfer more property to skip persons without generation-skipping transfer tax consequences. Note, however, that there are estate tax consequences for the non-skip holder of the general power of appointment. The generation-skipping transfer tax is fully discussed in Chapter 13.

Qualified Terminable Interest Property (QTIP) Trusts

A **QTIP trust**, which is typically created at the death of the first spouse to die, grants the surviving spouse a lifetime right to the income of the trust while transferring the remainder interest to individual(s) of the grantor's choosing. A QTIP trust qualifies for the unlimited marital deduction even though the spouse does not receive outright access to the assets. More information on QTIP trusts may be found in Chapter 10.

While most individuals create QTIP trusts after death, it is possible to create an inter vivos QTIP trust. While this type of planning is not common, it might be used to equalize vastly disproportionate amounts of wealth between spouses.

Grantor Retained Income Trusts (GRITs)

Grantor Retained Income Trusts (GRITs) are trusts created by a person who keeps an income interest in the trust or a right to use trust assets. Generally, the grantor will transfer property to the trust, retain some form of income or use interest for a period of time, and upon termination of the trust, transfer the remainder interest to a third party. Since the third party does not receive the immediate right to possess or enjoy the property, a discount on the value of the remainder interest is available due to the passage of time (referred to as a temporal discount). Historically, individuals wishing to transfer business or property interest at a discount would transfer the interest to the GRIT and retain an income interest from the trust which would be valued using very aggressive income payment rates. The increased value of the income interest would reduce the value of the remainder interest and the transfer would be subject to less transfer tax. After the transfer, the trustee of the GRIT would reduce the income payout from the trust by investing in non-income-producing property. The grantor would benefit from the increased value of the income interest for transfer tax purposes, but would not actually receive any income from the trust. The enactment of the anti-freeze rules of IRC Section 2701 eliminated a grantor's ability to benefit in this manner by placing requirements on the valuation of the income and remainder interests of trusts, and IRC Section 2702 specifically authorizes the four types of GRITs that may be established. These are Grantor Retained Annuity Trusts (GRATs), Grantor Retained Unitrusts (GRUTs), Qualified Personal Residence Trusts (QPRTs), and Tangible Personal Property Trusts (TPPTs).

Grantor Retained Annuity Trusts (GRATs)

Grantor Retained Annuity Trusts (GRATs) are a special type of GRIT created when the grantor funds a trust and retains a right to receive a fixed percentage of the initial contribution to the trust on an annual basis for a specified term of years. At the termination of the specified term of the trust, the assets remaining in the trust at that time pass to the remainder beneficiaries. GRATs are discussed in detail in Chapter 7.

Example 8.31

Jonathan transfers $11,580,000 to a 10-year GRAT in which he retains the right to receive a 6% annuity interest. Jonathan named his son and daughter as the remainder beneficiaries of the trust. Each year during the 10-year period, Jonathan will receive a distribution of $694,800 ($11,580,000 x 6%). When the 10-year period expires, the trust will terminate, and the assets in the trust at that time will pass to his son and daughter.

Grantor Retained Unitrusts (GRUTs)

As also detailed in Chapter 7, a Grantor Retained Unitrust (GRUT) is the second form of GRIT that is permissible under Chapter 14 of the Code. In substance, a GRUT has the same characteristics as a GRAT with one exception: the income stream received by the grantor is a fixed percentage of the annual value of the trust assets. Instead of fixing the dollar value of the distribution to the grantor, a GRUT provides a variable income stream that will increase as the value of the assets inside the trust increases, or decrease as the value of the assets in the trust decreases. GRUTs are not as effective as GRATs in transferring appreciation on a gift-tax free basis, since the appreciation is shared between the grantor and the remainder beneficiaries. The effects of a GRUT are generally contrary to the grantor's goals and are therefore created far less frequently than GRATs.

> **Key Concepts**
>
> 1. What type of property is contributed to a QPRT?
> 2. What type of property is contributed to a TPPT?
> 3. Identify the key differences between a Section 2503(b) trust and a Section 2503(c) trust.

Qualified Personal Residence Trusts (QPRTs)

A Qualified Personal Residence Trust (QPRT), as detailed in Chapter 7, is a GRAT in which the grantor contributes a personal residence to the trust and the retained income interest is the grantor's right to "use" the personal residence.

Tangible Personal Property Trusts (TPPTs)

Tangible Personal Property Trusts (TPPTs) are very similar to QPRTs, with one exception – personal property, not real property, is used to fund them. Grantor's of TPPTs usually transfer artwork, antiques, jewelry, and other items of personal property that have the potential to appreciate in value. A temporal discount is available due to the delay in the remainder beneficiary's use or enjoyment of the asset. Valuation of the retained interest, however, is difficult and the IRS will scrutinize the TPPT due to the difficulty of valuing the right to use a piece of tangible personal property.

Dynasty Trusts

Dynasty trusts are arrangements designed to last for very long periods of time (preferably forever, if created in a state that has abolished the rule against perpetuities). The primary advantage achieved through use of a dynasty trust is an ability to avoid transfer taxation at the death of each generation of the family. To the extent that assets are kept in the trust and are not distributed to the beneficiaries, the value of the assets will not be included in the beneficiary's gross estate even if the beneficiary has the right to use the assets. Dynasty trusts are discussed above and are covered in more detail in Chapter 13.

Grantor Trusts

Grantor trusts are trusts governed under Sections 671 to 679 of the Internal Revenue Code. When a grantor trust is created, the grantor, not the trust or its beneficiaries, will be subject to income tax on the trust income.

Grantor trusts have many names (mostly used for marketing purposes), and include "Intentionally Defective Grantor Trust (IDGT)" (sometimes pronounced "I-dig-it" or "Id-It" depending on your location in the country), "Defective Trust," and "Intentionally Defective for Income Tax Only Trust." The term defective merely means that, for income tax purposes, there is a defective provision in the trust requiring the grantor to pay tax on the trust income. "Defective" in this context does not imply that the trust will not be effective for estate, gift, or generation-skipping transfer tax planning purposes.

The concept of a grantor trust can be confusing if you think of the federal tax system as one tax system. There are three separate tax systems in the United States: (1) an income tax system, (2) an estate and gift tax system, and, (3) a generation-skipping transfer tax system. Each of these systems is separate and distinct, and it is possible to make a transfer that is complete for one system but incomplete (or defective) for another system.

For example, if an individual creates an irrevocable trust and does not retain an interest in the trust, a completed gift has been made for gift and estate tax purposes. At the time a transfer is made to the trust, gift tax may be due but the fair market value of the property in the trust at the date of the grantor's death will not be included in his gross estate. That same trust could contain a provision that would make it incomplete (or defective) for income tax purposes (such as a right given to the grantor to substitute assets in the trust with other assets of equivalent value), thereby triggering grantor trust status and requiring the grantor to pay the income tax on the trust income.

Several grantor trusts have been discussed throughout this text, namely revocable living trusts, GRATs, GRUTs, QPRTs, and TPPTs, but other types of trusts may also include provisions which will make the trust a grantor trust.

The circumstances requiring the grantor to be treated as owner of the trust for income tax purposes include situations where:

1. The grantor has a reversionary interest in the trust that exceeds five percent of the value of the trust upon creation or upon an additional contribution;

2. The grantor or a non-adverse party can revoke the trust acting alone or with the consent of a non-adverse party;
    - Whereas an adverse party is a person having a substantial beneficial interest in the trust which would be adversely affected by the exercise or nonexercise of the trust power he/she possesses, a non-adverse party is a person who is not an adverse party (IRC Section 672). Note that in a grantor trust situation, if the grantor or a non-adverse party (i.e., a party that would be subject to the control of the grantor) has the power to revoke the trust, the power is imputed to the grantor, creating a grantor trust. If the non-adverse party alone has the power to revoke, that power is attributed to the grantor, triggering grantor trust status.

3. The grantor or a non-adverse party (or both) can control the beneficial enjoyment of the trust;

4. The grantor retains certain administrative powers, including:
   - the right to purchase, exchange, deal with, or dispose of the principal or income of the trust for less than full and fair or adequate consideration;
   - the right to borrow principal or income without adequate security;
   - a power of administration exercisable in a nonfiduciary capacity by any person without the approval or consent of any person in a fiduciary capacity. (These powers include the power to vote stock of a corporation in which the grantor or the trust has a significant voting interest, the power to control investment of the trust funds, and the power to reacquire the trust corpus by substituting other property of equivalent value.);

5. The income of the trust, at the discretion of the grantor or a nonadverse party (or both), is or may be:
   - distributed to the grantor,
   - held or accumulated for future distribution to the grantor, or
   - applied to the payment of premiums on insurance policies on the life of the grantor or the grantor's spouse.

6. The income of the trust is distributed to the grantor's spouse, or held or applied for future distribution to the grantor's spouse, or applied to the payment of premiums on insurance policies on the life of the grantor's spouse.

A final grantor trust rule creates a trust where the beneficiary, not the grantor, becomes liable for payment of income tax on the trust income. Under this rule, if a person other than the grantor has the sole power to vest the principal or income of the trust in himself or herself, that person will be treated as owner of the principal, requiring the trust's income to be taxable to that individual. This type of trust is commonly referred to as a beneficiary defective trust, and is most commonly created when the trust grants the beneficiaries a Crummey right of withdrawal.

Recall that several of the powers listed above that create a grantor trust for income tax purposes may also run afoul of the retained interest rules for estate tax purposes, resulting in the fair market value of the trust assets being included in the gross estate of a decedent. When planning with grantor trusts, it is important to tread carefully and make sure that the grantor trust provisions employed do not trigger an estate tax inclusion for the client.

Incorporating a grantor trust power in a trust document that does not trigger inclusion in the gross estate for estate tax purposes, however, allows the grantor to make a series of tax-free gifts to the beneficiaries of the trust. Since the grantor will be responsible for paying the income tax on trust income, amounts that the trust or the beneficiaries would have otherwise had to spend to cover the tax liability will remain in the hands of the trust or its beneficiaries. The grantor, in paying the income tax, is paying an obligation imposed upon him or her by the Internal Revenue Code, and is therefore not deemed to be making a gift to the trust or its beneficiaries. In addition to making a gift-tax free indirect transfer to the trust beneficiaries, over time, as the grantor pays the income tax liability for the trust, he is also reducing the size of the taxable estate, saving at the highest marginal tax rate, 40 percent in estate taxes.

Example 8.32

Randy created a trust several years ago. The trust's terms permit Randy to acquire trust property by substituting property of equal value, a power that makes the trust a grantor trust. This year the trust earned $100,000 in ordinary income, and had no capital gains. Assume Randy is in the highest marginal ordinary income tax bracket, so he paid $37,000 in taxes on the trust income (37%). By paying the tax, Randy relieved the trust and the trust's beneficiaries of the $37,000 income tax liability (alternatively stated, Randy let the trust keep, for the benefit of the beneficiaries, the $37,000 it would have used to pay the income tax liability), and at the same time, removed the $37,000 from Randy's gross estate. If Randy dies after making the income tax payment, he will have saved $14,800 in estate taxes (40 percent of the value removed from his gross estate), making the net cost of paying the income tax equal to $22,200 ($37,000 - $14,800). As illustrated, over time Randy can make significant additional wealth transfers to the beneficiaries of the trust by simply paying the tax on trust income for them.

Trusts for Minors – Section 2503(b) and Section 2503(c) Trusts

Strictly speaking (from a legal perspective), minors are not permitted to own property. Property that is transferred to a minor must be either held in trust for the benefit of the minor, or must be held in a custodial account (such as the Uniform Gift to Minors Act Account (UGMA) or Uniform Transfers to Minors Act Account (UTMA) as discussed in Chapter 5).

If property is transferred to a trust for the benefit of a minor, the minor will not be able to legally access those funds until the later of (1) the date the minor reaches the age of majority, or (2) the date set forth in the trust instrument. Since the minor cannot receive a present right to enjoy or use the property, any gift to a trust for the benefit of a minor would be considered a future interest gift. As previously stated, a future interest gift does not qualify for the gift tax annual exclusion. Consequently, any transfer to a trust for a minor (even those under $15,000 in value, the 2020 gift tax annual exclusion) would require the donor to use part of his applicable gift tax credit amount or, if the applicable gift tax credit has been previously used, pay gift tax.

The Code does provide two exceptions to this otherwise harsh result, thus allowing the transfer to a trust for the benefit of a minor to qualify for the annual exclusion. Section 2503 of the Code states that if property is transferred to a trust for the benefit of a minor that meets the requirements of Section 2503(b) or 2503(c), the transfer will be treated as a present interest gift that qualifies for the gift tax annual exclusion even though, absent these provisions, the gift tax annual exclusion would not apply. In enacting Section 2503 of the Code, Congress recognized that individuals may wish to make transfers to minors in a way that would not result in using their applicable gift tax credit amount. Note that 203(b) and 2503(c) trusts are single beneficiary trusts.

2503(b) Trust

A **2503(b) trust** may hold property in trust for the lifetime of the beneficiary (or beneficiaries), but must make income distributions to the beneficiary (or beneficiaries) on an annual basis. This means, at a minimum, the interest and dividends received by the trust must be distributed. Once distributed, the income can be placed in a custodial account for the benefit of the child, or may be used for the child's benefit. Gifts made to a 2503(b) trust will partially qualify for the gift tax annual exclusion. The portion qualifying for the gift tax annual exclusion equals the present value of the income interest that the child will receive over the term of the trust.

2503(c) Trust

A **2503(c) trust**, unlike its counterpart the 2503(b) trust, allows income to be accumulated in the trust, and allows the grantor to qualify the entire gift to the trust up to the annual exclusion amount for the gift tax annual exclusion, but can have only one beneficiary. The trustee of the 2503(c) trust may, but is not required to, make principal and income distributions for the benefit of the child. In order to achieve these benefits, the trust must terminate when the child reaches age 21, or, at a minimum, the child must be given the right to receive the trust assets at age 21. A 2503(c) trust compares favorably with UGMA and UTMA accounts in states where a child would have access to custodial account funds at an age earlier than 21, but still places a substantial constraint on those who wish to avoid giving the minor a right to the property. Individuals who wish to fully utilize the gift tax annual exclusion for transfers to trusts for minors, and who wish to keep the property in trust after the child reaches age 21 without giving the child a right to access the funds should consider the creation of a standard Crummey trust.

Crummey Trusts

Crummey trusts, as discussed above, are trust agreements that allow the beneficiary to withdraw the contribution made by the grantor to the trust. These trusts are named for the taxpayer who successfully litigated a case in the tax court that held that the grant of the withdrawal right transforms a future interest gift in trust to a present interest gift that qualifies for the gift tax annual exclusion. The withdrawal right is generally limited to the gift tax annual exclusion amount. In granting the beneficiary a withdrawal right, however, a general power of appointment is conferred, and it is important to consider the lapsing issues under the five-and-five power created by the withdrawal right (discussed above).

Crummey trusts are often used as alternatives to Section 2503(c) trusts when the grantor wishes to keep the property in trust after the beneficiary reaches age 21. Crummey trusts are frequently associated with irrevocable life insurance trusts, since the grantor of an ILIT often wishes to make transfers to the trust without using any of his applicable gift tax credit amount.

Charitable Trusts

Charitably inclined individuals frequently use trusts to accomplish two objectives: (1) transfer assets to charity in a tax efficient manner, and (2) assist in estate planning by transferring assets to non-charitable beneficiaries. A full discussion of charitable trusts is included in Chapter 9, but a brief review of the available types of charitable trusts follows.

Charitable Remainder Trusts (CRTs) are created when the grantor transfers assets to a trust, retains an annuity or unitrust interest for a period of time or for his life, and the remainder value passes to a qualified charity. CRTs are often used to transform illiquid assets into a cash flow stream in a tax efficient manner while at the same time accomplishing the grantor's charitable objectives.

Charitable Lead Trusts (CLTs) are created when the grantor transfers assets to a trust, gives an income stream (which must be an annuity or unitrust interest to qualify for the income tax charitable deduction) to a charity for a fixed period of time followed by a transfer of the remainder interest in the trust to a third party or, possibly, back to the grantor. If a third party is named as remainder beneficiary of the trust, use of a CLT can achieve significant wealth transfer goals.

Private foundations may be structured as either corporations or trusts, but most family foundations use the trust form. A private foundation manages a family's social capital, and makes a distribution of at least five percent of its assets each year to charitable organizations or charitable causes. Private foundations are often coordinated with other charitable techniques, such as charitable remainder trusts and charitable lead trusts, to maximize the tax and charitable benefits available to the grantor.

Totten Trusts

As detailed in Chapter 4, **totten trusts** are not really trusts, but rather bank accounts that include payable on death beneficiary clauses (PODs). A bank account with a payable on death clause is transferred to the named beneficiary upon the death of the owner and escapes probate.

Blind Trusts

A **blind trust** is a revocable trust arrangement whereby an individual transfers property to the trust for management purposes when self-management of the assets might be deemed to be a conflict of interest. Blind trusts are commonly used by high ranking political officials to provide management of their assets during their term in office. For example, an individual who is elected as President of the United States has loftier concerns than asset management, and the decisions he makes as President may impact the price of securities owned in his personal portfolio. To avoid any appearance of impropriety, and to ensure that presidential decisions are made objectively, the President will transfer all of his assets to a blind trust before entering office, and the trustee manages those assets. Upon leaving office, the blind trust typically terminates and any assets revert to the grantor of the trust.

> **Quick Quiz 8.7**
>
> 1. A bypass trust can be created during a grantor's life.
>   a. True
>   b. False
> 2. The fair market value of the interest retained by the grantor of a GRAT is subject to gift tax.
>   a. True
>   b. False
> 3. Blind trusts are most commonly used by politicians.
>   a. True
>   b. False
>
> True, False, True.

Special Needs Trust

A **special needs trust** is a specific type of trust that is used to provide benefits to persons or beneficiaries with special needs. Typically, these trusts are established to ensure that benefits available from federal and state agencies are preserved and maintained. Federal benefits include available funds and healthcare, such as provided by Social Security disability, Medicaid, and the SSI (Supplemental Security Income) program through Social Security. Many of these programs will not pay benefits if the person has even limited resources. For example, to qualify for SSI, an individual cannot have more than $2,000 in assets and a couple cannot have more than $3,000.

While special needs trusts are used to improve the quality of life and to provide additional resources to the special needs person without interfering with available governmental resources, there are several types of special needs trusts that should be considered. While there are more than three, the more common special trusts are discussed here and include the Third Party Special Needs Trust, the self settled type trust that is established and exempt under 42 U.S.C. Sec. 1396p(d)(4)(A), and what is referred to as a pooled trust.

chapter 8

Third Party (Family) Special Needs Trust (SNT)

A **third party SNT** is sometimes referred to as a family trust because the trust is a receptacle for funds from a parent, guardian, or other family member. The assets of these trusts, if properly structured, are not counted or considered for purposes of available federal or state benefits for the beneficiary. These trusts make it possible to receive federal, state, and local funds.

These trusts can be funded by a parent or guardian during their life or at their death and are sometimes funded with the proceeds from a life insurance policy. The funds are contributed to a trust by the grantor or settlor for the benefit of the person with the special needs (beneficiary). The assets were never the property of, or owned by, the beneficiary and are therefore not counted as assets for purposes of federal or state benefits.

The trust provisions must be established so as to not provide food, shelter, or any asset that could be converted into food or shelter, such as cash. It may provide for other benefits, such as medical treatment, therapy, education, travel, computer equipment, etc. These types of benefits can improve the lifestyle of the beneficiary and not interfere with or reduce governmental benefits.

> ### Key Concepts
>
> 1. Explain the benefits for special needs trusts.
> 2. Identify and explain the three types of special needs trusts.
> 3. Identify the threshold dollar amount of assets to preserve federal and state benefits.
> 4. Describe the role of an advocate or guardian of a special needs trust.
> 5. Explain how ABLE accounts can be established to help disabled individuals.

For example, on the website for Social Security, under SSI, it states that "Money paid directly by someone to provide you with items other than food and shelter does not reduce your SSI benefits. (Items that are not "food or shelter" include medical care, telephone bills, education, entertainment, etc.)."

Assets exceeding $2,000 owned by or distributed to a person with a disability may jeopardize federal government benefits. A common way to structure assets either during life or at death that are intended to provide benefits for a disabled dependent is through the use of a special needs trust.

A special needs trust, created to hold contributed or inherited assets, or its trustee, is the legal owner of the trust property. The dependent special needs person is not the owner of these trust assets, but rather the beneficiary of such a trust. Special needs trusts are irrevocable. However, an irrevocable life insurance trust with a second-to-die life insurance policy insuring parents of a special needs dependent may satisfy this need. Also, a revocable living trust (inter vivos) may also satisfy this need as it will become irrevocable upon the death of the grantor (parent). In any case, the special needs trust may provide benefits for education, transportation, insurance, rehabilitation, and other life enhancing benefits. The trustee needs to have discretion over the distribution and management of income and assets, but should be explicitly prevented by trust provisions from any action that would jeopardize eligibility for government benefits. The remainder beneficiaries can be other children, grandchildren, or charities.

Exhibit 8.5 | Third Party (Family) Special Needs Trust

It is a good idea for the grantor of such a trust (generally the parent) to name an advocate (the advocate could be the guardian) for the dependent (beneficiary). The advocate is usually someone close to the dependent who understands both the grantor's wishes and the beneficiary's needs. The advocate works closely with the trustee in determining appropriate distributions that will maintain or improve the quality of life for the beneficiary without jeopardizing government benefits.

The grantor of a special needs trust can write a set of instructions to the advocate and to the trustee. This set of instructions frequently takes the form of a "letter of intent." While not legally enforceable, much like a side letter to a will, the letter of intent expresses the wishes of the grantor. Assuming that the guardian, advocate, and trustee are carefully selected, these wishes are likely to be followed.

Special Needs Trusts Under 42 U.S.C. Sec. 1396p(d)(4)(A)
Special needs trusts under 42 U.S.C. Sec. 1396p(d)(4)(A), which are considered to be self-settled in nature, are typically established by the special needs person's parent, grandparent, legal guardian, or by a court, and will avoid disqualification of Medicaid and SSI benefits. This law was effective with Omnibus Budget and Reconciliation Act of 1993 and permits individuals with special needs or disabilities to establish a trust on their behalf or to direct that settlement proceeds from a personal injury case be protected in a trust for their benefit and still qualify for benefits under Medicaid and SSI. Their statutory language for this section is:

> A trust containing the assets of an individual under age 65 who is disabled ... and which is established for the benefit of such individual by a parent, grandparent, legal guardian of the individual, or a court if the State will receive all amounts remaining in the trust upon the death of such individual up to an amount equal to the total medical assistance paid on behalf of the individual under a State plan under this subchapter.

The funds can be contributed to the trust and they can still qualify, but the assets remaining at the death of the beneficiary must be paid to the State to the extent funds and assistance from the State have been paid to or for the beneficiary.

It should be obvious that it would be better if the trust were not self-settled. However, in some cases, a beneficiary may receive an award from a litigation settlement or from proceeds from a life insurance policy or from an inheritance. If a financial planner were involved, the last two should be able to be paid into a third party trust. However, these funds, which are the property of the beneficiary, can be contributed to a trust as described above.

Pooled Trust (42 U.S.C. Sec. 1396p(d)(4)(C))

The other exception that resulted from the Omnibus Budget and Reconciliation Act of 1993 is a **pooled trust** that is managed by a nonprofit association. While each beneficiary will have their own account, the assets will generally be pooled and managed together for investment purposes. This type of trust can be funded by a parent, grandparent, legal guardian of the individual, or even by the beneficiary. These accounts must be established solely for the benefit of individuals who are disabled. To the extent that amounts remaining in the beneficiary's account upon the death of the beneficiary are not retained by the trust, the trust pays to the State, from such remaining amounts in the account, an amount equal to the total amount of medical assistance paid on behalf of the beneficiary under the State plan. In other words, the assets remaining at the death of the beneficiary will either go to the nonprofit association or to the State.

ABLE Accounts

The **Achieving a Better Life Experience Act of 2014** permits the states to create "ABLE" accounts for disabled individuals that provide some of the benefits of special needs trusts without the complexities typically associated with those trusts. ABLE accounts are very similar to 529 plans used to fund educational expenses for beneficiaries. Once established, a donor can contribute up to $15,000 to an ABLE account for the benefit of a disabled individual each year, and qualified expenses distributed from the accounts are not included in income. Starting in 2018, if the beneficiary works, the beneficiary can also contribute part or all of what they make to their ABLE account. This additional contribution is limited to the poverty line amount for a one-person household. However, the designated beneficiary is not eligible to make this additional contribution if their employer contributes to a workplace retirement plan on their behalf. In addition, starting in 2018, ABLE account beneficiaries can qualify for the Saver's Credit based on contributions they make to their ABLE accounts. Up to $2,000 of these contributions qualify for this special credit designed to help low- and moderate-income workers. Finally, some funds now may be rolled into an ABLE account from the designated beneficiary's own 529 plan or from the 529 plan of certain family members.

> **Quick Quiz 8.8**
>
> 1. A special needs trust allows family members to provide for a special needs person without adversely effecting government benefits.
>   a. True
>   b. False
>
> 2. The three types of special needs trusts identified in the chapter are the Third Party SNT, the SNT created from the Omnibus Budget Reconciliation Act of 1993 and the Pooled Trust.
>   a. True
>   b. False
>
> 3. Assets exceeding $2,000 owned by or distributed to a person with a disability may jeopardize federal government benefits.
>   a. True
>   b. False
>
> True, True, True.

The ABLE Act defined qualified expenses to include costs for transportation, housing, education, job training, and assistive technology, but also gave the IRS the ability to expand the definition of qualified expenses. In June of 2015 the IRS proposed regulations that suggested that the term qualified expenses should be broadly construed to permit inclusion of living expenses as well. Distributions from ABLE accounts that are not used to cover qualified expenses are subject to income tax and a 10 percent penalty. Up to $100,000 can be accumulated in an ABLE account without impacting the beneficiary's qualification for Supplemental Social Security income. Once the accumulation is over $100,000, Supplemental Social Security eligibility is suspended, but state Medicaid eligibility continues provided that the accumulation in the ABLE account stays below the state's 529 plan maximum amount.

Two features of ABLE accounts have the potential to make them less attractive when compared to traditional special needs trusts. First, the beneficiary has direct control over an ABLE account, and therefore does not receive the benefit of a third-party trustee overseeing distributions. This could, inadvertently, lead to income tax consequences for the beneficiary. Second, all amounts in ABLE accounts can be claimed by state Medicaid agencies upon the death of the beneficiary, an outcome that is typically avoided with a properly structured special needs trust. Despite these potential disadvantages, ABLE accounts provide some degree of additional flexibility when planning for individuals with special needs. As of 2018, almost all states have adopted legislation authorizing ABLE accounts.

IRAs in Estate Planning

By the end of 2019, individual retirement accounts (IRAs) assets totaled $9.9 trillion and was the largest component of the $32.3 trillion in retirement assets in the United States.[1] For many Americans, IRAs are a significantly large portion of their net worth. In some cases, IRAs may contain substantial balances and should be part of an overall estate plan. Consider the following exhibit depicting the number of IRAs with varying account balances.

> **Key Concepts**
>
> 1. Describe the risks of an inherited custodial IRA.
> 2. Explain the advantages of a trusteed IRA and a See-Through trust.

Exhibit 8.6 | High Balance IRA Accounts

IRA Balance	Number of Taxpayers (Estimate)	Total IRA Fair Market Value Balances (in Billions) (Estimate)
$1 million or less	42,382,192	$4,092
> $1 million to $2 million	502,392	$674
> $2 million to $3 million	83,529	$198
> $3 million to $5 million	36,171	$133
> $5 million to $10 million	7,952	$52
> $10 million to $25 million	791	$11
> $25 million	314	$81

Source: GAO Analysis of IRA Data | GAO 15-16 (latest data available at time of printing)

Traditionally, custodial IRAs are held at banks, brokerage companies, mutual funds, or other financial services companies. At the death of the IRA owner, the beneficiary takes control of the IRA assets. At that point, the IRA is called an inherited IRA. There are two significant risks that are associated with

---

1. ICI.org

inherited IRAs. These risks include the sudden depletion of the IRA assets and creditor risks associated with inherited IRAs.

One of the benefits of an IRA is the ability to stretch out the distributions over the life of two individuals (the owner and the beneficiary). This stretching of the IRA allows for larger tax-deferred growth and minimum required payouts. However, beneficiaries of IRAs have full control over the IRA assets and can take out more than the required minimum distributions or even completely liquidate the IRA. Taking larger than required distributions is very common and is often in conflict with the wishes of the IRA owner, who is now deceased. There is no mechanism to prevent a beneficiary from simply taking the money out of a traditional custodial IRA.

The second risk applies to non-spousal IRAs who have immediate or potential creditor problems. In the recent Supreme Court case, "Clark v. Ramaker," the court found that inherited IRAs are not protected or excluded in bankruptcy because they are not retirement assets. The decision dealt with a non-spouse beneficiary. It should be noted that spouses can roll over IRAs into their own name. While the Federal law may not protect inherited IRAs in bankruptcy, there are currently seven states that specifically exempt inherited IRAs from levy and seizure. These states also require the use of state exemptions in bankruptcy thus protecting these inherited IRAs in these states from creditors. However, the named beneficiary may not live in one of the seven states that explicitly protect inherited IRAs. There are two possible solutions to the above risks: the trusteed IRA and the "See-Through" Trust as a beneficiary to the IRA.

To understand how to resolve the above issues, it is important to realize how IRAs are set up. IRAs may be structured as a custodial IRA (under IRC Section 408(h)) or as a trusteed IRA (under IRC Section 408(a)). Custodial IRAs, which are most common today, can be set up with a see-through trust as a beneficiary. This type of arrangement creates a trust between the IRA and the beneficiary and resolves both of the above issues. The other alternative is to create a Trusteed IRA, which is effectively an IRA within a trust. Both of these alternatives resolve the two issues discussed above.

Trusteed IRAs

Trusteed IRAs, which can be either traditional or Roth IRAs, are trusts established within the United States. They are IRAs and trusts, and therefore, have the same advantages of IRAs, including creditor protection and tax deferral while the owner is alive, and the same advantages of trusts. The structure of the trust allows for the unique advantage of being able to control the distributions from the IRA after the owner dies, which provides creditor protection and reduces the likelihood of the assets being prematurely consumed.

When established, trusteed IRAs are structured to make pre-defined payments to beneficiaries. These amounts might be limited to:
1. The required minimum distribution.
2. The required minimum distribution plus additional amounts under an ascertainable standard for the benefit of the beneficiaries (generally for health, education, maintenance, or support).
3. The greater of income or the required minimum distribution.

> **Quick Quiz 8.9**
>
> 1. Inherited IRAs are protected in bankruptcy because they are IRAs.
>   a. True
>   b. False
> 2. Trusteed IRAs allow IRA owners to control how distributions from the IRA will be paid out and to whom the assets will pass after the death of the primary beneficiary.
>   a. True
>   b. False
>
> *False, True.*

In addition to controlling the distributions to beneficiaries, a trusteed IRA can be set up to control who receives the funds after the death of the primary beneficiary. Typically, the beneficiary of an inherited custodial IRA will choose the person to receive the assets after he or she dies.

Trusteed IRAs are established with an institutional trustee who will generally manage the trust and often the assets of the IRA. Trusteed IRAs are more expensive than custodial IRAs, but less expensive than a See-Through trust. There is often a 1.0 percent to 1.5 percent fee on the assets as well as a required asset minimum (generally $500,000 to $1 million).

> ## Quick Quiz 8.10
>
> 1. See-through trusts are the same as trusteed IRAs.
>   a. True
>   b. False
> 2. See-through trusts require RMD.
>   a. True
>   b. False
>
> *False, True.*

"See-Through" Trusts

Owners of custodial IRAs can name a **"see-through" trust** as a beneficiary. A see-through trust is a stand-alone trust used as a beneficiary of a retirement (IRA) account. The IRS has four minimum distribution trust rules that must be followed in naming a trust as the beneficiary of an IRA.
- The trust must be valid under state law.
- The trust is irrevocable or will by its terms, become irrevocable upon the death of the IRA owner.
- The beneficiaries of the trust are identifiable.
- A copy of the trust documents must be provided to the IRA custodian by October 31 of the year immediately following the year in which the IRA owner died.

A see-through trust allows the custodian to determine the required minimum distribution (RMDs) by looking through the trust to the life expectancies of the trust beneficiaries. The trust can have the strongest spendthrift provisions permitted by law. The trustee can be empowered to direct the custodian's investments and direct the custodian to distribute more but not less than the RMDs at the trustee's discretion.

Exhibit 8.7 | See-Through Trusts

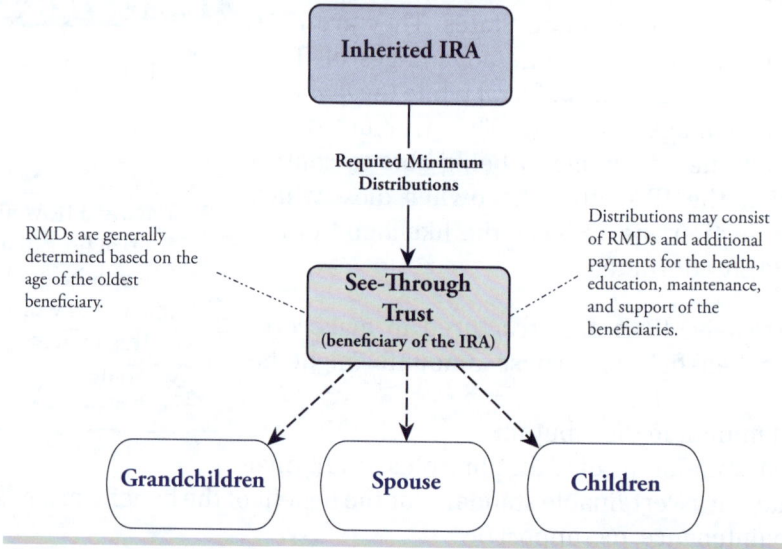

The see-through trust can be either a conduit trust (the distribution by the custodian is exactly the same amount distributed by trustee to beneficiary) or an accumulation trust. The accumulation trust is much more complex and requires specialized tax knowledge to properly draft. The accumulation trust is especially useful if the IRA is a Roth IRA and deferral and growth are objective as well as creditor protection. An accumulation trust can also be used as a special needs trust. However, it is important to keep in mind that the tax brackets for trusts are compressed with income above $12,950 taxed at 37 percent.

KEY TERMS

2503(b) Trust - A trust for the benefit of a minor designed to qualify the present value of the income interest of the trust for the annual exclusion. A 2503(b) trust must pay its income annually to the minor, but may hold the trust property for the minor's lifetime.

2503(c) Trust - A trust for the benefit of a minor designed to qualify the contribution to the trust for the annual exclusion. A 2503(c) trust must give the minor the right to receive the trust assets when he reaches age 21, but is not required to pay the income to the minor at any earlier time.

ABLE Accounts - Accounts for disabled individuals that provide some of the benefits of special needs trusts without the complexities typically associated with those trusts.

Beneficiary - The person(s) entitled to receive the death benefit of a life insurance policy at the insured's death. Also, the person(s) who hold(s) the beneficial title to a trust's assets.

Blind Trust - A revocable trust arrangement whereby an individual transfers property to the trust for management purposes when self-management of the assets might be deemed to be a conflict of interest.

Bypass Trust (also known as a Credit Shelter Trust or B Trust) - A trust created to ensure that an individual makes use of his applicable estate tax credit.

Charitable Lead Trust (CLT) – A trust in which a charitable organization receives the income interest and a non-charitable beneficiary (usually a family member) receives the remainder interest.

Charitable Remainder Trust (CRT) – A trust in which a non-charitable beneficiary receives the income interest and a charitable organization receives the remainder interest.

Complex Trust - A trust that does not meet the definition of a simple trust.

Distributable Net Income (DNI) - A tax concept that allocates taxable income between the trust and beneficiaries to ensure the trust income is subject to only one level of tax.

Estate Trust - A trust which grants the surviving spouse a testamentary general power of appointment over the trust assets. Because of the spouse's general power of appointment over the trust's assets, the fair market value of the trust will be eligible for the unlimited marital deduction at the death of the first-to-die spouse.

Fiduciary - A person who has a legal duty to act in the best interest of another as a result of holding a position of trust and confidence.

Grantor - The person who creates and initially funds a trust. The grantor is also known as the settlor or creator.

Grantor Retained Income Trust (GRIT) - A trust in which the grantor retains an income or use interest in the trust.

Income Beneficiary - The person or entity who has the current right to income from a trust, or the right to use the trust assets.

Inter Vivos Trust - A trust that is created during the grantor's lifetime.

Irrevocable Life Insurance Trust (ILIT) - An irrevocable trust that owns and holds life insurance on its grantor's life. An ILIT is also known as a wealth replacement trust (WRT).

Irrevocable Trust - A trust created by a grantor that cannot be revoked. The grantor cannot take back the property that was transferred to the trust.

Pooled Trust - An exception that resulted from the Omnibus Budget and Reconciliation Act of 1993; managed by a nonprofit association. While each beneficiary will have their own account, the assets will generally be pooled and managed together.

Pourover Trust - A trust that receives assets that "pour" into it from another source, generally the grantor's estate at the grantor's death.

Prudent Man Rule - A rule which requires a trustee, as a fiduciary, to act in the same manner that a prudent person would act if the prudent person were acting for his own benefit.

QTIP Trust - A trust that grants the surviving spouse a lifetime right to the income of the trust while transferring the remainder interest to individual(s) of the grantor's choosing, typically created at the death of the first spouse to die.

Remainder Beneficiary - The individual or entity entitled to receive the assets that remain in the trust at the date of the trust's termination.

Revocable Living Trust - A revocable trust that is managed by the grantor and is for the benefit of the grantor during his lifetime. The property transferred to the trust avoids the individual's probate estate, but is included in the individual's gross estate.

Revocable Trust - A trust created where the grantor of the trust retains the right to revoke the trust at any time prior to his incapacity or death.

Rule Against Perpetuities (RAP) - A common law rule which requires that all interests in a trust must vest, if at all, within lives in being plus 21 years.

See-Through Trust - A trust that is the beneficiary of a custodial IRA. It provides for more control over distribution of IRA assets after the owner's death, as well as providing increased creditor protection for the beneficiaries of the trust.

Self-Settled Trust - A trust where the beneficiary is also the grantor of the trust.

Simple Trust - A trust that requires all of the trust income to be distributed on an annual basis to the beneficiaries and does not have a charitable organization as one of its beneficiaries.

Special Needs Trust - A specific type of trust that is used to provide benefits to persons or beneficiaries with special needs.

Special Needs Trusts Under 42 U.S.C. Sec. 1396p(d)(4)(A) - Considered to be self-settled in nature, are typically established by the special needs person's parent, grandparent, legal guardian or by a court and will avoid disqualification of Medicaid and SSI benefits.

Spendthrift Clause - A clause in a trust document which does not allow the beneficiary to anticipate distributions from the trust, assign, pledge, hypothecate, or otherwise promise to give distributions from the trust to anyone. If such a promise is made, it is void and may not be enforced against the trust.

Standby Trust - A trust created during the grantor's lifetime that is either unfunded or minimally funded. A standby trust is also known as a contingent trust.

Testamentary Trust - A trust created after the death of the grantor. The grantor's will generally includes all of the trust provisions.

Third Party SNT - Sometimes referred to as a family trust because the trust is a receptacle for funds from a parent, guardian or other family member. The assets of these trusts, if properly structured, are not counted or considered for purposes of available benefits for the beneficiary, thus making possible federal, state, and local funds.

Totten Trust - Not a trust, but rather a bank account with a beneficiary clause.

Trust - A structure that vests legal title (the legal interest) to assets in one party, the trustee, who manages those assets for the benefit of the beneficiaries (who hold the equitable title) of the trust.

Trustee - The individual or entity responsible for managing the trust assets and carrying out the directions of the grantor that are formally expressed in the trust instrument.

Trusteed IRAs - A trust established within the United States that holds IRA assets, which is an alternative to a custodial IRA. It allows for ultimate control over the distribution of the IRA assets by the owner after his or her death and provides creditor protection for the beneficiaries.

Uniform Statutory Rule Against Perpetuities - A legislatively created alternative to the Common Law RAP that typically sets the perpetuities period at 90 years.

Wealth Replacement Trust (WRT) - An irrevocable trust that owns and holds life insurance on its grantor's life. A WRT is also known as an Irrevocable Life Insurance Trust (ILIT).

chapter 8

DISCUSSION QUESTIONS

SOLUTIONS to the discussion questions can be found exclusively within the chapter. Once you have completed an initial reading of the chapter, go back and highlight the answers to these questions.

1. Why are trusts used in estate planning?

2. What is a trust?

3. List the common parties of a trust.

4. Who is the fiduciary of a trust?

5. Explain the legal duties imposed on a fiduciary.

6. Describe the two most common types of beneficiaries.

7. List three reasons the use of a trust is beneficial to an estate plan.

8. What is a spendthrift clause and why is it included in a trust?

9. How can the creation of a trust reduce estate taxes?

10. What is the effect of the rule against perpetuities?

11. Under what circumstances will the fair market value of the assets of an irrevocable trust be included in the grantor's gross estate?

12. What are the most common reasons for using a revocable trust?

13. How is a testamentary trust created?

14. Explain the differences between an unfunded trust and a funded trust.

15. At the death of the grantor of a revocable trust, what controls the disposition of the trust's property?

16. Describe a Crummey provision and explain why a trust would contain a Crummey provision.

17. List and explain the three methods used to prevent estate tax consequences from the lapsing of a general power of appointment created by a Crummey power.

18. What is the purpose of an Irrevocable Life Insurance Trust (ILIT) and why is it created?

19. Under what circumstances will the death benefit of a life insurance policy owned by an ILIT be included in the insured's gross estate?

20. In the ideal estate plan, what amount would be transferred to a testamentary bypass trust?

21. List the various forms of Grantor Retained Income Trusts (GRITs).

22. What is the primary reason to use a GRAT for estate planning purposes?

23. List the primary difference between a GRAT and a GRUT.

24. How is a GRAT more effective in reducing the grantor's gross estate than a GRUT?

25. Discuss the consequences of a grantor dying during the term of a TPPT.

26. What is a dynasty trust and what is its primary purpose?

27. Who is subject to the income tax on the income of a grantor trust?

28. What is the primary purpose of using a 2503(b) or 2503(c) trust?

29. List the requirements of a 2503(b) trust.

30. Describe a Totten Trust and its benefits.

31. What are the three types of special needs trusts?

32. Describe a third party special needs trust.

33. What are some of the requirement for a special needs trust under 42 U.S.C. Sec. 1396p(d)(4)(A)?

34. Why are IRAs of interest in Estate Planning?

35. What is the purpose of a Trusteed IRA?

36. Does the IRS require the trustee of a See-Through Trust to provide the complete trust instrument to the custodian?

chapter 8

MULTIPLE-CHOICE PROBLEMS

A sample of multiple choice problems is provided below. Additional multiple choice problems are available at money-education.com by accessing the Student Practice Portal.

1. Which of the following is not a party to a trust?
    a. Trustee.
    b. Income beneficiary.
    c. Grantor.
    d. Principal.

2. A trustee is subject to which of the following?
    a. Prudent Man Rule.
    b. Trustee's Ethical Code.
    c. Uniform Trustee Provisions.
    d. Fiduciary Responsibilities Doctrine.

3. A spendthrift clause:
    a. Requires the fiduciary of a trust to make small distributions.
    b. Protects the trust assets from the claims of the beneficiary's creditors.
    c. Eliminates the problems associated with multiple beneficiaries.
    d. Prevents the lapse of a general power of appointment and its subsequent estate tax consequences.

4. Marcia contributed $600,000 to an irrevocable trust with no retained powers in 2018 and did not retain any powers over the transferred assets. She named her only daughter as the sole income and remainder beneficiary and paid gift tax at the date of the transfer of $25,000. In 2020, Marcia died of lung cancer. The fair market value of the property in the irrevocable trust was $3,000,000 at the date of her death. What amount of the trust assets are included in Marcia's gross estate?
    a. $0.
    b. $600,000.
    c. $625,000.
    d. $3,000,000.

5. A trust created in the will of a decedent is a:
    a. Standby trust.
    b. Testamentary trust.
    c. Trust by will.
    d. Decedent's trust.

QUICK QUIZ EXPLANATIONS

Quick Quiz 8.1
1. False. A trust may have only one beneficiary. Two beneficiaries are not required.
2. True.
3. False. The income beneficiary is entitled to receive the income or current distributions from the trust. The remainder beneficiary receives the corpus of the trust at the end of the trust's term.

Quick Quiz 8.2
1. False. One of the classic reasons for using a trust is to protect assets from the claims of the beneficiaries' creditors.
2. False. A spendthrift clause provides asset protection by legally restricting a beneficiary's ability to anticipate distributions from the trust. A properly constructed spendthrift clause will prevent creditors from being able to access trust assets unless they are distributed to the beneficiary.
3. True.
4. False. Since transfers to a revocable living trust are revocable, the property in the trust is included in the grantor's gross estate pursuant to the retained interest rule (Section 2038).

Quick Quiz 8.3
1. True.
2. True.
3. True.

Quick Quiz 8.4
1. False. DNI is a tax concept that maintains the character of the income that is distributed to the beneficiaries, and limits the beneficiary's exposure to income taxation on trust distribution. It is not necessarily required to be distributed to the trust beneficiaries.
2. False. Assets transferred to a trust are only excluded from the gross estate of the grantor if the trust is irrevocable and the grantor has not retained any interest in the trust that would require inclusion in the gross estate under the retained interest rules (Sections 2036-2038).
3. True.

Quick Quiz 8.5
1. False. Revocable trusts allow the grantor to take back the property that was transferred to the trust.
2. True.
3. False. A trust that requires all income to be distributed on an annual basis is a simple, not complex, trust.

QUICK QUIZ EXPLANATIONS

Quick Quiz 8.6
1. False. Revocable trusts cannot avoid estate taxes due to the grantor's retained right to revoke the transfer. The most common use for inter vivos revocable trusts is to avoid probate, not estate tax.
2. False. ILITs are used to exclude life insurance from a decedent's gross estate.

Quick Quiz 8.7
1. True.
2. False. The fair market value of the remainder interest in a GRAT is subject to gift tax when the GRAT is created.
3. True.

Quick Quiz 8.8
1. True.
2. True.
3. True.

Quick Quiz 8.9
1. False. The Supreme Court ruled in Clark v. Ramaker that inherited IRAs are not retirement plans and therefore, are subject to claims of creditors in bankruptcy.
2. True.

Quick Quiz 8.10
1. False. A see-through trust is a beneficiary of a custodial IRA, whereas a trusteed IRA is the IRA itself, as well as being a trust.
2. True.

9
CHARITABLE GIVING

LEARNING OBJECTIVES

1. Describe the general issues regarding charitable contributions and income, gift and estate taxation.
2. Identify and classify qualifying organizations.
3. Describe charitable gifts during life including gifts of cash, gifts of services, and gifts of property.
4. Identify the income tax treatment for various gifts of property depending on the donee, the donor's adjusted gross income, the type of property, and the donor's tax basis.
5. Describe the process of choosing the adjusted basis over the fair market value for charitable income tax deductions.
6. Identify the methods of valuation record keeping and reporting required by the IRS for charitable tax deductions.
7. Describe outright gifts to charities, bargain sales to charities, charitable gift annuities, and gifts of life insurance to charities.
8. Describe charitable gifts of a split interest including pooled income funds, charitable remainder trusts, and charitable lead trusts.
9. Understand the differences in requirements for charitable remainder trusts and charitable lead trusts.
10. Describe a wealth replacement trust.
11. Describe testamentary giving to charities.
12. Describe why charitable gifts made during life are more tax advantageous than charitable bequests made at death.

CFP Board Resource Document - Student-Centered Learning Objectives based upon CFP Board Principal Topics.

INTRODUCTION

Charitable giving is a way of life in America. According to National Philanthropic Trust, in 2016, American households donated over $390.05 billion to charity, and approximately 63 million Americans donated over 7.9 billion hours of their time to charity, worth an estimated value of $193 billion.[1] The most frequent contributors to charity include college graduates, retirees, and other households with incomes over $100,000. In 2016, the largest source of charitable giving came from individuals at $281.86 billion, or 72 percent of total giving.

---

1. National Philanthropic Trust, Charitable Giving Statistics.

chapter 9

Exhibit 9.1 | Charitable Giving (In Billions of Dollars)

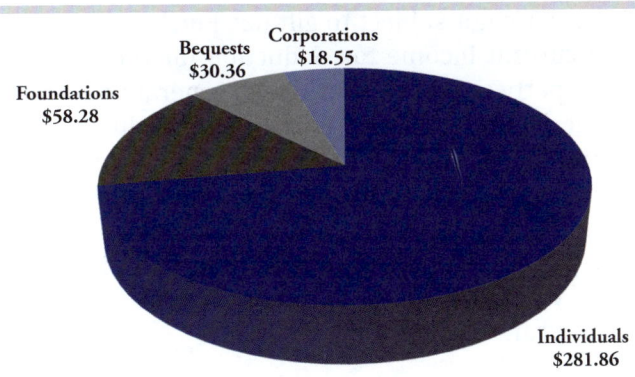

- Bequests $30.36
- Corporations $18.55
- Foundations $58.28
- Individuals $281.86

Many people use charitable trusts as part of their overall estate plan, which allows them greater flexibility and control over intended charitable contributions while still fulfilling philanthropic goals. The chart below depicts the assets held in charitable trusts in 2012.[1]

Exhibit 9.2 | Charitable Trusts

	Total Number	Assets (in Billions)
Charitable Remainder Unitrusts	91,244	$85.2
Charitable Remainder Annuity Trusts	14,616	$6.4
Charitable Lead Trusts	6,498	$23.7
Pooled Income Funds	1,324	$1.3

Charitable Trusts

1. Charitable remainder trusts (CRTs) allow donors to transfer assets to a trust and receive income over the life of the trust, in addition to a current income tax deduction. Remaining assets at the termination of the trust are transferred to charity.
2. Charitable lead trusts are often used to transfer assets to an heir in the future with minimal transfer tax.
3. Pooled income funds are similar in nature to CRTs except the funds from many donors are pooled together in one fund.

Source: IRS 2012 Tax Statistics & National Philanthropic Trust

Gifts to charity can be made during life (inter vivos) or at death (causa mortis). A donor needs to consider charitable objectives and the timing of the gift, in addition to the tax consequences of making a charitable donation. The character of the property given, the type of charity, the timing of the contribution, and, for inter vivos giving, the taxpayer's adjusted gross income (AGI) are all factors that can affect the tax consequences of charitable donations.

---

1. Latest information available at time of printing.

General Issues Regarding Charitable Contributions and Taxation

Charitable deductions of any size are not subject to gift tax. Furthermore, direct gifts to charities made during life usually generate a current income tax deduction for the donor. Under certain conditions, even a remainder interest in property given to a charity will generate a current income tax deduction for the donor. All bequests made at death to qualified charities are deducted from the decedent's adjusted gross estate to arrive at the taxable estate. The deduction is unlimited but is only available for those assets included in the decedent's gross estate. Bequests do not receive income tax benefits. If a donor makes a gift to a charity of a complete interest in property and has no other gifts that year, no gift tax return is required. However, a gift tax return is required for any split interest gift involving a qualifying charity and any other donee or where the donor is required to file a gift tax return as a result of non-charitable gifts made during the year.

Under certain conditions, the value of an otherwise lifetime gift to charity may be included in the decedent's gross estate. A like amount will also be deducted from the adjusted gross estate to arrive at the taxable estate. A common example is where the decedent had assigned the ownership of a life insurance policy to a qualified charity and the decedent died within three years of assigning the policy. Because the assignment was made within three years of the decedent's death, the death benefit must be included in the decedent's gross estate, but is also eligible as a charitable deduction from the adjusted gross estate to arrive at the taxable estate. There are some potentially unfortunate consequences from this type of a transaction which will be covered in Chapter 12, Post Mortem Elections. Other examples that may trigger this treatment include situations where the donor retains a general power of appointment over property that upon his death passes to a qualified charity, and when a donor creates a charitable remainder trust and possesses the right to receive income payments (at death) from the trust when he/she dies.

> **Key Concepts**
>
> 1. Identify the types of organizations that qualify for charitable status per the IRC.
> 2. List three examples of qualifying charities.
> 3. Which websites are available to provide more information on specific charitable organizations?

Qualifying Organizations

The Internal Revenue Code (Section 170(c)) defines the types of organizations that qualify for charitable status. They include:
1. A state, a possession of the United States, or any political subdivision (contribution must be solely for public purposes).
2. A corporation, trust, or community chest, fund, or foundation that is organized in the U.S. and is operated exclusively for:
    a. religious, charitable, scientific, literary, or educational purposes;
    b. fostering national or international amateur sports competition; or
    c. preventing cruelty to animals or children.
3. A post or organization of war veterans organized in the United States.
4. A domestic fraternal society, order, or association, operating under the lodge system, but only if the contribution is to be used for the purposes listed in 2 above.
5. A cemetery company (not deductible if the donation is limited to the maintenance of a specific cemetery plot).

Exhibit 9.3 | Charitable Organizations

Charities that would generally qualify under this definition include:	Charities that generally do NOT qualify under this definition include:
• Churches, temples, synagogues • Public parks • Colleges and universities • United Way • Boy Scouts and Girl Scouts of America • Salvation Army • American Heart Association • American Society for Prevention of Cruelty to Animals	• Foreign organizations • For-profit groups • Homeowners' associations • Political groups • Labor unions • Chambers of commerce • Social clubs • Individuals • Civic groups

There are three easy ways to determine if an organization qualifies as a charitable organization. The IRS Exempt Organization search page.[1] The IRS website (www.irs.gov) also lists the charitable organizations, and Guidestar, the National Database of Nonprofit Organizations (www.guidestar.org) allows you to verify the organization's status as well as view the organization's informational tax return, Form 990.

Example 9.1

Question: If an organization tells you that your contribution is tax deductible when, in fact, it is not, can you still take a deduction?

Answer: No. The burden is on the taxpayer to verify a qualifying organization's charitable status.

Types of Charitable Organizations

Charitable organizations can be categorized as public charities, private operating foundations, or private nonoperating foundations. The classification of the organization will affect the amount of income tax deduction allowed for the charitable contribution.

Public charities are those that receive broad support from the general public. Specifically, an organization must meet two tests. The first test, under Section 509(a)(2)(A) of the IRC, states that more than one-third of the organization's support must be from a combination of gifts, grants, contributions, membership fees, and gross receipts from sales in an activity which is not an unrelated trade or business. The second test, under Section 509(a)(2)(B), requires that not more than one-third of an organization's support can come from the sum of gross investment income plus unrelated business taxable income (reduced by related taxes).

---

1. The IRS Exempt Organization search page is located at https://apps.irs.gov/app/eos/

Exhibit 9.4 | Types of Charities

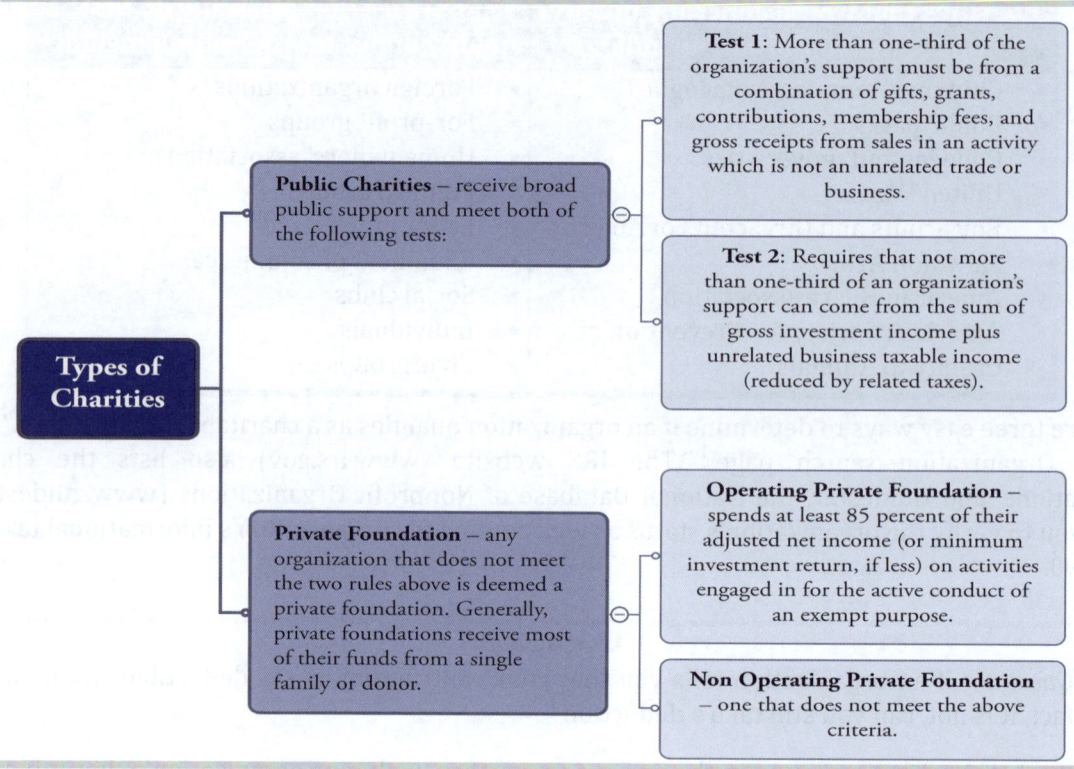

If an organization does not meet the two tests described above, it is considered to be a private foundation. **Private foundations** generally receive their support from a single individual or family and can be classified as either operating or nonoperating. **Private operating foundations** are those that spend at least 85 percent of their adjusted net income (or minimum investment return, if less) on activities engaged in for the active conduct of an exempt purpose. In addition, an assets test, endowment test, or support test must be met. (Although beyond the scope of this text, more information on this topic can be found in IRC Section 509.) If a private foundation does not meet the tests to be classified as operating, then it is deemed to be a **private nonoperating foundation**. Most family established foundations are private, nonoperating foundations.

Quick Quiz 9.1

1. A gift tax return must be filed whenever a gift is made to a public charity.
   a. True
   b. False

2. Gifts to the state of Texas qualify as deductible charitable gifts.
   a. True
   b. False

3. Public charities are for the benefit of the public, without a specific cause or beneficiary class.
   a. True
   b. False

False, True, False.

chapter 9

CHARITABLE GIFTS DURING LIFE

Generally, any gift to a charity of money, property (including tangible, intangible, or real property), or any right with value will qualify as a charitable contribution, and thus its value may be deductible for federal income tax purposes. While neither gifts of a partial interest nor services are typically deductible for federal income tax purposes, any out of pocket expenses directly related to a charitable activity are deductible for federal income tax purposes.

Gifts of Cash

Individuals may deduct cash contributions made to qualified charitable organizations subject to some limitations. The value of the cash contribution is reduced by any tangible benefit received by the donor from the donation.

> **Key Concepts**
>
> 1. Understand how much of a charitable deduction is allowed for contributions to universities to purchase athletic tickets.
> 2. Identify expenses that can be deducted in relation to gifts of services.
> 3. Identify the requirements of a contribution acknowledgment for contributions in excess of $250.
> 4. Know the IRS form used to report noncash contributions in excess of $500.

Example 9.2
Larry purchased a $150 per couple ticket to a fund raising dinner for the benefit of the local ballet company. The dinner served had a fair market value of $25 per person. Larry took his girlfriend Camille to the dinner. Larry's charitable deduction is $100 [$150 FMV - (2 x $25)].

For cash contributions to colleges and universities where the donor receives the right to purchase tickets to athletic events, none of the contribution is allowed as a charitable contribution.

Example 9.3
Mr. Crimson donates $1,000 to the Tide Pride fund at his college alma mater. In exchange, Mr. Crimson receives the right to purchase football tickets. Mr. Crimson's charitable deduction is $0.

If a taxpayer receives an item of low (de minimis) value that has the organization's name or logo on it, then the contribution is deductible in full.

Example 9.4
Sally makes a donation of $50 to her local public radio station. In return, Sally receives a mug with the station's call letters on it. Sally does not have to reduce the donation by the value of the mug - the entire $50 donation will qualify as a charitable contribution.

Gifts of Services

When donating services to a charitable organization, only the unreimbursed out-of-pocket expenses directly connected with the services are deductible. The value of the service itself is nondeductible.

Exhibit 9.5 | Examples Of Deductible Out-Of-Pocket Expenses

- Car expenses - direct expenses such as gas and oil (not depreciation or insurance), or alternatively the standard mileage deduction at 14 cents per mile can be taken.
- Support for foster children in excess of payments received, if no profit motive exists.
- Travel and transportation expenses incurred in connection with attending a convention on behalf of a qualified organization.
- Uniforms required to be worn while performing a charitable service.

Example 9.5

Mary volunteers as an aide at the local hospital. She is required to wear a special pink uniform. If she buys the uniform, the cost of her uniform is deductible as a charitable contribution.

Example 9.6

Sarah delivers Meals on Wheels to the elderly in her community. She drives 2,000 miles a year performing this service. Out-of-pocket expenses incurred in connection with the mileage include $167 in gas, $80 pro rata share of insurance, and a $25 parking fine. Sarah's maximum deduction is $280 (14 cents x 2000 miles). Actual expenses would only be $167, since the insurance and parking fine are not considered to be out-of-pocket charitable expenses.

Question: What if Sarah paid for the parking and avoided the fine?

Answer: She would consider the actual cost of parking as a charitable contribution.

Gifts of Property

Generally, the income tax charitable deduction for donated property is the fair market value of the property as of the date of the contribution, subject to AGI limitations. However, the taxpayer needs to consider the specific type of property (ordinary income, capital gain, or Section 1231) contributed to determine the deductible amount of the charitable contribution.

An easy way to determine the type of property donated is to determine the income tax consequences if that some property would have been sold. If the result of the sale would have been ordinary income or short-term capital gain, then such property is ordinary income property. Alternatively, if the sale of the property would have resulted in long-term capital gain or Section 1231 gain, then such property is capital gain property. A detailed discussion of the deductible amounts related to each type of property follows.

Ordinary Income Property

Ordinary income property is property that, if sold, would result in recognition of ordinary income. Examples include inventory, capital assets held one year or less, and works of art created by the donor.

The deduction for donated ordinary income property is equal to the fair market value of the property reduced by any ordinary income that would have resulted from its sale. As a result, the deductible amount is usually the adjusted basis of the property. In the event the fair market value is less than the adjusted basis (no ordinary income would result from this sale), the deduction is equal to the fair market value of the property itself.

Example 9.7

Robert donates a sculpture he created (adjusted basis $100, fair market value $500), painting supplies from his crafts store (adjusted basis $200, fair market value $100), and some Mackie Corporation stock which he has held less than one year (adjusted basis $1,500, fair market value $2,000) to the local art museum. Given this information, his charitable deduction is $1,700 as follows:

Sculpture	$100	The deduction for a work of art created by the donor is limited to adjusted basis.
Painting Supplies	$100	When the fair market value of the ordinary income property is less than the adjusted basis, the charitable deduction is limited to the fair market value.
Stock	$1,500	The deduction for a short-term capital asset is limited to its adjusted basis.
TOTAL	$1,700	

Capital Gain Property

Property that, if sold, would result in either capital gain or Section 1231 gain is considered to be **capital gain property**. A capital asset includes intangible property (e.g., stocks and bonds), tangible property (automobile), and real property. Section 1231 property is commercial in nature or used to generate income, must be held long term (greater than one year), and is eligible for depreciation. There is a special requirement for tangible property put to an unrelated use that is discussed further below. Otherwise, subject to the following two exceptions listed below, the charitable deduction for capital gain property is the property's fair market value.

Example 9.8

Assume the Mackie Corporation stock described in the example above was held long-term by Robert and donated to Robert's church. The charitable deduction in such a case would be $2,000, the fair market value of the stock.

Donation to a Private Nonoperating Foundation

There are two exceptions to the general rule that provides for a fair market value deduction for capital gain property. First, when capital gain property is donated to a private nonoperating foundation, the deduction is limited to the adjusted basis of the property.

> **Example 9.9**
> Robert donates the Mackie Corporation stock (held long-term) to Delle Foundation (a private nonoperating foundation, whose purpose is to promote medical research in the area of relieving stress for people who work with Type A individuals). Robert's charitable donation is limited to the adjusted basis of the stock, $1,500, because the donation is to a private nonoperating foundation.

Donation of Property for Unrelated Use

The second exception to the fair market value deduction for capital gain property applies to donations of **tangible property** (property that is not realty, is not permanently affixed to the land, has physical substance, and is capital in nature) put to an unrelated use. This includes art, jewelry, automobiles, books, etc. that are not created by the donor. When tangible property is donated to a public charity and is used in a manner that is unrelated to the exempt purpose of the charity, the deduction is limited to the donor's adjusted basis of the property. If the donation is made to a governmental entity, the donated property must be used exclusively for public purposes, or it will be considered "unrelated use" property. The assumption underlying this rule is that if the donated property is unrelated to the mission of the charity, the charity will sell the donated property shortly after the date of donation so the appropriate value of the charitable deduction would be the lesser of fair market value or the donor's adjusted basis. Furnishings that are contributed to a charity and are used in the offices that carry out the charitable objective are considered related use property.

> **Example 9.10**
> Paul has a valuable coin collection he has been managing for over 30 years. Paul has been a savvy investor, and the collection has a fair market value well in excess of Paul's adjusted basis. If Paul contributes the coin collection to the local museum, whose intent is to display the coin collection, Paul will have a charitable deduction equal to the fair market value of the coin collection. If, however, Paul contributes the coin collection to his church, it is hard to imagine a situation where the coin collection could be used for religious purposes. In this case, Paul's deduction would be limited to the lesser of the fair market value of the collection, or his adjusted basis in the coin collection. Even if the church sold the coin collection and used the proceeds for religious purposes, it would still be considered an unrelated use, and Paul's charitable deduction in this case would be limited to his adjusted basis in the coin collection.

The taxpayer must establish or be able to reasonably anticipate at the time of the donation that the property will not be put to an unrelated use. If one of these two requirements is met, the property is considered related use even if the charitable organization later sells or exchanges the property. No recapture provision at the lesser value would apply.

To ensure the availability of a charitable deduction equal to the fair market value of the donated property, a taxpayer may create a contract with the charitable organization requiring the charity to put the donated tangible property to a related use.

Example 9.11

Michael owns artwork with an adjusted basis of $100 and a fair market value of $100,000. He donates the artwork to Loyal University and contractually requires the university to display the artwork in the art department for 2 years for the educational purpose of art students. Because the artwork will be put to a related use of Loyal University, Michael will be able to deduct the fair market value of $100,000 (subject to AGI limitations).

Example 9.12

Question: If a taxpayer is holding property that has depreciated relative to its adjusted basis, is it better for the taxpayer to donate the property to a charitable organization, or sell it first and donate the proceeds from the sale?

Answer: Sell the property and donate the proceeds of the sale, otherwise the taxpayer will lose the capital loss deduction.

Contribution Base (Adjusted Gross Income) Limitations

Depending upon the classification of the charitable organization and the type of donated property, the IRC (Section 170(b)) prescribes an adjusted gross income (AGI) limitation for contributions. The income deduction limitation for individual contributions is either 20 percent, 30 percent, or 60 percent of the donor's contribution base, depending on the classification of the charitable organization and the type of property contributed.[1] Overall, the total deductible contributions for the tax year cannot exceed 60 percent of the donor's contribution base. A donor's contribution base is his/her AGI, not taking into account net operating loss carrybacks. Since most taxpayers do not have net operating loss carrybacks, when discussing the charitable deduction limitations in this chapter, we use AGI.

60 Percent Organizations

60 percent organizations include:
- Public charities (including churches, schools, hospitals),
- Private operating foundations, and
- Private nonoperating foundations that distribute their contributions to either public charities or private operating foundations within two and one-half months of their tax year-end (referred to as a pass-through private foundation).

If the donee organization is a 60 percent charity, then a donor can deduct charitable contributions to these charities up to a limit of 60 percent of his AGI. An exception exists for contributions of appreciated capital gain property, which are limited to 30 percent of AGI. Taxpayers are permitted to avoid the 30 percent ceiling on this type of property by electing to use the adjusted basis to determine the amount of the deduction instead of the fair market value. The contribution would then be subject to a 60 percent of AGI ceiling. In other words, for a contribution of appreciated property, a taxpayer has the choice of a deduction equal to the fair market value with a 30 percent of AGI limitation or a deduction equal to the adjusted basis with a 60 percent of AGI limitation.

---

1. TCJA 2017 increased the 50 percent limit to 60 percent.

30 Percent Organizations

Contributions to private nonoperating foundations that do not qualify as 60 percent organizations (i.e., those private foundations that do not distribute its income by the 15th day of the 3rd month of the organization's tax year-end) are subject to either a 20 percent or 30 percent of AGI limitation, depending on the type of property contributed. Contributions of cash and ordinary income property are subject to a 30 percent of AGI limitation, whereas contributions of long-term capital gain property are subject to a 20 percent of AGI limitation. While there is a lower percentage limitation that applies to gifts of long-term capital gain property, the donor will receive an income tax deduction equal to the full fair market value of the property without being required to recognize the gain on the property as income.

Special Rules and Carryforward of Disallowed Contributions

If a taxpayer makes donations to both 30 percent and 60 percent organizations during a year, the 60 percent donations are considered first. Any charitable contribution deductions disallowed because of the AGI limitations may be carried over for five years and are used in a first-in-first-out order. The carryover amounts retain their classifications as 20 percent, 30 percent, or 60 percent donations.

Exhibit 9.6 | Charitable Contribution Deductions (Percent of Taxpayer's AGI)

Type of Property Donated	Valuation for Purposes of Charitable Deduction	Ceiling for Public Charities, Private Operating Foundations and Certain Private Nonoperating Foundations	Ceiling for Other Private Nonoperating Foundations (PNOF)	
Cash	Fair Market Value	60%	30%	
Ordinary Income Property and Short-term Capital Gain Property	Lesser of the adjusted basis or the fair market value	60%	30%	
Long-term Capital Gain property: - Intangible	Fair market value	30%*	Adjusted Basis	20%**
- Tangible Personalty	Fair market value - (a) related use Adjusted basis - (b) unrelated use	30%* 60%		20%
- Real Property	Fair market value	30%*		20%

*Taxpayer has the option to use the adjusted basis and the 50% of AGI ceiling for regular charities.
**Certain contributions of qualified appreciated stock may use the fair market value.

Choosing the Adjusted Basis Over the Fair Market Value (Special Election)

The determination of whether to select the adjusted basis as the charitable deduction for each contribution instead of the fair market value should be made with great care. The factors to consider include:
- The donor's current AGI and the projected AGI for the next 5 years;
- The fair market value of the donated property;
- The adjusted basis of the donated property; and
- The time value of money.

chapter 9

Example 9.13

Suppose Jerry makes the following charitable contributions:

Type of Property	Basis	FMV	Donee
Stock (LT)	$35,000	$40,000	University
Stock (ST)	$10,000	$12,000	United Way

LT = Long-term   ST = Short-term

- Jerry's AGI is $100,000. His charitable contribution income tax deduction, not using the alternative adjusted basis/60% election is:

Type of Property	Adjusted Basis or FMV	Deduction	5-Year Carryover
Stock (LT)	$40,000 (FMV) limited to 30% of AGI	$30,000	$10,000
Stock (ST)	$10,000 (adjusted basis) limited to 60% of AGI	$10,000	$0
Total Deductible Contributions		$40,000	$10,000

Jerry's total deduction for the year is $40,000 which does not, in total, exceed 60% of Jerry's AGI or $50,000. Jerry would have a charitable contributions carryover of $10,000 that must be used within 5 years.

If Jerry had elected to use the adjusted basis for the long-term stock with a 60% of AGI ceiling, his deduction would be as follows:

Type of Property	Adjusted Basis or FMV	Deduction	5-Year Carryover
Stock (LT)	$35,000 (adjusted basis) limited to 60% of AGI	$35,000	$0
Stock (ST)	$10,000 (adjusted basis) limited to 60% of AGI	$10,000	$0
Total Deductible Contributions		$45,000	$0

Under these circumstances, Jerry would have a current $45,000 charitable contribution deduction. Since Jerry deducted the full adjusted basis of both assets in the first year, there is no carryover contribution for use in future years. Jerry would have to consider a number of factors to decide which option to take - the time value of money, his projected AGI over the next five years (will he be able to use the carryover?) and his immediate cash needs.

Charitable Gifts During Life

Example 9.14

Merrily has an AGI of $50,000 consisting entirely of taxable bond interest. She has a rare antique that her father bequeathed to her. Her adjusted basis in the antique is $200,000, and the antique has a fair market value of $1,000,000. Assuming that her AGI will remain at $50,000 for the next six years, which tax election (adjusted basis or fair market value) creates better tax benefits for her if she donates the antique to a museum in 2020?

Tax Year	AGI	Deductible Amount	
		Adjusted Basis (subject to 60% of AGI)	FMV (subject to 30% of AGI)
2020	$50,000	$30,000	$15,000
2021	$50,000	$30,000	$15,000
2022	$50,000	$30,000	$15,000
2023	$50,000	$30,000	$15,000
2024	$50,000	$30,000	$15,000
2025	$50,000	$30,000	$15,000
TOTALS	$300,000	$180,000	$90,000

Because of the five-year carry forward limit and the difference in AGI limitations, Merrily has a greater total deduction by electing to deduct the adjusted basis rather than the fair market value of the antique. By electing to deduct the adjusted basis of the antique, she can deduct 60% of AGI up to the adjusted basis of the antique rather than being limited to 30% of AGI up to the fair market value. Recognize that even with the election to deduct the property based upon the adjusted basis, Merrily will not be able to receive cumulative deductions equal to her adjusted basis in the antique, let alone the full fair market value, because of the AGI limitations. The situation would obviously be quite different if Merrily's adjusted basis in the antique was substantially lower, or alternatively, if Merrily were to have, and expect to continue to have, a much higher AGI.

Example 9.15

Assume instead Merrily has an AGI of $400,000 and donates the same antique with an adjusted basis of $200,000, and a fair market value of $1,000,000. Assuming that her AGI remains at $400,000 for the next 6 years, which tax election (adjusted basis or fair market value) creates better tax benefits for her?

Tax Year	AGI	Deductible Amount	
		Adjusted Basis (subject to 60% of AGI)	FMV (subject to 30% of AGI)
2020	$400,000	$200,000	$120,000
2021	$400,000	$0	$120,000
2022	$400,000	$0	$120,000
2023	$400,000	$0	$120,000
2024	$400,000	$0	$120,000
2025	$400,000	$0	$120,000
TOTALS	$2,400,000	$200,000	$720,000

Obviously, even though the deduction is limited to 30% of her AGI each year, Merrily should elect to deduct the fair market value of the antique as her charitable deduction as it produces a much greater overall deduction.

Valuation, Record Keeping, and Reporting

Determining the fair market value of donated property can be difficult. The fair market value of any property is the price at which a fully informed, willing seller and a fully informed, willing buyer will complete a transaction. IRS Publication 561, *Determining the Value of Donated Property*, as well as some third party publications, such as "blue books," may offer assistance in valuation. A qualified appraisal will also provide the determination of value, but the IRS only requires an appraisal for property donated with a value in excess of $5,000. The additional cost for the appraisal is a miscellaneous itemized deduction subject to the two percent of AGI floor.

When a taxpayer makes any charitable contribution in the form of cash or a canceled check, a detailed receipt (indicating the donee's name, the date, and the amount of contribution) should be retained by the taxpayer as supporting documentation.

Contemporaneous written acknowledgment by the donee organization is required when an individual contributes cash or property valued at $250 or more per donation. This is not aggregated. For instance, if a church-member gave $200 each week to the church as a charitable contribution over the course of the year, no written acknowledgment is required since each donation was less than $250. For donations over $250, the acknowledgment must include:
- The amount of cash or a description (but not value) of the property;
- Whether any goods or services were given in consideration of the donated property; and
- A good faith estimate of the value of the goods and services provided in consideration of the donated property.

> **Quick Quiz 9.2**
>
> 1. If a product or service is rendered in return for the charitable contribution, no portion of the contribution is deductible.
>   a. True
>   b. False
> 2. Gifts of services are fully deductible for the person performing the service.
>   a. True
>   b. False
> 3. An individual will always choose to deduct the fair market value of the contributed property.
>   a. True
>   b. False
> 4. It is the responsibility of the IRS to determine the value of contributed property.
>   a. True
>   b. False
>
> *False, False, False, False.*

If the value of a donated item is $5,000 or less, but more than $500, the donor must provide information on how and when the property was acquired, as well as its adjusted basis. This information, along with the donee's name and address, and the date of the contribution, must be provided on Form 8283, *Noncash Charitable Contributions*. Form 8283 must also be filed whenever the aggregate total of all non-cash contributions exceeds $500. Form 8283 must be filed with the donor's income tax return for the year in which the property was contributed and the deduction is first claimed.

If a donated item is valued at more than $5,000, and the item is neither cash nor a publicly traded security, then the donor must obtain a qualified appraisal on the property and the appraisal must be attached to the donor's tax return. If the donated property is a non-publicly traded stock, the donor is required to obtain an appraisal if the value is more than $10,000. The IRS maintains a list of approved appraisers, although the use of an approved appraiser does not guarantee that the IRS will not challenge the valuation.

Example 9.16

Question: Are appraisal fees deductible for federal income tax purposes as part of the charitable contribution?

Answer: No. However, appraisal fees can be deducted for federal income tax purposes as a miscellaneous itemized deduction subject to the 2% of AGI floor.

Exhibit 9.7 | Charitable Contributions/Reporting

Amount or Value of Donation	Cash	Property
Under $250	Canceled check	Receipt with donee name, date, description of property
$250-$500	Contemporaneous acknowledgment from donee organization	Contemporaneous acknowledgment from donee organization
Over $500, but no more than $5,000	Same as above	Same as above plus maintain records of how and when property was acquired, its adjusted basis and file Form 8283
Over $5,000 ($10,000 for non-publicly traded stock)	Same as above	Same as above plus must obtain qualified appraisal and attach appraisal to the return

When taxpayers donate art work that has been appraised at $50,000 or more, taxpayers may request a statement of value from the IRS. The statement of value can only be requested <u>after</u> the donation has been made, and the taxpayer is required to file the statement with the income tax return, whether the taxpayer agrees with the value or not. A minimum fee of $2,500 is imposed by the IRS for the statement of value with an additional $250 fee for each additional item over three. The statement of the value can provide the donor with a level of assurance at the time of filing that his deduction will not be subsequently disallowed or limited by the IRS.

OTHER OUTRIGHT GIFTS TO CHARITY

Bargain Sales of Property to Charities

Recall (from Chapter 7) that a person may sell property at a price below its fair market value to benefit a related party. Persons may also sell property to a charity at a price below its fair market value. When a bargain sale to a charity occurs, the transaction is split into two elements, a sale element and a charitable contribution element. The adjusted basis of the property is allocated pro rata between the sale element and the charitable contribution element.

Example 9.17

Donor sells real estate at a fair market value of $100,000 and with an adjusted basis of $100,000 to a charity for $60,000 cash. The transaction is split into two: a sale of $60,000 (less pro rata allocation of the property's adjusted basis, or $60,000 = no gain or loss) and a charitable contribution equal to the bargain on the sale of $40,000.

Bargain Sales of Appreciated Property to Charities

When a bargain sale of appreciated property to a charity occurs, the capital gain portion of the sale element should be considered for income taxation purposes. The capital gain portion is calculated as follows:

$$\text{Sale Component} - \left[\frac{\text{Sale Component}}{\text{Fair Market Value}} \times \text{Donor's Adjusted Basis}\right] = \text{Capital Gain}$$

Example 9.18

Referring to the last example and considering instead that the donor's adjusted basis of the property was $30,000, what is the result of the sale of $100,000 property to a charity for $60,000? The sale component of $60,000 is reduced by the proportional basis of $18,000 (60% x $30,000), creating a capital gain of $42,000 ($60,000 - $18,000). The charitable deduction remains, as in the last example, at $40,000. However, the ability to deduct the contribution is still subject to the AGI limits discussed above.

Charitable Gift Annuities

With the dramatic increase in individual retirement life expectancy, charities have been promoting charitable gift annuities. Donations can come in a variety of forms, including cash, securities, or property subject to the gift acceptance policy of the charity. This transaction involves an inter vivos transfer of property to a charity in exchange for the charity's promise to pay an annuity either to the donor, the donor and his spouse, or to another person. The charity keeps the principal, but is obliged to provide lifetime income to the annuitant.

The annuity paid to the donor is dependent upon the age of the donor (annuitant), or donors (annuitants) in the case of a joint life annuity. An older donor will receive a greater annuity percentage payout due to reduced life expectancy, but in either case the present value of the annuity will be less than the value of the property contributed to the charity in return for the annuity. For example, a charity that receives property from a 60-year old in exchange for an annuity may only pay the annuitant a 5.2 percent annuity, whereas an 82-year old transferring the same property will receive an 7.5 percent annuity from the same charity. The value of the property contributed less the present value of the annuity equals the charitable income tax deduction in the year of the transfer.

Exhibit 9.8 | Single Life Rate Guidelines[1]

Age	Annuity Rate	Age	Annuity Rate
30	2.8%	65	4.7%
35	3.0%	70	5.1%
40	3.3%	75	5.8%
45	3.5%	80	6.9%
50	3.7%	85	8.0%
55	4.0%	90+	9.0%
60	4.3%		

The charitable annuity can be created to provide either an immediate or a deferred benefit annuity. If the annuity is a single-life contract that is paid to the donor, the donor receives a charitable income tax deduction in the year of the transfer and removes the value of the asset from his gross estate. In the case of an annuity payable to another person, the donor receives a charitable income tax deduction equal to the present value of the remainder interest, the value of the property may not be included in his gross estate, and the donor has made a potentially taxable gift (equal to the present value of the annuity) to the person who receives the annuity.

> **Key Concepts**
>
> 1. How is a bargain sale of appreciated property to a charity treated for income tax purposes?
> 2. Why are charities promoting charitable gift annuities now more than in the past?
> 3. How is the value of a gift of encumbered property calculated?

Unlike transfers to qualified charitable remainder trusts (CRATs, CRUTs, and Pooled Income Funds - discussed below), an income tax liability may arise on the transfer of appreciated property in exchange for an annuity. Similarly, the bargain sale rules apply.

Benefits of charitable gift annuities to the donor include all of the following:
- simplicity
- low (or no) cost
- guaranteed fixed income for life
- provides an income tax charitable deduction to the donor
- annuity payments have a tax-free recovery of capital components
- principal is removed from the donor's estate

---

1. The American Council on Gift Annuities (ACGA) suggested maximum rate schedule. Effective January 1, 2020.

Example 9.19

Donor transfers property to XYZ charity in exchange for a life annuity to begin immediately. Information regarding the assets and transfer is as follows:

Date of Transfer	July 1, 2020
Fair market value of property	$200,000
Adjusted basis	$80,000
Annuity amount paid monthly	$404.71 (beginning August 1, 2020)
Section 7520 discount rate (assumed)	2% (0.1667%/month)
Table life expectancy (Table V Reg 1.72-9)	20 years
Present value of annuity payments	$80,000 (N = 240, i = 2%/12mo, PMT_{OA} = $404.71)

The donor must split the transaction into two elements:
1. the sale element
2. the charitable gift element

Sale Element

	$80,000	(PV of the annuity)
Pro rata adjusted basis	- $32,000	($80,000 x ($80,000/$200,000))
Capital gain portion	$48,000	

Charitable Gift Element

$120,000 ($200,000 - $80,000)

Over the life of the annuity the donor will collect:
240 monthly payments x $404.71 = $97,130.40 total amount received.

Broken down as:

Return of Capital	$32,000.00	
Capital gain amount	$48,000.00	
Ordinary income	$17,130.40	(interest component)
Total Amount Received	**$97,130.40**	

Each payment, as described in the previous example, will consist of three components: ordinary income to the extent of interest, capital gain, and return of capital (exactly as a purchased annuity). Once the sum of the return of capital components equals the purchase amount, any remaining payments are taxable since the return of capital component cannot exceed basis.

Example 9.20

The donor in the above example would have received five payments of $404.71. The ordinary income component would be calculated using an amortization table or calculator as follows:

Initial annuity obligation	$80,000.00	
End of year obligation	- $78,639.25	(N = 5, i = .2%/12mo., PV = $80,000, PMT_{OA} = ($404.71))
Principal reduction	$1,360.75	
Total annuity payments	$2,023.55	($404.71 x 5)
Less principal reduction	$1,360.75	
Equals interest earned	$662.80	Ordinary Income (taxable interest)
Principal reduction	$1,360.75	
Less basis recovery (40% x $1,360.75)	- $544.30	
Capital gain component (60% x $1,360.75)	$816.45	

Charitable Annuity of Encumbered Properties (Mortgaged)

A donor may transfer encumbered property directly to a charity in exchange for the charity's payment of an annuity to the donor. The annuity payments are a general obligation of the charity. As discussed above, a charitable annuity is treated as a bargain sale transaction. If the property is encumbered by a mortgage, the donor may be relieved of the obligation to pay the mortgage and receive a periodic annuity from the charity.

Calculation of the Donation

The donation equals the fair market value of the property minus the principal of the mortgage and the present value of annuity. The annuity is valued using Section 7520 interest rate (which is 120 percent of the federal midterm rate). A higher rate is more advantageous from the donor's perspective, since the charitable income tax deduction consists of the value of the contribution less the mortgage principal and the present value of the annuity stream.

Income Tax Consequences

Each benefit component (the relief of the mortgage and the annuity) receives a proportionate allocation of basis, potential capital gain, and ordinary income. Any capital gain and the ordinary income related to the mortgage must be recognized in the year of the transfer. The donor can avoid recognizing the ordinary income and capital gain associated with the annuity in the year of transfer if (1) the annuity is non-assignable to the charity, and (2) the donor or the donor and his designated survivor's trust are the only annuitants. Under these conditions, the annuitant will recognize return of capital, ordinary income, and capital gain ratably over the life of the annuity (life expectancy of donor, Table V of Treasury Regulation 1.72-9).

Example 9.21

Colin donates a building with a fair market value of $800,000, an adjusted basis of $250,000, and a mortgage of $200,000 to a charitable organization. In return for the donation, Colin receives an annuity for the remainder of his life of $32,000 per year from the charity.

Fair market value	$800,000
Adjusted basis	$250,000
Mortgage	$200,000
Annuity (annual)	$32,000
Section 7520 discount rate	10%
Life expectancy of donee	20 years

Step #1 - Calculate the present value of the annuity.

PMT_{OA}	$32,000
i	10%
N	20
PV	$272,434

Step #2 - Calculate charitable donation.
Fair market value of property - Principal of mortgage - Present value of annuity = Charitable Donation
$800,000 - $200,000 - $272,434 = $327,566

Step #3 - Calculate total capital gain.
Fair market value of property - Charitable donation - Adjusted basis = Capital gain
$800,000 - $327,566 - $250,000 = $222,434

Step #4 - Allocate capital gain between relief of debt and annuity.

Present value of annuity	$272,434	57.66%
Relief of debt	$200,000	42.34%
	$472,434	

57.66% x $222,434 = $128,255
42.34% x $222,434 = $94,179

Reconcile:

Donation	$327,566
Relief of debt capital gain	$94,179
Capital gain attributable to annuity	$128,255
Return of capital	$250,000
Total Value	**$800,000**

Colin would be required to recognize $94,179 of capital gain in the year of the donation related to the relief of debt. Colin would also recognize capital gain of $128,255 and interest income ratably over the life of the annuity.

Gifts of Life Insurance to Charities

Life insurance may be donated to charities and has certain advantages over other property. Assuming the policy is a permanent life insurance policy, the death benefit will be payable to the charitable organization at the insured's death as long as the premiums, which are generally paid on an installment basis, are paid. The amount of the gift can be leveraged if the insured dies prior to full life expectancy (i.e., the death benefit far exceeds the premiums paid plus an investment return).

Death proceeds from life insurance are received tax free to a charity and are received without delay of probate or other administrative processes by simply providing the insurer with a certified death certificate. Use of life insurance on charitable giving is particularly valuable if the donor anticipates that a will contest would void the charitable gift.

A gift of life insurance to a charity is valued according to general gift tax rules (fair market value at the date of gift). When life insurance is sold, any gain is ordinary gain, so a gift of life insurance is a gift of ordinary income property. Therefore, the charitable deduction is equal to the lesser of the donor's adjusted basis or the fair market value of the life insurance policy. See Chapter 11 for a complete, detailed discussion of gifts of life insurance.

> **Quick Quiz 9.3**
>
> 1. If an individual sells property to a charity at a bargain price, the individual will have a part sale and a part charitable contribution.
>   a. True
>   b. False
> 2. The donor of a charitable annuity receives an income tax deduction equal to the difference between the value of the annuity and the value of the property contributed for the annuity.
>   a. True
>   b. False
> 3. An individual may choose to gift a life insurance policy to a charity.
>   a. True
>   b. False
>
> True, True, True.

Group Term Life Insurance

Life insurance premiums paid by an employer for a group term life insurance policy (up to a face value of $50,000) are excluded from an employee's gross income. Any group term life insurance coverage in excess of $50,000 paid for by an employer will create taxable income based on the table life insurance rates under Section 72 (Table 1 found in Treasury Regulation 1.79-3). An employee can avoid such income inclusion by irrevocably naming a charitable beneficiary for any amount of employer provided life insurance in excess of $50,000.

CHARITABLE GIFTS OF A SPLIT INTEREST

A lifetime charitable gift may produce an income tax deduction, but if a charitable gift is made at an individual's death, no income tax deduction is available. However, there may be estate tax benefits. The date of the gift is determined by the date of irrevocability. If an individual makes a charitable gift at his death, the value of the asset is included in his gross estate, but the value of the asset is fully deducted from the adjusted gross estate (using the unlimited charitable deduction) to arrive at the taxable estate.

A charitable trust can be a useful vehicle for a donor who wants to make a donation to charity, but does not want to give an undivided interest to the charity. For example, a donor who owns appreciated stock, real property, or a business, and needs the income from the property for living or retirement expenses, but wishes that the ultimate ownership of the property will transfer to charity at a later date. Conversely, the donor might not currently need the income from the asset, but would like the stock, or other asset, to pass to a spouse or a child at the donor's death. A charitable donation of a split interest can provide a solution to these two scenarios and fulfill the donor's objective.

The advantages of charitable trusts created during life are that the donor gets a charitable income tax deduction at the time of the transfer, retains some right to enjoy the property, and reduces his taxable estate. To receive the current income tax deduction at the creation of a charitable trust, the trust must be in the precise form of one of the following:
- Pooled Income Fund
- Charitable Remainder Trust (Annuity or Unitrust)
- Charitable Lead Trust (Annuity or Unitrust)

IRC Section 664 delineates the requirements for charitable remainder annuity trusts and charitable remainder unitrusts. When the donor transfers property to an irrevocable charitable remainder trust, the trust provides an income interest (minimum rate of return of 5%) for the donor for some specified period of time, and at the end of that period, the trust corpus is paid to the named charity. In this case, the donor receives a charitable income tax deduction equal to the value of the remainder interest in the year the property is placed in the trust. Upon the death of the donor, the full fair market value of the trust property is included in the donor's gross estate, but is offset by the unlimited charitable deduction equal to the full fair market value of the property.

> **Key Concepts**
>
> 1. Identify three types of charitable trusts.
> 2. Why is a pooled income fund more advantageous than a CRAT for a small donor?
> 3. How is the value of the annuity interest of a CRAT calculated for gift tax purposes?
> 4. Who receives the annuity payment in a CLAT?

Pooled Income Funds (PIF)

Pooled income funds are analogous to a mutual fund provided by a charity. All donor contributions are pooled into a trust created and maintained by a single charity, and each donor receives an allocable share of the trust's income for life. No defined term trusts are allowed. The income stream can fluctuate based upon the underlying performance of the pooled income fund. Pooled income funds are also not permitted to invest in tax-exempt securities. As with the remainder trusts described in detail below, the donor receives a current income tax deduction for the present value of the remainder interest. Pooled income funds are advantageous for a small donor because the individual can receive the benefits of gifting the remainder interest in property without the legal expense of creating an individual charitable remainder trust. Furthermore, the pooling of funds creates additional investment diversification and protection for all donors in the pooled income fund.

Unlike CRATs and CRUTs, pooled income funds are subject to substantiation rules. The charity must provide written acknowledgment of the transfer of cash or property, state whether any goods or services were given to the donor in exchange, and indicate the donor's income interest in the fund.

Charitable Remainder Annuity Trust (CRAT)

A **charitable remainder annuity trust (CRAT)** is less flexible than a CRUT. CRATs provide a fixed annuity to the donor for an amount that is at least five percent (but not more than 50 percent for transfers after June 18, 1997) of the initial net fair market value of the property contributed to the trust. Even if the principal must be invaded, the annuity must be paid at least annually to the donor. The term of the annuity may be for life, or if for a certain number of years, must be no more than twenty years. The remainder interest is paid to a named charity, and once a CRAT is established, additional principal contributions are not allowed. The trustee of a CRAT can be given the right, known as a **sprinkling provision**, to make distributions to the income beneficiaries as he desires. Even though the trust is irrevocable, the donor does not have to notify the charity of its beneficial status, and the donor may reserve the right to change the designated remainder charitable beneficiary to another qualifying charitable organization without affecting the trust or its charitable status. Like charitable gift annuities, tax relief is greater for CRATs in a higher interest rate environment. The reason that the tax relief is greater in a higher interest rate environment is that the present value of the annuity will be lower resulting in a higher charitable deduction.

Charitable Remainder Unitrust (CRUT)

A **charitable remainder unitrust (CRUT)** provides more flexibility than a CRAT. The yearly pay out is a fixed percentage, or fraction, that is at least five percent (but not more than 50 percent for transfers after June 18, 1997) of the annual net fair market value of the assets. To determine the yearly cash payment, the assets are revalued annually. Unlike the CRAT, the CRUT payments may be limited to the income earned by the trust, with a catch up provision if the income later exceeds the current percentage payout. For example, if in Year 1 the payout should be $5,000 but the trust's income was only $4,500, the trust document could be written to limit the payment to the income, $4,500. If trust income is greater than $5,000 in a subsequent year, the $500 deficiency from Year 1 can be paid at that time. A CRUT that includes such language is often referred to as a **NIMCRUT,** a Net Income With Make-Up Trust. NIMCRUTs work well with deferred annuities since the trustee can trigger annuitization. Unlike a CRAT, the settlor of a CRUT may make additional principal contributions after the trust is established. The trustee of a CRUT can also be given a sprinkling provision to make distributions to the income beneficiaries as he desires. Other variations include NICRUTs and FlipCRUTs. NICRUTs pay the lesser of the percentage payout stipulated in the trust or the actual income generated. FlipCRUTs are unitrusts that start off as NIMCRUTs, but upon a triggering event they "flip" to a standard CRUT. After the flip, the makeup provision is lost. A FlipCRUT can be funded with a non-productive asset, such as raw land, that is anticipated to be sold. FlipCRUTs have strict standards. For instance, during the NIMCRUT phase, 90 percent of assets must consist of non-tradeable or fixed assets.

Exhibit 9.9 | CRAT and CRUT

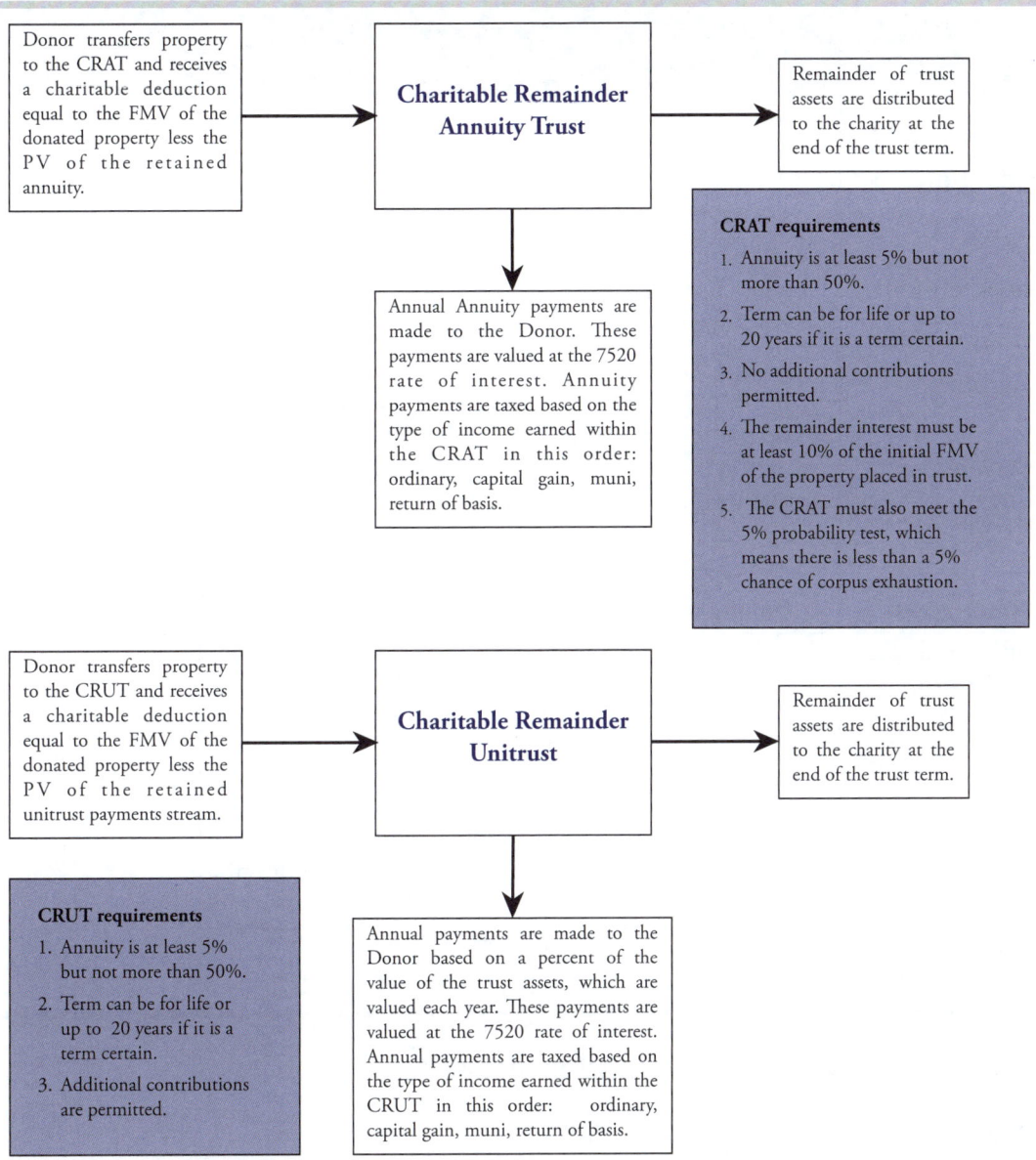

When drafting remainder trusts, care must be exercised in granting the trustee latitude in choosing investments. Treasury Regulation Section 1.664-1(a)(3) prohibits the trust from restricting the trustee in such a manner that endangers the trustee's ability to generate a reasonable amount of income. Restricting the investment of the trust to tax-exempt securities might violate these regulations. Several revenue procedures issued by the IRS provide sample trust provisions which state that nothing in the trust may restrict the trustee from an investment strategy that results in realization of a reasonable amount of income or gain. Inclusion of a similar provision in a charitable remainder trust is advisable.

Exhibit 9.10 | Summary of Characteristics of Charitable Remainder Trusts

	CRAT	CRUT	Pooled Income Funds (PIF)
Income Tax Deduction	Total value of property less present value of retained annuity payments	Total value of property less present value of retained unitrust payments	Total value of property less present value of retained income interest
Income Recipient	Non-charitable beneficiary (usually donor)	Non-charitable beneficiary (usually donor)	Non-charitable beneficiary (usually donor)
Income	At least 5% and no more than 50% of initial fair market value of assets paid at least annually for life or term ≤ 20 years (similar to fixed annuity)	At least 5% and no more than 50% of current fair market value of assets (revalued annually) paid at least annually for life or term ≤ 20 years (similar to variable annuity)	Trust rate of return for year
Remainderman	Qualified Charity	Qualified Charity	Qualified Charity
Additional Contributions Permissible	No	Yes	Yes
Sprinkling Provisions	Yes	Yes	No
When Income is Insufficient for Payment	Must invade corpus	Can pay up to income earned and make up deficiency in subsequent year	N/A
Can Invest in Tax-Exempt Securities	Yes	Yes	No

Calculation of the Gift and Remainder Interest

Charitable Remainder Annuity Trust (CRAT)

The calculation of the income (the annuity payment) and remainder interest of a charitable remainder annuity trust is fairly straightforward. The value of the income interest is derived by multiplying the annual annuity by a factor from the IRS Valuation Table S based on the Section 7520 rate (published monthly by the IRS) and the age of the annuitant at the date of the transfer. The income interest is then subtracted from the fair market value of the property contributed to the trust (at the contribution date) to determine the value of the remainder interest. As stated earlier, the value of the remainder interest qualifies as a current income tax deduction for the donor.

Example 9.22

Matteo, age 65, funds a Charitable Remainder Annuity Trust (CRAT) with $500,000 in cash and securities. In exchange, the trust provides for an annual annuity to Matteo of 7% of the initial fair market value of the assets. Assume a Section 7520 rate of 10%.

Income interest = 7.1213 (from Table S utilizing Matteo's age and the 10% Section 7520 rate) x $35,000 (the annuity) = $249,245.50

Remainder interest = $500,000 - $249,245.50 (the income interest) = $250,754.50

The implicit life expectancy is approximately 14 years ($500,000/$35,000).

Subject to AGI limitations, Matteo can deduct $250,754.50 in the year of the transfer as a charitable income tax deduction. If his charitable deduction is limited due to the AGI limitations, he may utilize the five-year carryover.

Probability of Exhaustion Test

In addition to the 5-50 percent payout requirement, the 10 percent remainder requirement, and the maximum term requirement (life of the beneficiary/beneficiaries or a fixed term no greater than 20 years), CRATs must also meet a probability of exhaustion test. The probability of exhaustion test was imposed by Treasury Regulations (not by statute), and can be found in Treas. Reg. Sec. 20.2055-2(d), which states:

> If, as of the date of a decedent's death, a transfer for charitable purposes is dependent upon the performance of some act or the happening of a precedent event in order that it might become effective, no deduction is allowable unless the probability that the charitable transfer will not become effective is so remote as to be negligible.

When issuing Revenue Ruling 70-452, 1970-2 C.B. 199, the IRS determined that a probability of exhaustion of five percent is not so remote as to be considered negligible. This five percent standard is consistent with statutory language covering the value of reversionary interests under IRC Sections 2037 and 2042. In Revenue Ruling 77-374, 1977-2 C.B. 329, the IRS ruled that the probability of exhaustion test applied to CRATs, and reaffirmed the five percent standard set forth in Revenue Ruling 70-452. Five years later, the Tax Court upheld the application of the probability of exhaustion test to CRATs in Estate of Moor v. Commissioner, T.C. Memo 1982-299. As a consequence of these rulings and cases, the income beneficiary of a Charitable Remainder Annuity Trust must have a five percent or less chance of outliving trust assets to qualify for a charitable income tax deduction.

The five percent probability of exhaustion test does not impose any design limitations for individual's creating CRATs structured to make payments annually when the valuation rate (the IRC Section 7520 rate) exceeds the payout rate on the trust (which must be between 5 and 50 percent of the initial contribution). When a CRAT makes payments more frequently than annually, however, it is possible to violate the five percent probability of exhaustion test even when all of the other requirements for a valid CRAT have been met.

Statutory law sets the minimum payout rate on a charitable remainder Trust at five percent. In low interest rate environments, when the 7520 rate falls below this amount, the probability of exhaustion test imposes significant limitations on the use of CRATs. In Rev. Proc. 2016-72 (issued on August 22, 2016), the IRS provided an example of how this can impact CRAT design:

> *Low interest rates in recent years have greatly limited use of a CRAT as an effective charitable-giving vehicle. For example, in May of 2016, the Section 7520 rate was 1.8 percent. At this interest rate, the sole life beneficiary of a CRAT that provides for an annual end-of year payment of the minimum allowable annuity (equal to 5 percent of the initial FMV of the trust assets) must be at least 72-years-old at the creation of the trust for the trust to satisfy the probability of exhaustion test. The Section 7520 rate has not exceeded the minimum five percent annuity payout rate since December of 2007, which has necessitated testing for the probability of exhaustion for every CRAT proposed since that time.*

As the IRS example illustrates, in a low interest rate environment it is difficult to impossible for any young individual to create a CRAT based on the lifetime of the income beneficiary without violating the probability of exhaustion test.

Due to this limitation, taxpayer interest in using CRATs for charitable giving may have declined. In an effort to address this issue, the IRS issued Rev. Proc. 2016-72 to provide an alternative to the five percent probability of exhaustion test to permit a broader range of taxpayers to employ CRATs in their charitable planning. Rev. Proc. 2016-72 provides specific language that can be included in a CRAT to elect into a new 10 percent termination test that will exempt the CRAT from the five percent probability of exhaustion test. The new 10 percent termination test requires early termination of a CRAT (and a distribution of the remaining assets to the charitable remainder beneficiary) once the trust balance falls to 10 percent of the initial trust corpus (with discounting at the initial applicable federal rate).

Individuals who create CRATs with lifetime payouts and who opt into the new 10 percent termination test must be aware, however, that (1) the CRAT may not provide lifetime payouts if the 10 percent termination test is triggered; and (2) the trust will terminate if the discounted trust value falls below 10 percent of the initial corpus, which is a much different measure than 10 percent of the initial corpus. To illustrate the application of the 10 percent termination test, the IRS provided the following example in Rev. Proc. 2016-72:

Example 9.23

On January 1, Year 1, Donor (S) transfers property valued at $1,000,000 to a Trust, an inter vivos trust providing for an annuity payment of $50,000 (5 percent of the value of the initial trust corpus) on December 31 of each year to S for S's life followed by the distribution of trust assets to Charity. Trust includes the precise language of the sample provision in section 5 of...[Rev. Proc. 2016-72] providing for an early termination contingency and specifies the Section 7520 rate in effect for January, Year 1, which is 3 percent. But for the early termination provision, Trust meets all of the requirements...[for a Charitable Remainder Trust]. In accordance with...[Rev. Proc. 2016-72], the IRS will treat the early termination contingency as a qualified contingency under Section 664(f). Therefore, the early termination provision does not cause Trust to fail to qualify as a CRAT under Section 664. In addition, Trust qualifies as a CRAT regardless of whether it passes the probability of exhaustion test on January 1, Year 1.

Each year, prior to payment of the annuity to S, the trustee performs the calculations required to determine if Trust will terminate early in accordance with the terms of the qualified contingency. In each year from Year 1 through Year 17, the trustee determines that the value of the trust corpus, minus the $50,000 annual payment, and then multiplied by the specified discount factor, is greater than 10 percent of the initial trust corpus. The value of the trust corpus as of December 30 in Year 18 is $210,000. Only in year 18 does the value of the trust corpus as of December 30, when reduced by the annuity payment and multiplied by the specified discount factor, fall below 10 percent of the value of the initial trust corpus. The calculations required to determine if Trust will terminate early in Year 18 are as follows:

1. $1,000,000 x 10 percent = $100,000
2. $210,000 - 50,000) x $[1 / (1 + 0.03)]^{18}$

   $160,000 \times (1/1.03)^{18}$

   $160,000 \times 0.0970874^{18}$

   $160,000 \times 0.0587397 = \$93,984$

Because the trust corpus ($210,000), when reduced by the annuity payment ($50,000) and then multiplied by the specified discount factor (0.0587397), is less than 10 percent of the value of the initial trust corpus ($100,000), Trust terminates on December 30, Year 18, and the principal and income remaining in Trust (including the annuity payment for Year 18 that otherwise would have been payable to S) then must be distributed to charity.

Note in the prior example that the charitable remainder beneficiary receives $210,000, or 21 percent of the initial contribution to the trust even though the 10 percent remainder interest requirement implies that the remainder interest should not go below 10 percent of the initial contribution to the trust, or, in this example, $100,000. While Rev. Proc. 2016-72 provides some relief in avoiding the five percent probability of exhaustion test, there is a cost in the sense that the remainder beneficiary may receive more, and the income beneficiary may receive less than each party would otherwise receive if the other qualification rules for charitable remainder trusts were strictly met. The operation of the 10 percent termination test may, itself, have a chilling effect on client willingness to use CRATs in their planning.

If the five percent probability of exhaustion test eliminates CRATS as a planning option, and the client is not satisfied with the economics of the CRAT under the 10 percent termination test of Rev. Proc. 2016-72, other alternatives are available. Charitable Gift Annuities provide cash flow over the life of the annuitant while providing a benefit for charity, and are not subject to the five percent probability of exhaustion test. While not always an optimal substitute for a CRAT, the economics of a Charitable Gift Annuity may trump the benefits provided under a CRAT opting into the 10 percent termination test of Rev. Proc. 2016-72. Another option, and one that may be particularly useful for younger donors, is to structure the Charitable Remainder Trust as a Unitrust (CRUT) instead of an annuity trust (CRAT). Since a CRUT pays out a fixed percentage of the annual value of the trust assets, it is impossible to exhaust the CRUT during the payout term. Stated differently, a CRUT will always have a zero percent probability of exhaustion, and, therefore, the five percent probability of exhaustion test becomes moot. When the investment portfolio of a CRUT is managed well, and the payout rate is on the lower end of the permissible scale (5%), a client creating a CRUT may expect to receive increasing cash flows over time without the need to force an early termination that may be required in a CRAT if the 10 percent termination test is used in the design of the CRAT.

The American College of Trust and Estate Counsel (ACTEC) has proposed an alternative fix to the five percent probability of exhaustion test, but this change would require Congressional action. ACTEC has suggested that IRC Sections 664(d)(1) and (d)(2) be amended to permit a minimum income payout for a charitable remainder trust to be the lesser of (1) the current Section 7520 rate, or (2) five percent. Provided that a CRAT is structured to provide annual payments, this proposal would allow individuals funding CRATs to opt out of the five percent probability of exhaustion test simply by choosing a payout rate that is equal to or lower than the Section 7520 rate used to value the trust. Of course, in the case of a CRAT, this would mean that the income beneficiary receives a lower payout rate, which offsets some of the allure of creating the CRT. This proposal, if accepted, would provide more flexibility for donors when choosing how to structure their charitable remainder trusts.

As interest rates rise, and the Section 7520 rate approaches the trust payout rate, more donors will be able to use CRATs without opting into the 10 percent termination test of Rev. Proc. 2016-72. Once the 7520 rate exceeds the trust payout rate (for a CRAT making annual payments), neither the five percent probability of exhaustion test, nor the 10 percent termination test will limit the donor's ability to create a CRAT.

Charitable Remainder Unitrust (CRUT)

Calculating the value of the remainder interest of a CRUT is more complex and beyond the scope of this text. IRS Publication 1458 provides the factors for valuing remainder interests in CRUTs, and further guidance is given in Treasury Regulation Section 1.664-4. The income tax deduction for a CRUT is usually determined using professional software, but the charitable income tax deduction will be less than the CRAT because of the flexibility available with the use of the CRUT.

Exhibit 9.11 | CRATs vs. CRUTs

Advantages	
CRATs	**CRUTs**
• Protects against declining balances • Provides a certain and fixed income stream	• Inflation protection • Can make subsequent contributions • Not subject to probability of exhaustion test
Disadvantages	
CRATs	**CRUTs**
• No inflation protection • Income stream percentage may be limited by 5% probability test • Subject to probability of exhaustion test	• Require annual revaluation • Have principal erosion risk

chapter 9

A CRT and Life Insurance for Wealth Replacement

For an inter vivos CRAT or CRUT, the disenfranchised parties, if any, would be the natural heirs of the donor (usually the donor's children). In such cases, the income tax savings created by the charitable deduction, in real dollar terms, can be used to purchase life insurance that can serve as a wealth replacement asset for the asset that was transferred to the charity.

Example 9.24

Recall Example 9.22, the charitable deduction was $250,754.50 (the remainder interest). Assume that Matteo's marginal total state and federal income tax rate is 40%. The total amount of tax savings is $100,302 ($250,754.50 x 40%). This tax savings could be used to fund a wealth replacement asset (life insurance policy on the donor). Assuming a rate of return of 9% (variable universal life insurance) for a period of 20 years (the assumed table life expectancy for a 65-year old) the cash value ignoring any insurance costs would be $562,132.

Non-Trust Split Interest Charitable Gifts

The most common forms of split interest charitable gifts are CRATs, CRUTs, and PIFs. An infrequently used split interest technique involves the transfer of a remainder interest in a personal residence or farm. The donor can donate the underlying ownership of the property to a charity, but reserve the right to enjoy the property for the remainder of his life or for a term of years. This is similar to a QPRT, but a charity is the remainder beneficiary instead of a loved one. As with the charitable trusts, the current income tax charitable contribution deduction is equal to the present value of the remainder interest. An added benefit is the removal of the asset (and all of its administrative burdens) from the probate estate of the owner.

The Treasury Regulations give guidance to determine whether property is considered a personal residence or a farm. A personal residence does not have to be the taxpayer's principal residence, but the taxpayer must have used the property as a personal residence (not rental property). Accordingly, a taxpayer's vacation home would qualify as a personal residence, as well as stock owned in a cooperative housing corporation where the taxpayer has a personal residence. Farms include any land (and improvements) used by the taxpayer (or tenant) in producing crops, fruits, other agricultural products, or for raising livestock. When determining the value of the remainder interest of a farm, any depreciation or depletion must be taken into account.

> **Quick Quiz 9.4**
>
> 1. Charitable bequests in a will do not produce any income tax benefits.
>   a. True
>   b. False
>
> 2. A pooled income fund is analogous to a mutual fund provided by a charity.
>   a. True
>   b. False
>
> 3. A CRAT provides an annuity to the grantor for a term defined by the grantor.
>   a. True
>   b. False
>
> 4. A CLAT provides an annuity to a charity for a term defined by the grantor.
>   a. True
>   b. False
>
> *True, True, True, True.*

Example 9.25

Question: How would appreciation, availability of the personal residence capital gain exclusion, and the health of the donor be factors in deciding to gift a remainder interest in a personal residence to a charity?

Answer: If the Section 7520 interest rate at the date of the transfer is less than the expected appreciation rate, the gift is beneficial. The personal residence capital gain exclusion can be used to offset any capital gain. The donor should be in good health.

Charitable Lead Trusts

Another split interest vehicle available for charitable donors is the **Charitable Lead Trust (CLT)**. The charitable organization receives the income interest during the term of the trust and a non-charitable beneficiary (usually a family member) receives the remainder interest. This vehicle is often used by high net worth individuals who do not need the current income from a particular asset or set of assets. It is most advantageous to fund a charitable lead trust with highly appreciating assets since future appreciation is effectively removed from the estate. The trust is often structured so that the present value of the annuity to the charity is equal to the full fair market value of the property transferred while the remainder interest is valued at zero to eliminate any taxable gift. Unlike charitable remainder trusts, charitable lead trusts are not tax exempt entities and not covered under Section 664.

Example 9.26

Brewster has substantial wealth and wants to transfer assets to his daughter, Amelia. Brewster sets up a CLAT and funds it with property worth $2 million. The CLAT provides for an annual annuity to the charity of $122,400. The term of the trust is 20 years and the 7520 rate is 2%. Based on these facts, the present value of the annuity to the charity equals slightly more than $2 million. Once the trust terminates, the remainder with go to Amelia. The value of the gift equals zero, because the value of the charitable annuity is over $2 million. Assuming that the underlying property appreciates annually at 5 percent, the value of the property will be over $5.3 million. None of this value will be included in Brewster's estate. However, he will have given $2,448,000 (20 payments) to charity over the term of the trust.

The charitable lead trust, which may take the form of annuity or unitrust (CLAT or CLUT), is an irrevocable trust, and if the grantor (donor) drafts the trust document to treat the trust as a grantor trust then the grantor will receive an income tax deduction at the inception of the trust. However, when the CLT qualifies the grantor for an income tax deduction (referred to as a qualified charitable lead trust), the grantor must subsequently recognize all income of the CLAT or CLUT. If an income tax deduction is desired, the trust must be designed as a grantor trust. The remainderman (non-charitable beneficiary) may either be the donor, in which case the grantor trust status is certain, or another family member (non-spouse) in which case there is a taxable gift equal to the fair market value of the remainder interest. Alternatively, a grantor may create a nonqualified CLT (any CLT which is not considered a grantor trust for income tax purposes), in which case the grantor will not receive a charitable income tax deduction and will not be required to include the income of the CLT on his own tax return. CLATs are particularly appealing in a low interest rate environment, since effectively they increase the value of the income interest to the charity which reduces the value of the remainder (taxable) interest.

chapter 9

TESTAMENTARY GIVING TO CHARITIES

As discussed in Chapter 6, a deduction is allowed from the gross estate for bequests to qualified charities. Generally, these are the same charities that qualify for an income tax charitable deduction with the exception of cemeteries. In addition, some foreign charities, which are not eligible for an income tax charitable deduction, are permitted donees for the estate tax charitable transfer deduction.

The methods of charitable transfers at death (testamentary) include the following:
1. A specific bequest or device
2. A general legacy of a particular percentage or dollar amount of a decedent's gross estate
3. A residuary bequest
4. A remainder interest in property - personal residence or farm
5. A split interest in a charitable trust, income or remainder interest

Requirements must be met to qualify for the estate tax charitable deduction. First, the bequest must be mandatory. If the decedent qualifies the charitable transfer upon some contingency, an estate tax charitable deduction is disallowed unless the possibility that the transfer will not occur is very remote. Second, the amount of the bequest must be ascertainable at the date of the decedent's death, and the asset must be included in the decedent's gross estate. The courts have disallowed estate tax charitable deductions where the executor was given the power to determine the amount of the contribution. In one case, the executor was given the power to make a bequest to the decedent's household employee, with the remainder going to a charity. The remainder amount was ruled to be uncertain and the estate tax charitable deduction was denied, since the value of the estate tax charitable deduction was dependent upon how much the executor decided to give to the employee.

> **Key Concepts**
>
> 1. List the requirements for a testamentary transfer to charity to qualify for the unlimited estate tax charitable deduction.
> 2. Identify the charitable transfers methods used at death.
> 3. How often must the value of the assets in a CRUT be determined?
> 4. Which IRC Section provides the directions to reform a disqualified split interest?

CASE STUDY 9.1

In **Estate of Belmont v. Commissioner (144 TC No 6)**, the Tax Court denied an estate a charitable estate deduction because the estate had not permanently set aside the funds for the charity. The estate used some of the funds to pay for litigation over the decedent's will. Thus, the Court held that the bequest was not mandatory (See Requirement #1 above).

A transfer to a testamentary trust created for the purpose of providing scholarship funds qualifies as a deductible charitable transfer for the estate tax calculation, however the wording of the trust instrument must be precise. An estate tax charitable deduction was disallowed in a case where the scholarship funds were limited to individuals with the same surname as the decedent. The IRS interpreted the language to be a requirement and disallowed the estate tax charitable deduction. In similar cases, estate tax charitable deductions have been allowed when the surname parameter was explicitly stated as a preference and not a requirement.

Some items are more beneficial (valuable) if given at death, rather than during the donor's life. An example would be a political figure who was contemplating contributing his personal papers to a museum. If he gives the papers during life, his income tax deduction is limited to his adjusted basis, which would be very low. If he waits and transfers his papers by will, the deduction from the gross estate will be the substantially higher (provided the papers appreciated in value) fair market value of the papers. Alternatively, the decedent could bequeath the papers to a non-charitable beneficiary who would then have the increased adjusted basis in the papers due to the "step-to" fair market value. The heir could then donate the papers to charity to receive a substantial income tax deduction.

As discussed in Chapter 2, a disclaimer clause in a will can provide that if an heir disclaims an interest in an asset, the asset will transfer to a specified charity. In such a case, the value of the asset that actually transfers to the charity will qualify for the unlimited estate tax charitable deduction.

ADVANCED FINANCIAL & ESTATE PLANNING TOPICS

Tangible Property

As detailed above, when tangible property is donated to a charity and the charity does not use the property for a related use, the charitable deduction is generally equal to the donor's adjusted basis. However, the taxpayer may contractually require the charity to put the donated property to a related use so that the taxpayer is able to deduct the fair market value of the property as opposed to the adjusted basis.

Recall Example 9.10 about the coin collector who donated his valuable coin collection to a museum and was able to deduct the fair market value of the coin collection. If the same contribution had been made to a university, and the donor contractually required the university (donee) to place the coin collection in the library for a period of two years for the purposes of students studying old coins (a related educational use), the deduction would also be equal to the fair market value of the coin collection. However, if the coin collection had been donated to the university so the university could sell the coin collection, the donor's deduction would only be the adjusted basis of the coin collection (the period of two years used in this example is not precise but goes to the facts and circumstances to establish related use).

chapter 9

Community Property

If community property is donated to a charity and the donor, or donors, retain an interest in the property, care must be exercised to avoid unwanted taxable results. For example, a transfer to a charitable remainder trust may be contemplated and funded using community property, but if the trust benefits only one spouse, the donee spouse has made a gift to the other spouse. If separate property is used to fund a trust that benefits both spouses, then a gift has occurred from the donee spouse to the other spouse. While there is no federal gift tax due because of the unlimited marital deduction, there may be a gift tax imposed by certain states that do not have an unlimited marital deduction for state estate tax and/or state inheritance tax.

Choosing Between the CRAT or the CRUT

If the client's primary objective is to maximize the income payments to the non-charitable beneficiaries, a CRUT is generally preferable to a CRAT, particularly if the trust assets are expected to appreciate. However, due to the guaranteed income payment from the CRAT, the non-charitable beneficiary would receive more from a CRAT than a CRUT if the value of the trust assets decline.

> **Quick Quiz 9.5**
>
> 1. A bequest to a charitable organization based on a contingency is not eligible for the charitable deduction.
>   a. True
>   b. False
> 2. A will cannot create a CRAT.
>   a. True
>   b. False
> 3. The remainderman of a pooled income fund is the grantor.
>   a. True
>   b. False
> 4. Tax-exempt securities are prohibited investments for CRUTs.
>   a. True
>   b. False
>
> True, False, False, False.

The CRAT has a significant cost advantage over a CRUT holding the same property if the underlying trust assets are not readily marketable and require a qualified annual appraisal. This is because the CRAT only requires one valuation at the funding of the trust and a CRUT requires yearly valuations. Yearly appraisals for property that is not readily marketable can be very expensive.

Example 9.27

A 60 year-old individual with property valued at $1,000,000 and with a $0 adjusted basis contributes property to a CRAT retaining a 6% annuity interest. The IRS factor rate for the date of the transfer is 9%.

$1,000,000	Fair market value
$0	Adjusted basis
6%	Annuity percentage (chosen by donor)
60	Age (single life annuity)
$60,000	Amount of annuity
8.3031	Factor (Table S at 9%) - Based on date of transfer
$498,186	PV of annuity
$501,814	Charitable remainder = FMV of trust - PV of annuity

As calculated here, the donor would receive an annuity of $60,000 (6% of the initial contribution) for the remainder of his life (single life annuity), and in the year of the contribution of the property, a charitable contribution deduction equal to $501,814.

Advanced Financial & Estate Planning Topics

To illustrate the effects of the grantor's choice of annuity, listed below are several annuity options at 7%, 8%, 9%, and 10%, and the corresponding charitable contribution of each.

Assumed Annuity Percentage	6%	7%	8%	9%	10%
	$60,000	$70,000	$80,000	$90,000	$100,000
Factor	8.3031	8.3031	8.3031	8.3031	8.3031
PV of Annuity	$498,186	$581,217	$664,248	$747,279	$830,310
Charitable Deduction	$501,814	$418,783	$335,752	$252,721	$169,690

The alternative to creating the CRAT could have been to sell the property, pay capital gains tax on its appreciation, and then reinvest the proceeds in a commercial annuity (9% for the date of the annuity). The following calculation illustrates this scenario:

```
$1,000,000
    x   85%   15% Federal Capital Gains Tax
  $850,000
    x    9%   Factor Rate at Date of the Annuity
   $76,500   Annuity
```

The individual would receive a $76,500 annuity for the remainder of his life but would not receive any charitable deduction. Contrast this with an 8% CRAT (as detailed above) which pays the individual an $80,000 annuity and allows the individual to take a charitable contribution of $335,752. There may also be a reduction for state tax on capital gains.

Reformation of Disqualified Split Interests

Unfortunately, advisors who create CRATs, CRUTs, CLATs, and CLUTs do not always fully comply with the specific requirements necessary for a donor to receive a charitable deduction. It also happens that a split gift interest is inadvertently created under certain conditions such as an election to take against the will.

It would be a harsh result indeed if due to a minor drafting flaw, oversight, or unexpected minor non-charitable beneficiary interest, the entire charitable deduction was disallowed. Section 2055(e)(3) of the Code outlines the procedure to correct the error to reduce this harsh treatment. The reformation must be commenced prior to the due date of the estate tax return or the trust's income tax return if no estate tax return is required. The details of the information are beyond the scope of this text.

Transfer of an Interest in an IRA by Taxpayers Over the Age of 70½ (QCDs)

The ATRA 2012 revived the ability of a taxpayer over the age of 70½ to donate up to $100,000 directly from an IRA to a charity without having to take the $100,000 distribution into income. The ATRA of 2012 made such transfers permissible until December 31, 2013. This provision was extended through 2014, but expired again January 1, 2015. The Consolidated Appropriations Act of 2016 made permanent qualified charitable distributions (QCDs). This avoids the inclusion of the IRA distribution made to a charity being included in the adjusted gross income of the taxpayer.

chapter 9

KEY TERMS

Capital Gain Property - Property that, when sold, results in either capital gain or Section 1231 gain.

Charitable Lead Trust (CLT) - A trust in which a charitable organization receives the income interest and a non-charitable beneficiary (usually a family member) receives the remainder interest.

Charitable Remainder Annuity Trusts (CRAT) - A trust that provides a fixed annuity to the donor (usually for life) for an amount that is greater than or equal to 5% of the initial net fair market value of the property contributed to the trust. The remainder interest of the trust passes to a named charitable organization.

Charitable Remainder Unitrust (CRUT) - A trust that provides a payment to the donor (usually for life) equal to a fixed percentage of the trust assets as valued annually. The remainder interest of the trust passes to a named charitable organization.

Net Income with Makeup Charitable Remainder Trust (NIMCRUT) - A CRUT that requires that a fixed percentage (minimum of 5%) of the annual value of trust assets be credited to the income beneficiary, or if less, the net income of the trust for that year, with any deficiencies to be made up in later years when trust income exceeds the required set percentage amounts for such years.

Ordinary Income Property - Property that, when sold, results in recognition of ordinary income.

Pooled Income Funds (PIF) - Donor contributions are pooled in a trust created and maintained by the charity. Each donor receives an allocable share of the income from the trust for his life.

Private Foundation - A charitable organization that receives its support from a single individual or family. It can be either a private operating foundation or a private nonoperating foundation.

Private Nonoperating Foundation - A charitable organization (private foundation) that does NOT spend at least 85% of its adjusted net income (or minimum investment return, if less) on activities engaged in for the active conduct of the exempt purpose.

Private Operating Foundation - A charitable organization (private foundation) that spends at least 85% of its adjusted net income (or minimum investment return, if less), on activities engaged in for the active conduct of the exempt purpose.

Public Charities - Charitable organizations that receive broad support from the general public.

Qualified Charitable Distributions (QCDs) - Distributions made after age 70½ that are not included in the AGI of the donor / taxpayer.

Sprinkling Provision - The trustee's right to make distributions to the trust beneficiaries at his discretion.

Tangible Property - Property that is not realty and may be touched.

DISCUSSION QUESTIONS

SOLUTIONS to the discussion questions can be found exclusively within the chapter. Once you have completed an initial reading of the chapter, go back and highlight the answers to these questions.

1. What factors must an individual consider before making a charitable gift?

2. Define "charitable organization" as detailed in the Internal Revenue Code.

3. Identify three ways to verify a charitable organization's qualifying status.

4. How does a private operating foundation differ from a private nonoperating foundation?

5. List at least three examples of deductible out-of-pocket expenses related to donating services to a charitable organization.

6. If ordinary income property is contributed to a charitable organization, what is the maximum deductible amount?

7. What does it mean for a charity to be a "60% organization?"

8. List the factors a donee must consider when electing to deduct the adjusted basis of donated property as opposed to electing to deduct the fair market value of the property.

9. If an individual donates property with a fair market value of $750, what information must the donor provide to the IRS and on what tax form is the information provided?

10. Why would a donor request a statement of value from the IRS?

11. If a charitable annuity pays the annuity to the donor, how is the value of the donor's charitable income tax deduction calculated?

12. Under what circumstances may the donor of encumbered property, donated in return for a charitable annuity, avoid recognizing the ordinary income and capital gain associated with the annuity in the year of the transfer?

13. Which charitable trusts provide the donor with an income tax deduction in the year the property is transferred to the trust?

14. Explain how a pooled income fund benefits a donor.

15. How is a Charitable Remainder Annuity Trust (CRAT) less flexible than a Charitable Remainder Unitrust (CRUT)?

16. If an individual donates the underlying ownership interest of his personal residence to a charity, but retains the right to live in the residence for the remainder of his life, how is the donor's charitable deduction calculated?

17. When a donor creates and funds a CLAT under the grantor trust provisions, how is the income of the trust treated for income tax purposes each year?

18. Under what circumstances is a testamentary charitable transfer deductible from a decedent's adjusted gross estate?

19. How may a testamentary charitable transfer be more beneficial to a donor than an inter vivos charitable transfer?

MULTIPLE-CHOICE PROBLEMS

A sample of multiple choice problems is provided below. Additional multiple choice problems are available at money-education.com by accessing the Student Practice Portal.

1. Terrence contributed $15,000 to a foreign charitable organization. At the time of the contribution, the organization told him that his contribution was tax deductible for income tax purposes. Ignoring any income limitations, how much of the $15,000 contribution is deductible?
    a. $0.
    b. $7,500.
    c. $10,000.
    d. $15,000.

2. The Organization to Prevent Cruelty to Animals receives contributions from the general public to fund programs to prevent cruelty to animals. Of its total support during the year, 75% of the funds are from contributions from supporting individuals. What type of charity is The Organization to Prevent Cruelty to Animals?
    a. Public Charity.
    b. Private Foundation.
    c. Private Operating Foundation.
    d. Public Nonoperating Charity.

3. Connie cooks and delivers meals for the homeless and the elderly at Thanksgiving. Connie spends $200 on food, she drives 300 miles, and she spends 15 hours of her time (valued at $10/hour) completing the charitable service each year. Of these expenses, how much will Connie deduct on her income tax return for the year?
    a. $0.
    b. $200.
    c. $242.
    d. $392.

4. Which of the following statements regarding life insurance is true?
    a. When an individual designates a charitable organization as the beneficiary of his life insurance policy, the individual can deduct the face value of the policy as a charitable contribution on his income tax return.
    b. If an individual designates a charitable organization as the beneficiary of his life insurance policy, but retains the right to change the beneficiary designation, the death proceeds of the life insurance policy will be included in his gross estate.
    c. If an individual designates a charitable organization as the beneficiary of his life insurance policy, and then dies without changing the beneficiary designation, the death proceeds of the life insurance policy will be included in his taxable estate.
    d. Transferring ownership of a life insurance policy to a charitable organization does not qualify for an income tax charitable deduction.

5. Four years ago, Walter created a charitable remainder trust with himself as the income beneficiary and a charity as the remainder beneficiary. In the current year, Walter would like to make an additional contribution to the trust. Which of the following charitable trusts would allow Walter to make an additional contribution during the year?
    a. CRAT.
    b. CRUT.
    c. CRET.
    d. CRIT.

QUICK QUIZ EXPLANATIONS

Quick Quiz 9.1
1. False. Gifts made to public charities, regardless of size, do not require the filing of a gift tax return.
2. True.
3. False. Public charities are often organized to benefit specific causes or beneficiary classes. Charities are classified as public charities based on their source of funding, not their charitable objectives.

Quick Quiz 9.2
1. False. When a product is donated, the lower of the donor's adjusted basis or the fair market value of the property is allowed as a deduction. While the value of services donated to a charity are not deductible, any costs incurred in performing those services (such as the cost of uniforms, mileage expenses, parking fees, and the like) that are not reimbursed may be claimed as a charitable deduction.
2. False. Gifts of services provide great value to charitable organizations, but do not qualify the donor for a tax deduction.
3. False. In some cases, electing to deduct cost basis may be more advantageous to a taxpayer. Since the value of gifts to charities may only be carried forward five years under the deduction limitations, when a donor has low income relative to the size of the gift, electing to deduct cost basis and moving to the 60% deduction limitation may maximize tax benefits. (See Examples 9.14 and 9.15)
4. False. The taxpayer has the burden of proving the value of the deduction for tax purposes.

Quick Quiz 9.3
1. True.
2. True.
3. True.

Quick Quiz 9.4
1. True.
2. True.
3. True.
4. True.

Quick Quiz 9.5
1. True.
2. False. Charitable Remainder Trusts (CRTs), in the form of CRATs and CRUTs, may be created during life or on a testamentary basis (by instructing the executor of the estate to create the trust after the testator's death).
3. False. The remainderman of a Pooled Income Fund (PIF) is the charity that sponsors and manages the fund. The grantor is only entitled to a pro-rata portion of the income generated by the pool of assets during his or her life.
4. False. Tax-exempt securities are permissible investments for CRTs. PIFs, however, may not invest in tax exempt securities.

10
THE UNLIMITED MARITAL DEDUCTION

LEARNING OBJECTIVES

1. Discuss the single economic unit theory as applied to married parties.
2. Discuss the advantages and limitations of the unlimited marital deduction.
3. Describe the requirements for qualification for the marital deduction.
4. Describe the terminable interest rule and identify its exceptions.
5. Identify them those three general ways for a bequest to a spouse to qualify for the unlimited marital deduction including outright gift, general power of appointment trusts, and qualified terminable interest property trust.
6. Describe the concept of portability as it applies to estate tax planning.
7. Describe planning for a non-citizen spouse including the use of the super annual exclusion of $157,000 per year.
8. Describe the use of a qualified domestic trust for a non-citizen spouse survivor.
9. Describe over and under qualification.
10. Describe the use of a bypass trust as an alternative to portability.
11. Describe the use of disclaimers and irrevocable life insurance trusts.

CFP Board Resource Document - Student-Centered Learning Objectives based upon CFP Board Principal Topics.

THE MARITAL DEDUCTION DEFINED

The Single Economic Unit

Historically, the amount of property that an individual could leave to his or her spouse without transfer tax consequences was limited. Prior to 1981, for example, only one-half of a deceased spouse's estate could qualify for the estate tax marital deduction.

Under current law, an individual is permitted to leave an unlimited amount of property to his citizen spouse at his death without incurring any estate tax. This approach is consistent with the gift tax rules, which allow an individual to make outright lifetime gifts of an unlimited amount of property to a citizen spouse without paying any gift taxes. The theory behind the **unlimited marital deduction** is that a married couple should be treated as a single economic unit for estate tax purposes. This theory applies to all legally married couples, regardless of sex. To the extent that property is consumed by either spouse during their lifetime, it should not be subject to gift or estate tax. Only the property owned by either spouse that remains after the death of the surviving spouse (or, in the eyes of the law, the termination of the economic unit), and that passes to some other party, should be subject to estate tax. Therefore, property that passes from one spouse to another citizen spouse is usually not subject to estate tax at the death of the first spouse, but if the surviving spouse does not consume the property before his or her death, the property will be subject to estate tax in the surviving spouse's estate.

chapter 10

Exhibit 10.1 | Benefits of the Unlimited Marital Deduction

1. Defers estate taxes until the death of the surviving citizen spouse.
2. May fund the applicable estate tax credit of the surviving spouse.
3. Ensures the surviving citizen spouse has sufficient assets to support his lifestyle.

Advantages of the Unlimited Marital Deduction

Use of the unlimited marital deduction can result in several benefits. First, using the marital deduction defers the payment of estate tax until the death of the surviving spouse. In some high-net worth planning situations, it may make sense to incur estate tax at the first death to increase the total tax savings for the family. The temporary repeal of the estate tax under EGTRRA 2001, and the new exemption portability rules and lower rates enacted as part of the Tax Relief, Unemployment Insurance Authorization, and Job Creation Act of 2010 (TRA 2010), encourages deferral for joint estates expected to fall below the applicable credit amount. ATRA of 2012 has made these provisions permanent.

Key Concepts

1. Identify the advantages of the unlimited marital deduction.
2. List the requirements of the unlimited marital deduction.
3. What are the consequences of utilizing the unlimited marital deduction for the first-to-die spouse?

Example 10.1

An elderly, married individual dies in early 2020 when the applicable estate tax credit equivalency is $11,580,000. The combined estate of the decedent and his surviving spouse is $13,580,000 (for purposes of this example, all assets are in the name of the decedent), and the surviving spouse is expected to die in 2022. If the decedent transfers $11,580,000 to a bypass trust (B Trust) at his death, and leaves $2,000,000 to his surviving spouse, use of the unlimited marital deduction will result in no federal estate tax for the family. No tax is due at the first spouse's death. Assuming that the applicable estate tax credit equivalency remains $11,580,000 at the surviving spouse's death in 2022, and that the $2,000,000 inherited by her is all that makes up her gross estate, no estate tax will be due at her death either.

A second advantage of the unlimited marital deduction is the opportunity to fund the applicable estate or gift tax credit of the surviving spouse. When one spouse is wealthy, and the other is not (the term wealthy, as used here, implies that a person has sufficient assets to fully use the applicable credit amount), assets can be transferred to the surviving spouse during life or upon the death of the wealthy spouse, such that the non-wealthy spouse can make full use of his/her own applicable estate or gift tax credit. This benefit is also illustrated in the example above. Since the surviving spouse had no assets, the applicable estate tax credit belonging to the second spouse would have been wasted if the decedent had not transferred sufficient property to the surviving spouse so that she could fully utilize (fund) the credit. Finally, and probably most importantly, the use of the marital deduction to transfer assets to the surviving spouse helps ensure that the surviving spouse will have sufficient assets to maintain his lifestyle after the death of the first spouse.

Exhibit 10.2 | Celebrity Estate Planning Mistake

Celebrity: Philip Seymour Hoffman (actor)
Estimated Estate Worth: $35 million
Mistake: Failing to marry his sweetheart

When actor, Philip Seymour Hoffman died in 2014, he left his $35 million estate to Mimi O'Donnell, his longtime partner and the mother of their three children. Because they were not married, O'Donnell's bequest did not qualify for the unlimited marital deduction. Although Hoffman will get the benefit of a $5.34 million lifetime exemption, the remaining $30 million will be fully taxable, up to a 40% rate. On top of that, New York state has its own 16% estate tax for non-spouses on any amount over its $1 million exemption. Forbes estimated that the Oscar winner's loved ones lost at least $15 million to the IRS and the state. If Hoffman and O'Donnell had been married, about $12 million more would have ended up in the hands of O'Donnell and their family rather than going to the IRS.

Exhibit 10.3 | Unlimited Marital Deduction Summary

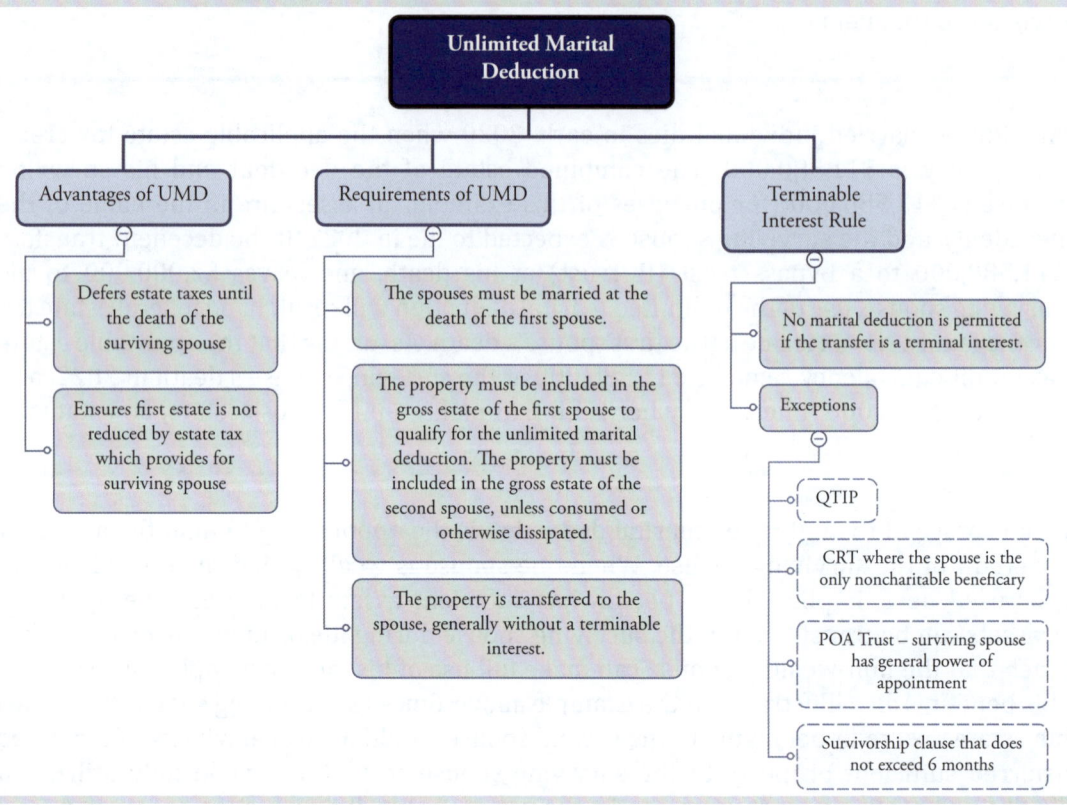

Chapter 10: The Unlimited Marital Deduction

Requirements of the Unlimited Marital Deduction

In order to claim a marital deduction, the decedent must have been married as of the date of his death and the surviving citizen spouse must receive property through the estate. As such, property left to a divorced spouse will not qualify for the marital deduction. If, however, the couple is separated but not yet divorced, property passing to the separated spouse will qualify for the unlimited marital deduction.

Limitations of the Unlimited Marital Deduction

To prevent abuse, the unlimited marital deduction is limited in two ways:
1. the property passing to the spouse must qualify for the marital deduction; and
2. only the net value of qualifying property that is left to a surviving spouse can be included as the marital deduction.

These qualification rules are discussed below. The term "net value" for marital deduction purposes equals the gross value of the qualifying property left to the surviving spouse less any taxes, debts, or estate administration expenses payable out of the spousal interest. If an individual gives his executor the authority to pay expenses and taxes out of the marital share, the marital deduction must be reduced by that amount even if the executor chooses not to use the marital share to pay for those expenses. The purpose of this rule is to prevent individuals who allocate taxes, debts, and administration expenses to the marital share from qualifying for the marital deduction for the taxes, debts, and expenses they incurred during lifetime or during the administration of their estate.

> **Quick Quiz 10.1**
>
> 1. Unless the inherited property has been consumed, a second-to-die spouse must include the property in his gross estate if the first-to-die spouse elected the marital deduction on the property.
>   a. True
>   b. False
>
> 2. Transfers to a divorced spouse qualify for the unlimited marital deduction. The only requirement is that the individuals were married within the last three years.
>   a. True
>   b. False
>
> 3. Use of the marital deduction will defer the payment of estate tax on property transferred to the surviving spouse until the surviving spouse's death.
>   a. True
>   b. False
>
> *True, False, True.*

Example 10.2

Derek died in 2020 with an estate valued at $14,830,000. Derek's will creates a credit shelter trust at his death and leaves all of his property in excess of the applicable estate tax credit equivalency amount to his spouse, Bob. The apportionment clause in his will allocates all debts to the marital share. Derek's debts were $250,000. The first $11,580,000 in Derek's estate will pass to the credit shelter trust, leaving only $3,250,000 for Bob. Since debts must be paid out of the property passing to Bob, Derek's estate will qualify for a marital deduction of $3,000,000 ($3,250,000 spousal share less $250,000 of debts equals the net value of qualifying property left to the surviving spouse).

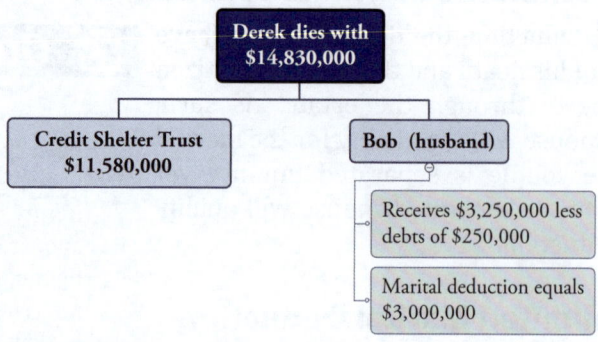

Note that the marital deduction does not avoid estate taxes; it merely postpones them. If a transfer of property to a surviving spouse qualifies for the marital deduction, the value of that property will be included in the surviving spouse's gross estate if the property has not been ultimately consumed by the surviving spouse. While the marital deduction may look enticing, care should be exercised in planning to prevent over-qualification of the marital deduction and an increase in the total estate taxes paid by a married couple.

If property is not transferred to the surviving spouse outright, special qualification rules must be met for that property to qualify for the marital deduction. There are primarily three ways to leave property to a spouse and qualify for the marital deduction. These three ways are summarized in the following chart and are discussed throughout this chapter.

Exhibit 10.4 | Alternatives that Qualify for the Unlimited Marital Deduction

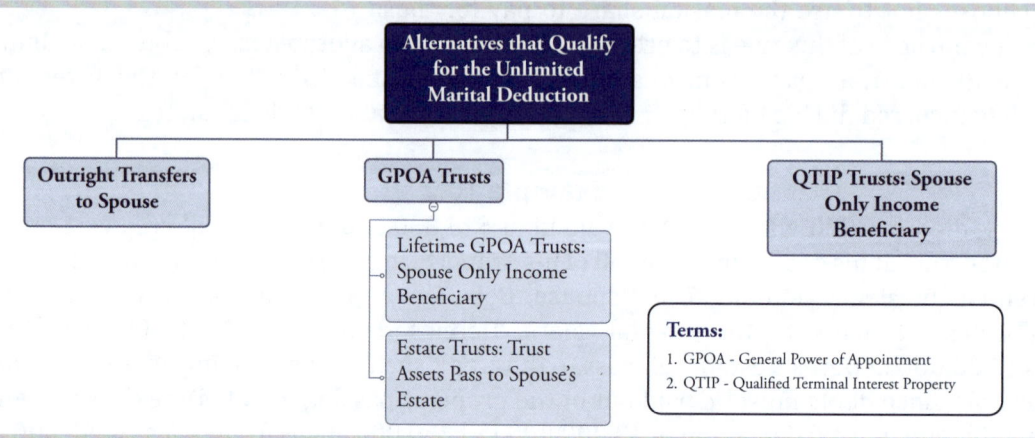

Community Property

Only half of the community property belongs to the decedent. Generally, the decedent's half will pass through probate. If the property is left to the surviving spouse in a qualifying manner, then the transfer will qualify for the unlimited marital deduction. It should also be noted that both halves of the community property are adjusted to the fair market value at the date of death of the first spouse.

chapter 10

QUALIFICATION FOR THE MARITAL DEDUCTION

For a transfer to qualify for the estate tax marital deduction, the property interest must meet three requirements. First, the property must be included in the decedent's gross estate. Second, the property must be transferred to the surviving spouse. Third, the interest must not be a terminable interest unless it meets one of the exceptions to the terminable interest rule.

If the surviving spouse is not a U.S. citizen, additional requirements must be met in order to qualify for the unlimited marital deduction. The special rules that apply to non-citizen spouses will be addressed later in this chapter.

Key Concepts

1. Identify the property transfers that qualify for the unlimited marital deduction.
2. What is the terminable interest rule and what is its impact on the marital deduction?
3. Identify the rules related to the survivorship clause and the time allowed to qualify the property transferred for the unlimited marital deduction.

Inclusion in the Decedent's Gross Estate

A general principal of taxation is that an individual cannot deduct something that is not first brought into the tax base. For example, an attorney who volunteers legal services to a charity cannot take a charitable deduction for the value of his time because he never reported the value of his time as taxable income. Likewise, if property is not included in the gross estate of the decedent, the decedent will not be permitted to deduct the value of that property from the gross estate as a marital deduction.

Example 10.3

Sal and Norma were married for 51 years when Sal died. Many years ago, Norma purchased a life insurance policy on Sal's life. Norma was the named owner and beneficiary of the policy, and made all of the premium payments. Upon Sal's death, Norma collected the $1,000,000 death benefit from the insurance company. Sal's estate will not be entitled to a marital deduction for the $1,000,000 of insurance proceeds because the insurance proceeds were not included in his gross estate as the policy was owned by Norma.

Example 10.4

Assume the same scenario as above, except that Sal created and funded an Irrevocable Life Insurance Trust (ILIT) that purchased a policy on his life. The ILIT was properly drafted and administered, and, as a result, the death benefit received by the ILIT was not included in Sal's gross estate. Even though Norma is the primary beneficiary of the ILIT and will receive all of the trust income for the rest of her life under the terms of the trust, the death benefit will not qualify for the marital deduction since it was not included in Sal's gross estate.

Property Transferred to a Surviving Spouse

In order to qualify for the unlimited marital deduction, the property must pass from the decedent to, and for the benefit of, the surviving spouse. If the property passes from someone other than the decedent to the surviving spouse, or if the property transferred by the decedent goes to someone who is not his surviving spouse, the marital deduction will not be available. If the decedent leaves property to his surviving spouse as trustee for some other individual, the surviving spouse does not have a beneficial interest in the property and the transfer will not qualify for the marital deduction.

Example 10.5
George died last month, leaving behind his wife, Laura, and two minor children. George's will creates a credit shelter trust for the benefit of his two minor children, and names Laura as the trustee of the trust. While Laura has legal title to the property inside the trust, she does not have beneficial title to the property, and therefore the money and property passing to the credit shelter trust do not qualify for the unlimited marital deduction.

Generally, property that is included in the decedent's gross estate and is transferred to the surviving spouse by any means will meet the "transferred to" requirement for the marital deduction, even if the decedent is not the person transferring the property.

Example 10.6
Shortly before her death, Valentina was estranged, but not divorced, from her husband, Felix. Valentina wrote a will leaving all of her property to her three children, including specific language disinheriting Felix. After Valentina's death, Felix elected against her will, and was awarded one-half of Valentina's estate, which represented his "elective" or "statutory" share. Despite the fact that Valentina tried to disinherit Felix, property in her gross estate passes to her surviving spouse, and therefore the property included in the gross estate that passes to Felix qualifies for the marital deduction.

Example 10.7
Jane owned a beach house that she transferred to her husband, Charlie, retaining the right to use the home for the rest of her life. Jane recently died, and the full fair market value of the beach home was included in her gross estate since she had retained the right to use the property. Since Charlie received the house, the fair market value of the house qualifies for the marital deduction.

Example 10.8
Lewis gave his son, David, a general power of appointment over farmland located in Long Island, New York. The power of appointment states that David can appoint the property to anyone he wishes, including himself, either during lifetime or at death. In the event that David does not exercise the power, the property will be transferred to David's spouse or, if David's spouse predeceases him, to David's children, per stirpes. David died last month and had never exercised the power during lifetime or through his will. Since David had a general power of appointment over the property the full fair market value of the property is required to be included in David's estate. Since the property is transferred to David's spouse at death, the value of the property qualifies for the unlimited marital deduction.

Example 10.9

Peg wrote her will at the height of the last bull market cycle. Since she was feeling wealthy and generous, she decided to leave $3,000,000 of her $6,000,000 estate directly to her children, with the remainder to her husband, Ed. After the will was written, the stock market crashed and when Peg died last month, her estate was only worth $2,900,000. As a result, under the terms of the will, Peg's children will receive the entire estate and Ed will receive nothing. The children decide to disclaim $2,000,000 of the property that would pass to them so that it will pass under the terms of the will to Ed. The $2,000,000 disclaimed by the children qualifies for the unlimited marital deduction.

The Terminable Interest Rule

The **terminable interest** rule is based on the premise that a marital deduction should only be permitted when property passing from the decedent spouse to a surviving spouse will be included in the surviving spouse's gross estate. The current unlimited marital deduction allows individuals to defer estate tax at the death of the first-to-die spouse but not avoid it entirely. Any property left by a decedent directly to his surviving spouse that is held until the surviving spouse's death is included in the surviving spouse's gross estate.

There are situations, however, where property left to the surviving spouse will not be included in the surviving spouse's gross estate. For example, if the decedent leaves property in trust for the benefit of the surviving spouse, and the trust gives the spouse the right to receive all income, the right to receive distributions for health, education, maintenance, and support, and the right to demand the greater of $5,000 or five percent of the trust corpus each year, the spouse will not have a sufficient ownership interest in the property to require an inclusion in her estate. The terminable interest rule is designed to prevent the use of the unlimited marital deduction in circumstances such as this where the surviving spouse will not have to include in his gross estate the value of certain property transferred from the deceased spouse.

Terminable Interest Defined

A terminable interest is any interest in property passing from a decedent to his surviving spouse where the surviving spouse's interest in that property will terminate at some point in the future. To be classified as a terminable interest, it does not matter how the interest terminates – whether by passage of time or upon the occurrence or non-occurrence of some contingency. All that matters is that the interest will terminate. If a contingency is attached to property resulting in a termination of the surviving spouse's interest, it will be considered a terminable interest if the contingency might occur.

> ### Quick Quiz 10.2
>
> 1. A transfer to a surviving spouse as trustee of a trust for the benefit of her children will qualify for the unlimited marital deduction.
>   a. True
>   b. False
>
> 2. A terminable interest is any interest in property passing from the decedent to his surviving spouse where the surviving spouse's interest in that property will terminate at some point in the future.
>   a. True
>   b. False
>
> 3. Only a terminable interest that terminates at a certain period of time will qualify for the marital deduction.
>   a. True
>   b. False
>
> 4. A terminable interest in a general power of appointment trust will qualify for the unlimited marital deduction.
>   a. True
>   b. False
>
> False, True, False, True.

Example 10.10
Jennifer, a famous musician, recently passed away leaving all of her property to her husband, Eric. In addition to Jennifer's tangible personal property, Eric inherited ownership of the copyrights on Jennifer's musical compositions. Copyrights protect property for a limited period of time, and, therefore, expire with the passage of time. The copyrights that Jennifer left to Eric are terminable interest property (but see **Example 10.13**).

Example 10.11
Ken recently died. Ten years before his death, he retired from his tenured faculty position at Home State University. Home State University's benefit package included a pension plan that provided a lifetime income for Ken, and a 50% survivor annuity for his wife, Liz, should Ken die before her. Liz is now entitled to receive 50% of the retirement income that Ken was receiving before his death for the rest of her life. Because the survivor annuity will terminate upon Liz's death, the annuity interest that Liz received from Ken's estate is a terminable interest (but see **Example 10.14**).

Example 10.12
Steve's will left his condo to his wife, subject to the condition that if his wife does not survive his sister, his sister will get the property. At the time of Steve's death, his sister had terminal cancer with two weeks to live, and his wife was very healthy. Shortly after Steve's death, his sister passed away. Despite the fact that it was unlikely that Steve's wife would predecease his sister, it was possible that his wife would predecease his sister, and therefore the bequest of the condo, subject to the survival contingency, is a terminable interest.

The Terminable Interest Rule and the Unlimited Marital Deduction
A terminable interest alone will not prevent the use of the unlimited marital deduction for the transfer. The marital deduction will not be available if the following three criteria are met:
1. a terminable interest is transferred to a surviving spouse, **and**
2. another interest in the same property passes from the decedent to someone other than the surviving spouse (a third party) for less than full and adequate consideration in money or money's worth, **and**
3. the third party may possess or use any part of the property after the interest of the surviving spouse terminates.

Example 10.13
Recall the facts from the Jennifer and Eric example (**Example 10.10**). When Jennifer died, she left all of her property to Eric. While the copyrights to her musical compositions were terminable interests, no person other than Eric had any interest in the property, since all rights under the copyrights were given to Eric. If Eric dies before the copyrights expire, the value of the copyrights will be included in his gross estate. Consequently, the transfer of the copyrights to Eric will qualify for the unlimited marital deduction.

chapter 10

Example 10.14

Recall the facts from the Ken and Liz example (**Example 10.11**). When Ken died, Liz received an annuity that paid 50% of Ken's pension benefit to her for the rest of her life. As noted above, the annuity Liz received was a terminable interest. Since no one other than Liz has an interest in the annuity and since no person can possess any part of the property after Liz's interest expires (the annuity payments terminate at Liz's death), the full value of the annuity Liz receives will qualify for the unlimited marital deduction.

Example 10.15

Andy's will gave his wife the right to use his beach house for life, and stated that the beach house would be transferred to his children at her death. The transfer to Andy's wife is a terminable interest. Andy's children received an interest in the property (remainder interest) that allows them to possess or use the property after the surviving spouse's death. Consequently, the value of the transfer to the surviving spouse (the right to use the property for the rest of her life) is a terminable interest that will not qualify for the unlimited marital deduction.

Example 10.16

Andy gave his beach house to his children, subject to the condition that he and his wife could use the house for the rest of their lives. When Andy died, the full fair market value of the house was included in his estate. Andy's wife still has the right to use the house for the rest of her life, which has been valued at 40% of the value of the house. Since Andy's children received an interest in the property that allows them to possess or use the property after his wife's death, the value of the life estate given to Andy's wife does not qualify for the unlimited marital deduction.

Example 10.17

Assume the same facts as above, except that Andy sold, at fair market value, the remainder interest in his beach house to his children, subject to the condition that he and his wife could use the beach house for the remainder of their lives. At Andy's death, the full fair market value of the house is included in his estate due to the retained interest. Because his children paid for their remainder interest in the house, the terminable interest given to his wife will qualify for the unlimited marital deduction since the children did not receive their interest for less than full or fair consideration.

The terminable interest rule has one additional caveat. If the deceased spouse's will directs his executor to use property included in the gross estate to purchase terminable interest property for the surviving spouse, the unlimited marital deduction is not available for that property.

Example 10.18

Fred and Betty have been married for 40 years. Fred has always taken care of the family finances, and was not sure if Betty would be able to handle them if he died first. Fred included a provision in his will directing his executor to purchase a life annuity for Betty so that she would not run out of money during her lifetime. The value of the annuity that is transferred to Betty through Fred's estate is a terminable interest that does not qualify for the unlimited marital deduction.

Example 10.19

Assume the same facts as above, except that, instead of having his executor purchase an annuity after his death, Fred purchases a deferred annuity contract naming Betty as the beneficiary. When Fred dies, Betty will receive an income stream for life. The value of the annuity is included in Fred's gross estate, it is a terminable interest (it will end at Betty's death), and it will qualify for the unlimited marital deduction because no one other than the surviving spouse received an interest in the annuity for less than adequate consideration allowing them to enjoy the property after Betty's interest expires.

Exceptions to the Terminable Interest Rule

The terminable interest rule prevents terminable interest transfers to the surviving spouse from qualifying for the marital deduction when another party receives an interest in the same property for less than adequate consideration. There are, however, several exceptions to the terminable interest rule. The exceptions include:

1. A survival contingency of no more than six months.
2. A terminable interest, either outright or in trust, over which the surviving spouse has a general power of appointment.
3. A Qualified Terminable Interest Property (QTIP) Trust.
4. A Charitable Remainder Trust (CRT) where a spouse is the only non-charitable beneficiary.

In planning large estates, contingency clauses are often used to ensure that the combined estates of a married couple make full use of their available applicable estate tax credits and to provide for the orderly disposition of the client's wealth.

Survivorship Clause

As discussed in Chapter 2, a **survivorship clause** included in a will creates a terminable interest. In such a situation, if the surviving spouse does not survive for the stated number of months, his interest terminates. For the terminable interest rule to apply there only has to be the possibility that the interest passing to the surviving spouse will terminate – certainty is not required.

> ### Quick Quiz 10.3
>
> 1. If the deceased spouse's will directs his executor to use property in the estate to purchase an annuity for the surviving spouse, the unlimited marital deduction is not available for that property.
>   a. True
>   b. False
>
> 2. If a will includes a survival contingency longer than six months, the unlimited marital deduction will not apply to the transfer.
>   a. True
>   b. False
>
> 3. If a survival clause requires the surviving spouse to outlive the decedent by more than 8 months, the property will not qualify for the marital deduction, even if the surviving spouse lives for 20 years after the death of the decedent.
>   a. True
>   b. False
>
> True, True, True.

While a survivorship clause creates a terminable interest that would not qualify for the unlimited marital deduction, an important exception applies. Provided that: (1) the survivorship clause does not require the surviving spouse to survive for more than six months after the decedent's death, and (2) the surviving spouse actually does survive the stated period, the transfer of property to the surviving spouse will qualify for the marital deduction. If the survival clause requires the spouse to survive for a period of more than six months after the decedent's death to inherit under the will, any transfers subject to the survival clause that pass to the surviving spouse will not qualify for the unlimited marital deduction.

Example 10.20
Gary's will creates a credit shelter trust at his death and directs his executor to fund the credit shelter trust with the maximum amount that can be transferred without increasing his federal estate tax liability. The remainder of Gary's gross estate is left to his wife provided that she survives him for five months, and, if she does not survive him, the property is transferred to The Gary Foundation. While the survival contingency creates the possibility of a terminable interest, it is not longer than six months. If Gary's wife survives the 5-month period, she will receive property and it will qualify for the marital deduction.

Example 10.21
Wally's will leaves all of his property to his wife if she survives him for nine months; and if she does not survive him, the property is transferred to his children, per stirpes. Since Wally's will creates the possibility of a terminable interest for his spouse and the survival contingency is more than six months, the transfer to his spouse will not qualify for the marital deduction. Even if Wally's wife survives him by nine months and takes all of the property, the marital deduction will not apply.

General Power of Appointment (GPOA)
The second exception to the terminable interest rule deals with terminable interests coupled with the surviving spouse having a general power of appointment. Once the surviving spouse has a general power of appointment over the property, the property will be included in the surviving spouse's gross estate under IRC Section 2042. Therefore, even though a terminable interest is created, the inclusion in the surviving spouse's gross estate due to the general power of appointment will allow the transfer to qualify for the marital deduction in the first spouse's gross estate. Typically, these transfers are completed by use of trust vehicles. The use of General Power of Appointment Trusts is discussed later in this chapter.

Qualified Terminable Interest Property (QTIP) Trust
The third exception to the terminable interest rule involves the use of a Qualified Terminable Interest Property Trust (QTIP Trust), which is discussed later in this chapter.

Charitable Remainder Trust (CRT)
The fourth exception to the terminable interest rule applies when a spouse is named as the only non-charitable income beneficiary of a Charitable Remainder Trust (CRT). (A full discussion of CRTs is included in Chapter 9.)

A Charitable Remainder Trust is structured to provide an income stream from the trust to the grantor or the grantor's designee, followed by a transfer of the remainder interest in the trust to a qualified charity when the income interest expires. The income stream can be structured as either an annuity interest or a unitrust interest. An annuity interest is a right to receive a fixed percentage of the initial contribution to the trust for the entire term of the income interest. Charitable Remainder Trusts that create an income stream in the form of an annuity are referred to as Charitable Remainder Annuity Trusts (CRATs).

Example 10.22

Alisha created a Charitable Remainder Annuity Trust (CRAT), naming her husband, Anton, as the income beneficiary for his lifetime, and the McFadden Foundation, a qualified charity, as the remainder beneficiary. Alisha funded the CRAT with $1,000,000 in highly appreciated stock, and set the income payout rate at 5%. Each year until his death, Anton will receive $50,000 from the CRAT. When Anton dies, the trust will terminate and the remaining principal will be distributed to The McFadden Foundation. Note that Alisha did not incur any gift tax in forming the CRAT, since she gave the income interest to her spouse, which qualifies for the gift tax marital deduction. The remainder interest that passes to the charity will qualify for the gift tax charitable deduction.

A unitrust interest is created by granting the income beneficiary a right to receive an income stream equal to a fixed percentage of the value of the trust assets as determined each year. When a unitrust income stream is used, the CRT is referred to as a Charitable Remainder Unitrust (CRUT).

Example 10.23

Randy created a Charitable Remainder Unitrust (CRUT) naming his wife, Kelly, as the income beneficiary for her lifetime, and The Jarvis Foundation, a qualified charity, as the remainder beneficiary. Randy funded the CRUT with $1,000,000 in highly appreciated stock, and set the income payout rate at 5%. In the first year of the trust's existence, Kelly will receive $50,000 from the CRUT ($1,000,000 x 5%). If, in year two, the value of the trust assets rises to $1,100,000, Kelly will receive an income distribution of $55,000 ($1,100,000 x 5%). If, in year three, the value of the trust assets falls to $950,000, Kelly will receive an income distribution of $47,500 ($950,000 x 5%). When Kelly dies, the trust will terminate and the remaining principal will be distributed to The Jarvis Foundation. Note that Randy did not incur any gift tax in forming the CRUT, since he gave the income interest to his spouse, which qualifies for the gift tax marital deduction. The remainder interest that passes to the charity will qualify for the gift tax charitable deduction.

In both of the examples above, the grantor of the CRT created an interest for his spouse during his lifetime. It is also possible to create a testamentary CRT by placing instructions in a will directing the executor of the estate to create and fund a CRT at the grantor's death. The spouse can be named as the income beneficiary of this testamentary CRT as well, but if the spouse is named as beneficiary of a testamentary CRT, a terminable interest is created since the spouse will only receive the income interest and, after the spouse's interest expires, a charity receives the remainder interest. Without a special exception to the marital deduction rules, the ability to treat the property as qualified terminable interest property would not be available to qualify the spouse's interest for the marital deduction since the CRT will only pay an annuity or unitrust amount, which is not the same as the requirement of distributing all income to the spouse when the QTIP election is made (discussed below). Congress recognized that some individuals might want to use a CRT in their estate plan to benefit both their surviving spouse and a charity, so they enacted a special provision in the IRC Section 2056 stating that when a spouse is named as the only non-charitable income beneficiary of a charitable remainder trust, despite the fact that the CRT income interest is a terminable interest, it will qualify for the marital deduction.

The CRT exception is consistent with the theory underlying the marital deduction and the terminable interest rule. Recall that the terminable interest rule was enacted to ensure that the property passing to the surviving spouse would be subject to tax either in the estate of the first-to-die spouse or in the estate of the surviving spouse. If a CRT is created, the remainder interest in the trust is permanently set aside for a qualified charity. As such, the remainder interest would not be taxed in either estate under normal estate tax principles since it qualifies for the charitable deduction. While the spouse will receive a terminable interest in the trust, the fact that a charity receives an interest in the trust after the spouse's term expires exempts the remaining value from estate tax. Therefore, allowing an income interest in a CRT to qualify for the marital deduction is consistent with the philosophy of treating the two spouses as a single economic unit, and allows property to pass to qualified charities without estate tax consequences.

OUTRIGHT BEQUESTS TO THE SPOUSE

The simplest way to qualify the transfer of property for the unlimited marital deduction is to transfer property directly to the surviving spouse. Many individuals prefer this method, since the surviving spouse has complete control over the property during his lifetime. To the extent that the surviving spouse does not consume the property received from the decedent, that property will be included and taxed in the surviving spouse's gross estate. Therefore, all outright transfers of property to the surviving spouse will qualify for the estate tax marital deduction. Standard "I Love You" wills make direct transfers of all of the decedent's property to his surviving spouse. In addition, any property which is jointly titled between the decedent and his spouse with a survivorship feature will, upon transfer to the surviving spouse, qualify for the unlimited marital deduction.

Limiting a Direct Transfer

While an outright transfer to the surviving spouse is simple and provides the surviving spouse with complete control over the property, it may be more appropriate to limit the surviving spouse's control over the property through the use of a trust. In situations where the surviving spouse is not capable of managing assets or may need protection from current and future creditors, a transfer in trust should be considered. Furthermore, if the deceased spouse would like to protect his property for his children and is concerned that the surviving spouse may remarry (making his assets available to the surviving spouse's new husband or wife), a trust may be preferred. Once a transfer to the surviving spouse is accomplished through the use of a trust, a terminable interest results, potentially disqualifying the transfer for the marital deduction. There are two types of trusts, General Power of Appointment Trusts and QTIP Trusts, which can be created to protect property for a decedent's heirs and still qualify for the unlimited marital deduction. These trusts are addressed below.

GENERAL POWER OF APPOINTMENT (GPOA) TRUSTS

A **General Power of Appointment (GPOA) Trust**, also known as an "A Trust," creates a terminable interest for a surviving spouse that will nevertheless require the unconsumed assets to be included in the surviving spouse's gross estate and thus qualify the transfer of the property to the trust for the unlimited marital deduction.

Qualifying a GPOA Trust for the Marital Deduction

To qualify for the marital deduction, the trust must grant to the surviving spouse a power to appoint the trust property to himself, his estate, his creditors, or the creditors of his estate. Possession of one or more of these rights requires the fair market value of the trust assets to be included in the surviving spouse's gross estate. Note that it is not necessary to give the surviving spouse the right to appoint the property to all of these individuals or entities – the right to appoint the property to one of them is sufficient. The power of appointment can be exercisable during the surviving spouse's lifetime, or only at the surviving spouse's death, or both during the surviving spouse's lifetime and at his death. Any such trust must meet the following additional requirements to qualify for the unlimited marital deduction:

1. The surviving spouse, and only the spouse, must be entitled to receive all of the income from the trust at least annually;
2. The general power of appointment granted to the surviving spouse must be exercisable by the surviving spouse alone; and
3. No person other than the surviving spouse may appoint any part of the property to anyone other than the surviving spouse during the life of the surviving spouse.

Example 10.24

Lee died last month. His will created a credit shelter trust to hold that portion of his gross estate that could be transferred without increasing his federal estate tax liability, and a trust for the benefit of his wife, Betty, to hold the remaining assets in his gross estate. The trust for Betty states that she is entitled to receive all of the income from the trust on a quarterly basis and that Betty has the right to appoint the principal of the trust during her lifetime or at her death to any of Betty and Lee's heirs or to her estate. In addition, Lee gave his brother a power of appointment over Betty's trust, allowing him to appoint the principal of the trust to Betty and Lee's issue solely to cover educational expenses. Since someone other than the surviving spouse can appoint property to someone other than the surviving spouse, the transfer in trust for Betty will not qualify for the unlimited marital deduction.

Estate Trusts

A general power of appointment trust that only grants the surviving spouse the power to appoint the property to his estate is referred to as an **estate trust**. Unlike a normal power of appointment trust, an estate trust does not require the annual distribution of income to the surviving spouse. Rather, an estate trust permits the trustee to distribute all, none, or some income to the spouse. Note, however, that if income is accumulated in an estate trust, the accumulated income is included in the surviving spouse's gross estate in addition to the original principal of the trust.

For the trust to qualify for the marital deduction, no one other than the surviving spouse can have a beneficial interest in the trust. Upon the surviving spouse's death, the trusts assets must pass to the spouse's estate. Estate trusts are useful for passing non-income producing property since there is no statutory requirement for the trust to produce income. The trustee controls the trust assets during the spouse's lifetime.

While an estate trust offers more creditor protection over assets during the surviving spouse's lifetime and allows for a more flexible disposition scheme (due to the ability to accumulate income), it is not the best option to use in all states. Some states may impose an inheritance tax on assets passing through an estate trust, and thus include those assets in the probate estate of the surviving spouse (thereby subjecting the assets of the trust to the creditors of the surviving spouse's estate), but will not subject a regular general power of appointment trust to inheritance tax or consider it part of the probate estate. A clear understanding of both the state and federal tax, transfer rules, and probate will allow a planner to structure the estate plan in the most effective way for the client.

QUALIFIED TERMINABLE INTEREST PROPERTY (QTIP) TRUSTS

In considering what transfers should be allowed to qualify for the unlimited marital deduction, Congress recognized that in certain circumstances, an individual may wish to qualify assets for the marital deduction while still retaining control over the ultimate disposition of those assets. All of the marital deduction techniques discussed to this point grant the surviving spouse the right to determine who ultimately receives the property. Use of a **Qualified Terminable Interest Property (QTIP) Trust**, also known as a "C Trust," allows a decedent to qualify a transfer for the marital deduction at his death yet still control the ultimate disposition of the property.

> **Key Concepts**
>
> 1. Describe the use of a QTIP Trust and its impact on the unlimited marital deduction.
> 2. Identify the requirements for a QDOT to qualify for the unlimited marital deduction.

A QTIP Trust holds property for the benefit of a surviving spouse and makes income distributions to the surviving spouse at least annually. At the surviving spouse's death, the trust property will be transferred to the remainder beneficiary selected by the grantor of the QTIP Trust (the first-to-die spouse). To qualify a trust as a QTIP Trust, the executor of the decedent's estate must make an election on the estate tax return to qualify the trust for the marital deduction. The election defers any estate tax on the property until the death of the surviving spouse. Even though it is a terminable interest, the QTIP Trust will qualify for the unlimited marital deduction since the surviving spouse will be required to include in his gross estate the fair market value of the assets in the trust. Despite the fact that the assets are taxed in the surviving spouse's gross estate, the assets will be transferred according to the terms of the trust created by the first-to-die spouse.

Qualifying as a QTIP Trust

In order to qualify as a QTIP Trust, the following requirements must be met:
1. The property transferred to the trust must qualify for the unlimited marital deduction. Consequently, it must be included the gross estate of the first-to-die spouse and must be transferred to the surviving spouse (in this case, in trust).
2. The surviving spouse is entitled to all of the trust income for her life, and that income must be paid at least annually. If the trust earns income during the surviving spouse's lifetime that is not distributed as of the date of the surviving spouse's death, the trust must distribute this income to the surviving spouse's estate (this is referred to as "stub income").

3. The surviving spouse must have the authority to compel the trustee to sell non-income producing investments and reinvest those proceeds in income-producing investments.
4. During the surviving spouse's lifetime, no one can have the right to appoint the property to anyone other than the surviving spouse.
5. The transferor or his executor must file an election to treat the trust as a QTIP Trust on the transferor's gift tax return (Form 709) or the decedent's federal estate tax return (Form 706).

The QTIP Trust as a Lifetime Transfer Device

Most QTIP elections are made at the death of the first spouse. However, it is possible to make lifetime transfers to a QTIP Trust. A lifetime QTIP trust may be useful when a wealthy spouse wishes to transfer sufficient assets to the less wealthy spouse to ensure that the less wealthy spouse has sufficient funds to make full use of his or her estate tax exemptions equivalent if the less wealthy spouse dies first. If the QTIP Trust meets all of the qualifications listed above, the current transfer to the trust would qualify for the unlimited gift tax marital deduction, and at the death of the donee spouse, the trust property will be transferred to the remainder beneficiary as designated by the donor spouse. Such a transfer assures that the assets are transferred to the party or parties chosen by the wealthy spouse, but makes use of the applicable estate tax credit equivalency of both spouses. Control over the ultimate disposition of the property afforded by a QTIP trust may be important even though there is portability of any unused estate tax exemptions between spouses.

Estate Taxes

Upon the death of the surviving spouse, the executor of the surviving spouse's estate may require the trustee of the QTIP Trust to pay, out of the trust assets, any estate taxes attributable to the inclusion of the trust assets in the surviving spouse's gross estate. This provision is included in the law to prevent one spouse from forcing the other spouse to pay estate taxes attributable to his assets.

Exhibit 10.5 | Form 706 Part 6

Form 706 (Rev. 8-2019)

Estate of: | **Decedent's social security number**

Part 6—Portability of Deceased Spousal Unused Exclusion (DSUE)

Portability Election

A decedent with a surviving spouse elects portability of the DSUE amount, if any, by completing and timely filing this return. No further action is required to elect portability of the DSUE amount to allow the surviving spouse to use the decedent's DSUE amount.

Section A. Opting Out of Portability

The estate of a decedent with a surviving spouse may opt out of electing portability of the DSUE amount. Check here and do not complete Sections B and C of Part 6 only if the estate opts **NOT** to elect portability of the DSUE amount. ☐

Section B. Qualified Domestic Trust (QDOT) | Yes | No

Are any assets of the estate being transferred to a QDOT? . . . .

If "Yes," the DSUE amount portable to a surviving spouse (calculated in Section C, below) is preliminary and shall be redetermined at the time of the final distribution or other taxable event imposing estate tax under section 2056A. See instructions for more details.

Section C. DSUE Amount Portable to the Surviving Spouse (To be completed by the estate of a decedent making a portability election.)

Complete the following calculation to determine the DSUE amount that can be transferred to the surviving spouse.

1	Enter the amount from line 9d, Part 2—Tax Computation	1
2	Reserved	2
3	Enter the value of the cumulative lifetime gifts on which tax was paid or payable. See instructions	3
4	Add lines 1 and 3	4
5	Enter amount from line 10, Part 2—Tax Computation	5
6	Divide amount on line 5 by 40% (0.40) (do not enter less than zero)	6
7	Subtract line 6 from line 4	7
8	Enter the amount from line 5, Part 2—Tax Computation	8
9	Subtract line 8 from line 7 (do not enter less than zero)	9
10	DSUE amount portable to surviving spouse (Enter lesser of line 9 or line 9a, Part 2—Tax Computation) . .	10

Section D. DSUE Amount Received From Predeceased Spouse(s) (To be completed by the estate of a deceased surviving spouse with DSUE amount from predeceased spouse(s))

Provide the following information to determine the DSUE amount received from deceased spouses.

A Name of Deceased Spouse (dates of death after December 31, 2010, only)	B Date of Death (enter as mm/dd/yy)	C Portability Election Made?		D If "Yes," DSUE Amount Received From Spouse	E DSUE Amount Applied by Decedent to Lifetime Gifts	F Year of Form 709 Reporting Use of DSUE Amount Listed in col. E	G Remaining DSUE Amount, if any (subtract col. E from col. D)
		Yes	No				
Part 1 — DSUE RECEIVED FROM LAST DECEASED SPOUSE							
Part 2 — DSUE RECEIVED FROM OTHER PREDECEASED SPOUSE(S) AND USED BY DECEDENT							
Total (for all DSUE amounts from predeceased spouse(s) applied) . .							

Add the amount from Part 1, column D, and the total from Part 2, column E. Enter the result on line 9b, Part 2—Tax Computation . . . . ▶

Qualified Terminable Interest Property (QTIP) Trusts

Example 10.25

Jim died leaving behind his wife, Carolyn, and their children, Jake and Hank. After Jim's death, Carolyn remarried and had children with her new husband. Jim's will created a QTIP Trust at his death that met all of the requirements for the marital deduction. The QTIP Trust requires all of the income to be paid to Carolyn during her lifetime and at her death, the trust assets are distributed to Hank and Jake, in equal shares, per stirpes. Upon Carolyn's death, Hank and Jake will receive the trust assets, less the estate tax attributable to those assets. If the QTIP Trust was not required to pay the estate taxes on the trust property, Carolyn's estate would have to pay those taxes, resulting in a reduction of the amount of property that can pass to her heirs, which may or may not include Jake, Hank, and her other children.

The surviving spouse can waive, in his will, the requirement that the QTIP Trust pay the estate taxes attributable to the QTIP Trust property. If the beneficiaries of both spouses' estates are the same, for example, it may be more appropriate for each spouse to waive his right to have the QTIP Trust pay estate taxes on trust property, since the property in the QTIP Trust may not be considered part of the probate estate and may result in providing additional creditor protection for the beneficiaries.

Portability

The Tax Relief, Unemployment Insurance Authorization, and Job Creation Act of 2010 (TRA 2010) introduced **portability** of the estate tax exemption amount between spouses. The American Taxpayer Relief Act of 2012 (ATRA 2012) made the exemption portability provisions permanent. For portability to apply, the executor of the deceased spouse's estate must elect to transfer the deceased spouse's unused exemption (DSUEA) to the surviving spouse on a timely filed estate tax return. This election is made on Part 6 of Form 706. The DSUEA is the lesser of the applicable exclusion amount (currently $11,580,000), or the applicable exclusion amount less the value of the deceased spouse's taxable estate plus adjusted taxable gifts.

When the election to transfer the unused exemption is made, the statute of limitations is suspended for purposes of determining the deceased spousal unused exemption amount available for use by the surviving spouse. This provision does not extend the statute of limitations for assessing tax in the deceased spouse's estate, but does permit the IRS to confirm (and possibly change) the value of the unused exemption amount that may be used in the surviving spouse's estate (or, if applicable, to make lifetime transfers). While this provision may impose some uncertainty for estates taking advantage of valuation discounts, most estates will probably not be affected by its provisions. Individuals with large estates may wish to consider the repositioning of assets that are subject to

> **Quick Quiz 10.4**
>
> 1. A QTIP Trust allows a decedent to qualify a transfer for the marital deduction at his death yet still control the ultimate disposition of the property.
>   a. True
>   b. False
>
> 2. Because a surviving spouse's interest in a QTIP Trust is a terminable interest, the surviving spouse's estate will not include the value of the trust property at her date of death.
>   a. True
>   b. False
>
> 3. The income from a lifetime QTIP Trust must be paid to the surviving spouse at least annually for the trust to qualify for the unlimited gift tax marital deduction.
>   a. True
>   b. False
>
> 4. A QTIP trust will allow a transfer to a non-U.S. citizen spouse to qualify for the unlimited marital deduction.
>   a. True
>   b. False
>
> True, False, True, False.

valuation discounts. To minimize uncertainty for the estate of the surviving spouse (at least to the extent of the amount of the deceased spouse's unused exemption amount), it may be wise to transfer discounted assets to the spouse using the marital deduction, while transferring assets that are not subject to valuation discounts to the heirs or the bypass trust to fix the value of the unused exemption amount.

One further limitation applies to the portability of the estate tax exemption between spouses. Portability is only permitted for the surviving spouse's "last deceased spouse." This limitation prevents stacking up the exemptions of multiple deceased spouses to effectuate a large estate-tax free transfer of wealth. The Joint Committee on Taxation clarified, in their technical explanation of the act, that this requirement applies even if the "last deceased spouse" had no unused exemption, or had not made a timely election to transfer unused exemption to the surviving spouse.

Example 10.26

David died in 2020 leaving his entire $4,000,000 estate outright to his wife, Tanya. In 2021, Tanya married Christopher, a long-time acquaintance who was not in good health. Christopher died in November of 2021, but did not have any assets to transfer at his death. Since Christopher did not have any estate tax liability, his executor never filed his estate tax return. Tanya died in December, 2021, leaving her entire $8,000,000 estate (including the $4,000,000 she received from David) to her children in equal shares per stirpes. Since Christopher was Tanya's last deceased spouse, and Tanya did not receive any of Christopher's unused exemption amount (an election was never made by the executor to transfer the unused exemption to Tanya), Tanya's estate is entitled to only the original $11,580,000 (as indexed) exemption. Tanya cannot use any of the exemption transferred to her by David since David was not Tanya's last deceased spouse, and the family will incur estate tax (after her credit equivalency).

A **privity** requirement also applies to the use of a deceased spouse unused exemption. Exemption amounts transferred by a deceased spouse to the surviving spouse cannot later be transferred to the surviving spouse's new spouse upon the death of the surviving spouse.

Example 10.27

Emil passed away in 2020 leaving his entire $2,000,000 estate to his wife, Roberta. Emil's executor elected, on a timely filed estate tax return, to transfer Roberts $11,580,000 exemption to Roberta. In 2021, Roberta married Luciano, and died later that year. Assuming that Roberta leaves all of her property to Luciano in a manner that qualifies for the marital deduction, the executor may elect to transfer Roberta's $11,580,000 exemption to Luciano, but cannot transfer Roberta's "deceased spouse's unused exemption amount" (Emil's exemption) to Luciano. Emil's exemption, in this case, is lost due to the privity requirement.

Current law provides for inflation indexing for the estate, gift, and generation skipping transfer tax exemption amounts. For example, wealthy individuals may wish to marry sickly, poor, dying people to take advantage of the estate exemption of the sick, dying individual that would otherwise go unused. One marriage such as this may permit the taxpayer to transfer $23,160,000 (2020) on a gift tax-free basis. Furthermore, widows and widowers need to think twice before getting remarried, particularly if any of their deceased spouse's unused exemption amount has been allocated to them. Remarriage, followed by the death of the new spouse, will prevent use of the first spouse's unused exemption amount.

An interesting feature of TRA 2010 is that the legislation authorizes indexing of the estate and gift tax exemption amounts beginning in 2012, but a deceased spouse's unused exemption allocated to the surviving spouse will not qualify for indexing. It is a static number determined upon the death of the first spouse to die. This could lead to some confusion among clients as the estate tax exemption amount begins to increase.

For purposes of lifetime gifting, a surviving spouse may use any ported amounts from a deceased spouse before using their own lifetime exemption. It is possible to have a ported amount of $11,580,000, use it as a gift, then remarry, and if the second spouse dies after the gift, have their ported amount also. Gifting by using the last deceased spouse's DSUEA may take place either before or after a subsequent marriage. It just needs to occur before the death of the second spouse or the original DSUEA is lost.

Extension of Time to File the Portability Election
On June 9, 2017, the IRS issued Revenue Procedure 2017-34, which extended the time available to make a portability election for estates that are not otherwise required to file a Federal estate tax return.

A decedent's estate is required to file an estate tax return if the gross estate exceeds the federal estate tax exemption amount, or $11,580,000 for 2020, even if no estate tax liability is due. The due date for the estate tax return is nine months after the decedent's death. While prior law permitted executors to extend the due date of the estate tax return, no extension was generally available for the portability election. Under Treas. Reg. Sec. 20.2010-2(a)(2), by filing a timely estate tax return, the executor of a decedent's estate will have elected portability of the decedent's DSUE amount unless the executor chooses not to elect portability.

Provided that a decedent's gross estate (including adjusted taxable gifts) falls below $11,580,000 (in 2020), the executor of the estate is not required to file an estate tax return, but may nevertheless choose to do so to elect portability of the deceased spouse's unused exemption (DSUE).

In the past, if an executor failed to file an estate tax return but could establish that he acted reasonably and in good faith, and that the granting of relief would not prejudice the interests of the government, taxpayers could request a private letter ruling from the IRS to permit the late filing of an estate tax return for purposes of electing portability. The Treasury and IRS received a considerable number of ruling requests for an extension of time to elect portability, which placed a significant burden on the Service. Accordingly, to simplify the procedure for obtaining an extension of time to elect portability for estates not required to file an estate tax return, and to reduce the burden on the Service, the IRS issued Revenue Procedure 2017-34. Ruling requests for extensions of time to make the portability election for estates that are not required to file an estate tax return and which meet the requirements set forth in Rev. Proc. 2017-34 will no longer be accepted by the Service.

Under Rev. Proc. 2017-34, an extension of time to file an estate tax return solely for the purpose of electing portability is automatically granted if the following conditions are met:

1. The decedent
   - Was survived by a spouse
   - Died after December 31, 2010; and
   - Was a citizen or resident of the United States on the date of his/her death;
2. The executor of the decedent's estate is not required to file an estate tax return under IRC Sec. 6018(a) as determined based on the value of the gross estate and adjusted taxable gifts and without regard to the need to file for portability purposes;
3. The executor did not file an estate tax return within the time required (9 months from date of death);
4. The person making the election (the executor) must file the estate tax return (Form 706) on or before the later of:
   - January 2, 2018 (for estates of decedents dying after December 31, 2010 that have not yet filed an estate tax return), or
   - The second anniversary of the decedent's date of death.
5. The estate tax return must include a caption at the top of the form that states, "FILED PURSUANT TO REV. PROC. 2017-34 TO ELECT PORTABILITY UNDER SECTION 2010(c)(5)(A)."

If all of these requirements are met, the Form 706 will be considered timely filed for purposes of electing exemption portability.

As a result of Rev. Proc. 2017-34, estates not otherwise required to file an estate tax return now have 2 years from the decedent's death to file the return (706) for purposes of electing portability without going through the time, hassle, and expense of obtaining a private letter ruling. The Service also granted retroactive relief (gave a second chance) to estates of decedents who died after December 31, 2010 by permitting them to file a portability election by January 2, 2018. These new portability extension rules create more flexibility for taxpayers, but still require the filing of a return in order to achieve portability of the DSUE. Even with small estates, surviving spouses and executors should consider making protective elections for portability of the DSUE just in case it might be needed to facilitate planning options available to the surviving spouse.

PLANNING FOR THE NON-CITIZEN SPOUSE

The unlimited estate tax marital deduction is not available for an outright bequest to a surviving spouse if the surviving spouse is not a U.S. citizen. For non-citizen spouses, there is a special annual exclusion amount of $157,000 (2020) available for lifetime transfers by a citizen spouse to a non-citizen spouse. As discussed above, Congress allows an unlimited marital deduction in the estate of the first-to-die spouse on the assumption that the property that has not been consumed will be subject to estate tax at the surviving spouse's death. If the surviving spouse is not a U.S. citizen, he could, after receiving the decedent's property, return to his country of origin with the property in hand. When this non-U.S. citizen spouse dies, the U.S. would not have jurisdiction over either the surviving spouse or the property, and therefore would not be able to collect the estate tax on the transfer of property at the surviving spouse's death. To prevent this from happening, special rules apply to transfers to non-U.S. citizen spouses.

> **Example 10.28**
> Gino, a U.S. citizen, recently died leaving behind his spouse, Blair, a citizen of the United Kingdom, and his children. Gino's will leaves all of his property to Blair. If the marital deduction applied to the transfer of Gino's property to Blair, and Blair returned to England after Gino's death with the property, the U.S. would not be able to tax the remaining property at Blair's death. Therefore, the unlimited marital deduction is not available for Gino's estate.

One remedy to this problem is having the non-U.S. citizen surviving spouse become a U.S. citizen before the due date of estate tax return and maintain residency in the United States following the death of the decedent-spouse. If both of these conditions are met, the transfer to the surviving spouse will qualify for the unlimited estate tax marital deduction. Upon the death of the surviving spouse, the U.S. will be able to collect an estate tax on the value of the remaining assets.

Qualified Domestic Trust

For individuals who do not wish to obtain U.S. citizenship, the citizen-spouse, or the executor of the citizen-spouse's estate, can create a **Qualified Domestic Trust (QDOT)**. A QDOT will allow the U.S. government to subject remaining assets to estate taxation upon the death of the non-citizen surviving spouse by maintaining jurisdiction over those assets. In order to qualify the QDOT for the unlimited marital deduction, the following requirements must be met:
1. at least one of the QDOT trustees must be a U.S. citizen or a U.S. domestic corporation;
2. the trust must prohibit a distribution of principal unless the U.S. citizen trustee has the right to withhold estate tax on the distribution;
3. the trustee must keep a sufficient amount of the trust assets in the United States to ensure the payment of federal estate taxes, or the trustee must have a minimum net worth sufficient to assure the payment of estate taxes upon the death of the non-citizen surviving spouse; and
4. the executor of the citizen-spouse's estate must elect to have the marital deduction apply to the trust.

> **Quick Quiz 10.5**
>
> 1. For direct transfers from a decedent's estate to qualify for the marital deduction, the property must transfer to a surviving spouse who is a U.S. citizen.
>   a. True
>   b. False
> 2. In order for transfers to a QDOT to qualify for the unlimited marital deduction, the executor of a citizen spouse's estate must elect to have the marital deduction apply.
>   a. True
>   b. False
> 3. A distribution to a surviving spouse of the principal of a QDOT will be subjected to estate tax.
>   a. True
>   b. False
>
> *True, True, True.*

If all of the requirements listed above are met, the transfer of property into the QDOT will qualify for the marital deduction in the citizen-spouse's estate, and the principal remaining in the QDOT at the date of the surviving spouse's death will be subject to estate tax. The surviving spouse is entitled to receive all of the income of the QDOT for life, but if the principal of the trust is distributed to the surviving spouse during lifetime, the distribution will be subject to estate tax. The estate taxes payable on lifetime or testamentary distributions of principal are equal to the amount of estate tax that would have been imposed had the property been taxed in the citizen-spouse's gross estate. If property passes to a non-citizen spouse in a QDOT, temporary regulations provide that a surviving spouse may elect portability. However, the surviving spouse may not use the ported exemption until the final distribution or termination of the QDOT. This means that the DSUEA will generally not be available to the surviving spouse during life, for gifting purposes. All income distributions, as well as distributions of principal on account of hardships, to the non-citizen surviving spouse are not subject to estate tax. However, all distributions of income from the QDOT to the surviving spouse are subject to ordinary income tax.

ALTERNATIVES TO QUALIFICATION

At first glance, the unlimited marital deduction appears to be a planning panacea – once you qualify for the marital deduction, there is no estate tax on the value of the property at the death of the first spouse. Remember, however, that the marital deduction is only a deferral device; it is available in the first spouse's estate only if the assets transferred will be available to be taxed in the surviving spouse's gross estate.

> **Key Concepts**
>
> 1. Describe overqualification and underqualification.
> 2. What is a bypass trust and why is it created?
> 3. Describe a disclaimer and its applications.
> 4. What are the estate tax consequences of an ILIT?

Overqualification

In 2020, an individual can pass up to $11,580,000 of assets to a non-spouse during lifetime or at death without triggering federal estate transfer tax. **Overqualification** of the marital deduction implies that a deceased individual transfers too many assets in a qualifying way to a surviving spouse, causing an increase in the overall estate taxes for the family.

The new exemption portability rules allow a deceased spouse's unused exemption (DSUEA) to be transferred to his or her unused estate tax exemption to the surviving spouse, at death. For couples who do not anticipate that their combined gross estates, including future appreciation in assets to surviving spouse's death, will exceed $23,160,000 (2020) and who do not anticipate remarrying after the death of the first spouse, overqualification of the estate is no longer an issue. When the combined gross estates of the spouses is anticipated to exceed $23,160,000 (2020), or when the surviving spouse may remarry, a transfer of too many assets to the surviving spouse may lead to an increase in overall family estate taxes.

> ### Example 10.29
> Erin and Orion have been married for 50 years. Over his years of service as a Chemistry professor, Orion has accumulated $4,000,000 in assets in his own name. Erin's net worth is approximately $4,000,000, which resulted from inheritances she received and her savings and investments made during her career as a civil engineer. They have two children, Odin and Ender, and three grandchildren. Erin and Orion do not anticipate any further increases in their net worth over time; and should one of them pass away, the other does not intend to get remarried. If Orion died, leaving his entire estate to Erin, and Orion's executor elects to transfer Orion's unused estate tax exemption to Erin, Erin would have an estate of $8,000,000 when she died, which could be fully shielded by her estate tax credit plus the DSUEA transferred to her by Orion's estate.

When there is a possibility that the surviving spouse will remarry, transferring unused estate tax exemption amounts to the surviving spouse may not be optimal from a tax planning standpoint.

Example 10.30

Matt, age 34, and Lisa, age 32, were married last year. In 6 months, they are expecting the first of what they hope will be several children. Both Matt and Lisa are independently wealthy, and each has a gross estate valued at $9,260,000. They enjoy a lavish lifestyle, and do not anticipate significant growth in their net worth over their lifetime (they plan to spend that growth). Matt died in a tragic car accident in 2020, and left his $9,260,000 estate to Lisa. Matt's executor elected to transfer Matt's unused estate tax exemption amount ($11,580,000) to Lisa. Presuming Lisa never remarried and the value of her estate did not grow, when she dies Lisa can leave $18,520,000 to her heirs estate tax free.

After a whirlwind romance, Lisa is swept off her feet by Leonardo, and they get married 9 months after Matt's death. Leonardo's first wife and the mother of his two children, Mona, had also passed away. Unfortunately, while skiing in the Alps on their honeymoon, Leonardo is killed by a sudden avalanche. His will transferred $5,790,000 to each of his children (which was shielded by his $11,580,000 estate tax exemption), and left the rest of his estate, totaling $2,000,000, to Lisa.

Lisa now has $20,520,000 in property (her original $9,260,000, plus the $9,260,000 from Matt, and $2,000,000 from Leonardo). Within a year of Leonardo's death, Lisa dies of a broken heart. The exemption portability rules only permit a surviving spouse to increase his or her estate tax exemption amount by the unused estate exemption amount of the last deceased spouse. Lisa's last deceased spouse was Leonardo; and Leonardo used his entire exemption at his death. Matt's unused exemption is lost to Lisa; and when Lisa's $20,520,000 estate is transferred to her children, $8,940,000 is taxable. In this case, Matt overqualified the marital deduction by transferring property to Lisa resulting in an overall increase in taxes for the family. Had Matt transferred his $9,260,000 directly to the children, or to a credit shelter (bypass) trust for the benefit of Lisa and the children, the family could have saved $3,704,000 ($9,260,000 x 0.40) in estate taxes. (This is before any funeral expenses.)

Note that in the above example, it may be possible for Lisa to preserve Matt's unused estate tax exemption amount by making lifetime gifts to the children before Leonardo's death (lifetime use of exemption portability was discussed in the Gift Tax Chapter), but there is a potential problem with this approach. The problem is illustrated by the example, when death is unexpected, the surviving spouse may not feel a compulsion to act. As long as Leonardo is alive, Lisa's last deceased spouse is Matt, and she holds Matt's unused exemption, which can be used to make either lifetime or testamentary transfers. Therefore, if Lisa had transferred money during her lifetime and before Leonardo's death, she could make use of Matt's unused exemption amount. From the taxpayer's perspective, it would be best to use the deceased spouse's unused exemption first, followed by the taxpayer's exemption. This would permit preservation of the deceased spouse's credit without having to make a large transfer ($11,580,000) of the surviving spouse's own assets.

This problem could have been avoided if Matt had created a bypass trust (discussed in detail below) and transferred his assets totaling $9,260,000 into the trust for the benefit of Lisa and the children. Matt would have used $9,260,000 of his $11,580,000 exemption, and his executor still could have elected to transfer the additional $2,320,000 unused exclusion amount to Lisa. Upon her death, Lisa would still have an estate tax to pay, since her assets in combination with those transferred to her from Leonardo exceed the $11,580,000 exemption, but the estate tax on Matt's assets would have been avoided, saving the family $3,704,000 ($9,260,000 x 0.40) in federal estate tax. Matt's failure to use a bypass trust, in conjunction with Lisa's subsequent marriage and the death of her second husband, resulted in an overqualification of the marital deduction by $9,260,000.

Underqualification

In contrast, the unlimited marital deduction can also be **underqualified**. Underqualification means that too much of the decedent's property was subject to estate tax at the death of the first spouse due to a failure to make adequate use of the unlimited marital deduction.

Example 10.31

Arden and Landry had been married for 40 years at the date of Landry's death. Arden and Landry have three children. The value of Arden's gross estate is $2,000,000, and the value of Landry's gross estate is $12,000,000. Landry's will leaves $12,000,000 to a bypass trust for the benefit of Arden and their children, and the rest of the estate outright to Arden. Since Landry's estate exceeds the applicable estate credit equivalency amount of $11,580,000 (2020), estate tax will be due on the $420,000 ($12,000,000 - $11,580,000) excess. Landry has underqualified the marital deduction in the estate. If Landry had left $11,580,000 to the bypass trust and $420,000 (the $420,000 that was originally going to the bypass trust) to Arden, the estate would not have a federal estate tax liability, and since Arden's gross estate will not exceed $11,580,000 (Arden's assets of $2,000,000 plus the $420,000 received from Landry's estate, assuming there is no growth in the value of the assets), Arden's estate would have no federal estate tax liability. Landry's underqualification of the marital deduction causes $420,000 of assets to be subject to estate tax that would have passed tax free to the children at Arden's death had the appropriate marital deduction been used. In this case, the underqualification of the marital deduction cost the family $168,000 ($420,000 x 0.40).

Exhibit 10.6 | Celebrity Estate Planning Mistake

Celebrity: James Gandolfini (actor)
Estimated Estate Worth: $70 million (at time of death)
Mistake: Failing to utilize unlimited marital deduction

At the time of his death, James Gandolfini's estate was worth approximately $70 million. While Gandolfini had a will in place, approximately 80% of his estate was not properly protected against estate taxes. His will left $1.6 million to various friends and relatives, and bequeathed land and property in Italy to his kids. The rest of the estate was divided so that 30% went to each of his two sisters, 20% to his wife and 20% to his daughter. While nothing was directly left to his son in the will, his son was the primary beneficiary on Gandolfini's substantial $7 million insurance policy.

By simply leaving a small percentage to his surviving spouse, Gandolfini missed out on the unlimited marital deduction. While his wife's 20% share was protected against federal and state estate taxes, the remaining 80% of the estate was not and led to approximately $30 million being owed to the government in taxes.

Bypass Trust

A **bypass trust** (sometimes referred to as a **credit shelter trust** or "B Trust") is used to ensure that an individual can make full use of his applicable estate tax credit amount. Instead of overqualifying the marital deduction by leaving all property to the surviving spouse or undertaking the risk that the deceased spouse's unused exemption amount will be lost if the surviving spouse remarries, a bypass trust is created to receive property with a fair market value equal to the decedent's remaining applicable estate tax credit equivalency ($11,580,000 in 2020) from the decedent's gross estate, while the remainder of the property passes to the surviving spouse (either outright, or through the use of a GPOA Trust or QTIP Trust). The portion of the gross estate that funds the bypass trust will be subject to federal estate tax, but the applicable estate tax credit will be available, eliminating any estate tax liability. As long as any remaining property passing to the surviving spouse qualifies for the estate tax marital deduction, no estate tax will be payable at the death of the first spouse.

For the Benefit of the Surviving Spouse

Many individuals wish to leave as much property to their surviving spouse as possible and may be uncomfortable with using a bypass trust since the assets in the trust will not be transferred to the spouse. While the surviving spouse will not own the assets transferred to the bypass trust, the trust may be established for the surviving spouse's lifetime benefit, followed by a remainder interest to the children (or other beneficiaries named in the trust). Typically, a bypass trust gives the surviving spouse the right to receive the trust income (by including a mandatory distribution clause or leaving the distribution to the discretion of the trustee). Furthermore, the trustee can be given the right to distribute the principal to the surviving spouse (or any other beneficiary) on a discretionary basis, or subject to an ascertainable standard. (If the trust document is written to allow distributions at the discretion of the trustee, the surviving spouse should not be the trustee to avoid the appearance of a conflict of interest, and the inclusion of the trust assets in the surviving spouse's estate.) An **ascertainable standard** allows distributions of any amount for the recipient's health, education, maintenance, or support. In addition, the surviving spouse can be given a right to demand the greater of (1) $5,000 or (2) five percent of the trust corpus on an annual basis. While these rights provide the surviving spouse with significant access to the trust assets during his lifetime, none of these rights are sufficient to constitute ownership of trust assets or require the surviving spouse to include the fair market value of the bypass trust's asset in his gross estate. Bypass planning may be important for any client where the combined estates of the married couple exceed the applicable estate tax credit equivalency.

Example 10.32

Recall the Matt and Lisa example (**Example 10.30**). Instead of leaving all of his assets to Lisa, Matt's will could have created a bypass trust at his death, and funded it with $9,260,000 of his assets. The $9,260,000 transferred to the bypass trust would not qualify for the marital deduction and would be subject to estate tax at Matt's death. Matt's applicable estate tax credit would shield this amount from estate tax. Matt would have no estate tax liability at his death. The bypass trust created under Matt's will could provide for Lisa, giving her (a) income from the trust, (b) distributions for health, education, maintenance, and support, and (c) the right to demand the greater of $5,000 or 5% of the trust corpus on an annual basis without causing an inclusion of the trust assets in Lisa's gross estate. At Lisa's death, the assets remaining in the bypass trust would pass to the children free of estate tax. If Lisa remarries and survives her new husband, the family will not lose $9,260,000.

The estate tax calculation for Matt's Estate follows:

Matt's Gross Estate	$9,260,000
- Funeral & Admin Expenses (assumed)	(0)
- Debts	(0)
- Taxes due at death	(0)
Adjusted Gross Estate	$9,260,000
- Marital Deduction	(0)
- Charitable Deduction	(0)
Taxable Estate	$9,260,000
+ Post '76 Gifts	0
Tentative Tax Base	**$9,260,000**
Tentative Estate Tax ($345,800+ ($8,160,000 x 0.40))	$3,649,800
- Applicable Estate Tax Credit	($3,649,800)
Total Estate Tax Liability	**$0**

Since Matt's tentative tax base is less than his applicable estate tax credit equivalency amount, he will not have to pay any estate tax on the assets used to fund the bypass trust. At Lisa's subsequent death, her estate tax calculation follows (assuming no growth in the value of the assets between the deaths):

	Current Example	Previous Example
Lisa's Gross Estate	$11,260,000	$11,260,000
Assets from Matt's Estate	0	$9,260,000
- Funeral & Admin Expenses (assumed)	($400,000)	($400,000)
- Debts	(0)	(0)
- Taxes due at death	(0)	(0)
Adjusted Gross Estate (AGE)	$10,860,000	$20,120,000
- Marital Deduction	(0)	(0)
- Charitable Deduction	(0)	(0)
Taxable Estate	$10,860,000	$20,120,000
+ Post '76 Gifts	0	0
Tentative Tax Base	**$10,860,000**	**$20,120,000**
Tentative Estate Tax	$4,289,800	$7,993,800
- Applicable Credit	($4,289,800)	($4,577,800)
Total Estate Tax Liability	**$0**	**$3,416,000** *

* Note that compared with **Example 10.30**, Lisa's tentative taxable estate is reduced by $9,260,000, representing the amount that Matt transferred to the bypass trust at his death. Since the assets transferred to the bypass trust at Matt's death were subject to estate tax (and covered by his applicable estate tax credit), they are not included in Lisa's gross estate in the current example. If those assets were included in Lisa's gross estate, those assets would be taxed twice, which would be inconsistent with the premise of treating a married couple as one economic unit. As this example illustrates, use of a bypass trust at the death of the first spouse saves estate taxes if Lisa dies in 2020 (a tax savings of $3,416,000, which is equal to the tax for the exemption equivalency of $8,540,000).

Lisa's gross estate is initially $11,260,000 ($9,260,000 plus $2,000,000) from Leonardo reduced by funeral and administrative costs of $400,000. Her credit is $4,577,800. Leonardo's unused credit is $0 ($11,580,000 - $11,580,000 x 0.40).

Graphically, Matt and Lisa's estate plan would look like this:

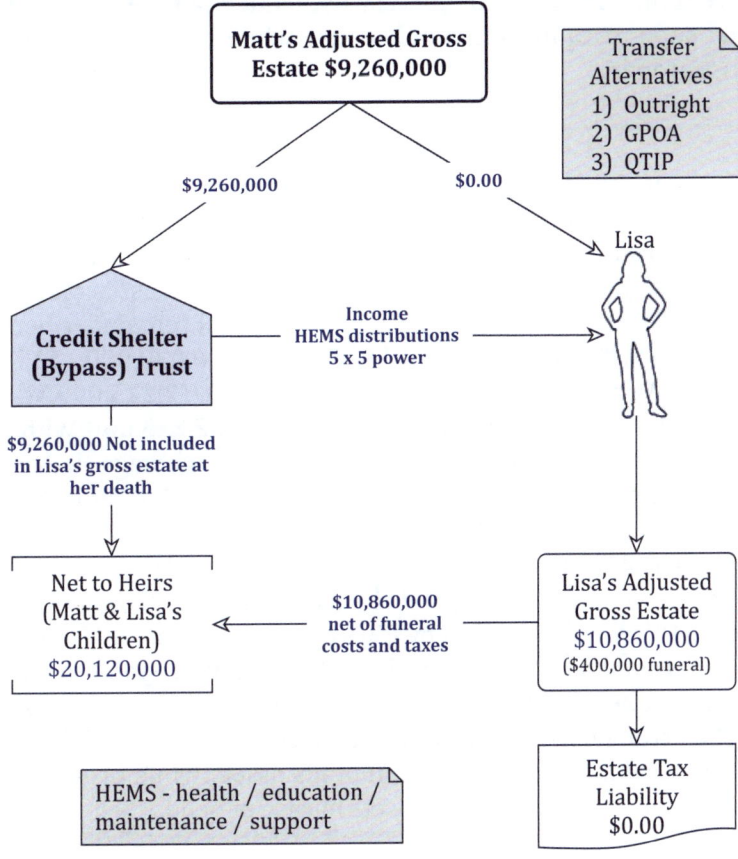

Common Trust Arrangements

A common testamentary trust arrangement includes the transfer of the remaining applicable estate tax credit equivalency to a bypass trust, also known as a B Trust, the transfer of a certain amount to a General Power of Appointment Trust, also known as an A Trust, and the transfer of the remaining balance to a QTIP Trust, known as a C Trust. The arrangement is often referred to as an **ABC Trust arrangement**.

With such an arrangement, a decedent can accomplish several objectives. First, the decedent can guarantee the full use of his applicable estate tax credit equivalency with the transfer to the B Trust. The decedent can also provide the necessary funds to his surviving spouse in several ways. The A Trust allows the spouse to receive income distributions as well as appoint the principal to herself. The B and C Trusts allow income distributions to the surviving spouse as well as the ability for the surviving spouse to receive principal distributions from the B and C Trusts for health, education, maintenance and support. In addition, the A Trust and C Trust qualify the transfers for the unlimited marital deduction. However, a key difference between the A and the C Trust is the selection of the ultimate beneficiaries of the trust property. Because the surviving spouse will have a GPOA over the trust property of the A Trust, the surviving spouse can choose the ultimate beneficiary of the trust property, whereas the decedent (grantor) will choose the remainder beneficiary of the C Trust.

Most often the ABC Trust arrangement is used in situations where the decedent and the surviving spouse's heirs are different individuals, as in the case of blended families. The ABC arrangement allows the decedent to provide support to his surviving spouse while maintaining control over the ultimate disposition of the C Trust property.

> **Example 10.33**
> Betty and Bill were married for ten years before Bill's death. Betty and Bill had three children together. Prior to his marriage to Betty, Bill had a child with his former wife. At Bill's death, his gross estate had a fair market value of $16,030,000 and Bill had not made any lifetime transfers. Bill's will included the common ABC Trust arrangement. The will directed $11,580,000 to the B Trust (bypass) for the equal remainder benefit of each of Bill's children (all four). The remainder of $4,450,000 ($16,030,000 - $11,580,000) was divided between the A Trust (Power of Appointment Trust), $2,225,000, which gave Betty a GPOA over the trust assets and the C Trust (QTIP trust), $2,225,000, with the remainder beneficiary designated as Bill's child from his previous marriage. Betty would be the income beneficiary of each of the A, B, and C Trusts for her life. With this arrangement, Bill's executor would make the QTIP election on the C Trust to qualify it for the unlimited marital deduction. The A Trust would qualify for the unlimited marital deduction because of the general power of appointment, and the assets transferring to the B Trust, would create an estate tax that would be offset by Bill's applicable estate tax credit. Thus, at Bill's death, no estate tax would be due. Furthermore, Betty would appoint the A Trust assets to their three children at her death, and Bill's child will receive the assets of the C Trust at Betty's death. The arrangement allowed Bill to be certain that his child from his former marriage would receive a pro rata allocation of his assets while providing his surviving spouse income and the ability to use the assets in case of need.

Disclaimers

Despite the tax savings that can be generated by using a bypass trust, many individuals are still uncomfortable with the prospect of keeping property away from their spouses. A disclaimer allows the surviving spouse to make a determination of how much property is needed after the first spouse dies.

A qualified disclaimer allows an individual to refuse property from the estate of a decedent. The disclaimer can include a particular asset, amount, fraction of an interest or all property the heir is entitled to receive. When a disclaimer is used, the property will pass to the next person eligible to receive it under the disclaimer clause of the decedent's will or, if no one is listed, under the state intestacy statute. As discussed in Chapter 2, to be valid, a disclaimer must be executed in writing within nine months of the decedent's death and the disclaimant must not have received any benefit from the disclaimed property.

Disclaimers and Bypass Trusts

An individual who is uncomfortable placing a large amount of money in a bypass trust could leave all of his property to the surviving spouse but include a provision in the will stating that if the surviving spouse disclaims any or all of the bequest, the disclaimed property will be placed in a bypass trust, thus giving the surviving spouse an income interest in the trust as noted above. Upon the death of the first spouse, the surviving spouse can assess his financial situation and to the extent that he does not need to receive the property directly, can disclaim his interest in the marital bequest in whole or in part. Once the disclaimer is made, the bequest will not qualify for the marital deduction, but it will qualify as a transfer offset by the applicable estate tax credit. Disclaiming the interest will allow the surviving spouse to prevent the property from being included in his gross estate, even though the surviving spouse will receive an interest in the bypass trust. Note that the property will pass to a trust benefiting the spouse as opposed to passing outright to some other beneficiary.

> **Quick Quiz 10.6**
>
> 1. A disclaimer filed 15 months after the decedent's date of death is valid.
>   a. True
>   b. False
> 2. When a disclaimer is used, the property will pass to the person chosen by the disclaiming party.
>   a. True
>   b. False
> 3. A properly created Irrevocable Life Insurance Trust (ILIT) will avoid inclusion in the decedent's gross estate and the surviving spouse's gross estate.
>   a. True
>   b. False
>
> False, False, True.

This result may seem surprising. Usually, for a disclaimer to be valid, the disclaimant cannot receive an interest in the disclaimed property. In this situation, the surviving spouse disclaims a bequest but nevertheless receives an interest in the trust that is created as a result of the disclaimer. There is a special exception in the law that allows a surviving spouse to execute a qualified disclaimer, yet receive a benefit from the property disclaimed if that property is transferred into a trust in which the surviving spouse receives an income interest, without requiring the value of the trust to be included in the surviving spouse's estate at his death. Anyone other than a surviving spouse executing a similar disclaimer would be deemed to have retained a lifetime right to the income from the property, thereby requiring the property to be included in the gross estate (IRC Section 2036).

Irrevocable Life Insurance Trust (ILIT)

Provided that a client is comfortable with limiting the amount of property that is transferred outright to a spouse, a myriad of planning options emerge. One of the most powerful is the use of an Irrevocable Life Insurance Trust (ILIT) to provide for the surviving spouse, prevent property from being included in the gross estate of either spouse, and protect assets from the claims of the beneficiaries' creditors (discussed in detail in Chapter 11).

A properly drafted ILIT can accomplish all of these objectives. By allowing the trustee of the ILIT to apply for and purchase a life insurance policy on the life of the insured/grantor of the ILIT, the insured will possess no incidents of ownership in the policy thereby keeping the policy out of his gross estate. The grantor of the ILIT can then name his spouse as the primary beneficiary of the trust, granting the surviving spouse:

1. the right to income;
2. the right to receive distributions for health, education, maintenance, and support; and
3. the right to demand up to $5,000 or five percent of the trust corpus each year without subjecting the principal of the ILIT to estate taxation in the surviving spouse's gross estate.

Since no estate tax inclusion results, the marital deduction is unnecessary. At the death of the surviving spouse, the ILIT can continue in existence for the benefit of the children, protecting the assets from the claims of the children's creditors, or can terminate and distribute any remaining principal to the children.

As use of an ILIT and bypass trust illustrates, certain structures can be created that allow the surviving spouse to receive benefits, even though the unlimited estate tax marital deduction does not apply to the transaction. When using these techniques, the transaction does not have to meet the requirements associated with qualifying for the unlimited marital deduction.

Using the Marital Deduction to save State Inheritance Taxes

After the enactment of the American Taxpayer Relief Act of 2012, the federal estate tax exemption was increased to $5,000,000 and became subject to inflation adjustments. In 2020, the exemption is $11,580,000 which exempts most estates from Federal estate taxation. Many states, however, have inheritance taxes that are imposed on much lower levels of wealth transfer. In Massachusetts, for example, transfers of property at death that exceed $1 million are subject to state inheritance tax. For individuals with taxable estates in excess of their state inheritance tax exemption, but below the Federal estate tax exemption level, it is possible to use the marital deduction to avoid state inheritance taxes by using the marital deduction at death. This technique is effective in any state that does not have a gift tax. Currently, the only state that imposes a gift tax is the State of Connecticut.

If a couple would like to avoid state inheritance/estate and transfer taxes at the death of the first spouse, yet still transfer some funds to non-spousal beneficiaries, their estate could be structured to leave the amount in excess of the state inheritance/estate tax exemption to the surviving spouse at death to qualify for both Federal and State estate/inheritance tax deductions. This should result in an avoidance of estate/inheritance taxes at death.

> **Quick Quiz 10.7**
>
> 1. An estate is overqualified when too many assets pass to a surviving spouse in a qualifying way.
>   a. True
>   b. False
> 2. A bypass trust is created to receive the property that does not transfer free from estate tax under the applicable estate tax credit.
>   a. True
>   b. False
> 3. A bypass trust can provide the surviving spouse with income for the rest of her life and avoid inclusion in the surviving spouse's gross estate.
>   a. True
>   b. False
>
> True, False, True.

Example 10.34

Amelie and Noah are residents of Massachusetts, and their combined net worth is $5 million. Amelie is several years older than Noah, and assets titled in her name total $3.0 million. The remaining assets (totaling $2 million) are titled in Noah's name. Amelie and Noah have one son, Ryan. Both Amelie and Noah would like to transfer as much of their wealth as possible to Ryan at each death, and both Amelie and Noah feel comfortable that they could maintain their current lifestyle on the assets they hold individually in their own names.

If Amelie dies this year, she will have a gross estate of $3,000,000. Regardless of how Amelie distributes the assets in her estate, there will be no federal estate tax since her gross estate is less than the Federal estate tax exemption amount available at death ($11,580,000 assuming that Amelie did not make any taxable gifts during her life). For Massachusetts, however, Amelie will be subject to an estate tax on $2 million ($3,000,000 gross estate less $1,000,000 exemption). Under current law, Massachusetts imposes an inheritance tax beginning at 0.8% and up to 16%, depending on the filing status of the decedent and the identity of the recipient of the property. Assume for this example that the Massachusetts estate tax rate that applies to Amelie is 5%. If Amelie left her entire $3 million estate to Ryan, the estate or Ryan would have to pay an estate tax of $100,000 ($2 million x 5%).

They could have avoided the $100,000 Massachusetts estate tax by structuring her estate so that the Massachusetts estate tax exemption amount of $1 million was transferred directly to Ryan, with the remaining $2 million transferred using the unlimited marital deduction to Noah. The $2 million that Noah receives will be shielded by the marital deduction, and Amelie's estate will not have to pay any estate tax to Massachusetts.

Once the state estate tax is avoided through use of the unlimited marital deduction, the surviving spouse could make a gift of the assets that he/she received from the deceased spouse to the intended beneficiary. If the amount of the gift exceeds the annual exclusion amount, a gift tax return must be filed, and an allocation of part of the Federal estate tax exemption will shield the transfer from Federal gift taxes. Provided that the state of residence does not have a gift tax, no transfer tax will be due to the state as a result of the gift.

Example 10.35

Continuing with the same facts from the example above, assume that Amelie's estate was structured to leave $1 million to Ryan at her death, with the remaining assets transferred outright to Noah. Shortly after Amelie's death, Noah gives Ryan the $2 million that he received from Amelie's estate.

For federal gift tax purposes, a taxable transfer results from this gift, but will not trigger any immediate gift tax due to the use of the applicable exclusion amount. The taxable gift that Noah made to Ryan was $1,985,000 ($2 million - $15,000 annual exclusion), which will use up $1,985,000 of Noah's applicable exemption amount. Noah still has over $9 million of his applicable exemption amount remaining, which is more than enough to cover his $2 million estate when he dies. Don't forget that the gift/estate tax exclusion amount is indexed for inflation. Even if Noah's estate increases in value between the time of the gift to Ryan and his death, as of the date of the gift, Noah has a significant buffer, plus the estate tax exemption will increase each year from annual inflation adjustments, thus, providing an additional buffer from the imposition of federal estate taxes at Noah's death.

Since Massachusetts does not have a gift tax, the gift of the $2 million from Noah to Ryan is not a taxable event. By structuring her estate to take advantage of the marital deduction and then have Noah transfer the excess assets by gift to Ryan, Amelie avoids the $100,000 estate tax that she would have had to pay had she left the assets outright to Ryan.

The avoidance of state estate tax at Amelie's death in the prior example is not the only benefit that Amelie, Noah, and Ryan receive. By transferring the excess assets to Ryan, Noah removes the growth on those assets from his estate, thereby avoiding exposure of that growth to Federal estate taxes and state estate taxes at his death. Of course, using the facts set forth in the example, Noah will be subject to Massachusetts estate tax at his death if his estate exceeds $1 million and he has not remarried. Exposure to the state estate tax at Noah's death can be minimized by reducing the size of his estate either by employing additional transfer tax planning techniques or, possibly, a reduction in estate value through consumption of some of his assets prior to his death. If Noah did not make the gift of the excess assets that he received from Amelie's estate to Ryan, all of the growth on that $2 million in assets, plus the $2 million received from Amelie, would be included in his estate and would be subject to state estate tax. Without the gift, the use of the marital deduction delays the payment of the state estate tax, but does not assist in reducing or eliminating exposure to that state estate tax.

As our discussion illustrates, the high federal estate tax exemption eliminates the need for federal estate tax planning for many. However, the use of the federal exemption in combination with state estate tax rules can result in state estate tax savings for those with more modest estates.

chapter 10

COMPREHENSIVE EXAMPLE

Mike has an estate valued at $13,000,000. In addition, there is a fully paid-up life insurance policy on Mike's life that has a $1,500,000 death benefit. Mike is married to Mary and has two children. Mike is expected to die before Mary, who is substantially younger than him. Mike and Mary have asked you to help them with their estate planning and would like you to consider the following three alternative scenarios:

Assume for each scenario funeral and administrative expenses of $100,000.

Scenario 1

Assume that all of Mike's assets, including the death benefit on the life insurance policy he owns on his life, pass to Mary. When Mike dies in early 2020, the estate tax calculation is as follows:

Mike's Gross Estate (Estate plus Life Insurance)	$14,500,000
- Funeral & Admin Expenses	($100,000)
- Debts	(0)
- Taxes due at death	(0)
Adjusted Gross Estate	$14,400,000
- Marital Deduction	($14,400,000)
- Charitable Deduction	(0)
Taxable Estate	$0
+ Post '76 Gifts	0
Tentative Tax Base	$0
Tentative Estate Tax	$0
- Applicable Estate Tax Credit	(0)
Total Estate Tax Liability	$0

Mike's gross estate includes the $13,000,000 in assets that he held at the date of his death, plus the $1,500,000 death benefit from the life insurance policy Mike owned on his life at the time of his death. Since all of Mike's assets, including the death benefit on the life insurance policy, pass to Mary, his estate qualifies for a $14,400,000 marital deduction, resulting in a taxable estate of $0. Note that Mike has not made use of his applicable estate tax credit nor did his executor elect to transfer his unused estate exemption to Mary (they failed to elect portability). Assuming that Mary dies later in the year (2020), and that Mary's only assets are those that she inherited from Mike and that the value of the assets that she inherited did not change, Mary's estate tax calculation would be as follows:

Comprehensive Example

Mary's Gross Estate	$0
Assets from Mike's Estate	$14,400,000
- Funeral & Admin Expenses	($100,000)
- Debts	(0)
- Taxes due at death	(0)
Adjusted Gross Estate	$14,300,000
- Marital Deduction	(0)
- Charitable Deduction	(0)
Taxable Estate	$14,300,000
+ Post '76 Gifts	0
Tentative Tax Base	$14,300,000
Tentative Estate Tax ($345,800 + ($13,300,000 x 0.40))	$5,665,800
- Applicable Estate Tax Credit	($4,577,800)
Total Estate Tax Liability	$1,088,000

The net result of Scenario 1 is that Mike and Mary pay total federal estate taxes of $1,088,000 on the $14,500,000 estate, or approximately 9% percent of the gross estate in estate taxes. Mike and Mary's heirs receive $13,212,000 ($14,500,000 - $100,000 - $100,000 - $1,088,000) assuming that there is no additional tax levied by their state of residence. The cost of poor planning was $1,088,000, the tax that they had to pay because they failed to use or transfer Mike's credit equivalency of $11,580,000.

Scenario 2

Mike creates an ILIT to own the life insurance on his life. For this scenario assume that Mike was able to fund the ILIT using annual exclusion gifts subject to a Crummey right of withdrawal. In this case, the $1,500,000 death benefit is excluded from Mike's gross estate because he did not possess at his death (or in the three years immediately preceeding his death) any incident of ownership in the life insurance policy. Instead, the life insurance policy was owned by the trustee of the ILIT. The results of the estate planning of Scenario 2 are as follows:

At Mike's death, the $1,500,000 life insurance proceeds are paid to the ILIT. The trust grants Mary the right to receive the trust income and the right to principal distributions for her health, education, maintenance, and support. Effectively, all of these assets are available for Mary in the event she will need them during her lifetime. At Mary's death, any amounts remaining in the ILIT are split equally among Mike and Mary's children. Mike's estate tax calculation is as follows:

chapter 10

Mike's Gross Estate (Assets)	$13,000,000
- Funeral & Admin Expenses	($100,000)
- Debts	(0)
- Taxes due at death	(0)
Adjusted Gross Estate	$12,900,000
- Marital Deduction	($12,900,000)
- Charitable Deduction	(0)
Taxable Estate	$0
+ Post '76 Gifts	0
Tentative Tax Base	**$0**
Tentative Estate Tax	$0
- Applicable Estate Tax Credit	(0)
Total Estate Tax Liability	**$0**

Note that Mike's gross estate is $1,500,000 less than it was in Scenario 1 due to the exclusion of the life insurance proceeds. However, again, Mike has failed to use or transfer his applicable estate tax credit in his estate planning process (failed to elect portability). Assuming that Mary dies later this year (2020), and assuming that the assets that Mike bequeathed to Mary remained at the same value and that these are the only assets included in Mary's gross estate, Mary's estate tax calculation would be as follows:

Mary's Gross Estate	$0
Assets from Mike's Estate	$12,900,000
- Funeral & Admin Expenses	($100,000)
- Debts	(0)
- Taxes due at death	(0)
Adjusted Gross Estate	$12,800,000
- Marital Deduction	(0)
- Charitable Deduction	(0)
Tentative Tax Base	$12,800,000
+ Post '76 Gifts	0
Tentative Tax Base	**$12,800,000**
Tentative Estate Tax ($345,800 + ($11,800,000 x 0.40))	$5,065,800
- Applicable Estate Tax Credit	($4,577,800)
Total Estate Tax Liability	**$488,000**

Note that by transferring the life insurance into the ILIT, the family saves $600,000 (0.40 x $1,500,000) in taxes. The total estate tax, as a percentage of the gross assets transferred, is approximately 4.4 percent, and Mike and Mary's children will receive $13,812,000 ($14,500,000 - $100,000 - $100,000 - $488,000). While the results of Scenario 2 are certainly better than the results of Scenario 1, additional planning can further reduce Mike and Mary's estate taxes.

Scenario 3

Assume that Mike moves the life insurance policy into an ILIT so that the death benefit will remain outside of his estate and that he makes full use of his applicable estate tax credit. For this scenario, assume that Mike was able to fund the ILIT using annual exclusion gifts subject to a Crummey right of withdrawal. In this case, the $1,500,000 death benefit will be excluded from Mike's gross estate because he did not own, at his death (or in the three years immediately preceeding his death), any incident of ownership in the life insurance policy. Instead, the life insurance policy was owned by the trustee of the ILIT.

At Mike's death, the $1,500,000 life insurance proceeds are paid to the ILIT. The trust grants Mary the right to receive the trust income and the right to principal distributions for her health, education, maintenance, and support. Effectively, all of these assets are available for Mary in the event that she needs them during her lifetime. At Mary's death, any amounts remaining in the trust are split equally among Mike and Mary's children.

Mike's will directs his executor to create a bypass trust and to fund it with the maximum amount that can be transferred without increasing Mike's estate tax. Since Mike has not made any taxable transfers during his lifetime, the full applicable estate tax credit equivalency of $11,580,000 is available. Therefore, Mike's executor transfers $11,580,000 in assets to the bypass trust. During her lifetime, Mary will have the right to receive the trust income and the right to receive distributions of principal for her health, education, maintenance, and support. Similar to the ILIT, the assets of the bypass trust are available to Mary should she need them during her lifetime. At Mary's death, any amounts remaining in the bypass trust are split equally among Mike and Mary's children. By using a bypass trust, Mike and Mary are avoiding the possible loss of Mike's exemption if the executor elected to transfer it to Mary, and she remarried after Mike's death and survived her second husband.

Mike's estate tax calculation follows:

Mike's Gross Estate	$13,000,000
- Funeral & Admin Expenses	($100,000)
- Debts	(0)
- Taxes due at death	(0)
Adjusted Gross Estate	$12,900,000
- Marital Deduction	($1,320,000)
- Charitable Deduction	(0)
Taxable Estate	$11,580,000
+ Post '76 Gifts	0
Tentative Tax Base	**$11,580,000**
Tentative Estate Tax	$4,577,800
- Applicable Estate Tax Credit	($4,577,800)
Total Estate Tax Liability	**$0**

Unlike Scenario 1 or Scenario 2, Mike has made full use of his applicable estate tax credit equivalency ($11,580,000 in 2020) to reduce the overall estate taxes paid by Mike and Mary. Assuming that the assets that Mike bequeathed to Mary are the only assets included in Mary's gross estate, and they did not appreciate or depreciate and that Mary died later in 2020, Mary's estate tax calculation would be as follows:

Mary's Gross Estate	$0
Assets from Mike's Estate	$1,320,000
- Funeral & Admin Expenses	($100,000)
- Debts	(0)
- Taxes due at death	(0)
Adjusted Gross Estate (AGE)	$1,220,000
- Marital Deduction	(0)
- Charitable Deduction	(0)
Taxable Estate	$1,220,000
+ Post '76 Gifts	0
Tentative Tax Base	**$1,220,000**
Tentative Estate Tax	$433,800
- Applicable Estate Tax Credit	($433,800)
Total Estate Tax Liability	**$0**

By using both the ILIT and his applicable estate tax credit, Mike has been able to reduce the estate taxes paid on the property from $1,088,000 (Scenario 1) to $0 (Scenario 3), a savings of $1,088,000. The percentage of the assets utilized to pay estate taxes is 0 percent. The additional amount that the heirs received is due solely to the estate tax savings resulting from the use of the ILIT and the bypass trust. As these scenarios illustrate, good estate planning can save large amounts of transfer tax dollars. The same result may have been accomplished if Mike's executor had elected to transfer any of Mike's unused estate exemption to Mary (portability).

Reconciliation of Net to Heirs		Change in Net to Heirs Scenario 1 to 3	
Total Estate*	$14,500,000	Scenario 3	$0
Less Funerals	$200,000	Scenario 1 (tax)	$1,088,000
	$14,300,000	Tax Cost	($1,088,000)
Estate Taxes	$0	From ILIT (save)	($600,000)
Net to Heirs	**$14,300,000**	From Bypass Trust	($488,000)
		Total Savings	**($1,088,000)**

* $13,000,000 Assets + $1,500,000 Life Insurance

Reconciliation of Scenario 1 to 3 Estate Tax		
Estate Tax Scenario 1	$1,088,000	
Savings from ILIT	($600,000)	($1,500,000 x 0.40)
Savings from Bypass Trust	($488,000)	($1,220,000 x 0.40)
Estate Tax Scenario 3	**$0**	

KEY TERMS

ABC Trust Arrangement - A common trust arrangement that utilizes a bypass trust (the B Trust), a GPOA Trust (the A Trust), and a QTIP Trust (the C Trust) to provide the necessary support to a surviving spouse while maximizing the use of the decedent's applicable estate tax credit and providing the decedent the ability to determine the ultimate beneficiary of most of his assets at the death of the surviving spouse.

Ascertainable Standard - An objective standard for allowing distributions defined in the Internal Revenue Code as distributions for health, education, maintenance, or support (HEMS).

Bypass Trust (also known as a Credit Shelter Trust or B Trust) - A trust created to ensure that an individual makes use of his applicable estate tax credit.

Estate Trust - A trust which grants the surviving spouse a testamentary general power of appointment over the trust assets. Because of the spouse's general power of appointment over the trust's assets, the fair market value of the trust will be eligible for the unlimited marital deduction at the death of the first-to-die spouse.

General Power of Appointment Trust (A Trust) - An irrevocable trust that can be created either during an individual's lifetime or at an individual's death that gives the agent the right to appoint the settlor's assets.

Overqualified - A decedent's taxable base is less than the applicable estate tax credit equivalency because too many assets have passed to a surviving spouse.

Portability - The ability of the executor of an estate to timely file Form 706 to transfer the decedent's unused credit exclusion to the surviving spouse.

Privity - The prohibition of a surviving spouse transferring his or her inherited or donated unused exemption amount to his or her next spouse at the surviving spouse's death. The privity requirement prohibits the accumulation of exemptions through remarriage.

Qualified Domestic Trust (QDOT) - A trust created for the benefit of a non-citizen spouse which has enough transfer stipulations to allow the U.S. government to subject assets remaining at the death of the non-citizen surviving spouse, as well as distributions of principal, to estate taxation. Assets transferred to a QDOT qualify for the unlimited marital deduction.

Qualified Terminable Interest Property Trust (QTIP Trust or C Trust) - A trust which allows a decedent to qualify a transfer for the marital deduction at his death yet still control the ultimate disposition of the property.

Survivorship Clause - A clause included in a will requiring that the legatee survive for a specific period in order to inherit under the will. The bequest will qualify for the marital deduction if the property transfers to the surviving spouse and the time period of the survivorship clause is six months or less.

Terminable Interest - An interest that terminates at some point.

Underqualified - When too much of a decedent's property is subject to estate tax at the death of the first spouse due to improper use of the unlimited marital deduction.

Unlimited Marital Deduction - Because a married couple is viewed as one single economic unit for estate and gift tax purposes, an individual receives a deduction from his gross gifts or from the adjusted gross estate for transfers to a spouse. Hence, transfers to a spouse are not subject to estate or gift tax.

DISCUSSION QUESTIONS

SOLUTIONS to the discussion questions can be found exclusively within the chapter. Once you have completed an initial reading of the chapter, go back and highlight the answers to these questions.

1. Explain the theory behind the unlimited marital deduction.

2. List three benefits of the unlimited marital deduction.

3. Discuss the following statement: "The use of the unlimited marital deduction does not avoid estate tax, it merely postpones it."

4. List the three most common methods of leaving property to a spouse and qualifying the transfer for the marital deduction.

5. What are the three requirements for a transfer of property to qualify for the unlimited marital deduction?

6. Define terminable interest.

7. List the exceptions to the terminable interest rule.

8. Since community property is owned between a married couple, will it receive an automatic allocation of the unlimited marital deduction on the federal estate tax return?

9. Identify the requirements necessary for a General Power of Appointment (GPOA) Trust to qualify for the unlimited marital deduction.

10. Identify the requirements necessary for a QTIP Trust to qualify for the unlimited marital deduction.

11. Discuss the alternatives available for paying the estate taxes incurred at the death of the surviving spouse attributable to the QTIP Trust property.

12. Identify the requirements necessary for a Qualified Domestic Trust (QDOT) to qualify for the unlimited marital deduction.

13. How is a bypass trust used in estate planning?

14. What is a qualified disclaimer and how is it used?

15. Describe how the portability of exemptions works.

chapter 10

MULTIPLE-CHOICE PROBLEMS

A sample of multiple choice problems is provided below. Additional multiple choice problems are available at money-education.com by accessing the Student Practice Portal.

1. Jeremy and Rosa were married forty years ago after meeting on the beaches of Cozumel. Rosa moved to the U.S. with Jeremy, but she never applied for U.S. citizenship. If Jeremy is concerned about using the marital deduction for the fair market value of the property he bequeaths to Rosa, which of the following techniques could he use?
    a. Qualified Terminable Interest Trust (QTIP).
    b. Section 2503(b) Trust.
    c. Section 2503(c) Trust.
    d. Qualified Domestic Trust (QDOT).

2. An executor may elect the unlimited marital deduction for which of the following transfers?
    1. Decedent's will directs the creation of a CRAT and the decedent's nonresident alien spouse is the income beneficiary. The trustee of the CRAT is a citizen of the United Kingdom.
    2. Bequest to U.S. citizen spouse of the right to use property for the remainder of her life. Executor has elected QTIP on the property.
    3. A payment of $650,000 to fulfill a specific bequest to decedent's U.S. citizen spouse. Decedent's spouse became a U.S. citizen two months before the filing of the decedent's estate tax return.
    4. A payment of $250,000 to fulfill a specific bequest to decedent's resident alien spouse.
        a. 2 only.
        b. 2 and 3.
        c. 3 and 4.
        d. 1, 2, and 3.

3. If a decedent bequeaths the outright ownership of his house to his children subject to his wife's right to live in that house for the remainder of her life, which of the following statements is correct?
    a. If the wife disclaims her interest in the house, the house is not included in the decedent's taxable estate.
    b. If the children disclaim their interest in the house, the house will automatically transfer to the decedent's spouse as the life estate beneficiary.
    c. If the decedent's wife is a resident alien of the U.S., a QTIP election over the property will allow a marital deduction equal to the fair market value of the property.
    d. If the executor makes a QTIP election on the house, the house is not included in the decedent's taxable estate.

4. Of Pablo's $10,000,000 federal gross estate, his will includes one specific bequest of $7,500,000 to his wife, Ariana, and directs the debts and other expenses of $1,000,000 to be payable from the residuary of the estate. The residuary heirs are Pablo's children. What is the amount of the marital deduction included on Pablo's federal estate tax return?
   a. $0.
   b. $6,500,000.
   c. $8,500,000.
   d. $7,500,000.

5. Jeff died in the current year. He had inherited the following property from his wife in 1999:

Asset	Fair Market Value at Wife's Date of Death	Fair Market Value at Jeff's Date of Death
Life Estate* in Home	$240,000	$600,000
Cash	$450,000	$250,000
1991 Chevrolet	$14,000	Sold in year 2000
IRA	$380,000	$500,000

   *No QTIP election.

   Considering only the property listed above, what is the value of the property included in Jeff's gross estate?
   a. $250,000.
   b. $704,000.
   c. $750,000.
   d. $1,350,000.

chapter 10

QUICK QUIZ EXPLANATIONS

Quick Quiz 10.1
1. True.
2. False. Transfers to a divorced spouse never qualify for the unlimited marital deduction.
3. True.

Quick Quiz 10.2
1. False. A transfer of property to a surviving spouse as trustee for the benefit of the children will not qualify for the marital deduction. As trustee, the surviving spouse will have a fiduciary duty to the trust beneficiaries, and while he will hold legal title to the trust assets, beneficial title belongs to the beneficiaries. As such, the trust property will not be included in the surviving spouse's estate, and the transfer will not qualify for the marital deduction.
2. True.
3. False. Generally, terminable interests do not qualify for the marital deduction. There are four primary exceptions to this rule: (1) six month survival contingencies; (2) terminable interests over which the surviving spouse has a general power of appointment; (3) QTIP Trusts; and (4) CRTs where the only non-charitable beneficiary is the surviving spouse. To qualify for the marital deduction, one of these four exceptions must be met. The period of time in which a terminable interest terminates is irrelevant.
4. True.

Quick Quiz 10.3
1. True.
2. True.
3. True.

Quick Quiz 10.4
1. True.
2. False. To qualify the trust as a QTIP trust, and obtain a marital deduction in the estate of the first spouse to die, the executor must elect to treat the trust as a QTIP trust, which requires the surviving spouse to include the remaining assets of the QTIP trust in his or her estate when the surviving spouse dies. Despite the terminable interest held by the spouse in the QTIP, the full fair market value of the remaining assets will be included in the surviving spouse's estate at death.
3. True.
4. False. A QTIP election cannot be made to qualify a transfer to a non-U.S. citizen spouse for the unlimited marital deduction. Deferral of estate taxes can be achieved, however, through use of a Qualified Domestic Trust (QDOT) for the benefit of the surviving non-citizen spouse.

QUICK QUIZ EXPLANATIONS

Quick Quiz 10.5
1. True.
2. True.
3. True.

Quick Quiz 10.6
1. False. To be valid, a disclaimer must be made within nine months of the decedent's death.
2. False. When an individual disclaims property, the property will pass in accordance with the terms of the decedent's will, by intestacy, or to the successor beneficiary in a transfer by contract scenario. The disclaimant may not direct the disposition of the property.
3. True.

Quick Quiz 10.7
1. True.
2. False. Bypass trusts are used to hold property that will transfer free of estate tax through use of the applicable estate tax credit.
3. True.

11
LIFE INSURANCE IN ESTATE PLANNING

LEARNING OBJECTIVES

1. Discuss the objective of using life insurance in estate planning.
2. Discuss the advantages of using life insurance in estate planning.
3. Understand the use of life insurance and buy-sell agreements.
4. Recognize the complications for a closely held business upon the death of an owner and the need for buy-sell agreements.
5. Distinguish between the three most common types of buy-sell agreements: cross-purchase agreements, entity agreements, and wait and see agreements.
6. Describe the types of life insurance.
7. Identify the parties to a life insurance policy.
8. Summarize the income tax treatment of life insurance when owned by the insured, when transferred for value, and when transferred or assigned as a gift.
9. Describe the income tax treatment of a modified endowment contract.
10. Explain Section 1035 exchange treatment for life insurance and annuities.
11. Describe a chronically ill individual and a terminally ill individual as these terms relate to qualified viatical settlements and accelerated death benefit clauses.
12. Explain the gift tax treatment of life insurance including valuation.
13. Summarize the estate tax treatment of life insurance on the decedent's life and life insurance owned by the decedent on other person's lives.
14. Describe the three year look back rule.
15. Explain the process of creating an irrevocable life insurance trust.

CFP Board Resource Document - Student-Centered Learning Objectives based upon CFP Board Principal Topics.

INTRODUCTION

One of the great uncertainties in life is that, usually, one does not know exactly when he or she will die. At any point in time, individuals may want to achieve goals and objectives that require financial resources beyond that which they have already accumulated. Life insurance is a tool that can be used to ensure that a person will have the capital to fund all of his important goals, even if he dies before acquiring sufficient resources to fund those goals himself. Viewed in this context, life insurance is a hedge against the untimely death of the income earner and the resulting shortfall of resources that may result from early death.

Many misconceptions surround the use of life insurance, and some individuals engaged in the financial and estate planning process do not fully comprehend the need for life insurance protection. For persons who have modest estates and who have achieved most of their goals during their lifetime (for example, retiring the mortgage on a principal residence, funding their children's education, and saving for an adequate retirement income), large amounts of life insurance may not be necessary. Most individuals, however, should consider using life insurance in their estate plans. For individuals with estates in excess of the applicable estate tax credit equivalency amount ($11,580,000 for 2020), and for individuals who have not accumulated sufficient financial resources to fund all of their estate planning goals, life insurance is an essential part of the estate planning process because it provides estate liquidity and in a timely manner.

chapter 11

OBJECTIVE OF LIFE INSURANCE

Depending upon the goals and current financial situation of the person, life insurance can be used to provide for several personal objectives. Common objectives that can be served by using life insurance include protecting the income stream of the person's family, providing liquidity at the insured's death, providing a source of retirement income, funding the children's education, creating or sustaining family wealth, and funding buy-sell agreements. Keep in mind that while there are no absolutes in financial planning, the general rule with regard to ownership of life insurance is that if the purpose of the life insurance is to provide estate liquidity and benefits to heirs, the insured need not own the policies. If on the other hand, life insurance is intended to be used during the insured's life for education or retirement (by accessing policy cash values generally through loans), the insured will need to own the policy, thus causing inclusion of any death benefit in the insured's gross estate at death.

Protect Income Stream for Beneficiaries

One of the most important issues that an individual faces in the estate planning process is ensuring that surviving family members have an adequate income stream to maintain their standard of living. This need is particularly acute for young individuals who have not had time to accumulate a significant estate and for individuals who are the sole breadwinner of their family.

> **Key Concepts**
>
> 1. What are the common objectives of life insurance?
> 2. Identify the four main types of life insurance policies and their characteristics.
> 3. Identify and define the parties to a life insurance contract.

Several issues should be considered when funding this goal of income stream protection. The most obvious is the need to replace the lost income stream due to the death of one spouse. Even where both spouses are working, the loss of one income stream can present a significant financial hardship on the family. Expenses beyond normal recurring expenses may be incurred by the surviving spouse, particularly when children are still at home, since the decedent's domestic services will no longer be available to the family. In determining the appropriate dollar amount of life insurance to carry, consider the amount of income needed on an inflation-adjusted basis to allow the surviving spouse and any dependent children to maintain their current standard of living.

The amount of life insurance necessary to adequately insure a person may be determined using a needs analysis, a human value method, or a capitalized income model. The needs approach and human value approach are covered in insurance textbooks. The capitalized income approach is fairly straightforward and is calculated as follows.

$$\text{Life insurance needed} = \frac{\text{Gross income - Adjustments}}{\text{Riskless rate adjusted for inflation}}$$

Example 11.1

Jack, age 40, makes $100,000 per year of which 30% represents taxes. Jack personally consumes 20% of the remainder. Jack is married to Jill, age 40, who has no investment experience. They have three small children. The current and projected long-term Treasury Bond is returning 6% and inflation is projected to be 2.5%.

$$\frac{\$100{,}000 - 30\%\,(\$100{,}000) - 20\%\,(\$70{,}000)}{(1.06/1.025) - 1} = \frac{\$56{,}000}{0.03415 \text{ (rounded)}} = \$1{,}639{,}824$$

The amount of life insurance needed to fully insure Jack's life is estimated to be $1,639,824 producing perpetual income at the riskless rate (Treasury bond) of $93,389 in the initial year following death. Jill would then spend ($56,000 x 1.025%) $57,400 in the first year and reinvest the $40,989 back into principal leaving her with a riskless inflation adjusted annuity equal to $56,000 (as indexed for inflation).

The amount of annual income a family needs may include allowances for day-to-day spending, maintaining mortgage payments and real estate taxes on family residences, credit card and consumer loan payments, and primary and secondary school tuition payments for the children. Note that some of these expenses could be relieved at the death of the first spouse by ensuring that the death benefit is sufficiently large to allow the payment of the decedent's outstanding debts including any mortgage.

Example 11.2

David, a 42-year old father of three, recently died. He was married to Martha, age 39. All of their children are under age 18. Upon the birth of their third child, David and Martha purchased a new home. The home was worth $350,000 when David died, and the outstanding mortgage balance was $225,000. Monthly payments on the mortgage were $1,900. As part of his estate plan, David purchased a life insurance policy to ensure his family would have enough money in the event of his untimely death. David purchased enough insurance so that if he died, the mortgage on the house could be paid off in full. As a result of the mortgage being paid off, Martha's monthly expenses have declined by $1,900.

One benefit of paying off outstanding debts at the death of the first spouse is that the surviving spouse will not have the burden of servicing the outstanding debt. This strategy may be particularly helpful if the surviving spouse is not skilled at managing finances.

A Source of Funds for Education

One of the family objectives most frequently cited in the financial planning process is a desire to assist children in obtaining a college education. The extent of desired funding for this goal may differ from client to client, but it is not uncommon for parents to want to provide their children with a college education.

Assuming that the client will live beyond the children's graduation from college, a funding plan can be established that calls for saving a specific amount on a monthly or annual basis. Since most individuals do not immediately have the resources to set aside a lump sum to cover the total for educational costs, the untimely death of the client may result in a shortfall in educational funding. Life insurance can be used in the estate planning process to ensure that the desired level of funding for education is available. This illustrates the need to coordinate estate planning with the traditional lifetime financial planning needs of the client.

Provide Liquidity at Death

One of the classic reasons for using life insurance in an estate plan is to create immediate liquidity at the decedent's death. If the decedent was the primary breadwinner of the family, this is particularly important to the survivors.

Depending upon the structure of the estate plan, there may be a time delay in transferring assets to family members. For example, if the decedent's property is being transferred via the probate process, months may pass before the probate property is made available to the family. During this period, the family will need money to pay the mortgage, buy clothes for the children, pay school tuition, and possibly, if the surviving spouse is not working, provide for living expenses. The funeral expenses of the decedent must be paid (usually before the funeral), as well as any outstanding medical and hospital bills incurred during the decedent's last illness. It may be either desired or advantageous to provide sufficient liquidity at death to pay off all outstanding liabilities, such as any mortgage on the residence, credit card debt, and consumer loans. When these debts are extinguished quickly after the decedent's death, the administration of the estate often moves faster and the surviving spouse is no longer burdened with the monthly task of servicing the debt, allowing him or her to focus on caring for the family.

For individuals with large estates or closely held businesses, liquidity may be essential to provide the funds for the payment of estate and inheritance taxes. Federal estate taxes are due nine months after a person's death. Most states have a similar time frame for the payment of state estate or inheritance tax. Because the federal tax, if due, tends to be large, it is not always easy to pay that tax from the decedent's assets without having to sell assets. In the case of having to sell a closely held business owner, this could be fatal. If the business is sold quickly in a "fire-sale" fashion, the family may realize far less than the fair market value of the business. An effective solution to this problem is to purchase life insurance coverage sufficient to cover not only the debts of the decedent and the cash flow needs of the family immediately after death, but also any expected estate taxes that will be due within nine months. If the individual has partners, he may wish to have a buy-sell agreement with the partners that is funded with insurance. A buy-sell agreement allows the parties to require the surviving partners to buy out the deceased partner's share and is generally funded with life insurance. Ensuring that the cash is available to cover all of these expenses will allow a more orderly administration of the estate and a more efficient disposition of the decedent's assets. Insurance to be used for paying estate taxes is usually placed in an irrevocable life insurance trust (ILIT) so that there are no transfer taxes on the proceeds. ILIT's are discussed in more detail later in this chapter.

A Source for Retirement Income

In addition to the income stream for survivors, educational needs of children, and liquidity needs of the estate are provided for, there may still be a need for additional income for the surviving spouse. Life insurance can provide a lump-sum dollar amount at death that will satisfy the needed capital to provide income for the surviving spouse.

In constructing a financial plan for a client, a central issue typically addressed is providing for an adequate retirement income for the client and his spouse. Usually, a plan is established where the client saves a specific dollar amount on a weekly, monthly, or annual basis that will, when combined with future investment earnings, provide for the desired level of retirement income. If an individual dies before this goal is fully funded, a shortfall may result for the surviving spouse. Life insurance can provide a lump sum that can be set aside to make up for the loss of annual contributions by the deceased spouse, providing financial security for the surviving spouse.

If life insurance is purchased to fund the client's financial and estate planning objectives, it may also be useful for funding retirement needs even if a death does not occur before retirement. When a cash-value life insurance policy is purchased, and the premium is paid on a regular basis, and the life insurance cash value grows over time. If by the time the client retires, the mortgage on the home has been paid off, the children's education has been paid for, and an adequate retirement income has been funded, the death benefit of the life insurance policy may be more than necessary to fund remaining liquidity needs. In this case, the owner of the policy could take tax-free distributions up to his adjusted basis in the life insurance policy by taking loans from the cash value of the life insurance policy to supplement retirement income. If the client's estate will not have significant liquidity needs at death, the policy could be surrendered. The surrender of a life insurance policy will subject any gain in excess of the adjusted basis in the policy to ordinary income taxation, but the proceeds could be used to supplement retirement income.

Keep in mind, that if the client wants control over loans or access to cash values during life to fund education or retirement needs, the client must own the life insurance policy. For estate planning purposes of income replacement for survivors and estate liquidity, the client generally will not want ownership of the life insurance policy because such ownership will cause inclusion of the proceeds in the decedent's gross estate.

To Create or Sustain Family Wealth

Some individuals have estate planning objectives that are beyond providing for their individual needs and the needs of their children. Individuals who tend to think of wealth maximization for the family in the long-run may wish to create pools of capital that can be used by future family members such as grandchildren, great-grandchildren, and so on. Some common examples of planning techniques for these individuals include the use of dynasty trusts, Generation-Skipping Trusts, and foundations (all of these techniques are covered elsewhere in this book). A significant amount of capital may be needed to ensure that these arrangements can be created to benefit future generations of the family.

Quick Quiz 11.1

1. Life insurance is often used in educational funding plans.
   a. True
   b. False

2. A whole life insurance policy is a life insurance contract that does not accumulate cash value and states that if the insured dies within the term of the contract, the insurance company will pay the stated death benefit.
   a. True
   b. False

3. Generally, as an individual gets older, the mortality cost of a term life insurance policy increases.
   a. True
   b. False

4. A term life insurance policy is more appropriate for short-term needs than a whole life insurance policy.
   a. True
   b. False

5. The insured is the person whose life is covered by the life insurance policy.
   a. True
   b. False

True, False, True, True, True.

Life insurance may be the ideal funding arrangement for individuals with these types of goals. Even if an individual has not yet accumulated a large net worth, long-range goals could be funded appropriately as long as there is sufficient income to pay the life insurance premiums. When the client dies, the life insurance company will pay the death benefit to the accumulation vehicle (usually a trust) and the client's long-range objectives can be satisfied. Some individuals feel that life insurance is the best way to fund these vehicles, since all of the client's assets, aside from those used to pay the life insurance premiums, are available for use of the client and his or her family during their lifetime, and the life insurance death benefit will "create" the wealth necessary to satisfy the long-run client objectives at death.

Life insurance also presents an opportunity for wealthy individuals and families to sustain family wealth. For example, assume that as part of his estate planning, a grandparent created a dynasty trust for his family. Throughout the lifetime of the beneficiaries, the dynasty trustee distributes some of the income and assets of the trust to the family members. If the trustee had purchased a life insurance policy on the life of each beneficiary of the trust, upon the death of each beneficiary the trust would receive a capital infusion that may partially or wholly reimburse the trust for the distributions made to that beneficiary during his lifetime. When used in this way, life insurance ensures that current generations of the family enjoy the family's accumulated wealth without depriving future generations of the family of that wealth.

To Fund Buy-Sell Agreements

Closely-held business interests often represent a considerable portion of business owner's net worth and gross estate at the death of the owner. These business interests are generally illiquid, which creates a need for liquidity within the estate and often for a surviving spouse. Life insurance can be used to fund buy-sell agreements for closely held and family-owned business owners. While a complete discussion of buy-sell agreements and their tax consequences is beyond the scope of this chapter, an overview of this common planning technique is warranted.

Buy-sell agreements are legal arrangements that require the sale of securities owned by one individual to another individual or entity upon a specified triggering event. Buy-sell agreements are commonly used by business owners to plan for the orderly transfer and control of a business interest, to create a market for stock that is not traded on securities exchanges, and to plan for liquidity in the estate of a deceased business owner.

The most common triggering event that invokes obligations under a buy-sell agreement is the death of the business owner. A properly structured buy-sell agreement requires the estate of the business owner to sell the decedent's business interest to another entity or person, who is often a family member or close business associate of the decedent. Since an obligation to purchase a business interest is triggered at the death of the owner, life insurance is an ideal funding vehicle for buy-sell agreements triggered at death. Typically, either the business itself, or the individual or entity who is obligated to purchase the decedent's business interest will hold a life insurance policy on the decedent's life that has a death benefit sufficient to cover the purchase price of the decedent's business interest.

Key Concepts

1. Highlight the parties to an entity agreement versus a cross-purchase agreement.
2. Distinguish between an entity agreement, a cross-purchase agreement, and wait-and-see buy-sell agreement.
3. Explain why life insurance is a perfect hedge for buy-sell agreements that are triggered on the death of the owner.

Other triggering events for buy-sell agreements include disability, divorce, retirement, and withdrawal from the business, but a full discussion of these is beyond the scope of this chapter.

Buy-sell agreements generally are of one of three types:
- entity purchase (sometimes referred to as redemption agreements)
- cross-purchase agreements
- wait-and-see agreements

Entity (Redemption) Agreements

The simplest form of buy-sell agreement is the **entity purchase**, or redemption, agreement. This type of buy-sell agreement obligates the business entity to purchase an owner's interest in the entity upon that owner's death. This type of buy-sell agreement works well for organizations that have a separate legal existence from their owners but would not be appropriate for a sole proprietorship. Sole proprietorships are wholly owned by one person, and when that person dies, so does the proprietorship. The business of a sole proprietor may be transferred to another person or entity at the death of the sole proprietorship through a cross-purchase agreement (discussed below), but the proprietorship cannot purchase itself.

Example 11.3

Cecil is part owner of a luxury resort hotel, Fawlty Towers. Fawlty Towers is organized as a C corporation, and the corporation is wholly owned by members of Cecil's family. To ensure that the ownership of the hotel stays within the family and to make sure that Cecil's estate has sufficient liquidity to cover its expenses at his death, Cecil enters into a buy-sell agreement with Fawlty Towers, Inc. whereby Cecil (through his estate) agrees to sell, and Fawlty Towers agrees to purchase his stock when he dies. The agreement between Cecil and Fawlty Towers is an entity purchase buy-sell agreement.

To fund the purchase obligation under an entity-purchase buy-sell agreement, the business can acquire a life insurance policy on the owner's life with a death benefit sufficient to cover the purchase amount. Life insurance is an ideal vehicle to use for this purpose, since it provides funds at the exact time they are needed (the death of the insured). Furthermore, using the death benefit to meet the purchase obligation under the buy-sell agreement does not affect cash holdings or other assets that the company may need for continued business operations.

What type of life insurance policy should be purchased to fund the buy-sell agreement? The answer, of course, depends on the facts. If the business is family owned, and the owner of the interest is a family member, or if there has been a long-term relationship between the owner and the business with no definitive date when that relationship will end (such as a retirement date), a permanent life insurance policy should be considered. Permanent life insurance costs more up front but provides protection for longer periods of time with guarantees from the insurance company. Using term life, universal life, or variable universal life may be risky, since those policies will only remain in force as long as there is money to pay premiums or in the policy cash value to pay the annual mortality and expense charges. Permanent life insurance guarantees that the money needed to buy the business interest will be there no matter how long the owner lives or continues to be involved in the operation of the business activity.

Disadvantages
While entity buy-sell agreements have the advantage of simplicity, there is at least one disadvantage to using this structure.

If an entity buy-sell agreement is used, and the surviving owners plan to sell their business interests after the death of the first owner but prior to their own deaths, the entity buy-sell agreement will increase their taxable gain upon sale of their interests. Of course, this would not be an issue for family businesses that are not sold during the lifetimes of the family members. This first disadvantage of entity buy-sell agreements is easily remedied by using a cross-purchase buy-sell agreement.

Cross-Purchase Agreements
A **cross-purchase buy-sell agreement** is an arrangement between individuals who agree to purchase the business interest of a deceased owner. Unlike an entity-type agreement, which involves the business itself, a cross-purchase agreement only involves the owners of the business.

Example 11.4
Cecil and his sister, Sybil, are equal owners of a luxury resort hotel, Fawlty Towers. Fawlty Towers is organized as a C corporation, and the corporation has been wholly owned by members of Cecil & Sybil's family since it began. Neither Cecil nor Sybil are married, and neither has any children. To ensure that the ownership of the hotel stays within the family, and to make sure that their estates have sufficient liquidity to cover expenses at death, Cecil and Sybil enter into a buy-sell agreement whereby the first sibling to die agrees to sell (through her estate), and the surviving sibling agrees to purchase the decedent's interest when she dies. The agreement between Cecil and Sybil is a cross-purchase buy-sell agreement.

To fund a cross-purchase buy-sell agreement with life insurance, each party to the agreement purchases a life insurance policy on the life of all of the other parties to the agreement so that the death benefit is sufficient to purchase the interest of any deceased owner. If there are only two parties, this approach is relatively straightforward – each party purchases one policy on the life of the other. When more than two owners are involved, however, things can get complicated, and as the number of owners grows, so does the complexity of the arrangement and the number of life insurance policies that must be purchased.

Example 11.5
Bertie, Claude, and Eustice are equal owners of Wooster Enterprises, Ltd. They have entered into a cross-purchase buy-sell agreement triggered upon death. If Bertie dies first, his 1/3 interest would have to be purchased by Claude and Eustis in equal shares. To fund the agreement, both Claude and Eustice should purchase a life insurance policy on Bertie's life that will pay a death benefit equal to 1/6 (1/3 x 1/2) of the value of the company. Bertie and Claude should each purchase a life insurance policy on Eustice's life for the same amount (in case Eustice dies first), and Eustice and Bertie should purchase a life insurance policy on Claude's life in case Claude dies first. As this example illustrates, for a three-owner agreement, six life insurance policies would have to be purchased to fund this buy-sell agreement.

The number of cross purchase policies needed to fully fund the buy-sell agreement can be calculated by using the formula:

$$\text{Number of policies} = N(N-1)$$

Where N = the number of owners subject to the agreement. The greater the number of owners, the greater the number of life insurance policies that should be purchased. For example, four owners would require twelve policies or 4(4-1).

While applying for a large number of life insurance policies does somewhat complicate the administration of a cross-purchase agreement, the real issues emerge in the annual maintenance of the agreement. Each year, each of the owners will pay the premiums on policies they own covering the lives of other owners in order to keep those policies in force. If just one owner fails to pay the premium and another owner dies, the benefits of entering into the buy-sell agreement may be in jeopardy.

An entity agreement is a simple arrangement in which only one policy is purchased on the life of each owner and the premiums are paid by the entity. A cross-purchase agreement is much more complex than an entity agreement.

One of the advantages to a cross-purchase agreement is the ability to increase the surviving owner's basis in his or her shares of the business entity. When life insurance death benefits are received (on a tax-free basis), and are used to purchase the business interest of a deceased owner, each surviving owner's share of the business increases, but so does his or her basis in the business entity. Basis is that portion of the sale proceeds not subject to income tax, so a higher basis results in a higher after-tax benefit to the taxpayer. This benefit is unavailable with entity buy-sell agreements and is often the reason that financial advisors prefer cross-purchase arrangements.

Example 11.6

Bertie, Claude, and Eustice are equal owners of Wooster Enterprises, Ltd. The adjusted basis for each 1/3 interest is $100,000. They have entered into a cross-purchase buy-sell agreement triggered upon death. Bertie passed away, and his 1/3 interest in Wooster enterprises was valued at $334,000. The entire business was worth $1 million, leaving $333,000 each for Claude and Eustice. As specified in the buy-sell agreement, Claude and Eustice each purchase half of Bertie's 1/3 interest in Wooster Enterprise, Ltd. for $167,000. After the purchase, Claude's and Eustice's ownership percentages increased from 33% to 50%. Their basis in the ownership interests increased from $100,000 to $267,000 each ($100,000 original adjusted basis + $167,000 paid for acquisition of the interest from Bertie's estate). If Claude and Eustice immediately sold Wooster Enterprises, Ltd. for $1 million, each of them would receive $500,000 (1/2 the proceeds) and would have to pay income tax on a capital gain of $233,000 ($500,000 amount realized - $267,000 adjusted basis).

How would this result differ if the buy-sell agreement was structured as an entity buy-sell, and Claude and Eustice sold the business after Bertie died? As described above, Claude and Eustice would each receive $500,000 (1/2 the proceeds) but would have to pay income tax on a capital gain of $400,000 ($500,000 amount realized - $100,000 adjusted basis). In this instance, the basis of the surviving shareholders is not affected because the corporation, not the individual shareholders, purchased the shares from Bertie's estate.

Cross-purchase agreements are typically preferred from a tax planning standpoint because:
1. they permit the surviving shareholders to increase their basis in the business interest;
2. the death benefit on life insurance owned by individuals is not subject to the possible imposition of the alternative minimum tax; and
3. life insurance owned by business owners outside of a corporation does not trigger any potential accumulated earnings tax.

Wait-and-See Buy-Sell Agreements

Wait-and-see buy-sell agreements are a cross between entity and cross purchase buy-sell agreements. Using this approach, the business has the first option to purchase the interest of a deceased owner. If the business entity chooses not to purchase the interest, the surviving owners of the company are given the opportunity to purchase the deceased owner's interest in proportion to his or her ownership interest. If the surviving owners do not exercise their right to purchase the interest, any interest remaining is purchased by the business.

By giving both the company and the owners the right to purchase an interest, the wait-and-see buy-sell maintains flexibility between the simplicity of the entity agreement and the tax advantages of the cross-purchase agreement. Both the company and the surviving owners can assess their respective situations when the death of an owner occurs and act in a way that maximizes their combined benefits.

Wait-and-see buy-sell agreements are very useful for C corporations with large amounts of retained earnings. When retained earnings are distributed to shareholders, they are usually treated as dividend distributions and are subject to income tax. If a corporation redeems shares from the estate of a deceased owner, and the redemption does not exceed the estate and inheritance taxes plus funeral expenses incurred by the deceased owner's estate, the redemption is typically exempt from income tax. This approach results in a reduction in retained earnings at the corporate level (IRC Sec. 303). The reduction in retained earnings reduces the amount of future corporate distributions that are subject to taxes as dividends, which is a significant benefit for C corporations and their surviving shareholders. Under a wait-and-see buy-sell agreement, the corporation will typically exercise its first option to purchase the number of shares necessary to effectuate a Sec. 303 redemption (thereby reducing its retained earnings) and give the surviving shareholders the option to purchase the remaining interest. If the surviving shareholders exercise this option, they will receive an increase in their basis in the business interest, which will reduce their taxable gain in the business entity should they decide to sell their interests before their deaths.

> ### Quick Quiz 11.2
> 1. A cross purchase agreement will increase the income tax basis of survivors/owners.
>   a. True
>   b. False
> 2. The number of policies for 5 equal partners in an entity approach to buy/sell is 20.
>   a. True
>   b. False
> 3. The number of policies for 5 equal partners in cross-purchase arrangement to buy/sell is 20.
>   a. True
>   b. False
>
> True, False, True.

While wait-and-see buy-sell agreements are often used for C corporations, they are not frequently used for S corporations, partnerships, limited liability companies, or limited liability partnerships. Only C corporations issue taxable dividends, so the tax features of the wait-and-see buy-sell agreements are applicable only to C corporations. Wait-and-see buy-sell agreements could still be used with other types of business entities if the primary objective is to maintain flexibility in the repurchase of interests.

Life Insurance is the Perfect Hedge for a Buy-Sell Agreement Triggered at Death

As illustrated in the discussion above, life insurance is a perfect hedge for buy-sell agreements that are triggered on the death of the owner. If life insurance is purchased on the owner's life, the proceeds can be used to purchase the business interest from the decedent owner's estate. This facilitates effective transfer of ownership and control of the business entity and provides liquidity for the deceased owner's estate so that estate and inheritance taxes, funeral expenses, and end-of-life medical care costs can be paid.

Exhibit 11.1 | Objectives of Life Insurance

- Protect income stream for beneficiaries.
- Source of funds for education.
- Provide liquidity at death.
- Source for retirement income.
- Create or sustain family wealth.
- Fund buy-sell agreements.

TYPES OF LIFE INSURANCE

Several types of life insurance policies exist in the market today. Many contracts have unique features that may prove valuable in a given planning situation. It is important to remember, however, that life insurance is not a one-size-fits-all product. What works for one client's plan may not be the best solution for another client. The planner should always try to fit the characteristics of the contract to the planning issues being addressed. The basic types of life insurance are summarized below.

Term Insurance

A **term insurance policy** is a life insurance contract that states if the insured dies within the term of the contract, the insurance company will pay the stated death benefit. The premium on a term insurance policy reflects the actuarial risk that the insured will die during the term of the contract. Some commentators refer to the premium on a term insurance policy as the "pure cost of life insurance protection" since none of the premium dollars are allocated to a savings account (as is the case in universal life, whole life, and variable universal life insurance policies).

The premium on a term insurance policy will likely be significantly lower than the alternative permanent policies available, since there is no cash accumulation account to be funded. This may be advantageous in certain circumstances. For example, a young individual who has not had time to accumulate much wealth may need a large amount of life insurance protection to provide an income stream for the surviving spouse, pay off the mortgage on the principal residence, pay for children's education, and so on. Because the individual is young, however, the pure cost of insurance is low, which allows him or her to purchase the necessary coverage at a relatively reasonable cost. As the client's income increases and the needs being funded by the life insurance become more permanent (for example, liquidity to pay death taxes), the term insurance contract may be converted to a permanent type of policy.

One point of caution should be noted, however. Many individuals have been taught that "buying term and investing the difference" is always an optimal strategy. This is not the case. When an individual has a permanent need for life insurance protection, buying term and investing the difference can be a disaster. As the individual gets older, the pure cost of the insurance protection (the premium on a term policy) increases exponentially. At advanced ages, the annual cost of the insurance policy may be prohibitive and if the premium is not paid, the policy will lapse. With life expectancies increasing, this may prove to be a significant problem. When choosing the most appropriate policy, consider the use of permanent insurance for permanent needs.

Term insurance is appropriate for funding temporary needs. For example, a young couple who wishes to ensure that there will be sufficient money to send the children to college in the event of their premature death could purchase a term insurance policy to cover this need (perhaps a 30 year level term insurance contract). Once the children graduate from college, the need for the insurance disappears and the policy can be canceled. Term insurance may also be useful as a hedge when engaging in sophisticated estate planning involving the use of GRATs, GRUTs, QPRTs, and other transfers that may result in estate tax inclusion. All of these techniques pose a risk of estate tax inclusion for a period of time and term insurance can be purchased to cover the estate taxes due in the event that the insured dies before the transfers are complete for estate planning purposes.

Universal Life

Universal life insurance is, in essence, a term insurance policy with a cash accumulation account attached to it. One of the advantages of universal life insurance is that the premium is flexible – if the owner of the policy has extra income in a particular year, he can make additional contributions to the policy. If money is tight in another year, no premium has to be paid as long as there is enough in the cash accumulation account to pay that year's premium. All of the premiums paid go into the cash accumulation account, and each month or year the insurance company will take the pure cost of insurance protection out of the cash value. As long as there is sufficient money in the cash account to pay the current year premium, the policy remains in force. The money inside of the cash accumulation account grows on a tax-deferred basis depending on the investment returns.

Like a term insurance policy, the pure cost to maintain the policy increases as the insured's age increases. The insurer typically does not guarantee that the universal life policy will remain in force as long as a certain premium is paid. Instead, the policy will remain in force only as long as there is enough cash in the accumulation account to pay the increasing pure insurance premium. This type of policy is probably best suited to cover temporary needs and a permanent type of life insurance protection should be used when the client's need for life insurance is permanent.

Variable Universal Life

Variable universal life insurance policies are simply universal life insurance policies (described above) with one added feature – the insured can choose how to invest the cash in the cash accumulation account. Usually, the insurer will offer several different investment choices in the form of mutual funds including equity funds, bond funds, and money market funds. Variable universal life insurance policies do not provide guarantees like whole life policies do, and will remain in force only as long as there is sufficient value in the investment account to pay the annual pure insurance premium. Variable universal life insurance policies are a good option for younger clients with a higher risk tolerance for investments, since the accumulation of funds inside of the policy over the long-run can be significant.

Whole Life

Whole life insurance provides guarantees from the insurer that are not found in term insurance and universal life insurance contracts. As long as the insured pays a stated premium each year, the insurer guarantees that the life insurance policy will remain in force. Part of each premium is allocated to a cash savings account that will grow over time. The cash that is accumulating in the contract is used to pay the higher costs of life insurance protection when the insured reaches advanced ages. Even if the cash account runs out, the life insurance is guaranteed to remain in force provided that the insured pays the premium. Whole life insurance policies are useful when the client wants such guarantees, and for middle-aged and older clients who are obtaining life insurance protection. The cash value of a whole life policy is invested by the insurer and usually has a minimum guaranteed return.

Second-to-Die

A second-to-die policy has two insureds, and may be issued as a permanent (cash value) policy, or a term policy. The advantage of a second-to-die policy is that one of the parties (usually spouses) may be uninsurable, but the insurance company will still issue the policy since the policy pays the death benefit at the death of the second spouse. Usually the objective of second-to-die insurance is to provide estate liquidity to pay estate taxes at the death of the second spouse. Consequently, a second-to-die policy is usually owned by an irrevocable life insurance trust (ILIT).

Exhibit 11.2 | Types of Life Insurance

- Term
- Universal Life
- Variable Universal Life
- Whole Life
- Second-to-Die

PARTIES TO A LIFE INSURANCE POLICY

Before examining the tax consequences of holding life insurance, it is important to distinguish between the owner of the policy, the insured of the policy, and the beneficiary of the policy. It is possible that different people will occupy each of these positions for a single life insurance policy. The tax ramifications of policy ownership are often dependent on the identification of the parties to the life insurance policy.

Owner

The **owner** of the policy is the person who has title to the contract. The owner may or may not be the insured, and may or may not be the beneficiary. The owner is the person who can exercise control over the economic rights of the policy. For example, the owner can borrow from the cash value of the policy, can pledge the policy for a loan, and can increase or decrease the premium payments made on the policy (depending upon the type of policy and the current funding status).

Insured

The **insured** is the person whose life is insured by the contract. When the insured dies, the life insurance company will pay the death benefit to the beneficiary named in the policy.

Beneficiary

The **beneficiary** is the person entitled to receive the death benefit once the insured dies. The owner of the life insurance policy can designate the beneficiary on a form provided by the life insurance company. In the event that no beneficiary is named, the owner of the policy will receive the death benefit. In the event that the owner of the policy was also the insured, the owner's estate will receive the death benefit. It is always advantageous to make sure that beneficiary designations are on file with the insurance company and that the appropriate party is named as the beneficiary. When there is a named beneficiary for the life insurance policy, the death benefit will avoid probate and will generally avoid income taxation.

Exhibit 11.3 | Parties to a Life Insurance Policy

Owner - the person who has title to the contract.
Insured - the person whose life is insured by the contract.
Beneficiary - the person entitled to receive the death benefit once the insured dies.

INCOME TAX TREATMENT OF LIFE INSURANCE

General Approach

Internal Revenue Code (IRC) Section 61(a)(10) states that "income from life insurance and endowment contracts" is subject to income tax. For federal income tax purposes, any accretion to wealth constitutes taxable income and a life insurance contract results in an accretion to wealth for the beneficiary of the policy. Absent a provision to the contrary, therefore, the death benefit of a life insurance contract would be taxable to the beneficiary of the policy.

> **Key Concepts**
>
> 1. What is the general rule regarding the income tax treatment of life insurance?
> 2. What is the transfer-for-value rule?
> 3. What are the settlement options available to beneficiaries of a life insurance policy?

Section 101(a) of the Code provides an exception that states "Except as otherwise provided...gross income does not include amounts received (whether in a single sum or otherwise) under a life insurance contract, if such amounts are paid by reason of the death of the insured." Therefore, as a general rule, the death benefit paid on a life insurance policy will escape income taxation in the hands of the beneficiary. The transfer-for-value rule is the only exception to this general rule.

Transfer for Value

While the death benefit on a life insurance policy is not typically subject to income taxation, the death benefit in excess of the transferee's adjusted basis will be subject to income tax if the life insurance policy is transferred for valuable consideration (The Transfer for Value Rule).

The condition that subjects the policy death benefit subject to tax is a **transfer for value**. The life insurance policy must be exchanged for valuable consideration in order for the transfer-for-value rule to apply. Consider the following examples:

Example 11.7

Five years ago, Mila purchased a life insurance policy on her life and named herself as the owner and beneficiary of the policy. She recently learned that the death benefit will be subject to estate taxation, since she is both the insured and the owner of the policy. To avoid estate taxation of the death benefit, Mila gave the policy to her spouse, Milan, who is now listed as the sole owner and beneficiary of the contract. When Mila dies, Milan will not have to pay income tax on the death benefit because Mila made a gratuitous transfer of the policy to Milan; she did not give Milan the policy in return for valuable consideration.

Example 11.8

Jessie has had a very bad year. His spouse, Finley, left him and took everything he owned except for a life insurance policy he has on Finley's life. The life insurance policy has a cash value of $50,000 and a death benefit of $500,000. Jessie owes Margie, the meanest banker in town, $200,000. Jessie has considered filing for bankruptcy. During a recent meeting, Margie discovered that Jessie had the insurance policy and offered to forgive the debt he owed her in exchange for the policy. Margie's reasoning was that the $50,000 cash value was better than nothing and she might hang on to the policy until Finley died to receive the death benefit. Jessie happily agreed to the exchange. This exchange is an example of a transfer for value because the policy was exchanged for extinguishment of debt. Margie will have an adjusted basis in the policy of $200,000 (the amount of debt forgiven). If she were to cash in the policy today she would have a $150,000 loss and if she waits until the death benefit is paid she will have a taxable gain of $300,000.

Example 11.9

John, Randy, Tom, and Keegan are partners in the XYZ partnership. They decide to enter into a cross-purchase buy-sell agreement to ensure that their families will receive full value for their partnership interest when they die. Under a cross-purchase agreement, they will each have to purchase a policy on everyone else's life, requiring a total of 12 life insurance policies. To simplify the arrangement, they decide to create a trust that will hold one life insurance policy on each partner's life. As each partner dies, the trust will purchase the deceased partner's business interest with the life insurance proceeds. When the first partner dies, everything works as planned, with one exception. A transfer for value has occurred, since the ownership of the remaining three policies on the lives of the survivors has shifted from 4 partners to three. Initially, each partner owned (indirectly) 25% of each policy, but after the first death, each of the surviving partners owns 33% of each policy. This was not a gratuitous transfer, but rather a transfer for valuable consideration because there was an economic reason behind the buy-sell agreement.

Even if the transfer-for-value rule applies, certain exceptions to the rule will prevent the death benefit in the policy from being subject to income tax. Alternatively stated, if an exception to the transfer-for-value rule applies, we go back to the general rule that states that the death benefit paid by reason of the insured's death is not subject to income tax. IRC Section 101(a)(2) states that the transfer-for-value rule will not apply when there is a transfer of a life insurance policy to any of the following individuals:
1. the insured
2. a partner of the insured
3. a partnership in which the insured is a partner
4. a corporation in which the insured is a shareholder or officer
5. a transferee who takes the transferor's basis in the contract

Therefore, when planning a transaction that could be considered a transfer for value, it is important to structure the transaction so that it meets an exception to the transfer-for-value rule so that the death benefit will not be subject to income taxation. Consider the following examples:

Example 11.10
Randy is a key employee at a large international manufacturing company. The company purchased a life insurance policy on Randy's life several years ago to provide compensation to the company for the loss of Randy's services in the event of his early death. Randy is retiring this month and the company no longer needs the life insurance policy on Randy's life. Randy, however, could use the policy for estate planning purposes. The value of the policy is $65,000. If Randy purchases the policy from the company for $65,000, a transfer for value has occurred, but the death benefit will not be subject to income tax because the life insurance policy was transferred for valuable consideration to the insured.

Example 11.11
Assume the same facts as above, except that instead of purchasing the policy himself, Randy has the trustee of an irrevocable grantor trust (of which he is the grantor) purchase the policy for $65,000. Randy does this to ensure that the death benefit will not be subject to estate tax at his death. The transaction constitutes a transfer of a life insurance policy for valuable consideration, but the death benefit will not be subject to income tax because the transferee (the irrevocable grantor trust) is considered to be the same as the transferor. This result is attained because, for income tax purposes, Randy is considered to be the owner of the assets inside of the irrevocable grantor trust he created and therefore the sale is treated in the same manner as a sale of the policy to the insured.

Example 11.12
Recall the XYZ Partnership example stated above, where John, Randy, Tom, and Keegan enter into a trusted cross-purchase buy-sell agreement. While a transfer for value occurs at the death of the first partner, the death benefits on the remaining three life insurance policies held by the trust will not be subject to income taxation because the transfer was to a partner of the insured, (an exception to the transferfor-value rule). Note that if XYZ was a corporation, no exception to the transfer-for-value rule would apply, since the

transfer is not made to a corporation in which the insured was a shareholder or officer, but was made to the remaining shareholders.

Example 11.13

John, Randy, Tom, and Keegan are all equal shareholders in the XYZ Corporation. The shareholders decide to enter into an entity-type buy-sell agreement where the corporation agrees to purchase the shares of a deceased shareholder. The corporation will fund the buy-sell agreement with life insurance. Keegan owns several life insurance policies on his own life and the total death benefit is significantly higher than what is necessary to satisfy his estate planning goals. Keegan sells one of his life insurance policies to the corporation at fair market value. While a transfer for value has occurred, the corporation will not have to pay income tax on the death benefit in excess of basis since the transferee was a corporation in which the insured was a shareholder or officer.

The transfer-for-value rule can be a serious trap for the unwary. It is important to consider the income tax implications of any transfer of life insurance that is not considered a gratuitous transfer before entering into such a transaction. The "transfer-for-value rule" subjecting the death benefit to income taxation cannot be avoided by having the parties cancel the transaction at a later time.

Settlement or Cash Surrender

When the insured dies, the beneficiary can choose to receive the policy benefits in one of several different ways, referred to as **settlement options**, assuming the owner had not previously established an irrevocable settlement option. One option, of course, is a **lump-sum death benefit**. (As previously stated, the death benefit itself is exempt from income tax provided that there has been no transfer of the policy for valuable consideration.) As an alternative, the beneficiary can choose to keep the life insurance proceeds on deposit at the insurer and receive the interest that accrues on the balance on a regular basis. Some life insurance policies offer various annuity options as well.

While the death benefit on the policy is typically income-tax free, any interest accumulated on the death benefit is subject to ordinary income tax. If a beneficiary elects, for example, to leave the death benefit on deposit with the insurance company and receive distributions of the interest credited to the death benefit, the interest payments will be taxed as ordinary income. If an annuity option is chosen, the rules under Section 72 of the IRC (the exclusion ratio) are used to determine what portion of each payment is treated as a nontaxable return of adjusted basis, and what portion is taxable income.

> **Quick Quiz 11.3**
>
> 1. The transfer-for-value rule subjecting the death benefit of a life insurance policy to income taxation can be avoided by having the parties cancel the transaction at a later point in time.
>   a. True
>   b. False
>
> 2. The owner of a life insurance policy can select the settlement option that will be payable to the beneficiary.
>   a. True
>   b. False
>
> 3. If the death benefit of a life insurance policy payable to a beneficiary is left on deposit with the insurance company, the beneficiary will receive tax-exempt interest on the policy proceeds.
>   a. True
>   b. False
>
> 4. The surrender value of a term life insurance policy increases each year the premium is paid.
>   a. True
>   b. False
>
> False, True, False, False.

The income tax implications should be considered by the owner or by the beneficiary when selecting a particular settlement option.

Even if a beneficiary elects to take a lump-sum distribution, part of the distribution will be subject to income tax. The life insurance policy matures on the date the insured dies and the death benefit becomes payable on that date. To collect the death benefit, the beneficiary of the policy must notify the insurance company of the insured's death, provide proof of death (usually a certified copy of the death certificate), and comply with the insurance company's requests for information. The insurance company could pay quickly or the claim could take some time. It is not unusual for several months to pass before the beneficiary receives the payment for the death benefit especially if the cause of death is suspect. Interest on the death benefit accrues, however, from the date of the insured's death. Therefore, when the beneficiary receives the death benefit, he will also receive fully taxable interest on the death benefit that accrued from the time of the decedent's death to the date the insurance company actually paid the claim.

Instead of waiting for the life insurance policy to mature, the owner of the policy could surrender it and receive the "surrender value" of the contract. The **surrender value** is generally the cash value of the contract less a surrender charge which is governed by the contract or by state law. If the owner of the policy surrenders it to the insurance company and receives an amount that is greater than his adjusted basis in the policy, the difference between the amount received and the owner's adjusted basis is considered taxable income. In this instance, the policy benefit was not paid by reason of the death of the insured, and therefore did not qualify for the income tax exclusion offered in the IRC. Any amount received in excess of the owner's adjusted basis in the policy will be taxed as ordinary income.

Policy Dividends

Policy dividends issued on a life insurance policy are not like cash dividends issued on stock. When a corporation distributes a cash dividend to its shareholders, the dividend represents a distribution of the earnings and profits of the corporation and is fully subject to income tax. A dividend on a life insurance policy, however, is not treated as a distribution of profits, but rather as a return of the policy owner's adjusted basis.

In pricing a life insurance policy, actuaries assume that the pool of individuals being insured will experience a specified rate of mortality. If, on average, the individuals in the pool live longer than the actuaries estimate, the insurance company imposed a higher than appropriate mortality charge when issuing the policy. To compensate a policy holder for this overcharge, the insurance company issues a policy dividend which returns the overcharge to the policy owner. Consequently, since the policy owner is receiving a return of his adjusted basis in the contract, no taxable income is recognized. Note, however, that the issuance of a policy dividend decreases the policyholder's adjusted basis in the contract, and, if the contract is surrendered at a later time, a greater gain in the policy may result, increasing the ordinary income tax due at that time.

Some individuals choose to keep policy dividends on deposit with the insurer, in return for which the insurer pays interest on the balance. The interest earnings on the dividends are taxable to the owner of

> **Key Concepts**
>
> 1. What are the key points of policy dividends and how are they taxed?
> 2. Identify the availability of loans from a life insurance policy.
> 3. Describe MECs and the taxability of the policy.
> 4. What are the rules for policy exchanges under Section 1035?
> 5. What are the rules associated with accelerated death benefits?

the policy even if the interest is not distributed to the owner on an annual basis. The individual may also choose to purchase additional life insurance with the policy dividends. In such a case, the individual's adjusted basis would be reduced by the dividend payment and then subsequently increased by the additional purchase. The net effect to the owner's adjusted basis would be zero, or in other words the owner's adjusted basis would not change.

Loans

One of the benefits of using a cash value life insurance policy in an estate plan is that the cash value of the policy is available through loans to the policy owner if needed. The owner of the policy can borrow from the cash value of the policy at a favorable interest rate specified in the contract. Unlike other loans the owner may be able to obtain, the loan from the life insurance policy need not be paid back. If the loan is not paid back, interest will accrue at the specified rate until the death of the insured.

Generally, no income tax consequences result from taking a loan from the policy cash value. It may appear that the owner of the policy has constructive receipt over the cash value and that by exercising the borrowing privilege he is withdrawing part of the growth in the policy. While constructive receipt of income typically results in immediate taxation of income, in the case of a life insurance policy loan a substantial risk of forfeiture exists. When the policy owner takes a loan from the policy, the outstanding loan balance plus the accumulated interest due will reduce the death benefit payable from the policy dollar-for-dollar. The substantial risk of forfeiture prevents the owner of the life insurance policy from being taxed on the income until the policy lapses.

If the life insurance policy **lapses**, the gain in the policy will include the outstanding loan, and will be subject to ordinary income tax. From a planning perspective, individuals usually do not take policy loans unless (1) they expect to repay them, or (2) if the loan will not be repaid, the policy will remain in force until the death of the insured.

These rules only apply when the contract meets the definition of life insurance as provided by the Internal Revenue Code. If the contract is funded in a way that violates the definition of life insurance, it is considered a **modified endowment contract (MEC)** and will lose some of its tax deferral features.

MECs

Prior to 1986, life insurance contracts were sometimes used as tax-deferral investment vehicles. While the product purchased was called life insurance, the contract was being used merely to defer taxable income to another tax year. To illustrate, assume that Harry has received a large inheritance from the estate of his uncle and is 10 years away from retirement. Harry would like to invest the proceeds, but would like to avoid paying income tax on the investment income until after retirement, when he will be in a lower income tax bracket. Since the rules governing retirement plan contributions limit the amount that can be contributed on an annual basis, it would not be possible to put the entire inheritance into retirement planning vehicles. Instead, Harry purchases a single-premium life insurance policy with his inheritance and invests the cash value of the policy in several mutual funds offered by the insurer. Over the last 10 years of Harry's working life, none of the gains will be subject to income tax since they are inside the income-tax free life insurance contract. When Harry retires, he can begin to take policy loans from the contract, paying no income tax on the distributions. If the policy ever lapses, Harry will have to pay income tax on the gain, but the tax would have been deferred for many years to a time when he will be in a lower tax bracket. Harry never intended to use the life insurance policy as life insurance, but rather as a tax-free/tax-deferred investment accumulation device.

In 1986, Congress defined life insurance for federal income tax purposes. In doing so, Congress focused on the funding of the contract. Since most of the abusive uses of life insurance involve situations where all of the premium is paid in the first few years of the contract's existence, a policy that has its premium payments front-loaded will not be eligible to receive the tax benefits traditionally associated with life insurance. In particular, if the owner of the policy attempts to borrow from the policy cash value, the loan will be considered a taxable distribution to the policy holder to the extent of any gain in the contract. The death benefit received by the beneficiary will continue to be income-tax free to the extent that the policy has not been transferred for value.

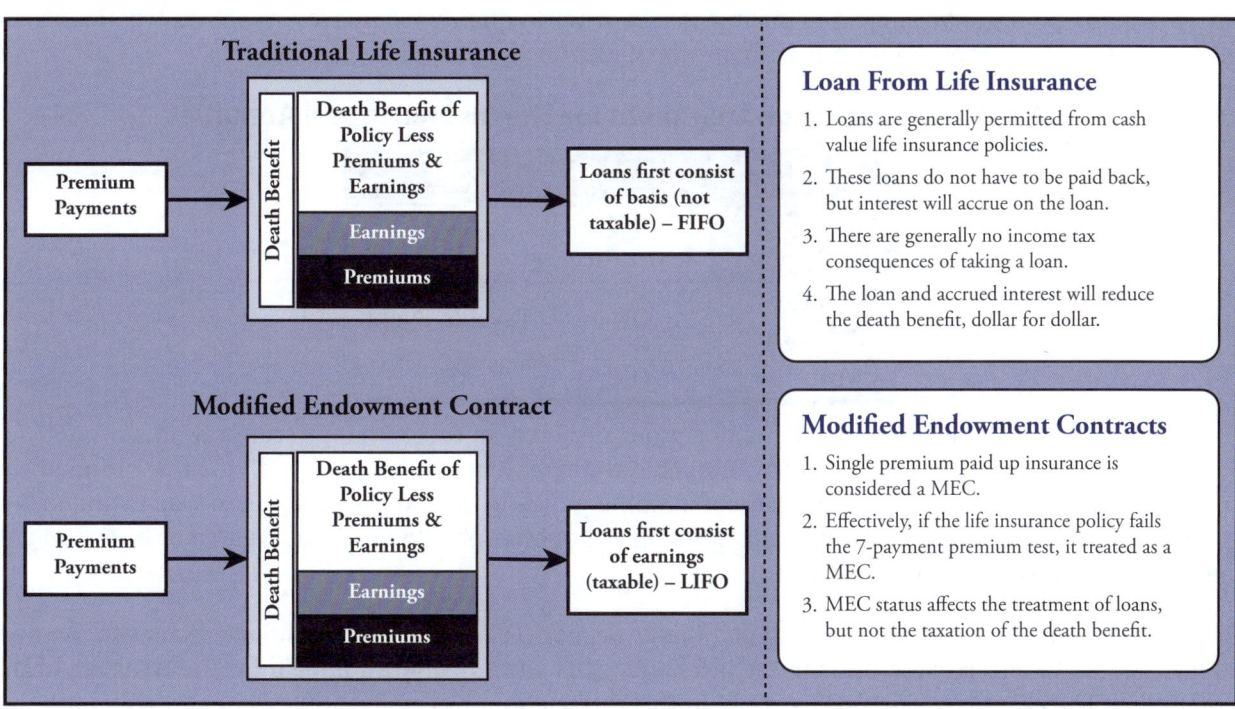

Exhibit 11.4 | Life Insurance Treatment of Loans

Example 11.14

Patrick purchased a single premium life insurance policy on his life 10 years ago for $100,000 (the single premium feature requires the contract to be treated as a MEC). The current value of the policy is $275,000. Patrick needs some cash to put a down payment on a vacation home, so he borrows $50,000 from the policy. The gain inherent in the policy is $175,000 ($275,000 - $100,000), and, therefore, the $50,000 loan will be treated as a 100% taxable distribution to Patrick. If Patrick dies next year, the beneficiary of the policy will receive the net death benefit free of federal income tax.

In adopting the MEC rules, Congress set forth two tests that determine whether a life insurance policy will be considered a modified endowment contract. These tests, the corridor test and the premiums paid test, are more appropriately covered in an insurance course. If the policy is paid up before it is seven years old, it will generally be treated as a modified endowment contract and the owner of the contract will not enjoy the lifetime tax benefits associated with traditional life insurance policies because the policy has been deemed an investment rather than insurance. MEC status only affects loans, not the taxation of proceeds at death.

Policy Exchanges 1035

IRC **Section 1035** allows the owner of a life insurance contract to exchange the contract for another life insurance contract, an endowment contract, or an annuity contract on the same insured without causing any gain in the policy to be subject to income tax. In order to qualify for this favorable tax treatment, the existing policy must be exchanged directly for the new policy.

Exhibit 11.5 | Exchange Treatment for Life Insurance and Annuities

	Exchange From	
Exchange To	**Life Insurance**	**Annuity**
Life Insurance	OK	Taxable Event
Annuity	OK	OK

To the extent that the owner receives cash or other property in the exchange (referred to as "boot" for income tax purposes), gain in the policy is taxable to the extent of boot received. If, at the time of the exchange, the owner of the policy had an outstanding policy loan, and the policy loan was extinguished as a result of the exchange, the principal amount of the outstanding loan will be treated as boot and will therefore be subject to income taxation.

When a life insurance contract is exchanged under Section 1035, the owner's adjusted basis in the new policy is equal to his adjusted basis in the old policy plus any consideration paid for the issuance of the new policy. The carryover basis rules apply to this transaction. Normally, however, basis will not be an issue with life insurance policies unless (1) the policy is a modified endowment contract and the owner is taking a distribution or borrowing money from the policy, or (2) the policy is surrendered before the death of the insured triggering income taxation on the policy gain.

There are a few additional rules that are important to note when considering a 1035 exchange. First, two individual life insurance policies cannot be exchanged for one joint life policy insuring both lives. Second, Section 1035 does not apply to an exchange of life insurance if the insured is not a United States citizen.

Accelerated Death Benefits

Some life insurance companies allow insureds who are terminally or chronically ill to receive an **accelerated death benefit** under the contract. Essentially, the owner surrenders the life insurance contract in return for a payment that is less than the death benefit (and greater than the cash value) and the proceeds are typically used to pay for the medical care of the insured. Recall that only amounts received under a life insurance contract by reason of the death of the insured are exempt from income tax (IRC Section 101(a)). Absent some other statutory provision, receipt of an accelerated death benefit would trigger taxable income for the owner of the policy.

The Code (Section 101(g)) states, however, that amounts received under a life insurance contract on the life of an insured individual who is chronically or terminally ill may be excluded from gross income. For individuals who are chronically ill, however, the nontaxable portion is limited to the amounts incurred by the payee (that are not reimbursed by insurance) for qualified long-term care services provided for the insured.

A **chronically ill individual** is a person who is not terminally ill but has been certified by a licensed health care provider as being unable to perform, without assistance, at least two activities of daily living for at least 90 days, or a person with a similar level of disability. Activities of daily living, as defined in IRC Section 7702(B)(c)(2)(B), are (1) eating, (2) toileting, (3) transferring, (4) bathing, (5) dressing, and (6) continence.

A **terminally ill individual** is a person who has been certified by a licensed health care provider as having a condition or illness that can reasonably be expected to result in death within 24 months. (IRC Section 101(g)(4)(A)).

The income tax exclusion found in IRC Section 101(g) also applies to sales of life insurance by chronically or terminally ill individuals to **qualified viatical settlement providers** or companies that purchase life insurance policies from terminally and chronically ill individuals. Prior to accepting an accelerated death benefit from the life insurance company, it would be wise to determine if selling the policy to a qualified viatical settlement provider would provide more income for the owner.

While these rules were enacted in order to provide a source of funds for chronically and terminally ill individuals to pay for medical expenses, they can be used effectively for estate planning purposes as well. This is particularly true when the insured is the owner of the life insurance policy and is in a high estate tax bracket, as illustrated in the next example.

> **Quick Quiz 11.4**
>
> 1. Dividends issued on life insurance policies are distributions of the earnings and profits of the insurance company.
>   a. True
>   b. False
> 2. The beneficiary of a life insurance policy can take a loan for an amount up to the cash value of the life insurance policy.
>   a. True
>   b. False
> 3. If a life insurance policy is determined to be a MEC, any loans against the policy are taxable to the extent that the owner has gain in the policy.
>   a. True
>   b. False
> 4. IRC Section 1035 allows the owner of a life insurance contract to exchange the contract for another life insurance contract, an endowment contract, or an annuity contract on the same insured without any tax consequences.
>   a. True
>   b. False
> 5. Surrender payments from a life insurance contract to an insured individual who is chronically or terminally ill may be excluded from gross income.
>   a. True
>   b. False
>
> False, False, True, True, True.

Example 11.15

Elizabeth is a 92-year old widowed great-great grandmother, who has recently been diagnosed as terminally ill. Her physicians expect her to live no more than six months. She has 6 children, 18 grandchildren, and 36 great-grandchildren. Elizabeth owns a life insurance policy on her life with a death benefit of $1,000,000. Her gross estate (including the life insurance death benefit) is expected to be well over $11,580,000. If Elizabeth dies owning the life insurance policy, the $1,000,000 death benefit will generate a $400,000 federal estate tax (in 2020), leaving only $600,000 of the death benefit for her heirs. Instead, Elizabeth could sell the life insurance policy to a viatical settlement provider and receive $800,000. If Elizabeth used the proceeds to make annual exclusion gifts to her descendants (a total of 60 people), she could immediately remove up to $840,000 from her estate. Her heirs would be better off by $200,000 ($400,000 of tax - $200,000 cost of viatical settlement). As a result of this planning, Elizabeth's family receives more, and the federal government receives less, of her accumulated wealth.

GIFT TAX TREATMENT OF LIFE INSURANCE

In estate and financial planning, life insurance is often gifted directly or indirectly to individual family members or charities. An understanding of the gift tax treatment of life insurance is important when planning for these transfers.

> ### Key Concepts
> 1. Describe the gift tax treatment of life insurance policies.
> 2. What are the benefits, particularly in terms of income tax, of donating a life insurance policy to charity?

A life insurance policy is a unique form of property because several parties can hold an interest in the policy. While the insured is alive, the owner of the policy can exercise all of the economic rights over the policy, such as borrowing from the policy cash value or pledging the policy as collateral for a loan. Once the insured dies, the death benefit is paid to the beneficiary named on the policy, which may or may not be the policy owner. These different economic interests may be gifted or transferred to different individuals, but often with gift tax consequences. If the owner of the policy is also the insured, estate tax consequences may result. This section reviews the common types of transfers of life insurance that may trigger gift tax liability.

Changing the Beneficiary on the Life Insurance Policy

The individual, trust, or entity that owns a life insurance policy will also often be named as the beneficiary of the policy. Some individuals mistakenly believe that by filing a change of beneficiary form with the life insurance company, ownership of the policy has been transferred.

If a change of beneficiary is made, a completed gift does not occur for federal gift tax purposes. When the insured dies, whoever is named as the beneficiary of the policy will receive the death benefit, but until the insured's death, the original owner may still exercise all economic rights over the policy, including the right to change the beneficiary in the future. Even if an irrevocable beneficiary designation is made with the insurer, the owner of the policy will still be able to exercise all economic rights over the policy until the insured's death, except to name a different beneficiary, and therefore a completed gift has not been made.

Planners should tread cautiously when changing the beneficiary of a life insurance policy without transferring ownership. If the insured is also the owner of the policy, the IRC (Section 2042) will require the death benefit to be included in his federal gross estate and any beneficiary can be named on the policy without triggering a gift tax. If the owner is not the insured, however, and the owner designates a third party as the beneficiary of the policy, a completed gift is made when the insured dies. The value of the gift is the death benefit of the policy. This unintended consequence may result in serious gift tax problems for the owner of the policy.

Example 11.16

Ken and Greg are brothers. Greg purchased a $1,000,000 life insurance contract on Ken's life, and was initially designated as both the owner and the beneficiary of the policy. Both brothers have enjoyed financial success in their careers. Jodie, Ken and Greg's sister, has recently fallen on hard times and Greg decides to name Jodie as the beneficiary of the life insurance policy he owns on Ken's life. No taxable gift occurred at the time the beneficiary was changed. One year after the beneficiary change became effective, Ken unexpectedly died, and the insurance company paid the $1,000,000 death benefit to Jodie. Because Greg owned the policy, and the death benefit was paid to Jodie, Greg will be deemed to have made a $1,000,000 gift to Jodie for federal gift tax purposes. The gift to Jodie will qualify for the annual gift tax exclusion ($15,000), but this will be a small consolation for Greg, who has now used up $985,000 of his applicable gift tax exemption amount.

The same result would occur if a husband was to transfer a policy to his wife while remaining the insured, and the wife names the daughter as the beneficiary. In this instance, if the husband died within three years of the transfer, the entire death benefit would be included in his gross estate and subject to an estate tax. The entire death benefit would also be subject to gift tax, since the payment of the death benefits is treated as a gift from the wife to the daughter. This is referred to in the profession as the "unholy trinity."

Outright Gift of a Life Insurance Policy

When the owner of a life insurance policy transfers ownership of the policy to another by gift, a gift tax may result. To transfer the ownership of the policy, appropriate change of owner forms must be filed with the life insurance company that issues the contract; as discussed earlier, a mere change of beneficiary is not sufficient. If ownership is formally transferred, the gift of the policy will be considered a present interest gift and will qualify for the gift tax annual exclusion. If the value of the policy is less than the gift tax annual exclusion, there will be no gift tax consequence and a gift tax return does not need to be filed. If the value of the policy exceeds the gift tax annual exclusion, however, a taxable gift results, requiring the donor to allocate a portion of his applicable gift tax credit amount to the transaction or, if the applicable gift tax credit has already been used up, pay gift tax on the transfer.

For gift tax purposes, the value of the policy depends on whether the policy is still in premium pay status or is already paid up.

A life insurance policy is in **premium pay status** if premiums are currently being paid on the policy. For a policy in pay status, the value for gift tax purposes is the sum of the policy's **interpolated terminal reserve** plus any unearned premium. The interpolated terminal reserve is the amount the insurance company has actuarially booked as a reserve liability for this policy. The insurance company that issued the policy will provide this value upon request. When requesting a value from the insurance company, it is important to make sure that the value of the policy is calculated as of the date of the gift.

A **paid-up policy** is either a policy where premiums are no longer necessary to keep the policy in force, or a policy that cannot accept additional premiums without causing the policy to become a modified endowment policy. The gift tax value of a paid-up policy is the replacement cost of the policy, which equals the present cost charged by the insurance company to issue a similar contract. Once again, this value can be requested from the issuer.

There is one exception to the valuation rule for gifts of life insurance policies: If a physician has determined that the insured has a physical condition that is terminal, the value of the policy will be the death benefit, discounted for the predicted life expectancy of the insured. When the insured is known to have a terminal condition, the normal actuarial tables cannot be used to approximate the value of the policy.

Example 11.17

Assume the same facts as **Example 11.16**. Here, instead of simply naming Jodie as the beneficiary of the policy, Greg formally transferred ownership and filed the appropriate forms with the insurer. At the time Greg transferred ownership, Ken had not been diagnosed as terminally ill, and the policy was in pay status. The insurance company reported that the interpolated terminal reserve plus unearned premium on the policy as of the date of the gift was $10,500. Upon transfer of ownership, Greg made a completed gift of a present interest to Jodie that will qualify for the gift tax annual exclusion. Since the value of the policy was less than the annual exclusion amount ($15,000 for 2020), Greg will not have to pay any gift tax and will not have to file a gift tax return with the IRS. When Ken dies, Greg will not be deemed to have made a gift of the death benefit to Jodie, since Jodie is the owner of the policy.

Gifts of Premiums

Sometimes, it may make sense to have a single individual or entity own and be the beneficiary of a life insurance policy, but perhaps that person or entity does not have sufficient resources to make the premium payments. In many planning situations, for example, life insurance on the lives of senior generation family members may be owned by junior generation family members or by an entity created for their benefit. Family wealth typically resides with the senior generation family members. A simple way to resolve this problem involves a cash gift made to the junior family members or entity equal to the premium due on the policy. The junior member would then pay the premium. The cash gift is considered a gift for gift tax purposes, so, ideally the premium is less than the annual exclusion.

When life insurance policies are owned outright by individuals, gifts of cash that qualify for the gift tax annual exclusion can be made to the policy owner at the time the premium is due. If a trust is the owner of the life insurance policy, a gift of the premium to the trust that includes a **Crummey provision** (a general power of appointment over the contribution to the trust given to the beneficiaries of the trust) will qualify such gift for the gift tax annual exclusion. A more detailed review of life insurance trusts will be addressed later in this chapter.

Gifts of Life Insurance to Charities

Life insurance is often the object of charitable gifts. An individual with charitable intent may find that a gift of excess life insurance to a charitable organization can generate current tax benefits. Some individuals with modest means may want to make a sizable gift to charity and may use life insurance as a way of creating a legacy for a specific charitable cause. Other clients may anticipate a will contest after their death and would like to ensure that a certain amount of money will be transferred to a charitable organization. A successful will contest could have the effect of disinheriting a charitable beneficiary, but the death benefit paid to a charitable beneficiary of a life insurance policy are not usually successfully challenged by disgruntled heirs.

Life insurance is generally considered ordinary income property. Thus, gifting life insurance policies to a charity will follow the income tax charitable deduction rules for ordinary income property. The deduction for donated ordinary income property is equal to the fair market value of the property reduced by any ordinary income that would have resulted from its sale. The net deduction is usually the adjusted basis of the property. In the event the fair market value is less than the adjusted basis (no ordinary income would result from this sale), the deduction is equal to the fair market value of the property itself. If the policy is "paid up" (i.e., no premiums remain to be paid), the fair market value is equal to the policy's **replacement value**. If premiums remain unpaid on the policy, the fair market value is the policy's interpolated terminal reserve value. If the donor continues to pay the premiums on any policy donated to a charity, those premium payments are an additional tax-deductible charitable gift.

> **Quick Quiz 11.5**
>
> 1. When the owner of a life insurance policy designates the beneficiary of the policy, he has made a taxable gift equal to the present value of the expected future death benefit to the beneficiary.
>   a. True
>   b. False
>
> 2. For gift tax purposes, the value of a life insurance policy in pay status is the replacement cost of the policy plus the present value of any outstanding premiums.
>   a. True
>   b. False
>
> 3. When a life insurance policy is donated to a charity, the donor may deduct the fair market value of the policy as a charitable deduction on his income tax return (subject to income limitations).
>   a. True
>   b. False
>
> *False, False, True.*

The income tax charitable deduction for a gift of an existing life insurance policy is limited to 50 percent of the donor's contribution base (which is adjusted gross income not taking into consideration net operating loss carrybacks) if the policy is given to a public charity and 30 percent of the donor's contribution base if the policy is given to a private charity. Simply naming the charity as the beneficiary or making the charity the irrevocable beneficiary of the policy is not sufficient to generate a current income tax deduction, since the owner (not the charity) will be able to exercise economic rights over the policy and could possibly prevent the charity from receiving anything. The ownership of the policy must be transferred to the charity if the donor wishes to qualify the gift for the income tax charitable deduction.

A potential estate tax issue arises when the owner/insured transfers a life insurance policy to a charity and dies within three years of the transfer. While the charity is the owner and beneficiary of the policy, the insured had incidents of ownership in the policy within three years of death, requiring an inclusion of the death benefit in the insured's gross estate. When this occurs, the entire death benefit would qualify for the estate tax unlimited charitable deduction, resulting in no additional estate tax. Note, however, that if the insured/decedent was also a business owner and was planning on a Section 303 redemption, a Section 6166 deferral of estate taxes, or a Section 2032A Special Use Valuation, the inclusion of the death benefit in the gross estate may prevent use of these favorable elections.

If the donor/insured lives for more than three years after the transfer, the death benefit proceeds on the policy are removed from his gross estate. The three-year rule of the IRC (Section 2035) is discussed in more detail in the next section. The gift of the policy to the charity will not be considered an adjusted taxable gift, since the annual exclusion and the gift tax charitable deduction apply to the transfer.

After a life insurance policy is given to a charity, the donor typically continues to make the premium payments on the policy. The amount of the premium payment will be deductible as a charitable gift, subject to the 30 percent of adjusted gross income limitation if the recipient is a public charity and 20 percent if the recipient is a private charity. If the donor would like to qualify for the higher 50 percent of adjusted gross income limitation, he could make a gift of cash to the charity and allow the charity to pay the premium on the policy directly.

FEDERAL ESTATE TAX TREATMENT OF LIFE INSURANCE

Life Insurance on Someone Else's Life

When an individual dies owning a life insurance policy on the life of another person, the value of the life insurance policy will be included in his gross estate (IRC Section 2033). The value of the policy for estate tax purposes is generally the interpolated terminal reserve plus any unearned premium when the policy is in in-pay status. Otherwise, it will be replacement value.

Key Concepts

1. When would a life insurance policy be included in the gross estate?

Example 11.18
Ted recently died. One of his assets was a life insurance policy on the life of Ted's friend Ron, who is still living. The interpolated terminal reserve plus unearned premium of the policy on Ron's life was $26,000 as of the date of Ted's death. Therefore, $26,000 will be included in Ted's gross estate.

Life Insurance on the Insured/Decedent's Life

The IRC (Section 2042) states that if a decedent owns a life insurance policy on his own life, or possesses any incidents of ownership in the policy on the date of his death, the policy death benefit will be included in his gross estate. While the beneficiary will receive the death benefit free of income tax (as set forth in IRC Section 101), the insured will have to include the death benefit proceeds of the policy in his gross estate.

Example 11.19
Barbara recently died. She owned a life insurance policy on her own life in the amount of $1,000,000. Barbara's sister, Rita, was named as the beneficiary. Rita received the death benefit income-tax free, but because Barbara owned the policy, the full death benefit is included in her gross estate.

An **incident of ownership in a life insurance policy** is the ability to exercise any economic right in the policy. Incidents of ownership include, but are not limited to, the right to borrow from the cash value in the policy, the right to assign the policy for a loan, and the right to change the beneficiary of the policy. The right to pay the premiums on a life insurance policy is not considered an incident of ownership in the policy. If an insured/decedent possessed any incident of ownership in a life insurance policy on his life at the time of death, the policy death benefit will be included in his gross estate.

> ### Quick Quiz 11.6
>
> 1. Life insurance proceeds payable to the estate of a decedent are included in the decedent's federal gross estate.
>   a. True
>   b. False
> 2. The owner of a life insurance policy will include the value of the life insurance policy in his federal gross estate if he dies before the insured.
>   a. True
>   b. False
> 3. The three-year rule does not apply to the sale of a life insurance policy.
>   a. True
>   b. False
> 4. The three-year rule requires inclusion of the death benefit of any life insurance policy transferred within three years of the death of the insured in the insured/owner's federal gross estate.
>   a. True
>   b. False
>
> *True, True, True, True.*

Example 11.20
Last year, Jim transferred ownership of the life insurance policy on his life to his son, Chris. Jim frequently invests in real estate ventures and occasionally needs a quick source of cash. Therefore, he retained the right to borrow against the cash value of the policy he transferred to Chris. Jim recently died and as of the date of his death, he still had the right to borrow from the cash value of the policy. The full policy death benefit will be included in Jim's gross estate.

Example 11.21
Five years ago, Jim transferred complete ownership of his life insurance policy (insuring Jim) to his son, Chris. The value of the policy as of the date of the transfer was less than the gift tax annual exclusion amount. Jim recently died. At the time of his death, Jim did not possess any incident of ownership over the policy and therefore the death benefit will not be included in his gross estate.

The Three-Year Look Back Rule

The death benefit on a life insurance policy once owned by the decedent may be included in his gross estate even if he does not own an interest in the policy as of the date of his death. IRC Section 2035 gives us the **three-year rule**, which states that if an individual gratuitously transfers ownership (or any incident of ownership) of a life insurance policy on his life within three years of death, the death benefit of the policy is included in his gross estate.

The three-year rule applies when the insured gifts a policy or incidents of ownership in a policy on his life within three years of his death. If the owner of the policy is not the insured and the owner gives the policy to another party, the three-year rule does not apply. The gift of the policy will, however, be subject to gift tax. To the extent that the value of the policy exceeds the annual exclusion, it will be considered an adjusted taxable gift and will therefore be added back to the taxable estate for purposes of calculating any estate tax due.

Example 11.22

Two years ago, Roger gifted a life insurance policy he owned on the life of Connie to their son, Glen. The value of the policy at the time of the gift was $60,000. The transfer of the life insurance policy was a present interest gift qualifying for the gift tax annual exclusion. The adjusted taxable gift that Roger made was therefore $45,000 ($60,000-$15,000). Roger allocated part of his applicable gift tax credit to the transfer, and therefore paid no gift tax. Roger died this year, and was survived by Connie and Glen. The value of the policy is not included in his gross estate, because the policy insured Connie, not Roger, and therefore the three-year rule does not apply. The adjusted taxable gift of $45,000 will, however, be added back to Roger's taxable estate to determine how much estate tax he must pay. [Note that if Roger had paid gift tax on the transfer of the policy, in addition to the inclusion of the adjusted taxable gift in his gross estate, the gift tax paid would be added back into his gross estate because Roger died within three years of making the gift.]

Note that the three-year rule applies only to gratuitous transfers (gifts) of life insurance policies or incidents of ownership in life insurance policies. It does not apply to a sale of a life insurance policy. Of course, if a life insurance policy is sold for valuable consideration, the transfer-for-value rule applies, causing the death benefit to be subject to income taxation in the hands of the beneficiary. By taking advantage of the exceptions to the transfer-for-value rule, it may be possible to remove the death benefit of a policy owned by the insured from his gross estate. For planning purposes, the following exceptions to the transfer-for-value rule are relevant in this context: a transfer to (1) a partner of the insured, (2) a partnership in which the insured is a partner, (3) a corporation in which the insured is a shareholder or officer, and (4) a transferee who takes the transferor's basis. A sale of a life insurance policy from the insured to any of these individuals or entities will avoid both the transfer-for-value rule and the three-year rule.

From a planning point of view, if a client is healthy and is not at an advanced age the risk of dying within three years of transfer is generally small. In the case of a party who is insurable, the planner must weigh the cost of creating a new policy (generally expensive for permanent policies but inexpensive for term) with the risk of the three-year look back rule.

Example 11.23

Quinn owns a cash value life insurance policy with a death benefit of $1,000,000 on her life that was purchased several years ago to pay off her mortgage and put her children through college in the event of her early death. The cash value of the policy is $65,000. Her mortgage is paid off and all of the children have completed both college and graduate school. After retiring from her position as head of security of a national pharmaceutical firm, Quinn created a security consulting partnership with a former colleague, Elliott. Elliott and Quinn have just entered into a cross-purchase buy-sell agreement requiring the surviving partner to purchase a deceased partner's interest. Elliott purchased Quinn's life insurance policy for $65,000, and will use the death benefit to fund his obligations under the buy-sell agreement. Because Elliott is Quinn's partner, the sale of the policy meets an exception to the transfer-for-value rule. Since the policy was not gifted to Elliott, the three-year rule does not apply, and the death benefit will be immediately removed from Quinn's estate.

Example 11.24

Many years ago, Sam purchased a life insurance policy on his own life. Never envisioning that she would have a taxable estate, she owned the policy and named her spouse, Marlowe, as the beneficiary. Business has been very kind to Sam and she would be subject to the highest marginal estate tax bracket if she died today. The policy has a value of $83,000 and a death benefit of $1,000,000. Sam created an irrevocable trust that qualifies as a grantor trust for income tax purposes. The trust purchased the life insurance policy from Sam. If Sam dies immediately following the sale, the death benefit will be excluded from her estate, because the three-year rule only applies to gratuitous transfers of life insurance. The trust will also receive the death benefit income-tax free, and the transfer-for-value rule does not apply since all transactions between a grantor trust and the grantor are ignored for income tax purposes. Because the grantor trust is irrevocable and Sam has not retained any rights that would cause inclusion, the value of the trust will not be included in Sam's gross estate.

CREATION OF A LIFE INSURANCE TRUST (ILIT)

Life insurance death benefits are exempt from income taxes (provided there has been no transfer for value), but are subject to estate taxes if the policy is owned by the insured. This can pose a significant tax problem in estate planning. One solution to this problem is to have a trust own the life insurance policy so that the insurance proceeds will not be subject to estate tax at the insured's death. These trusts are often referred to as irrevocable life insurance trusts (ILITs) or Wealth Replacement Trusts (WRTs).

> **Key Concepts**
>
> 1. Describe the ILIT and its benefits.
> 2. When would the death benefit be included in the gross estate assuming the life insurance policy is owned by an ILIT?

The concept of the ILIT is relatively simple. Instead of having the insured own the life insurance policy on his own life, thus causing estate tax inclusion, the insured can create a separate trust whose trustee will own and have all incidents of ownership in the life insurance policy. The insured avoids inclusion of the policy proceeds in his gross estate since he neither owns the policy nor has any incident of ownership over the policy. If the trust owns the policy, the proceeds will not be included in the insured's gross estate even though the insured created the trust and set forth the terms for distribution of trust assets (the death benefit on the life insurance policy) to the beneficiaries.

Using the Annual Exclusion

An ILIT can get a bit complex when we consider the funding of the life insurance premiums. Typically, the insured/grantor of the trust will make annual gifts to the trust so that the trustee can pay the premiums on the life insurance policy. Generally, all gifts to irrevocable trusts are considered future interest gifts and therefore do not qualify for the gift tax annual exclusion. However, the future interest characterization of the gift can be transformed into a present interest by the inclusion of a Crummey provision in the trust document. A Crummey provision states that the annual contribution made to the trust may be withdrawn by the beneficiaries for a specified period (usually 30 days) after the contribution is made. The trustee must give the beneficiaries notice of their right to withdraw their pro rata share of the annual contribution. Because the beneficiaries have the right to reduce the contribution to the trust to their possession, and use the funds in any way they see fit, the future interest gift in trust is transformed into a present interest gift that qualifies for the gift tax annual exclusion. To the extent that the gift to the trust does not exceed the gift tax annual exclusion multiplied by the number of beneficiaries of the trust, the donor will not have to use up any of his applicable gift tax credit when funding the trust.

Crummey Powers

As discussed previously, a Crummey power allows the beneficiary of a trust to withdraw the annual contribution. In other words, the beneficiary has a right to appoint the annual contribution to himself. Whenever an individual has the right to appoint property to himself, he possesses a general power of appointment. General powers of appointment are usually included in the gross estate of the person holding the power if the power holder dies while holding the power. While the Crummey power allows the donor to make a transfer under the annual exclusion rather than utilize his applicable gift tax credit, a beneficiary who holds a Crummey power may, as a result of that power, be required to include part of the trust assets in his gross estate.

If an individual has a general power of appointment over the annual contribution made to the trust, and the value of the general power of appointment does not exceed the greater of (1) $5,000, or (2) five percent of the trust corpus, the general power of appointment is ignored, and the beneficiary will not trigger gift tax if there is more than one party to the trust. This exception is often referred to as the **Five-and-Five rule**. Technically, a general power of appointment lapses to the extent that its value does not exceed $5,000 or five percent of the trust corpus in order to maximize the tax benefits of Crummey trusts, therefore, the contribution made to the trust should not exceed (1) $5,000 per beneficiary or (2) five percent of the trust corpus times the number of beneficiaries. When this convention is followed, the grantor will qualify gifts made to the trust for the gift tax annual exclusion and the beneficiaries will not have any inclusion in their gross estates by reason of possessing a general power of appointment over the contribution made to the trust, as long as the power lapses before the power holder dies.

Once the beneficiary's withdrawal right from the trust exceeds the greater of $5,000 or five percent of the trust corpus, there will be estate tax consequences for the beneficiary who dies after the Crummey power lapses.

Example 11.25
Pat created an irrevocable life insurance trust with Crummey demand rights to hold a policy on his life. The beneficiaries of the trust are his four children. Pat transferred $16,000 to the trust this year to fund the annual premium. The trustee notified each of the beneficiaries (or their guardians) of their right to withdraw their pro rata share of the contribution, $4,000. Because each beneficiary's Crummey power (general power of appointment) is less than $5,000, there will be no inclusion in any of the beneficiary's estates as a result of the Crummey power if a beneficiary dies after the Crummey power lapses.

Example 11.26
Fifteen years ago, Pat created an irrevocable life insurance trust, with Crummey demand rights, to hold a policy on his life. The current value of the trust is $150,000. The beneficiaries of the trust are his four children. This year, Pat transferred $25,000 to the trust to pay the annual premium on the life insurance policy. Upon receiving the contribution, the trustee notified the beneficiaries of their right to withdraw $6,250 each from the trust. While the Crummey demand right (general power of appointment) exceeds the $5,000 limit, no beneficiary has the right to withdraw more than 5% of the trust corpus ($7,500). Therefore there will be no inclusion in the beneficiary's gross estates if a beneficiary dies after the Crummey power lapses.

Other Objectives

While the primary purpose of an ILIT is to exclude the death benefit of a life insurance policy from an insured's federal gross estate, the trust can be used for other estate planning objectives as well. First, the trust document will govern the disposition of the property. Instead of leaving a large death benefit to a family member, the trust will provide for management and conservation of the funds for the benefit of the family members. Second, the trust provides a degree of asset protection for the insured and the insured's family. During the insured's lifetime, the cash value of the policy is protected from the insured's creditors. After the insured's death, to the extent that the death benefit remains in the trust and is managed for the benefit of the beneficiaries, the funds are protected from the claims of the beneficiaries' creditors.

Life Insurance Proceeds Made Available to the Executor of the Insured's Estate

Since the objective of a life insurance trust is typically to provide liquidity for the estate while keeping the policy death benefit out of the insured's estate, it is important to avoid situations that will trigger inclusion by having incidents of ownership. Recall that the IRC requires the death benefit of a life insurance policy on the insured to be included in the insured's gross estate when:
1. The insured owns the policy at any time within the three-year period before his death;
2. When the insured possesses any incident of ownership over the policy at any time within the three-year period before his death; and
3. When the proceeds of the policy are made available to the executor.

Proceeds of the policy are deemed to be made available to the executor of the insured's estate when the proceeds are required to be or may be used by the executor to pay the insured's estate taxes or administration expenses. A life insurance trust that mandates the payment of the insured's estate taxes, for example, will cause the death benefit of the policy owned by the ILIT to be included in the insured's gross estate, thereby defeating the purpose of the life insurance trust. It is important in drafting a life insurance trust to ensure that the trust does not require the trustee to pay estate taxes or administration expenses of the estate.

Example 11.27
John, a personal injury attorney, drafted an ILIT to hold a new life insurance policy on his life for the benefit of his wife, Patty, and their children. John was not experienced in drafting estate planning documents, but became aware of the desirability of excluding the death benefit on life insurance policies from estate taxation. In drafting the ILIT, John copied the trustee powers section from a revocable trust form that he had in his forms library. Like most revocable trusts, the trustee was given the power to pay estate taxes and administration expenses of the grantor (in this case, the grantor is also the insured). Upon John's death, the death benefit will be considered available to the executor and the full death benefit will be taxed in John's estate.

Providing Liquidity to the Estate

Two provisions are commonly found in life insurance trusts that allow the trust to provide the needed liquidity for the insured's estate while, at the same time, preventing the policy death benefit from being subject to estate tax. These provisions include:
1. Giving the trustee of the life insurance trust the right to purchase assets from the estate of the insured; and
2. Giving the trustee of the life insurance trust the right to loan money to the estate of the insured.

> **Quick Quiz 11.7**
> 1. By creating an ILIT, the insured eliminates any risk created by the three-year rule.
>   a. True
>   b. False
> 2. Irrevocable life insurance trusts are primarily designed to ensure that the death benefit is excludable from the insured's federal gross estate.
>   a. True
>   b. False
>
> *False, True.*

Frequently, estates have little or no liquidity, and if forced to liquidate assets, the sale would cause a substantial loss. Both of these provisions require the estate to trade something of value (assets or a promissory note) in return for access to the policy death benefit and are therefore considered to be arm's-length transactions. The life insurance trust should not require the trustee to purchase assets or make a loan to the estate and the decedent's will should not require the estate to sell assets to the life insurance trust or borrow money from the trust. The reason for this is that any such requirement may be construed as the insured or his estate having an incidents of ownership in such a policy thus causing the proceeds to be included in the gross estate. After the death of the insured, the executor of the insured's estate and the trustee of the life insurance trust should determine whether or not a sale of assets or a loan should be made.

Example 11.28
Tom, a tax attorney, drafted an ILIT to hold a new life insurance policy on his life for the benefit of his wife and children. The life insurance trust gave the trustee the authority to purchase assets from his estate and the authority to make loans to his estate, but specifically prohibited the trustee from directly paying estate taxes or administration expenses of Tom's estate. Upon Tom's death, the proceeds of the life insurance policy will not be deemed to be available to the executor and will therefore be excluded from his taxable estate.

It is not uncommon to encounter situations where the beneficiary of a life insurance policy on the decedent's life or the trustee of an ILIT holding a life insurance policy on the decedent's life is also the executor of the decedent's estate. If the executor receives the policy death benefit in an individual capacity and there is no express or implied requirement for the executor, as an individual, to use the death benefit to pay estate taxes or administration expenses, the death benefit will not be deemed "payable to the executor," and will not be included in the insured's estate.

Example 11.29
Arturo is the original owner and beneficiary of a life insurance policy on the life of his father, Angelo. There is no express or implied agreement that Arturo will use the proceeds of the policy to pay estate taxes or administration expenses of Angelo's estate. Angelo's will names Arturo as the executor of his estate. When Angelo dies, the death benefit on the life insurance policy paid to Arturo will not be considered "payable to the executor" and will not be included in Angelo's estate.

Likewise, if the trustee of an ILIT holding a life insurance policy on the life of the insured is also executor of the insured's estate, the policy proceeds are not deemed to be "payable to the executor" solely because the executor is also serving as trustee. The terms of the ILIT must make the policy proceeds available for the payment of estate taxes and/or administration expenses of the insured to trigger estate tax inclusion.

Example 11.30
Lewis is the executor of David's (his father's) estate. Lewis is also the trustee of an ILIT that David created for estate liquidity purposes. The ILIT allows Lewis, as trustee, to purchase assets from David's estate, or to loan money to David's estate. The ILIT prohibits Lewis, as trustee, from directly paying estate taxes and administration expenses in David's estate. The proceeds will not be considered to be "payable to the executor" despite the fact that Lewis is serving both as trustee and executor, and will therefore not be subject to estate taxation.

The purpose of the ILIT is to remove the proceeds of life insurance from the insured's estate, provide estate liquidity at death, and to avoid inclusion of the proceeds in the surviving spouse's estate while making the income from such trust available to the surviving spouse and providing the trustee with the power to invade the corpus for health, education, or maintenance of any beneficiary (a limited power of appointment subject to an ascertainable standard).

Exhibit 11.6 | Visual Depiction of an Irrevocable Life Insurance Trust (ILIT)

chapter 11

KEY TERMS

Accelerated Death Benefit - A reduced payment of the death benefit of a life insurance policy paid to the insured during the insureds lifetime in return for a surrender of the life insurance contract.

Beneficiary - The person(s) entitled to receive the death benefit of a life insurance policy at the insureds death. Also, the person(s) who hold(s) the beneficial title to a trust's assets.

Buy-Sell Agreements - Arrangements that require the sale and purchase of securities owned by one individual to another following a specified triggering event, such as the death of a business owner.

Chronically Ill Individual - A person who has been certified by a licensed health care provider as being unable to perform, without assistance, at least two activities of daily living for at least 90 days, or a person with a similar level of disability.

Cross-Purchase Buy-Sell Agreement - An arrangement between individuals who agree to purchase the business interest of a deceased owner.

Crummey Provision - The explicit right of a trust beneficiary to withdraw some or all of any contribution to a trust for a limited period of time after the contribution. A Crummey provision converts what otherwise would have been a gift of a future interest (not eligible for the annual exclusion) to a gift of a present interest, eligible for the annual exclusion.

Entity Purchase (Redemption) Agreement - Type of buy-sell agreement that obligates the business entity to purchase an owner's interest in the entity upon that owner's death.

Five-and-Five Rule – The lapse of a general power of appointment, like the release of such a power, results in a transfer for gift tax purposes. This rule applies only to the extent the value of the property subject to the lapsed powers exceeds the greater of $5,000 or 5 percent of the aggregate value of the assets out of which the powers could have been satisfied.

Incident of Ownership in a Life Insurance Policy - The ability to exercise any economic right in a life insurance policy.

Insured - The person whose life is insured by the life insurance contract.

Interpolated Terminal Reserve - The amount the insurance company has actuarially booked as a reserve liability for a policy.

Lapse - When a power or right ends because of time or circumstance.

Lump-Sum Death Benefit - A single payment of a life insurance death benefit to a beneficiary.

Modified Endowment Contract (MEC) - A life insurance policy that appears to function like an investment contract because the policy is paid up in just a few payments. MECs function like other life insurance policies except for the tax treatment of loans from the policy.

Owner - The person who holds title to a life insurance contract.

Paid-Up Policy - A life insurance policy where no more premium payments are necessary to keep the life insurance policy in force, or a life insurance policy that cannot accept additional premiums without causing the life insurance policy to become a modified endowment contract.

Policy Dividends - Refunds of overcharged premiums to life insurance policy owners. The payments are treated as a return of the policy owner's adjusted basis.

Premium Pay Status - Premiums are currently being paid on the life insurance policy.

Qualified Viatical Settlement Provider - A state licensed business that is regularly engaged in the business of buying life insurance policies from the policy owners.

Replacement Value - The fair market value of a "paid-up" life insurance policy (no premiums remain to be paid).

Section 1035 Exchange - A tax-free exchange of a life insurance contract for another life insurance contract, a modified endowment contract, or an annuity contract on the same insured.

Settlement Options - The beneficiary's available options when receiving the death benefit, usually either lump sum or annuity.

Surrender Value - The cash value of the life insurance policy less a surrender charge which is governed by the policy or state law.

Term Insurance Policy - A life insurance contract which states if the insured dies within the term of the contract, the insurance company will pay a stated death benefit.

Terminally Ill Individual - A person who has been certified by a licensed health care provider as having a condition or illness that can reasonably be expected to result in death within 24 months.

Three-Year Rule - If an individual gratuitously transfers ownership of a life insurance policy on his life, or any incident of ownership in a policy on his life within three years of his date of death, the death benefit of the policy is included in his federal gross estate.

Transfer for Value - A transfer of an asset by means of a sale, exchange or any transfer which includes valuable consideration. If a life insurance policy is transferred for value, the death benefit in excess of the transferor's adjusted basis will be subject to income tax, unless the transfer meets certain exceptions.

Universal Life Insurance - A term insurance policy with a cash accumulation account attached to it.

Variable Universal Life Insurance - A universal life insurance policy with investment options available for the cash accumulation account.

Whole Life Insurance - A permanent insurance policy which guarantees that the policy will remain in force as long as the premium is paid. The policy has a cash account attached to it which grows tax deferred.

chapter 11

DISCUSSION QUESTIONS

SOLUTIONS to the discussion questions can be found exclusively within the chapter. Once you have completed an initial reading of the chapter, go back and highlight the answers to these questions.

1. List the five most common objectives of using life insurance in an estate plan.

2. When selecting the amount of life insurance needed to protect the income stream of beneficiaries, what should be considered?

3. What is the advantage of paying off debt at the death of the first spouse?

4. How is life insurance included in a plan for funding college education?

5. Why is liquidity an issue when a decedent's assets pass through the probate process?

6. Why is liquidity an issue for a large estate?

7. How can life insurance provide financial security for a surviving spouse in retirement?

8. How can life insurance fund retirement needs while the insured is still alive?

9. List the basic types of life insurance.

10. Define a term life insurance policy.

11. Why is the premium on a term insurance policy lower than the premium on a permanent policy?

12. Why is the strategy of "buy term and invest the difference" not an optimal strategy for people who have a permanent need for life insurance protection?

13. How is a term insurance policy used when an estate plan includes a GRAT?

14. How does a universal life insurance policy differ from a term life insurance policy?

15. What guarantee does the insurer give the insured under a whole life insurance policy?

16. How is the cash value of a whole life insurance policy invested?

17. In general, how does a variable universal life insurance policy differ from a universal life insurance policy?

18. Identify the parties to a life insurance policy.

19. In the event that a life insurance policy does not have a named beneficiary, who receives the death benefit?

20. Briefly describe the transfer-for-value rule.

21. List the exceptions to the transfer-for-value rule.

22. List the settlement options available for life insurance policies.

23. Discuss the tax consequences to a beneficiary who chooses to leave the life insurance proceeds on deposit at the insurer.

24. How is the surrender value of a life insurance policy calculated?

25. If an owner elects to receive the surrender value of the life insurance policy, why might it be taxable?

26. How do dividends from corporations differ from dividends on a life insurance policy?

27. List some of the advantages and disadvantages of taking a loan from a life insurance policy.

28. The designated beneficiary of a life insurance policy will receive the death benefit of the policy at the death of the insured. Why is the designation of the beneficiary not a completed gift for federal gift tax purposes?

29. In general, how is the value of a life insurance policy in pay status determined for federal gift tax purposes?

30. In general, how is the value of a paid-up life insurance policy determined for federal gift tax purposes?

31. How can the owner of a life insurance policy receive a current income tax deduction for the value of the life insurance policy?

32. If the owner of a life insurance policy gifts ownership of the policy to charity, what is the effect of the owner continuing to pay the premiums?

33. Define "incident of ownership" in a life insurance policy and give an example.

34. With regards to the federal estate tax and life insurance, what is the three-year rule?

35. What provision allows the gift of premium payments to an ILIT to be eligible for the annual exclusion?

36. What is the structure and purpose of an entity purchase, or redemption, buy-sell agreement?

37. What is the structure and purpose of a cross-purchase buy-sell agreement?

38. What are the tax differences between entity and cross-purchase buy-sell agreements?

chapter 11

MULTIPLE-CHOICE PROBLEMS

A sample of multiple choice problems is provided below. Additional multiple choice problems are available at money-education.com by accessing the Student Practice Portal.

1. Jack purchased a life insurance policy on his own life and never designated a beneficiary. In this case, the life insurance policy death benefit is:
    a. Included in Jack's federal gross estate if Jack dies within three years of the initial premium payment.
    b. Included in Jack's federal gross estate if Jack paid the premiums until his death.
    c. Never included in Jack's federal gross estate.
    d. Always included in Jack's federal gross estate.

2. Carol and Joe, unrelated business partners, began operating a drug store in southern Florida. They funded a buy/sell agreement with a cross-purchase life insurance arrangement. Carol purchased a life insurance policy with Joe as the insured, and Joe purchased a life insurance policy with Carol as the insured. If Carol dies, which of the following is/are true?
    1. The death benefit of the life insurance policy on Carol's life, owned by Joe, is excluded from Carol's federal gross estate.
    2. The death benefit of the life insurance policy on Carol's life, owned by Joe, is included in Carol's federal gross estate if Carol owns 50% or more of the stock of the drug store.
    3. The value of the life insurance policy on Joe's life, owned by Carol, is included in Carol's federal gross estate.
    4. The death benefit of the life insurance policy on Carol's life, owned by Joe, is included in Carol's federal gross estate.
        a. 1 only.
        b. 1 and 3.
        c. 1, 2, and 3.
        d. 1, 2, 3, and 4.

3. Louie gave a $1,000,000 life insurance policy on his own life to his brother. At the date of the gift, the life insurance policy was valued at $200,000. Which of the following statements regarding the gift of this life insurance policy is correct?
    a. If Louie dies two years after this gift, his federal gross estate will include $200,000.
    b. If Louie dies four years after this gift, his federal gross estate will include $200,000.
    c. If Louie dies two years after this gift, his federal gross estate will include $1,000,000.
    d. If Louie dies four years after this gift, his federal gross estate will include $1,000,000.

4. Which of the following statements regarding term life insurance is correct?
   a. The premium on a term life insurance policy reflects the actuarial risk that the insured will die during the term of the contract.
   b. The cash accumulation account of a term life insurance policy is invested in the bond portfolios of the insurer.
   c. The cash accumulation account of a term life insurance policy is invested in individual stocks selected by the insured.
   d. The premium of a term life insurance policy will decrease as the pure cost of life insurance increases.

5. Jim purchased a yacht from Ronald for $200,000 seven years ago. The terms of the sale included a note of $50,000 and cash for the remaining amount. Ronald had a zero basis in the yacht. Immediately after purchasing the yacht, Jim's business began to fail and Jim could no longer make the payments. In exchange for the note, Jim gave Ronald a life insurance policy on his life with a face value of $50,000. This year, Jim died and Ronald received the death benefit as the designated beneficiary of the policy. How much of this death benefit is taxable to Ronald?
   a. $0.
   b. $50,000.
   c. $150,000.
   d. $200,000.

QUICK QUIZ EXPLANATIONS

Quick Quiz 11.1
1. True.
2. False. A whole life insurance policy will pay the stated death benefit if the insured dies while the policy is in force. It also creates a cash value pool that can be used to pay for future increases in mortality charges. Whole life insurance policies provide guarantees that if the stated premium is paid, the policy will remain in force until the insured dies.
3. True.
4. True.
5. True.

Quick Quiz 11.2
1. True.
2. False. An entity approach buys one policy per owner, therefore 5 policies not 20.
3. True.

Quick Quiz 11.3
1. False. The transfer-for-value rule imposes income tax on the death benefit of a life insurance policy that has been transferred for valuable consideration once the transfer for value occurs. Subsequently canceling the transfer for value will not invalidate this tax result.
2. True.
3. False. While the death benefit on a life insurance policy is typically received income-tax free, interest earnings on death benefits remaining on deposit with the life insurance company are subject to income tax.
4. False. The surrender value of a term insurance policy is merely the unearned premium on the policy, which is reduced to zero each year. Therefore, there is no accumulation of surrender value from year to year in a term insurance policy.

Quick Quiz 11.4
1. False. Unlike corporate dividends, which represent a distribution of earnings and profits that are subject to tax, dividends on a life insurance policy represent a return of part of the insured's capital, and are therefore not subject to income tax.
2. False. If a loan is taken for the full cash value, the policy will lapse since there will be no cash left to cover policy expenses. Each insurance contract has rules governing the amount of loans that may be taken against the cash value of the policy.
3. True.
4. True.
5. True.

QUICK QUIZ EXPLANATIONS

Quick Quiz 11.5
1. False. Naming a beneficiary on a life insurance policy is not considered a completed gift, since the owner has the right to change the beneficiary. As such, no gift tax would be due upon changing the beneficiary of a life insurance policy.
2. False. The gift-tax value of a life insurance policy in pay status is the interpolated terminal reserve plus the unearned premium. If the policy was paid up, its value for gift tax purposes would be the replacement cost.
3. True.

Quick Quiz 11.6
1. True.
2. True.
3. True.
4. True.

Quick Quiz 11.7
1. False. Creation of an ILIT does not eliminate the estate inclusion risk associated with the three year rule. If the insured gratuitously transfers his or her life insurance policy to the ILIT, and dies within three years, the three-year rule of Section 2035 will require the death benefit to be included in the insured's gross estate. If, however, an ILIT is created, and the ILIT applies for and purchases a policy in the life of the grantor (so that the grantor never possesses any incidents of ownership in the policy), the ILIT can be used to keep the death benefit out of the grantor's estate.
2. True.

12
SPECIAL ELECTIONS & POST MORTEM PLANNING

LEARNING OBJECTIVES

1. Identify the liquidity needs of a decedent's family.
2. Determine liquidity sources and their implications.
3. Describe a IRC Section 303 redemption.
4. Identify the income tax issues relating to a decedent's final income tax return.
5. Identify the elections associated with a decedent's final income tax return.
6. Explain the election to split gifts between spouses for the year of death of a decedent spouse.
7. Describe the valuation of assets for a decedent including the date of death value, and the election for the alternative valuation date.
8. Describe installment payments of estate tax under IRC Section 6166.
9. Explain special use valuation under IRC Section 2032A.
10. Discuss the value of disclaimers for post mortem planning.
11. Describe the use of a qualified terminable interest property election.
12. Explain the portability of a deceased spouse's estate tax exemption.

CFP Board Resource Document - Student-Centered Learning Objectives based upon CFP Board Principal Topics.

INTRODUCTION

Proper financial and estate planning can result in an estate plan that minimizes transfer taxes and is tailored to a person's needs. However, changes to the person's circumstances often occur after the plan has been adopted. Even individuals who periodically revise and update their estate plan may end up with planning that does not necessarily fit their needs when they die. After the death of a person, there are several issues that need to be addressed, as well as techniques that are available to the executor to modify the lifetime planning completed by the decedent so as to better reflect the needs of the decedent's family. This chapter reviews common estate issues that arise when an individual dies, as well as the elections available to modify the decedent's pre-death estate plan.

LIQUIDITY NEEDS

Access to readily available cash is vitally important in the administration of a decedent's estate. Having sufficient liquid resources available to pay for estate and inheritance taxes, medical expenses, funeral expenses, administration costs, and the needs of surviving family members during the estate administration process is paramount. Since most individuals do not regularly maintain sufficient cash and liquid assets in their investment and banking portfolios to cover all of these costs and expenses, life insurance is often used to provide the needed liquidity. As discussed in prior chapters, an ideal way to hold life insurance is in an irrevocable life insurance trust (ILIT) so that the dollar amount of the death benefit of the policy is not included in the decedent's gross estate but is available to provide liquidity to the estate.

Last Medical Costs

Most of an individual's lifetime medical expenses are incurred within the last three months of life. As people age and medical needs increase, this reality becomes more evident. Many medical costs are covered by insurance (private health insurance, Medicare, Medicare supplement, and retiree health insurance), but those costs not covered by insurance become a debt of the estate. In the administration of a decedent's probate estate, medical costs (debts) must be paid before any distributions are made to beneficiaries, and such costs in extreme circumstances could deplete the entire estate. Maintaining proper medical insurance coverage until death helps minimize estate costs (by transferring the payment responsibility to the insurance company) and may help preserve the assets of the estate for heirs. Medical expense insurance reduces the liquidity needs of the estate by providing an outside source of funding for these expenses.

Funeral Costs

Funerals can be expensive and prices of funerals are continuing to increase. A burial of a decedent's remains costs on the average $6,000 to $20,000, depending upon the level of service selected and the cost of materials used. Cremations can also be expensive, but are typically less expensive than burial. In either case, these costs must usually be paid shortly after the decedent's death and prior to the service being rendered. If the decedent did not have sufficient liquid funds on hand at death to cover the expenses, life insurance proceeds are often used to cover these expenses since insurance death claims are usually paid shortly after the decedent's death. Often, a family member advances a deposit for the funeral service, or pays for the entire service and is reimbursed by the estate when the estate generates sufficient liquidity for reimbursement.

> ### Key Concepts
>
> 1. Why must an estate have cash during its administration?
> 2. Identify three common estate administrative costs.
> 3. When is a decedent's estate tax return due?

An alternative to having the estate pay for the funeral expenses is to have the decedent pre-arrange and pre-fund the funeral during his life. This can be achieved either formally (by making arrangements with a funeral director and paying for the services in advance) or informally (by leaving instructions for the heirs along with sufficient cash to cover the expenses). If a funeral is pre-arranged and pre-funded, these administrative burdens are relieved and the estate's liquidity needs are reduced.

Transition or Adjustment Period Costs

A decedent's surviving family members need cash to cover living and other normal expenses, often referred to as transition or adjustment period costs, during the estate administration process. This is particularly true when a person dies unexpectedly, when the decedent is young, or when the surviving spouse and the dependent children do not have independent sources of funds.

To the extent that the decedent held cash accounts as joint tenancy with rights of survivorship with his surviving spouse, the surviving spouse should be able to immediately access those funds to cover living expenses. If all of the liquid accounts were titled solely in the name of the decedent, the funds are typically frozen by the financial institution and then transferred to the estate upon presentation of a certified death certificate and letters testamentary or letters of administration.

In determining the appropriate amount of life insurance to place on a person's life, transition and adjustment expenses should be considered. Including these expenses in the plan for a working individual is even more important, since a significant source of income for the family disappears when the decedent dies. Estate administration can extend from approximately nine months to several years depending upon the size and complexity of the estate, and longer periods of estate administration will increase the liquidity needs for the decedent. Without proper planning for transition expenses, the surviving spouse and dependent heirs may not have access to any of the estate's funds during this administrative period.

Administrative Costs

Administrative costs for the estate include executor's and attorney's fees, fees for preparation of the estate and inheritance tax returns, and fees for appraisal reports and the opinions of experts. For complex estates, these costs can be substantial and must normally be paid as incurred. Consequently, the estate will need to have a liquid source of funds to cover these expenses.

Planning to provide liquidity is even more important for a decedent's estate that consists of a large number or percentage of hard to value assets. Assets that are difficult to value include artwork, jewelry, antiques, commercial real estate, and closely held business interests. All of these types of assets must be appraised to determine the value included in the gross estate. Appraisals can be complex and expensive, and involve the time of experts, which is also typically expensive. Factoring these costs into the liquidity needs of large estates is an important consideration for an estate planner.

> ### Quick Quiz 12.1
>
> 1. Most individuals die with the cash necessary to cover all of the costs and taxes associated with their death.
>   a. True
>   b. False
> 2. Funerals are expensive and can be pre-funded to reduce the expense burden for the family and the estate.
>   a. True
>   b. False
> 3. Administrative expenses of an estate include the expense of the preparation of the estate tax return.
>   a. True
>   b. False
> 4. The administration of an estate is usually quick and easy.
>   a. True
>   b. False
>
> *False, True, True, False.*

Income, Estate, and Generation-Skipping Transfer Taxes

Taxes are a fact of both life and death. Federal estate taxes and generation-skipping transfer taxes occasioned by the decedent's death are due nine months after the decedent's date of death. Most states impose a similar time frame for payment of any state inheritance and estate taxes. Any gift taxes generated by the decedent's gifts prior to death will be due April 15th of the year following the decedent's death, and income taxes on income generated by the estate will be due on an annual basis during the estate administration. Having a source of funds to pay these taxes is critical in the estate administration process. In some special circumstances, it may be possible to defer payment of some of these taxes, but that deferral is not without cost. Once taxes are due, interest begins to accrue if the tax is not paid in full by the due date of the tax return.

chapter 12

LIQUIDITY SOURCES AND IMPLICATIONS

Sale of Assets

One way to generate liquidity to pay estate taxes and administrative expenses is to sell some of the decedent's assets. If the assets are liquid, or easy to sell, this can be effective. While a sale may require effort from the executor or administrator (and may therefore increase the administration expenses), assets that are easy to liquidate (such as stocks and bonds) can generally be sold at fair market value.

> **Key Concepts**
>
> 1. Identify three ways an executor can generate liquidity for an estate.
> 2. Identify the parties involved in a split-dollar life insurance arrangement.
> 3. How much of a stock redemption must the executor complete to receive the special capital gains treatment of Section 303?
> 4. Is the interest on a loan used to pay estate taxes deductible?

Selling assets is not an attractive alternative when a significant portion of the decedent's gross estate consists of hard-to-value assets (such as artwork and jewelry, business interests, or real estate). Not only is it difficult to determine the fair market value of these assets, but it is also very difficult to find a buyer who is willing to pay fair market value shortly after the decedent's death. When these types of assets need to be liquidated to pay the estate taxes and the administration expenses, they are often sold for less than fair market value, resulting in a loss for the heirs. Whenever a taxable estate includes illiquid assets, other methods of generating liquidity should be considered.

Life Insurance

Using life insurance to generate estate liquidity matches the need for funds at death with the availability of funds. When an insured decedent dies and incurs estate taxes and administration expenses, the life insurance policy will mature, making a large amount of cash available to cover those expenses. One disadvantage to life insurance is that if the decedent owns the policy, the death benefit will be included in the gross estate. The traditional technique used to avoid estate taxation of the death benefit is the use of an irrevocable life insurance trust (ILIT). Some business owners and corporate executives may also use a split-dollar life insurance arrangement.

Irrevocable Life Insurance Trust (ILIT)

An **irrevocable life insurance trust (ILIT)** is an irrevocable trust that is funded by the grantor and which owns life insurance on the grantor's life. Typically, the grantor makes annual contributions to the trust to pay the life insurance policy premium and the beneficiaries of the trust are given a Crummey power over the annual contribution to qualify the gifts for the gift tax annual exclusion. Once the grantor dies, the trustee collects the life insurance death benefit proceeds and uses or distributes them in accordance with the terms of the trust document.

As discussed in Chapter 6, when using an ILIT, it is important to avoid estate tax inclusion rules (under Section 2042) which require the life insurance policy death benefit to be included in the insured's gross estate. The requirements state that the death benefit of a life insurance policy is included in the decedent's gross estate if:
1. the decedent owned the policy at the time of his death;
2. the death benefits are made available to the executor or the estate; or
3. the decedent had any incident of ownership in the policy at the time of his death.

A grantor should also be concerned with the three-year lookback rule (IRC Section 2035) which states that if the decedent transferred the life insurance policy or any incident of ownership in the life insurance policy within three years of his death, the full death benefit is subject to estate taxation. An often overlooked application of this rule states that if the death benefit is made available to the executor of the estate for the purpose of paying death taxes, the full death benefit is subject to estate taxation. In other words, if an ILIT allows the trustee to pay the estate taxes and administration expenses of the decedent's estate, or gives the executor of the estate the right to demand a distribution from the ILIT for that purpose, the death benefit will be subject to estate tax even though the policy was not owned by the decedent.

There are two ways to address this issue. Instead of making the proceeds available to the estate, the ILIT could give the trustee the discretion to make loans (bearing an adequate interest rate and backed up with security) to the decedent's estate, or to purchase property from the decedent's estate. The decedent's will should contain similar language allowing the executor or administrator of the estate to sell assets to any party, including the ILIT, or to borrow money from any source, including the ILIT. Since the decedent's estate and the ILIT created by the decedent are two separate entities, as long as an arm's-length transaction is entered into to provide liquidity for the estate, the proceeds of the life insurance policy are not deemed to be made available to the estate, thereby escaping inclusion in the decedent's gross estate.

Split-Dollar Life Insurance Arrangements

Split-dollar life insurance is not a type of life insurance, but rather a form of ownership for a life insurance policy. When a split-dollar arrangement is created, two parties have an ownership interest in one life insurance policy. One party typically owns the death benefit protection, while another party owns the cash value. Split-dollar arrangements are often established to allow executives and business owners the opportunity to purchase life insurance at a reduced out of pocket cost. In an employer-employee context, a traditional split-dollar arrangement would provide death benefit protection to the employee while the employer would have an interest in the policy cash value to the extent of its share of the premium payments. The employee would typically pay the portion of the premium reflecting the pure cost of insurance protection, and the employer would pay the portion of the premium reflecting the increase in the cash value of the policy. A reverse split-dollar plan is an arrangement where the employee owns the cash value, and the employer owns the pure death benefit protection provided by the policy.

When a split-dollar arrangement is established, the employee often transfers his portion of the policy (typically the pure death benefit protection) to an ILIT so that the death benefit received will be excluded from his gross estate. To the extent that an ILIT is used to hold a portion of the policy, the issues discussed above are relevant. If the insured owns a portion of the policy directly, that portion of the death benefit will be included in his gross estate, and can therefore be used to pay estate taxes and administration expenses.

Tax-Advantaged Accounts

Some individuals have large accumulations in their tax-advantaged accounts (qualified plans and individual retirement accounts) and believe that these accounts will provide the liquidity needed to pay estate taxes and administration expenses at their death. This is particularly true for those individuals whose estates consist primarily of qualified plans and IRAs. While it is possible for the estate to access these types of accounts to generate cash needed by the estate, pension plans and IRAs are not the most efficient source of funds for estate liquidity purposes.

Perhaps the most important feature of a tax-advantaged account is that it provides deferral of income tax. Assets placed in a tax-deferred account do not incur income tax on income as it is earned, but rather defer that income to a future tax year (presumably when the client retires). If the client died after making a deferral decision, but before he took the money out of the tax-deferred account, and could receive a step-up in basis on the deferred account at his death, the income that was transferred to the deferred account will forever escape income taxation. To combat this potential for abuse, Congress created the Income in Respect of a Decedent (IRD) rules.

The IRD rules state that when an individual has chosen to defer income during his lifetime, the value of those deferrals at death will not qualify for a step-up in basis. Instead, whoever receives the decedent's income tax-deferred accounts must pay income tax on the distributions received from the accounts. However, if the IRD causes the estate to be subject to estate tax (because it is included in the decedent's gross estate), the beneficiary of the tax-advantaged account will be eligible for a deduction in the form of a miscellaneous itemized deduction not subject to the two percent of AGI floor. The amount of the deduction is equal to the estate tax attributable to the net IRD.

If the executor or administrator of the decedent's estate takes a distribution from a tax-advantaged account to pay the estate taxes and administration expenses, the distribution is taxable income to the estate. The executor can take a distribution equal to the amount necessary to pay the estate taxes and the administration expenses plus the income tax liability generated by the distribution, but this may result in a significant reduction in the amount of assets available for the heirs.

For individuals whose gross estate consists primarily of tax-advantaged accounts and who are insurable, a better approach may be to take distributions from the qualified plan or IRA during their lifetime and transfer the funds to an ILIT holding a life insurance policy. The ILIT can be used to provide liquidity for the estate. This approach will minimize the distributions from the tax-advantaged plan necessary to cover the estate's liquidity needs, and allow those plans to achieve further income tax deferral by stretching out the distributions after the decedent's death over the lifetime of the beneficiaries.

Corporate Redemption from Closely Held Businesses

Owners of closely held and family C corporations have yet another source of funds to cover estate liquidity needs – the corporation itself. A corporate redemption of some or all of the decedent's stock at death can transform an illiquid asset (a closely held business interest) into a liquid asset (cash).

A corporate redemption is a sale of company stock from a shareholder back to the issuing corporation. Federal tax law requires all partial redemptions of corporate stock to be treated as a dividend distribution unless an exception can be found in the Code. Despite the fact that stock is sold to the corporation, the entire amount distributed to the shareholder is generally treated as a dividend distribution subject to ordinary income tax. Usually, the sale of an asset results in a capital gain, which allows the seller to take into consideration his adjusted basis when determining the amount subject to the capital gains tax, but corporate redemptions do not allow the shareholder to take his or her basis into account, subjecting the entire distribution to dividend tax treatment.

A major exception to the treatment of a partial redemption as a dividend distribution is found in **IRC Section 303**. IRC Section 303 states that the estate of a deceased shareholder may redeem enough shares to cover the death taxes (federal and state estate, inheritance, and generation-skipping transfer taxes), funeral expenses, and administrative expenses of the decedent, and the shares redeemed for this purpose will qualify for capital gains tax treatment. The imposition of Section 303 will usually result in the avoidance of income tax on the redemption, since the redemption occurs after death, and at death, the decedent's estate receives a step up in the adjusted basis of the shares equal to their fair market value at the decedent's date of death. If the redemption occurs shortly after death, a Section 303 redemption essentially allows the estate of a deceased shareholder to receive cash from the corporation in a tax-free exchange, and allows the corporation to reduce its earnings and profits (the accumulated earnings of the corporation that are typically subject to dividend taxation when distributed) which also benefits the surviving shareholders.

To qualify for a Section 303 redemption, more than 35 percent of the decedent's adjusted gross estate must consist of the closely held business interest. In the event that the decedent owned interests in several closely held businesses, the fair market value of all of the closely held business interests can be aggregated to meet the 35 percent test provided that the decedent owned at least 20 percent of each company's outstanding stock. In addition, the shareholder redeemed must be responsible for the payment of the estate taxes, administration expenses, and funeral expenses.

Example 12.1

Roger died last month, leaving an adjusted gross estate valued at $2,000,000. One of the assets in his estate was an interest in a closely held business valued at $800,000. The tax apportionment clause of Roger's will allocated all taxes and expenses to his residuary estate, which will be distributed to his three children in equal shares. Roger's will also included a specific bequest of the closely held business stock to his son. Roger's son received the entire interest in the closely held business, but would not be responsible for paying the estate taxes and administration expenses for the estate (all three children are responsible, per the will), and therefore Roger's estate will not qualify for a Section 303 redemption.

Example 12.2

Don died last month, leaving an adjusted gross estate of $2,000,000 including a closely held interest in a C corporation valued at $900,000. Don's will leaves all of his property with the exception of his closely held business interest to two of his children in equal shares. The business interest, as part of Don's residuary estate, will pass to his third child. According to the tax apportionment clause in the will, all estate taxes and administration expenses are allocated to the residuary estate. Since Don's third child will receive only the net value of the closely held business after the estate taxes and administration expenses have been paid, Don's third child is responsible for the payment of estate taxes and administration expenses. Don's estate will qualify for a Section 303 redemption, since more than 35% of his adjusted gross estate ($2,000,000 x 35% = $700,000) consists of the closely held C corporation stock.

When a Section 303 redemption is used, only the amount necessary to cover estate taxes, administration expenses, and funeral expenses of the decedent may be redeemed at favorable capital gains tax rates. To the extent that the estate redeems an amount in excess of the taxes and expenses of the estate, the redemption must meet the Code requirements to achieve capital gains tax treatment (i.e., there must be a complete redemption, or a substantially disproportionate redemption) or the excess amount will be treated as a dividend distribution to the estate, subject to tax at ordinary rates.

Distribution of Assets

In some cases, the executor or administrator of an estate will distribute the estate's assets in lieu of a cash payment to creditors and those providing estate administration services. However this is not be possible for the payment of taxes – both the federal and state governments require a cash payment within nine months of the decedent's date of death.

When an asset is distributed in lieu of a cash payment, the estate must recognize any gain on the asset to the extent that the fair market value of the asset at the date of distribution exceeds the estate's adjusted basis in the asset (generally the fair market value at the decedent's date of death). If the payment requires the recipient to report income upon receipt (payment for performance of services), the recipient will have to pay income tax on the fair market value of the asset at the time of distribution.

Loans for Payments of Taxes and Other Costs

If liquidity is needed, and all else fails, the estate may borrow money to cover the estate taxes and administration expenses of the decedent. If there is not an adequate source of funds available (such as from a life insurance policy), borrowing to cover taxes and expenses may be the most prudent approach.

> **Quick Quiz 12.2**
>
> 1. Selling an estate's assets is the best way to generate the cash necessary to cover the administration expenses of the estate.
>   a. True
>   b. False
>
> 2. Estate planning should always ensure that the decedent owns his life insurance policy.
>   a. True
>   b. False
>
> 3. Distributions from qualified plans are subject to ordinary income tax.
>   a. True
>   b. False
>
> 4. An estate may not take a loan to pay its estate tax.
>   a. True
>   b. False
>
> False, False, True, False.

Borrowing to cover taxes and administration expenses is an attractive alternative for several reasons. First, borrowing may prevent the need for a fire-sale of the assets, thereby protecting the value of the estate for the heirs and giving the executor or administrator more time to find a purchaser willing to pay the true fair market value of the assets. Second, the interest incurred on the note is a tax-deductible expense for the estate. Particularly for estates that have significant amounts of taxable income, the interest deduction may offset taxable income at the high estate income tax rates (due to the compressed rate brackets for estates and trusts).

INCOME TAX ISSUES AND ELECTIONS ON DECEDENT'S FINAL INCOME TAX RETURN (1040)

After an individual dies, a final income tax return (Form 1040) must be prepared and filed. The final return will include all of the decedent's taxable income and deductions until the date of his death. At the decedent's death, the decedent's estate is created and the estate will pay income tax on the income it receives to the extent that income is not distributed to the decedent's heirs by filing a Form 1041 (fiduciary return).

Exhibit 12.1 | Post Mortem Timeline

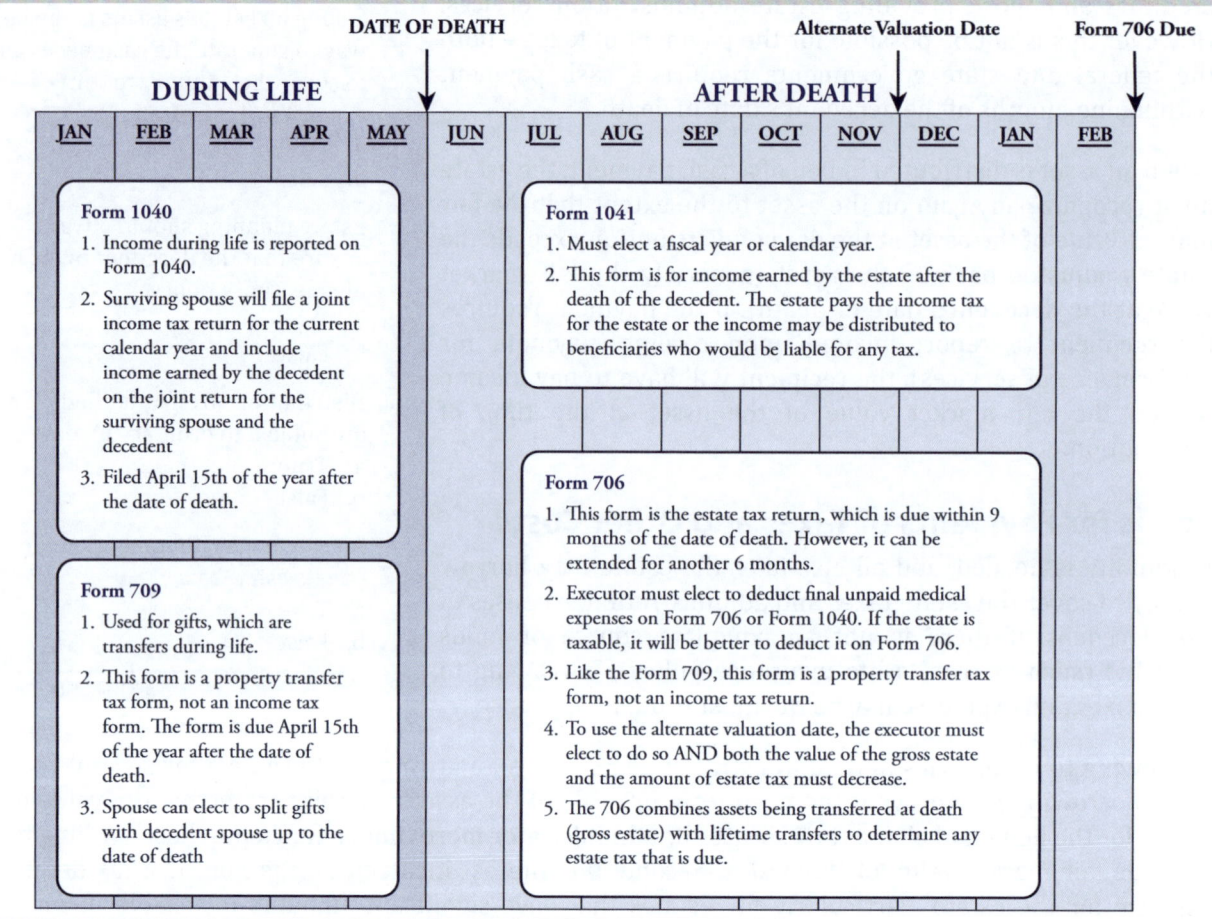

Joint or Separate Final Return

For the year of the decedent's death, if the decedent was married and is survived by a spouse, the decedent's final income tax return may be filed as married filing separately or married filing jointly. Generally, it is more advantageous to file as married filing jointly due to the more favorable income tax rate schedules and the income splitting benefits of joint returns. However, if the surviving spouse has concerns about a joint filing, or if the executor determines that filing separately would make more economic sense, separate returns are permitted.

A surviving spouse may file as a qualified widow(er) for two years following the decedent's death and enjoy the lower tax rates applicable to joint returns provided that:
1. the surviving spouse has not remarried, and
2. the surviving spouse is maintaining a home for one or more dependent children. (Note that if the surviving spouse remarries, he will be entitled to the married filing jointly lower rates if the new couple files their income tax returns as married filing jointly.)

Passive Losses

If the decedent had income tax losses from prior tax years that were suspended due to the application of the passive activity loss rules, those losses can be claimed on the decedent's final income tax return. To the extent that the decedent had passive loss carryforwards, it may be more advantageous to file the final return as married filing jointly due to the possibility of offsetting not only the decedent's taxable income, but also the spouse's taxable income with the passive loss carryforwards.

Expense Elections

Certain deductible expenses can be claimed either on the decedent's final income tax return (Form 1040) or on the estate tax return (Form 706).

The executor or administrator of the estate may elect to deduct unpaid medical expenses as of the date of the decedent's death either on the decedent's final income tax return (1040) or on the estate tax return (706). Of course, the executor cannot elect to deduct the expenses on both returns. As a general rule, if the decedent's estate is not subject to estate tax (either because the taxable estate is less than the applicable estate tax credit equivalent amount or estate taxes have been avoided through use of the unlimited marital or unlimited charitable deduction), the expenses should be deducted on the decedent's final income tax return (1040). Medical expenses are deductible on the final income tax return only to the extent that they exceed 7.5 percent in 2017 and 2018 and then 10 percent of AGI, thereafter. If the election is made to include the medical expenses on the final income tax return, the nondeductible portion is not permitted

Key Concepts

1. Identify the requirements for a surviving spouse to file as a qualifying widow.
2. Which expenses can be deducted on the estate tax return or the decedent's final income tax return?
3. What is the threshold for deducting medical expenses on the decedent's final income tax return?

Quick Quiz 12.3

1. A surviving spouse must file as a qualifying widow for the tax year of her husband's death.
   a. True
   b. False
2. Any passive loss carryforwards are deductible on the decedent's final income tax return.
   a. True
   b. False
3. A decedent's last medical expenses cannot be deducted on the estate tax return unless they exceed 7.5 percent of the adjusted gross estate.
   a. True
   b. False

False, True, False.

to be deducted on the estate tax return. When a decedent has a taxable estate, it is usually more advantageous to deduct the medical expenses from the estate tax return (706), because the lowest estate tax rate is higher than the highest income tax rate, and will generate a bigger tax benefit and there is no AGI floor for estate tax purposes, allowing the entire amount of medical expenses to be deductible. The executor may elect to deduct a portion of the medical expenses on the decedent's estate tax return, and the remaining portion of the medical expenses on the decedent's final income tax return if this yields a better overall tax result (unlikely).

INCOME TAX ISSUES AND ELECTIONS REGARDING THE ESTATE FIDUCIARY INCOME TAX RETURN (1041)

Selection of Tax Year

Since an estate is not a natural person, it is not required to use a calendar year for income tax purposes. The executor can elect to have the estate's income tax year end on the last day of any month during the year. When the executor elects to have the estate's income tax year end on the last day of any month other than December, the estate is said to have a fiscal year for income tax purposes.

Whether a fiscal year is elected by the executor often depends upon the expectation of the timing of the receipt of estate income. By electing a fiscal year, it is possible to control the timing of income recognition, and thereby minimizing the income tax the estate has to pay by keeping the income in a lower tax bracket or matching income with deductible expenses.

> **Key Concepts**
>
> 1. Identify a reason an executor may choose a fiscal year-end for the income tax purposes of the estate.
> 2. Why would an executor choose to waive his executor's fee?
> 3. How would the marginal income tax bracket of the heirs affect an executor's decision to make distributions to the heirs?

Expense Elections

Expenses of administering the decedent's estate and any casualty losses suffered during estate administration may be deducted on either the fiduciary income tax return for the estate (Form 1041), or the decedent's estate tax return (Form 706), but not both. The executor may elect to deduct some of the expenses on the income tax return and some of the expenses on the estate tax return if this yields a better overall tax result.

Like the deduction for medical expenses, to the extent that the decedent's estate is subject to estate taxes, it is usually better to deduct administrative expenses or casualty losses on the decedent's estate tax return, since the lowest estate tax rate is higher than the highest income tax rate. In the event that the estate is not subject to federal estate taxes (i.e., the tentative tax is less than the applicable estate tax credit amount, or estate taxes have been avoided through use of the unlimited marital or unlimited charitable deduction), an income tax deduction should be claimed.

Waiver of Executor's Fees

Executor's fees are deductible either on the fiduciary income tax return (Form 1041) or on the estate tax return (Form 706), but not on both. Executor's fees are taxable income to the recipient and require the recipient to pay income, and potentially, self-employment taxes on the amount received. (If paid to a professional executor or administrator, self-employment tax may apply to such fees. For a nonprofessional executor or administrator (a person serving in such capacity in an isolated instance, such as a friend or relative of the decedent), self-employment tax only applies if a trade or business is included in the estate's assets, the executor actively participates in the business, and the fees are related to the operation of the business.

In many cases, the executor of the estate is also an heir or legatee of the estate. No income tax consequences are triggered when an heir or legatee receives a distribution from an estate. Therefore, an executor who is also an heir of the estate should consider whether or not to waive the executor's fee. If the executor decides to waive the fee, a waiver should be executed early in the estate administration process to prevent the IRS from arguing that the executor had constructive receipt of the executor's fee and thus taxable income.

For relatively small estates, a waiver of the executor's fee usually makes financial sense. If the total value of the estate is less than the applicable estate tax credit equivalency amount, a deduction for the executor's fee will not reduce the estate taxes due (no estate taxes will be due). By waiving the fee, the executor will avoid the recognition of taxable ordinary income (potentially subject to self-employment tax as discussed previously) on the distribution and will receive the inheritance free of income taxes. An exception to this rule may apply when the estate is in a high income tax bracket, the executor is in a lower income tax bracket, and the executor's earnings already exceed the Social Security taxable wage base. In such a circumstance, it is necessary to calculate the benefits of the executor taking the fee as compared to receiving an inheritance and then choose the course that results in the greatest overall tax savings.

> **Quick Quiz 12.4**
>
> 1. An executor must file a fiduciary income tax return (1040) for the estate on a calendar year basis.
>   a. True
>   b. False
>
> 2. An executor may choose to waive his/her executor's fee.
>   a. True
>   b. False
>
> 3. A casualty loss, if permitted, may be deducted on the fiduciary income tax return (1041) or on the estate tax return (706).
>   a. True
>   b. False
>
> 4. U.S. savings bonds do not receive a step-to fair market value at the decedent's date of death. When redeemed, all interest is subject to ordinary income tax.
>   a. True
>   b. False
>
> False, True, True, True.

For larger estates, accepting an executor's fee may produce a more attractive tax benefit, since estate tax rates are higher than fiduciary income tax rates. This may not be true for estates that are subject to the lower marginal tax rates or in situations where the executor will have to pay self-employment taxes on the income. Again, a mathematical calculation is necessary to determine what course of action is most appropriate.

In situations where there are multiple heirs/legatees of an estate and the executor is also a heir/legatee, waiving the executor's fee may result in the executor receiving less, not more, of the property. This can happen when all of the heirs/legatees share the estate equally. If the executor waives the fee, the amount that would have been paid to the executor is split up among all of the heirs. In this circumstance, the executor may be better off by taking a fee, even if it creates taxable income. Receiving an executor's fee, however, may create a conflict between the executor and the other heirs who may feel that the executor is receiving part of their inheritance. To avoid this type of conflict, as discussed in Chapter 2, a will should include a discussion of the executor selection and the determination of the executor's fee and duties.

Exhibit 12.2 | Summary of Alternative Income and Estate Tax Deductions

	Decedent's Income Tax Return Form 1040	Estate Income Tax Return Form 1041	Estate Tax Return Form 706	Notes
Unpaid Medical Expenses	Yes	No	Yes	Not both, but may split > 10% AGI
Casualty Losses	Yes During Life	Yes After Death	Yes After Death	Not both, but may split >10% AGI if occurred before death
Executor Fees (Taxable Income to the Executor)	No	Yes	Yes	May be waived for better tax result

U.S. Savings Bonds and Income in Respect of Decedent (IRD) Assets

U.S. savings bonds are income in respect of decedent assets. IRD assets do not receive a step to fair market value in basis at the owner's date of death. U.S. savings bonds are treated in this way because usually income tax is not paid on the interest as it accrues – it is paid when the owner redeems the bond. If the estate redeems the bond, the estate will have to pay income tax on the interest income or, if circumstances dictate, distribute the income to the heirs and allow them to pay the income tax. In either case, whoever receives the income may receive a corresponding IRD deduction (a deduction equal to the estate tax attributable to the value of the IRD asset). Other IRD assets include qualified plan accounts, IRAs, annuitized annuities, installment notes, accrued dividends, accrued rent, and wages owed to the decedent at the time of his death.

If the decedent has made any charitable bequests in his will, it may be wise to satisfy those bequests with any U.S. savings bonds or IRD assets held by the estate. While the charity will recognize income upon the receipt of the asset, no income tax will be paid because charitable organizations are exempt from income tax.

Exhibit 12.3 | Partial List of IRD Assets

- Qualified Plans
- IRAs
- U.S. Savings Bonds
- Installment Notes
- Annuitized Annuities
- Accrued Dividends
- Accrued Wages

chapter 12

Distributions and Income Tax Bracket Analysis

During the administration of an estate, it is important to keep the marginal estate and income tax bracket of the estate and the marginal income tax bracket of the heirs in mind. In most cases, the estate will be in a higher marginal income tax bracket due to the compressed rate brackets that apply to trusts and estates (see **Exhibit 8.2**) in Chapter 8 for the trust and estate income tax rates).

> **Key Concepts**
>
> 1. How does a couple make the election to split gifts for the tax year?
> 2. What is the "fair market value" of an asset?
> 3. Identify the qualification requirements to utilize IRC §6166.
> 4. Identify the qualification requirements of a special use valuation.
> 5. How does the availability of a QTIP election benefit the decedent?

If the estate is in a higher marginal income tax bracket than the heirs, the executor should consider distributing the income of the estate to the heirs (in the manner provided for in the decedent's will). The income will pass through to the heirs and they will pay income tax on that income at their lower income tax rates.

If all heirs are in the same income tax bracket as the estate, or in a higher tax bracket, distribution of income will not be necessary for income tax savings and the executor may wish to retain the income to ensure that the estate has sufficient liquidity to meet its expense needs. To the extent that the estate is holding assets that have appreciated from the date of the decedent's death and the heirs are in a higher income tax bracket than the estate, it may be wise to consider selling the assets prior to making distributions to heirs so that the overall income tax liability is minimized. In such a case, the estate would pay the tax on the gain rather than the heirs.

GIFT TAX ISSUES AND ELECTIONS

Election to Split Gifts for the Year of Death

Many individuals use lifetime gifting as a key component of their estate planning strategy. By giving assets during their lifetime, not only is the asset removed from their gross estate (at least the portion that qualifies for the gift tax annual exclusion), the future appreciation of the asset is transferred to the donee. Once an individual begins gifting property, annual gifts frequently continue until the individual's death. When a couple decides to begin gifting property to heirs, they will usually first make use of the annual exclusion, and only after exhausting the annual exclusion will they make transfers subject to gift tax. One of the ways a married couple can make full use of their annual exclusions is to elect to split gifts of separate property made during the year. The gift-splitting election treats a gift of separate property as being made one-half from each spouse, thereby allowing the use of each spouse's annual exclusion for the gift. The election is made on each spouse's annual gift tax return, requires each spouse to sign the other's gift tax return, and applies to all gifts made by either spouse during the year.

If a decedent made gifts during the last income tax year before his death, those gifts must be reported on a timely filed gift tax return. The decedent will obviously not be available to sign the gift tax return for gift-splitting purposes with his spouse. The IRC allows a surviving spouse, however, to elect gift-splitting on the gifts made by the decedent before his death in the decedent's final tax year. This can be a valuable planning tool and can help preserve the decedent's applicable estate tax credit amount for testamentary transfers from his estate. The spouse must not have remarried in the year of the gift.

Example 12.3

Michael has a wife and two children. Michael's daughter, Maureen, graduated from college in May and began a career as an elementary school teacher. Michael decided to reward Maureen for her hard work and he purchased a new car for her that cost $21,000. The funding for the car came from Michael's separate (not marital) assets. Since the gift exceeded the gift tax annual exclusion amount ($15,000), the excess ($6,000) would have reduced Michael's applicable gift tax credit amount by the corresponding gift tax. If Michael's wife, Diane, elects to split gifts with Michael for Michael's final tax year, the $21,000 gift to Maureen is treated as if one-half was made by Michael and one-half was made by Diane. Under the gift-splitting election, neither party gave Maureen an amount in excess of the gift tax annual exclusion. Michael's applicable gift tax credit amount will not be reduced as a result of the gift, and as a result, more property can pass to Michael's heirs without being subjected to gift or estate tax.

BASIC ESTATE PLANNING ISSUES AND ELECTIONS (POST MORTEM)

Valuation of Assets

As discussed in Chapter 6, a decedent's assets are included in his gross estate at their fair market value. Fair market value is the value that would be paid for the property in an arm's-length transaction where there is a willing buyer and willing seller, where neither party is acting under compulsion, and where both parties have full knowledge of the facts. "Fair Market Value" is the value that the asset would trade at in the ideal world.

Small estates will be encouraged to overstate the value of its assets, while large estates will tend to understate the value of its assets. A small estate (one that does not have to pay estate tax), may benefit by assigning higher values to its assets, since the value of the assets included in the gross estate receive a step-up in basis for the heirs. The heirs of a small estate will have a smaller taxable capital gain for income tax purposes to the extent that the adjusted basis of the assets is higher. Larger estates (estates that have to pay estate taxes) would rather undervalue the assets and save on estate taxes, even if this means that heirs have higher capital gains taxes to pay later. Larger estates have a tendency to understate values because estate tax rates are significantly higher than capital gains rates. The IRS scrutinizes estate tax returns for exaggerations or minimizations in asset valuation.

Selection of Valuation Date

Generally, the value of property included in a decedent's gross estate is determined as of the date of the decedent's death. However, requiring the valuation date to be the date of the decedent's death may result in a hardship for some estates. This is particularly true when the estate consists primarily of illiquid assets and the value of those assets depreciates, instead of appreciates, during the estate administration process. In such a circumstance, the executor or administrator of the estate can elect to use the alternative valuation date for valuation purposes on the estate tax return (Form 706).

chapter 12

Alternate Valuation Date

If the executor or administrator elects to value the estate's assets on the **alternate valuation date**, the fair market value of the assets six months after the decedent's date of death is included in the gross estate. To be eligible to elect the alternate valuation date, both of the following conditions must be met:
1. the value of the assets included in the gross estate six months after decedent's date of death must be lower than the value of the assets on the date of death; and
2. there must be a reduction in the total estate tax due as a result of the election.

Note that one impact of these two requirements is to prevent small estates (estates that do not have an estate tax liability) from electing the alternate valuation date to increase the value of the assets included in the gross estate, thereby increasing the step-up in basis for heirs. If an additional step-up in basis could be achieved with no estate tax cost, income tax savings would result for the beneficiaries of the estate due to decreased capital gains.

Estates that are subject to the estate tax would not elect the alternative valuation date if the election would result in an increase in estate taxes, since the estate tax is more expensive than the capital gains tax. From a practical standpoint, therefore, the alternate valuation date election is available only for estates subject to estate tax, and only when estate tax savings can result.

> **Quick Quiz 12.5**
>
> 1. A couple who elects to split gifts must agree to split all gifts made during the year.
>   a. True
>   b. False
> 2. A decedent's assets are included in his gross estate at the fair market value at his date of death or the alternate valuation date.
>   a. True
>   b. False
>
> True, True.

Exhibit 12.4 | Alternate Valuation Date (AVD)

To Qualify
1. The total value of the gross estate must depreciate after the date of death; and
2. The total estate tax must be less than the estate tax calculated using the date of death values.
Valuation if properly elected
1. All assets are valued at the alternate valuation date
2. Except: • Assets distributed before 6 months from the date of death which are valued at the date of distribution or sale; and • Wasting assets (annuitized annuities, patents, royalties, installment notes, lease income) which must be valued at the date of death.

Basic Estate Planning Issues and Elections (Post Mortem)

Installment Payments of Estate Tax (IRC Section 6166)

Closely held business owners often face a severe liquidity problem at death. Their largest and most valuable asset is usually their business interest. The inclusion of the value of the business interest in the decedent's gross estate may result in a large estate tax liability that is due nine months after the date of death, but it is often difficult to liquidate the business interest in such a short period of time, or it may be imprudent to liquidate the business interest if, as a result, the owner group or family will lose control.

To help closely held business owners resolve this problem, Congress enacted **IRC Section 6166**, which allows for the deferral of estate taxes attributable to the closely held business interest. When the executor of the estate elects to make installment payments of estate tax under IRC Section 6166, it is possible to extend the payment of estate taxes attributable to the closely held business over 14 years. The first four years of payments are interest-only, followed by 10 payments that amortize the estate tax liability over the payment period (although may be paid over a shorter period). If the family of the decedent wishes to keep the business interest, an installment payment of estate taxes will allow the estate taxes to be paid with the ongoing earnings of the business, thereby relieving the estate of the obligation to pay a large amount of cash for taxes shortly after the decedent's death.

To qualify for an IRC Section 6166 deferral of estate tax, three requirements must be met (in addition to filing an extension on Form 4768):
1. the value of the business interest must exceed 35 percent of the value of the decedent's adjusted gross estate;
2. the business interest must be a closely held business (a sole proprietorship; a partnership if at least 20 percent of the total capital interest is included in the decedent's gross estate; a partnership with 45 or fewer partners; a corporation if at least 20 percent of the voting stock is included in the decedent's gross estate; a corporation with 45 or fewer shareholders); and
3. the entity must have been actively engaged in the conduct of a trade or a business at the date of the decedent's death.

The interest paid on the deferred tax is two percent on the tentative tax generated on $1,570,000 (indexed annually for inflation) plus the applicable estate tax credit equivalency amount for the year of death, less the applicable estate tax credit for the year of death. For 2020, the two percent rate would apply to the tentative tax generated on $13,150,000 [$1,570,000 (indexed number for 2020) + $11,580,000 (applicable estate tax credit equivalency amount for 2020)] less $4,577,800 (applicable estate tax credit for 2020), or the estate tax due of $628,000 [$13,150,000 generates an estate tax of $5,205,800 less $4,577,800]. If the amount of estate tax attributable to the closely held business is less than the amount computed above, the two percent portion applies to the lesser amount. If the balance of the unpaid estate taxes exceeds this amount, the excess is subject to an interest rate up to 45 percent of the regular underpayment rate.[1]

Neither the two percent interest nor the interest on the excess portion are deductible on the decedent's estate tax return.

---

1. IRC §6601(a) and 6601(j).

Special Use Valuation (IRC Section 2032A)

Generally, fair market value implies the value of a property in its highest and best use. Over the years, the highest and best use of a particular piece of property may change. For example, 50 years ago, the use of property outside of a city for farming purposes may have been the highest and best use of the land, but as the city expands, the highest and best use of the property may shift from farming activities to a residential subdivision or office complex. For estate tax purposes, the fair market value (i.e., the highest and best use value) of the property must be included in the gross estate; the value of the land in its current use does not matter. If an individual is using a piece of real property as a farm or in another trade or business that is not employing the property at its highest and best use, the value of the property may be higher than the value of the property in its current use. This may create an estate tax that could be much larger than an estate tax based on the value of the property utilizing its current use value. As a result, the farming operation or business enterprise may not be able to continue, since the real estate it is using must be sold to pay the estate taxes it has generated. To help provide relief in cases such as this, Congress enacted the Special Use Valuation provisions under **IRC Section 2032A**. If special use valuation is elected, the value included in the decedent's gross estate will be the current use value of the property, subject to a limitation that the highest and best use value cannot be reduced by more than $1,180,000 in 2020.

In order to qualify for special use valuation, the following conditions must be met:
1. the decedent was at the time of his death a citizen or resident of the U.S.;
2. the property must be used in a farming operation or trade or business that was actively managed by the decedent or the decedent's family for five out of the eight years immediately preceding the decedent's death;
3. the value of the real and personal property used in a qualifying manner must equal or exceed 50 percent of the decedent's gross estate (as adjusted only for secured mortgages for property included in the gross estate);
4. the value of the real property used in a qualifying manner must equal or exceed 25 percent of the value of the gross estate (as adjusted only for secured mortgages for property included in the gross estate);
5. the qualifying property must be located in the U.S. and must pass to qualifying heirs (a member of the decedent's family who acquires the property from the decedent) who must actively participate in the farming activity or trade or business; and
6. the executor must file the election with the estate tax return, complete with a recapture agreement.

Subsequent to the transfer of the property to the qualifying heirs, the qualifying heirs must continue to use the property in its qualified use, as stated in the election included with the estate tax return, for a period of at least 10 years following the decedent's death. If the heirs stop using the property in a qualifying manner, or the property is sold during the 10-year period following the decedent's death, an additional tax is imposed. The amount that is imposed is the lesser of:
1. the estate tax savings from special use valuation, or
2. an amount equal to the proceeds from the sale of the property less the special use valuation amount.

While special use valuation is available to business owners and farmers, it is rarely used. The qualification requirements are strict, and even if they can be met, the ongoing requirements necessary to avoid recapture of the estate tax savings place real restrictions on the heir's use of the property. When possible, it is usually more advantageous to use other estate planning techniques to deal with the property than attempt to maintain qualification for special use valuation over long periods of time.

Exhibit 12.5 | Summary of Elections Available for Closely Held Business Interests

Installment Payment of Estate Tax
IRC Section 6166

- 14 annual installments
  - Payments 0 - 4: Interest-only payments
  - Payments 5 - 14: Interest and Estate Tax
  - 2% interest on first $628,000 (2020) of estate tax due attributable to the closely held business
- Eligibility
  - Value of closely-held business interest > 35% of the AGE
  - If more than one business, they can be aggregated if the AGE includes ≥ 20% of the capital interest in the closely held business
    - if corporation with ≤ 45 shareholders, or
    - if partnership with ≤ 45 partners
- Closely held business actively engaged in trade or business

Special Use Valuation
IRC Section 2032A

- Reduce the fair market value of real property up to $1,180,000 (2020)
- Eligibility
  - Business real property must be used in farm or business activity managed by the decedent or the decedent's family for 5 out of the 8 years prior to the decedent's death
  - Value of business real and personal property must be ≥ 50% of the GE as adjusted
  - Values of business real property must be ≥ 25% of the GE as adjusted
  - Real property must pass to qualifying heirs
  - Executor must file election with the estate tax return
  - Heirs must use property in business for at least 10 years

Election to Disclaim

As discussed in Chapter 2, a **disclaimer** is an irrevocable and unqualified refusal to accept a gift or bequest. To be considered qualified for estate tax purposes, the disclaimer must meet the following requirements:
1. the disclaimer must be in writing,
2. the disclaimer must be made within nine months of the date on which the transfer creating the interest was made or the day on which the disclaiming party reaches the age of 21,
3. the disclaimant cannot specify the party to whom the property will be transferred as a result of the disclaimer, and
4. the disclaimant cannot accept any interest or benefit in the property prior to disclaiming.

The availability of a disclaimer exists because an individual cannot be forced to accept a gift or bequest. By executing a qualified disclaimer, the disclaimant can prevent the property from being transferred to him.

By the Surviving Spouse

A special rule exists for surviving spouses. A surviving spouse may disclaim a bequest yet still receive benefits in the disclaimed property. Use of this provision adds flexibility to an estate plan by allowing the surviving spouse to make determinations regarding the size of the deceased spouse's taxable estate after the decedent has died.

Example 12.4
Philip died leaving his entire $9.5 million dollar estate to his wife, Elizabeth. Philip's will states that if Elizabeth disclaims any portion of the property left to her, that property is transferred to a bypass trust that makes income distributions to Elizabeth and allows principal distributions for Elizabeth's health, education, maintenance, and support (an ascertainable standard), with the remainder of the trust transferred to the children at Elizabeth's death. Elizabeth has a sizable estate of her own, and together Philip and Elizabeth have four children. If Elizabeth disclaims the amount that can pass through Philip's estate without triggering a federal estate tax, the disclaimer will be a qualified disclaimer even though Elizabeth will receive benefits from the disclaimed property. In this case Elizabeth would disclaim the amount necessary to create a $11,580,000 (2020) taxable estate. This amount would pass to the bypass trust.

In Favor of Surviving Spouse

In some situations, disclaimers are used to transfer property to the surviving spouse. This situation occurs when the property passing to the surviving spouse is insufficient, and the other heirs of the estate (usually the children) want to sufficiently provide for their surviving parent. To the extent that a disclaimer is executed and, as a result, property passes to the surviving spouse, the property passing as a result of the disclaimer will qualify for the estate tax marital deduction and will not be construed as a gift from the disclaimant to the spouse.

Example 12.5

At the time David wrote his will, the market was strong, and his net worth was high. He left a substantial portion of his estate directly to his children in the form of specific bequests, with the remainder to his wife, Lisa. In the event that any of his children predeceased him, the child's share would be transferred first to Lisa in the form of a QTIP trust, and, upon Lisa's death, to the child's issue, per stirpes. Unfortunately, David's portfolio declined in value very quickly as the stock market declined, and David died without changing his will. If the terms of his will are strictly adhered to, his children will receive all of his estate, and his wife, Lisa, will receive nothing. Since the children do not want to leave their mother destitute, they decide to disclaim a portion of their inheritance (in aggregate, an amount equal to the excess over what can be transferred through David's estate without triggering any estate tax liability). All of the requirements for a qualified disclaimer are met, and the property passes to Lisa in the form of a QTIP trust. Since the property passed to the surviving spouse in a qualified way, David's estate would be entitled to a marital deduction for a like amount.

In Favor of Charities

If a disclaimer is executed and, as a result, the property is transferred to a charity under the terms of the decedent's will, the charitable transfer will qualify for the unlimited charitable deduction in the transferor's estate.

By Others Ignoring the Marital Deduction

In the event that an individual disclaims property and the property does not pass to the surviving spouse or a qualified charity, no estate tax savings will result in the transferor's estate. Overall family transfer tax savings may result, however, by preventing the inclusion of that property in the gross estate of a family member who does not need to receive it.

Example 12.6

Lewis, a widower, died recently. He left his entire estate to his children, per stirpes. Isaac, Lewis' youngest child, is independently wealth and would prefer not to receive the inheritance from his father's estate. Lewis is not otherwise using his generation-skipping transfer tax exemption on any lifetime or death-time transfers. Isaac disclaims, and the property passes to his children (under the terms of Lewis' will and not under direction by Isaac), and the executor of Lewis' estate elects to allocate Lewis' generation-skipping transfer tax exemption to the transfer. While there will be no estate tax savings (or additional transfer tax cost) in Lewis' estate, when Isaac dies, none of the property will be subject to estate tax, since he does not own it. Transfer tax savings result for the next generation.

Powers of Appointment

If the disclaimant has the authority to designate the recipient of the property as occurs with a general power of appointment, a qualified disclaimer of the bequest cannot be made. When such a situation exists, the original beneficiary has been granted a power of appointment over the property. The power of appointment will be considered a general power of appointment, since the original beneficiary would receive the property if he does not specify that the property will be transferred elsewhere.

Consequently, the value of the property subject to the general power of appointment is subject to transfer tax in the hands of the beneficiary. While it is possible to plan for future disclaimers by having the decedent include a disclaimer clause in his will, naming the appropriate parties as alternate takers, care should be taken to avoid granting a general power of appointment, since this will result in transfer tax consequences for the beneficiary.

Qualified Terminable Interest Property (QTIP) Election

One form of marital deduction transfer involves the use of the qualified terminable interest property (QTIP) election, which is discussed in depth in Chapter 10. While an individual can express a desire that his executor elect to qualify certain transfers for the unlimited estate tax marital deduction by making a QTIP election, the ultimate decision of whether to make the election rests with the executor or administrator of the estate. The determination as to how much property should be qualified for the election is also made by the executor or administrator of the estate. As such, the QTIP election is a post mortem planning device, since the decisions are made after the decedent's death.

As discussed above, it is possible to allow the surviving spouse to determine the value that will qualify for the unlimited estate tax marital deduction by leaving property to the surviving spouse and allowing the surviving spouse to disclaim all or a portion of that property. This planning relies, however, on the judgment of the surviving spouse. If the surviving spouse is not versed in the intricacies of estate planning, or is not in the best position to make a decision due to the emotional stress caused by loss of a spouse, the anticipated estate planning benefits could be lost.

Use of a QTIP election can assist in meeting the objectives of the decedent. First, an independent party, the executor, is able to make a decision concerning the amount of property that will qualify for the marital deduction. The surviving spouse is relieved of this burden (unless, of course, the surviving spouse is also the executor of the estate), and the decision likely considers the interests of all of the beneficiaries of the estate (not just the surviving spouse). Furthermore, if a spousal disclaimer plan is used, the spouse has only nine months to make the disclaimer decision. The executor does not have to make the QTIP election until the due date of the estate tax return, including extensions. Since the executor can file for an automatic six month extension for the estate tax return, the executor has a total of 15 months (nine months for normal due date, plus a six month extension of time to file) to determine the applicability of the QTIP election. This may be particularly important if the surviving spouse is in ill health. If the surviving spouse dies during the 15 month period after the first spouse's death, the executor can consider the overall tax impact on both estates before making the QTIP election.

Qualified Domestic Trust (QDOT) Election

In the case of a non-citizen surviving spouse, a Qualified Domestic Trust (QDOT) can be created to qualify the estate for the marital deduction properly passing to the non-citizen spouse. QDOTs are discussed in detail in Chapter 10.

Portability of a Deceased Spouse's Estate Tax Exemption Election

The Tax Relief, Unemployment Insurance Authorization, and Job Creation act of 2010 (TRA 2010), enacted on December 17, 2010, introduced portability of a deceased spouse's estate tax exemption amount. ATRA 2012 made this provision permanent. Congress accomplished this by amending Section 2010(c) of the Code, which defines the applicable estate tax exclusion amount as the sum of:

1. the basic exclusion amount ($11,580,000 for 2020), and
2. for a surviving spouse, the "deceased spousal unused exclusion amount."

Details on the application of the portability feature were covered in Chapters 5 (Gift Tax), 6 (Estate Tax) and 10 (Marital Deduction).

To effectuate a transfer of a deceased spouse's unused exclusion amount to the surviving spouse, the executor of the deceased spouse's estate must file an election on a timely filed estate tax return. Under prior law, only gross estates that exceeded the exemption amount were required to file an estate tax return. Beginning in 2011, however, gross estates below the exemption should file an estate tax return to transfer any unused exemption from the deceased spouse to the surviving spouse. Even if the executor believes that the gross estate of the surviving spouse will not exceed the estate tax exemption amount, it may be prudent to file the election to cover the potential for unexpected windfalls the surviving spouse may receive.

> **Quick Quiz 12.6**
>
> 1. Section 2032A allows the executor to extend the payment of the estate tax over a maximum of 14 years.
>   a. True
>   b. False
>
> 2. To reap the full benefits of special use valuation, the heirs of the property must use the property in the same use as the decedent for at least ten years after the decedent's date of death.
>   a. True
>   b. False
>
> 3. A disclaimer must be filed within six months of the decedent's date of death.
>   a. True
>   b. False
>
> False, True, False.

Generation-Skipping Transfer Tax Elections

The executor will also elect any allocation of the generation-skipping transfer tax (GSTT) exemption and if appropriate, a Reverse QTIP election so that the decedent remains the transferor of this QTIP property for GSTT purposes after the death of the surviving spouse, even though the property is included in the surviving spouse's gross estate for estate tax purposes (see Chapter 10 and Chapter 13).

Exhibit 12.6 | Summary of Elections

Election - Income Tax
1. Joint tax return
2. Catch-up for passive losses
3. Expenses elections (medical, casualty)
4. Executor fees
5. U.S. savings bonds
6. Fiscal vs. calendar year for 1040

Election - Gift Tax
1. Split gifts

Election - Estate Tax
1. Valuation date of death or alternate valuation date
2. Installment payments
3. Special use assets
4. Disclaimers
5. QTIP
6. QDOT
7. Portability of unused exemption
8. 303 stock redemption

Election - Generation Skipping Transfer Tax
1. Reverse QTIP

KEY TERMS

Alternate Valuation Date - An alternate date, other than the date of death, to value a decedent's gross estate. The alternate valuation date is either six months after the date of death, or if the asset is disposed of within six months of the date of death, the asset's disposition date.

Disclaimer - An heir or legatee's refusal to accept a gift or bequest. The disclaimer allows assets to pass to other heirs or legatees without additional transfer tax.

IRC Section 2032A - Special use valuation provision that allows the value included in the decedent's gross estate to be the current use value of the property, subject to a limitation that the highest and best use value cannot be reduced by more than $1,180,000 in 2020.

IRC Section 303 - Allows the estate of a deceased shareholder to redeem enough shares to cover the death taxes (federal and state estate, inheritance, and generation-skipping transfer taxes), funeral expenses, and administrative expenses of the decedent, and the shares redeemed for this purpose will qualify for capital gains tax treatment.

IRC Section 6166 - Allows for the deferral of estate taxes attributable to the closely held business interest over a 14-year period. The first four years of payments are interest-only, followed by 10 payments that amortize the estate tax liability over the payment period (although may be paid over a shorter period).

Irrevocable Life Insurance Trust (ILIT) - An irrevocable trust that owns and holds life insurance on its grantor's life. An ILIT is also known as a wealth replacement trust (WRT).

Split-Dollar Life Insurance - A single life insurance policy in which two parties have an ownership interest. One party typically owns the death benefit, while the other party owns the cash value.

chapter 12

DISCUSSION QUESTIONS

SOLUTIONS to the discussion questions can be found exclusively within the chapter. Once you have completed an initial reading of the chapter, go back and highlight the answers to these questions.

1. Why is it important for an estate to have cash?

2. How can an individual potentially reduce the medical expenses to be paid by his estate?

3. How can an individual reduce the funeral expenses that his estate will have to pay?

4. List three common administration costs of an estate.

5. Why should selling an estate's assets to generate the liquidity necessary for the estate taxes generally be the last option?

6. List three methods that an executor can use to reduce the liquidity requirements of an estate.

7. How can an ILIT be used to generate liquidity for an estate without requiring the value of the ILIT to be included in the decedent's gross estate?

8. Even if qualified plans are payable to the decedent's estate, why should the executor seek alternative means of meeting the cash requirements of the estate before taking distributions from the qualified plans?

9. Explain the tax benefit allowed by a Section 303 stock redemption.

10. What requirements must an estate meet to benefit from Section 303 stock redemption?

11. List two reasons why borrowing cash is an attractive option for the executor of an illiquid estate.

12. In the year of a decedent's death, what are his surviving spouse's filing status options?

13. What requirements must be met for a surviving spouse to file as a qualifying widow/widower?

14. Unpaid medical expenses of a decedent are deducted on which form, the estate tax return or the final income tax return?

15. When is the tax year-end of an estate for income tax purposes?

16. When would an executor choose to deduct an estate's administrative fees on the fiduciary income tax return?

17. Why might an executor choose to waive his executor's fee?

18. Why do small estates generally overvalue the fair market value of assets in the gross estate?

19. What are the two requirements for electing the alternate valuation date?

20. List the three requirements necessary for an estate to elect IRC Section 6166.

21. Explain why the government would allow an estate to utilize the special use valuation as a property's fair market value in the gross estate.

22. Why is the special use valuation rarely used?

MULTIPLE-CHOICE PROBLEMS

A sample of multiple choice problems is provided below. Additional multiple choice problems are available at money-education.com by accessing the Student Practice Portal.

1. Which of the following is not a typical reason an estate will have liquidity concerns?
    a. To meet specific bequests.
    b. To pay taxes.
    c. To pay life insurance premiums on the decedent's life.
    d. To pay funeral and administrative expenses and the executor's fee.

2. Which of the following statements regarding selling an estate's assets to generate cash is not correct?
    a. The estate may have income tax consequences.
    b. The assets may not be sold at full, realizable fair market value.
    c. Any losses on the sale of the assets are deductible as losses on the estate tax return.
    d. Any selling expenses are deductible on the estate tax return.

3. Josh was a majority owner in a closely held business. He had an adjusted basis in his interest of $400,000, and at his death this year, the fair market value reported on his estate tax return was $6,000,000. Like most majority owner's in closely held businesses, Josh did not have much liquidity in his estate and his executor was forced to redeem some of his interest in the business. If Josh's executor redeemed 30% of Josh's interest for $2,500,000 to pay the estate tax and administration fees, how much is subject to capital gains tax?
    a. $0.
    b. $700,000.
    c. $2,100,000.
    d. $2,500,000.

4. Mary Jane's husband died in October of 2020. Which filing status will Mary Jane probably use on her 2020 income tax return?
    a. Single.
    b. Head of household.
    c. Married filing jointly.
    d. Qualifying widow.

5. Before his death in 2020, Melvin, age 66, incurred $65,000 in medical bills. Melvin's taxable estate at his death was $675,000 and his adjusted gross income for 2020 was $100,000. How much of Melvin's medical expenses will be deducted on his estate tax return?
    a. $0.
    b. $57,500.
    c. $65,000.
    d. $100,000.

QUICK QUIZ EXPLANATIONS

Quick Quiz 12.1
1. False. Most individuals do not have sufficient liquidity at death to cover expenses, taxes, and provide for surviving family members.
2. True.
3. True.
4. False. Typically administration of an estate takes at least 9 months, and can go on for several years for large estates.

Quick Quiz 12.2
1. False. Selling assets often results in realizing less than the fair market value of the property. Generally, other ways of generating liquidity should be considered.
2. False. Generally, a life insurance policy should be held in an ILIT to avoid estate taxation at the decedent's death.
3. True.
4. False. Borrowing money is a common way of generating liquidity for an estate.

Quick Quiz 12.3
1. False. For the year of the husband's death, a surviving spouse may file married filing jointly or married filing separately.
2. True.
3. False. When medical expenses are deducted on the estate tax return, no percentage limitations apply.

Quick Quiz 12.4
1. False. Fiduciary income tax returns may be filed on a fiscal year basis.
2. True.
3. True.
4. True.

Quick Quiz 12.5
1. True.
2. True.

Quick Quiz 12.6
1. False. Section 2032A allows the executor to include property in the gross estate at its current use value as opposed to its fair market value. IRC §6166 allows the executor to extend the payment of estate taxes over a maximum of 14 years.
2. True.
3. False. A disclaimer must be filed within nine months of the decedent's death in order to be effective.

13
GENERATION-SKIPPING TRANSFERS

LEARNING OBJECTIVES

1. Discuss generation-skipping transfer tax.
2. Identify the parties involved in generation-skipping transfers.
3. Identify a skip person, either lineal descendant or non-lineal descendant.
4. Discuss the predeceased ancestor exception.
5. Describe the three types of taxable transfers associated with generation-skipping transfers.
6. Identify the exceptions exclusions and exemptions associated with generation-skipping transfer tax.
7. Describe the process of allocation of the GST exemption.
8. Identify the rate associated with generation-skipping transfer tax transfers.
9. Identify filing requirements and returns for generation-skipping transfers.
10. Describe Dynasty trusts and their purposes, advantages and disadvantages.

CFP Board Resource Document - Student-Centered Learning Objectives based upon CFP Board Principal Topics.

INTRODUCTION

In addition to the estate and gift tax systems, a third, separate, transfer tax system exists known as the generation-skipping transfer tax system (GSTT). The GSTT is an excise tax, imposed in addition to any gift or estate tax, on the transfer of property to a donee other than a spouse who is two or more generations younger than the donor.

The first GSTT was enacted by The Tax Reform Act of 1976 to remedy what Congress perceived as an abusive use of trusts to benefit several generations while avoiding estate and gift taxes. The 1976 GSTT was extremely complex, and it was widely criticized as conceptually flawed, unworkable, and ineffective. As a result, the 1976 GSTT was retroactively repealed by The Tax Reform Act of 1986 and replaced by a new GSTT system. Unlike the estate tax system, which is a progressive tax, the GSTT rate is a flat tax rate equal to the maximum estate tax rate (40% in 2020) in effect at the time of the generation-skipping transfer (GST). This difference in the GSTT system coupled with the ability to elect the use of the GST exemption (discussed below) causes the calculation of GSTT to be different than the estate and gift tax calculations. The GSTT calculation is also discussed below.

Like the estate and gift tax systems, the GSTT system has an annual exclusion ($15,000 in 2020), a lifetime exemption($11,580,000 in 2020 and is indexed to inflation, per ATRA 2012), and an exemption for qualified transfers. The following exhibit identifies the similarities and differences among the GSTT, estate tax, and gift tax regimes that are covered throughout this chapter.

Exhibit 13.1 | Comparison of the Gift, Estate, and GSTT Tax Systems

Features	Gift Tax Transfers	Estate Tax Transfers	Generation-Skipping Transfer Tax	
			Gifts	Bequests
Applies to	Lifetime Transfers	Transfers at Death	Lifetime Transfers to Skip Persons	Transfers at Death to Skip Persons
Calculation of Transfer Includes	Value of Lifetime Transfers, plus any GSTT Paid	Value of Transfers at Death, plus any GSTT Paid	Value of Lifetime Transfers to Skip Persons	Value of Transfers at Death to Skip Persons
Annual Exclusion (2020)	$15,000	N/A	$15,000	N/A
Lifetime Exemption (2020)	$11,580,000 Cannot allocate	$11,580,000 Note: Includes Gift Transfers*	$11,580,000 Can Allocate	$11,580,000 Note: Includes GST Gifts*
Nature of Tax Rate	Progressive	Progressive	Highest Gift Tax Rate (Flat) 40% for 2020	Highest Estate Tax Rate (Flat) 40% for 2020
Annual Exclusion Available for Transfers under Crummey Power	Yes	N/A	Yes for Outright Transfers Possible for Transfers in Trust (See Annual Exclusions)	N/A

N/A = Not applicable   * Lifetime

PARTIES INVOLVED IN GENERATION-SKIPPING TRANSFERS

When discussing generation-skipping transfers, it is important to understand how each individual involved in the transaction is associated with the transfer and their impact on the GSTT system. Accordingly, the parties involved are specifically defined for GSTT purposes.

Transferor

Whether or not a transfer is subject to GSTT depends on whether the transferor is two or more generations older than the transferee. Thus, in order to determine the GSTT consequences of a particular transfer, one must first identify the transferor. When property is transferred during life and is subject to gift tax, the transferor is the donor. When the property is transferred at death and is subject to estate tax, the transferor is the decedent. If the property is subject to estate tax or gift tax at some future time, usually a new transferor is determined.

Example 13.1

Theresa creates an irrevocable trust with income for life to her daughter, Catherine. When Catherine dies, the remainder will transfer to her daughter, Haley. If Catherine was given a general power of appointment over the trust assets, then the trust assets would be included in Catherine's gross estate when Catherine dies. Since the trust is an irrevocable trust, Theresa's transfer to create the trust was subject to gift tax. Therefore, Theresa is the original transferor of the trust assets for GSTT purposes. However, upon Catherine's death, Catherine becomes the transferor of the trust assets because the assets are included in Catherine's gross estate (due to the general power of appointment she held at her death) and subject to estate tax.

Transferee

The transferee is the individual who receives the property. For GSTT purposes, individuals are categorized into two groups: (1) non-skip persons and (2) skip persons. Broadly defined, non-skip persons are those individuals to whom transfers do not result in generation-skipping transfer tax consequences, whereas skip persons are those individuals to whom the same transfers would result in GSTT consequences.

> **Key Concepts**
> 1. Describe who is a skip person and who is not a skip person for both lineal and non-lineal descendants.
> 2. Explain the predeceased ancestor exception.

Skip Person

A skip person, or the person to whom a transfer may result in a generation-skipping transfer tax, is broadly defined as a transferee who is two or more generations younger than the transferor. When determining whether an individual is a skip person, the Code treats lineal and non-lineal descendants differently.

The IRC defines a skip person as any one of the following:
1. Any lineal descendant of the transferor's grandparent (or the transferor's spouse's grandparent) who is two or more generations younger than the transferor. (Certain exclusions may apply and are discussed below.)
2. Any person who is not a lineal descendant (as described in #1 above), is not the spouse of the transferor, and is more than 37½ years younger than the transferor.

For the purpose of applying these rules, any spouse or former spouse of a transferor and all charitable organizations are always considered to be in the same generation as the transferor. Also, adopted relatives are considered the same as blood relatives.

Lineal Descendants

To determine if an individual is considered a lineal descendant, consider the family tree below. The tree only considers those individuals who are descendants of the transferor's grandparent (up to two generations back from transferor). Age is irrelevant for purposes of lineal descendants. **Exhibit 13.2** illustrates those individuals who are skip persons (two or more generations younger than the transferor) in relation to the transferor; the 1st cousins twice removed and 1st cousins thrice removed, the grand and great-grand niece and nephew and the grand and great-grandchild. Note that an adopted great-grand niece/nephew is considered to be in the same category as a nonadopted great-grand niece/nephew. Also, spouses and former spouses of each of these individuals are placed in the same age category as their spouse.

Exhibit 13.2 | Table of Consanguinity (Lineal Descendants)

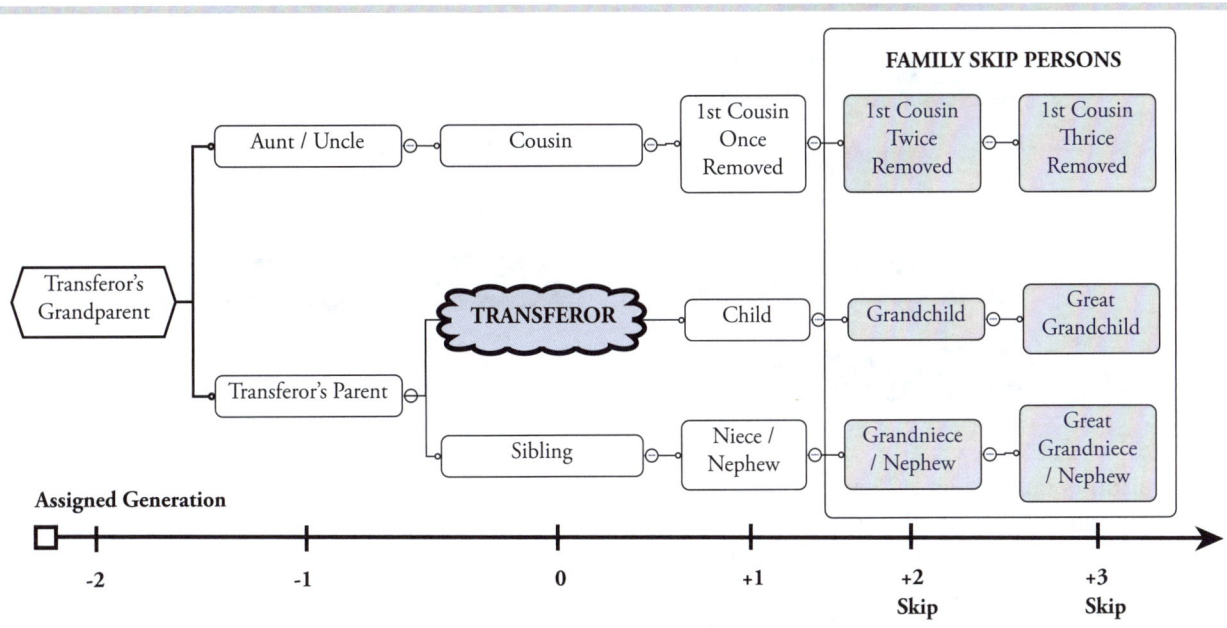

All listed individuals in the lineal line follow the lineal rules.
Individuals are skip persons based on lineal lines of the transferor identified and assigned to a generation that is two or more generations below the generation of the transferor.
Skip persons are identified in blue.

Unrelated and Non-Lineal Descendants for GSTT Purposes

Unrelated individuals are those individuals who are not related to the transferor. Non-lineal descendants, for GSTT purposes, are relatives who are more distant than the lineal descendants of the transferor's grandparents. To determine whether unrelated individuals or non-lineal descendants are skip persons, the individual's age is the only relevant factor; where the individual falls in relation to the transferor's family tree is irrelevant.

Exhibit 13.3 | Identifiable Relatives Not Part of Lineal Descendant Rules for GSTT

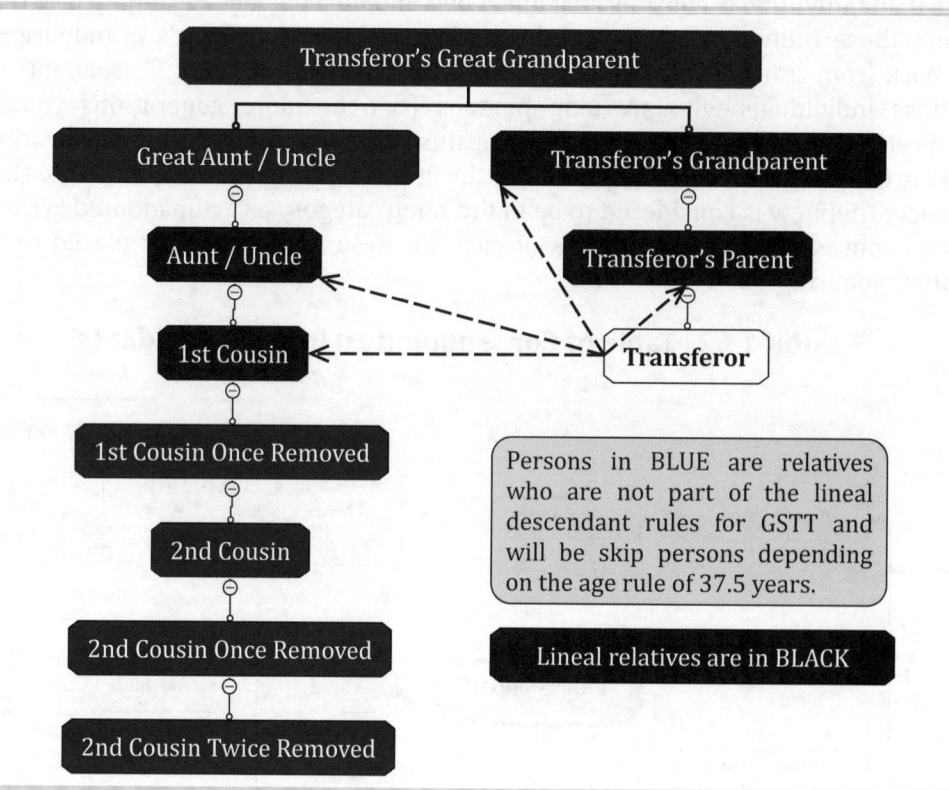

A generation is defined as a 25-year time period. Exhibit 13.4 illustrates an 80-year-old transferor. His generation would include all individuals 12½ years older than him and 12½ years younger than him. The next generation includes all individuals born within the next 25 years below the first 12½ years. Therefore, all individuals between the ages 67½ and 42½ would be one generation below the transferor. Since neighbor is 67 (13 years younger than transferor), neighbor is one generation below transferor. Friend, age 55, also falls one generation below transferor. Individuals between the ages of 42½ and 17½ are two generations below transferor, and are therefore skip individuals. Thus, both neighbor's son and friend's son are skip persons, and any transfer from transferor to neighbor's son and/or friend's son are generation-skipping transfers.

If transferor had a child the same age as neighbor's son, the child would not be considered a skip person because the child is a lineal descendant. As detailed above, lineal descendants are deemed skip persons based on the transferor's family tree. Therefore, transferor may have a child the same age as neighbor's son, and transferor's child would not be a skip person even though neighbor's son would be a skip person.

Exhibit 13.4 | Unrelated Persons and Nonlineal Descendants

Trusts

A trust may also be considered a skip person (1) if all interests in the trust are held by skip persons, or (2) if the trust distributions can only be made to skip persons. For purposes of the first definition, a person is deemed to have an interest in a trust if he has the present right to receive income or principal distributions from the trust.

Example 13.2
Anthony recently established an irrevocable trust for his grandson, Allen. The trust will pay income to Allen for his life, and at Allen's death the remaining trust assets will be distributed to Allen's children. Since Allen and his children are all skip persons and they are the only individuals that can receive distributions, the trust is also a skip person.

Example 13.3
Beau created an irrevocable trust to pay income to his daughter, Joann, and his grandson, David. In this instance the trust is not a skip person because Joann, who is not a skip person holds a present right to receive distribution from the trust. Remember that if you have one person holding an interest in the trust that is not a skip person then the trust will NOT be a skip person for GSTT purposes until the last non-skip beneficiary's interest expires.

As mentioned, charitable organizations are considered to be in the same generation as the transferor. If a charitable organization holds an interest in a trust, then the trust cannot be a skip person. For this purpose, a charitable organization is deemed to have an interest in a trust (1) if it has a present, non-discretionary right to receive income or principal, or (2) if the organization is the remainder beneficiary of a qualified charitable remainder trust or pooled income fund (as defined in Chapter 9).

Example 13.4
Brett decided to participate in a pooled income fund benefiting his local church (a qualified charitable organization). Brett's grandson, Blake, will receive an annuity for his life, and the remainder will be paid to the church. Because of its remainder interest, the church has an interest in the pooled income fund and the pooled income fund is not considered a skip person since the charity is deemed to be in the same generation as the transferor.

Example 13.5
Brett decided to create a charitable remainder trust naming his grandson, Blake, as the income beneficiary and giving the trustee the discretion to select the remainder charitable beneficiary. Because a specific charitable organization has not been declared, no charitable organization has an interest in the trust. Therefore, the trust would be considered a skip person.

Predeceased Ancestor Exception
If a child of the transferor is deceased at the time of a transfer, then that child's descendants move up one generation when determining if the transfer is a GST. As a result, certain transfers that, absent this rule, would be GSTs, will not be treated as GSTs.

Example 13.6
Terrell gave $100,000 to his grandson, Willie. At the time the gift is made, Terrell's child, Charlotte, who is also Willie's mother, is deceased. For GSTT purposes, Willie is treated as being in Charlotte's generation (i.e., Willie is treated as being Terrell's child rather than Terrell's grandchild) and the $100,000 gift from Terrell to Willie is not a GST.

Example 13.7
Margaret establishes an irrevocable trust for the benefit of her granddaughter, Sally. The trust instrument provides that Sally is to receive all of the trust's annual income until she reaches age 35, at which time the trust will terminate and distribute its principal to Sally. At the time Margaret establishes the trust, Margaret's child, Maxwell, who is also Sally's father, is dead. Therefore, for GSTT purposes, Sally is treated as Margaret's daughter rather than granddaughter, and neither the initial transfer to the trust nor any distributions from the trust to Sally are GSTs.

Example 13.8

Assume the same facts as the above example, except that Celeste, Maxwell's surviving spouse, is the income beneficiary of the trust for her life. Upon Celeste's death, the trust will terminate and distribute its principal to Sally. Because Maxwell was dead at the time the trust was created, the termination of Celeste's interest in the trust will not be a GST.

Example 13.9

Assume the same facts as the above example, except that Maxwell was living at the time the trust was created, but died before Celeste's interest in the trust terminated. Because Maxwell was alive at the time the trust was created, the termination of Celeste's interest in the trust at Celeste's death will be a GST.

The predeceased ancestor exception may also apply to transfers made to the transferor's grandniece(s) and/or grandnephew(s) if, at the time of the transfer, the transferor has no living lineal descendants.

The predeceased ancestor exception only applies if there is a death in an intervening generation. The exception will not apply to a "deemed death" for transfer purposes such as when an intervening generation executes a qualified disclaimer.

Non-Skip Person

A non-skip person is any person or trust that is not a skip person. Therefore, any lineal descendant less than two generations below the transferor (based on the family tree) are non-skip persons, and non-lineal descendants and unrelated parties that are not more than 37½ years younger than the transferor are non-skip persons. Also, a transferor's spouse, or former spouse, is always considered a non-skip person because they are considered to be in the same generation as the spouse.

> ### Quick Quiz 13.1
>
> 1. Anyone who is less than two generations younger than the transferor is a skip person.
>   a. True
>   b. False
> 2. If a parent disclaims the property bequeathed to them, then the predeceased parent rule will apply if the assets are transferred to the children instead.
>   a. True
>   b. False
>
> False, False.

A trust is a non-skip person if any non-skip person holds an interest in the trust. Also, if no person has an interest in the trust, but a distribution may be made to a non-skip person, the trust is a non-skip person. Refer to **Exhibit 13.2**, **Exhibit 13.3**, and **Exhibit 13.4** for a visual depiction of who is a skip person and who is a non-skip person.

Qualified Disclaimers

As discussed in prior chapters, qualified disclaimers allow property to pass to someone other than the primary beneficiary named in the decedent's will or under the state's intestacy laws. When the heir of an estate executes a qualified disclaimer, he is deemed, for estate tax purposes, to predecease the decedent. The property the disclaimant would have received will be transferred to the alternate beneficiary named under the will or, if there is no will, to the decedent's other heirs according to state intestacy law. Use of a qualified disclaimer prevents the property passing from the decedent, being included in the disclaimant's gross estate.

A qualified disclaimer by a parent cannot be used to avoid GSTT. The predeceased parent exception to the generation-skipping transfer tax applies only when the parent actually dies, thus "presumed death" for estate tax purposes will not suffice.

> **Example 13.10**
> Morris recently died, leaving his entire estate to his son, Junior, and daughter, Barbara, in equal shares, per stirpes. Barbara has been very successful in her career and has accumulated substantial personal wealth. If Barbara disclaims her inheritance from Morris, the property she would have received from the estate will be transferred to her children (grandchildren of Morris). For estate tax purposes, Barbara is deemed to predecease Morris, allowing her children to take her share without any adverse gift tax imposed on Barbara. Since Barbara has not actually died, however, the transfer of property from Morris's estate to the grandchildren is a GST and will be subject to GSTT. Morris's executor can allocate part of Morris's GST exemption (if any remains) to the transfer to offset the GSTT due.

TYPES OF TAXABLE TRANSFERS

GSTT applies to three types of taxable transfers: (1) direct skips, (2) taxable distributions, and (3) taxable terminations. The amount of GSTT due on a taxable transfer, and the person liable for the tax, depends on the classification of the taxable transfer as a direct skip, a taxable distribution, or a taxable termination. Thus, it is important to understand the differences between these taxable transfers and to identify how and when each type may occur.

Direct Skip

Definition
A **direct skip** is an outright transfer of property to a skip person that is subject to estate or gift tax. An outright gift to a grandchild or a trust that is a skip person during life or at death is a direct skip.

> **Example 13.11**
> Clyde's great-grandson, Brandon, wanted a new car for his 16th birthday. Clyde bought him a brand new red convertible and parked it in the driveway on Brandon's birthday. Since Clyde gave Brandon an outright gift, and Brandon is a skip person, the gift is a direct skip. Note that even though Brandon is more than two generations below Clyde, the transfer is only taxed once because transfers to direct skips are only subject to GSTT once regardless of the number of generations skipped.

Taxation Issues on Direct Skips
The GSTT on a direct skip is imposed on the value received by the transferee. The transferor is liable for the GSTT on a direct skip, unless the direct skip is made from a trust. In the trust instance, the trustee is liable for the GSTT. Unless the transferor's will or the applicable trust document directs otherwise by specific reference to the GSTT, the property transferred in a GST is charged with any GSTT imposed on the transfer.

Taxable Termination

Definition
A **taxable termination** is any termination of a trust interest unless at the termination of the trust, the trust property transferred is subject to (1) federal estate or gift tax, (2) a non-skip person receives an interest in the property transferred out of the trust, or (3) the distribution from the trust will never be made to a skip person.

> **Key Concepts**
>
> 1. What are direct skips, taxable terminations, and taxable distributions?
> 2. Who is liable for the GSTT on a direct skip, taxable termination, and taxable distribution?

Example 13.12
Terrence established an irrevocable trust to benefit his son, Tyler. The trust will pay income to Tyler for his life and the remainder will transfer to Tyler's children at Tyler's death. When Tyler dies, a taxable termination has occurred because skip persons, Tyler's children, receive an interest in the trust at its termination.

Taxation of Taxable Terminations
The taxable amount of a taxable termination equals the value of the trust property transferred less any expenses, indebtedness, and taxes attributable to the taxable termination. The trustee is responsible for paying (from the trust) the GSTT on a taxable termination.

Taxable Distribution

Definition
A **taxable distribution** is any distribution from a trust to a skip person that is not a taxable termination or a direct skip.

Example 13.13
Bobby established a revocable trust under which the trust income is payable to Bobby's child, Carolyn, for life. When Bobby's grandchild, Alex, attains 35 years of age, Alex is to receive one-half of the principal. The remaining one-half of the principal is to be distributed to Alex on Carolyn's death. Assume that Carolyn survives until Alex attains the age of 35. When the trustee distributes one-half of the principal to Alex on his 35th birthday, the distribution is a taxable distribution because it is a distribution to a skip person and is neither a taxable termination nor a direct skip.

Taxation of Taxable Distributions

The amount received by the transferee in a taxable distribution, reduced by any expenses incurred by the transferee in connection with the GSTT, is the taxable amount of the distribution. Unlike direct skips and taxable terminations, the transferee is liable for the GSTT on a taxable distribution. Therefore, if the trust pays the GSTT instead of the transferee, another taxable distribution occurs for an amount equal to the GSTT paid because the transferee was responsible for the tax, and the payment by the trust is considered a gift from the trust to the transferee. The GSTT rules dictate that the additional distribution for the taxes paid is treated as being made on the last day of the calendar year in which the original taxable distribution occurred. This occurs even if the actual tax payment occurs in a subsequent calendar year.

> **Quick Quiz 13.2**
>
> 1. Any distribution from a trust to a skip person other than a direct skip is a taxable termination.
>   a. True
>   b. False
>
> 2. The beneficiaries of a trust are liable for the GSTT on a taxable termination.
>   a. True
>   b. False
>
> *False, False.*

Example 13.14

Assume that Angie has already used up her lifetime GST exclusion ($11,580,000 for 2020) and this year she has already gifted the annual exclusion amount to her grandson, Wade. She established an irrevocable trust under which the trust income is payable to Angie's daughter, Maria, for life. When Angie's grandson, Wade, turns 25-years-old, Wade is to receive $1,000,000 of principal and the trustee is directed to pay all taxes associated with the transfer. The remaining principal will be distributed to Wade on Maria's death. When the trustee distributes the $1,000,000 of principal to Wade on his 25th birthday (that is a taxable distribution to a skip person), Wade is liable for the GSTT on the distribution. Since the trust pays the tax of $400,000 (40% of $1,000,000) it must be added to the gift for gift tax purposes. In total, the trust will have to pay out $1,960,000 (GST of $400,000 plus gift tax of $560,000 plus the $1,000,000 equals total cash outlay of $1,960,000) in order to give Wade a sum of $1,000,000.

chapter 13

EXCEPTIONS, EXCLUSIONS, AND EXEMPTION

Like the gift and estate tax systems, the GSTT System also has exceptions, exclusions, and an exemption amount.

> **Key Concepts**
> 1. Identify the effective dates for the GSTT.
> 2. How do qualified transfers affect the GSTT?
> 3. Identify the requirements to qualify a gift for the GST annual exclusion.
> 4. When must an individual allocate his GST exemption to a transfer?
> 5. Who allocates a decedent's GST exemption?

Exceptions

The original GSTT system was retroactively repealed in 1986 and was replaced with a new GSTT system. Therefore, the current GSTT only applies to transfers made after the date of enactment, October 22, 1986, although certain transfers made between September 25, 1985 and October 23, 1986 are subject to GSTT. Transfers between these dates will not be subject to GSTT if:

- The transfer was to an irrevocable trust that was in existence on or before September 25, 1985, to the extent no additions were made to the trust after September 25, 1985.
- The transfer was pursuant to certain wills and revocable trusts executed before October 22, 1986 and the decedent died before January 1, 1987.
- The transfer was from a person who was suffering from a mental disability and as such could not change the disposition of his property beginning October 22, 1986 and continuing until the date of his death.

Specifically, the exception applies to trusts that were grandfathered at the time and trusts where the grantor was unable to change the trust due to mental capacity.

Exclusions

The GSTT system has both an exclusion available for qualified transfers and an annual exclusion of $15,000 (for tax year 2020).

Medical and Educational Payments - Qualified Transfers

The direct payment of tuition to a qualified educational institution (see Chapter 5) or the direct payment of qualified medical expenses (see Chapter 5) to a medical care provider on behalf of a skip person is not subject to GSTT. The exclusion from GSTT also applies if the payments are made from a trust.

Example 13.15
Tony established a trust for the benefit of his grandchildren. The trust instrument authorizes the trustee to pay tuition and medical expenses for any grandchild. If the trustee makes a tuition payment to a qualified educational organization for one of the grandchildren the distribution from the trust is not subject to GSTT because it is a qualified transfer.

Annual Exclusion

Similar to the gift tax system, an annual exclusion of $15,000 per donee per donor for present interest gifts is available for GSTs. The application of the GST annual exclusion depends on the type of transfer. For transfers that constitute direct skips, the application of the annual exclusion is applied in the same manner as the annual exclusion for gift tax (as discussed in Chapter 5). Thus, a direct skip is a nontaxable gift for GSTT purposes to the extent the transfer is excluded from taxable gifts under the annual gift tax exclusion.

Example 13.16
Last Christmas, Claude gave his grandson Darryl $15,000 outright. As discussed in Chapter 5, $15,000 is the gift tax annual exclusion, resulting in a nontaxable transfer for gift tax purposes. For GSTT purposes, the gift is also a nontaxable gift because the gift is not taxable under the gift tax system.

Example 13.17
Assume in the example above that Claude gave his grandson Darryl $20,000 outright. Again, the $15,000 would be excluded from gift tax and GSTT. The remaining $5,000 would be subject to both gift tax and GSTT.

For gifts in trust, the gift tax annual exclusion and the GST annual exclusion differ. To qualify a gift in trust for the gift tax annual exclusion, the beneficiaries of the trust must have a present interest in the trust (which is often accomplished by giving the beneficiaries a Crummey power over the contributions made to the trust). Transfers to a trust deemed a skip person are nontaxable gifts for GSTT purposes only to the extent the transfer is equal to or less than the annual exclusion and the following requirements are met:
1. The beneficiaries are given a Crummey power over the contribution to the trust;
2. The trust assets can only be distributed for the benefit of the beneficiary during the beneficiary's lifetime; and
3. If the trust does not terminate before the beneficiary's death, the assets must be included in the beneficiary's gross estate.

Example 13.18
Assume the same facts as above except that instead of giving Darryl the money outright, Claude established an irrevocable trust for Darryl with a contribution of $15,000. The trust requires the income to be distributed to Darryl for his life and the remainder to be distributed to Darryl when he attains the age of 30. The trust also gives Darryl a Crummey power. If Darryl dies before attaining the age of 30, his estate will receive the remainder of the trust. Since the trust only pays to Darryl, a skip person, and all benefits must be paid to him or his estate, the $15,000 transfer will qualify for the GST and gift tax annual exclusion and thus is a nontaxable gift for both gift tax and GSTT purposes.

Split Gifts

Gift splitting (discussed in Chapter 5), also applies to transfers subject to GSTT. Gift splitting enables a spouse to treat gifts of separate property as being made one-half from each spouse, allowing each spouse to use the other's annual exclusion. This enables an individual to transfer $30,000 (the combined annual exclusion for the two spouses) to an individual without incurring gift tax or GSTT. When an individual elects on the gift tax return (Form 709) to split gifts for gift tax purposes, any GSTs are also deemed split gifts.

Example 13.19

Harry gives $20,000 to his grandson and $20,000 to his granddaughter in a calendar year. Katie, Harry's wife, consents to have the gifts treated as made one-half by her for gift tax purposes (a split gift election). As a result, Katie is also treated as the transferor for GSTT purposes of one-half of the gifts (i.e., Katie is treated as the transferor of $10,000 to the grandson and $10,000 to the granddaughter). While these gifts are made to a skip person, the GSTT annual exclusion applies to these transfers, eliminating the GSTT.

Exemption

Every individual is allowed a lifetime tax credit for gift, estate, and generation skipping transfer taxes ($4,577,800 for 2020). The credit equivalent in taxable gifts, taxable estate transfers, or generation skipping transfers is $11,580,000 (2020). In other words, the tax that is avoided on a transfer of $11,580,000 is $4,577,800.

Allocation Rules

The applicable gift, estate, and GST tax credit equivalency is applied automatically to transfers until it is depleted. Since it is possible that a transferor may wish to save his or her GSTT credit for other transfers, the law permits the transferor to opt out of the automatic allocation provisions by including an election statement on the transferor's gift or estate tax return.

The transferor or his executor may affirmatively allocate the GST exemption any time between the date of the transfer and the due date, including extensions, of the transferor's federal estate tax return. If an estate tax return is not required and the automatic allocation provisions do not apply, the GST exemption must be allocated before what would have been the due date of the estate tax return, including extensions. When the GST exemption is allocated on a timely filed gift tax return, the allocation is effective as of the date of the transfer. An allocation after the due date is considered a late allocation and will require the use of the GST exemption for the property's fair market value at the date of the late allocation.

Allocation of the Exemption for Direct Skips During Life

If a direct skip occurs during a transferor's lifetime, the transferor's GST exemption that has not been used is automatically allocated to the direct skip. If the transferor does not want to use his GST exemption, the transferor must:
1. describe on a timely filed federal gift and GSTT return (Form 709) the transfer and the extent to which the automatic allocation does not apply; or
2. timely file the federal gift and GSTT return (Form 709) with the payment of the GSTT due without the automatic allocation.

Allocation of the GST Exemption for Taxable Terminations and Taxable Distributions

If any GST exemption remains after the allocation to any direct skips, the exemption is allocated pro rata to any taxable terminations or taxable distributions from the decedent. The allocation, included on the transferor's gift tax return, must detail the name of the trust, the amount of the allocation, the value of the trust's assets at the date of the allocation, and the inclusion ratio (discussed below) of the trust after the allocation.

When an individual allocates the GST exemption to a trust in excess of the amount necessary to create a zero inclusion ratio (discussed below), the allocation of the excess exemption amount is void and available for subsequent allocation. However, in the case of a Charitable Lead Annuity Trust (CLAT), an allocation of GST exemption in excess of the amount necessary to obtain a zero inclusion ratio for the trust is not void and may not be restored to the transferor. As a result, an excess allocation of GST exemption to a CLAT wastes the transferor's GST exemption.

The **Estate Tax Inclusion Period (ETIP)** rule prevents a grantor from allocating any of his GST exemption to a transfer that would result in estate tax inclusion for the grantor if he died after the transfer. This rule prevents the grantor from allocating his GST exemption to the remainder interest in GRATs, GRUTs, QPRTs, and CLATs prior to the expiration of the retained interest term.

Allocation of the GST Exemption for Transfers at Death

When an individual dies with unused GST exemption, the executor of his estate allocates the GST exemption on the decedent's federal estate tax return (Form 706). This allocation may be for a testamentary GST or a late allocation to a lifetime transfer. In either case, the allocation is effective once the federal estate tax return (Form 706) is filed.

As with the allocation of the GST exemption to lifetime transfers in trust, the allocation at death must identify the name of the trust, the allocation to the trust, the fair market value of the trust's assets at the date of the allocation, and the trust's inclusion ratio after the allocation. Any allocation for a trust that will not be a GST trust is void and the GST exemption is available for subsequent allocation.

When an individual makes a generation-skipping transfer in the year of his death, the executor will be responsible for filing the decedent's gift tax return and allocating any GST exemption on that gift tax return.

Quick Quiz 13.3

1. The GSTT only applies to transfers after October 22, 1986.
   a. True
   b. False

2. A direct skip is a nontaxable gift for GSTT purposes to the extent the transfer is excluded from taxable gifts under the annual exclusion.
   a. True
   b. False

3. Qualified transfers are not subject to GSTT.
   a. True
   b. False

False, True, True.

chapter 13

APPLICABLE RATE, INCLUSION RATIO, AND APPLICABLE FRACTION

After it has been determined that a GST has occurred (whether a direct skip, taxable termination, or taxable distribution) the value of the GST is then multiplied by the **applicable rate**. The applicable rate is the maximum estate tax rate in effect at the time of the GST (40% for 2020) times the **inclusion ratio**, which is the difference between the applicable fraction (defined below) and one. The calculation and examples are provided below.

The applicable fraction is calculated by dividing the applicable GST exemption allocated to the transfer by the value of the transfer reduced by any federal estate tax or state death tax incurred by reason of the GST that is chargeable to the trust and is actually recovered from the trust, the amount of any charitable deduction allowed, and the value of the transfer that is a nontaxable gift (i.e., annual exclusion and qualified transfers).

The inclusion ratio is then determined by subtracting the applicable fraction from one. The inclusion ratio is then multiplied by the maximum transfer rate (40% for 2020) to calculate the applicable rate which is multiplied by the value of the GST to determine the GSTT due.

> ### ✏️ Quick Quiz 13.4
>
> 1. The inclusion ratio is determined by subtracting the applicable fraction from one.
>   a. True
>   b. False
> 2. The 2020 lifetime GST exemption is $4,577,800.
>   a. True
>   b. False
>
> True, False.

Exhibit 13.5 | The Applicable Fraction Formula

$$\text{Applicable Fraction} = \frac{\text{GST Exemption Allocated}}{\text{Value of Property Transferred} - \text{Estate Taxes} - \text{Charitable Deductions} - \text{Nontaxable Gift Portion}}$$

Inclusion Ratio = 1 − Applicable Fraction

Applicable Rate = Inclusion Ratio × Maximum Transfer Tax Rate

Example 13.20

In 2020, Cindy gave her granddaughter Marsha $12,015,000 outright. Cindy made no previous gifts and allocated her entire GST exemption to this transfer. As the calculation below illustrates, the transfer is subject to both gift tax and GSTT. After using her entire gift tax applicable credit amount and her entire GST exemption, the transfer tax cost of transferring $12,015,000 to Marsha is $403,200 ($168,000 + $235,200).

GSTT Calculation		Notes:
Applicable Fraction (AF)	0.9650	$11,580,000/($12,015,000 - $15,000)
Inclusion Ratio (IR)	0.0350	1- AF
Applicable Rate	0.0140	IR x Max Transfer Rate (40%)
GST	$12,015,000	
Less: Annual Exclusion	($15,000)	
Taxable GST	$12,000,000	
Times: Applicable rate	0.0140	
GSTT	**$168,000**	

While the above formula is the appropriate calculation utilizing the applicable rate, the following calculation can be used for simple GSTT calculations involving direct skips.

GST	$12,015,000	
Less: Annual Exclusion	($15,000)	
Less: GST Exemption	($11,580,000)	
Taxable GST	$420,000	
Times: GSTT Rate	40%	
GSTT	**$168,000**	

Gift Tax Calculation		
Gift	$12,015,000	
Plus GSTT Paid	$168,000	The GSTT paid is considered a gift.
Less: Annual Exclusions	($15,000)	
Less: Qualified Transfers	$0	
Less: Marital Deductions	$0	
Equals: Total Taxable Gifts	**$12,168,000**	
Add: Previous Taxable Gifts (post 1976)	$0	
Equals: Tentative Tax Base (TTB)	$12,168,000	
Tentative Tax (TT)	$4,813,000	[($345,800 + 0.40($11,168,000)]
Less: Gift Tax Deemed Paid	$0	
Less: Applicable Gift Tax Credit	($4,577,800)	
Equals: Gift Tax Liability	**$235,200**	

Generation-Skipping Transfer Tax and QTIPs

The election of the GST exemption may be complicated by the QTIP election when the fair market value of the decedent's transfers in a QTIP Trust to the surviving spouse is greater than the applicable estate tax credit equivalency. To remedy this situation, a Reverse QTIP election can be made. A Reverse QTIP election is a QTIP election that is made for estate tax purposes but not for GSTT purposes. Thus, the assets would qualify for the unlimited marital deduction for estate tax purposes (requiring all of the unused assets in the QTIP Trust at the surviving spouse's death to be included in his or her estate) while using the GST exemption of the first spouse to die to avoid future imposition of the GSTT. Since a partial Reverse QTIP election is not permitted, an executor may wish to create two QTIP Trusts for the same spouse and make a Reverse QTIP election for one of them so as to accomplish two goals: (1) elimination of estate tax at the death of the first spouse, and (2) full use of the decedent's GST exemption.

Example 13.21

Decedent, age 60 has a gross estate in 2020 of $12,580,000 and wishes to leave $11,580,000 to a credit shelter trust. The income and remainder beneficiaries are his son, age 34, and his daughter, age 25, from his previous marriage. The balance of the estate, $1,000,000, will pass to two QTIP Trusts. The income beneficiary of the QTIP Trust is his current spouse Joy, age 28, a known spendthrift, and the remainder beneficiary is Jordan, the decedent's newborn grandchild.

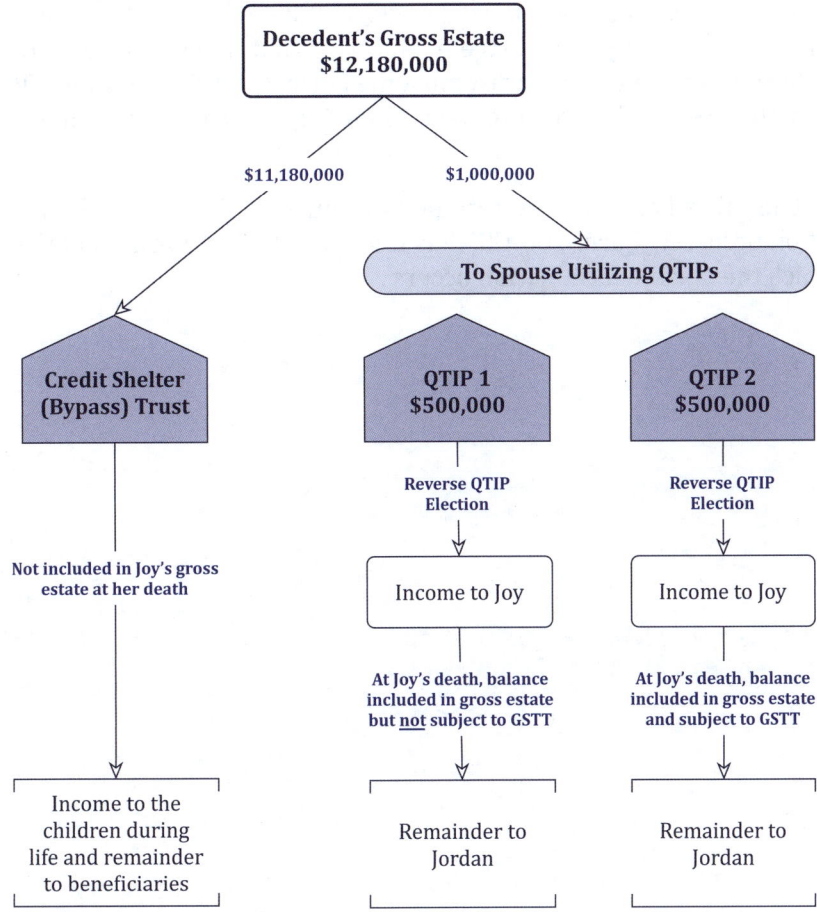

Applicable Rate, Inclusion Ratio, and Applicable Fraction

To minimize any estate tax due and to fully use the decedent's GST exemption of $11,580,000, the executor would elect to treat property equal to $1,000,000 as QTIP in two QTIP Trusts, "QTIP 1" and "QTIP 2." The executor would than make a Reverse QTIP election for GSTT purposes for QTIP 1 using the decedent's GST exemption. At the death of the surviving spouse, Joy, the assets in QTIP 1 and 2 would be included in Joy's gross estate for estate tax purposes, but only QTIP 2 would be included in her gross estate for GSTT purposes. (As noted earlier, partial Reverse QTIP elections are not permitted necessitating the use of the two trusts.) At Joy's death, she can use her GST exemption for QTIP 2.

FILING REQUIREMENT AND RETURNS

Inter vivos direct skips are reported on Form 709, United States Gift and Generation-Skipping Transfer Tax Return, which is due on or before April 15 of the year following the calendar year in which the direct skip occurs. Direct skip transfers at death are reported on Schedule R or R-1 of Form 706, which is due nine months after the transferor's date of death.

Quick Quiz 13.5

1. When a GSTT is reported on a Form 709, the form is due within three months of the date of transfer.
   a. True
   b. False

False.

Taxable distributions are reported on Forms 706-GS(D-1) and 706-GS(D), and taxable terminations are reported on Form 706-GS(T). Form 706-GS(D-1) is filed by the trustee of any trust that makes a taxable distribution. Anyone who receives a taxable distribution from a trust must file Form 706-GS(D). Forms 706-GS(D-1) and 706-GS(D) are due on or before April 15 of the year following the calendar year in which the taxable distribution is made.

The trustee of any trust that has a taxable termination must file Form 706-GS(T) for the tax year in which the termination occurred. Form 706-GS(T) is due on or before April 15 of the year following the calendar year in which the taxable termination occurs.

Exhibit 13.6 | GSTT Summary

Key Points
- Designed to tax large transfers between skipped generations (i.e., grandparent to grandchild).
- It is separate from, and additional to, the gift and estate tax systems.

Transfers Subject to GSTT
- Direct skips.
- Taxable termination.
- Taxable distribution.

GSTT Rate
- The GSTT rate is the highest marginal rate for the unified gift and estate tax rates (40% for 2020).
- Any GSTT paid will be added to the fair market value of the gift to determine total taxable gifts for the federal gift tax.

Exceptions to GSTT
- GSTT annual exclusion is $15,000 per donee per donor, gift splitting is available if both spouses elect.
- Crummey power can qualify a gift in trust for the GSTT annual exclusion if additional requirements are met.
- Indexed, but $15,000 for 2020.
- The predeceased parent rule applies for direct skips to lineal descendants and collateral heirs if the decedent does not have any direct lineal descendants (children, grandchildren). Use of a disclaimer will not invoke the predeceased parent exception.
- Lifetime exemption available during life or at death equals $11,580,000 for 2020.
- Qualified transfers are excluded.

AN OVERVIEW OF GENERATION-SKIPPING TRUSTS

Property transferred to a member of the next generation, and then later transferred to that person's heirs, is generally taxed twice, once each time the property is transferred. Over the years, estate planners have devised techniques to minimize transfer taxation by failing to give some generations an ownership interest in property. The generation-skipping trust has been used in estate planning to pass property ultimately to a generation at least two levels younger than the grantor of the trust while allowing the intervening generation some income benefits from the property on an estate tax-free basis.

Use of a generation-skipping trust allows the planner to split legal ownership of assets (ownership is held by the trust) from the use of assets (the beneficiaries of the trust may use the trust assets). If the beneficiaries do not have legal title to the trust assets when they die, the beneficiary cannot transfer anything in the trust at his death, and therefore no part of the trust will be included in the beneficiary's gross estate. Using a generation-skipping trust to avoid estate tax inclusion for descendants of the grantor can substantially increase the wealth that is transferred to future generations of the family because the estate tax paid at each generation is eliminated.

INTRODUCTION TO DYNASTY TRUSTS

Dynasty trusts are generation-skipping trusts created in perpetuity. Once created, a dynasty trust provides for trust beneficiaries, but avoids transfer taxation in the individual beneficiary's estate by restricting ownership of trust assets. When properly drafted, a dynasty trust will not vest ownership of trust property in any individual beneficiary. If a beneficiary is not deemed to own the trust assets, those assets cannot be included in the beneficiary's gross estate at death. Each time a property "vests" it is drastically reduced when it passes to the next generation, since estate taxes are payable from the property. According to Jesse Dukeminier, Maxwell Professor of Law at the University of California Los Angeles School of Law, a nationally recognized expert on the Rule Against Perpetuities, "A dynasty trust, free of estate, gift, and GST taxes for its duration, is a most valuable device for protecting the settlor's descendants from federal transfer taxes for a very long time. A $1,000,000 dynasty trust should be considered by every millionaire with descendants" because the long-term wealth accumulation potential of these trusts is significant. Assuming the trust will last for 120 years, if $1,000,000 is transferred to the trust shielded by the grantor's GST exemption, at an eight percent compounded growth rate per year, the value of the trust at termination will be $10,252,992,943.

> **Key Concepts**
>
> 1. What was the original purpose of the Rule Against Perpetuities?
> 2. How are dynasty trusts taxed for income tax purposes?
> 3. How are the assets of a dynasty trust protected from the claims of a beneficiary's creditors?
> 4. Identify several types of dynasty trusts.

The Rule Against Perpetuities

At common law, any restraint on the alienation of property was considered void. As a result, trusts could not be created because they had the potential of restraining the disposition of property. Common law judges sought to ensure that property could be used in its most productive use and believed that allowing individuals to retain the right to use property led to inefficiency.

The Duke of Norfolk's case changed the rules. The Duke of Norfolk's case involved a situation where the Duke, whose oldest son and heir was "non compos mentis" (i.e., incompetent), attempted to transfer all of his property to a trust. Under the terms of the trust, the trustee was prohibited from selling the property, but could manage it for the benefit of the Duke's heirs in perpetuity. After about a century of litigation, including a review by the English House of Lords, Lord Chancellor Nottingham articulated "the Rule Against Perpetuities," which states "No interest [in real or personal property] is good unless it must vest, if at all, not later than twenty-one years after some life in being at the creation of the interest." The Rule Against Perpetuities was interpreted to mean that an interest in trust must terminate within lives in being plus 21 years in order to be valid. Note that this does not mean that a trust must terminate within lives in being plus 21 years, but rather that the interest vests, resulting in a termination of the trust no later than the expiration of all life estates vesting within the perpetuities period.

In its common law form, the Rule Against Perpetuities has created a tremendous amount of confusion. Volumes have been written trying to interpret its exact application, and many variations and interpretations have been set forth. Much of the confusion has been clarified by modern statutes setting forth the rules of construction for interpreting the Rule Against Perpetuities.

Some states have adopted The Uniform Statutory Rule Against Perpetuities (USRAP). Under USRAP, an interest in trust will be valid if it:
1. will vest or terminate within lives in being plus 21 years (the common law Rule Against Perpetuities); or
2. the interest vests or terminates within 90 years of the creation of the trust.

USRAP Section 1(e) prohibits a settlor from creating a trust for the longer of the common law perpetuities period or the 90-year period provided for in USRAP. The IRS and Treasury have accepted the 90-year perpetuities period provided for in USRAP, but conditioned their acceptance upon the condition that a trust settlor cannot create the trust with language that defines the trust duration as the longer of the common law perpetuities period or the 90-year perpetuities period.

A growing trend among the states is to abolish the Rule Against Perpetuities. The purpose of the Rule Against Perpetuities was to (1) ensure that property is freely alienable, and (2) prevent the dead hand from controlling the lives of the living. To address these concerns, states that have abolished the Rule Against Perpetuities typically require the property transferred in trust to be freely alienable by the trustee. Since most dynasty trusts use powers of appointment and/or give the trustee the discretionary power to terminate the trust upon changes in law or taxation, the influence of the dead hand is minimized, thereby addressing the second purpose of the Rule Against Perpetuities. Many states have abolished the Rule Against Perpetuities, but three states, Delaware, Alaska, and South Dakota, do not assess a state tax on trust income. As a result, Delaware, Alaska, and South Dakota are the states where most individuals create dynasty trusts.

Taxation of Dynasty Trusts

Once established, a dynasty trust, which is a complex trust, pays tax on its income to the extent that the income is not distributed to the beneficiaries.

Trust situs for income tax purposes is not always the same as trust situs for perpetuity purposes. If the grantor trust rules apply, the trust may be subject to taxation in the state where the grantor is domiciled. This result typically occurs when the dynasty trust has been set up as an **Intentionally Defective Grantor Trust (IDGT)**, a trust which gives the grantor sufficient control to be considered the owner for income tax purposes, but not so much control to require the trust property to be included in the transferor's gross estate. The grantor must be aware of potential income tax issues upon creation and during administration of the trust.

To achieve transfer tax objectives, the dynasty trust must have a zero inclusion ratio for GSTT purposes. Property in the dynasty trust will not be included in the estate of the beneficiaries of the trust, thereby avoiding estate taxation. A zero inclusion ratio for GST purposes results in a GSTT rate of zero.

Basic Structure and Types of Dynasty Trusts

Dynasty trusts are usually set up as family trusts that grant the trustee discretion to pay income and corpus among members of the family (usually defined as the lineal descendants of the grantor). The grantor usually funds the trust with personal (not real) property.

The trust document usually designates the state whose laws will govern the validity and construction of the trust, and will name the individual or corporation who will serve as trustee. It is not usually necessary for the grantor to reside in the state in which the trust is governed. In many instances, it is desirable to have the grantor be a resident of another state, since some states do not tax the trust income of non-residents. If the trustee maintains a place of business within the selected state, and the assets of the trust are administered in that state, a substantial relationship is established that is usually sufficient to guarantee that the trust will be enforced. For long-term trusts, like dynasty trusts, it is usually wise to allow the trustee to change the situs of the trust in the event of adverse legal or tax changes.

Unless the trust has a corporate fiduciary, it is usually wise to name two independent trustees. Some individuals include a clause that sets the age that individual trustees (with the exception of family members) must resign and transfer trusteeship to others. Dynasty trusts typically name two or more "Trust Protectors," who are individuals that are not beneficiaries of the trust with the authority to remove the trustee. The grantor should never serve as trustee or trust protector of a dynasty trust.

Due to their very long duration, the trust instrument often gives the trustee the authority to terminate the trust in whole or in part if it is appropriate to do so. This may be necessary due to a change in tax law that makes the trust a hindrance, rather than a benefit.

A possible alternative to termination of the trust is making another dynasty trust the discretionary beneficiary of the trust assets. In this instance, the trustee will be able to pay over all of the trust assets to another trust upon the occurrence of adverse events.

The trustee is typically empowered to purchase assets for the beneficiary's personal use. If the trustee exercises this option, the assets are protected from the claims of the beneficiary's creditors, and will not be included in the beneficiary's estate for federal estate tax purposes. The purchase of assets inside of the trust can also protect those assets from the claims of a beneficiary's spouse, and in this way the trust can be used as an alternative to a premarital agreement. A beneficiary's spouse will generally not be able to demand assets held by the trust in the event of divorce. If a beneficiary is given the use of an asset owned by the trust, such as a piece of artwork, trust documents usually require the beneficiary to purchase an insurance policy on the property to reimburse the trust in the event of the asset's destruction.

Note that the right to use assets cannot extend to the grantor of the trust. If the grantor receives income from, or use of assets held by the trust, the assets will be included in the grantor's gross estate, even if the grantor had no legal entitlement to such income or use.

Usually, the trust is drafted to require that beneficiaries pay for their own consumable and wasting assets, such as vacations, food, and transportation. Assets purchased inside the trust are typically permanent assets that tend to appreciate over time.

The trustee should be required to refuse contributions to the trust not shielded by the grantor's GST exemption.

Dynasty Trusts and Business Succession Planning

A dynasty trust can be used to acquire and hold closely held or family business stock. Once the stock is in the trust, the family can maintain control of the business for multiple generations, and avoid transfer taxation on the value of the business as long as the trust holds the interest. If the trust is used to hold family business interests, the trustee should be given the authority to split the trust into sub-trusts, with the beneficiary of the sub-trust holding the business interest named as investment trustee of the sub-trust. As noted above, use of a dynasty trust provides creditor protection, avoidance of transfer taxation at each generational level on the value of the business, as well as protection from the claims of a divorcing spouse.

chapter 13

Types of Dynasty Trusts

Pot Trusts

A **pot trust** is created as a single trust and remains a single trust during the period of its administration. These trusts are easily administered and the trustee has the flexibility to treat all beneficiaries equally, as opposed to basing beneficial interest in the trust on degree of relationship to the grantor (which is the result when a per stirpital trust is created).

Disadvantages of the pot trust include:
1. that "equal" treatment may lead to conflict between or within various generations of the family; and
2. this structure does not encourage beneficiaries to make additional contributions to the trust, since all trust assets benefit all individuals with an interest in the trust, including remote relatives (cousins many times removed).

Significant benefits can be achieved if several generations of family members make contributions to the trust, shielded by their GST exemption. Successive generations may be hesitant to do so, however, unless the contributions they make will directly benefit their heirs.

Generational Sub-Trusts

Another common structure for dynasty trusts is a series of **generational sub-trusts** within the larger family trust. A sub-trust is created on the birth of the first member in a generation, or at the death of the surviving member of a generation.

Generational sub-trusts can avoid potential conflict between siblings or conflict between or within various generations of the family. As the number of sub-trusts rise, however, trust administration expenses increase.

Generational sub-trusts may encourage additional contributions, since the contributors know that the contributions will be earmarked for a specific branch of the family.

Funding the Trust

A dynasty trust is typically funded with cash or personal property. Due to the anti-alienation provisions enacted by states that have abolished the Rule Against Perpetuities, real property should not be placed in the trust. Instead, real property can be placed inside of a limited liability company (or family limited partnership), followed by a transfer of the limited liability company (or family limited partnership) interest to the dynasty trust. When selecting assets to transfer to a dynasty trust, highly appreciating assets are preferred if the GST exemption is going to be applied.

The trust can also be funded with a life insurance policy. Life insurance is an ideal asset for a dynasty trust since, during the accumulation phase, the growth in the cash value is shielded from income taxation. Furthermore, life insurance can be used to leverage the value of the trust, which can be particularly attractive with a GST trust. For example, if the settlor is age 50 and a standard risk, a $1,000,000 premium can purchase $6,500,000 worth of life insurance; if the settlor is age 60, the trustee can buy a policy paying $4,000,000. If the spouses are younger, for example, age 35, the trustee could buy, with a single premium payment of $2,000,000, a policy paying $62,000,000 on the death of the second to die.

Even if life insurance is not used, the value of the trust can grow significantly over time. If a $1,000,000 trust is invested in common stocks, which appreciate in value at the same rate stocks have appreciated over the 20th century, the original trust corpus of $1,000,000 will grow to over $200,000,000 in 100 years (or, inflation adjusted, to $10,000,000). If the settlor and spouse have created a life insurance trust, a $10,000,000 death benefit may grow to $2,000,000,000 upon the termination of the trust (or, adjusted for inflation, to $100,000,000).

General Drafting Issues for Dynasty Trusts

Powers of Appointment

Whenever a long-term trust is created, flexibility becomes important because, over time, tax laws, family situations, and economic environments change. To create flexibility, the trust document may grant certain beneficiaries the authority to change the dispositive provisions of the trust to better reflect current circumstances through the use of a power of appointment.

If a power of appointment is granted to a beneficiary of the trust, it should be a limited power of appointment to ensure that the trust assets are not included in the beneficiary's estate. A limited power of appointment can be very broad, and can give the holder the authority to appoint the trust assets to anyone in the world other than himself, his creditors, his estate, or the creditors of his estate. Instead of granting a power to a single individual, the trust document may grant a power to a committee of the heirs, who, by majority vote, may determine those matters specified in the power.

For tax purposes, a limitation is applied to powers of appointment. If the trust is set up as a perpetual trust, the donee of a special power of appointment cannot exercise the power after the common law perpetuities period has expired if the donee wants to continue to use the transfer tax exemption. This rule is commonly referred to as "The Delaware Tax Trap." The flexibility lost by use of a power of appointment can be offset by creating discretionary powers in trustees after the expiration of the perpetuities period.

> ### 📝 Quick Quiz 13.6
>
> 1. Dynasty trusts are against the law and subject to penalties.
>   a. True
>   b. False
>
> 2. The grantor of a dynasty trust often gives the trustee the authority to terminate the trust.
>   a. True
>   b. False
>
> 3. A pot trust is a pool of many trusts for different individuals.
>   a. True
>   b. False
>
> 4. Dynasty trusts should always include spendthrift clauses.
>   a. True
>   b. False
>
> False, True, False, True.

Termination of the Trust

Typically, dynasty trusts are structured to terminate upon the death of the last lineal descendant of the grantor.

If a generational sub-trust approach is used, the trust should provide an allocation formula for distribution of the assets of a trust for the benefit of a family line with no living issue. The distribution among the remaining sub-trusts can be pro rata, based upon degree of relationship, or can be structured as an equal distribution.

In the event that all beneficiaries die with no lineal descendants, and all collateral branches of the family have been provided for, it is generally advisable to name a charity as the final repository of the principal. If the family also has a private foundation, the private foundation may be the ultimate beneficiary. If a private family foundation will not be used, the grantor should specify which charities should receive the funds, and should grant the trustee the right to distribute those funds to charities with like goals and objectives in the event the charity named is no longer in existence at the time of the termination of the trust.

Dynasty trusts often give the trustee or a committee of the heirs the authority to terminate the trust, if desirable, due to size (the trust is too small to justify administration expenses), tax reasons, or otherwise. When a termination provision is included in the document, it is often coordinated with powers of appointment granted to trust beneficiaries.

Broad Investment Powers
The trustee should be granted broad investment powers, including, if applicable:
1. the ability to invest in international securities;
2. a waiver of diversification requirements, especially if the trust will be used to hold family business interests; and
3. the ability to consider other trusts or resources in establishing the investment goals of the trust.

Spendthrift Clause as a Protective Provision
A spendthrift clause should always be included in a dynasty trust to prevent the garnishment of trust proceeds.

Definitions of Terms Used in the Trust Document
While certain terms are taken for granted in casual discussion, it is important to define those terms in a dynasty trust. The dynasty trust is designed to last for a very long time, and the common use of various terms changes over time. To ensure that the intent of the grantor is followed, the trust instrument should define important terms.

The term "ISSUE" should be specifically defined in the trust. The grantor should consider whether he wants issue to include illegitimate or adopted children, children conceived by artificial insemination after the death of the grantor or one of the beneficiaries, and, with modern technology, whether clones of beneficiaries will be eligible for distributions from the trust.

The term "SPOUSE" should also be specifically defined in the trust. Spouse should be defined to take into consideration divorce and remarriage without impacting the spendthrift clause. Some trust documents define "spouse" as the person to whom the beneficiaries are married from time to time. This implies that the only time an in-law is entitled to distributions from the trust is when he is married to the heir. Once the marriage terminates, for whatever reason, the in-law's interest in the trust terminates.

Summary of Dynasty Trusts
Dynasty trusts are perhaps the ultimate tool in transfer tax planning, since they allow assets to pass from one generation to the next without the imposition of gift, estate, or GST taxes. Dynasty trusts are not for everyone, however. Many individuals do not wish to tie up their property for long periods of time and would rather allow their heirs to have outright access to the property even if it will require paying more in transfer taxes. Like any other estate planning tool, a dynasty trust must be consistent with the goals and objectives of the client to be effective.

KEY TERMS

Applicable Rate - The maximum estate tax rate in effect at the date of the GST multiplied by the "inclusion ratio."

Direct Skip - A transfer of property or an interest in property to a skip person that is subject to estate or gift tax in the hands of the transferor.

Dynasty Trust - Generation-skipping trust created in perpetuity. Once created, a dynasty trust provides for trust beneficiaries, but avoids transfer taxation in the beneficiaries' gross estates by restricting ownership of trust assets.

Estate Tax Inclusion Period (ETIP) - The period during which, should the transferor or the transferor's spouse die, the fair market value of the transferred property would be included in the gross estate of the transferor or the transferor's spouse.

Generational Sub-Trust - Trust created on the birth of the first member in a generation, or at the death of the surviving member of a generation. A sub-trust can avoid potential conflict between siblings or conflict between or within various generations of the family.

Inclusion Ratio - Ratio determined by subtracting the applicable fraction from one.

Intentionally Defective Grantor Trust (IDGT) - A trust which gives the grantor sufficient control to be considered the owner for income tax purposes, but not so much control to require the trust property to be included in the transferor's gross estate.

Pot Trust - A trust created as a single trust and remains a single trust during the period of its administration. The trustee has the flexibility to treat all beneficiaries equally, as opposed to basing beneficial interest in the trust on the degree of relationship to the grantor.

Taxable Distribution - Any distribution from a trust to a skip person other than a taxable termination or a direct skip.

Taxable Termination - The termination of an interest in property held in trust *unless*: (1) a transfer subject to federal estate or gift tax occurs with respect to the property held in the trust at the time of the termination; (2) immediately thereafter a non-skip person has an interest in the property; or (3) *no* distributions may be made at any time thereafter to a skip person.

chapter 13

DISCUSSION QUESTIONS

SOLUTIONS to the discussion questions can be found exclusively within the chapter. Once you have completed an initial reading of the chapter, go back and highlight the answers to these questions.

1. Define skip person.

2. To which type of transfers does the GSTT apply?

3. Who is liable for the GSTT on a direct skip?

4. Define taxable distribution.

5. Who is liable for the GSTT on a taxable distribution?

6. List the characteristics of a termination of an interest in property held in trust that does not create a taxable termination.

7. Who is liable for the GSTT on a taxable termination?

8. What is the GSTT rate?

9. How much can an individual transfer to a skip person during his lifetime, or at his death, without incurring any GSTT?

10. When must the allocation of the GST exemption take place?

11. Explain the predeceased ancestor exception.

12. What is a qualified transfer and what are its GSTT implications?

13. What is the estate tax inclusion period?

14. How are lifetime direct skips reported to the IRS?

15. What are the benefits of using a generation-skipping trust?

16. What is the Uniform Statutory Rule Against Perpetuities?

17. Who pays the income tax on the income generated within a dynasty trust?

18. Why should a dynasty trust give some beneficiaries a limited power of appointment?

MULTIPLE-CHOICE PROBLEMS

A sample of multiple choice problems is provided below. Additional multiple choice problems are available at money-education.com by accessing the Student Practice Portal.

1. To which of the following transfers does the GSTT not apply?
    a. A taxable termination.
    b. A taxable distribution.
    c. A direct skip.
    d. A skip-over.

2. Mel has never made any gifts subject to GSTT. He is single and would like to transfer as much as he possibly can during the year to his grandchild without triggering any GSTT. How much can Mel transfer to his grandchild this year and meet his goal?
    a. $15,000.
    b. $4,577,800.
    c. $11,580,000.
    d. $11,595,000.

3. Many grandparents name their grandchildren as the beneficiaries of their life insurance policies. How should the life insurance policies for the benefit of grandchildren be held?
    a. A revocable life insurance trust should be established and funded with a transfer of the life insurance policy.
    b. The grandparent should be the owner with the grandchild as the listed beneficiary.
    c. An irrevocable life insurance trust should be created for the benefit of the grandchild.
    d. The ownership of the policy should be transferred to the grandchild.

4. Justin transfers $2,000,000 in 2020 to an irrevocable trust providing that income is to be accumulated for 22 years. At the end of 22 years, the accumulated income is to be distributed to Justin's child, Chip, and the trust principal is to be paid to Justin's grandchild, Beau. Justin allocates $800,000 of his GST exemption to the trust on a timely filed gift tax return. What is the GSTT rate applicable to the trust?
    a. 20.00%.
    b. 24.00%.
    c. 40.00%.
    d. 60.00%.

5. Upon what form is a lifetime GST reported?
    a. Form 1040.
    b. Form 709.
    c. Form 706.
    d. Form 1041.

chapter 13

QUICK QUIZ EXPLANATIONS

Quick Quiz 13.1
1. False. While a person two or more generations below the transferor is generally considered a skip person, exceptions such as the predeceased ancestor exception may change this result.
2. False. While the impact of executing a disclaimer is to allow property to pass as if the disclaimant had predeceased the transferor, since the disclaimant has not actually died, the disclaimer is ignored for generation-skipping transfer tax purposes.

Quick Quiz 13.2
1. False. A taxable termination occurs when the last non-skip beneficiary dies or when the trust actually terminates. Usually, distributions from a trust to a skip person are considered to be taxable distributions.
2. False. When a taxable termination occurs, the trustee pays the GSTT due from the trust assets. The beneficiaries of the trust are not directly liable for paying the GSTT.

Quick Quiz 13.3
1. False. The GSTT applies to some transfers made before October 22, 1986 if specific requirements imposed by law have not been met.
2. True.
3. True.

Quick Quiz 13.4
1. True.
2. False. The lifetime exemption amount for the GSTT is $11,580,000 (2020).

Quick Quiz 13.5
1. False. Form 709, the Federal Gift and Generation-Skipping Transfer Tax Return, is due on or before April 15th of the year following the calendar year in which the direct skip occurs.

Quick Quiz 13.6
1. False. Dynasty trusts are legitimate planning vehicles used to avoid the imposition of future transfer taxes.
2. True.
3. False. A pot trust is a dynasty trust that keeps all of its assets in one account, which can be contrasted with a separate share trust, which has an account for each beneficiary.
4. True.

14

BASIC ESTATE PLAN

LEARNING OBJECTIVES

1. Describe the estate planning process and develop a basic estate plan.
2. Describe a revocable life insurance trust, a bypass trust, and a marital trust.
3. Identify the parts of an estate planning checklist.
4. Prepare the solutions to the comprehensive cases.

CFP Board Resource Document - Student-Centered Learning Objectives based upon CFP Board Principal Topics.

THE ESTATE PLANNING PROCESS

Chapter 1 introduced the seven basic steps in the estate planning process. As you may recall, they are:
1. Gather and analyze the information necessary to understand the client's personal and financial circumstances, including the client's current financial statements and existing estate planning documents.
2. Identify and select the client's transfer objectives, including family and charitable objectives.
3. Analyze the client's current estate plan and potential alternative courses of action.
4. Develop a comprehensive plan of transfers consistent with all information and objectives.
5. Present the estate planning recommendations.
6. Implement the estate planning recommendations.
7. Review the estate plan periodically and update the plan when necessary (especially for changes in family situations).

The first two steps were discussed in Chapter 1. The remaining steps are discussed in this chapter.

Determine the Client's Financial Situation

Once the client and family information is collected, the planner can begin to determine the financial situation of the client. The planner should define any areas of concern, including liquidity issues, potential excessive taxes or costs, and other situational needs, such as disability of an identified heir or blended family. The planner should also estimate the current value of the estate and liquidity needs now and at five-year intervals forward for the full life expectancy of the transferor, including estate transfer costs. Based on the client's objectives and priorities, the planner should make realistic judgments regarding the feasibility of meeting those objectives.

chapter 14

Develop the Estate Plan
When contemplating the design of a simple estate plan, the following steps should be considered:
1. Identify the potential inheriting parties in terms of assets, competence, and relation to the transferor.
2. Identify all property interests in terms of value and property ownership type.
   - Identify any existing beneficiary designations.
   - Identify joint property owners and percentage of contribution to original purchase price of property. Also determine the basis of certain assets, such as business interests or other high-valued assets.
   - Verify how life insurance is owned.
3. Have all documents prepared - will, durable power of attorney for both property and health care, and advance medical directives.
   - Identify legatees.
   - Identify property transferring to trusts.
4. Review any inter vivos trusts.
   - Identify property transferring to a trust or from a trust and its beneficiaries.
5. Verify use of the applicable estate tax credit.
6. Optimize use of the unlimited marital deduction/consider portability of unused exemption.
7. Select use of the unlimited charitable deduction.

While the development of the estate plan should be specific to the client, common planning techniques are generally used for particular parties. The more common parties and devices used with each are discussed below. In addition, an estate planning checklist is provided below. This list is not exhaustive and should only be used by the planner to develop their own check list to use when creating the estate plan.

Spouse
If the individual is not married, step six, optimizing the use of the unlimited marital deduction and strategizing with the portability of decedent's unused exemption amount is not available. However, if the individual is married, the surviving spouse's needs and desires (which will vary in each individual case) must be considered in the estate planning process. Ideally, a plan would transfer sufficient assets to non-spouse heirs so as to utilize the unified gift and estate tax credit and transfer the remainder of the estate's assets to the surviving spouse to qualify for the unlimited marital deduction. This strategy presumes that the surviving spouse has no need of the assets transferred to the non-spouse heirs. If the spouse has such a need, it may be better to consider using a bypass trust with the spouse as the income beneficiary. Portability could also be considered if all the assets are left to the surviving spouse.

An individual could choose to leave all of his property to his surviving spouse outright and allow the surviving spouse to disclaim the undesired property interest(s). The individual's will would contain a provision to direct the disclaimed property to children or other heirs thus fulfilling the use of the applicable estate tax credit and covering any needs and desires of the surviving spouse. However, this method does not guarantee use of the applicable estate tax credit, as the surviving spouse may not choose to disclaim a proper amount. Therefore, many individuals choose to use one of the following transfer methods which qualify for the unlimited marital deduction: (1) GPOA Trust or (2) QTIP Trust. Any combination of these methods, coupled with outright transfers, may also be used, as in the case of the ABC Trust arrangement discussed in Chapter 10. The ABC Trust arrangement is frequently used in blended family situations to maximize the use of the unlimited marital deduction, the applicable estate tax credit, and to give the testator the power to control the ultimate disposition of his property. Now with the advent of the concept of inter-spousal portability of the decedent's exemption amount, opportunities abound for well-planned tax savings.

Non-Citizen Spouse
Recall that transfers to a surviving spouse who is not a U.S. citizen do not qualify for the unlimited marital deduction. So, in the case of an individual who would like to qualify transfers to his non-citizen spouse for the unlimited marital deduction, the individual will have to either use a QDOT or have his surviving spouse become a U.S. citizen.

Children
When an individual has children, one must consider an individual's desires to transfer assets to his children, regardless of the reasons. Most often, when property is transferred to, or for the benefit of minor children, the transfer is made in trust, which provides for the management and protection of the funds. If an individual dies with adult children, he may still consider the use of a trust, but in either case, the individual may also transfer assets outright to his children.

If a trust is desired, a bypass trust may be appropriate. If the child is a minor, the 2503(b) or (c) trust, or a Crummey trust, can be used to maximize the use of the annual exclusion. If the client desires to give property outright to a minor child, particular attention should be given to state law to determine the ability of minors to own property. Custodial accounts under UGMA or UTMA may also be appropriate.

Grandchildren
Grandchildren present additional opportunities to transfer wealth through a gifting program, but they also increase the risk of inadvertent tax consequences because of the GSTT system. The planner should determine if a lifetime gifting program is appropriate for the client to make use of the GST annual exclusion of $15,000 (2020) and qualified transfer exclusions. In addition, a Reverse QTIP election may be considered to make use of the GST exemption of $11,580,000.

Trusts
Trusts should be used in two distinct situations - when there is a split interest in property (i.e., income interest to spouse with remainder interest to children) and when the individual has reservations about the heir's ability to manage, control, or preserve the assets.

Irrevocable Life Insurance Trust
As discussed throughout this text, an insured should not possess any incidents of ownership in the life insurance policies on his life unless the insured intends to use the cash value of the policy during his life for other financial planning purposes (e.g., educational funding or retirement funding). If the proceeds of the life insurance policy will be income replacement for the insured's beneficiaries or will be used to pay estate taxes, the insured should not own the policy. As you may recall, such an arrangement may be accomplished either through the purchase of a new policy by the beneficiaries or by the trustee of an irrevocable life insurance trust (ILIT), or, alternatively, if a policy is already in existence, the policy may be assigned (transferred) to a named beneficiary or to the trustee of an ILIT.

The general problem with direct beneficiary ownership is that there is no assurance of management, no creditor protection, and it is difficult to accomplish a split asset arrangement. If there is a single mature beneficiary, direct ownership or assignment may be cost effective, but whenever there is a need for a split interest (see **Exhibit 14.1**), an ILIT is recommended.

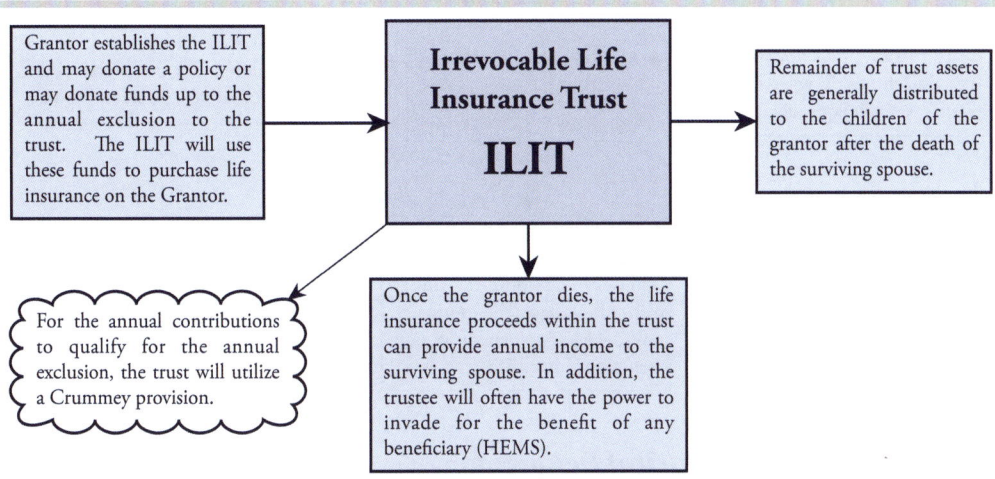

Exhibit 14.1 | Visual Depiction of an ILIT

For example, suppose that the client did not know while planning the estate whether the spouse would need the income from the life insurance policy. It would seem prudent to set up the life insurance within an ILIT with the trust provisions calling for income to the spouse for life (note this does not utilize the marital deduction nor does it cause the insurance to be included in either spouse's gross estate) and the remainder to the insured's children. The trustee may also be given the power to invade for health, education, maintenance, or support (HEMS) for any beneficiary of the trust. The surviving spouse, upon the death of the first-to-die spouse, may disclaim the income interest while continuing to enjoy the discretionary power of the trustee to invade for HEMS if the surviving spouse needed such invasion. In other words, the use of an ILIT allows the surviving spouse to decide if she needs the income from the life insurance policy, or whether it should transfer directly to the children at the death of the first-to-die spouse.

Unified Gift and Estate Tax Credit

To provide for use of the unified gift and estate tax credit equivalency ($11,580,000 for 2020), the testator could make lifetime taxable gifts of up to $11,580,000. The advantage of such an arrangement is that any future appreciation of the assets gifted during life is completely removed from the transferor's gross estate. The disadvantage created when the appreciation is removed from transferor's gross estate is (1) that the transferor loses control of the property transferred and (2) such transfers may adversely affect the recipient (recipient may not be capable of handling wealth).

Alternatively, an amount equal to the applicable estate tax credit equivalency can be transferred at the transferor's death directly to his children. However, if the surviving spouse has a need to use some or all of the assets, such an arrangement will not be appropriate because the surviving spouse will not have a right to the assets.

Once again, the formation of a bypass trust (credit equivalency trust) will provide the transferor and his heirs' flexibility. The ILIT and the bypass trust are quite similar. Generally, the only difference is that the assets in the bypass trust are included in the gross estate of the decedent, but the proceeds from the insurance policy owned by the ILIT are not included in the decedent's gross estate.

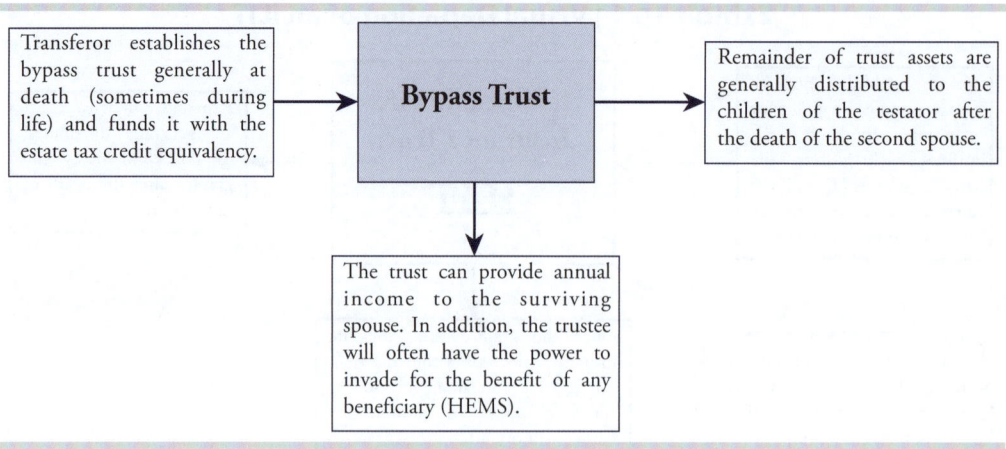

Exhibit 14.2 | Visual Depiction of a Bypass Trust ($11,580,000 in 2020)

Optimize Use of the Unlimited Marital Deduction

As previously discussed, there are several qualifying ways to leave assets to a surviving spouse and eliminate the estate tax at the death of the first spouse. The decision between transferring property to a GPOA Trust or the QTIP Trust is dependent upon the testator's desire to retain control of the ultimate remainderman of the property. Generally, the GPOA Trust gives the surviving spouse a general power of appointment over the trust assets which gives the surviving spouse the power to name the ultimate remainder beneficiary of the property after her death. If the testator desires to retain control of the ultimate disposition of the property, perhaps in the case of different beneficiaries than the surviving spouse, a QTIP Trust is used. The QTIP Trust gives the testator the ability to preselect the ultimate remainder beneficiary of the trust property. Also, as noted above, the combination of these trusts is quite often used with the ABC Trust arrangement.

Quite a few things can derail an otherwise good plan. For example, any assets that qualify for the unlimited marital deduction at the death of the first-to-die spouse will be included in the surviving spouse's gross estate to the extent that they are not consumed. Therefore, if the surviving spouse dies soon after his spouse, there may be a bunching of assets in the second estate. Bunching of assets in the second estate where the second spouse dies shortly after the death of the first spouse no longer creates a significant issue since the second spouse is able to make use of the deceased spousal unused exemption, through the use of portability.

The usual objective is to treat spouses as one economic unit and push as many assets to lower generations without transfer taxes. This objective is accomplished through transfers for support, utilizing qualified transfers, utilizing annual exclusion gifts, utilizing the uniform credit during life or at death, electing to split gifts, and utilizing the GST exemption.

Portability

TRA 2010 introduced portability of a deceased spouse's unused tax exemption amount and ATRA 2012 made portability permanent. By affirmative election on a timely filed estate tax return, an executor, on behalf of a deceased spouse, can donate or allocate the deceased spouse's unused estate exemption to the surviving spouse. Therefore, a surviving spouse could shield up to $23,160,000 (2020) (her own $11,580,000 exemption amount and her deceased spouse's donated $11,580,000 exemption amount) from being subjected to any transfer tax.

Portability solves the problem of failure to plan and provides for the unused spousal exemption by the surviving spouse. The concept of portability, however, is not without its drawbacks. Portability does not protect against estate taxes for the state, nor does it allow for GSTT planning since the GSTT exemption is not portable. It also does not address non-tax related issues, such as families with children from a prior marriage or heirs who are not sufficiently mature enough to handle money. Its existence does not mean that the use of bypass trusts and marital deduction planning is anachronistic.

In addition, in the event the surviving spouse remarries and the subsequent spouse dies, this will preclude the surviving spouse from using her first deceased spouse's exemption. The requirement of privity precludes the surviving spouse from, at her death, donating her deceased spouse's unused exemption to her new spouse. She many only donate her original, unused exemption. Another issue that has been addressed by the IRS is the ordering of exemptions used by a surviving spouse, who during her life has her deceased spouse's exemption, in addition to her own. The spouse can make use of the DSUE amount before her own lifetime exemption.

Example 14.1
Susie inherits her deceased spouse's entire unused exemption, which is added to her entire unused exemption. When Susie makes a taxable gift, which exemption applies – hers or the one transferred to her by the deceased spouse? The spouse can make use of the DSUE amount before her own lifetime exemption.

Select Use of Charitable Deduction
If the desire is to transfer assets to qualifying charities, it is usually wise to consider transferring tax-advantaged funds (IRAs, annuities) to these charities because these funds do not receive a step-to fair market value in adjusted basis at the decedent's death and are considered taxable income eligible for the Income in Respect of the Decedent deduction to taxable recipients. Moreover, newly enacted legislation keeps alive, for now, the specific exclusions from income tax on an otherwise taxable distribution if the IRA account holder is at least 70½ and distributes directly to a charity. The charitable organization, as a tax exempt organization, would receive the assets income-tax free. After the charitable aspirations are satisfied, the remaining assets are distributed to the spouse and the remaining heirs.

Gifting Program
If the client has substantial assets, a lifetime gifting program may be considered to make use of the annual exclusion of $15,000 (2020). Depending on the number of descendants and the number of years in which the donor can utilize the plan, a substantial amount of wealth can be transferred. If the donor is married, a split gift election should also be considered to make use of the non-donor spouse's annual exclusion. Qualified transfers during life to education and medical institutions may also be considered especially in the case of gifts to grandchildren to avoid the GSTT.

Implement the Plan

Once the plan has been designed, the planner should present the plan to the client, ensure the client understands all aspects of the plan, and following their approval, assist in implementing the plan. Unlike other areas of estate planning, the implementation generally involves a substantial amount of initial work, and very little subsequent work. The creation of the trusts and estate planning documents, the retitling of the assets and the selection of the beneficiaries are completed during implementation. Unless changes are needed, very little work is done until the client's death unless the planner's assistance is required in the interim.

The financial planner's involvement in the actual implementation of the plan will vary depending on the financial planner's education, experience, and comfort level. In the case of an experienced financial planner specializing in estate planning, much of the plan implementation may be done with the assistance of or by the planner. The planner may draft the estate planning documents if the planner is also an attorney, or seek the assistance of an attorney to draft these documents. (Generally, planners work closely with a particular firm or designated attorneys.) The planner may also sell (if properly licensed) the client the necessary insurance policies, execute the required investments, secure the necessary beneficiary designation forms, and help the client change title to property if needed. If trusts are used, the planner may continue to work with the client to ensure appropriate investments are made, Crummey provisions are handled appropriately, and tax returns are filed.

Alternatively, if the planner is not experienced in the estate planning field, he may outsource much of the work to other professionals. In this case, he may truly act as the team captain giving the client instructions on people to see and things to do and leave a majority of the work to the client and other professionals. The extent of the planner's involvement and the client's expectations of the planner should be detailed in the client engagement letter.

Monitor the Plan

The estate plan should be reviewed periodically and updated when necessary. Typically, changes to the estate plan will occur when there has been a change in the family situation, usually a death, marriage, divorce, birth, or adoption. Good estate plans are created such that they anticipate some changes in family situations, for example births of children or grandchildren, but all changes cannot be foreseen. In addition, changes in the client's financial situation may also change the need for lifetime gifting programs and estate planning devices. The planner may wish to provide the client with specific situations in which they should return to update their estate plan, particularly marriages and divorces, moving from one state to another, or threshold changes in net worth. Because clients may forget to tell the planner of substantial changes over the years, the planner should meet with the client at least every five years to ensure necessary changes are addressed.

Exhibit 14.3 | Estate Plan Checklist

☐ Yes ☐ No	Is the will properly prepared and updated?	
If no, why: _____		

☐ Yes ☐ No	Have appropriate provisions been implemented to account for all children?	
If no, why: _____		

☐ Yes ☐ No	Have disinherited heirs been addressed in the will?	
If no, why: _____		

☐ Yes ☐ No	Have the executor and successor executors been named and notified?	
If no, why: _____		

☐ Yes ☐ No	Have the trustee and successor trustees been named and notified?	
If no, why: _____		

☐ Yes ☐ No	Have guardians and successor guardians for children been named and notified?	
If no, why: _____		

☐ Yes ☐ No	If desired, have appropriate steps been taken to avoid probate (e.g., revocable living trusts, titling, designated beneficiaries)?	
If no, why: _____		

☐ Yes ☐ No	Will the appropriate property interests be transferred to the proper heirs?	
If no, why: _____		

☐ Yes ☐ No	Is the general power of attorney and/or power of attorney for health care properly prepared and updated?	
If no, why: _____		

☐ Yes ☐ No	Is the Living Will properly prepared and updated?	
If no, why: _____		

☐ Yes ☐ No	Have all beneficiary designations for life insurance, retirement accounts, etc. been changed?	
If no, why: _____		

☐ Yes ☐ No	Have all life insurance policies been transferred from the estate (unless the cash value is needed by the insured to pay for education or retirement)?	
If no, why: _____		

☐ Yes ☐ No	If an ILIT is used, does the trustee have the power to (but is not required to) loan money to and purchase assets from the estate?	
If no, why: _____		

Exhibit 14.4 | Estate Plan Checklist (Continued)

☐ Yes ☐ No	Will the gift and estate tax applicable credit be fully utilized?
If no, why: _____	

☐ Yes ☐ No	Will the unlimited marital deduction be properly utilized?
If no, why: _____	

☐ Yes ☐ No	Will the client make optimal use of annual exclusion gifts and qualified transfers during life?
If no, why: _____	

☐ Yes ☐ No	If the client is married, will the client make appropriate use of gift-splitting?
If no, why: _____	

☐ Yes ☐ No	If the client is married and the assets owned by each spouse are disproportionate, have appropriate measures been taken to ensure that the applicable estate tax credit of both spouses is utilized?
If no, why: _____	

☐ Yes ☐ No	If the client is married to a non U.S. Citizen, has appropriate planning been utilized?
If no, why: _____	

☐ Yes ☐ No	Have charitable intentions and desires been fulfilled?
If no, why: _____	

☐ Yes ☐ No	If appropriate, has the use of a Family Limited Partnership, QPRT, or GRAT been implemented?
If no, why: _____	

☐ Yes ☐ No	Do trusts include appropriate Crummey provisions?
If no, why: _____	

☐ Yes ☐ No	Should the executor make timely portability election to transfer the deceased spousal unused exclusion to surviving spouse?
If no, why: _____	

☐ Yes ☐ No	Has the executor provided basis information to heirs and the IRS?
If no, why: _____	

Exhibit 14.5 | Post Mortem Checklist

☐ Yes ☐ No	Has the appropriate valuation date been selected (date of death or alternate valuation date)?	
If no, why: _____		
☐ Yes ☐ No	Have appropriate disclaimers been used?	
If no, why: _____		
☐ Yes ☐ No	Have appropriate expense allocations been made between the Forms 1040, 1041, and 706?	
If no, why: _____		
☐ Yes ☐ No	Have appropriate Section 303 redemptions been completed?	
If no, why: _____		
☐ Yes ☐ No	If appropriate, was the Section 6166 election to pay by installments made?	
If no, why: _____		
☐ Yes ☐ No	Have appropriate 2032A special use elections been made?	
If no, why: _____		
☐ Yes ☐ No	Have appropriate QTIP elections been made?	
If no, why: _____		
☐ Yes ☐ No	Have appropriate Reverse QTIP elections for GSTT purposes been made?	
If no, why: _____		
☐ Yes ☐ No	If the decedent was married to a non U.S. Citizen, has a QDOT been utilized?	
If no, why: _____		
☐ Yes ☐ No	If needed, were extensions to file tax returns filed with the IRS?	
If no, why: _____		
☐ Yes ☐ No	Have all necessary income, gift, estate, and fiduciary tax returns been prepared, reviewed, and filed?	
If no, why: _____		
☐ Yes ☐ No	Has the probate process been completed and assets distributed?	
If no, why: _____		
☐ Yes ☐ No	Has the executor made the election for portability of the deceased spousal unused exemption (DSUE) amount?	
If no, why: _____		

COMPREHENSIVE CASE EXAMPLE

The Gail and Tony case illustrates the basic estate planning concepts and calculations discussed throughout the text.

GAIL AND TONY BACKGROUND

Gail and Tony have been married for 42 years. Gail is currently in good health, but due to a severe heart attack last year, Tony is only expected to live a few more years. They have the following children and grandchildren:

Children	Ages	Grandchildren
Shami	39	2 children
Lisa	36	5 children
Mary	30	4 children
Monica	29	3 children
Rick	25	No children

All of their daughters are healthy, employed, and married. Rick, their only son, is single and does not have any children.

Tony and Gail own Tony's Video and Games, a family-owned video and game store that has been very popular. Tony wants to sell half of the business to his key employee, Hari, and he wants to sell the other half to his oldest daughter, Shami, the CFO of the store.

Tony's grandson Philip, Monica's youngest child, was born with a serious physical disability. To provide additional support for Philip, Tony created an irrevocable trust with a $2,500,000 transfer on January 1, 2008. The trust met the requirements of 2503(b). At the time of the transfer (2008), the GST exemption was $2,000,000, the GST rate was 45 percent, and the annual exclusion was $12,000.

Tony also made the following additional lifetime transfers:
- On January 2, 2009, Tony gave each of his five children $200,000 of his separate property (assume the annual exclusion was $13,000).
- On January 1, 2012, Tony gave each of his five children $100,000 of his separate property. The annual exclusion at that time was $13,000.

Gail has never made any taxable gifts during her lifetime nor has she agreed to split any of Tony's separate property gifts.

Tony and Gail each have a simple will which leaves most probate assets to each other and also includes a six-month survivorship clause. Each will also declares that debts are to be paid from the residual estate, and taxes are to be paid by the children's share of the estate.

Tony and Gail estimate the following at each of their deaths:
1. The last illness and funeral expenses are expected to be $250,000 per person.
2. Estate administration expenses are estimated at $200,000 per person.

WILL

Selected clauses from Tony's Statutory Last Will and Testament:

I, Tony, being of sound mind and wishing to make proper disposition of my property in the event of my death, do declare this to be my Last Will and Testament. I revoke all of my prior wills and codicils.

1. I have been married but once, and then to Gail with whom I am presently living. Out of my marriage to Gail, five children were born, namely Shami, Lisa, Mary, Monica, and Rick. I have adopted no one nor has anyone adopted me.

2. I give my deferred annuity to David's Charity, a qualified charitable organization.

3. I leave Auto 1 to my favorite grandchild, Don.

4. I give the residual of my estate to Gail, my wife.

5. In the event that Gail predeceases me or fails to survive me for more than six months from the date of my death, I give any interest of my estate determined to be payable to her to my children in equal and 1/5 shares.

6. In the event that any of the named legatees should predecease me, die within six months from the date of my death, disclaim, or otherwise fail to accept any property bequeathed to him or her and said legatee has no descendants, his or her share of all of my property of which I die possessed shall be paid equally among their surviving named legatees.

7. I name my best friend Gary to serve as the executor of my succession with full seizin and without bond.

8. I direct that the expenses of my last illness, funeral, and the administration of my estate shall be paid by my executor as soon as practicable after my death and allocated against the residual estate.

9. Since I have made numerous lifetime gifts to my children, all inheritance, estate, succession, transfer, and other taxes (including interest and penalties thereon) payable by reason of my death shall be allocated to the children's share, regardless of whether my spouse survives me.

Exhibit 14.6 | Statement of Financial Position (Tony & Gail) (July 31, 2020)

ASSETS		LIABILITIES AND NET WORTH	
Cash/Cash Equivalents		**Liabilities**	
JT Cash	$100,000	Current Liabilities	
Total Cash/Cash Equiv.	**$100,000**	W Credit card 1	$1,000
		W Credit card 2	15,000
Invested Assets		**Total Current Liabilities**	**$16,000**
JT Tony's Video and Games	$5,000,000		
W Gail's Portfolio	500,000	Long-Term Liabilities	
H Deferred Annuity	233,047	JT Mortgage - Primary	$258,630
H 401(k) Plan	600,000	JT Mortgage - vacation 1	369,428
H Profit Sharing Plan	526,382	JT Mortgage - vacation 2	687,444
H Tony's Portfolio	4,000,000	**Total Long-Term Liabilities**	**$1,315,502**
JT Commercial Property A	1,500,000		
Total Investments	**$12,359,429**		
		Total Liabilities	**$1,331,502**
Personal Use Assets			
JT Primary Residence	$1,300,000		
JT Vacation Home 1	800,000		
JT Vacation Home 2	700,000		
JT Personal Property	875,000	**Net Worth**	**$15,087,927**
H Auto 1	80,000		
H Auto 2	55,000		
W Auto 3	40,000		
W Yacht	110,000		
Total Personal Use	**$3,960,000**		
Total Assets	**$16,419,429**	**Total Liabilities and Net Worth**	**$16,419,429**

Notes to Financial Statements:
1. Assets are stated at fair market value (rounded to even dollars).
2. Liabilities are stated at principal only (rounded to even dollars).
3. The adjusted basis of Tony's Video and Games is $1,000,000.
4. The 401(k) and the Profit Sharing Plan have the children designated as equal beneficiaries (with the consent of Gail). Tony has never designated a beneficiary of the deferred annuity. No other item has designated beneficiaries or automatic survivorship features unless specifically indicated.
5. Property Ownership:
    - JT - Joint tenancy with right of survivorship. Gail and Tony are joint tenants of all property owned JT.
    - H - Husband separate.
    - W - Wife separate.

Estate Plan Exercise

Assuming the facts given and that Tony died on July 31, 2020, answer the following questions. Use the gift and estate rates and exclusions at the time of any transfer. Use 2020 exclusions, credits, and tax rate for the estate tax.

1. Calculate the gift tax and GSTT consequences of the gift to Philip made on January 1, 2008.

2. Calculate the annual exclusion and gift tax due on the gifts (to children) made during 2009.

3. Calculate the annual exclusion and gift tax due on the gifts made during 2012.

4. Calculate the total of the assets that will pass through Tony's probate estate assuming he died on July 31, 2020.

5. Calculate the estate tax due at Tony's death assuming he died on July 31, 2020. Assume $0 state death tax credit, $0 credit for prior transfers and $0 foreign death tax credit. (Hint: Use the layout provided in your book.)

6. Assume that Tony did not die on July 31, 2020. Discuss possible options for the transfer of Tony's Video and Games from Tony and Gail to Hari and Shami.

7. What trust options would you recommend as part of Tony and Gail's overall estate plan?

8. What additional planning advice would you give Tony and Gail regarding their estate plan that has not been addressed?

Estate Plan Solutions

The following are model solutions to the estate planning exercise. Note numbers are rounded for presentation but unrounded numbers were used for calculations.

1. Calculate the gift tax and GSTT consequences of the gift to Philip made on January 1, 2008.

The GSTT and gift tax consequences are calculated as follows:

GSTT Calculation

		Notes:
Applicable Fraction (AF)	0.8039	$2,000,000/$2,488,000
Inclusion Ratio (IR)	0.1961	1- AF
Applicable Rate	0.0883	IR x Max Transfer Rate of 45%

GST	$2,500,000
Less: Annual Exclusion	($12,000)
Taxable GST	$2,488,000
Times Applicable rate	8.83% (rounded)
GSTT	**$219,600**

Transfers to a 2503 (b) trust are eligible for the annual exclusion
Numbers are rounded for convenience, but unrounded numbers were used throughout the calculation

Since the entire 2008 GST Exemption is used, the problem could be calculated as follows:

GST	$2,500,000	
Less: Annual Exclusion	($12,000)	
Less: Applicable GST Exemption	($2,000,000)	
Taxable GST	$488,000	
Times Tax Rate	45%	
GSTT	**$219,600**	The same as the tax calculated above.

Gift Tax Calculation

		Notes:
1 Total Current Year Gifts	$2,500,000	Gift to Philip
Plus GSTT Tax Paid	$219,600	GSTT paid is a taxable gift.
2 Less Annual Exclusion	($12,000)	
3 Total Current Year Taxable Gifts	$2,707,600	
4 Plus Taxable Gifts from Prior Years	$0	
5 Total Taxable Gifts	**$2,707,600**	
6 Tax on Total Taxable Gifts	$1,099,220	[$780,800 + 0.45(707,600)]
7 Tax on Prior Gifts	$0	
8 Balance	$1,099,220	
9 Applicable Credit	$345,800	The 2008 Applicable Gift Tax Credit
10 Applicable Credit Against Tax for all Prior Periods	$0	
11 Balance (subtract 10 from 9)	$345,800	
12 Applicable Credit (smaller of 8 or 11)	$345,800	
13 Total Gift Tax (8 minus 12)	**$753,420**	

Note: In 2008, the gift tax exclusion amount was $1,000,000 and the higest marginal gift tax rate was 45%

2. Calculate the annual exclusion and gift tax due on the gifts made in 2009.

The gift tax consequences are calculated as follows:

Gift Tax Calculation		Notes:
1 Total Current Year Gifts	$1,000,000	$200,000 to each of his 5 children
2 Less Annual Exclusion	($65,000)	$13,000 to each of 5 children - Gail did not split gifts
3 Total Current Year Taxable Gifts	$935,000	
4 Plus Taxable Gifts from Prior Years	$2,707,600	
5 **Total Taxable Gifts**	**$3,642,600**	
6 Tax on Total Taxable Gifts	$1,519,970	[$780,800 + 0.45($1,642,600)]
7 Tax on Prior Gifts	$1,099,220	[$780,800 + 0.45($707,600)]
8 Balance	$420,750	
9 Applicable Credit	$345,800	The 2009 Applicable Gift Tax Credit
10 Applicable Credit Against Tax for all Prior Periods	$345,800	
11 Balance (subtract 10 from 9)	$0	
12 Applicable Credit (smaller of 8 or 11)	$0	
13 **Total Gift Tax (8 minus 12)**	**$420,750**	(also 45% of $935,000)

Note: In 2009, the gift tax exclusion amount was $1,000,000 and the higest marginal gift tax rate was 45%

3. Calculate the annual exclusion and gift tax due on the gifts made during 2012.

The gift tax consequences are calculated as follows:

Gift Tax Calculation		Notes:
1 Total Current Year Gifts	$500,000	$100,000 to each of his 5 children
2 Less Annual Exclusion	($65,000)	$13,000 to each of 5 children - Gail did not split gifts
3 Total Current Year Taxable Gifts	$435,000	
4 Plus Taxable Gifts from Prior Years	$3,642,600	
5 **Total Taxable Gifts**	**$4,077,600**	
6 Tax on Total Taxable Gifts	$1,407,960	[$155,800 + 0.35($3,577,600)]
7 Tax on Prior Gifts	$1,255,710	[$155,800 + 0.35($3,142,600)]
8 Balance	$152,250	
9 Applicable Credit	$1,772,800	The 2012 Applicable Credit
10 Applicable Credit Against Tax for all Prior Periods	$345,800	The Applicable Credit Used in Prior Periods
11 Balance (subtract 10 from 9)	$1,427,000	
12 Applicable Credit (smaller of 8 or 11)	$152,250	
13 **Total Gift Tax (8 minus 12)**	**$0**	

Note: In 2012, the gift tax exclusion amount was $5,120,000 and the higest marginal gift tax rate was 35%

chapter 14

4. Calculate the total value of the assets that will pass through Tony's Probate Estate, assuming he died on July 31, 2020. Assume any gift tax paid is more than 3 years ago.

The total value of the assets that will pass through probate is calculated as follows:

Asset	Owned	Full Value	Tony's Interest	Probate Estate	Gross Estate	Marital Deduction
Cash	JT with Spouse	$100,000	$50,000	$0	$50,000	$50,000
Tony's Video and Games	JT with Spouse	$5,000,000	$2,500,000	$0	$2,500,000	$2,500,000
Gail's Portfolio	Wife only	$500,000	$0	$0	$0	$0
Deferred Annuity	Husband only	$233,047	$233,047	$233,047	$233,047	$0
401(k) Plan	Husband only	$600,000	$600,000	$0	$600,000	$0
Profit Sharing Plan	Husband only	$526,382	$526,382	$0	$526,382	$0
Tony's Portfolio	Husband only	$4,000,000	$4,000,000	$4,000,000	$4,000,000	$4,000,000
Commercial Property A	JT with Spouse	$1,500,000	$750,000	$0	$750,000	$750,000
Primary Residence	JT with Spouse	$1,300,000	$650,000	$0	$650,000	$650,000
Vacation Home 1	JT with Spouse	$800,000	$400,000	$0	$400,000	$400,000
Vacation Home 2	JT with Spouse	$700,000	$350,000	$0	$350,000	$350,000
Personal Property	JT with Spouse	$875,000	$437,500	$0	$437,500	$437,500
Auto 1	Husband only	$80,000	$80,000	$80,000	$80,000	$0
Auto 2	Husband only	$55,000	$55,000	$55,000	$55,000	$55,000
Auto 3	Wife only	$40,000	$0	$0	$0	$0
Yacht	Wife only	$110,000	$0	$0	$0	$0
Gift Tax Paid within 3 years	Husband only	$0	$0	$0	$0	$0
Total		**$16,419,429**	**$10,631,929**	**$4,368,047**	**$10,631,929**	**$9,192,500**

Reconciliation of Gross Estate to Marital Deduction:

Tony's Gross Estate		$10,631,929
Less Gross Estate Items:		
To David's Charity per Will	$233,047	
401(k) to Children	$600,000	
Profit Sharing Plan to Children	$526,382	
Auto per Will	$80,000	
Gift Tax Gross Up for Gifts Made within 3 Years	$0	
		$1,439,429
Assets Qualifying for Marital Deduction		$9,192,500

Expenses Allocated to the Marital Portion:

Qualified Marital Deducation		$9,192,500
Less Expenses:		
Last Illness and Funeral Expense	$250,000	
Estate Administration Expenses	$200,000	
Debt on Property Received by Gail (1/2 of $1,315,502)	$657,751	
		$1,107,751
Marital Deduction		$8,084,749

Comprehensive Case Example

5. Calculate the estate tax due at Tony's death assuming he died on July 31, 2020. (Hint: Use the layout provided in Chapter 6.)

   The estate tax is calculated as follows. The answer provided for question #4 details the determination of the available amount for the marital deduction, the net amount passing to the spouse.

Gross Estate		$10,631,929	Gross Estate
Less Deductions:			
Last Medical/Funeral	($250,000)		
Administrative Costs	($200,000)		
Debts	($657,751)		
Losses During Estate Administration	$0	($1,107,751)	Deductions
Equals: Adjusted Gross Estate		**$9,524,178**	Adjusted Gross Estate
Less: Charitable Deduction	($233,047)		
Less: Marital Deduction	($8,084,749)		
Less: State Death Tax Credit	$0	($8,317,796)	
Equals: Taxable Estate		**$1,206,382**	Taxable Estate
Add: Previous Taxable Gifts (post-1976)		$4,077,600	Post-1976 Gifts
Equals: Tentative Tax Base		**$5,283,982**	Tentative Tax Base
Tentative Tax [$345,800 + (0.40 x $4,283,982)]		$2,059,393	Tentative Tax
Less: Credits			
Previous Gift Tax Paid ($1,174,170)	($1,174,170)		
Applicable Estate Tax Credit	($885,223)		
State Death Tax Paid	$0		
Prior Transfer Credit	$0		
Foreign Death Tax Credit	$0		
Total Tax Credit		($2,059,393)	
Equals: Federal Estate Tax Liability (Refund)		**$0**	Federal Estate Tax Liability

Note: $3,692,577 remains in unused credit ($4,577,800 - $885,223).

6. Assume that Tony did not die on July 13, 2020. Discuss possible options for the transfer of Tony's Video and Games from Tony and Gail to Hari and Shami.

Because Tony's Video and Games is titled joint tenancy between Tony and Gail, both should agree on a plan to transfer the business. Nonetheless, if they could agree to transfer 50 percent of the business to Hari, the only real options would be either an outright sale or an installment sale. Since Hari is not a relative, neither Tony nor Gail would have any desire to transfer any of the business interest to Hari at less than its fair market value. In fact, if they sold the business to Hari via an installment sale, a market rate of interest would be charged. Of course, Tony and Gail will be subjected to capital gains taxes on the sales price above their adjusted basis of $1,000,000.

Tony may decide to sell the business through a direct sale to Shami also, but more likely Tony will transfer his interest in the other 50 percent to Shami utilizing either a SCIN or private annuity. Either of these options may create the possibility that a portion of the business may transfer to Shami for an amount less than fair market value because Tony, as the facts tell us, is in poor health and for both transfer devices the required installment payments cease at Tony's death. Gail would most likely transfer her interest in the business to Shami through a direct sale or installment sale as Gail is in good health. If Gail sold her interest to Shami through the SCIN, Shami would likely overpay for the asset (compared to current fair market value) by an amount equal to the SCIN premium. If Gail utilized an installment sale, she could charge Shami the IRS imputed interest rate.

The options detailed above are not all inclusive, but are meant to be illustrative of a few various options.

7. What trust options would you recommend as part of Tony and Gail's overall estate plan?

   Tony and Gail should consider using each of the following trusts:
   - Revocable Living Trusts - to avoid assets transferring through probate.
   - QPRT - to potentially transfer the vacation homes at a reduced transfer tax cost.
   - GRAT - to potentially transfer any property to heirs at a reduced transfer tax cost.
   - ILITs - to create additional funds at either Tony's or Gail's death through the payment of the death benefit.

   Again, these options are illustrative, as the expense of creating and maintaining a trust should be weighed against the client's needs.

8. What additional planning advice would you give Tony and Gail regarding their estate plan that has not been addressed?

For all clients, planning advice should be customized to the client and their circumstances. Below are just a few recommendations that could be made, although additional information may be needed.
- Begin using the annual exclusion. Gail should agree to split Tony's gifts. If Tony and Gail utilized their annual exclusions ($15,000 for 2020) each year together they could transfer $150,000 ($30,000 x 5) to their children, an additional $420,000 ($30,000 x 14) to their grandchildren, and an additional $112,000 ($30,000 x 4) to their sons-in-law, completely transfer tax free each year.
- Consider the availability of any qualified transfers (education or medical) - especially for Philip - to transfer additional assets without transfer tax costs.
- Create TOD and POD accounts to avoid probate.
- Ensure Will, Living Wills/Advance Medical Directives, and any Powers of Attorney are complete and up-to-date.
- Designating Gail as the beneficiary of the 401(k) and the profit sharing plan as Gail may be able to roll the assets into her own IRA and further delay the recognition of any income tax on the assets.
- Add beneficiary to deferred annuity and modify will accordingly.
- Make sure to elect portability by filing the 706.

BENNY AND MARTHA FRANKLIN CASE

Benny and Martha Franklin have come to you for help with their estate plan.

Personal Background and Information

Benny and Martha Franklin are 55-years-old and have been happily married for 35 years. They are both in excellent health and expect they will live well into their 90s. They live in Virginia and have three children and six grandchildren. The Franklins plan to retire at age 65. The chart below depicts their family as of today.

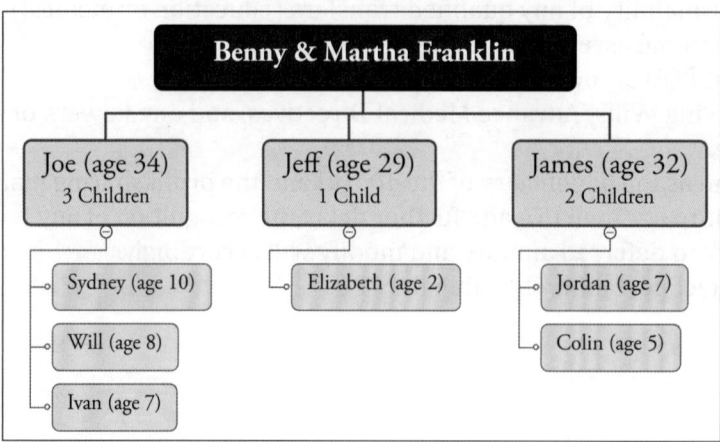

Joe and James are both married and work in the family businesses. Jeff is a lawyer and is recently divorced with custody over his daughter, Elizabeth. Joe's youngest child, Ivan, was born as a special needs child who needs full time care. Benny and Martha have a great relationship with their daughter-in-laws and consider them part of the family.

Benny graduated from MIT and is an aerospace engineer. He started and owns three companies that produce components for various weapons systems for the United States Department of Defense. Joe and James both graduated from West Point Academy and spent several years in the military. They have been working for Benny in various roles for the last couple years.

The three businesses are structured as C corporations and are owned entirely by Benny and Martha. The three businesses have appreciated over the last five years at an annual compound rate of growth of 10 percent. Benny expects this rate of growth to continue indefinitely.

Martha majored in communications at Boston College and has been a stay-at-home mom. She now helps with the grandchildren regularly and volunteers with the Wounded Warrior Project.

Education Information

Benny and Martha believe strongly in education and would like their five grandchildren to all attend MIT. Ivan is not expected to attend college. The current cost of undergraduate studies at MIT is $63,000 per year. Tuition has been increasing at an average rate of seven percent and is expected to continue at that rate.

Vacation Home
Benny and Martha used to spend summers with friends at a home on Martha's Vineyard. They had such fond memories that once they became successful, they decided to purchase a home on Martha's Vineyard. They spend a substantial amount of time with their children and grandchildren at the vacation home every summer.

Life Insurance
The life insurance policy is a second-to-die policy on the lives of Benny and Martha. The policy has a death benefit of $2 million. Assume the replacement value of the policy is $200,000. The policy is currently owned by Benny and the three boys are the beneficiaries.

Investment Real Estate
The investment real estate includes several pieces of commercial real estate held in separate entities. The value is expected to increase at an average rate of 10 percent per year.

Estate Planning Documents
Benny and Martha have basic wills that make optimal use of testamentary bypass trusts and the marital deduction. The wills were designed to avoid all estate tax at the death of the first spouse and to make use of their lifetime exemptions.

They also have durable powers of attorney for health care, advanced medical directives and financial powers of attorney.

Prior Gifts
In 2000, Benny established a Charitable Remainder Annuity Trust and funded it with highly appreciated publicly-traded stock worth $1,000,000. Benny and Martha were the income beneficiaries and the Wounded Warrior Project was the remainder beneficiary. The trust was set up with a ten-year term.

In 2009, Benny established an irrevocable trust for each of the three boys and funded each trust with $1 million. The trusts were set up in such a way as to allow the trustee of each trust to provide for the health, education, maintenance and support of the beneficiary. The trusts were established as simple trusts. The trustee is directed to not terminate the trust until the beneficiary turns age 45. The trusts were not set up as crummy trusts. The trusts name the children (born and unborn) of each of the boys as the contingent beneficiaries for each trust.

In 2012, Benny gave Uncle George a gift of $1,013,000 in cash. His uncle had been inspirational when Benny was a kid and has fallen on hard times.

Martha has not made any taxable gifts in her past.

Goals: Prepare a Proper Estate Plan

1. Minimize estate taxes.
2. Fund college education for the five grandchildren.
3. Set up a special needs trust for Ivan's future needs.
4. Ensure that the vacation home is a permanent family home for children and grandchildren.
5. Keep 100 percent of business interests in the family.
6. Maintain control of the business until retirement at which time James and Joe will take over.
7. Transfer an additional $2 million to the Wounded Warrior Project some time in the future.

Financial Statements

Balance Sheet

ASSETS		LIABILITIES AND NET WORTH	
Cash/Cash Equivalents		**Liabilities**	
JT Checking and Savings	$1,000,000	Current Liabilities	
Total Cash/Cash Equiv.	**$1,000,000**	JT Credit Card	$100,000
		Total Current Liabilities	**$100,000**
Invested Assets			
JT Marketable Securities	$6,000,000		
JT Business Interests	6,000,000	**Long-Term Liabilities**	
H 401(k) Plan	1,250,000	JT Mortgage - Primary	$1,000,000
JT Investment Real Estate	3,000,000	**Total Long-Term Liabilities**	**$1,000,000**
Total Investments	**$16,250,000**		
Personal Use Assets		**Total Liabilities**	**$1,100,000**
JT Primary Residence	$2,000,000		
JT Vacation Home	1,500,000		
JT Autos	100,000		
JT Household Furnishings	500,000	**Net Worth**	**$20,450,000**
H Life Insurance	200,000		
Total Personal Use	**$4,300,000**		
Total Assets	**$21,550,000**	**Total Liabilities and Net Worth**	**$21,550,000**

Statement of Income and Expenses

Statement of Income and Expenses
Mr. and Mrs. Franklin
Statement of Income and Expenses for Past Year

CASH INFLOWS		Totals
Salaries		
Income	$900,000	
Investment Income	$400,000	
Total Cash Inflows		**$1,300,000**
CASH OUTFLOWS		
Lifestyle Needs (includes debt repayment)	$500,000	
Income Taxes	$400,000	
Property Taxes	$100,000	
Homeowner's Insurance	$25,000	
Health Insurance	$25,000	
Long-term Care Insurance	$25,000	
Disability Insurance	$25,000	
Life Insurance	$100,000	
Total Fixed Outflows		**$1,200,000**
Excess Cash Flow		**$100,000**

Case Assumptions

1. They want to make maximum use of their annual exclusions.
2. They want to maintain total control over their business interests until retirement.
3. They are willing to fully utilize their gift and estate applicable credits any time to accomplish the best plan.
4. The long-term AFR is 3%.
5. Any minority transfer of business interests will receive a 25% discount.
6. Their life expectancies for GRAT or QPRT purposes are as follows:

	Him	Her
95%	5 years	5 years
75%	20 years	25 years
50%	30 years	35 years
25%	35 years	40 years

7. Their principal residence and the vacation home are appreciating at 10% per year and are expected to continue to grow at that rate.

Directions for the Case

1. What are the steps Benny and Martha should take immediately and over the long-term to reduce their gross estate and achieve their goals. Be specific and quantify the impact of each recommendation.
2. Prepare the gift tax returns for 2009 and 2012, as well as for the current year, based on recommendations. The applicable credit amount for gift tax purposes was $345,800 in 2009, $1,772,800 in 2012, and $4,577,800 in 2020. The annual exclusion was $13,000 in 2009 and 2012, and is $15,000 in 2020.
3. Prepare an estate tax return for Benny as of the end of the current year after any recommended transfers. Assume he dies on December 31 of the current year. Assume the combined last medical and funeral costs are $100,000 and the estate administration cost is $150,000.

Case Appendix

Exhibit 14.7 | Tax Rate Schedule for Taxable Gifts and Estates (2009)

Over $0 but not over $10,000	**18%** of such amount.
Over $10,000 but not over $20,000	$1,800 plus **20%** of the excess of such amount over $10,000
Over $20,000 but not over $40,000	$3,800 plus **22%** of the excess of such amount over $20,000
Over $40,000 but not over $60,000	$8,200 plus **24%** of the excess of such amount over $40,000
Over $60,000 but not over $80,000	$13,000 plus **26%** of the excess of such amount over $60,000
Over $80,000 but not over $100,000	$18,200 plus **28%** of the excess of such amount over $80,000
Over $100,000 but not over $150,000	$23,800 plus **30%** of the excess of such amount over $100,000
Over $150,000 but not over $250,000	$38,800 plus **32%** of the excess of such amount over $150,000
Over $250,000 but not over $500,000	$70,800 plus **34%** of the excess of such amount over $250,000
Over $500,000 but not over $750,000	$155,800 plus **37%** of the excess of such amount over $500,000
Over $750,000 but not over $1,000,000	$248,300 plus **39%** of the excess of such amount over $750,000
Over $1,000,000 but not over $1,250,000	$345,800 plus **41%** of the excess of such amount over
Over $1,250,000 but not over $1,500,000	$448,300 plus **43%** of the excess of such amount over
Over $1,500,000 but not over $2,000,000	$555,800 plus **45%** of the excess of such amount over
Over $2,000,000	$780,800 plus **45%** of the excess of such amount over

Exhibit 14.8 | Tax Rate Schedule for Taxable Gifts and Estates (2012)

Over $0 but not over $10,000	**18%** of such amount.
Over $10,000 but not over $20,000	$1,800 plus **20%** of the excess of such amount over $10,000
Over $20,000 but not over $40,000	$3,800 plus **22%** of the excess of such amount over $20,000
Over $40,000 but not over $60,000	$8,200 plus **24%** of the excess of such amount over $40,000
Over $60,000 but not over $80,000	$13,000 plus **26%** of the excess of such amount over $60,000
Over $80,000 but not over $100,000	$18,200 plus **28%** of the excess of such amount over $80,000
Over $100,000 but not over $150,000	$23,800 plus **30%** of the excess of such amount over $100,000
Over $150,000 but not over $250,000	$38,800 plus **32%** of the excess of such amount over $150,000
Over $250,000 but not over $500,000	$70,800 plus **34%** of the excess of such amount over $250,000
Over $500,000	$155,800 plus **35%** of the excess of such amount over $500,000

Exhibit 14.9 | Tax Rate Schedule for Taxable Gifts and Estates (2020)

Over $0 but not over $10,000	**18%** of such amount.
Over $10,000 but not over $20,000	$1,800 plus **20%** of the excess of such amount over $10,000
Over $20,000 but not over $40,000	$3,800 plus **22%** of the excess of such amount over $20,000
Over $40,000 but not over $60,000	$8,200 plus **24%** of the excess of such amount over $40,000
Over $60,000 but not over $80,000	$13,000 plus **26%** of the excess of such amount over $60,000
Over $80,000 but not over $100,000	$18,200 plus **28%** of the excess of such amount over $80,000
Over $100,000 but not over $150,000	$23,800 plus **30%** of the excess of such amount over $100,000
Over $150,000 but not over $250,000	$38,800 plus **32%** of the excess of such amount over $150,000
Over $250,000 but not over $500,000	$70,800 plus **34%** of the excess of such amount over $250,000
Over $500,000 but not over $750,000	$155,800 plus **37%** of the excess of such amount over $500,000
Over $750,000 but not over $1,000,000	$248,300 plus **39%** of the excess of such amount over $750,000
Over $1,000,000	$345,800 plus **40%** of the excess of such amount over

APPENDIX A
GLOSSARY

A

Abatement – The reduction in assets transferring to a legatee because the estate has insufficient assets to satisfy all of the legatees.

ABLE Accounts - Accounts for disabled individuals that provide some of the benefits of special needs trusts without the complexities typically associated with those trusts.

ABC Trust Arrangement – A common trust arrangement that utilizes a bypass trust (the B Trust), a GPOA Trust (the A Trust), and a QTIP Trust (the C Trust) to provide the necessary support to a surviving spouse while maximizing the use of the decedent's applicable estate tax credit and providing the decedent the ability to determine the ultimate beneficiary of most of his assets at the death of the surviving spouse.

Accelerated Death Benefit – A reduced payment of the death benefit of a life insurance policy paid to the insured during the insured's lifetime in return for a surrender of the life insurance contract.

Actual Contribution Rule – The value of a decedent's joint interest in property is based on the actual percentage of the original purchase price contributed by the decedent – not the decedent's ownership percentage.

Ademption – Extinction of a legacy because an asset, specifically bequeathed to a legatee, has been disposed of prior to death.

Adjusted Gross Estate – The adjusted gross estate is equal to the gross estate less any deductions for funeral expenses, last medical expenses, administrative expenses, debts, and losses during the administration of the estate.

Administrator – A person, usually a relative of the deceased, appointed by the probate court to oversee the probate process when an executor is not named in the will.

Advance Medical Directive/Living Will – Legal document expressing an individual's last wishes regarding life sustaining treatment.

Alternate Valuation Date – An alternate date, other than the date of death, to value a decedent's gross estate. The alternate valuation date is either six months after the date of death, or if the asset is disposed of within six months of the date of death, the asset's disposition date. Wasting assets do not qualify to use the alternative valuation date.

American Taxpayer Relief Act (ATRA 2012) – Tax act signed by President Barack Obama in January of 2013. The act reunified estate and gift tax with a $11,580,000 exemption and a 40 percent marginal rate (2020).

Ancillary Probate – Concurrent second probate process conducted in a non-domiciliary state in which the decedent owns property, which often requires the service of an attorney from that state, and separate court fees.

Annual Exclusion – An exclusion from gift taxes for present interest transfers less than or equal to $15,000 per year per donee.

Applicable Federal Rate (AFR) – Rates published monthly by the IRS for federal income tax purposes, in accordance with section 1274(d) of the Internal Revenue Code. Interest rates on loans should not be less than the AFR for the loan to be considered a taxable event and not a gift by the IRS.

Applicable Rate – The maximum estate tax rate in effect at the date of the GST multiplied by the "inclusion ratio."

Appointment of Executor Clause – A clause in a will that identifies the executor and any successor executor. This clause may also define the extent of the executor's powers and may grant specific or general powers.

Arm's-Length Transaction – A transfer generally between unrelated parties in the form of a sale, an installment sale, or an exchange.

Glossary

Ascertainable Standard – An objective standard for allowing distributions defined in the Internal Revenue Code as distributions for health, education, maintenance, or support (HEMS).

Attestation Clause – Witness clause stating that the testator is of sound mind and that he signed the document in the witness' presence.

Attorney in Fact – Agent or power holder of a power of attorney.

B

Beneficiary – The person(s) entitled to receive the death benefit of a life insurance policy at the insured's death. Also, the person(s) who hold(s) the beneficial title to a trust's assets.

Bequest Clause – Directs the distribution of property, whether cash, tangible property, intangible property, or real property.

Blind Trust – A revocable trust arrangement whereby an individual transfers property to the trust for management purposes when self-management of the assets might be deemed to be a conflict of interest.

Blockage Discount – A reduction in the fair market value of a large block of stock because the transfer of a large block of stock is less marketable than other transfers of smaller amounts of stock.

Buy-Sell Agreements - Arrangements that require the sale and purchase of securities owned by one individual to another following a specified triggering event, such as the death of a business owner.

Bypass Trust (also known as a Credit Shelter Trust or B Trust) – A trust created to ensure that an individual makes use of his applicable estate tax credit.

C

Capital Gain Property – Property that, when sold, results in either capital gain or Section 1231 gain.

Charitable Lead Trust (CLT) – A trust in which a charitable organization receives the income interest and a non-charitable beneficiary (usually a family member) receives the remainder interest.

Charitable Remainder Annuity Trusts (CRAT) – A trust that provides a fixed annuity to the donor (usually for life) for an amount that is greater than or equal to 5% of the initial net fair market value of the property contributed to the trust. The remainder interest of the trust passes to a named charitable organization.

Charitable Remainder Trust (CRT) – A trust in which a non-charitable beneficiary receives the income interest and a charitable organization receives the remainder interest.

Charitable Remainder Unitrust (CRUT) – A trust that provides a payment to the donor (usually for life) equal to a fixed percentage of the trust assets as valued annually. The remainder interest of the trust passes to a named charitable organization.

Chronically Ill Individual – A person who has been certified by a licensed health care provider as being unable to perform, without assistance, at least two activities of daily living for at least 90 days, or a person with a similar level of disability.

Codicil – A document that amends a will. A codicil is prepared subsequent to and separate from the will to modify or explain the will.

Community Property – A regime in which married individuals own an equal undivided interest in all of the property accumulated, utilizing either spouse's earnings, during the marriage.

Complex Trust – A trust that does not meet the definition of a simple trust.

Consideration – Payment or transfer of property in return for other property.

Contingent Legatee Clause – A clause in a will that names a secondary person to inherit if the original legatee is dead or disclaims the property.

Cross-Purchase Buy-Sell Agreement - An arrangement between individuals who agree to purchase the business interest of a deceased owner.

Crummey Provision – The explicit right of a trust beneficiary to withdraw some or all of any contribution to a trust for a limited period of time after the contribution. A Crummey provision converts what otherwise would have been a gift of a future interest (not eligible for the annual exclusion) to a gift of a present interest, eligible for the annual exclusion.

D

Date of Declaration – The date a board of directors approves and declares a dividend to be paid to its shareholders.

Date of Record – The date that a dividend paying company determines the owners of its stock who are entitled to a dividend (regardless of whether or not the individual owns the stock as of the payment date).

Deceased Spouse's Unused Exclusion (DSUE) – The portion of the $11,180,000 (2018) transfer tax exemption that is not used by a deceased spouse to shield transfers from estate tax that is transferred to the surviving spouse pursuant to an election made by the deceased spouse's executor on a timely filed estate tax return.

Declaration Clause – A clause in a will which states this is the last will and testament of the testator.

Devisee - A person names to receive real estate under the will.

Digital Assets - An electronic record of which an individual has a right or interest, may include information stored on a user's computer and other digital devices, social media accounts, information uploaded to websites, and catalogs of the content of electronic communications.

Direct Gift – A direct payment of cash or transfer of property to a donee.

Direct Skip – A transfer of property or an interest in property to a skip person that is subject to estate or gift tax in the hands of the transferor.

Disclaimer Clause – An heir or legatee's refusal to accept a gift or bequest. The disclaimer allows assets to pass to other heirs or legatees without additional transfer tax.

Distributable Net Income (DNI) – A tax concept that allocates taxable income between the trust and beneficiaries to ensure the trust income is subject to only one level of tax.

Domicile – Where a person lives, the location of their home.

Donee – The person who receives the gift.

Donor – The person who gives the gift.

Double-Basis (or Bifurcated Basis) Rule - When the fair market value of the property at the date of the gift is less than the donor's adjusted basis. In this case, the donee will have one basis for gains and one basis for losses.

Durable Feature – Allows a power of attorney to survive incapacity and/or disability.

Durable Power of Attorney Issued Either for Health Care or for Property – A written document enabling one individual, the principal, to designate another person(s) to act as his "attorney-in-fact." A durable power of attorney survives the incapacity and/or disability of the principal.

Glossary

Dynasty Trust – Generation-skipping trust created in perpetuity. Once created, a dynasty trust provides for trust beneficiaries, but avoids transfer taxation in the beneficiaries' gross estates by restricting ownership of trust assets.

E

Economic Growth and Tax Relief Reconciliation Act of 2001 (EGTRRA 2001) – Tax act signed by President George W. Bush in June of 2001. The act phases in a repeal of the estate and generation-skipping transfer tax. It also creates separate applicable credits for gift tax and estate tax.

Effective Transfer – A transfer of a person's assets to the person or charitable institution intended by that person.

Efficient Transfer – A transfer that occurs when transfer costs are minimized consistent with the greatest assurance of effectiveness.

Entity Purchase (Redemption) Agreement - Type of buy-sell agreement that obligates the business entity to purchase an owner's interest in the entity upon that owner's death.

Equitable Ownership – Possession of the economic right to property.

Escheat - The reversion of an heirless, intestate decedent's property to the state.

Estate Administration or Succession – The passing of property at death to surviving heirs/legatees.

Estate Planning – The process of accumulation, management, conservation, and transfer of wealth considering legal, tax, and personal objectives.

Estate Tax Inclusion Period (ETIP) – The period during which, should the transferor or the transferor's spouse die, the fair market value of the transferred property would be included in the gross estate of the transferor or the transferor's spouse.

Estate Tax Liability - The amount equal to the tentative tax less any applicable credits available to a decedent's estate.

Estate Trust – A trust which grants the surviving spouse a testamentary general power of appointment over the trust assets. Because of the spouse's general power of appointment over the trust's assets, the fair market value of the trust will be eligible for the unlimited marital deduction at the death of the first-to-die spouse.

Exchange – A mutual transfer of assets with equal fair market values between individuals.

Executor – Estate representative designated in the will by the decedent. An executor may serve without bond if the bond is waived by the decedent.

F

Family Limited Partnership (FLP) – A limited partnership created under state law with the primary purpose of transferring assets to younger generations using minority and marketability discounts to create reduced gift tax valuations.

Fee Simple Ownership – The complete individual ownership of property with all the rights associated with outright ownership.

Felonious Homicide Statutes – Statute that prevents heirs who feloniously participated in the decedent's death from inheriting via the will or state intestacy laws.

Fiduciary - A person who has a legal duty to act in the best interest of another as a result of holding a position of trust and confidence.

Five-and-Five Lapse Rule – The lapse of a general power of appointment, like the release of such a power, results in a transfer for gift tax purposes. This rule applies only to the extent the value of the property subject to the lapsed powers exceeds the greater of $5,000 or 5 percent of the aggregate value of the assets out of which the powers could have been satisfied.

529 Plan - A tax-advantaged savings plan designed to encourage saving for future college costs.

Forced Heirship – A state requirement that a certain portion of the decedent's estate be transferred to a spouse and, in some instances, children.

Future Interest – An interest which is limited in some way by a future date or time. A gift of a future interest does not qualify for the annual exclusion.

G

General Power of Appointment Trust (A Trust) – An irrevocable trust that can be created either during an individual's lifetime or at an individual's death that gives the agent the right to appoint the settlor's assets.

Generational Sub-Trust – Trust created on the birth of the first member in a generation, or at the death of the surviving member of a generation. A sub-trust can avoid potential conflict between siblings or conflict between or within various generations of the family.

Gift – A voluntary transfer, without full consideration, of property from one person (a donor) to another person (a donee) or entity.

Grantor – The person who creates and initially funds a trust. The grantor is also known as the settlor or creator.

Grantor Retained Annuity Trust (GRAT) – An irrevocable trust that pays a fixed annuity to the grantor (settlor) for some defined term, and pays the remainder interest of the trust to a non-charitable beneficiary.

Grantor Retained Income Trust (GRIT) – An irrevocable trust in which the grantor retains an income interest in the trust for the term of the trust. Thus, the grantor will donate property to the trust and the income from the asset will be distributed to the grantor during the term of the trust. At the end of the trust term, the remaining property is distributed to the beneficiary (remainderman).

Grantor Retained Unitrust (GRUT) – A irrevocable trust that annually pays a fixed percentage of the value of its assets (as revalued on an annual basis) to the grantor or (settlor) for some defined term, and pays the remainder interest of the trust to a non-charitable beneficiary.

Gross Estate – The gross estate consists of the fair market value of all of a decedent's interests owned at the decedent's date of death plus the fair market value of certain property interest the decedent transferred during his life, in which he retained some rights, powers, use, or possession.

Guardianship Clause – A clause in a will which allows the testator to identify an individual(s) to raise any minor children.

H

Heir – One who inherits under state law.

Holographic Will – Handwritten will.

I

In Trust For (ITF) Accounts - A bank account utilizing a beneficiary designation.

Incident of Ownership in a Life Insurance Policy – The ability to exercise any economic right in a life insurance policy.

Inclusion Ratio – Ratio determined by subtracting the applicable fraction from one.

Income Beneficiary – The person or entity who has the current right to income from a trust, or the right to use the trust assets.

Glossary

Income in Respect of Decedent (IRD) Assets - Assets that, as a result of income deferral, have built in income that must be recognized by the beneficiary of the asset.

Incomplete Transfer – Any transfers that include a revocable beneficiary designation or a transfer to a revocable trust. Incomplete transfers are not considered gifts for gift tax purposes.

Indirect Gift – A payment, or transfer, to a third party on behalf of a donor for the benefit of the donee.

Installment Sale – A sale of property that includes a note from the buyer to the seller. The buyer pays the seller the full valuable consideration of the property over a specified set of terms.

Insured – The person whose life is insured by the life insurance contract.

Intangible Personal Property – Property that cannot truly be touched such as stocks, bonds, patents, and copyrights.

Intentionally Defective Grantor Trust (IDGT) – A trust which gives the grantor sufficient control to be considered the owner for income tax purposes, but not so much control to require the trust property to be included in the transferor's gross estate.

Inter Vivos Trust – A trust that is created during the grantor's lifetime.

Interpolated Terminal Reserve - The amount the insurance company has actuarially booked as a reserve liability for a policy.

Intestacy – To die without a valid will or to die with a will that does not distribute all property.

Introductory Clause – A clause in a will which identifies the testator.

IRC Section 2032A - Special use valuation provision that allows the value included in the decedent's gross estate to be the current use value of the property, subject to a limitation that the highest and best use value cannot be reduced by more than $1,180,000 in 2020.

IRC Section 303 Redemption - Allows the estate of a deceased shareholder to redeem enough shares to cover the death taxes (federal and state estate, inheritance, and generation-skipping transfer taxes), funeral expenses, and administrative expenses of the decedent, and the shares redeemed for this purpose will qualify for capital gains tax treatment.

IRC Section 6166 - Allows for the deferral of estate taxes attributable to the closely held business interest over a 14-year period. The first four years of payments are interest-only, followed by 10 payments that amortize the estate tax liability over the payment period (although may be paid over a shorter period).

Irrevocable Life Insurance Trust (ILIT) – An irrevocable trust that owns and holds life insurance on its grantor's life. An ILIT is also known as a wealth replacement trust (WRT).

Irrevocable Trust – A trust created by a grantor that cannot be revoked. The grantor cannot take back the property that was transferred to the trust.

J

Joint Tenancy (with Right of Survivorship) – An undivided interest in property held by two or more related or unrelated persons, generally includes a right of survivorship.

Joint Will – One will executed by two or more individuals jointly that transfers their common interest in property.

K

Key Person Discount – A reduction in the fair market value of transferred stock due to an economic reality that the value of the stock will decline if a key person, such as the founder, dies or becomes disabled.

L

Lack of Marketability Discount – A reduction in the fair market value of a transferred asset because the interest is more difficult to sell to the public.

Lapse – When a power or right ends because of time or circumstance.

Legal Ownership – Possession of legal title to the property.

Legatee – One who inherits under the will.

Letters of Administration – A legal document that affirms the power of the administrator to act as the agent of the probate court.

Letters Testamentary – A legal document that affirms the power of the executor to act as the agent of the probate court.

Life Estate – An interest in property that ceases upon the death of the owner of a life interest or estate and provides a right to the income or the right to use property or both.

Living Will/Advance Medical Directive – Legal document expressing an individual's last wishes regarding life sustaining treatment.

Lump-Sum Death Benefit – A single payment of a life insurance death benefit to a beneficiary.

M

Medicaid – A state and federal assistance program that pays for medical care and most long-term care expenses for eligible persons with low incomes and limited assets.

Medicare – A federal program that pays for healthcare for persons over age 65 and for people under age 65 with disabilities.

Minority Discount – A reduction in the fair market value of a transferred interest in property because the interest is not a controlling interest.

Modified Endowment Contract (MEC) – A life insurance policy that appears to function like an investment contract because the policy is paid up in just a few payments. MECs function like other life insurance policies except for the tax treatment of loans from the policy.

Mutual Will – Two or more identical wills that leave all assets to the reciprocal party.

N

Net Gift – A gift that requires the donee to pay the gift tax. The gift tax is based on the value of the transfer less the gift tax.

Net Income with Makeup Charitable Remainder Trust (NIMCRUT) - A CRUT that requires that a fixed percentage (minimum of 5%) of the annual value of trust assets be credited to the income beneficiary, or if less, the net income of the trust for that year, with any deficiencies to be made up in later years when trust income exceeds the required set percentage amounts for such years.

No-Contest Clause – A clause in a will that discourages heirs from contesting the will by substantially decreasing or eliminating bequests to them if they file a formal legal contest to the will.

Nuncupative Will – Oral will consisting of dying declarations.

O

Ordinary Income Property – Property that, when sold, results in recognition of ordinary income.

Overqualified – A decedent's taxable base is less than the applicable estate tax credit equivalency because too many assets have passed to a surviving spouse.

Owner – The person who holds title to a life insurance contract.

P

Paid-Up Policy – A life insurance policy where no more premium payments are necessary to keep the life insurance policy in force, or a life insurance policy that cannot accept additional premiums without causing the life insurance policy to become a modified endowment contract.

Pay-on-Death Bank Account (POD) – A bank account utilizing a beneficiary designation.

Per Capita – Sometimes called "by the head" allows the deceased person's heirs to move into the generational slot of the deceased heir and inherit accordingly.

Per Capita at Each Generation - Directs equal shares to each living member of the same generation.

Per Stirpes – Sometimes called "taking by representation" directs that the deceased person's designated share of an estate is transferred to his heirs.

Physician Orders for Life Sustaining Treatment (POLST) - A document, constituting a physician's order, detailing the types of medical treatments an individual wishes to receive when they are within a year or so of death. The POLST is part of the patient's medical record, and is used to minimize the potential for medical errors in providing treatment.

Policy Dividends – Refunds of overcharged premiums to life insurance policy owners. The payments are treated as a return of the policy owner's adjusted basis.

Pooled Income Funds (PIF) – Donor contributions are pooled in a trust created and maintained by the charity. Each donor receives an allocable share of the income from the trust for his life.

Pooled Trust - An exception that resulted from the Omnibus Budget and Reconciliation Act of 1993; managed by a nonprofit association. While each beneficiary will have their own account, the assets will generally be pooled and managed together.

Portability – The ability of the executor of an estate to timely file Form 706 to transfer the decedent's unused credit exclusion to the surviving spouse.

Pot Trust – A trust created as a single trust and remains a single trust during the period of its administration. The trustee has the flexibility to treat all beneficiaries equally, as opposed to basing beneficial interest in the trust on the degree of relationship to the grantor.

Pourover Trust – A trust that receives assets that "pour" into it from another source, generally the grantor's estate at the grantor's death.

Power of Appointment – The power to name who will enjoy or own property.

Power of Attorney – Legal document that authorizes an agent to act on a principal's behalf.

Power of Attorney for Property - A special Power of Attorney designed for a specific purpose.

Premium Pay Status – Premiums are currently being paid on the life insurance policy.

Present Interest – An unrestricted right to the immediate use of property. A present interest gift qualifies for the annual exclusion.

Principal – The grantor giver of a power of attorney.

Private Annuity – The annuitant sells an asset to a buyer in exchange for an unsecured promise from the buyer to make fixed annual payments to the annuitant for the remainder of the annuitant's life.

Private Foundation – A charitable organization that receives its support from a single individual or family. It can be either a private operating foundation or a private nonoperating foundation.

Private Nonoperating Foundation – A charitable organization (private foundation) that does NOT spend at least 85% of its adjusted net income (or minimum investment return, if less) on activities engaged in for the active conduct of the exempt purpose.

Private Operating Foundation – A charitable organization (private foundation) that spends at least 85% of its adjusted net income (or minimum investment return, if less), on activities engaged in for the active conduct of the exempt purpose.

Privity – The prohibition of a surviving spouse transferring his or her inherited or donated unused exemption amount to his or her next spouse at the surviving spouse's death. The privity requirement prohibits the accumulation of exemptions through remarriage.

Probate Process – The legal proceeding that serves to prove the validity of existing wills, supervise the orderly distribution of decedent's assets to the heirs, and protect creditors by ensuring that valid debts of the estate are paid.

Prudent Man Rule – A rule which requires a trustee, as a fiduciary, to act in the same manner that a prudent person would act if the prudent person were acting for his own benefit.

Public Charities – Charitable organizations that receive broad support from the general public.

Q

QTIP Trust – A trust that grants the surviving spouse a lifetime right to the income of the trust while transferring the remainder interest to individual(s) of the grantor's choosing, typically created at the death of the first spouse to die.

Qualified Charitable Distributions (QCDs) - Distributions made after age 70½ that are not included in the AGI of the donor / taxpayer.

Qualified Domestic Trust (QDOT) – A trust created for the benefit of a non-citizen spouse which has enough transfer stipulations to allow the U.S. Government to subject assets remaining at the death of the non-citizen surviving spouse, as well as distributions of principal, to estate taxation. Assets transferred to a QDOT qualify for the unlimited marital deduction.

Qualified Personal Residence Trust (QPRT) – A special form of a GRIT in which the grantor transfers his home to the QPRT and receives "use" of the personal residence as the annuity. The remainder interest of the trust passes to a non-charitable beneficiary.

Qualified Terminable Interest Property Trust (QTIP Trust or C Trust) – A trust which allows a decedent to qualify a transfer for the marital deduction at his death yet still control the ultimate disposition of the property.

Qualified Transfers – A payment made directly to a qualified educational institution for tuition, excluding room and board, or a payment made directly to a medical institution for the qualified medical expenses of someone else. Qualified transfers are excluded from gift tax.

Qualified Viatical Settlement Provider – A state licensed business that is regularly engaged in the business of buying life insurance policies from the policy owners.

Quasi-Community Property – Property that would be community property had the married couple been living in the community-property state at the time of acquisition (applies to married couples who move from a common law (separate property) state to a community-property state).

R

Real Property – Property that is land and buildings attached to the land.

Reciprocal Will – Two or more identical wills that leave all assets to the reciprocal party.

Remainder Beneficiary – The individual or

entity entitled to receive the assets that remain in the trust at the date of the trust's termination.

Replacement Value - The fair market value of a "paid-up" life insurance policy (no premiums remain to be paid).

Residence Domiciliary – An individual's legal state of residence.

Residuary Clause – A clause in a will which directs the transfer of the balance of any assets not previously bequeathed or distributed.

Reversionary Interest – Interests that have been transferred and subsequently revert back to the transferor. Also, includes a possibility that the property transferred by the decedent may return to him or his estate and a possibility that property transferred by the decedent may become subject to a power of disposition by him.

Revocable Living Trust – A revocable trust that is managed by the grantor and is for the benefit of the grantor during his lifetime. The property transferred to the trust avoids the individual's probate estate, but is included in the individual's gross estate.

Revocable Trust – A trust created where the grantor of the trust retains the right to revoke the trust at any time prior to his incapacity or death.

Rule Against Perpetuities (RAP) – A common law rule which requires that all interests in a trust must vest, if at all, within lives in being plus 21 years.

S

Sale – The direct transfer of property to another for a note, money, or property of equal fair market value.

Section 1035 Exchange – A tax–free exchange of a life insurance contract for another life insurance contract, a modified endowment contract, or an annuity contract on the same insured.

Section 7520 Rate - To be used to value certain charitable interests in trusts. Pursuant to IRC 7520, the interest rate for a particular month is the rate that is 120 percent of the applicable federal midterm rate (compounded annually) for the month in which the valuation date falls. That rate is then rounded to the nearest two-tenths of one percent. For example, if the rate that is 120 percent of the applicable federal rate (compounded annually) for specific month is 1.28 percent. That rate is then rounded to the nearest two-tenths of one percent or 1.2 percent for purposes of IRC 7520.

See-Through Trust - A trust that is the beneficiary of a custodial IRA. It provides for more control over distribution of IRA assets after the owner's death, as well as providing increased creditor protection for the beneficiaries of the trust.

Self-Cancelling Installment Note (SCIN) – An installment sale that terminates at the earlier of the (1) death of the seller or (2) the term set forth in the installment note.

Self-Proving Clause – A clause in a will which involves the notary signing a notarized declaration that he/she witnessed the testator and witnesses sign the will.

Self-Settled Trust – A trust where the beneficiary is also the grantor of the trust.

Settlement Options – The beneficiary's available options when receiving the death benefit, usually either lump sum or annuity.

Side Instruction Letter – Also known as a personal instruction letter, details the testator's wishes regarding the disposition of tangible possessions (household goods), the disposition of the decedent's body, and funeral arrangements. A side instruction letter is not legally binding, but generally followed.

Simple Trust – A trust that requires all of the trust income to be distributed on an annual basis to the beneficiaries and does not have a charitable organization as one of its beneficiaries.

Simultaneous Death Clause – A clause in a will that establishes a presumption of which person died first in simultaneous death situations.

Situs – The place, generally referring to the state, where property is located.

Sole Ownership - The complete ownership of property by one individual who possesses the property fee simple meaning all ownership rights associated with the property, including the right to use, sell, gift, alienate, convey, or bequeath the property.

Sound Mind – A person's mental capacity.

Special Needs Trust - A specific type of trust that is used to provide benefits to persons or beneficiaries with special needs.

Special Needs Trusts Under 42 U.S.C. Sec. 1396p(d)(4)(A) - Considered to be self-settled in nature, are typically established by the special needs person's parent, grandparent, legal guardian or by a court and will avoid disqualification of Medicaid and SSI benefits.

Spendthrift Clause – A clause in a trust document which does not allow the beneficiary to anticipate distributions from the trust, assign, pledge, hypothecate, or otherwise promise to give distributions from the trust to anyone. If such a promise is made, it is void and may not be enforced against the trust.

Split-Dollar Life Insurance – A single life insurance policy in which two parties have an ownership interest. One party typically owns the death benefit, while the other party owns the cash value.

Split Gift Election – An election available to a donor of separate property which allows him to utilize his spouse's annual exclusion and transfer up $28,000 per year per donee without incurring gift tax.

Springing Power – The agent's power "springs" into existence upon some defined event or determination.

Sprinkling Provision – The trustee's right to make distributions to the trust beneficiaries at his discretion.

Standby Trust – A trust created during the grantor's lifetime that is either unfunded or minimally funded. A standby trust is also known as a contingent trust.

Statute of Limitations - The period of time allowed for the IRS to assess any additional gift tax, generally three years, unless the gift is not adequately disclosed on a filed gift tax return. If the gift is not adequately disclosed, the statute of limitations will never expire.

Statutory Will – A will meeting state statutes generally drawn up by an attorney and signed in the presence of witnesses.

Straight Single Life Annuity – An annuity for a term equal to the annuitant's life.

Surety Bond – A bond posted by the administrator or the executor of the estate to protect creditors, heirs, and legatees from losses created by the administrator or executor.

Surrender Value – The cash value of the life insurance policy less a surrender charge which is governed by the policy or state law.

Survivorship Annuity – An annuity that provides payments to one person, and then provides payments to a second person upon the death of the first.

Survivorship Clause – A clause included in a will requiring that the legatee survive for a specific period in order to inherit under the will. The bequest will qualify for the marital deduction if the property transfers to the surviving spouse and the time period of the survivorship clause is six months or less.

Glossary

Sweetheart Will – Two wills executed by spouses that leave all assets to the other spouse.

T

Tangible Personal Property – Property that is not realty and may be touched.

Tangible Personal Property Trusts (TPPT) – A special form of a GRAT in which the grantor transfers tangible personal property to the TPPT and receives "use" of the property as the annuity. The remainder interest transfers to a non-charitable beneficiary.

Tangible Property – Property that is not realty and may be touched.

Tax Cuts and Jobs Act of 2017 (TCJA) - Tax act signed in December 2017 by President Donald Trump that increased the transfer tax exemption to $11,580,000 for 2020 (and increased that exemption for inflation after 2018).

Tax Relief, Unemployment Insurance Authorization, and Job Creation Act of 2010 (TRA 2010) – Tax act signed December 2010 that extended various income and estate tax provisions of EGTRRA, set the tax credit equivalency amount for gift, estate, and generation skipping purposes at $5,000,000 for 2011 and 2012, set the maximum transfer tax rate at 35%, and introduced portability.

Tax-Appointment Clause – A clause in a will directing which assets will bear the payment of any debts and estate taxes.

Taxable Distribution – Any distribution from a trust to a skip person other than a taxable termination or a direct skip.

Taxable Estate – The adjusted gross estate less the available unlimited marital and unlimited charitable deductions.

Taxable Gift - A gift in excess of the annual exclusion. Does not create a tax liability until the lifetime exemption for taxable gifts is exhausted. A taxable gift does not include any qualified transfers.

Taxable Termination – The termination of an interest in property held in trust unless: (1) a transfer subject to federal estate or gift tax occurs with respect to the property held in the trust at the time of the termination; (2) immediately thereafter a non-skip person has an interest in the property; or (3) no distributions may be made at any time thereafter to a skip person.

Tenancy by the Entirety – A JTWROS that can only occur between a married couple.

Tenancy in Common – An undivided interest in property held by two or more related or unrelated persons.

Tentative Tax – The estate tax calculated on the tentative tax base.

Tentative Tax Base – The tentative tax base equals the taxable estate plus all post–1976 taxable gifts.

Term Insurance Policy – A life insurance contract which states if the insured dies within the term of the contract, the insurance company will pay a stated death benefit.

Term Interest – An interest in property that ceases after a defined period of time.

Terminable Interest – An interest that terminates at some point.

Terminally Ill Individual – A person who has been certified by a licensed health care provider as having a condition or illness that can reasonably be expected to result in death within 24 months.

Testamentary Trust – A trust created after the death of the grantor. The grantor's will generally includes all of the trust provisions.

Testate – When a decedent dies with a valid will.

Testator – Writer of a will.

Third Party SNT - Sometimes referred to as a family trust because the trust is a receptacle for funds from a parent, guardian or other family member. The assets of these trusts, if properly structured, are not counted or considered for purposes of available benefits for the beneficiary, thus making possible federal, state, and local funds.

Three-Year Rule – If an individual gratuitously transfers ownership of a life insurance policy on his life, or any incident of ownership in a policy on his life within three years of his date of death, the death benefit of the policy is included in his federal gross estate.

Totten Trust – Not a trust, but rather a bank account with a beneficiary clause.

Transfer Costs – Includes the gift and estate taxes and the costs of avoiding taxes, such as the cost of documents, planning, trusts, and other professional fees.

Transfer for Value – A transfer of an asset by means of a sale, exchange or any transfer which includes valuable consideration. If a life insurance policy is transferred for value, the death benefit in excess of the transferor's adjusted basis will be subject to income tax, unless the transfer meets certain exceptions.

Transferee - A person who receives a transfer (a donee receives a gift, a buyer receives property, an heir or legatee receives property from a decedent).

Transfer-on-Death Account (TOD) – An investment account utilizing a beneficiary designation.

Transferor - A person who makes a transfer (a donor makes a gift, a seller transfers, a decedent leaves property to others).

Trust – A structure that vests legal title (the legal interest) to assets in one party, the trustee, who manages those assets for the benefit of the beneficiaries (who hold the equitable title) of the trust.

Trustee – The individual or entity responsible for managing the trust assets and carrying out the directions of the grantor that are formally expressed in the trust instrument.

Trusteed IRAs - A trust established within the United States that holds IRA assets, which is an alternative to a custodial IRA. It allows for ultimate control over the distribution of the IRA assets by the owner after his or her death and provides creditor protection for the beneficiaries.

2503(b) Trust – A trust for the benefit of a minor designed to qualify the present value of the income interest of the trust for the annual exclusion. A 2503(b) trust must pay its income annually to the minor, but may hold the trust property for the minor's lifetime.

2503(c) Trust – A trust for the benefit of a minor designed to qualify the contribution to the trust for the annual exclusion. A 2503(c) trust must give the minor the right to receive the trust assets when he reaches age 21, but is not required to pay the income to the minor at any earlier time.

U

Unauthorized Practice of Law – The proffering of legal advice or services by one who is not a licensed attorney.

Underqualified – When too much of a decedent's property was subject to estate tax at the death of the first spouse due to improper use of the unlimited marital deduction.

Uniform Electronic Wills Act - A Uniform Law proposed in 2019 that permits electronic execution and storage of Wills. The act attempts to modernize the will creation process by permitting the creation and storage of a valid will through electronic means.

Glossary

Uniform Fiduciary Access to Digital Assets Act - A Uniform law that recognizes digital assets as a form of intangible personal property that can be held, managed, conserved, and transferred by the owner. The act provides methods for digital asset owners to grant fiduciary access to their digital assets that held by custodians even when the custodian's terms of service agreements would otherwise deny access to the assets.

Uniform Probate Code - A Uniform Law that provides rules for inheritance and the management of decedent's estates in the United States. The purpose of the act was to standardize probate court procedures across the states.

Uniform Statutory Rule Against Perpetuities - A legislatively created alternative to the Common Law RAP that typically sets the perpetuities period at 90 years.

Universal Life Insurance – A term insurance policy with a cash accumulation account attached to it.

Unlimited Marital Deduction – Because a married couple is viewed as one single economic unit for estate and gift tax purposes, an individual receives a deduction from his gross gifts or from the adjusted gross estate for transfers to a spouse. Hence, transfers to a spouse are not subject to estate or gift tax.

Usufruct – A Louisiana device similar to a life estate which provides the holder with the right to use property and/or the right to income from the particular property.

V

Variable Universal Life Insurance – A universal life insurance policy with investment options available for the cash accumulation account.

W

Wealth Replacement Trust (WRT) – An irrevocable trust that owns and holds life insurance on its grantor's life. A WRT is also known as an Irrevocable Life Insurance Trust (ILIT).

Whole Life Insurance – A permanent insurance policy which guarantees that the policy will remain in force as long as the premium is paid. The policy has a cash account attached to it which grows tax deferred.

Will – A legal document that provides the testator, or will maker, the opportunity to control the distribution of property, appoint an executor and avoid the state's intestacy law distribution scheme.

X

X Dividend Date – The date the market price of a stock adjusts for a declared dividend (i.e., the market price of the stock is reduced approximately by the amount of the dividend).

APPENDIX

B

INDEX

A

A Trust 307, 388
Abatement 107
ABC Trust Arrangements 403
ABLE Accounts 317–318
Accelerated Death Benefits 442–444
Actual Contribution Rule 74
Ademption 107
Adjusted Basis 158–160
    Bequests 212–215
    Community Property 215
    Gifts 158
        Appreciated Property 159
        Double Basis Rule 158
    Heirs 212–215
    Holding Period 212
    IRD Assets 213
    Reporting Requirements 213
    Surviving Owner 214
Adjusted Gross Estate 200–202
    Deductions From
        Charitable Deduction 203, 334, 352
        Unlimited Marital Deduction 203
Administrator 20, 104
    Duties 105
Advance Medical Directive 54–56
    Do Not Resuscitate Order 55
Alimony 148
Alternate Valuation Date 199–200, 481
American Taxpayer Relief Act of 2012 (ATRA) 124, 162
    Portability 139–141, 207–208, 306, 366, 375, 488
Anatomical Gift 55
Ancillary Probate 19, 70, 100
Annual Exclusion 133–134
    Generation-Skipping Transfer Tax 508
    Present and Future Interests 141
    Trusts 451
Annuities
    Straight Life Annuity 187
    Survivorship Annuity 187
Anti-Freeze Compliance 308
Anti-Lapse Statutes 43
Applicable Estate Tax Credit 205
Applicable Gift Tax Credit 137
Appointment of Executor Clause 27
Arm's-Length Transactions
    Exchange 233
    Installment Sale 230
Ascertainable Standard 400, 485
Assets
    Nonprobate 108, 109–110
        Annuities 109
        ITF Accounts 110
        Life Insurance 109
        POD Bank Accounts 110
        Retirement Plans 110
        TOD Accounts 110
        Totten Trust 110, 314
    Transfer of 97
    Valuation of 193–200
Attestation Clause 28
Attorney-In-Fact 44

B

B Trust 306, 400, 405
Bargain Sales 346, 347
Basis. See Adjusted Basis
Beneficiary 281–283
    Life Insurance 435
Beneficiary Designation 109
    Irrevocable 130
    Life Insurance 444
    Revocable 130
Bequests 166
Bequests Clause 26
Blind Trust 314
Blockage Discount 194
Business Agreements
    Buy-Sell Agreements 427–432
    Family Limited Partnership (FLP) 252
Business Disability Coverage 7
Business Transfers 148
Buy-Sell Agreements 425, 427–432
    Cross Purchase Agreements 429–431
    Entity (Redemption) Agreements 428–429
    Wait-and-See Buy-Sell Agreements 431
Bypass Trust 306, 400, 405

C

C Trust 308, 389, 487
Capital Gain Property
    Charitable Contributions 339
Carryover Basis 158
Case Study
    Estate of Belmont v. Commissioner 363
    Estate of Elkins v. Commissioners 193
    Estate of James Gandolfini 400
    Estate of Michael Crichton 40, 43
    Estate of Philip Seymour Hoffman 376
    Obergefell v. Hodges 3
    Steinberg v. Commissioner 133
Cash Surrender Value 198
Charitable Giving 332–366
    Bargain Sales 346, 347
    Charitable Annuity of Encumbered Properties 350–352
    Charitable Deduction 149
    Charitable Deductions 342–345
    Charitable Gift Annuities 347–350
    During Life 337–346

Gifts of a Split Interest 352
Gifts of Cash 337
Gifts of Property 338
Gifts of Services 337
Income Tax Issues 334, 341
Organizations 334
Tangible Property 364
Testamentary 363–364
Types of Charities 335–336
    Private Foundations 335
    Public Charities 335
Valuation 345
Charitable Remainder Annuity Trust (CRAT)
    Probability of Exhaustion Test 357
Charitable Trusts 313, 352–362
    Charitable Lead Trust (CLT) 313, 362
    Charitable Remainder Trusts (CRT) 313
        Charitable Remainder Annuity Trust (CRAT) 354, 356, 365
        Charitable Remainder Unitrust (CRUT) 354, 356, 360, 365
        Summary 356
    Pooled Income Funds 353
Child Support 147
Chronically Ill 443
Closely Held Business
    Buy-Sell Agreements 427–432
    Valuation 194–195
        Key Person Discount 195
        Minority Discount 194
Codicil 40
Community Property 76–79, 83, 215, 378
    Charitable Contributions 365
Completed Transfer 130
Complex Trust 298
Consideration 128
Contingent Legatee Clause 31–34
    Per Capita 31
    Per Capita at Each Generation 32
    Per Stirpes 31
Contribution Base 341
Credit for Tax on Prior Transfers 208
Credit Shelter Trust 306, 400, 405
Creditor Protection 283
    Probate 96–99
    Self-Settled Trust 284
    Spendthrift Clause 284
Crummey Provision 143–145, 301–305
    5-and-5 Power 303, 452
    Five-and-Five Power 144, 190, 302–305, 313, 452
    Irrevocable Life Insurance Trust (ILIT) 451
Crummey Trusts 313
Curtesy 181

D

Debts 202
Deceased Spousal Unused Exemption Amount (DSUEA) 140–141, 207–208, 392–394
    Privity 393
Declaration Clause 26
Deductions
    Adjusted Gross Estate 200–202
    Charitable Deduction 203
    Determine Taxable Estate 203
    Unlimited Marital Deduction 203
Defective Trust 310
    Intentionally Defective for Income Tax Only Trust (IDIOT) 310
    Intentionally Defective Grantor Trust (IDGT) 310, 517
Defense of Marriage Act (DOMA) 101–102
Deferral of Estate Tax (IRC §6166) 482
Descendents 19, 31, 264
    Lineal 499
    Non-Lineal 499
Developing the Estate Plan 529
Devisee 24, 97
Digital Assets 57, 68
Direct Skip 504
Disability Insurance 7
Disclaimer 30, 404, 485–487
Discount
    Key Person Discount 195
    Minority Discount 194
Disinheritance 263
Distributable Net Income 290
Distributing the Probate Estate 106
Divorce Statutes 42
Do Not Resuscitate Order (DNR) 55
Domicile 19, 104
Donee 127
Donor 127
Double Basis Rule 158
Dower 181
Durable Power of Attorney 47, 51
    For Health Care 52–53
Dying with Dignity 54
Dynasty Trust 309, 516–521
    Basic Structure 517
    Business Succession Planning 518
    Drafting Issues 520
    Funding the Trust 519
    Perpetuities 516
    Pot Trust 519
    Taxation of 517
    Termination 520
    Types 519

E

Economic Growth and Tax Relief Reconciliation Act of 2001 (EGTRRA 2001) 4, 123–124, 138
Effective Transfer 5
Efficient Transfer 5
Electronic Wills 23
Equitable Ownership 81
Estate Administration Expenses 201
Estate Equalization 265
Estate Liquidity 466–473
Estate of Belmont v. Commissioner 363
Estate of Elkins v. Commissioners 193
Estate Plan Checklist 535
Estate Planning
    Definition 5
    Establishing Goals with the Client 5
    Estate Planning Process 7
    Post Mortem 480–490
        Liquidity Needs 466–473
    Process 528
    Reform 4
    Specific Trusts Used 298
    Team 9
    The Financial Planner's Role 9
    Who Needs It 6
Estate Planning Documents 18–64
    Digital Assets 57
    Health Care Directives 52–55
    Other Documents 57
    Power of Appointment 44–47
    Power of Attorney 44–53
    Wills 18–43
Estate Planning for Small Estates
    Estate Equalization 265
Estate Planning for Small Estates.See Small Estates 264
Estate Returns
    Estate Tax Return (Form 706) 200
        Filing Requirements 210
        Penalties 212
        Tax Liability 209
    Income Tax Returns
        Decedent's Final Income Tax Return (Form 1040) 474
        Estate Income Tax Return (Form 1041) 476–479
Estate Tax Calculation
    Adjusted Gross Estate 200
    Alternate Valuation Date 199–200
    Credits
        Applicable Estate Tax Credit 205
        Prior Transfer Credit 208
    Credits From the Tentative Tax 205–209
    Deductions from the Adjusted Gross Estate 203
        Unlimited Charitable Deduction 203
        Unlimited Marital Deduction 203
    Deductions from the Gross Estate
        Administrative Expenses 201
        Debts 202
        Funeral Expenses 201
        Last Medical Expenses 201
        Losses During Estate Administration 202
        State Death Tax 203
    Estate Tax Liability 209
    Gross Estate 179, 179–193
        Dower 181
        Gifts Made Within Three Years of Death 182–183
        Proceeds of Life Insurance 191–192, 448–451
        Transfers With a Retained Life Estate 183
    Inclusions and Exclusions 179
    Installment Payments of Tax 482
    Portability 207–208
    Taxable Estate 203
    Tentative Tax 204–205
    Tentative Tax Base 204
Estate Trust 307
Exchange
    Life Insurance 442
Executor 20, 104
    Duties 105
    Fees 476
    Reporting 213

F

Family Limited Partnership (FLP) 252–256
Fee Simple 70
Felonious Homicide Statutes 42
Fiduciary 280
    Duties 280
    Selection 280
Financial Securities 195–198
    Accrued Dividends 196
    Accrued Interest 195
    Not Traded on Valuation Date 197
Five-and-Five Lapse Rule 144, 190, 302–305, 313, 452
Forced Heirship 42
Foreign Death Taxes 209
Form 1041 (Estate Income Tax Return) 476–479
Form 4768 211
Form 706 178, 210, 391
Form 709 135, 149, 155
Funeral Expenses 201
Future Interest 141, 142

G

Generation-Skipping Transfer Tax (GSTT) 496–521
    Annual Exclusion 508
    Applicable Fraction 511
    Applicable Rate 511
    Direct Skip 504
    Elections 488

Exceptions 507
Exclusions 507
Exemption 509
Filing Requirement 514
Inclusion Ratio 511
Non-Skip Person 503
Parties 497–504
Qualified Disclaimers 503
Qualified Transfers 507
Reverse QTIP 513
Skip Person 498
Taxable Distribution 505, 506
Taxable Termination 505
Generation-Skipping Trusts 515
Gift
    Adjusted Basis 158–160
        Appreciated Property 159
        Double Basis Rule 158
    Characteristics 127–132
    Community and Joint Property 135
    Complete Transfer 130
    Consideration 128
    Crummey Provision 143–145, 301–305
    Definition 127
    Elements 127
    Exclusions and Exemptions 133–141
    Future Interest 142
    Incomplete Transfer 130
    Loan 129
    Net Gifts 132
    Present Future Interest 141
    Present Interest 141
    Qualified Transfers 146
    Reversionary Interest 131
    Strategies 161–166
    Valuation 132
Gift Strategies 161–167
    Appreciating Property 162
    Bequests 166
    Fair Division Among Heirs 285, 403
    Gift Splitting 134
    Gifts of Appreciating Property 161
    Gifts to Minors 162
    Gifts to Spouses 162
    Gift-Splitting 134, 479
    Lifetime Transfers 166
    Multiparty Gifts 163
    Single Party Gifts 162
    Suitability of Gifting 161
    Tax Implications 157
    Techniques for Gift Giving 165
Gift Tax
    Adjusted Basis 158
    Calculation 149, 150–155
        Annual Exclusion 133–134
        Applicable Gift Tax Credit 137
        Form 709 135
        Prior Taxable Gifts 153
        Qualified Transfers 146
        Split Gifts 134, 479
        Tax Liability 126, 205, 555
    Form 709 149, 155
    Gross-Up Rule 182
    Life Insurance 444–448
    Lookback Provision 182–183
    Nontaxable Transfers 146–149
        Charitable Transfers 149
        Gifts to Spouses 148
        Payments Between Divorcing Spouses 148
        Payments for Support 147
        Political Organizations 146
        Qualified Transfers 146
        Transfers within a Business Setting 148
    Statute of Limitations 150
    Tax Paid 182
Gifting Strategies for Small Estates 266
Grantor 279
Grantor Retained Income Trusts (GRIT) 244
Grantor Trusts 297, 310
    Defective Grantor Trusts 310, 517
    Grantor Retained Annuity Trust (GRAT) 245–248, 308
        Valuation of Remainder Interest 246
    Grantor Retained Income Trust (GRIT) 308
        Anti-Freeze Compliance 308
    Grantor Retained Unitrust (GRUT) 248, 309
    Intentionally Defective Grantor Trust (IDGT) 249–250
    Qualified Personal Residence Trust (QPRT) 251
    Tangible Personal Property Trust (TPPT) 252
Gross Estate 179–193
Guardianship Clause 27

H

Health Care
    Durable Power of Attorney 52–53
Health Care Directives 52–57
    DNRs 55
    Durable Power of Attorney 52–53
    Living Wills 54–56
    Physician Orders for Life Sustaining Treatment (POLST) 57
Heirs 6, 8, 24, 97
Holding Period 212
Holographic Wills 22

I

In Trust For (ITF) Accounts 110
Incapacity Planning 54, 268
    Accelerated Death Benefits 442–444
    Durable Power of Attorney 48

Guardians as Fiduciaries 280
Health Care Directives 52–55
Insurance Arrangements 7
Power of Attorney 44–53
Viatical Settlement 443
Incident of Ownership in a Life Insurance Policy 449
Income Beneficiary 281
Income in Respect of a Decedent (IRD) 213, 470, 478
    Income Tax Deduction 478
Income Tax
    Charitable Contributions 334, 341
    Estates and Trusts 289
    Life Insurance 435–444
    Private Annuity 238
    SCIN 240
    Trusts 288–296
        Distributable Net Income 290
        Gift Tax 292
        Simple and Complex Trusts 289
Income Tax Return 475
Incomplete Transfer 130
Intangible Property 68
Intentionally Defective for Income Tax Only Trust (IDIOT) 310
Intentionally Defective Grantor Trust (IDGT) 249–250, 310, 517
Inter Vivos Trust 297, 301
Inter Vivos Trusts 298–305
Intestate 19, 96
    Sample Distribution Scheme 20
Intra-Family Transfers 233–257
    At Death 261–264
    DSUEA 392–394
    Family Limited Partnership (FLP) 252–256
    GRAT 245–248
    GRIT 244
    GRUT 248
    IDGT 249–250
    In Trust 234
    Not Subject to Gift Tax 233
    Partial Sale-Gift 235
    Private Annuities 236–239
    QPRT 251
    SCIN 239–243
    TPPT 252
Introductory Clause 26
IRC §2032A (Special Use Valuation) 483
IRC §6166 (Deferral of Estate Tax) 482
IRC Section 1014 266, 267
IRC Sections 2033-2044 180
IRC Sections 2036-2038 267
IRC Sections 673-677 249
Irrevocable Life Insurance Trust (ILIT) 305, 405, 451–456, 469, 530
Irrevocable Trust 296

J

Joint Tenancy with Right of Survivorship (JTWROS) 73, 82
Joint Wills 23

K

Key Person Discount 195

L

Lack of Marketability Discount 194
Lapse of Life Insurance Policy
    Effect on Loans 440
Last Medical Expenses 201
Legal Ownership 81
Legatees 8, 24, 97
Letters of Administration 105
Letters Testamentary 104
Life Estate 80
    Inclusion in Gross Estate 183
    Usufruct 80
Life Insurance 191
    Beneficiary Designation 444
    Buy-Sell Agreements 427–432
    Cash Surrender Value 180, 198
    Crummey Provision 446
    Estate Tax Treatment 448–451
    Exchange 442
    Gift Tax Treatment 444–448
    Gifts of Premiums 446
    Gifts to Charities 447
    Gross Estate Inclusion 180, 191
    Income Tax Treatment 435–444
    Interpolated Terminal Reserve 445
    Loans 440
    Objectives 423–432
    Paid-up Policy 446
    Parties 434
        Beneficiary 435
        Insured 435
        Owner 434
    Policy Dividends 439
    Premium Pay Status 445
    Proceeds 191–192, 453
    Replacement Value 447
    Second-to-Die Policy 434
    Settlement Options 438
    Three-Year Look Back Rule 449
    Transferred Within Three Years 183
    Types 432–434
        Term Insurance Policy 432
        Universal Life Insurance 433
        Variable Universal Life Insurance 433
        Whole Life Insurance 434
Unholy Trinity 445

Life Insurance Trusts (ILIT) 305, 405, 451–456, 469
Lifetime Planning Techniques 479
    Split Gifts 479
Lifetime Transfers 166, 228
Liquidity Needs 466–473
    Sources
        Life Insurance 469
        Sale of Assets 469
        Split-Dollar Life Insurance 470
Living Will 54–56
    Do Not Resuscitate Order 55
    Instruction Directive 54
    Natural Death Act 54
    Natural Death Declaration 54
Loans
    From Life Insurance Policy 440
Long-Term Care Insurance 7
Losses During Estate Administration 202
Lump Sum Death Benefit 438

M

Marital Agreements
    Divorce Statutes 42
    Family Limited Partnership (FLP) 252–256
    QTIPs for Blended Families 389
    Spouse of Trust Beneficiary 518
Marital Deduction 374–413
    DSUEA 392–394
    Terminable Interest 382
Marital Share 42
Marketability Discount 194
Marriage Equality 3
Medicaid 7
Medicaid Planning 257–261
Medicare 257
Medicare Surtax 289
Minority Discount 194
Modified Endowment Contract (MEC) 440
Mutual Wills 23

N

Natural Death Act 54
Net Gifts 132
No-Contest Clause 34
Noncitizen Spouse 395
Non-Traditional Relationships 3, 245
Nontraditional Relationships 43, 101–102
Nuncupative Wills 22

O

Obergefell v. Hodges 3
Operating Foundations 336
Oral Wills 22

Ordinary Income Property
    Charitable Giving 338
Overqualification 30

P

Partial Intestacy 19
Pay-on-Death (POD) Bank Accounts 110
Penalties 212
Per Capita 31
Per Capita at Each Generation 32
Per Stirpes 31
Perpetuities, Rule Against 287
Perpetuity Clause 287
Personal Representative 104
    Duties 105
Physician Orders for Life Sustaining Treatment (POLST) 57
Planning Considerations
    Children 530
    Grandchildren 530
    Noncitizen Spouse 530
    Spouse 529
    Trusts 530
Policy Dividends
    Insurance 439
Political Organizations 146
Pooled Income Funds (PIF) 353
Pooled Trust 317
Portability 139–141, 207–208, 375, 392–394, 397–399, 488, 529, 532–533
Post Mortem
    Checklist 537
    Liquidity Needs 466–473
    Planning Techniques 480–490
Post-1976 Taxable Gifts 204
Pot Trust 519
Pourover Trust 297
Power of Appointment 385, 486
    General 45
    Gross Estate Inclusion 189
    Limited 46
    Trust 307
Power of Appointment Trust 388
Power of Attorney 44–53
    Disadvantages of 51
    Durable Feature 47
    For Health Care 52–53
    For Property 50
    General 44
    Limited 45
    Springing Power 48
Present Interest 141
Principal 44
Prior Transfer Credit 208
Private Annuities 236–239

Private Foundations 314, 336
    Nonoperating Foundations 341
    Operating Foundations 336
Privity 393, 533
Probability of Exhaustion Test 357
Probate Avoidance
    Revocable Living Trust 286
    Trusts 298
Probate Court 104
Probate Process 5, 103–108
    Abatement 107
    Ademption 107
    Administrator 104
    Advantages 97–99
    Ancillary Probate 100
    Assets Subject to 108
    Creditors 96–99
    Defined 96
    Disadvantages 99–101
    Domicile 104
    Executor 104
    Intestate vs. Testate Succession 96
    Letters of Administration 105
    Letters Testamentary 104
    Probate Court 104
    Situs 100
    Succession 104
    Surety Bond 106
    Techniques of Avoiding 108–111
Property
    Digital Assets 68
    Intangible Property 68
    Ownership 69–79, 81–86
        Community Property 76–79, 83
        Equitable Ownership 81
        Fee Simple 70
        Joint Tenancy with Right of Survivorship (JTWROS) 73
        JTWROS 82
        Legal Ownership 81
        Sole Ownership 82
        Tenancy by the Entirety 75, 82
        Tenancy in Common 71, 82
    Partial Ownership Interests 80–81
        Life Estate 80
        Term Interest 81
        Usufruct 80
    Real Property 68
    Special Forms of Ownership 80–81
    Tangible Property 68
    Titling 82–89
    Transfer
        State Contract Law 108–109
    Types 68
Property Titling 69–81, 81–86
    Life Estate 80
    Term Interest 81
    Usufruct 80
Prudent Man Rule 280
Public Charities 335

Q

QTIP 389–392
Qualified Domestic Trust (QDOT) 396, 487
Qualified Personal Residence Trust (QPRT) 251, 309
Qualified Terminable Interest Property (QTIP) Trusts 308, 389, 487
Qualified Transfers 146
    Generation-Skipping Transfer Tax 507
Qualified Viatical Settlement Provider 443
Quasi-Community Property 78

R

Real Property 68
Reciprocal Will 23
Remainder Beneficiary 281
Residence Domiciliary 70
Residuary Clause 26
Retained Interest Transfers for Small Estates 267
Retained Interests 184
Reverse QTIP 513
Reversionary Interest 130, 131, 185
Revocable Living Trust 286
Revocable Trusts 296
Rule Against Perpetuities 287, 516

S

Same-Sex Relationships 3, 101–102, 245
Second-to-Die Policy 434
Section 1035 (Exchange of Life Insurance) 442
See-Through Trusts 320
Self Proving Clause 28
Self-Cancelling Installment Notes (SCIN) 239–243
Settlement Options 438
Settlor 279
Side Instruction Letter 41
Simple and Complex Trusts 289
Simple Trust 298
Simple Will 23
Simultaneous Death Clause 28
Situs 19, 100
Small Estates 264–268
    Gifting Strategies 266
    Incapacity Planning 268
    Need to Plan 268
    Retained Interest Transfers 267
Social Security Disability Benefits 7
Sole Ownership 70, 82
Sound Mind 24
Special Needs Trust 314–317

Special Use Valuation (IRC §2032A) 483
Spendthrift Clause 521
Split Gifts 134, 479
Split-Dollar Life Insurance 470
Spousal Gifts 148, 162
Springing Power 48
Standby Trust 297
State Death Tax 203
State Inheritance Tax 203
Statute of Limitations 150, 235
Statutes Affecting Wills 42
    Anti-Lapse Statutes 43
    Divorce Statutes 42
    Felonious Homicide Statutes 42
    Forced Heirship 42
    Marital Share 42
Statutory Will 22
Steinberg v. Commissioner 133
Straight Life Annuity 187, 191
Succession 104
Surety Bond 106
Surrender Value 439
Surviving Owner 214
Survivorship Annuity 187
Survivorship Clause 29
    Marital Deduction 384
Sweetheart Will 23

T

Tangible Personal Property Trust (TPPT) 252
Tangible Personal Property Trusts (TPPT) 309
Tangible Property 68
    Charitable Contributions 340, 364
Tax Cuts and Jobs Act of 2017 (TCJA 2017) 5, 124, 264, 266, 341
Tax Rate Schedule
    Estates and Trusts 289
    Gift and Estate 205, 555
    Gifts and Estates Rates 126
Tax Relief 392–394
Tax Relief, Unemployment Insurance Authorization, and Job Creation Act of 2010 (TRA 2010) 124–126, 139–141, 162, 375, 397–399, 532–533
    Portability 207–208, 488
Taxable Distribution 505–506
Taxable Estate 204
Taxable Termination 505
Tax-Appointment Clause 27
Tenancy by the Entirety 75, 82
Tenancy in Common 71, 82
Tentative Estate Tax 204
Term Insurance Policy 432
Terminable Interest 381- 382, 385, 389
    Defined 381
    Exceptions 384

Terminally Ill 443
Testamentary Trust 297
Testate 19, 96
Third Party (Family) Special Needs Trust 315
Three-Year Rule 449
Totten Trust 110, 314
Transfer-on-Death (TOD) Accounts 110
Transfers
    At Death 261–264
        By Contract 263
        By Operation of Law 263
        Charitable Transfers 264
    By Will 262
        Disinheritance 263
        Per Capita 262
        Per Stirpes 262
    Full Consideration 236
    In Trust 234
    Not Subject to Gift Tax 233
    Partial Sale-Gift 235
    Private Annuities 236–239
    SCIN 239–243
    To Charities 261
    To Loved Ones 233–257
    Transfer Costs 6
Trustee Selection 280
Trusteed IRAs 319
Trustor 279
Trusts
    ABC Arrangement 403
    Ascertainable Standard 400
    Definition 279
    Disclaimers 404
    Duration 287
    Income Taxation 288–296
        Distributable Net Income 290
        Exclusion from Gross Estate 292, 293
        Gift Tax 292
        Inclusion from Gross Estate 292, 293
        Simple and Complex Trusts 289
    Parties 279–283
        Beneficiary 281–283
        Grantor 279
        Income Beneficiary 281
        Remainder Beneficiary 281
        Trustee 280
    Perpetuities 287, 516
    Prudent Man Rule 280
    Reasons to Use 283
        Avoiding Probate 286
        Creditor Protection 283
            Self-Settled Trust 284
            Spendthrift Clause 284
        Minimizing Taxes 286
        Split Interests in Property 285

Trustee Selection 280
Types
    2503(b) Trusts 312
    2503(c) Trusts 312
    Blind Trust 314
    Bypass Trusts 306, 400, 405
    Charitable Trusts 313
    CLTs 362
    Complex 298
    CRATs 354, 356, 365
    Crummey Trusts 313
    CRUTs 354, 356, 360, 365
    Dynasty Trusts 309, 516–521
    Generation-Skipping Trusts 515
    GPOA 388
    Grantor Trusts 297, 310
    GRATs 308
    GRITs 308
    GRUTs 309
    Inter Vivos 297
    Inter Vivos-Irrevocable 301
    Inter Vivos-Revocable 298
    Irrevocable Trusts 296
    Life Insurance Trusts (ILIT) 305, 405, 451–456, 469
    Pooled Income Funds (PIF) 353
    Pourover Trusts 297
    Power of Appointment Trusts 307
    QDOTs 396, 487
    QPRTs 309
    QTIP 389–392
    QTIP Trusts 308, 487
    Revocable Trusts 296
    See-Through Trusts 320
    Simple 298
    Special Needs Trust 314–317
    Standby Trusts 297
    Testamentary Trusts 297
    TPPTs 309
    Trusteed IRAs 319

U

Unauthorized Practice of Law 10
Underqualified 399
Unemployment Insurance Authorization, and Job Creation Act of 2010 (TRA 2010) 392–394
Uniform Gifts to Minors Act (UGMA) 162
Uniform Transfers to Minors Act (UTMA) 162
Universal Life Insurance 433
Unlimited Marital Deduction 374–387
    Advantages of 375
    Limitations of 377
    Noncitizen Spouse 395
    Optimal Use 532
    Outright Bequests to the Spouse 387

    Overqualification 397
    Power of Appointment Trust 388
    QDOT 396, 487
    QTIP 389–392
    Terminable Interest 382
    Underqualification 399
Usufruct 80

V

Valuation
    Alternative Valuation Date 199–200
    Closely Held Business 194–195
    Estate 193–200
    Financial Securities 195–198
    Gift 132
    Life Insurance 198
Valuation Discount
    Key Person Discount 195
Variable Universal Life Insurance 433
Viatical Settlements 443

W

Wealth Replacement Trust 305, 405, 451–456, 469
Whole Life Insurance 434
Will Contests 25, 43
    Avoiding Will Contests 299
Wills
    Administrator 20
    Advance Medical Directive 54–56
    Advantages 21
    Ancillary Probate 19
    Avoiding Will Contests 34, 43, 101–102
    Clauses
        Appointment of Executor Clause 27
        Attestation Clause 28
        Bequests Clause 26
        Contingent Legatee Clause 31–34
        Declaration Clause 26
        Disclaimer Clause 30
        Guardianship Clause 27
        Introductory Clause 26
        No-Contest Clause 34
        Residuary Clause 26
        Self Proving Clause 28
        Simultaneous Death Clause 28
        Survivorship Clause 29
        Tax-Appointment Clause 27
    Codicil 40
    Devisee 24
    Domicile 19
    Executor 20
    Heirs 24

Intestate 19
    Sample Distribution Scheme 20
Legal Requirements 24
Legatees 24
Limitations 21
Living Will 54–56
Revoking and Changing 39
Side Instruction Letter 41
Situs 19
Statutes Affecting Wills 42
Testate 19
Types
    Electronic 23
    Holographic Will 22
    Joint Will 23
    Mutual Wills 23
    Nuncupative Wills 22
    Reciprocal Will 23
    Simple Will 23
    Statutory Will 22
    Sweetheart Will 23